GW01048700

PRESS LAW AND PRACTICE

A Comparative Study of Press Freedom in European and Other Democracies

An ARTICLE 19 Report

March 1993

Reprinted August 1994

© ARTICLE 19

Printed in the United Kingdom

ISBN 1 870798 07 4

TABLE OF CONTENTS

NOTE TO READERS

ANALYSIS OF PRESS LAW BY COUNTRY

Each of the country chapters has been arranged in the following 22 categories to facilitate comparative analysis:

1. Relevant Constitutional Provisions
2. Distribution of Powers between Central and Regional Government
3. Role of the Courts
4. Status of International Human Rights Treaties in National Law
5. Statutory Framework
6. Regulation of Ownership
7. Registration Requirements
8. Regulation of Import and Export of Publications
9. Mechanisms of Press Self-Regulation
10. Defamation
11. Invasion of Privacy
12. Right of Reply and/or Correction
13. Insults to Government Institutions or Officials
14. Official Secrecy and Access to Government-Held Information
15. Access to and Disclosure of Court Documents and Proceedings
16. Access to and Disclosure of Legislative Documents and Proceedings
17. Commercial Secrecy and Access to Information held by Private Parties
18. Prior Restraints
19. Protection of Sources
20. Restrictions on Offensive Language against Identifiable Groups
21. Blasphemy, Obscenity and Protection of Public Morals
22. Restrictions on Advertising

ACKNOWLEDGEMENTS

Press Law and Practice was edited by Sandra Coliver, ARTICLE 19's Law Programme Director. Patrick Merloe, Special Counsel to ARTICLE 19, and Ann Naughton, Programme Coordinator, were contributing editors.

Susan Hay and Elizabeth Schofield proofread the text. Susan York designed and typeset the study. Thanks are also due to Birgit Friedl and Kathryn Klingenstein, legal interns, for their assistance.

We wish to thank the authors of the various chapters for their time, effort and expertise (individually acknowledged in Notes on Contributors). We also thank the many other experts who provided information and comments on the text, particularly Juan Cebrián, Emmanuel Derieux, Helmut Kohl, Wolfgang Libal, David Pannick, Sven Egel Omdal, Arne Ruth, Jeroen Schokkenbroek and Julianne Schultz.

We gratefully acknowledge the support of UNESCO and the Council of Europe. The ideas and opinions expressed in this publication are those of the authors and do not necessarily represent the views of UNESCO or the Council of Europe.

ABBREVIATIONS

ACHR	American Convention on Human Rights
CERD	Committee on the Elimination of Racial Discrimination
CSCE	Conference on Security and Cooperation in Europe
EC	European Communities
ECHR	European Convention on Human Rights
ICCPR	International Covenant on Civil and Political Rights
UDHR	Universal Declaration of Human Rights
UN	United Nations

ARTICLE 19, International Centre Against Censorship
Lancaster House, 33 Islington High Street
London N1 9LH
Tel. (44) 71 278 9292
Fax. (44) 71 713 1356

INTRODUCTION

The primary purpose of this comparative study of press laws in eleven selected democracies is to illustrate how these countries balance the rights to press freedom and access to information against other social and individual interests. It is intended in particular to assist legislators, press freedom advocates and human rights campaigners engaged in drafting, amending or commenting on constitutional provisions, laws and regulations which affect the functioning of the press. The focus on laws and practice in European and other Western democracies is intended to be of immediate and practical use to those groups in Central and East Europe at present involved in building a free press. The study will also be a powerful aid in demonstrating evolving state practice in cases before the European Court and Commission of Human Rights. *Press Law and Practice* undoubtedly will prove an important resource for academics, journalists and lawyers interested in the relationship between laws, their implementation and the vitality of the press in different countries.

The countries included in this study were selected for the different traditions and approaches to press freedom they represent. The seven civil law countries (Austria, France, Germany, Netherlands, Norway, Spain, Sweden) reflect certain similarities as well as significant variations; in particular, the power of courts in Austria, France (to a limited extent), Germany and Spain to interpret statutes to be consistent with the constitution or else to declare them unconstitutional has increased the role of case-law in those countries. The voluntary press council systems in the Netherlands, Norway and Sweden are well respected by the press and public and often provide an effective alternative to the courts concerning many press-related disputes. The common law countries (Australia, Canada, the US and the UK) offer distinctive features. The US offers some of the most extensively reasoned judgments in support of strong constitutional protections. The UK and Australia have the dubious distinction of being the only two countries studied which lack a (written) constitutional protection of freedom of expression; the standard of press protection is correspondingly low (as evidenced, for example, by libel laws which heavily favour the plaintiff and poor protection for the confidentiality of journalists' sources). The efforts of the Australian Press Council to promote press freedom are thus particularly noteworthy.

The country chapters have been written by national experts and each is organized according to 22 categories ranging from relevant constitutional provisions to mechanisms of self-regulation and protection of journalists' sources in order to facilitate comparison of the ways in which different countries approach the same issues. Each contributor describes the requirements of relevant laws and regulations, summarizes the case-law and other evidence of how the laws have been applied in practice, and evaluates the impact of the laws on the press' effectiveness in informing the public about matters of legitimate public interest and in serving as a "public watchdog". The concluding comparative analysis chapter highlights the prevailing patterns concerning, as well as unusual approaches to, the different aspects of press freedom examined in the country chapters.

A number of expert readers provided helpful comments, many of which have been incorporated. ARTICLE 19 also undertook some additional research. Nonetheless, the country chapters reflect the research and analysis of the contributors, and do not necessarily reflect the views of ARTICLE 19.

ARTICLE 19 does not suggest any models for emulation or adoption by other countries. Far from it. First, national legislatures must adopt ways to protect press freedom which reflect their own traditions, culture and patterns of social interaction. Second, none of the countries surveyed offers an ideal approach. It should be noted for example, that the systems of press promotion and regulation in most countries studied have evolved over a period of more than a century. Thus, in most countries, laws affecting the press are scattered throughout the general laws, creating, in some countries, a complicated patchwork of laws and precedents. With the opportunity of creating a system of press protection and promotion, newly emerging democracies may well be able to craft a more unified and simplified system of fundamental principles, laws and measures of self-regulation.

This study arose from a recognition of the woeful lack of detailed information on laws which affect the press and their application and it is hoped that this will be only the first of a continuing series of regional reports on how the press works. ARTICLE 19 intends to research and document information on press laws and practice and to ensure that a body of material and expertise is easily available to a wider audience. It is also intended to use this study as a basis for regional workshops which will examine existing and proposed national practices regarding the press. As a campaigning organization, ARTICLE 19 hopes, by the publication of this and future reports, to generate greater awareness of and vigilance about the diverse ways in which press laws can restrict both press freedom and freedom of expression in general.

Press Law and Practice has been supported by grants from UNESCO and the Council of Europe and, as part of this project, a comprehensive set of national laws, collected by ARTICLE 19, will be available from UNESCO's Communication Division. This study follows on from UNESCO's *1991 Study on Broadcasting Laws in Selected Western European and North American Countries.*

Frances D'Souza
Executive Director, ARTICLE 19
12 March 1993

Chapter 1

PRESS LAW IN AUSTRALIA

David Flint

INTRODUCTION

Australia, first inhabited by the Aboriginal people, was acquired by the British in 1788. By the middle of the nineteenth century, Australia comprises six autonomous, internally self-governing colonies. Australia has had an unbroken experience of democratic government longer than most countries, and initiated, or was an early adherent of, such democratic reforms as the secret ballot and the vote for women. Essentially an immigrant society, its multicultural character has been reinforced by substantial non-British European immigration after the Second World War, followed by Asian immigration.

1. RELEVANT CONSTITUTIONAL PROVISIONS

There is no provision in either Australia's Federal Constitution or in any of the state constitutions which explicitly guarantees freedom of speech and of the free press. Australia inherited the traditional English view that freedom of speech was best protected by the common law. There have been unsuccessful attempts to incorporate a guarantee of free speech, alone or with other human rights, into the Australian Constitution. The Constitution, however, is notoriously difficult to amend.

Nonetheless, there have been three recent developments of interest. Although the ratification of treaties, for example the International Covenant on Civil and Political Rights (ICCPR), does not create rights and duties under Australian law without enabling legislation, there is some support for the proposition that the courts should have regard to international human rights norms in limited circumstances, including in resolving ambiguities in the statutory law or where there is no binding case-law authority.[1]

Second, there have been proposals by the Australian Press Council and others for the inclusion of a guarantee of freedom of expression in state constitutions, and the question is under consideration by the Queensland Electoral and Administration Review Committee.

Third, it is arguable that the Constitution includes some implied guarantees of free speech. In a recent case, the Australian High Court ruled that freedom of political communication is protected by implication by the Constitution's commitment to representative government

---

[1] *See Mabo v. State of Queensland* (1992) 66 ALJR 408, 422 (H.C); *Derbyshire County Council v. Times Newspapers Ltd* (1992) 3 WLR 28 (London Court of Appeal).

through elections.[2] Also, Section 92 of the Constitution, which declares that trade and intercourse among the states must be free, may have an impact on free speech.

2.   DISTRIBUTION OF POWERS BETWEEN CENTRAL AND REGIONAL GOVERNMENT

The Commonwealth of Australia, a constitutional monarchy, is a federation of six states (New South Wales, Queensland, South Australia, Tasmania, Victoria and Western Australia), and several territories (of which two, the Northern Territory and the Australian Capital Territory, have a degree of self-government that in some respects is state-like). The Australian Constitution grants certain limited exclusive powers to the Commonwealth (Cth); other powers enumerated in the Constitution are shared concurrently with the states. Under Section 109 of the Constitution, in the event of an inconsistency between federal and state law, federal law prevails.

The power of the Federal Parliament to enact laws directed only at the press is limited. The press, however, is subject to a number of federal laws of general application which come within one or other of the areas of power granted to the Parliament, including taxation, defence, corporations, interstate and overseas trade and commerce. The press is also subject to aspects of the common law (originally inherited from England, now declared by the Australian courts), which is uniform throughout the country. The law of contempt, for example, is essentially found in the common law.

3.   ROLE OF THE COURTS

Australia has both federal and state courts. In each state and territory there is a Supreme Court sitting in both civil and criminal jurisdictions, together with lower courts. At the federal level, there is a High Court of Australia which operates both as a constitutional court and as a final appellate court which, within its discretion, may decide to hear appeals from the Supreme Courts of the states and territories as well as the Federal Court. The Federal Court deals with actions under federal law. As a result of cross-vesting provisions, problems of demarcation between the jurisdiction of state and federal courts have been effectively overcome.

Australia is a common law jurisdiction, and case-law from other common law jurisdictions is of persuasive value, particularly decisions of English and New Zealand courts.

---

[2] *Australian Capital Television Pty Ltd v. The Commonwealth* and *New South Wales v. The Commonwealth (No.2)* (1992) 66 ALJR 695. The High Court invalidated federal legislation restricting political advertising on radio and television during election and referendum campaigns, and ruled that there is an implied guarantee of freedom of political communication in the Constitution which restricts the power, at least, of the Federal Parliament. *See also Nationwide News Pty v. Wills* (1992) 66 ALJR 658, in which the High Court invalidated, on similar grounds, a provision that limited robust criticism of a statutory body, the Industrial Relations Commission.

4. STATUS OF INTERNATIONAL HUMAN RIGHTS TREATIES IN NATIONAL LAW

Australia is a party to the ICCPR, and in 1991 it acceded to its First Optional Protocol which enables individuals to file complaints with the UN's Human Rights Committee. The ICCPR has not been enacted into domestic (municipal) law.

Ratified treaties not expressly enacted into Australian federal law have limited status in the courts. A Human Rights Commission was established in 1981 and was reconstituted as the Human Rights and Equal Opportunity Commission under the Human Rights and Equal Opportunity Commission Act, 1986 (Cth). Its purpose is to encourage observance in Australia of Australia's international human rights obligations. Various international human rights instruments, including the ICCPR, are included in the five schedules to the Act.

5. STATUTORY FRAMEWORK

There is no press law as such in Australia. The electronic media is governed by the Australian Broadcasting Services Act, 1992 (Cth).

6. REGULATION OF OWNERSHIP

Australia has experienced a gradual but dramatic reduction in the number of newspaper titles. In 1923, there were 26 metropolitan daily newspapers in Australia owned by 21 proprietors. By 1950, the number had fallen to 15 metropolitan dailies having 10 owners. By 1987, there were only three major proprietors of the metropolitan dailies: Herald and Weekly Times Limited, News Limited, and John Fairfax Group Pty Limited. In 1987, there was a take-over battle between News Limited and the Fairfax Group for the ownership of Herald and Weekly Times Limited. Notwithstanding the strenuous opposition of the Australian Journalists' Association and certain individuals, News Limited was successful and, subject to certain divestments, the take-over was approved by the Trade Practices Commission. Mr Rupert Murdoch's involvement, as an American citizen, in News Limited necessitated consideration by the Foreign Investment Review Board, an advisory body to the Commonwealth Government. The Government subsequently approved the proposal. There was no opposition to the take-over from the Australian Council of Trade Unions nor from the major political parties, neither at the federal nor at the state level.

Since 1986, some 17 daily and Sunday papers have closed. With the exception of Sydney and Melbourne, no capital city now has more than one daily paper. There are only two national dailies, *The Australian* and *The Australian Financial Review*. News Limited controls just over 70 per cent of total metropolitan daily circulation, while Fairfax, partially owned by Conrad Black (who holds major interests in papers in London, Jerusalem and Canada), controls 21 per cent. Only two major metropolitan daily papers, *The Canberra Times* and *The West Australian*, are controlled by proprietors independent of either News Limited or the Fairfax

Group. A major influence in magazine circulation is Australian Consolidated Press under the control of Mr Kerry Packer, which divested itself of newspaper titles in the 1980s.

Since 1987, most newspapers have divested themselves of significant interests in the electronic media, and restrictions now apply in relation to cross-media ownership between television and newspapers.[3] In contrast to the shrinking newspaper market, Australia's broadcast and electronic media are growing.[4]

Apart from the restrictions on cross-media ownership, the only restrictions on concentration of press ownership are the general ones contained in the Trade Practices Act, 1974 (Cth), which sets out Australian anti-trust law and applies to all industries. Section 46 proscribes the abuse of monopoly power through predatory practices. Section 50 proscribes the attainment or increase of a dominant position in a market. However, these may be authorized if there is a public benefit in the take-over. The Trade Practices Commissioner's view is that the product market for the press is the newspaper industry, not all media, and that for most metropolitan newspapers the market is limited to the state concerned.

A report of a parliamentary committee in 1992 found no abuses of concentration and made no recommendations concerning initiatives to create new newspapers.[5] However, all members of the committee agreed that "concentration of ownership is potentially harmful to plurality of opinion and increases the potential risk that news may be distorted" and accordingly urged that the risk of further concentration "should be minimised".[6] The report seemed to accept that, if new newspapers were created, there would be a market battle that would result in only one newspaper emerging. It recommended that the test in Section 50 of the Trade Practices Act be amended to return to the pre-1977 proscription of take-overs which would result, or be likely to result, in a substantial lessening of competition. The Government has since indicated that it will amend the Act accordingly.

---

[3] Broadcasting Services Act, 1992, Sections 59, 60, 61. The Act prohibits control of both a television station and a newspaper 50 per cent of whose circulation is in the relevant viewing area. An owner with a 15 per cent interest in a company is regarded as being in a position to control that company unless the Australian Broadcasting Authority determines otherwise (*Id.* at Schedule 2).

[4] Australia has an increasing number of radio stations, commercial and, at the national level, public, and five television networks, three commercial networks and two public national networks. Some satellite services are available, and restrictions on new technological developments, including cable television are being relaxed. Australia has one wire service, Australian Associated Press, which is under the joint control of News and Fairfax.

[5] *News and Fair Facts: The Australian Print Media Industry* (Canberra:1992). It should be noted that a minority of the committee members concluded that "there was a connection between the unprecedentedly high concentration of media ownership and the lack of diversity of information and ideas in the Australian press, and that the former is likely to be a significant cause of the latter." *Id.* at p. xxii. The Press Council's submission to the committee may be found in *Australian Press Council News* (November 1991), and its response in *Australian Press Council Annual Report* (1992), 20.

[6] *Supra, News and Fair Facts.*

7.   REGISTRATION REQUIREMENTS

There is no licensing system as such or any requirement of government approval to launch a newspaper or other press enterprise.[7] All states and territories other than South Australia require newspaper printing houses to include their name and address and the name and address of the publisher in the newspaper; some states also require registration.[8]

Section 201 of the federal Copyright Act, 1968 (Cth), requires that one copy of all printed material published in Australia be sent to the National Library in Canberra. In addition, each state requires that one copy of material published in the state be sent to the relevant state library.

8.   REGULATION OF IMPORT AND EXPORT OF PUBLICATIONS

There are no restrictions on import and export of publications apart from those relating to obscenity, violence, the promotion or incitement of terrorism, and the use of certain drugs.[9]

9.   MECHANISMS OF PRESS SELF-REGULATION

9.1   The Australian Press Council

The Australian Press Council, a voluntary body established in 1976 by the Australian Journalists' Association, three publishing associations (Country Press Australia, Australian Suburban Newspapers Association Ltd. and Regional Dailies of Australia Ltd.) and Australia's major publishers, is the principal body which promotes press ethics in Australia. It consists of a Chairman, ten representatives of the constituent organizations, two journalists, one member from a panel of editors, seven public members and 20 alternate members.[10]

---

[7] A British Colonial Governor of New South Wales in the nineteenth century did attempt to control the press by legislation and taxation. His recall to England was greeted with fireworks, bonfires and parties all over Sydney in 1831; no government has since attempted a direct assault on freedom of the press. Robert Pullan, *Guilty Secrets: Free Speech in Australia* (1986), 97.

[8] *See, e.g.,* Printing and Newspapers Act, 1973 (NSW); Printing and Newspapers Act, 1981 (Qld); Printers and Newspapers Act, 1911 (Tas); Printers and Newspapers Act, 1958 (Vic); Newspaper Libel and Registration Act, 1884 (WA); Printing and Newspapers Ordinance, 1961 (ACT); Printing and Newspapers Act, 1884 (NT).

[9] *See* Customs Act, 1901 (Cth), Sec. 50; Customs (Prohibition Imports) Regulations, 1956 (Cth), Reg. 4A (1A) and (2).

[10] Vacancies for public members and alternates are advertised. A selection committee advises the Chairman, who makes nominations to the Council. Most publishers' organizations send representatives who themselves have achieved eminence as editors and journalists. Equally, the editorial member, chosen from the panel of former editors, and the journalists are also eminent and acknowledged as independent. The public members are men and women of standing in the community who have rendered community service and who, as a body, are meant to provide a balanced representation of Australians, having regard to gender, ethnicity, geography and readership interests

The objects of the Press Council include the maintenance of the character of the Australian press in accordance with the highest journalistic standards and the preservation of the press' established freedom. The Press Council has a specific mandate to consider, investigate and deal with complaints about the conduct of the press as well as the conduct of persons and organizations towards the press.

The Council is based on the proposition that the freedom of the press to publish is the freedom of the people to be informed, and that press freedom includes "the right of the newspaper to publish what it reasonably considers to be news, without fear or favour, and the right to comment fairly upon it". The Council believes that press freedom is necessary to the fulfilment of the press' function as "public watchdog" and to the public's right to receive information of public interest.

The Council is funded by its constituent bodies, with the associations (country, regional and suburban) paying a certain percentage of the annual budget, and the balance being divided among publishers based on a proportional basis calculated on the circulation of all metropolitan dailies in Australia.

The Council provides an independent, efficient and free facility for hearing complaints against the press. In so doing, the Council gives first and dominant consideration to what it perceives to be the public's interest. The Council is guided by 12 basic principles contained in its Statement of Principles which, however, is not meant to be a precise or exhaustive formula. The 12 principles concern honesty and fairness; privacy; trust; rumour; the obtaining of news by dishonest and unfair means; the necessary distinction to be made between fact and opinion; gross breaches of taste; sexual, racial and other discrimination; opportunity to reply; corrections and apologies; as well as the obligation of newspapers to give prominence to adverse adjudications against them.

9.2   Complaint Procedures

The Council's complaints procedure involves the potential mediation of disputes. The Executive Secretary in effect performs the functions of a press ombudsman, settling complaints by mediation and referring some to third-party adjudication by the Complaints Committee and the Council. About 18 per cent of complaints are resolved by mediation.

The procedure is relatively simple, and telephone costs are reduced by access to a free phone and occasional sittings in places outside of Sydney. A complaint must be in writing. If mediation does not seem possible, the complaint is referred to the newspaper and the newspaper's reply is referred to the complainant.

If the complaint alleges defamation, the Council normally requires the complainant to sign a waiver stating that he or she will not take the case to court if dissatisfied with the Council's decision. Dissatisfied complainants rarely go to court, and the validity of the waiver has never

---

(metropolitan and provincial).

been tested. Only a small number of complainants were unwilling to sign the waiver and instead chose legal action.

If the complainant is not satisfied by the reply, the matter is referred to the next hearing of the Complaints Committee. A lesser used procedure involves having an assessor or panel of assessors hear a complaint. Attendance by either or both parties at a hearing is not mandatory but is useful. Hearings are informal and, at the opening, both the complainant and newspaper may, if they wish, speak briefly. Members of the Committee then pose questions, and there is a final opportunity for brief comments by the newspaper and the complainant.

The Complaints Committee consists of a majority of public members with one journalist and one publisher's representative. It drafts an adjudication which is then submitted to the full Council, which meets approximately ten times each year. In 1992, 421 complaints were received, of which 69 were adjudicated. Of those, 31 were upheld in whole or in part. All adverse adjudications were published by the publication involved.

The sanction of the Council lies in publication by the newspaper concerned of adjudications which are wholly or in part adverse to it; the essential points of the adjudication must be given prominence but, unlike under the British Press Complaints system, the adjudication does not have to be printed in full. From 1990 through 1992, only one adjudication has not been published; in that case the newspaper concerned argued that, because the complainant was another publisher, the dispute was between proprietors and thus not within the Council's jurisdiction. Concerning another adjudication, one media commentator argued that the paper concerned had not adequately reported it.

9.3   Role in Public Policy Formation

The Council, through its Freedom of Speech Committee, plays an important role in promoting press freedom, and free speech generally, by contributing to public policy debates. The Council frequently makes representations on various aspects of laws and other restrictions on free speech. These have included comments on defamation law reform, contempt law, "whistleblower" protection, the protection of journalists' confidential sources through "shield laws", proposals for constitutional guarantees of free speech at both the federal and state level, and action against the ban on political advertising in the electronic media.

The opinions of the Council are sought by government and private bodies, and by the media. The Council makes its views known in its quarterly newsletter, *Australian Press Council News*, and in its annual report, as well as by issuing frequent press releases. The Council also conducts conferences and seminars, and publishes conference reports in a series, the *Australian Press Council Conference Papers*.

The Council cooperates and shares information with a network of similar bodies and with others interested in freedom of speech and the press. The Chairman of the Australian Press Council also chairs a *pro tem* committee of the World Association of Press Councils to draft a constitution for the organization, and chairs the Executive Council, which was established in October 1992.

9.4 Australian Journalists' Association

The Australian Journalists' Association (AJA) is the professional association of Australian journalists as well as its trade union. It has recently merged with other organizations of media workers to become the Media, Entertainment and Arts Alliance (the "Media Alliance"). Matters relating to journalism are now the province of a division of the Alliance so that the AJA effectively continues within the larger organization.

The Media Alliance, as a professional association, has long been concerned with the ethics of journalism. It was the leading proponent for the establishment of the Press Council, and makes provision under its registered rules for the observance by its members of a Code of Ethics. The Code is enforced by branch Judiciary Committees from each of which appeal lies first to a branch Appeal Committee and finally to the Federal Council of the Media Alliance.

The rules compel attendance by a member when summoned to appear before a Judiciary Committee, and allow for the imposition of sanctions, including fines, suspension and even expulsion. Given that most journalists belong to the Media Alliance, these sanctions can be significant. Proceedings must be conducted fairly, and may not be published without the specific authorization of the Federal Executive or Federal Council. There are proposals to add a lay member to each Judiciary Committee and to publish the committees' findings in order to increase awareness of this facility which is not well-known among the public.

10. DEFAMATION

Each state and territory in Australia has its own defamation laws, all of which share four main features. First, defamation is a tort of strict liability; the media defendant's lack of knowledge concerning a statement's falsity is irrelevant when determining whether material is defamatory, though it may affect the amount of damages awarded. Second, defamatory material is presumed to be false, and the media defendant has the burden of proving its truth. On the other hand, the fact that a statement is false does not necessarily mean that it is defamatory. Third, it is sufficient that a statement had the *potential* to defame the plaintiff, the plaintiff does not need to prove that anyone actually lowered his or her opinion of the plaintiff as a result.

10.1 Civil and Criminal Actions

A person whose reputation has been injured by the press may bring a civil action for defamation to clear his or her name. In addition, in most jurisdictions defamation is also a criminal offence punishable by fine or imprisonment. In some jurisdictions, statutes provide that anyone who maliciously publishes a libel may be fined and imprisoned for up to one year, or up to two years if the person knew the material was untrue. There do not appear to have been any convictions of a newspaper or journalist for criminal defamation in recent times.

Federal law provides for the civil action of injurious falsehood. Under this cause of action, a plaintiff must show that a written or oral statement about him was untrue, caused him actual monetary loss, and was actuated by malice. Due to the difficulty of proving malice, actions against the press for injurious falsehood are uncommon.

The common law in Australia distinguishes between libel and slander. Libel (written defamation) is actionable even without proof that the plaintiff suffered financial loss, while to establish slander a plaintiff must show that he or she suffered actual monetary damage. This distinction has been abolished in Queensland, Tasmania and the Australian Capital Territory.

Queensland and Tasmania have codified their defamation laws and the codes amount to a complete statement of the law in these jurisdictions.[11] Western Australia also has a code, although its application is limited to civil actions. In New South Wales, South Australia, Victoria, the Australian Capital Territory and the Northern Territory, defamation law is based on the common law as modified by legislation.

10.2   What Constitutes Defamation

Whether a statement is defamatory involves determining what the statement means or "imputes", and then assessing whether that meaning or imputation satisfies the definition of defamation. What the defendant intended his or her words to convey is generally irrelevant; rather, most courts will apply the meaning that the ordinary, reasonable person would draw from the material.

In the common law jurisdictions, defamatory imputation is defined as: "matter ... calculated to injure the reputation of another, by exposing him to hatred, contempt or ridicule".[12] The definition of defamatory matter in the codes of Queensland and Tasmania is: "imputation concerning any person, or any member of his family, whether living or dead, by which the reputation of that person is likely to be injured, or by which he is likely to be injured in his profession or trade, or by which other persons are likely to be induced to shun or avoid or ridicule or despise him".[13]

10.3   Liability

Any person who intentionally or negligently takes part in, or authorizes, the publication of defamatory material is liable to be sued for defamation.[14] Thus in the case of a newspaper, the editor, writer, publisher, printer and proprietor are all potentially liable. "Innocent"

---

[11] Defamation Act, 1987 (Tasmania); Criminal Code, 1899 (Queensland), Sections 368-389.

[12] *Parmiter v. Coupland* (1840) 6 M & W 105 at 108.

[13] Criminal Code, 1899 (Queensland), Sec. 366; Defamation Act, 1957 (Tasmania), Sec. 5.

[14] *Webb v. Block* (1928) 41 CLR 331, at 362-366.

distributors are not liable, but a distributor is not considered innocent if he or she knew, or should have known, that a document contained defamatory material. Knowledge may be inferred if the allegedly defamatory material appeared in a publication with a reputation for publishing such material.

An action for defamation may be initiated anywhere the allegedly defamatory material was published. Publication is said to occur in each place where the material is read, seen or heard by a person other than the person defamed.[15] Thus if a publication is read in more than one state or territory, the plaintiff may sue in the jurisdiction which offers the best advantages. National publications must constantly try not to run afoul of any of the eight different defamation laws operating in Australia.

10.4   Defences

Australian jurisdictions recognize a number of defences to defamation actions, since it is recognized that the importance of protecting an individual's reputation must be balanced against the public interest in freedom of speech. The elements of the defences, and their availability, vary between jurisdictions. The principal defences include justification, fair comment, absolute privilege, qualified privilege, unintentional defamation, triviality and apology.

The defence of justification is satisfied in half of the jurisdictions (South Australia, Victoria, Western Australia and the Northern Territory) by proving the truth of the defamatory imputation. In the other jurisdictions (Queensland, Tasmania and the Australian Capital Territory) the defendant must also demonstrate that the defamatory imputation was published for the "public benefit" and, in New South Wales, that it relates to a matter of "public interest".[16]

The defence of fair comment is available at common law in South Australia, Victoria and the ACT. The law has been partially codified in New South Wales, and is fully codified in Queensland, Tasmania and Western Australia, although in the latter state there is authority that the common law defence also continues to be available. All jurisdictions require that the comment must be: (a) fair (*i.e.*, a person could honestly hold that opinion); (b) concerning a matter of public interest (the private life of a public official is not a matter of public interest unless it is material to his or her fitness for office); and (c) based on facts which are (i) stated or indicated in the material, and (ii) true or absolutely privileged.

That information shown to be false was published in the public interest is a defence in several jurisdictions. For instance, in New South Wales, material published for the information of the public may enjoy a statutory qualified privilege under Section 22 of the Defamation Act, 1974 (NSW). However, the publisher must be able to establish that he acted reasonably in believing

---

[15] *Hewitt v. West Australian Newspapers Ltd.* (1976) ACTR 15 at 20.

[16] Defamation Act, 1974 (NSW), Sec. 15; Criminal Code, 1899 (Qld), Sec. 376; Defamation Act, 1957 (Tas), Sec. 15; Defamation Act, 1901 (NSW), Sec. 6.

the information to be true. To do so, he may need to disclose a confidential source. Since few publishers are willing to do so, it becomes exceedingly difficult to establish this defence.

10.5   Public Figures

Neither in the common law nor in any of the codes are politicians or other public officials required to sustain a greater burden of proof concerning criticisms of their public functions than are private individuals. In practice, most defamation actions are brought by public figures (in large measure because of the high costs of litigation), and most concern statements regarding public affairs. To some extent, the defence of fair comment protects newspapers against claims from public figures; nonetheless, public figures win a significant number of cases and this undeniably must have some chilling impact on papers, especially the smaller regional ones which cannot so easily afford to defend, let alone lose, a libel suit.

10.6   Remedies and Costs

The principal remedy available to a plaintiff who wins a defamation action is an award of damages. An injunction may also be sought either as an interim measure to restrain the defendant from publishing material until the case is tried or on the application of a successful plaintiff. However, courts rarely order either interim or final injunctions.

The sums awarded by juries in defamation actions have grown very large, particularly in New South Wales. For instance, in 1989 the proprietor of a Sydney seafood restaurant was awarded A\$100,000 (US\$ 70,000) after a negative review by the food critic of the *Sydney Morning Herald*.

The losing party normally must pay an assessed proportion of the other party's costs, which normally are high (comparable to costs in England). The high cost of civil litigation is an important issue, and one which is the subject of a Senate inquiry. Legal aid is not normally available for defamation or malicious falsehood, and contingency fees are not allowed. However, government ministers have sometimes had their costs underwritten.

10.7   The Sociology of Defamation

A recent study comparing US and Australian litigation concluded that Australians, who are otherwise less litigious than Americans, instituted substantially more defamation suits per capita than Americans.[17] This was particularly so in Sydney where the caseload was up to 80 times higher per capita than in the US.

Despite the absence of a public figure defence in Australia (which logically would encourage Australian politicians to bring more suits), in fact the proportion of suits instituted by politicians was about the same in the two countries. However, the grounds of defamation actions by politicians in Australia were less serious than in the US; a statement that a

---

[17] M Newcity, "The Sociology of Defamation in Australia and the United States", 26 *Texas Int'l L J* (1991), 1-69.

politician was incompetent would be far more likely to sustain a defamation verdict in Australia than in the US.

While many more cases in the US are settled in pre-trial procedures, of those which proceed to trial in both countries about two thirds result in verdicts favourable to the plaintiff. On appeal, slightly more than 60 per cent of verdicts against defendants are overturned in the US, a success rate far higher than Australian defamation defendants can expect.

10.8 Proposals for Reform

Australia's defamation laws have been criticized for procedural complexities and inconsistencies among states. Notwithstanding recommendations for reform and uniformity, especially by the Australian Law Reform Commission of 1979[18], neither has yet been realized. The three eastern state Attorneys-General are considering proposals for reform, and law reform bills are also under consideration.

Arguing that the pendulum had swung too far towards protecting private reputations rather than the public interest, the Press Council issued a seven-point proposal for reform[19]: 1) where the plaintiff is a public figure, different considerations should apply in determining the balance between public interest and the protection of reputation (as recognized by the jurisprudence of the European Court of Human Rights and the US); 2) constitutional, or at the very least, legislative guarantees of free speech, including ones at the state level, should be introduced; 3) consideration should be given to whether the plaintiff should be required to prove fault or bad faith on the part of a media defendant; 4) a request for a retraction or opportunity to reply should be a pre-requisite to a defamation action; 5) where the press merely quotes statements of others (such as public figures), it should be a defence that the sources are identified and the matter is of public interest (the "attributed statement" or "neutral reportage privilege" defence); 6) consideration should be given to instituting a fast-track procedure for plaintiffs interested in a speedy remedy, whereby the sole remedy would be a declaratory judgment; and 7) the wider use of methods of alternative dispute resolution, other than resort to the courts, should be encouraged.

---

[18] Australian Law Reform Commission, *Report No. 11 - Unfair Publication: Defamation and Privacy* (1979).

[19] *Australian Press Council General Press Release* 145, see also *Australian Press Council Annual Report* 15, 1991 and *Australian Press Council News*, May, August 1992.

11.　INVASION OF PRIVACY

Under Australian law, there is no general tort of privacy. However, the laws relating to nuisance, trespass, breach of confidence and the use of listening devices provide a measure of relief for certain intrusions into privacy.

In 1988 the Commonwealth Parliament enacted the *Privacy Act* 1988 (Cth) which established the office of Privacy Commissioner.[20] The Commissioner may take privacy protection measures in relation to Commonwealth departments and agencies. The Act establishes rules of conduct for the disclosure of personal information about individuals, but these apply only to Commonwealth departments and agencies.[21] New South Wales, under the Privacy Committee Act, 1975 (NSW), Section 5, established a Privacy Committee which mediates complaints of unjustifiable invasions of privacy. It also engages in research and education and promotes law reform. Its sanction is to publish the names of "offenders" in its report to the Parliament.

In 1991, a Privacy Bill to create a tort of privacy was introduced into the South Australian Parliament.[22] After some debate, the Bill was re-submitted in 1992; its new version would not create a tort of privacy but rather would create a Privacy Committee along the lines established in New South Wales which could mediate complaints and take measures to protect personal information about individuals held by government departments.

12.　RIGHT OF REPLY AND/OR CORRECTION

There is no right of reply or correction in Australian law.

13.　INSULTS TO GOVERNMENT INSTITUTIONS OR OFFICIALS

There are no special causes of action for, or laws prohibiting, insults against the Head of State or other government officials or institutions.

---

[20] Privacy Act 1988 (Cth) Pt IV.

[21] *Id.* at Pts. III, IV, V.

[22] The Press Council argued that this would impose a chill on investigative reporting. *See Australian Press Council General Press Releases* 137 and 138; *Australian Press Council Annual Report* (1992), 37-40.

14. OFFICIAL SECRECY AND ACCESS TO GOVERNMENT-HELD INFORMATION

The Freedom of Information Act, 1982 (Cth) gives members of the public a right of access to documents held by government departments and agencies. The Act provides that every person has a legally enforceable right of access to government documents unless the documents fall within one of the exempt categories. The exempt categories include documents affecting national security, international relations, defence, enforcement of the law, protection of public safety, the national economy, personal privacy and commercial secrecy, as well as Cabinet documents and internal working documents.

A government agency may refuse to allow access to documents only if doing so would "substantially and unreasonably divert the resources of the agency from its operations or interfere substantially and unreasonably with the performance of the Minister of his functions".[23] Agency decisions against access to information must be accompanied by reasons, and appeals may be taken to the Administrative Appeals Tribunal and from there, to the Federal Court.

Since 1982 a number of amendments have strengthened the Act. The 1983 Amending Act, among other changes, provided an additional "public interest" test for several of the exemptions. The common law also acknowledges that information obtained in breach of a duty of confidentiality to the government should only be restrained if the public interest so requires.[24] Although the public interest may be a defence to charges of breach of confidentiality, no laws provide additional protection to government "whistleblowers" who reveal information of government wrongdoing or inefficiency from discharge or other employment discipline. Legislation is, however, being considered in at least Queensland and New South Wales.

There are approximately 180 secrecy clauses in other federal acts which further limit the freedom of information legislation. For instance, under the Crimes Act, 1914 (Cth) a Commonwealth officer is guilty of an offence if he or she communicates information which that person has a duty to treat as a secret to someone who is not authorized to receive it (Section 79). A journalist who receives such information and publishes it is guilty of an offence if he or she had reason to believe it was communicated in contravention of this provision. It is a criminal offence to publish such information regardless of whether the disclosure of the information would harm the public.

---

[23] *Id.* at Article 24.

[24] *Attorney-General v. Jonathan Cape Ltd* (1976) QB 752; *Commonwealth v. John Fairfax and Sons Ltd* (1980) 147 CLR 39 51-53 (per Mason J); *Attorney-General (UK) v. Heinemann Publishers Australia Pty Ltd* (1987) 8 NSW LR 341; *Attorney-General (UK) v. Heinemann Publishers* (1988) 78 ALR 449.

In *Commonwealth v. John Fairfax and Sons Ltd*[25], the High Court of Australia denied the government's request for a permanent injunction to prohibit two newspapers from publishing extracts from a book which disclosed a number of documents given to the book's authors by a government agent. The Court was not satisfied that restraint of publication was in the public interest; the likelihood that the Australian government would be embarrassed in its relations with other governments was not in itself a sufficient argument for the Court to issue an injunction.

Although in the *Spycatcher* case the Australian courts refused to restrain publication of a book by a former high-ranking officer of the British Security Service which the UK courts had banned, this was based on a refusal to apply foreign law rather than on a more liberal approach to freedom of the press.[26]

Several federal laws prohibit the publication of material deemed to affect Australia's national security or defence. For example, it is a serious criminal offence to disclose the identity of a member of the Australian Security Intelligence Organisation (ASIO). In September 1988, the Attorney General obtained injunctions preventing information about the identity and activities of an ASIO officer being published in the magazine, *The Eye*.

Australia established a "D" notice system in 1952, whereby notices are issued to media organizations by the federal Defence, Press and Broadcasting Committee listing subjects concerning defence and security measures that editors are requested not to publish. Compliance with the "D" notice system is voluntary; however, failure to comply is likely to be "punished" by removal of the publication from the government's list of publications which receive early notice of stories.

## 15.	ACCESS TO AND DISCLOSURE OF COURT DOCUMENTS AND PROCEEDINGS

### 15.1	Access to Court Hearings

Under the common law in Australia, court proceedings are usually open to the press and public. All information before a court is made available to those present[27], and the press is entitled to publish reports of court proceedings and public documents so long as "fair and accurate". Exceptions to the open court rule include cases involving family law matters and children. In some jurisdictions cases involving children or sexual offences are closed to the public, as may be criminal proceedings involving inquests or inquiries. Courts may issue suppression orders prohibiting the publication of evidence.

---

[25] (1980) 147 CLR 39 at 49-50.

[26] *Attorney-General (UK) v. Heinemann Publishers, supra* note 24.

[27] *Re Andres Dun* (1932) S R Q at 16 (per Henchman, J.), at 17 (per Douglas, J).

An important and as yet unsettled question is whether the media have standing to argue the public interest when a suppression order is proposed or requested in court. There are conflicting decisions. The Supreme Court of Western Australia has ruled that the media does have standing;[28] the Supreme Court of New South Wales has ruled to the contrary.[29]

15.2   Contempt of Court

The law of contempt of court aims to prevent the publication of material which risks prejudicing a fair trial or breaches a court order. Australia has no statutory definition of contempt of court. There are four forms of common law contempt.

First, *sub judice* contempts, which are criminal in nature, involve the publishing of information either with the intent to interfere with the course of justice or which has a tendency to interfere with the course of justice. Examples of this form of contempt include publishing material that may prejudice jurors or the judge, influence witnesses or prejudge an accused's innocence or guilt.

Second, contempt of court may be charged for publishing information which tends to interfere with the administration of justice as a continuing process. Such acts as scandalizing a court, revealing jurors' deliberations, revealing what has taken place in court, revealing information concealed from those present at court proceedings and alleging without grounds that a judge is biased in favour of or against a particular litigant fall within this category. At issue is whether the material is such that it tends to impair public confidence in the judicial proceedings.

Third, improper behaviour in court may be found to be contempt. As applied to journalists, this law may be invoked if a journalist refuses to give evidence on the ground that doing so would cause him to reveal the identity of confidential sources of information.[30]

Finally, contempt may stem from breaching an undertaking to a court or disobeying a court order. A media organization could be held in contempt if it published material in violation of a court order.

---

[28] *Re Bromfield; Ex parte West Australian Newspapers Ltd* (1991) 6 WAR 153.

[29] *John Fairfax Group Pty Ltd v. Local Court (NSW)* (1991) 26 NSWLR 131.

[30] *See infra* Section 19 for a discussion of protection of journalists' sources.

16. ACCESS TO AND DISCLOSURE OF LEGISLATIVE DOCUMENTS AND PROCEEDINGS

The common law doctrine of contempt of Parliament allows the two Houses of Parliament to restrict the content and timing of publication of reports on their actions and the actions of their members and committees. Contempt of Parliament is any act or omission that directly impedes the function of Parliament. Contempt of Parliament includes publication of the following types of material: 1) inaccurate reports of debates or proceedings of a House or committee; 2) articles "reflecting" on a House; 3) materials concerning a committee's proceedings before they have been presented to the relevant House; and 4) information that deters a witness from giving evidence.

17. COMMERCIAL SECRECY AND ACCESS TO INFORMATION HELD BY PRIVATE PARTIES

The courts have general jurisdiction to grant relief for a misuse of confidential information. In an action for breach of confidence, a plaintiff must show that a media organization divulged information that had a "quality of confidence about it", that was imparted in circumstances importing an obligation of confidence, and that there had been an unauthorized use of the information to the detriment of the party communicating it.[31]

Actions have been brought for disclosure of information regarding trade secrets; personal secrets (marital confidences and information about sexual conduct); tribal, cultural or religious secrets; and secret government information.

Where a media organization knows, discovers, or ought to have known that a person supplied it with information obtained in confidence, the organization is liable for breach of confidence if it publishes the information.[32]

There is a public interest defence where information divulged exposes an "iniquity" that is a crime, fraud or misdeed.[33] It is not clear whether the concept of "iniquity" is limited only to the disclosure of serious crimes.[34] It may be that the Australian courts will follow those English courts which have changed the defence into a balancing test.[35]

---

[31] *Coco v. A N Clark (Engineers) Ltd* (1969) RPC 41.

[32] *Seager v. Copydex Ltd* 1967 All ER 415.

[33] *Initial Service Ltd v. Putterill* (1968) I QB 396, 405 (per Lord Denning).

[34] *A v. Hayden* (1984) 156 CLR 532, 545-546 (per Gibbs CJ, Wilson and Dawson JJ).

[35] *See Woodward v. Hutchins* (1977) 1 WLR 760, 764 (per Lord Denning); *Attorney-General (UK) v. Heinemann Publishers Australia Pty Ltd* (1987) 8 NSW LR 341, 382 (per Powell J). In *Westpac Banking Corporation v. John Fairfax Group Pty Ltd* (1991), AIPC para 90.805, lawyers' letters relating to certain foreign currency loans were leaked to newspapers which were enjoined from publishing them. Powell J. refused to discharge the injunction;

18. PRIOR RESTRAINTS

Injunction is available as a remedy in civil cases, and there is no general doctrine against prior restraints on publication. However, interlocutory injunctions (pending a full hearing on the merits) are rarely issued in defamation actions. Courts are reluctant to grant injunctions which would have the effect of restraining the discussion of matters of public interest.[36]

Courts are more willing to issue injunctions in actions involving information which the plaintiff claims is confidential, so long as the plaintiff has not made otherwise private affairs public by seeking publicity.[37] The publication of government information will be restrained only if it is established that non-publication is in the public interest.[38] Embarrassment to Australia's foreign relations is insufficient reason to restrain publication.[39]

19. PROTECTION OF SOURCES

Australian law does not specifically protect the confidentiality of journalists' sources. The code of ethics of the Australian Journalists' Association, however, states: "In all circumstances the [journalists] shall respect all confidences received in the course of their calling."

Journalists cannot claim professional privilege to avoid disclosing their source of information if they are called before courts, Royal Commissions or parliamentary inquiries. In December 1989, Tony Barass, a Western Australian journalist, was jailed for seven days for refusing to disclose to a court the name of the person who had sent him confidential records from the Australian Taxation Office relating to a prominent public figure. In 1992 Joe Budd, a Queensland journalist then residing in the United States was jailed for 14 days for refusing to disclose the source of an article about a court case.[40]

---

it had been argued that the confidential information related to an impropriety and therefore ought in the public interest to be exposed. He observed that appropriate disclosure might be to a strictly limited group, such as the regulatory authorities, rather than by publication in the mass media.

[36] *Chappel v. Channel 9 Pty Ltd* (1988) Aust. Torts Rep. 80-187.

[37] *Lennon v. News Group Newspapers Ltd* (1978) FSR 573.

[38] *Commonwealth v. John Fairfax and Sons Ltd, supra* note 24. For criticism of the use of injunctions to restrain the publication of government information when confidentiality is claimed, *see Australian Press Council Annual Report* (No. 7, 1983); *Annual Report* (No. 13, 1989).

[39] *Id. at* 51-53.

[40] The Australian Press Council has called on both federal and state governments to introduce shield laws to effect recognition of the principle of respect for the confidentiality of journalists' sources. The Council prefers the American approach and proposes that, to obtain the identity of a source, a party must show that: 1) there is probable cause to believe that the newspaper has information that is clearly relevant to a specific probable violation of the law; 2) the information sought cannot be obtained by alternative means less destructive of freedom of speech and of the press; and 3) the interest in obtaining the information is compelling.

20. RESTRICTIONS ON OFFENSIVE LANGUAGE AGAINST IDENTIFIABLE GROUPS

Australia adopted the Racial Discrimination Act in 1975 which makes discrimination on the grounds of race, colour, descent and national or ethnic origin unlawful. Clause 8 of the Australian Press Council's Principles states that "a newspaper should not place gratuitous emphasis on the race, nationality or colour of individuals or groups". The AJA's Code of Ethics contains a similar provision.

New South Wales passed the first law in Australia to declare vilification on the ground of race unlawful. Under Section 20C(1) of the Anti-Discrimination (Amendment) Act, 1989, it is "unlawful for a person, by a public act, to incite hatred towards, serious contempt for, or severe ridicule of, a person or group of persons, on the ground of the race of the person or members of the group". There are three categories of acts that are exempted from civil liability, the one of primary relevance to the media being "a fair report of a public act". The subjectivity inherent in such a notion of fairness leaves room for the media to report without close attention to the potential for promoting negative stereotypes and inciting ridicule or contempt.

Anti-vilification legislation was also introduced in Western Australia under the Criminal Code Amendment (Incitement to Racial Hatred) Act, 1989.

21. BLASPHEMY, OBSCENITY AND PROTECTION OF PUBLIC MORALS

Publication of an "obscene libel" is a common law misdemeanour. Australia has adopted the English test for determining whether a publication is obscene: "whether the tendency of the matter charged as obscenity is to deprave and corrupt those whose minds are open to such immoral influences, and into whose hands a publication of this sort might fall".[41]

In addition, the courts assess whether the material is offensive or indecent in the sense that it outrages public decency, and whether it offends community standards of decency in the circumstances and in the manner in which it is presented. Whether the material is distributed to the general public or only to a small, distinct group is also a relevant factor.

Though most prosecutions for libel deal with sexual matters, depictions of violence, cruelty and harmful drug taking may be found libellous as well. Most states and territories have created statutory offences to supplement the common law misdemeanours. Several have established classification schemes, which may operate to prohibit or restrict access to the displaying and advertising of printed material. The legislation typically refers to "obscene or indecent" material, which is interpreted to mean offensive to contemporary community standards. The censorship laws administered through the Office of Film and Literature Classification place the burden on the publisher of a potentially obscene work to first submit it to the censorship authorities and to obtain an appropriate classification.

---

[41] *R v. Hicklin* (1868) LR 3 QB 360 at 371, per Cockburn, CJ.

It is also a common law offence to publish blasphemous material, meaning material that is offensive to the Church of England. The manner in which a comment is made, rather than the nature of the comment, determines whether it is blasphemous. For instance, a comment denying or attacking the fundamental doctrines of Christianity will not be an offence if expressed in a temperate manner. There have been no prosecutions for blasphemy in Australia for many years. In 1992, the New South Wales Law Reform Commission recommended abolition of the crime of blasphemy.[42]

22. RESTRICTIONS ON ADVERTISING

The Smoking and Tobacco Products Advertisements (Prohibition) Act, 1989 (Cth) prohibits cigarette and tobacco advertising in the print media. The ban has been criticized as discriminatory in that it exempts advertising in newspapers printed or published outside of Australia which are brought into Australia for sale, free distribution or personal use.

In 1991, the federal government introduced legislation to proscribe political advertising on radio and television. This attracted widespread opposition, not only by political parties but also the Human Rights Commission and the Press Council. The Bill was amended to restrict advertising only during election and referendum campaigns. The High Court invalidated the legislation in August 1992.[43]

CONCLUSION

In its long and unbroken traditions as a democracy, Australia has been well served by its press. The Australian press' ethical standards and objectivity are equal to the best in the world. Concern in recent years about its financial state have been allayed to some extent, and a number of papers continue to compete in the national market, although most regions have only one main paper. Concerns about the increasing concentration of press and cross-media ownership have been addressed in part by application of the anti-trust provisions of the Trade Practices Act, restrictions on cross media ownership in the Broadcasting Services Act, the considerable diversity and internal competition between publishing groups, and the growing proliferation of electronic sources of information and analysis.

It is nevertheless unfortunate that competition from this proliferation has had the effect of reducing the number of newspapers in Australia. Afternoon newspapers have been particularly affected. The mainly broadsheet morning newspapers maintain high standards of quality, but only the two largest cities having a second newspaper, each the result of the merging of a

---

[42] The Australian Press Council supported the observations of Law Reform Commissioner Professor David Weisbrot that "Blasphemy is an anachronistic and uncertain offence which is more likely to cause problems between groups than to prevent them." *Australian Press Council News* (May 1992).

[43] *See supra* Section 1.

morning and an afternoon title. While there are two national newspapers, the loss of titles, of separate editorial perspectives and of employment is to be regretted. It is to be hoped that the growth of the specialized and local press can balance this.

Good, serious reporting continues, although some journalists argue that less investigative work is being done than previously. This is said to be primarily due to costs but there also is an impression among those journalists that management is coolly disposed towards investigative reporting. On the other hand, it is pointed out that the mass media (including radio and television) have uncovered corruption and mismanagement in government as well as big business, under both conservative (National Party) and Labour governments.

The defamation and contempt laws, and especially the number of successful defamation suits by public figures, undeniably has had some chilling effect on reporting and editorials, particularly by mid-sized and smaller papers.[44] It probably has not had a great impact on quality investigative reporting, owing to the fact that investigative reporters generally are committed to ascertaining and double-checking the truth of their stories.

The Freedom of Information Act works reasonably well, although obtaining documents can often involve substantial costs and delays and even the initiation of legal action. There is a need for freedom of information acts at the state level.

The greatest threat to media freedom is the absence of an express guarantee of freedom of expression, press freedom or access to information in the federal constitution or any of the state constitutions. Thus, an aggregation of otherwise well meaning measures, as well as those aspects of statutory and common law which come from a more restrictive era, can deleteriously effect the full exercise of press freedom in Australia.

---

[44] *See* Newcity, "The Sociology of Defamation", *supra* note 17.

Chapter 2

PRESS LAW IN AUSTRIA

Walter Berka

INTRODUCTION

The constitutional basis of Austria is the Federal Constitution of 1920 (*Bundes-Verfassungsgesetz*). The Constitution is guided by the rule of law and based on republican, democratic and federal principles as well as on the strict division of legislative, executive and judicial powers.

The constitutional guarantee of basic rights draws on a tradition that is more than a century old. Most of the basic rights and freedoms were first guaranteed in the Basic Law of 1867, which is now included in the Federal Constitution of 1920. Since 1945, the most important change in the Austrian law concerning human rights was Austria's ratification and incorporation in 1958 of the European Convention on Human Rights (ECHR), followed in 1964 by full incorporation of the Convention into the Constitution. These developments have deeply influenced the legal system's protection of fundamental rights including, in particular, freedom of expression and freedom of the press.[1]

1.   RELEVANT CONSTITUTIONAL PROVISIONS

In Austria, the right to freedom of expression, as well as the right of the press to be free from prior censorship and from any form of licensing, is expressly guaranteed. Article 13 of the Basic Law provides:

> Everyone has the right to express his opinion freely, within the limits established by law, in speech, in writing, in print or in pictorial form.

> The press may neither be subject to censorship nor to the licence system. Administrative postal prohibitions cannot be extended to apply to printed matter in the country.

---

[1] For more extensive discussions of Austria's law and practice concerning the press *see*: W Berka, *Das Recht der Massenmedien* (The Law on the Mass Media) (Wien, Köln, Graz: Böhlau Verlag, 1989); W Berka, "Die Kommunikationsfreiheit in Österreich" (Freedom of Communication in Austria), *Europäische Grundrecht-Zeitschrift* (1982), 413-27 (a revised and updated version of this article will be published in 1993 by Engel Verlag (Strasbourg) in a reader on fundamental rights in Austria; R Hartmann & S Rieder, *Kommentar zum Mediengesetz* (Commentary on the Media Act) (Wien: Manz Verlag, 1985). Information about developments in Austrian media law and important decisions of the courts may be found in the periodical, *Medien und Recht* (Wien).

This constitutional provision was supplemented after World War I by a resolution of the Provisional National Assembly (*Provisorische Nationalversammlung*), which has constitutional status as well, affirming the freedom of the press and the prohibition of censorship.

The practical importance of these constitutional rules was rather restricted until a few years ago because the guaranteed freedoms were only rights "within the framework of law". The Constitution gave Parliament the competence to determine the scope and limits of freedom of expression. The only restriction which was binding on Parliament was the prohibition of censorship in advance of publication. Laws which set up procedures for censoring cinema and theatre performances were invalidated by the Constitutional Court.[2] Other legal restraints, however, remained outside the scope of the constitutional guarantee, even if statutes put unreasonable or excessive restrictions on press freedom.

Over the last few decades, the significance of the constitutional guarantee of freedom of expression has been steadily growing. As already mentioned, this is partly due to the fact that the rights and freedoms of the ECHR have become part of the Austrian Constitution and supplement the old Austrian civil liberties. In addition, the fact that the Constitutional Court has shown an increasingly rights-oriented approach has also accorded more importance to the right to freedom of expression. Finally, the Austrian courts have displayed a growing readiness to follow the relevant case-law of the European Court of Human Rights to meet a common European standard of human rights protection.[3] Thus, for instance, the decision of the European Court in the frequently cited *Lingens* case has prompted a change in the law of libel, although some aspects of libel law may still fall short of Article 10's requirements.[4]

In its present day practice the Constitutional Court applies Article 13 of the 1867 Basic Law and Article 10 of the Convention together and unites the guaranteed freedoms under the notion of "freedom of communication".[5] The reliance on Article 10 of the Convention has led to an extension of the scope of the guaranteed freedom in more than one respect:

(a)   Freedom of communication now includes the right to receive information set forth in Article 10. Journalists may invoke this basic right, for example, if they are prevented

---

[2] VfSlg (Decisions of the Austrian Constitutional Court) 552/1926, 630/1926, 949/1928, 1089/1928, 1829/1949, 1830/1949, 1846/1949. The prohibition of censorship is still taken very seriously. *See* Section 18, *infra*.

[3] For instance, the Constitutional Court cited the *The Sunday Times* case, regarding the importance of press freedom, in VfSlg 11.297/1982 *(Hainburg* case), *see* note 24 *infra*. The Constitutional Court also referred to various decisions of the European Commission of Human Rights in VfSlg. 10.948/1986 (*Die ganze Woche* case), *see* note 31 *infra*.

[4] *Lingens,* Judgment of 8 July 1986, Series A no. 103 (ruling that the limits of acceptable criticism regarding politicians in their public capacities are wider than regarding private citizens and that a defamation defendant must not be required to prove the truth of a value-judgement). The courts have cited *Lingens* in a number of decisions. *See, e.g.,* the decisions of the Supreme Court, 18 March 1987, 9 Os 18, 19/87; and 27 Jan. 1986, Evidenzblatt 1987/126; and the decision of the Vienna Court of Appeal, 2 Dec. 1986, 27 Bs 545/66, in *Medien und Recht* (1986), 11.

[5] The text of Article 10 is set forth in Appendix A.

from getting information by acts of the police or other public authorities (*see* Section 14 *infra*).

(b) Freedom of communication now also includes the freedom to impart information, whereas previously it was restricted to the expression of value judgments and opinions.

(c) The expression of value judgments has received additional protection, so that journalists no longer have to try to establish the truth of their opinions (*see* Section 10.2 *infra*.)

(d) Commercial speech is no longer excluded from the constitutional protection (*see* Section 22 *infra*).

(e) Most importantly, acts of Parliament restricting freedom of expression or press freedom are no longer sacrosanct but instead are subject to a very meticulous judicial review by the Constitutional Court under Article 10. This includes a necessity-test which inquires whether a restriction upon freedom is necessary in a democratic society. Since the concept of necessity implies the existence of a pressing social need, it also includes the principle of proportionality which has become the main battlefield of judicial review under Article 10. Thus, the Constitutional Court in recent years has invalidated laws that had placed unreasonable limits on the distribution of newspapers or the mailing of printed materials.[6]

2. DISTRIBUTION OF POWERS BETWEEN CENTRAL AND REGIONAL GOVERNMENT

Austria is a federal parliamentary democracy, comprised of nine *Länder* (provinces). Laws which affect the press are enacted and executed by the federation; the *Länder* do not have any relevant competencies in this field.

3. ROLE OF THE COURTS

The Austrian judicial system has three branches: the *Verfassungsgerichthof* (Constitutional Court) reviews the compatibility of legislative and administrative acts with the Constitution; the *Verwaltungsgerichtshof* (Administrative Court) examines matters affecting the legality of administration; and the *Oberster Gerichtshof* (Supreme Court) hears appeals from the judicial courts, both criminal and civil. The judicial courts include local courts, provincial and district courts, and four higher provincial court in Vienna, Graz, Innsbruck and Linz.

---

[6] See VfSlg 11.314/1987.

The Constitutional Court is the main guardian of constitutional rights. Anyone who feels that his or her basic rights have been infringed by an administrative act may appeal to this court. Furthermore, the Court has the power to declare invalid any statute which is incompatible with the basic rights set forth in the Constitution, including the rights and freedoms set forth in the European Convention. Decisions of the penal and civil courts cannot be appealed to the Constitutional Court; however, these courts can refer a law to the Constitutional Court when they believe that it violates a basic right.

Although the Constitutional Court is the main arbiter of constitutional rights, the other courts no longer hesitate to apply constitutional guarantees in civil or criminal cases. It is a broadly accepted principle that all legal provisions must be interpreted in accordance with the jurisprudence of the Constitutional Court concerning fundamental rights, including the principles of necessity and proportionality. This trend, however, has only emerged within the last decade; previously, the courts considered their only task to be to apply the criminal or civil law without regard to constitutional principles.

Because laws which affect the press are found in criminal as well as civil law, the jurisdiction of both the criminal and civil courts is important. Several provisions of the Media Act (for instance, concerning the right of reply and compensation claims for libel and invasion of privacy), although belonging to civil law in substance, are applied by criminal courts which employ their own specialized "media judges".[7]

4.   STATUS OF INTERNATIONAL HUMAN RIGHTS TREATIES IN NATIONAL LAW

The European Convention on Human Rights, ratified by Austria in 1958, was directly incorporated into Austrian constitutional law in 1964. Everyone is entitled to rely on the Convention's substantive protections, and the courts and administrative authorities must observe its obligations directly. Austria has also accepted the obligation under Article 25 to allow individuals to file applications against Austria with the European Commission of Human Rights.

Austria ratified the International Covenant on Civil and Political Rights (ICCPR) in 1978, and ratified its First Optional Protocol in 1987, thereby granting individuals the right to file complaints against Austria with the UN Human Rights Committee. However, the Covenant has not been incorporated into Austrian constitutional law and is not directly applicable by the courts. Compared to the European Convention, its practical importance is negligible.

---

[7] *See* Media Act, Article 41(2).

5. STATUTORY FRAMEWORK

The most important law concerning the press is the Media Act (*Mediengesetz*) of 1981.[8] This law replaced the Austrian Press Act (*Pressegesetz*) of 1922 and created a much more liberal legal framework for the press.

In principle, the Media Act applies to all the mass media. Thus, some of its provisions affect broadcasting, although there also exists a separate Radio and Television Act.[9] As concerns the press, several provisions of the Media Act (discussed below) are particularly important: regulatory provisions for printed publications; the right of reply; legal protection of the personality (libel and privacy) which complement the relevant criminal and civil law provisions; special criminal procedural provisions with reference to criminal offences involving the media (called *Medieninhaltsdelikte*), such as concerning confiscation of publications; protection of the editor's privilege; and protection of sources.

Various other laws, discussed throughout this chapter, also affect the press.

6. REGULATION OF OWNERSHIP

Concentration of ownership in the newspaper market is extraordinarily high. According to an international study, Austria at the beginning of the 1970s already had the second highest concentration of ownership of daily papers among the industrial nations. Since then the process of "newspaper-dying" has continued. Currently, only about a dozen independent dailies are still published. The three papers with the largest circulations account for two thirds of the total market, and the German "WAZ" group owns nearly 50 per cent of the two largest papers published in Vienna.[10] The media giant - comprising WAZ, the two largest papers published in Vienna, and a number of controlled enterprises -- also owns several periodicals, including *Profil* and *Wochenpresse* (in which it has a 50 per cent interest), the two most influential political magazines in Austria, as well as several popular magazines.

---

[8] *Bundesgesetz vom 12 June 1981 über die Presse und andere publizistische Medien (Mediengesetz)* BGBl 1981/314, as last amended by BGBl 1988/233.

[9] *Bundesgesetz über die Aufgaben und die Einrichtung des Österreichischen Rundfunks (Rundfunkgesetz — RFG)*, BGBl 1984/379, as last amended BGBl 1987/606. The Austrian government has always maintained a monopoly on radio and television broadcasting. Only the Austrian Broadcasting Corporation (ORF), an independent public enterprise, is entitled to broadcast radio and television programmes. Objective and impartial reporting, representation of a wide variety of opinions, balanced programming and complete independence for the staff is guaranteed by constitutional and legal provisions. Foreign programmes can be received by cable or satellite without interference. The European Commission of Human Rights declared admissible several applications challenging the Austrian broadcasting monopoly (applications no. 13914/88, 15041/89, 15717/89, 15779/89, 17Z07/90) which have not yet been decided. A bill providing for the licensing of private local radio stations is expected to be adopted in 1993.

[10] These are the *Neue Kronen-Zeitung* (with a daily circulation of nearly 1 million) and the *Kurier* (with a daily circulation of more than 400,000). Together they account for more than 80 per cent of the circulation of all dailies in Vienna and more than 50 per cent of the circulation of dailies throughout Austria.

Foreign, in particular German, companies hold substantial interests in some papers. For example, the German publisher Springer holds controlling interests in two dailies, *Der Standard* and *Tiroler Tageszeitung*, as well as in the *News*, a new weekly magazine.

The economic health, especially of the smaller newspapers, is precarious. Newspapers owned by political parties, which previously were very important, are steadily diminishing in number owing to financial difficulties.

The government administers an extensive press promotion system whereby it gives subsidies to *all* daily newspapers.[11] In recent years, the same amount has been given to each paper (including market leaders) and the total amount of subsidies has reached more than AS 100 million (US$ 9.1 million) annually. The aim of the subsidies is to promote the survival of as many newspapers as possible in order to maintain a correspondingly wide range of editorial opinion.

In addition to this general promotion scheme, there is a special promotion system by which the government provides subsidies to a few "smaller newspapers that are of particular importance in shaping political opinion".[12] This system may have minimized the trend towards press concentration, but has not stopped it.

Of greater economic impact than the subsidy systems are the reduced postage fees available to daily papers. The government also provides subsidies to printing enterprises.

As of the end of 1992, an amendment to the anti-trust law was under discussion which would require all mergers involving media enterprises to be submitted to the Anti-Trust Authority, which would be able to forbid any merger that would endanger the plurality of editorial opinions. It would also prevent any cross-ownership of a newspaper and a radio station which would create a local media monopoly (there are plans to begin licensing private radio stations for the first time in 1993). Some critics point out that this amendment offers too little, too late, especially because it would not require a break-up of any of the existing media enterprises.

The Media Act obliges the publisher of periodicals to publish annually the status of ownership and any existing inter-connections with other media enterprises.[13]

---

[11] Press Promotion Act of 1985 (*Presseförderungsgesetz*) 1985 BGBl 228, as last amended, BGBl 1992/465. *See also* the Periodical Promotion Act (vgl BGBl 1984/39, as last amended BGBl 1991/628), which promotes periodical publications in the field of culture and politics.

[12] Report of the Austrian Government to the UN Human Rights Committee, UN Doc. No. CCPR/C/51/Add.2 (9 Nov. 1990), para. 208.

[13] Media Act, Article 25.

7.   REGISTRATION REQUIREMENTS

There is no obligation to register the publication of a newspaper with any authority or to obtain a licence. Any such duty would be considered an infringement of the constitutional guarantee of press freedom.

It is necessary to get a trading licence in order to publish or trade in books, wholesale newspapers, or operate printing offices. The publishing of newspapers is exempted from this requirement.[14]

Newspapers and other printed material must contain an imprint which shows the names and addresses of the publishers and printers. All publications, including newspapers, must deposit several copies with public libraries free of charge; this requirement is not a measure of control but rather is intended to ensure the public's access to all publications published in Austria.[15]

8.   REGULATION OF IMPORT AND EXPORT OF PUBLICATIONS

There are no restrictions on the import and export of publications beyond those contained in the general customs laws. The right to freedom of information as guaranteed in Article 10 of the Convention also protects the right to receive newspapers from abroad without restrictions (other than those placed on the circulation of domestic papers). Although the police and customs authorities may seize foreign publications without a court order where there has been inadequate time to obtain a court order, confiscation without a basis in law violates the Constitution, according to a 1989 decision of the Constitutional Court.[16]

9.   MECHANISMS OF PRESS SELF-REGULATION

The Austrian Press Council was founded in 1961 by the Association of Austrian Newspaper Publishers and the Austrian Journalists' Union in order to provide a mechanism of voluntary self-regulation. The Council consists of 10 representatives from each organization. According to its statute, the Council aims to ensure that the press fulfils its professional obligations, and that the freedom of the press is not violated. It is responsible for maintaining the press' reputation and for determining and preventing abuses. It is also the responsibility of the Council to represent the interests of the press before Parliament, the administration and the public.

Anyone may turn to the Press Council if he or she believes that an article represents an affront to public decency, intrudes into the private sphere or disregards the obligation to

---

[14] Industrial Code (*Gewerbeordnung*) of 1973, Article 2(1) no. 18.

[15] Media Act, Articles 24 and 43.

[16] *See* VfSlg 12.104/1989 (*Demokratischer Informationsdienst* case).

provide honest and accurate reporting or any other principle of journalism. The council has drawn up a catalogue of such principles, the *Grundsätze für die publizistische Arbeit — Ehrenkodex der österreichischen Presse* (Code of Ethics).

The Council has no legal enforcement power. Its only sanction is the publication of a judgment; the Council may also direct an offending paper to publish the Council's negative judgment, but it has no power by which to compel publication. Although most of the press publications respect and publish the Press Council's findings, the most powerful Austrian newspaper, the *Neue Kronen-Zeitung*, against which there have been many negative judgments, refuses to do so. The Press Council is also criticized for having only publishers and journalists as members and for not including impartial experts or representatives of the general public. As a consequence, the public is largely unaware of the Press Council's work and it is viewed by many as having little authority.

10.   DEFAMATION

The influence of criminal law is still dominant for offences against honour and reputation, although recently there has been a trend towards greater application of civil law.

10.1   Differences between Criminal and Civil Actions

Criminal libel suits against the press are generally based on Article 111 of the Criminal Code.[17] Article 111 provides that anyone who publicly accuses another of having a contemptible character or attitude or of behaving contrary to honour or morality in such a way as to make him contemptible or otherwise lower him in public esteem shall be liable to a fine or to imprisonment for up to one year. Imprisonment in practice is virtually never ordered; in recent memory there have been no cases of imprisonment even for a few days.

If a mass media organ publishes an insult punishable by Article 111 of the Criminal Code, the aggrieved persons can claim compensation from the criminal court for the suffering (Media Act, Article 6). Compensation currently is limited by statute to AS 100,000 (US$ 9,100); an increase in this limit is expected because it is considered to be too low.

In a civil suit for libel, on the other hand, only material damage can be claimed, as well as retraction or correction of the defamatory statement.[18] In a few cases the amounts awarded can reach rather high levels (up to AS 1 million) but, because there is no compensation for non-material damage and because the insulted person has to prove the falsity of the statement,

---

[17] Bundesgesetz vom 23 Jan. 1974 über die mit gerichtlicher Strafe bedrohten Handlungen (Strafgesetzbuch — StGB) BGBl 60, as last amended BGBl 1991/628. On occasion, Article 115 of the Criminal Code, which prohibits different types of libel offences, is used.

[18] Article 1330 of the Civil Code (Allgemeines Bürgerliches Gesetzbuch vom 1 June 1811 JGS 946, as last amended BGB1 1989/656).

civil defamation has been less important than criminal defamation until recently. Nowadays civil actions are becoming more common; the mere threat of a civil action can put the journalist under pressure owing to the high cost of litigation and thus can have a negative impact on press freedom.

10.2   Defences

Previously, the only defence to criminal libel was that the statement was in fact true or, regarding an accusation which was not widely published, that the speaker reasonably believed that the statement was true. By Article 29 of the Media Act this strict burden of proof has been relieved; journalists now are not guilty of libel if they are able to establish both that they observed journalistic care (*Beweis der Wahrnehmung der journalistischen Sorgfalt*) and that there was a major public interest in the publication.

Concerning statements detrimental to business enterprises, the strict standards of competition law and unfair business practices are applied. Freedom of speech is, accordingly, severely restricted and the fact that the statement may promote a general social interest is no defence. Thus, for instance, an anti-smoking association was convicted and fined for distributing stickers which read "Only a Camel would go miles for a cigarette."[19]

10.3   Value Judgments and Public Figures

Article 111 of the Criminal Code and Article 1330 of the Civil Code apply to value judgments as well as to statements of fact. The severe case-law of the Austrian courts concerning offensive value judgments has been attenuated in the last few years as a result of decisions of the European Court of Human Rights[20] and, in general, has become more oriented towards the values of freedom of expression. In this context the status of the insulted person is considered and the courts have shown a readiness to require politicians to suffer a greater degree of criticism and scrutiny regarding matters which may affect their qualifications for public service than private persons. Nevertheless, some courts in recent decisions have remained very rigid; they treat allegations on the borderline between value-judgments and factual statements as factual statements requiring proof of truth or journalistic care, and may convict a person for a value-judgment which the court considers "excessive".

---

[19] *See* the decision of the Supreme Court, 13 Sept. 1988 (*Camel* case), published in *Medien und Recht* (1988), 194. The European Commission of Human Rights was of the opinion that the conviction did not violate Article 10 of the ECHR and thus declared the application (no. 17200/90) inadmissible.

[20] *See Lingens v. Austria*, Judgment of 8 July 1986, Series A no. 103; *Oberschlick v. Austria*, Judgment of 23 May 1991, Series A no. 204; *Schwabe v. Austria*, Judgment of 28 Aug. 1992, Series A no. 242-B.

11. INVASION OF PRIVACY

The Media Act of 1981 introduced a separate cause of action for invasion of privacy: Article 7 provides that a media organ is obliged to grant compensation if matters concerning the private life (*höchstpersönlicher Lebensbereich*) of a person are presented in such a way as to degrade him or her in public opinion. Publication is permitted in any case where there is a "connection with public life".[21] Very little use has so far been made of Article 7 and it thus appears that it will not inhibit reporting on matters of legitimate public interest.

Article 78 of the Copyright Act forbids the publication of pictures which violate legitimate interests of the person pictured. A few courts have found that there was no violation where pictures were of "public figures"; this "public figure" doctrine has not yet, but may eventually, have an impact on defamation law.

Article 113 of the Criminal Code prohibits a person from reproaching another for having committed a criminal offence in respect of which the sentence has already been served or provisionally suspended, or in respect of which the determination of the sentence has been provisionally adjourned. Reproach is only justified, pursuant to Article 114, if required by a legal duty, protected by a legal right, or compelled for special reasons within the meaning of Article 113. In the case of *Schwabe v. Austria*,[22] the European Court of Human Rights recently ruled that a conviction under Article 113 violated Article 10 of the ECHR because the Austrian courts refused to consider as a defence that the reproach was in the public interest (namely, that a politician's prior conviction for a driving accident which resulted in a death could be relevant to his fitness for political office).

12. RIGHT OF REPLY AND/OR CORRECTION

Under the 1922 Press Act, any person who had been the subject of an incorrect statement in the press was granted the right to publish a reply free of charge without having to establish the reply's accuracy; the responsible editor was criminally liable if he refused to publish the reply. The right of reply was fundamentally reformed by the Media Act of 1981 (Article 9), which extended the right to all mass media, and established that any mass media organ may refuse to publish a reply if it is untrue. This reform constitutes a substantial improvement; however, the complicated procedural rules for establishing both the right of reply and the right not to publish a reply are still criticized. If a media organ refuses to publish a legitimate reply the offended person can sue for a penalty (and may be awarded increasing amounts if the media defendant continues to refuse.)[23]

---

[21] For more information about the right to privacy *see*: G Hager, "Persönlichkeitsschutz im Straf- und Medienrecht", (1991); G Korn & J Neumayer, "Persönlichkeitsschutz im Zivil- und Wettbewerbsrecht", (1991).

[22] Judgment of 28 Aug. 1992, Series A no. 242-B.

[23] For more information about the right of reply, *see* B Weis, "Handbuch der Entgegnung", *Medien und Recht* (1989).

If a libel suit is filed against a newspaper, it can be obliged to publish a statement announcing the filing of such an action, or else risk having the offending issue confiscated (*see* Section 18, *infra*).

13.   INSULTS TO GOVERNMENT INSTITUTIONS OR OFFICIALS

Certain public authorities and institutions (including the federal Parliament and the national army) are protected against defamation by Article 116 of the Criminal Code. (Members of Parliament and other public officials must rely upon Article 111, *see* Section 10 *supra*.) Public disparagement of the Austrian state and its national symbols is punishable pursuant to Article 248. Treason and sedition constitute crimes if violence is applied or threatened (Article 242). None of these provisions has been used inappropriately against the press in the last few decades.

14.   OFFICIAL SECRECY AND ACCESS TO GOVERNMENT-HELD INFORMATION

Article 20(4) of the Federal Constitution obliges the government and all the other administrative authorities to make available to all citizens information about all matters concerning their areas of activity. It reads, in relevant part:

> All federal, state and local government bodies and all corporations under public law must give information on affairs within their responsibility unless laws protecting confidentiality provide for non-disclosure . . . ..

This right is granted to every citizen, not only to journalists. More detailed provisions are set forth in the federal and *Länder* Freedom of Information Acts (*Auskunftspflichtgesetze*). If information is denied, the person seeking information can appeal to the Administrative Court.

The right of access to information is restricted by the provisions concerning official secrecy, also anchored in the Federal Constitution (Article 20(3)). Whereas the government previously asserted that a great deal of information was protected by official secrecy, nowadays there is a tendency towards a more liberal approach.

If a civil servant makes information public by breaching a legal duty of confidentiality, only the civil servant will be found responsible. Journalists and other members of the media are not prevented from, and are not liable for, publishing such information. In fact during the last few years significant information about government wrongdoing and the internal workings of the state was published without any consequences to the press.

It is a crime to disclose official secrets if disclosure would risk severe damage to national defence or the international relations of the Austrian Republic (Section 255 of the Criminal Code). The law has been applied so as adequately to balance the right to freedom of expression and national security interests; within the last decades, only a very few charges have been filed against the mass media.

The right to receive information further means that the government may not interfere with the collection of information by journalists when they are in places where they are entitled to be. Thus, the police's destruction of photographs of a demonstration was declared unconstitutional.[24]

15. ACCESS TO AND DISCLOSURE OF COURT DOCUMENTS AND PROCEEDINGS

Court hearings are public in principle. The public and the press may be excluded from parts of a trial only in very limited situations when necessary to protect the interests of juveniles, the rights of the parties or public order. There are no restrictions on the reporting of public hearings, except that radio and television transmission are not permitted.

On the other hand, police investigations and preliminary proceedings are confidential. Until 1981, criminal provisions strictly prohibited the publication of documents concerning these confidential proceedings. Since the Media Act of 1981 abolished these provisions, newspapers have been unscrupulous in publishing confidential information. Not only lawyers but also some journalists are of the opinion that the media very often exceed the limits of legitimate reporting and threaten the presumption of innocence by conducting a "trial by the press". In order to safeguard the presumption of innocence, Article 23 of the Media Act prohibits publications which are apt to influence the outcome of a criminal proceeding. But this rule is formulated so narrowly that there is still a very broad margin for reporting, and only excessive violations are punishable.

Various reform proposals are currently being discussed; while a return to the previous criminal prohibitions is rejected, it is proposed to add to the Media Act a provision forbidding the publication of the names of persons who are suspected or convicted of having committed a crime. Identification of a person would be admissible in any case where the person's identity would be of public interest.

16. ACCESS TO AND DISCLOSURE OF LEGISLATIVE DOCUMENTS AND PROCEEDINGS

Proceedings of Parliament are public, and reporting of these proceedings is privileged by law (Article 33 of the Constitution). The Constitution permits the exclusion of the public only in narrowly defined circumstances. In contrast to this general principle, the consultations of parliamentary committees are confidential. However, a journalist who receives information about such consultations may neither be prevented from nor punished for reporting the information.

---

[24] VfSlg 11.297/1987 (*Hainburg* case).

For the last several years, representatives of the mass media have been entitled to attend the consultations of parliamentary investigating committees. This right has been very important in informing the public and generating discussion about significant public affairs.

17. COMMERCIAL SECRECY AND ACCESS TO INFORMATION HELD BY PRIVATE PARTIES

Employees are obliged not to disclose the business secrets of their companies (Article 11 of the Law on Competition). This obligation does not apply once the employment contract terminates, and it is generally held that this provision does not prevent the disclosure of information about illegal actions. The press may not be penalized if it publishes confidential information about a company which it received in violation of this duty of confidentiality.

At present, there is no law requiring private companies to disclose information of any kind to the public (except obligations provided by commercial law, for instance, to publish annual reports or balance sheets). This applies also for information which may be relevant to the environment. However, in this respect a law is currently under discussion to implement the EEC Directive on the Freedom of Access to Information about the Environment.[25]

18. PRIOR RESTRAINTS

Prior restraints are unconstitutional under Article 13 of the 1867 Basic Law. It is not clear if the prohibition of preventive measures also applies to interlocutory orders in the field of civil law. In practice such orders have been considered valid.

If there is a concrete suspicion that a publication violates a criminal law (such as libel under Article 111 of the Criminal Code), the publication can be confiscated; if the publication is a newspaper, all copies of the allegedly libellous issue may be seized (Article 36 of the Media Act). An independent judge decides whether confiscation is necessary based on a balancing of interests. The confiscation is only to be executed after the distribution has started. Confiscation, however, is very rare because it can be avoided if the newspaper publishes a statement that an action for libel has been initiated (Article 37 of the Media Act). The procedure represents an improvement over the previous law, which permitted the confiscation of newspapers relatively often.

The case-law has established that all media are protected against preventive measures. Thus, even a provision to evaluate films before their first public performance in the interests of protecting youth was ruled unconstitutional.[26] The Constitutional Court has further declared

---

[25] 90/313/EEC, OJ No L 158, 23 June 1990, 56.

[26] VfSlg 8461/1978.

unconstitutional a provision requiring the consent of the Labour Office for the publication of job-announcements for employment abroad.[27]

19. PROTECTION OF SOURCES

Article 31 of the Media Act provides strong protection for the confidentiality of journalists' sources. Publishers, editors, journalists and other employees of a media enterprise who are called as witnesses before a court or administrative authority have the right to refuse to answer questions referring to the author, contributor or source of information, or to the contents of information disclosed to them in regard to their professional activities. Furthermore, the Media Act prohibits the surveillance of telecommunications facilities of media enterprises except on the strength of a court order in the context of an investigation of a crime which carries a sentence of at least ten years' imprisonment.

20. RESTRICTIONS ON OFFENSIVE LANGUAGE AGAINST IDENTIFIABLE GROUPS

Article 283 of the Criminal Code made it a crime publicly to incite the commission of hostile activities against a religious, national or ethnic group. There are special criminal provisions against Nazi-propaganda. These have been amended recently to make possible the more effective prosecution of racist and national socialist activities.[28] Complaints are sometimes filed with the Press Council against publications for spreading racist prejudices.

21. BLASPHEMY, OBSCENITY AND PROTECTION OF PUBLIC MORALS

It is a criminal offence to publish certain kinds of pornographic and other materials which infringe public morality.[29] In the light of the present, rather liberal views, they are not very important for daily newspapers; for the most part only certain specialized periodicals are affected.

Blasphemy itself is not punishable under Austrian law. However, Article 188 of the Criminal Code makes it a crime publicly to discredit persons, objects, beliefs or institutions worshipped by a church or religious community recognized in Austria, under circumstances in which the public display is likely to cause justified disapproval or a disturbance of the religious peace. Problems of freedom of expression have been encountered in the context of the confiscation

---

[27] VfGH 19 June 1990, ÖJZ 1992, 38.

[28] Verbotsgesetz vom 8 May 1945 StGB1 13, as last amended BGB1 1992/48.

[29] *See* Criminal Code, Arts. 218, 219, 220; *see also Pornographiegesetz* BGB1 1950/97, as last amended BGB1 1988/599.

of films,[30] but there have not been reports of any proceedings against the press in recent years.

22.   RESTRICTIONS ON ADVERTISING

Unlike broadcasting, where legal restrictions on alcohol and tobacco advertising exist, there are no restrictions on advertising in newspapers. There currently is discussion as to whether cigarette advertising should be completely forbidden.

As far as competition law is concerned, the situation is more difficult. For instance, until recently the courts ruled invalid all forms of comparative advertising (that is, advertising which states that the advertised product is better than another named product). However, courts are now beginning to change their opinions, especially since the Constitutional Court recognized that advertising comes within the protection of Article 10 of the European Convention.[31] Certain kinds of comparative advertisements are now tolerated, so long as they are neither misleading, deprecating, insulting nor offensive.[32] The Constitutional Court declared restrictions on advertising by lawyers and tax consultants unconstitutional.[33]

CONCLUSION

In Austria press freedom is protected to a significant extent by the Constitution and by the European Convention on Human Rights which has constitutional status; moreover, all courts may apply the constitutional protections (although only the Constitutional Court may invalidate a legislative action) and individuals may file complaints (after exhausting domestic remedies) with the European Commission on Human Rights.

Freedom of the press was substantially extended by the Media Act of 1981. Since this law was sustained as valid, investigative journalism in Austria has noticeably improved and it can now truthfully be said that the press serves in practice as a "public watchdog". The two most important reforms introduced by the Media Act were, first, the liberalization of the standard of proof in defamation actions so that press defendants now only have to prove that they fulfilled the requirements of journalistic care (rather than having to prove a statement's truth); and (2) the introduction of protection for the confidentiality of journalists' sources which is

---

[30] *See, e.g.,* the confiscation of a film called *Das Liebeskonzil* (The Council of Love) which is subject of an application declared admissible by the European Commission of Human Rights (*Preminger v. Austria,* 12 April 1991, application no. 13470/87).

[31] VfSlg 10.948/1986 (*Die ganze Woche*).

[32] *See, e.g.,* the decision of the Supreme Court, 26 June 1990 (*Media-Analyse 1988* case), published in *Medien und Recht* (1990), 144.

[33] *See, e.g.,* the decision of the Constitutional Court, 27 Sept. 1990, VfSlg 95, 96.

as strong as any in Europe. A reform fostered to a large extent by the judgments of the European Court of Human Rights was the increase in protection afforded to value judgments so that now harsher criticism is tolerated, especially in the context of political debates. As a result, a "constitutionalization" of the Austrian libel law has been started, based on the relation between freedom of expression and the requirements of democracy.

On the other hand, according to many critics, the media does not adequately respect the privacy of individuals. This applies, in particular, to reports about criminal investigations and trials, concerning which the yellow press regularly exceeds the limits of morality and fairness. Because the Press Council has failed to promote responsible reporting in this area, proposals to prohibit identification of criminal suspects in press coverage are being discussed.

The weakest aspect of the Austrian Press is the extremely high concentration of ownership of daily newspapers. As a consequence, two jointly controlled mass circulation newspapers occupy a quasi-monopolistic position. The smaller newspapers and some of the quality newspapers are suffering financially. The government has attempted to address this trend towards concentration by proposing amendments to the anti-trust law and granting subsidies to publications on unsteady financial ground which contribute to the formation of political opinion. It is difficult to judge whether these efforts will be effective.

Chapter 3

PRESS LAW IN CANADA

Jan Bauer

INTRODUCTION

Canada is one of the world's oldest and most vibrant democracies. The right to freedom of expression, including freedom of the press, is widely respected. The Canadian press functions independently of government, and there is no government censorship of political discourse in the press.[1]

There are nonetheless significant issues facing the Canadian press. Press freedom is not adequately protected at the provincial level. Increasing media concentration poses genuine concerns. Indeed, economic pressures appear to have led to incidents of self-censorship regarding the critical issue of reaching a new constitutional accord. The unwillingness of government officials to provide information under the Access to Information Act substantially hinders the press in fulfilling its role as "public watchdog". Despite shortcomings, however, the press plays a vital role in Canada's democracy.

1. RELEVANT CONSTITUTIONAL PROVISIONS

With the adoption of the Canadian Charter of Rights and Freedoms in 1982, freedom of expression was constitutionally established.[2] Section 2(b) of the Charter guarantees everyone freedom of thought, belief, opinion and expression "including freedom of the press and other media of communication". These rights, however, are not absolute. They are subject to "such reasonable limits prescribed by law as can be demonstrably justified in a free and democratic society", under Section 1 of the Charter. Moreover, Section 33(1), commonly referred to as the "notwithstanding clause", provides for derogation from these and other rights should the Parliament or a provincial legislature pass an act expressly declaring that the act shall operate in violation of Section 2. Such laws lapse, unless renewed, after five years.

---

[1] For more extensive discussions of the laws and jurisprudence which affect the press in Canada *see* P Anisman and A Linden (eds.), *The Media, the Courts and the Charter* (Toronto: Carswell, 1986); R Martin and G Adam (eds.), *A Sourcebook of Canadian Media Law* (Carleton University Press, 1991); *The Canadian Encyclopedia* (Edmonton: Hurtig Publishers, 1985).

[2] The Charter of Rights and Freedoms was adopted as part of the Constitution Act of 1982, enacted as Schedule B to the Canada Act of 1982 (U.K.), Ch. 11, which formally recognized Canada's autonomy from the United Kingdom. Prior to 1982, the only protection available for freedom of the press was the Canadian Bill of Rights at the federal level and court interpretations of the division of powers under the British North America Act.

Given that the Charter has steadily gained in importance, the political costs attached to invoking the "notwithstanding clause" would be considerable. The clause has never been used by the federal government and only rarely by provincial governments. Only Quebec has used it to infringe freedom of the press. Since Quebec did not sign the 1982 Constitution Act, it invoked Section 33 regarding all its laws relating to rights guaranteed under Section 2, including press freedom.

2. DISTRIBUTION OF POWERS BETWEEN CENTRAL AND REGIONAL GOVERNMENT

In Canada, the division of powers and jurisdictions is complex and often problematic. In certain areas, such as culture and immigration, Quebec is given powers that other provinces do not enjoy. There are ongoing discussions about the status and administration of the Yukon Territory and the Northwest Territories as well as about the degree to which Canada's aboriginal peoples are entitled to sovereignty and self-determination. While the Constitution Act of 1982 made some progress in defining jurisdictions and powers, the failure of the Meech Lake Accord reopened many of the more contentious issues. Subsequent efforts to resolve Canada's ongoing constitutional crisis were further complicated by the negative vote in the October 1992 national referendum.

The Constitution Act of 1867 (formerly known as the British North America Act) gave the federal government exclusive law-making power over criminal law and criminal procedure as well as sole responsibility and power to legislate in the national interest. The federal government was not given power, however, over the criminal courts. That, as well as the law-making power in matters affecting the administration of justice, property and civil rights was given to the provinces.

3. ROLE OF THE COURTS

Since 1982, the courts have gradually shifted towards acting as guardians of the rights and freedoms guaranteed in the Charter. It would be fair to say, however, that the process has been uneven. With the exception of Quebec, where civil matters are governed by its civil code, the provincial and federal courts follow the common law system that evolved from English royal courts of justice.

Section 24(1) of the Charter ensures that: "Anyone whose rights or freedoms, as guaranteed by this Charter, have been infringed or denied may apply to a court of competent jurisdiction to obtain such remedy as the court considers appropriate and just in the circumstances." Federal and provincial courts are competent to consider constitutional questions, including challenges to federal legislation. Ultimately, the Supreme Court of Canada may pronounce the final judgment on such issues. The Court also has the power to advise the federal and provincial governments on questions of law and fact concerning interpretations of constitutional provisions, the legitimacy of federal or provincial legislation, and the powers of Parliament and the provincial legislatures.

4. STATUS OF INTERNATIONAL HUMAN RIGHTS TREATIES IN NATIONAL LAW

Both federal and provincial statutes were amended to bring them into accord with the standards defined by the International Covenant on Civil and Political Rights (ICCPR), which Canada ratified in 1976. Canada acceded to the ICCPR's First Optional Protocol at the same time, which permits individuals to file complaints against Canada with the Human Rights Committee. Several cases have been brought against Canada, including one involving the right to use English in exterior commercial signs in Quebec (where all external signs are required to be in French only).[3] Canadian courts often cite the ICCPR as providing guidance in construing corresponding rights in the Charter, and the Human Rights Law Section of the Department of Justice is charged with ensuring that Canadian laws (both federal and provincial) are consistent with ratified international instruments.

5. STATUTORY FRAMEWORK

There is no comprehensive press act in Canada. A number of statutes, discussed below, at both the federal and provincial levels affect the press. Moreover, as a common law jurisdiction, both federal and provincial court decisions help shape laws affecting press freedom.

6. REGULATION OF OWNERSHIP

The daily press in Canada is predominantly provincial in distribution. The main national paper is a national edition of the *Globe and Mail*; the *Financial Post* also distributes nationally.

Two corporations controlled approximately 60 per cent of the English-language circulation by 1980. By 1985, with the exception of Ontario, Quebec and Nova Scotia, publishing chains controlled two-thirds or more of the circulation in other provinces. The trend toward concentration has led to a *de facto* monopolization of certain areas of publishing, such as trade, lifestyle and the arts.

Media ownership remains highly concentrated despite two federal reviews, including the 1981 Royal Commission on Newspapers which concluded that the degree of concentration then existing already posed a threat to press freedom and recommended that some newspaper groups should be required to sell some of their newspaper interests in areas where concentration was most extreme.

While the government has restricted cross-media ownership, it has not acted on recommendations to limit press ownership beyond a certain market share. It is within the

---

[3] In *Ford v. Quebec* (1988), the Supreme Court of Canada found that this "French-only" law infringes Quebec's anglophone and other minorities' right to free expression under Section 2(b) of the Charter. As of this writing, the case is still pending before the Human Rights Committee.

power of the government, however, to review ownership under the Combines Investigation Act, when formation of a monopoly might be to the detriment of Canadian society. Such interventions must be designed to ensure market choices or to protect effective competition.

The Investment Canada Act sets conditions for reviewing applications by non-Canadians to acquire controlling interest in Canadian companies.[4] Generally, applications concerning companies, including newspapers, with a value greater than $5 million must be reviewed. In practice, applications are seldom refused.

7. REGISTRATION REQUIREMENTS

There are no requirements to register newspapers. All businesses, including newspapers, must be either federally or provincially incorporated but there are no special corporate requirements for newspaper companies.

8. REGULATION OF IMPORT AND EXPORT OF PUBLICATIONS

Import and export of goods is federally regulated. The criminal code places some controls on exports, but there have been no problems connected with the export of newspapers.

Section 43 of the Post Office Act contains provisions that broadly apply to the importation of published materials, but this has not affected newspapers. All goods imported into Canada are classified according to the Tariff Code. As a result, the Prohibited Importations Unit of Customs and Excise at Revenue Canada has an impact on determining which published materials may not be allowed into the country. In general, Tariff Code 9956 of Schedule VII prohibits the importation of hate propaganda or material considered to be obscene, treasonable or seditious.

To facilitate enforcement of Tariff Code 9956, Canada Customs operates under its own Memorandum D9-1-1, which sets forth criteria to be used when judging if a publication is objectionable. Customs agents, however, have been criticized for arbitrarily excluding material under the Memorandum. In recent years, material for gay and lesbian bookshops have been particularly targeted and a Charter challenge to the seizure of such literature is planned.

---

[4] Investment Canada Act: R.S.C. 1985, c. 20.

9.   MECHANISMS OF PRESS SELF-REGULATION[5]

9.1   General Considerations

There is no national press council in Canada. There are five provincial councils (in British Columbia, Alberta, Manitoba, Ontario and Quebec) and one regional organization, the Atlantic Press Council (for the provinces of Newfoundland, Prince Edward Island, Nova Scotia and New Brunswick). Presently, there are no press councils in Saskatchewan, the Yukon or Northwest Territories. In addition to the provincial press councils there are a number of community councils and a Parliamentary Press Gallery.[6] In all instances, membership is voluntary.

The councils' effectiveness depends on their ability to review the conduct of newspapers, comment on that conduct, and exert pressure on those which offend professional and ethical standards. While there is no enforcement mechanism as such, the requirement that any newspaper named in a complaint must publish the council's determination has proven to be a fairly effective means for upholding high standards of conduct.

The press councils' complaint process is generally respected by the press. Equally, since the memberships of most councils are fairly balanced between representatives of the press and public, their findings tend to command a good deal of respect from the public. Rather than serving as a mechanism of self-censorship, the councils encourage newspapers to be accurate, fair, thorough and thoughtful.

9.2   The Ontario Press Council: A Representative Model

While each press council is set up to respond to the needs of its own community and region, the Ontario Press Council is similar in many respects to most of them.

As of 1992, the Council consisted of some 120 member newspapers. There are 21 directors who are responsible for considering complaints. The Chairman must not have any connections with the press. The remaining positions are divided equally between the public and press industry representatives. The public members must not have any professional links with the media and must broadly represent Ontario's diverse society and geographical areas. The other positions are held by representatives of participating newspapers, with a balance between publishers, editors, reporters and other employees. All appointments are made by a two-thirds vote of the Council. Terms are for two years and no one may sit on the Council for more than eight years.

---

[5] For a thorough and insightful examination of press councils *see* J A Taylor (then Chairman of the Ontario Press Council), "The Role of the Press Council", in *The Media, the Courts and the Charter*, *supra* note 1.

[6] The Parliamentary Press Gallery is a loosely knit association of media workers assigned by media organizations to cover Parliament and government. The Gallery facilitates news coverage, arranges news conferences or access to information and is also responsible for disciplining its own members.

Anyone may register a complaint with the Council. There is no cost to the complainant beyond sending the original letter; the Council meets all other expenses. The Council will not, however, automatically hear all complaints, and its discretion is absolute.

A complaint must be specific. The newspaper against which the complaint has been lodged must have had a prior opportunity to provide satisfactory redress. Normally, the Council will not hear a complaint involving events that took place more than six months before the complaint was received. Neither will the Council consider a complaint that involves actual or potential litigation. In some instances it may insist on a waiver of subsequent legal action. The Council will not consider a complaint relating to an internal grievance covered by a collective bargaining agreement or Ontario labour legislation. Lastly, it will not hear a complaint against a non-participating newspaper unless that paper agrees.

After receiving a complaint, an Inquiry Committee comprising five members (of whom three, including the Chairman, are public members), conducts a detailed examination of the allegations. The complainant and newspaper are invited to submit written summaries of evidence and argument and to attend an informal hearing. Neither party may be represented or accompanied by legal counsel. There are no pleadings or cross-examinations. No one is sworn, and a verbatim record of proceedings is not kept. The complaining party speaks first, followed by the newspaper, and both parties are given a chance for rebuttal. Either party may call witnesses. A final written submission is not required. The Council sends each party's full submission to the other in order to ensure full disclosure.

The full Council makes the determination, after reviewing the Inquiry Committee's draft decision. In those instances where the complaint is against a Council member's own newspaper, that member may not participate in either the Inquiry Committee or the Council's decision. Complaints are always considered to be against a newspaper, not a member of its staff. The Council's determination is announced in a press release. It names the complaining party and newspaper, but the names of employees are generally not included. As a condition of participation in the Press Council, the newspaper involved has an obligation to publish the Council's findings.

The Ontario Press Council has not drawn up a code of ethics or other guide to journalistic conduct. Rather, its comments in case decisions have developed a core of basic ethical obligations. The nature of complaints are varied but nearly half involve news stories and allege bias, dishonesty, distortion, falsification, incompetence, sensationalism or similar charges. Other complaints concern cartoons, headlines, photographs, and opinion pieces.

The Ontario Press Council will also consider complaints concerning conduct of individuals and organizations against the press. While infrequent, these complaints generally relate to situations limiting press access. For example, in 1973 the Press Council upheld a complaint by the *Ottawa Citizen* which challenged a decision of the Ottawa-Carleton regional planning committee to draft the region's official plan in secret sessions, thereby denying access to the press and the public.

10. DEFAMATION

10.1 General Considerations

Canadian courts generally accept that, in matters concerning defamation and its sub-categories of libel (written defamation) and slander (oral defamation), the press does not enjoy any privileges or freedoms beyond those of private individuals.

Most defamation actions against the press are filed in provincial or territorial courts and are civil in nature.[7] With the exception of Quebec, the law of defamation generally depends on the common law. Each province and territory has its own libel, slander or defamation act and ordinances. Most follow the English Defamation Act of 1952.

It is generally agreed that Ontario, which has the largest circulation and greatest number of newspapers, is the jurisdiction in which it is most difficult to defend against a charge of defamation. Questions arising from Ontario's libel law led the Attorney General of Ontario in 1989 to appoint an Advisory Committee on the Law of Defamation. The Advisory Committee agreed in its Final Report that "the defence of justification should be easier to use, that fair report and fair comment should be expanded, and the opportunities for retraction by publishers or for the publication of reply by complainants should be made more accessible".[8] Media and writers' groups have called for further reforms, including the addition of a defence of honest or reasonable belief in the accuracy of published information, and the extension of absolute privilege to accurate reports of municipal council meetings and quasi-judicial proceedings.

10.2 Public Officials

Public officials are required to suffer a greater degree of criticism and scrutiny than private persons; nonetheless, the burdens of proof that politicians are required to meet remain relatively low and politicians frequently win defamation actions.

In *Vander Zalm v. Times Publishers*[9], the Minister of Human Resources of British Columbia claimed that a political cartoon published on the editorial page of the *Victoria Times* portrayed him as "a person of cruel and sadistic nature". The trial court rejected the defence of fair comment and awarded damages of $3,500 against the defendants. The Court of Appeal (British Columbia's highest court), noting that the Minister had made provocative statements likely to cause a public response, concluded that the press defendants had established the defence of fair comment and accordingly dismissed the action against them.

---

[7] Some federal statutes have provisions which impact on defamation law but the press is not significantly affected by these provisions.

[8] Report of the Advisory Committee on the Law of Defamation (Toronto: Ontario Ministry of the Attorney General, 1990).

[9] (1980), 18 B.C.L.R. 210 (B.C.C.A).

By comparison, in *Vogel v. CBC*[10], the Canadian Broadcasting Corporation was ordered to pay the Deputy Attorney General of British Columbia $125,000, plus costs, for declaring that he had used his position improperly to interfere in the judicial process on behalf of friends. The court disallowed the defence of justification when it became clear that a civil servant had used the reporter to attack his administrative superior without grounds, the reporter had failed to check the reliability of his source, and the editor had failed to check the facts and screen the story for bias.

10.3   Chilling Effect of Court Actions

It appears that in some instances the possibility of a defamation action by a public official or public figure has led to a decision not to publish. In Ontario, in the last few years, there have been a number of actions launched by wealthy individuals or corporations who are able to afford the costs of pursuing one or more cases concurrently. Most of these cases have been settled out of court. In at least one instance this happened in part because both the writer and the publication named in the action had exhausted all financial resources, including those provided by libel insurance.

In one instance in Ontario in 1992 a libel action was threatened before a book was even written. Lawyers acting on behalf of a corporation wrote to the publisher that, if plans proceeded to publish a book by a journalist who had written a number of articles for a major Canadian newspaper critical of the corporation, the corporation was likely to sue for defamation. The publisher decided not to publish but in so doing made public both his response to the lawyers and the initial letter threatening action. Public outcry forced the corporation to soften its stance, and the publisher subsequently indicated a willingness to reconsider its decision.[11]

To the extent that "libel chill" exists, it is caused as much by concerns over the costs of defending against defamation suits as by the size of damage awards. Damage awards granted in Canada are more modest than those granted in the United States or Britain. The award of $135,000 in *Snyder v. The Montreal Gazette Ltd.* is generally said to be the largest ever in a Canadian libel case.[12] In an Ontario trial court, an award of $883,000 was granted in *Walker and Walker Brothers Quarries Ltd. v. CFTO*,[13] but the Court of Appeal ordered a new trial to reassess damages, finding the original award seriously out of line with custom. In Quebec, awards tend to fall within a range of $5,000 to $15,000. In other provinces awards tend to be in the range of $3,500 to $35,000.

---

[10] (1982), 21 C.C.L.T. 105.

[11] *See* "Publisher abandons unseen manuscript: letter cautions Macmillan chief", *Globe and Mail* (24 Jan. 1992) at A1.

[12] (1988) Supreme Court of Canada (unreported).

[13] *Walker and Walker Brothers Quarries Ltd. v. CFTO Limited et al.* (1987), 19 O.A.C. 10 at 16 (Ont. C.A.).

In response to a concern that awards may eventually follow the trend in the United States, some commentators have suggested that the courts should fix a ceiling for non-pecuniary damages (that is, damages for hurt feelings and other non-material harm). It has been suggested that the limits might follow those determined by the Supreme Court of Canada in 1978 regarding personal injury cases; in such cases awards for recovery of non-pecuniary loss may not exceed $100,000.[14]

11. INVASION OF PRIVACY

The Charter of Rights and Freedoms does not contain a specific right to privacy. Federal legislation on privacy includes the Privacy Act of 1982, which was enacted as part of the Access to Information Act.[15] The 1982 Privacy Act does not create a right to privacy, but rather establishes the right of individuals to apply for access to information about themselves that is held by the state. The Protection of Privacy Act,[16] an amendment to the Criminal Code, makes it an indictable offence to intercept private communications. Issues of privacy may also be considered on other grounds, such as trespass and theft, but there is no federal common law tort of invasion of privacy.

Quebec is the only province which specifically guarantees the right to privacy in its Charter of Rights. British Columbia, Manitoba, Newfoundland and Saskatchewan all passed privacy acts, which create a right of action for invasions of privacy without the need for the plaintiff to prove any damage. To date, no cases have been heard under the statutes of Newfoundland or Saskatchewan. Cases brought in Manitoba and British Columbia have been defeated on various grounds, including defamation defences and a public interest defence.[17]

12. RIGHT OF REPLY AND/OR CORRECTION

Publication of a reply or a correction is an available remedy in defamation suits; it is most frequently used, however, as part of out-of-court settlements. An apology or statement of correction generally results in a reduction of damage awards. Under Ontario law, if an apology is printed within three days of the defendant being notified of the action, any subsequent award is limited to actual (or pecuniary) damages.

---

[14] *Andrews v. Grant & Toy Alberta Ltd.*, [1978] 2 S.C.R. 229; *Thornton v. Board of School District No. 57* (Prince George), [1978] 2 S.C.R. 267; *Arnold v. Teno*, [1978] 2 S.C.R. 287.

[15] Privacy Act: R.S.C. 1985, c.P-21; Access To Information Act: S.C., 1980-81-82-83, c.111; R.S.C. 1985, c.A-1.

[16] S.C. 1973-4, c.50; 1976-7 c.53.

[17] *See, e.g., Wooding v. Little* (1982) 24 C.C.L.T. 37 (B.C.S.C.); (publication of an individual's confidential medical reports was not considered an invasion of privacy, because the publication was privileged under defamation law); *Belzberg v. BCTV Broadcasting System Ltd.* (1981) W.W.R. 85 (B.C.S.C.) and *Silber v. BCTV Broadcasting System Ltd.* (1986) 69 B.C.L.R. 35 (S.C.) (the defence of public interest defeated the claim of invasion of privacy).

13. INSULTS TO GOVERNMENT INSTITUTIONS OR OFFICIALS

Seditious libel is defined in Sections 59 to 62 of the Criminal Code. Section 60 specifically exempts certain kinds of expression, including, amongst others, communications made in good faith to point out errors or defects in the government or constitution of Canada or a province, the Parliament of Canada or the legislature of a province, or the administration of justice.

As the Law Reform Commission pointed out in its Working Paper 49,[18] the crime of seditious libel remains problematic, despite Section 60, because the phrase "seditious intention" is not adequately defined in the Criminal Code. The Law Reform Commission referred to the 1950 case of *Boucher v. The King*,[19] in which the defendant was charged with distributing a pamphlet likely to incite or promote public disorder. On appeal, the Supreme Court of Canada stated:

> The use of strong words is not by itself sufficient nor is the likelihood that readers of the pamphlet ... would be annoyed or even angered, but the question is, was the language used calculated to promote public disorder or physical force or violence.

In that case, the question of good faith was brought to bear directly on the question of how to define seditious intention. Ultimately the Supreme Court quashed the original conviction and a new trial was ordered.

The Law Reform Commission observed that, following *Boucher*, there no longer appeared to be a separate offence of seditious libel, because the conduct that would be proscribed by it could just as easily be addressed under provisions related to incitement, conspiracy, contempt of court, or hate propaganda. The Commission, therefore, urged that the Criminal Code be revised to reflect this. No action has yet been taken on the recommendation.

---

[18] Ottawa, 1986.

[19] (1950) 1 D.L.R. 657 (S.C.C.).

14. OFFICIAL SECRECY AND ACCESS TO GOVERNMENT-HELD INFORMATION

14.1 Access to Information

The federal Access to Information Act took effect in 1983.[20] The Act entitles individuals to have access to certain kinds of government information and, at least theoretically, requires public authorities to respond to requests for information in a timely fashion and to impose only reasonable costs. The Act extends to all federal government departments, institutions and crown corporations.

The Act has been criticized in a number of areas, including that the grounds for exemption are neither limited nor specific. One of the main criticisms focuses on the government's absolute privilege concerning "Cabinet confidences" and its nearly absolute power to declare any document a "Cabinet document". The Act also specifies five areas of mandatory exemptions, which at least are subject to judicial review. In addition, there are twelve discretionary exemptions.

The requester may appeal a denial of access to the Information Commissioner. The Commissioner has the right to enter any government office, the right to study all documents and information (except for those protected under the absolute privilege of Cabinet confidences), and the power to recommend that information be released or withheld. If the requester disagrees with the Commissioner's decision not to recommend the disclosure, the matter may be taken to the Federal Court. Similarly, the Commissioner may take a government department to the Federal Court, if it does not comply with a recommendation to disclose information.

The government still today and historically has been extremely reluctant to make information available. Many commentators believe that, while the present Access to Information Act is important, the exemptions and general provision for "Cabinet confidences" have gutted it of much of its meaning and intent.

The provinces of Nova Scotia, New Brunswick, Newfoundland, Ontario and Quebec have freedom of information acts. Other jurisdictions have conducted studies on the subject but have not yet enacted legislation. The criticisms of the federal act's restrictions also generally apply to the provincial acts.

The public is entitled to information on test results of consumer products and the environment, but information on environmental testing is not available if the tests were done by a government department for a fee and as a service to a third party. Third party information may be disclosed, however, on consent or if public interest in such a disclosure clearly outweighs any financial gain or loss to the third party.

---

[20] R.S.C. 1985, c.A-1.

Section 74 of the Act states that a public servant who discloses a record, whether or not the record involves private party information, in good faith and in a way that is consistent with the Act cannot be prosecuted.

14.2 Official Secrets

Canada's Official Secrets Act was enacted in 1939.[21] Very few of the nearly two dozen prosecutions under the Act affected the press. The most notable case related to publication by the *Toronto Sun* of a document outlining suspected spying activities in Canada.[22] The document had been designated "top secret", and charges were brought against both the publisher and editor. During the preliminary inquiry, the court concluded, however, that earlier disclosures of the same information had brought the document into the public domain and dismissed the case.[23]

15. ACCESS TO AND DISCLOSURE OF COURT DOCUMENTS AND PROCEEDINGS

Section 11(d) of the Charter stipulates that a person charged with an offence has a right to be presumed innocent until proven guilty in a fair and public hearing by an independent and impartial tribunal. The phrase "public hearing" implies that the business of the courts is also the public's business, and that the media should have access to proceedings. There are, nonetheless, a number of rules affecting press coverage of court proceedings which attempt to strike a balance between the rights of the accused and freedom of expression.

Section 11 of the Uniform Defamation Act of 1978 provides that fair and accurate reports of court proceedings held in public are absolutely privileged, unless a person involved with the proceedings has requested publication of a statement of explanation or contradiction which the publication has refused to publish.[24]

Sections 9 and 10 of the Criminal Code address contempt. Contempt of court, however, is not statutorily defined in Canada. The law of contempt is generally addressed under two "headings". The first, *in facie* contempt, occurs in the court and involves such questions as a reporter disobeying an order to disclose the sources for a story. The second, *ex facie* contempt, occurs outside the court and involves issues such as "scandalizing the court", saying

---

[21] S.C. 1939, as amended R.S.C. 1985, c.O-5.

[22] *R. v. Toronto Sun Publishing Ltd.* (1979) 98 D.L.R.(3d) 524, 525. *See* W Tarnopolsky, "Freedom of the Press", in *Newspapers and the Law* (Toronto: Minister of Supply and Services Canada, 1981), at xi, 19-21.

[23] For the journalist's perspective of that incident, see Sawatsky, "John Sawatsky Stakes Out The High Ground", 29 *Bulletin of the Centre for Investigative Journalism* 11 (1986).

[24] To date only Alberta, Manitoba and the Yukon have enacted the Uniform Defamation Act. *See* R E Brown, *The Law of Defamation in Canada* (Toronto: Carswell, 1987), 7, 9.

that a judge is corrupt, or involves publication of materials or facts in defiance of an order not to publish. A judge may also cite a member of the press for violating the *sub judice* rule, for publishing a story containing an opinion, or an editorial, that in some way may prejudice proceedings (for example, by communicating a presumption of guilt before the trial has been completed).

A finding of contempt of court or a violation of the *sub judice* rule is left to an individual judge's summary ruling. Such findings may be appealed. A summary conviction, however, does not necessarily lead to punishment. A number of factors, such as the nature of a breach of the rule, whether the case is to be decided solely by a judge or involves a jury, and where the publication occurred, may be considered in deciding what penalty, if any, should apply.

The question of court access sometimes arises in federal proceedings under the Young Offenders Act.[25] Under the Act, information identifying an involved person (either the accused, a witness, or a victim) may not be published.

Access may also become an issue under Section 14(2) of the Official Secrets Act, which gives the courts discretion to hold closed trials at the request of the prosecution. The rationale used in these instances is that public disclosure of evidence would be prejudicial to the interests of the state. Publication bans on evidence heard at extradition hearings, preliminary inquiries, and applications for changes of venue have also been held to be reasonable limitations on freedom of the press.[26]

16. ACCESS TO AND DISCLOSURE OF LEGISLATIVE DOCUMENTS AND PROCEEDINGS

It has become common practice to televise the proceedings of both the federal and provincial legislatures. In addition, verbatim accounts of parliamentary proceedings at both the federal and provincial level are published in the *Hansard* and include records of all parliamentary committees and sub-committees. Similar records of the proceedings of municipal and regional councils are published unless the council concerned has taken the decision to hold closed meetings. Any citizen may acquire copies of *Hansard* or may receive, on request, selected records on specific questions debated in the relevant legislative assemblies, municipal or regional councils.

---

[25] S.C. 1980-81-82, c.110.

[26] *See* A M Linden, "Statutory Restrictions on Freedom of the Press in the Criminal Process", from "Limitations on Media Coverage of Legal Proceedings: A Critique and Some Proposals for Reform", in *The Media, the Courts and the Charter*, *supra* note 1, at 301-30.

17. COMMERCIAL SECRECY AND ACCESS TO INFORMATION HELD BY PRIVATE PARTIES

Information held by private parties is protected from compulsory disclosure to the press. Such information reported to the government is generally protected from disclosure under provisions of the Access to Information Act.

18. PRIOR RESTRAINTS

Interlocutory injunctions may be used to enforce press bans in Canada, particularly in situations where the plaintiff charges that publication would constitute defamation. Historically, injunctions have most often been requested when the subject or information in question is both controversial and of public concern. Interlocutory injunctions generally are not granted if the defendant shows that he has a plausible chance of establishing a defence of justification. Similarly, injunctions are rarely granted if the defendant can establish that sufficient grounds exist for a case to go to trial by jury. *Ex parte* injunctions may be granted for short periods, even though the defendant is not present to claim justification or other defences if the plaintiff shows imminent danger of irreparable harm.

The impact of interlocutory injunctions on the print media was well illustrated by the 1979 case of *Lorcon Inc. v. Kozy Insulation Specialists Ltd.*[27] In that case, a permanent injunction was granted preventing publication of "any reports by government or an independent body" on the potential harm of formaldehyde foam (commonly used as insulation in both residential and business properties). This injunction has been severely criticized as an unreasonable limit on the press, which resulted in vital information not being available to the public. Serious harmful health effects from the product later were acknowledged by government, manufacturers, and installers. This case reinforces the argument that such injunctions pose an unreasonable limit on press freedom.

19. PROTECTION OF SOURCES

Journalists have no statutory right to protect the confidentiality of their sources and the courts have refused to recognize anything more than a rather weak privilege. A qualified privilege has been acknowledged by some courts at the pre-trial stage under the so-called "newspaper rule". This rule provides that, at the discovery stage of a libel action, the press cannot be compelled to identify informants, even where such information is relevant. If the matter

---

[27] Ontario High Court of Justice, 14 Feb. 1979 (unreported decision granting temporary injunction); 26 Feb. 1979 (unreported decision extending temporary injunction); 25 Sept. 1979 (unreported decision imposing permanent injunction).

proceeds to trial and the informant's identity is still a relevant issue, disclosure must then be made.[28]

In some instances, where privilege was not granted and the journalist was found to be in contempt of court, fines have been levied.[29] In one case, a journalist was briefly imprisoned for refusing to be sworn before a municipal fire commission to answer questions relating to a story involving a person who claimed to be a terrorist.[30]

In *Pacific Press Limited v. The Queen*,[31] a search warrant was granted to search the offices of *The Vancouver Sun* and *The Vancouver Province* to obtain evidence of an offence to which the press were only witnesses. The trial court noted that issuing a search warrant against a newspaper is a serious matter, especially when its issuance may impede publication. It concluded that there had not been "reasonable information" to show whether a "reasonable alternative source" for the information was available and, if available, whether "reasonable steps" had been taken to obtain it from that source. The court ruled that in such circumstances it was improper to issue the warrant.

The Supreme Court of Canada ruled in November 1991 that Radio-Canada had to hand over to police videotapes that its crews had filmed of violent labour disputes. In a majority opinion, which did not declare newsrooms off-limits to reasonable police searches, the court enumerated three factors which justices of the peace and lower court judges should weigh before issuing such warrants: 1) such circumstances as whether the material being sought has already been published or broadcast; 2) whether a proper balance has been struck between the interests of the state in investigating crime and the right of the media to privacy while gathering and disseminating news (the seriousness of the crime being a factor for consideration); and 3) whether police have provided judges with sufficient details of all known circumstances of the case, including whether they exhausted all other reasonable efforts to gather the evidence from other sources.[32]

---

[28] *See* S N Lederman, P O'Kelly and M Grottenhaler, "Confidentiality of News Sources", in *The Media, the Courts and the Charter, supra* note 1, at 227, 233.

[29] *See generally* R Martin, "Criticising the Judges", 28 *McGill Law Journal*, 1, 13020, for a discussion of such cases; e.g., $4,000 fine in one and 10 days imprisonment in another.

[30] It is possible that imprisonment would not have been ordered had he appeared, taken the oath, and, in response to specific questions, refused to disclose the source or sources of his information. *See* W Kesterton, *The Law and the Press in Canada* (Toronto: McClelland & Stewart, 1976) 32-39.

[31] *Pacific Press v. The Queen* (1977), 38 C.R.N.S. 295 (B.C.S.C.).

[32] *Canadian Broadcasting Corporation v. Lessard* (1991) 3 S.C.R. 421; *Canadian Broadcasting Corporation v. New Brunswick (Attorney General)* (1991) 3 S.C.R. 459; *see also* 19th Annual Report, 1991, The Ontario Press Council, at 58-59. In a dissenting opinion, Madam Justice B McLachlan said she would have quashed the warrants because police had not shown the evidence could not be obtained from other sources.

In 1992, in an attempt to use the media to assist in the identification of criminal suspects, the police served warrants on nine media outlets in Toronto. The warrants, served on newspapers and television broadcasters, sought negatives and film of a Toronto riot. All of the media affected chose to cooperate with police. Several of them, however, are presently considering a legal challenge to the warrants, but to date no action has been filed.

20. RESTRICTIONS ON OFFENSIVE LANGUAGE AGAINST IDENTIFIABLE GROUPS

Multiculturalism is fully entrenched at both the federal and provincial levels of Canadian government. Governmental policy recognizes, and to some degree protects and promotes, the uniqueness of the cultures and traditions of all identifiable groups of people within the general population. The federal and provincial governments have enacted legislation criminalizing racist speech and propaganda.[33] Sections 318 and 319 of the Criminal Code address hate propaganda.[34] Other sections of the Criminal Code augment these provisions; Section 181, which criminalizes "spreading false news", has particular import for the press.

On 27 August 1992, in a 4-3 ruling,[35] the Supreme Court of Canada overturned the conviction of a pro-Nazi pamphlet publisher on a charge of knowingly spreading false news about the Holocaust. The Court said that provisions in Criminal Code Section 181, relating to spreading false news, imposed an unjustifiable limit on Section 2(b) of the Charter's guarantee of free speech.[36]

Canadian media have become increasingly sensitive to the issues of gender equality, race, and ethnicity and are more conscious of the potential for injury that an ill-considered use of

---

[33] In addition, the Canada Human Rights Act operates at the federal level, allowing complaints before the Canadian Human Rights Commission. Provincial human rights acts also exist, creating human rights commissions in most provinces to enforce the legislation.

For a thorough discussion of Canadian law related to hate speech, see J Manwaring, "Legal Regulation of Hate Propaganda in Canada", and I Cotler, "Principles and Perspectives on Hate Speech, Freedom of Expression and Non-discrimination: The Canadian Experience as a Case-Study in Striking a Balance", both in S Coliver (ed.), *Striking a Balance: Hate Speech, Freedom of Expression and Non-discrimination* (London: ARTICLE 19, 1992), 106-22 and 122-29, respectively.

[34] Section 318 criminalizes advocacy or promotion of genocide. Section 319 criminalizes incitement and promotion of hatred, in defined circumstances, against any section of the public distinguished by race, colour, religion or ethnic origin (defined as an "identifiable group").

[35] *R. v. Zundel* (1987) 35 D.L.R. (4th) 338.

[36] There is public pressure calling on the Attorney General of Ontario to lay charges on the basis of promoting hatred under Section 319(2) of the Criminal Code, relating to wilfully promoting hatred against identifiable groups, which the Supreme Court has approved in other cases. *E.g., R. v Keegstra* [1990] 3 S.C.R. 697 and *R. v Andrews* [1990] 3 S.C.R. 870. The Attorney General has taken the case under advisement and is also considering taking up the question with the attorneys-general of other provinces to work with the federal government to amend Section 181 to address the Court's concerns.

language or image can cause. Many of the major newspapers have an ombudsman to deal with this, amongst other issues. The press councils will also hear complaints on these grounds.

21. BLASPHEMY, OBSCENITY AND PROTECTION OF PUBLIC MORALS

Section 296 of the Criminal Code defines blasphemous libel as the "expression in writing of an opinion upon a religious question in bad faith and in language offensive and injurious to the religious convictions of those who do not share those convictions and of such a nature that it may lead to a disturbance of the public peace". The press has not been charged in a case of blasphemous libel since 1935.[37]

Sections 163 to 169 of the Criminal Code prohibit, among other actions, the publication and distribution of obscene materials.[38] Section 166(1) provides, in part, that it is an offence to publish, import, export, or advertise "anything that depicts a child performing a sexual act or assuming a sexually suggestive pose while in a state of undress". Section 166(1)(a) could have a significant effect on newspapers. In publications of court proceedings, this section prohibits inclusion of "any indecent matter or indecent medical, surgical or physiological details ... that, if published, are calculated to injure public morals". There, however, have been no recent cases against the press under Section 166 (1)(a).

22. RESTRICTIONS ON ADVERTISING

Canadian courts have generally adopted the attitude that commercial speech is not protected by Section 2(b) of the Charter.[39] The federal government enacted legislation prohibiting tobacco advertising, though the legislation may be challenged in the courts. Commercial speech may fall under the purview of libel if a company uses comparative advertising that implies a competitor's product is inherently inferior. Similarly, truth in advertising is legally required.

Sections 70.1(1) and 72 of the Canadian Elections Act, which prohibited anyone other than nominated candidates and registered parties from incurring election expenses or placing political advertisements during an election campaign, was successfully challenged in 1984,

---

[37] *See R. v. Rahard* (1935) 65 C.C.C. 344.

[38] The Law Reform Commission of Canada has recommended that obscenity be decriminalized on the ground that ample remedies are available in civil law to address this area. *See* Law Reform Commission of Canada, *Working Paper 10: Limits of Criminal Law; Obscenity: A Test Case* (Ottawa, 1975).

[39] In *Ford v. Quebec (Attorney General)*, [1989] 1 C.S.R. 103, however, the Supreme Court invalidated a law that restricted the use of English-language signs in commercial establishments, holding that both "speakers" and "listeners" are entitled to engage in commercial expression under Section 2(b) of the Charter. The Court noted that commercial speech plays a significant role in enabling consumers to make informed economic choices.

in the case of *National Citizens Coalition v. Attorney-General for Canada*.[40] The court held that the sections were inconsistent with Section 2(b) of the Charter and, therefore, of no force or effect. As a result, private interests, including corporations, are entitled to advertise their views on political issues in both the print and broadcast media.

CONCLUSION

The adoption of the Charter of Rights and Freedoms significantly advanced the cause of press freedom. In addition, the Canadian press is reasonably vigorous in resisting erosion of its rights. Similarly, the press is actively addressing complaints of press abuses through the press councils and seems to be taking to heart the need for more precision in its use of language and image.

At the same time, concentration of ownership, limited market size and resources leave the Canadian press at a comparative disadvantage to the press in the United States and a number of other countries. For example, the *Globe and Mail*, Canada's only nationally distributed general newspaper, depends on wire services for much of its reportage. While the Canadian Press wire service helps to balance sources, the *Globe* and most other newspapers depend on stories carried by the major US wire services and occasional stories from European services. It can, therefore, be argued that Canadians do not always receive a Canadian perspective from their own press.

Equally if not more worrisome is a decision taken by some media owners and managers voluntarily to limit coverage of the debates and discussions surrounding Canada's latest effort to reach a constitutional accord. In an article with the headline "Media muzzle the voices they fear",[41] Klaus Pohle reported that the president of Baton Broadcasting declared he does not want "to support the people who support separation". He reportedly said that these individuals "won't get on the air" at his stations.

Similarly, the publisher of the *Ottawa Citizen*, the leading newspaper in the nation's capital, informed a parliamentary committee last year that journalists had deliberately suppressed "major stories" that could have had a negative impact on Canadian unity.[42] This view apparently sees such limits as simply a question of economics (that is, a united Canada is better for business and "generates advertising dollars"). Following this reasoning, it would appear that, for some in the media, the public interest is equated with the need to maximize profits.

As Klaus Pohle points out, the media "would excoriate -- and rightly so -- any government that dared even to propose legislation prohibiting or limiting news coverage of Quebec

---

[40] (1984) 11 D.L.R. (4th) 481 (Alta. Q.B.).

[41] *The Toronto Star* (1 Aug. 1992), at B2.

[42] *Id.*

nationalism. They would call such a law an unconscionable intrusion into freedom of the press." Pohle also notes:

> To argue that separatism is bad for Canada is to miss the point ... . The issue is the public's right to hear, discuss and debate all points of view, however unpleasant or unpalatable they may be. That is what the constitutional protection of freedom of the press is supposed to be all about.[43]

Given the excess of statutory limitations, the concentration of ownership, and the limited resources of even major media outlets, the task of building a robust press seems difficult. That the media itself should cooperate in limiting public discourse on one of the most fundamental questions facing Canada only increases the enormity of the task of ensuring lively and continuous public disclosure and discussion of issues affecting all Canadians. Nonetheless, the Canadian press possesses the legal structure, the tradition and the will to meet its tasks as public watchdog and provider of information essential to democratic debate.

---

[43] *See id.*

Chapter 4

PRESS LAW IN FRANCE

Roger Errera

INTRODUCTION

This chapter does not aim, for obvious reasons of space, at presenting an exhaustive and complete analysis of the French law of the press as it stands today. Rather, it focuses on what seems to be the most relevant aspects and issues, namely, the constitutional and international law framework, the role of the courts, libel and privacy, and access to and disclosure of court proceedings and documents. References to the recent case-law have been provided wherever possible. For further information, several sources are suggested.[1]

1. RELEVANT CONSTITUTIONAL PROVISIONS

Freedom of expression and communication is a constitutional right under French law, entrenched in two provisions of constitutional stature. First, Article 11 of the 1789 Declaration of the Rights of Man and the Citizen, incorporated into the Preamble of the 1958 Constitution, provides:

> Free communication of thoughts and opinion is among the most precious rights of man. Thus all men may freely speak, write and publish, provided they be responsible for any abuse of this freedom in cases determined by law.[2]

In addition, freedom of expression and communication is one of the "fundamental principles guaranteed by the laws of the Republic" which, according to the case-law of the *Conseil constitutionnel* (CC), have constitutional value.

---

[1] Two basic texts in French are C A Colliard, *Libertés publiques*, 7th ed., (Dalloz, 1989), at 536 *et seq.;* and J Robert et J Duffar, *Libertés publiques et droits de l'homme*, 4th ed., (Paris, 1988), at 463 *et seq*. Unfortunately, very little has been written in English. Following are the titles of several articles and book chapters which I have written in English: "Balancing Legitimate Rights: Freedom of the Press and Other Rights in French Law," *Communications Lawyer* (Spring 1991), 13; "Recent Developments in the French Law of the Press in Comparison with Britain," in D Kingsford-Smith and D Oliver (eds.), *Economical with the Truth: the Law and the Media in a Democratic Society* (Oxford: ESC Publishing Ltd, 1990), 67; "The Freedom of the Press: The United States, France and Other European Countries," in L Henkin and A J Rosenthal (eds.), *Constitutionalism and Other Rights: The Influence of the United States Constitution Abroad* (New York, 1990); "Press Law in France," in P Lahav (ed.), *Press Law in Modern Democracies: A Comparative Study* (New York and London, 1985).

[2] Article 11 is often applied by the courts: *see, e.g.,* Paris Cour d'appel, 13 Jan. 1992, *X et al. v. Y,* in a case relating to the criticism of school textbooks.

The *Conseil constitutionnel*, in affirming the constitutional status of freedom of expression and freedom of the press, has stated that these freedoms constitute one of the essential safeguards of the other rights and liberties.[3] Moreover, the *Conseil constitutionnel* has affirmed that these freedoms apply not only to those who write, edit and publish, but also to those who read the press; the public's right to be able to choose from a diversity of views thus necessitates a degree of pluralism, at least for general dailies. Such a pluralism is also an aim of constitutional value.[4]

2.   DISTRIBUTION OF POWERS BETWEEN CENTRAL AND REGIONAL GOVERNMENT

France is divided into regions, *départements* and municipalities (*communes*). Only the national government has authority in matters affecting the press.

3.   ROLE OF THE COURTS

The French judicial and legal system has two branches. On the one side, ordinary courts (*tribunaux judiciaires*) have jurisdiction over disputes relating to civil, commercial and criminal law. The *Tribunal de grande instance (TGI)* is the trial court, the *Cour d'appel* is the intermediate appellate court and the *Cour de cassation* is the supreme court of this branch. On the other side, all litigation relating to the exercise of public authority (including by the central government and all local authorities) is governed by administrative law. Administrative law is applied by administrative courts (*jurisdictions administratives*), including 27 *tribunaux administratifs* (lower courts), five *cours administratives d'appel* (courts of appeal) and, at the top, the *Conseil d'Etat*. The decisions of the *Cour de cassation* and the *Conseil d'Etat* bind lower courts.

Press cases may be decided by civil courts (*e.g.* privacy cases), criminal courts (defamation, which under French law is both a criminal offence and a tort) and administrative courts (*e.g.*, the decision to ban a foreign publication).

The *Conseil constitutionnel*, France's constitutional court, is empowered to declare a statute invalid as contrary to the Constitution, and its decisions are final and binding on all authorities and powers. However, it may decide the constitutionality of a statute only when a statute passed by Parliament and not yet promulgated is referred to it by 60 members of Parliament, the President of the Republic, the Prime Minister, the President of the National Assembly or the President of the Senate. Courts may not refer statutes to the *Conseil constitutionnel*, nor may they themselves declare statutes unconstitutional. An administrative court, however, may quash a *regulation* if it finds it to be unconstitutional.

---

[3] *See* CC, 10-11 Oct. 1984, at 78.

[4] *See, e.g.,* CC, 29 July 1986, at 110.

4. STATUS OF INTERNATIONAL HUMAN RIGHTS TREATIES IN NATIONAL LAW

According to Article 55 of the French Constitution, international treaties, once signed, ratified and published, take precedence over domestic statutes. This applies irrespective of the kind of treaty (bi- or multilateral, human rights or other) and of the date of the statute (be it anterior or posterior to the treaty). France is thus a "monist" country. This principle is applied by the *Cour de cassation* and the *Conseil d'Etat*. All courts are thus empowered to construe and apply treaties, as long as they are self-executing[5], and to set aside a domestic statute if it is contrary to a treaty. Since courts are not empowered to set aside statutes as contrary to the Constitution, the result is that treaties enjoy a stronger protection than the Constitution vis-à-vis conflicting statutes.

When the *Conseil constitutionnel* has been asked to decide the constitutionality of a statute adopted by Parliament, it has so far refused to review its conformity with treaties on the ground that treaty review is the province of *all* the courts.[6]

Under Article 54 of the Constitution, the same authorities that may refer a statute to the *Conseil constitutionnel* (see above) may, before a treaty is ratified, refer it to the *Conseil constitutionnel* to check whether its ratification necessitates a revision of the Constitution. If so, the Constitution must be revised before the treaty is ratified. This procedure was followed in 1992 before ratification of the Maastricht Treaty.

France has ratified all relevant international human rights instruments including the European Convention on Human Rights (ECHR), the International Covenant on Civil and Political Rights (ICCPR) and its First Optional Protocol (authorizing individual complaints to the Human Rights Committee). It has also accepted the right of individual petition to the European Commission on Human Rights.

French courts have cited Article 10 of the ECHR (guaranteeing freedom of expression) in a number of cases. Although only one case involves the press, all are relevant in demonstrating the respect French courts generally accord to Article 10 and to the judgments of the European Court of Human Rights.

- In 1988, several Catholic associations asked the Paris civil court to ban Martin Scorsese's film, *The Last Temptation of Christ*. The Paris *Cour d'appel* quoting Article 11 of the 1789 Declaration of the Rights of Man and the Citizen as well as Article 10 of the ECHR, refused to ban the film. To account for religious

---

[5] To be self-executing, a treaty must reflect, either by its language or its drafting history, that its clauses are directly applicable in domestic courts, and the treaty must impose obligations which are specific, mandatory and capable of implementation without further acts of Parliament.

[6] *See* CC, decision of 15 Jan. 1975, at 19.

sensibilities, it ordered that all advertisements relating to the film should contain a warning about the film's fictional nature.[7]

- The *Conseil d'Etat* held that banning the public display of certain journals, their sale to minors and publicity for them was a permissible limitation on press freedom within the scope of paragraph 2 of Article 10 (which permits limitations on freedom of expression where "necessary in a democratic society, ... for the protection of health or morals").[8] The *Conseil* failed to inquire, as indeed it should have done, whether the ban respected the principle of proportionality contained in the European Court's case-law. In view of the *Conseil*'s subsequent case-law in cases relating to the application of the ECHR, this must be regarded as an isolated judgment.

- In 1991 the Paris civil court heard an action brought by the Moroccan Government against one television and two radio stations. The Moroccan Government argued that the stations had presented a book by G Perrault, *Notre ami le roi* (which strongly criticizes human rights violations in Morocco, including the widespread use of torture and detention camps, and implicates the responsibility of the King) in an unbalanced manner, without offering any criticism or opposing views. The State Prosecutor, usually silent in purely civil litigations, mentioned Article 10 and the *Lingens* judgment[9] in his opinion. The court ruled in favour of the radio and TV stations.

5.   STATUTORY FRAMEWORK

The Act of 1881 constituted, when it was adopted, a genuine code of freedom of expression: it applied not only to the printed press but also to the entire range of printed expression (including printers, bill posters, books and vendors). It thus covered all existing means of expression at the time.

In addition to proclaiming the principle of freedom of the press, the Act contained criminal provisions and a special code of criminal procedure relating to press offences. In the past 110 years, the law has been amended several times, mostly on a piecemeal basis. No general overhaul has ever been attempted. Regulations relating to the press have been inserted elsewhere either in codes (including the Criminal, National Service and Public Health Codes) or in special statutes (such as the 1949 law on publications addressed to young readers).

---

[7] Paris *Cour d'appel*, 27 Sept. 1988, *Gaz. Pal.*, 21 Oct. 1988.

[8] Conseil d'Etat, 9 Jan. 1990, *Société des éditions de la Fortune*.

[9] *Lingens v. Austria*, Judgment of 8 July 1986, Series A no. 103 (ruling that limits of acceptable criticism regarding politicians in their public capacities are wider than regarding private citizens, and that requiring a defamation defendant to prove the truth of an opinion infringes the right to impart ideas as well as the public's right to receive them).

In 1992, the government completed a codification of the existing law, called *Code de la communication*. Although it does not contain a systematic restatement and updating of the law applicable to the press, it does present the extant law in a more orderly fashion. Parliament could adopt it by as early as the end of 1992.

6.   REGULATION OF OWNERSHIP

Concentration of press ownership is regulated by the Act of 1 August 1986, as amended by the Act of 27 November 1986. The Act of August was referred to the *Conseil constitutionnel*, which affirmed that pluralism of dailies is, *per se*, an objective of constitutional value and accordingly ruled unconstitutional a clause (Article 11) of the Act which allowed *greater* concentration than the previously controlling Act of 1984. This in turn led to Parliament's adoption of the amending Act of 27 November.[10]

Article 11 of the present law makes it unlawful to buy or take over control of a general (that is, a non-specialized) daily if, as a result, a person or group of persons (physical or legal) would own or control, directly or indirectly, daily papers whose combined circulations would exceed 30 per cent of the circulation of all such dailies throughout France. Any contract which would lead to such a result is void, and breach of Article 11 is a criminal offence.

The present law imposes several other requirements. Press companies must follow a number of rules relating to such matters as the sale of their shares and the publication in each issue of certain information about the company. Foreigners may not, since the law's entry into force, own or acquire more than 20 per cent of a press company, although this restriction would be changed if France accepted an international obligation requiring equal treatment of nationals and non-nationals in this regard.

Beginning in the 1980s, concentration of press and cross-media ownership increased with the result that five media groups -- Hachette, Havas, Hersant, Groupe de la Cité and Filipacchi -- now dominate all media markets. The Hersant group, for example, as of early 1992 owned more than two dozen dailies, a dozen periodicals and seven monthly papers, in addition to more than 80 radio stations. While Hersant and the others have not significantly altered the editorial positions of the publications they acquired, the acquisitions have undeniably diminished readers' choice in regional markets. A few national papers -- notably *Le Monde*, *Libération* and some weeklies -- continue to offer high quality reporting on both national and international affairs.

State subsidies for general information dailies, begun in 1974, constitute one of several additional mechanisms which aim to preserve diversity. Public assistance to the press includes tax concessions and special mail and telephone rates.

---

[10] CC, 29 July 1986, *supra* note 4.

7. REGISTRATION REQUIREMENTS

Prior to the commencement of publication of any daily or periodical, a declaration must be made to the State Prosecutor's office, indicating the title, name and address of the director and that of the printer (Article 7 of the 1881 Act).

Under Article 10 of the 1881 Act, a number of copies of each issue of a newspaper or periodical must be deposited at the moment of publication with various authorities (generally two at the State Prosecutor's office or town hall, and 10 at the *préfet*'s and *sous-préfet*'s office).

The authorities do not have the power to refuse to register a paper, and the registration requirements have never been used as a form of censorship.

8. REGULATION OF IMPORT AND EXPORT OF PUBLICATIONS

There are no regulations applying to the export of publications and, in fact, the government provides some financial incentives to increase the circulation of French publications in foreign countries.

Under Article 14 of the 1881 Act, as amended in 1939, the Minister of the Interior is empowered to ban the distribution, circulation or sale of any writing in a foreign language or of "foreign origin", even if published in France by a French company. It is an offence to distribute or reproduce banned writings with knowledge that they have been banned. When a newspaper or a book has been banned under these regulations, the police may seize any copy or issue that they find. Article 14 is an archaic as well as an illiberal provision, inherited from the pre-World War II period and widely used until the end of the 1970s. It was used during the Cold War against the foreign communist periodicals, and currently is used against extreme forms of pornography and anti-Semitic and "revisionist" literature (including a foreign edition of the *Protocols of the Elders of Zion*). It has also been used from time to time at the request of some African governments to ban African opposition newspapers published in France. During the Gulf War, two Arabic-language papers published in London (*Al-Arab and Al-Dustur*) and one Arabic-language daily published in Paris (*Kol al-Arab*) were banned on the grounds that they defended interests contrary to those of France and that their circulation could, in the circumstances, disturb public order.

The notion of a writing of "foreign origin" is both broad and unclear. It applies not only to the French translation of foreign works, but also to writings, the "inspiration" of which is deemed to be foreign or whose author or publisher received foreign assistance of some kind.[11] For instance, the government tried in vain to use the law to ban a book published in

---

[11] Conseil d'Etat, 4 June 1954, *Jouloux et Riaux*, 435; *S*. 1954.3.87, upholding the banning of *La Tour de Garde*, the periodical published by the Jehovah's Witnesses; 2 Feb. 1958, *Société des éditions de la terre de feu, D.* 1958. 570, upholding the banning of Henry Miller's *Sexus*; 2 Nov. 1973, *Librairie F. Maspero*, 611; *JCP.* 1974. 17642 (concl. Braibant, note Drago), upholding the banning of *Tricontinental*, a French periodical published in Paris

France by a French author and publisher relating to the author's experience in Africa when he was a Guinean national.[12]

Article 14 says nothing about the grounds on which a ban may be ordered. The *Conseil d'Etat* has ruled that bans may be imposed on a broad range of grounds, including: foreign relations considerations[13], public order[14], national defence[15], and protection of the reputation of a public institution (in this case, the *Cité Universitaire*, an international students' residence in Paris)[16].

Two procedural protections are granted: first, before the authorities may issue a ban, the publisher or editor must be notified and (since 1983) must be given the opportunity to argue his case in writing and, second, the ban (since 1979) must state reasons of fact and law. Until 1973 review was extremely restricted. Since 1973 it includes review of a "manifest error of appreciation" (not unlike "unreasonableness"), in addition to error in law and, of course, validity under the treaties in force in France. The *Conseil d'Etat* has applied this standard on the theory that a fuller review is not required since the bannings concern only "foreign" authors or publishers and the Act is silent on the point.

Whatever one thinks of such considerations, which belong to the past, they are now clearly inconsistent with Article 10 of the ECHR and the European Court's relevant case-law which require full judicial review as well as the application of the concept of proportionality. A 1985 decision of the *Conseil d'Etat* may indicate a shift towards application of a broader standard of review.[17]

---

which reproduced the contents of a Cuban periodical of the same name, itself banned in 1968, and the banning of which had been upheld by the Paris Administrative Court (2 July 1969, p. 646).

[12] The book was J P Alata's *Prisons d'Afrique* (Editions du Seuil). The Conseil d'Etat refused to order a stay of execution of the ban pending its final decision on the merits (28 Feb. 1978, *Alata*, p. 193, and *AJDA* 1987, p. 398); and upheld the lower court's quashing of the ban on the ground that there was no evidence that the book had been written using "foreign documentation" or had "foreign inspiration" (9 July 1982, *Ministre de l'Intérieur c. Editions du Seuil et autre*, p. 281).

[13] In *Ministre de l'Intérieur c. S.A. Librairie F. Maspero*, 30 January. 1980, p. 53, *AJDA*, 1980, p. 242 (concl. Genevois), the Conseil d'Etat upheld the government's banning of J Chomé's book *L'Ascension de Mobutu* (1974), reversing the Paris Administrative Court's ruling that diplomatic considerations could not justify a ban in the absence of a threat to public order (Paris Administrative Court, 5 July 1978, *Librairie F. Maspero, AJDA*, 1978, p. 50).

[14] 2 Nov. 1973, *supra* note 11.

[15] 4 June 1954, *supra* note 11.

[16] *Monus*, 18 July 1973, 527.

[17] The Conseil d'Etat upheld the quashing of a ban by the lower Paris Administrative Court in its decision of 17 April 1985, *Ministre de l'Intérieur et de la décentralisation c. Société des éditions des Archers*, p. 100, (concl. Stirn), *Revue de droit public* (1985), 1363. The ban was directed against a new edition, published in Belgium, of the French edition of the German military propaganda magazine *Signal* which had been published during the war. The Minister invoked two grounds: (a) the magazine's circulation was such as to be likely to develop a renewal of Nazi

9.   MECHANISMS OF PRESS SELF-REGULATION

In France, there is neither a Press Council nor any other mechanism of press self-regulation. There are unions of journalists and unions of newspaper owners (for Paris dailies and provincial ones), and, in addition, a number of journalists' associations. In a daily like *Le Monde*, the journalists' associations play a very influential role, especially in the choice of the editor.

Ethical standards contained in international press declarations or national documents (such as the 1918 Charter of the Professional Duties of Journalists, amended in 1938) have no legal or binding value and do not seem to be used or even mentioned in court.

10.   DEFAMATION

In French law, defamation is both a tort (a civil wrong) and a criminal offence.[18] It consists of any allegation of *fact* which constitutes an attack on the honour or reputation of a person (Article 29 of the 1881 Act). If found guilty, the editor, publisher or author may be ordered to pay a criminal fine to the State in addition to civil damages to the aggrieved party. The civil and criminal action take place before the same court at the same time. There is no jury.[19] The two main defences are truth and good faith.

A journalist (or other defendant) may establish a defence if he or she can prove good faith, that is, that he or she proceeded with care, checked the facts, tried to contact the interested person, etc. Some court decisions mention the "presumption of bad faith" and a few balance this against the right and duty of the press to inform the public. For example, a Paris civil court rejected a libel action against two newspapers and a journalist filed by a Swiss lawyer based on articles stating that he belonged to the board of a company accused of laundering narcotics money.[20] Although truth could not be proven, the court accepted evidence of the defendants' good faith. The court stated:

> Although belief in the reality of the alleged facts and an absence of animosity
> or personal interest are not enough to set aside the presumption of bad faith,
> the legitimate motivation arising from *the right and duty to inform* allows the

---

ideology, and (b) it created a danger for public order. The Conseil noted that these two grounds were, in principle, lawful but found the public order ground manifestly wanting. Turning to the first ground, the Conseil concluded that had it been the only one, the Minister would not have taken the decision. This is a typical example of judicial review of the grounds of a decision when there is a plurality of grounds, one of which is unlawful.

[18] In French law, there are three degrees of criminal offence: a *contravention* (infraction), *e.g.,* for minor traffic violations; a *délit* (offence) for moderately serious crimes such as theft, burglary and defamation; and a *crime* (serious crime), such as murder and publication of official secrets.

[19] There are no jury trials in civil cases; only defendants charged with serious crimes are entitled to jury trials.

[20] *See, e.g.,* the decision of the Paris TGI of 19 Dec. 1990, reported in *Le Monde*, 23-24 Dec. 1990.

journalist to invoke his good faith as long as he establishes not only the seriousness of his inquiry, but also his prudence and objectivity. (Emphasis added.)

Despite the outcome in the above case, in general the case-law tends to impose a heavy burden on the press, as shown by the following examples:

• The fact that the plaintiff was accused before a court of having committed grave acts related to those mentioned in the allegedly defamatory article did not absolve the newspaper of its responsibility to check carefully those assertions that might have been prejudicial to his honour or reputation.[21]

• Good faith was not shown where the defendant re-published rumours originating in old books without conducting an independent inquiry into their credibility.[22]

• The author was found to have acted in bad faith when he published an article based on insufficient information and did not engage in any research to substantiate his statements.[23]

• Mistaking one person for another automatically excludes the possibility of good faith.[24]

Truth is a defence except in three situations: when the facts are older than ten years; when they infringe upon privacy; or when they relate to an offence which has been pardoned, which is older than the time-limit set in the statute of limitations, or which involves a person who has been rehabilitated.[25]

To prove truth is no easy task and acquittals on this ground are rare.[26] The burden rests on the defendant and relates only to the facts. In 1985 the courts considered an interesting case. A daily and a weekly paper published articles on M Le Pen, accusing him of having participated in torture in Algeria and of having personally executed a "suspect". Truth was not permitted to be proved because the facts at issue were older than ten years. M Le Pen sued for libel. The lower court rejected his action on the ground that he had publicly

---

[21] Paris TGI, 24 Jan. 1990, *X v. Y et al.*

[22] Paris TGI, June 1992, reported in *Le Monde*, 13 June 1992.

[23] Paris TGI, 27 Feb. 1992, reported in *Le Monde*, 29 Feb. 1992.

[24] Cass. Crim., 8 July 1986.

[25] Article 35 of the 1881 Act.

[26] For a recent and topical example, see Paris TGI, 17 Sept. 1992, reported in *Le Monde*, 19 Sept. 1992. The newspaper hailed the decision as a "victory of the rule of law against *raison d'Etat*".

condoned the use of torture to obtain information from terrorists and consequently could not claim that an accusation of torture against him constituted libel. The court found that the journalist had established his good faith concerning the execution claim.[27] The court of appeal reversed and ruled that the articles were libellous; whether or not M Le Pen had condoned the use of torture in Algeria, he had never acknowledged having used it himself. As to the execution claim, the court found that the journalist had not established good faith.[28]

10.1 Damages and Fines

Awards vary according to the circumstances. While the trend has been for the courts to award ever larger sums, the amounts on the whole are modest and do not begin to approach the amounts awarded by juries in countries such as the United States and Britain. The total burden for the newspaper or publisher is the sum of (civil) damages, a (criminal) fine, the cost of publishing the judgment in a number of newspapers, and of course the publication's own legal and other costs. Following are a few examples of typical damage awards:[29]

- A retired member of the Paris court of appeal was ordered to pay FF 100,000 (approximately US$ 19,000) for publishing a book which libelled one of his former colleagues.[30]

- The magazine *Elle* was ordered to pay FF 100,000 for libelling the wife of Prince Norodom Sihanouk, of Cambodia; good faith was rejected.[31]

- *Le Monde* was ordered to pay FF 40,000 to a Moroccan refugee for publishing an article, while a proceeding to expel him (reportedly initiated by a request from the Moroccan Government) was pending, in which it was suggested that he might be a dubious character or even an informant of the Moroccan police. The source of the accusations was a government official who had access to confidential information in the government's file on the refugee.[32]

---

[27] Paris TGI, 18 April 1985, *Le Pen v. Fressoz, Gaz. Pal.*, 13-14 Nov. 1985, note J P D; same court, 4 July 1985, *Le Pen et al. v. July* and *Le Pen v. July, D.* 1985. 5 (note Agostini); also reported in *Le Monde*, 6 July 1985.

[28] Paris Cour d'appel, 15 Jan. 1986, reported in *Le Monde*, 17 Jan. 1986.

[29] Criminal fines are generally smaller than civil awards.

[30] Rouen Cour d'appel, 9 Sept. 1991, reported in *Le Monde*, 20 Sept. 1991.

[31] Paris TGI, 11 June 1992, reported in *Le Monde*, 13 June.

[32] Paris TGI, 27 Feb. 1992, *supra* note 23.

10.2   Persons Performing a Public Function

Ministers, members of Parliament, civil servants and any public agent or person performing a public duty, even on a temporary basis (such as a member of a jury or a witness giving evidence in court) must meet a higher standard of proof in prosecuting a defamation claim. This is so in order to ensure that free and fair discussion of matters of public interest is not discouraged. Political leaders who do not fall into one of the above categories also tend to be required to meet a higher standard of proof in prosecuting defamation claims regarding their public functions.[33]

11.   INVASION OF PRIVACY

Initially a creation of the case-law of the civil courts during the 1960s, privacy is now a right under Article 9 of the Civil Code. Neither the Civil Code nor the case-law give a comprehensive definition of the limits of privacy, and rightly so. Any attempt at defining privacy would be bound to result in a definition that was either too minimal or too broad. Privacy is only a tort, unlike defamation (which may also be a criminal offence). Neither truth, nor good faith, nor the public interest provides a defence.

Although the *Conseil constitutionnel* has not yet decided a case concerning privacy, it is certainly arguable that the right to privacy has now acquired constitutional status and is protected as such, being one of the fundamental principles recognized by the laws of the Republic. Moreover, privacy is protected as a fundamental right by both the ECHR and the ICCPR.

Courts rarely order the seizure of a book or the complete edition of a periodical in a summary proceeding in advance of a full determination on the merits, in view of the significant infringement of press freedom that such a measure would constitute. They have, however, ordered such measures in extreme cases of deliberate and outrageous violation of privacy when summary seizure offered the only adequate remedy.[34]

---

[33] However, the French courts have not expressly adopted the rule set forth by the European Court of Human Rights in its *Lingens* judgment that politicians are required to sustain a higher degree of criticism regarding their public functions than private persons.

[34] For a discussion of the case-law and a bibliography, *see* R Errera, "Recent developments in the French law of the Press in comparison with Britain," in *Economical with the Truth: the Law and the Media in a Democratic Society*, edited by D Kingsford-Smith and D Oliver (Oxford: ESC Publishing Ltd, 1990), at 68.

12. RIGHT OF REPLY AND/OR CORRECTION

The French law on the press includes a right of reply (Article 13 of the 1881 Act). Such a right belongs to any person, natural or legal, mentioned or clearly alluded to in an article; whether the article is accurate or not, or libellous or not is of no relevance. The right has been held to be a fundamental right of the person; hence, it may be exercised only by the very person concerned or the person's legal representative.[35] Daily newspapers are bound to publish the reply within three days, and periodicals must publish in the next issue. The right of reply was extended by the Act of 4 January 1993 on criminal procedure so that it now is expressly available, for a period of three months following acquittal or a decision of non-presentation, to any person who has been acquitted of a crime or, following an investigation, has not had charges against him presented to a court for trial.

There are a number of limits to the right, some of which relate to the length of the reply, and others, to its substance. The most important substantive restrictions are that the reply may not contain any material which violates the interests of third parties (since the editor is liable for *everything* that is published in a newspaper without exception), which constitutes an attack upon the integrity or honour of the journalist, or which is unlawful (*e.g.*, libellous).[36]

An accelerated judicial procedure exists to compel compliance where the newspaper or periodical refuses or delays. It is even swifter, for obvious reasons, during election campaigns. The right of reply forms one of the oldest clauses of the French law of the press. It is widely accepted; journalists and newspaper associations do not complain about it and it has had no "chilling effect" on reporting.[37] The fact that a right of reply has or has not been used in a given case does not affect other available actions or remedies.

In addition to the general right of reply, editors are bound by law to publish any correction (*rectification*) submitted by any public servant (*lato sensu*) when acts relating to his or her duties or functions have been mistakenly reported (Article 12 of the Act). There exists very little case-law on this provision, which is rarely used.

---

[35] Paris Cour d'appel, 21 April 1988, *X v. Y.*

[36] *See* Paris TGI, 28 Oct. 1987, *Société le nouvel Economiste*; and Cass. crim., 15 April 1982, *Casanovas, D.* 1984, 358 (note Damerat).

[37] *See* G Biolley, *Le droit de réponse en matière de presse* (Paris, 1963), reviewed by R Errera in *Revue de science criminelle* (1964), 952.

13. INSULTS TO GOVERNMENT INSTITUTIONS OR OFFICIALS

Libel against any State institution (such as the courts, the army and public administration at large) is a criminal offence under Article 30 of the 1881 Act. In addition, libel against a minister, a member of Parliament, or any civil servant or public agent concerning his or her public duties or capacity is a separate offence under Article 31 (*see* Section 10, *supra*). Insult (*offense*) to the President of the Republic is an offence under Article 26.

Two other archaic provisions exist: insult to foreign heads of state and ministers of foreign affairs, and outrage to foreign ambassadors or diplomatic agents. These clauses do not seem to be used any more.

The prohibition of incitement to treason or to espionage (Article 24) has not been used against the press for at least several decades.

14. OFFICIAL SECRECY AND ACCESS TO GOVERNMENT-HELD INFORMATION

14.1 Access to Information

The Act of 17 July 1978 created the right of everyone to have access to public documents, subject to certain enumerated exceptions. The Act sets forth eight broad areas of exception; the administration may refuse to make available the contents of a document where to do so would impair: (1) the secrecy of the deliberations of the government and of the authorities exercising the power of the executive; (2) the secrecy of national defence and foreign policy; (3) the currency and public credit; (4) the security of the State and public safety; (5) the operation of the courts and pre-trial procedures, except where leave has been given by the competent authority; (6) the secrecy of personal and medical files; (7) the secrecy of commercial and industrial matters; and (8) investigations by the authorized services into infringement of tax and customs law.

A special committee, the *Commission d'accès aux documents administratifs* (CADA), examines complaints and difficulties concerning access. Its annual report is a good source of all sorts of information on the actual working of the system. CADA also publishes valuable studies and monographs, including a useful guide on access to administrative documents.[38]

To challenge a decision to withhold a document, a person must first seek CADA's opinion; most difficulties are dealt with at this level and the administration usually complies with CADA's opinions. If the person remains dissatisfied, he or she may petition the local administrative court to quash the refusal as unlawful *(recours pour excès de pouvoir)*. There is already a substantial case-law on this matter. The press does not seem to be among the

---

[38] CADA, *Guide de l'accès aux documents administratifs* (Paris: La Documentation Française, 1990).

main users of this right, perhaps because of the considerable delay involved in obtaining documents.[39]

14.2 Criminal Disclosure of Government Information

The Penal Code prohibits several forms of disclosure of information which might harm national security (Articles 74 *et seq.*). Of relevance to the press are Article 76, which makes it a crime for an unauthorized person to acquire or publish secret defence information, and Article 78, which prohibits disclosure to the public or an unauthorized person of secret military information which is manifestly likely to harm national security.

14.3 Whistleblowers

According to civil service regulations, all civil servants are bound by law to observe professional secrecy. There is no right to make public information about government wrongdoing. However, Article 40 of the Code of Criminal Procedure states that any civil servant who, in the course of his duties, acquires the knowledge of a crime or an offence is bound to inform the State Prosecutor and to transmit to him all relevant information.

15. ACCESS TO AND DISCLOSURE OF COURT DOCUMENTS AND PROCEEDINGS

The principle under French law is that court proceedings are public and that the press may freely report on them. The 1881 Act grants certain immunities to the press, including for good faith reporting of libel proceedings and of statements made in open court. There are several exceptions to the principle of public access and free reporting, primarily to protect the rights of litigants, the integrity of court proceedings, and privacy, particularly of minors.

To protect what Article 10(2) of the ECHR calls "the authority and impartiality of the judiciary" as well as the rights of criminal defendants to a fair trial, it is forbidden to publish information about the *in camera* deliberations of juries and courts (Article 39(4) of the 1881 Act), as well as about indictments or other documents relating to criminal proceedings before they are read in open court (Article 38(1)). Civil courts also are empowered to forbid the disclosure of court proceedings (Article 39(3)), although such power does not seem to be used.

Article 9(1), added to the Civil Code on 4 January 1993, requires measures to safeguard the presumption of innocence of criminal defendants. It provides:

> Every person is entitled to respect for the presumption of his innocence. When a person is, before any conviction, publicly presented as guilty of facts investigated by the police or by the investigating judge, the courts may, even

---

[39] *See* R Errera, "Access to administrative documents in France: Reflections on reform," in N Marsh (ed.), *Public Access to Government-held Information* (London: Stevens, 1987), 87.

in interlocutory proceedings, order the press to publish a rectification or a communique in order to put an end to the breach of the presumption. In addition, the person is entitled to make use of the normal civil actions for damages and interlocutory orders.

Moreover,

> During the investigation conducted by an investigating judge or the *chambre d'accusation* [a special division of the court], the judge of the court may order the publication of
> - the decision by which the person is *not* sent before the court, or
> - a communique summing up the reasons for such a decision.

Various kinds of court proceedings, held *in camera*, may not be reported in the interests of personal privacy. These include proceedings relating to family matters such as divorce, child custody, legitimacy and separation (Article 39(1)). Rape and related criminal proceedings may be held *in camera* whenever the victim so requests although the court may decide nonetheless to admit the press (Article 306 of the Criminal Procedure Code). The press may not publish the surname of the victim or any information allowing her identification unless express consent is given in writing (Article 39 quinquiès).

Juvenile courts sit *in camera*. It is forbidden to publish an account of court proceedings or, indeed, any information or illustration relating to the identity or the personality of a minor brought before such courts (*Ordonnance* of 2 February 1945, Article 14(2)). Court decisions may be published so long as no mention is made of the minor's name. The 1881 Act forbids, in Article 39*ter*, the publication of any text or illustration relating to the suicide of a minor.

In 1984 the Minister of Justice created a committee, chaired by this chapter's author, to inquire into the general state of relations between the press and the judiciary. The committee's report,[40] published in 1985, contains a thorough examination of the law and practice in this area as well as a series of proposals for reform, a number of which were included in the Act of 4 January 1993 on reform of the Code of Criminal Procedure.

---

[40] *Rapport de la commission presse-justice* (Paris, 1985).

16. ACCESS TO AND DISCLOSURE OF LEGISLATIVE DOCUMENTS AND PROCEEDINGS

Legislative proceedings are public and may be freely reported. Certain permanent and select committees of the National Assembly and the Senate also conduct their hearings in public.

Article 41 of the 1881 Act confers total immunity for speeches made in Parliament, for documents and reports made public by Parliament, and for good faith reporting of public sessions of Parliament. Parliament has no authority to penalize anyone. There is no offence of "contempt of Parliament".

Parliament may create special committees (*commissions de contrôle*) whose workings are secret (under the *Ordonnance* of 17 November 1958). All persons participating in the work of such special committees are bound to secrecy and publication of information relating to their work or to their non-published reports is an offence. There do not seem to be any cases concerning this offence.

17. COMMERCIAL SECRECY AND ACCESS TO INFORMATION HELD BY PRIVATE PARTIES

Access to and disclosure of information held by private parties may be restricted under the following provisions.

It is an offence for an employee of a company to disclose trade secrets to a third party (Penal Code, Article 148). What constitutes a trade secret has been defined by the case-law. Access to public documents contains an exception relating to matters covered by trade secrets. The reason is that companies are required by law to provide the administration with a growing volume of information, and access to administrative documents should not become an easy method of commercial or industrial espionage. The *Guide de l'accès aux documents administratifs*, published by CADA (*see* Section 14, *supra*) includes a chapter on CADA's policy on industrial and commercial secrecy, defined to encompass three kinds of information: manufacturing processes (*secrets des procédés*), economic and financial information, and commercial strategies.[41]

There is no law which protects "whistleblowers" (i.e., employees who disclose information about their employer's wrongdoing) from termination or discipline.

The publication by the press of confidential information about a company may, depending on the circumstances, be either a libel or a tort.

---

[41]   *See* "Le secret en matière industrielle et commerciale", in CADA, *supra* note 38, at 85.

18.   PRIOR RESTRAINTS

Summary measures may be taken to seize publications or prevent their distribution in advance of a full court hearing to protect a number of interests, although in practice such measures are rare. The most common ground is to protect privacy; the civil courts are empowered to take any steps to prevent or put a stop to an attack on core privacy interests (*l'intimité de la vie privée*) protected by Article 9 of the Civil Code.[42]

The police are authorized, when they believe that public morals are *immediately* threatened, to seize any materials or to destroy or cover posters. This power does not apply to books which bear the name of the author and publisher and which have been deposited with the National Library in compliance with regulations on *dépôt légal* (Penal Code, Article 290).

The administration is empowered to seize any foreign publication banned under Article 14 of the 1881 Act (*see* Section 8, *supra*), and any publication likely to incite hatred against a national, religious, racial or ethnic group (*see* Section 20, *infra*).

Under emergency law -- either under Article 16 of the Constitution, a state of siege (under the 1849 Act), or a state of emergency (under the Act of 1955) -- the administration is given broad powers to engage in censorship.

A recent decision of the Paris civil court in interlocutory proceedings typifies the way in which courts handle requests for prior restraints in practice. *L'évènement du jeudi*, a Paris weekly, had published excerpts of a telephone conversation between a reporter from *Le Monde* in Paris and the lawyer of Dr Garretta, a French physician recently sentenced to four years in jail for his responsibility in the blood transfusion scandal, in Boston. The conversation had been intercepted by a CNN reporter in Boston using a scanner. Dr Garretta asked the court to order the seizure of the newspaper on the grounds that the article interfered with his privacy, his rights before the courts and also with the professional secrecy owed him by his lawyer. The court rejected the application for an immediate seizure on the ground that there had been no intrusion upon "core" privacy interests. Although privacy had been invaded, which might allow the physician to recover damages after a full court hearing on the merits, and although *L'évènement du jeudi*'s actions were unlawful on the three grounds Dr Garretta raised, the situation did not create the "intolerable" situation necessary to justify such an extreme step as seizure. *Le Monde* severely castigated the conduct of *L'évènement du jeudi* and the CNN reporter, and compared the reporter's behaviour to the worst police habits.[43]

---

[42] *See* Section 11, *supra*, for a discussion of the substantive law of privacy.

[43] Paris civil court, 4 Nov. 1992, reported in *Le Monde*, 6 Nov. 1992.

19. PROTECTION OF SOURCES

Article 378 of the Penal Code forbids members of certain professions (including physicians, barristers, priests and others) to breach professional secrecy and makes it an offence to do so.[44] However, the duty of professional secrecy does not apply to journalists.

Any person called before a court (civil or criminal) is under an obligation to give evidence, unless the court recognizes that there is a legitimate reason for not doing so. Journalists may be questioned regarding their sources of information. Refusal to appear or to answer is an offence punishable by a fine or jail sentence. In practice very few courts or investigative *magistrats* (which, in French law, does not mean a magistrate, but instead designates a *juges d'instruction*, the State Prosecutor or a judge) ever go so far as to ask a journalist to disclose his or her sources. When this is done, the journalist generally declines to answer, invoking professional custom, and the court refrains from ordering sanctions. Journalists have been sanctioned in only one or two cases in recent memory.

The law on protection of sources and confidential information was substantially revised by adoption of the Act of 4 January 1993 amending the Code of Criminal Procedure.

Newly added Article 109(2) now provides that :

> Any journalist who appears as a witness concerning information gathered by him in the course of his journalistic activity is free not to disclose its source.

Concerning searches of media offices, Article 56(2) now provides:

> Searches of the premises of a press or broadcasting company may be conducted only by a judge or a State prosecutor, who must ensure that the investigations do not endanger the free exercise of the profession of journalism and do not obstruct or cause an unjustified delay to the distribution of information.

---

[44]   On professional secrecy in French law, *see* F Warenbourg-Auque, "Reflexions sur le secret professionnel en droit français," in Travaux de l'Association H Capitant, 23, *Le secret et le droit* (Paris, 1974), 105; B Decheix, *Un droit de l'homme mis à mal: le secret professionnel*, D. 1983, 133.

20. RESTRICTIONS ON OFFENSIVE LANGUAGE AGAINST IDENTIFIABLE GROUPS[45]

The Act of 1 July 1972 which, in amended form, remains today the basis of current French law on group libel and racial incitement, makes discrimination on ethnic, national, racial or religious grounds an offence, unless justified by a *motif légitime* (legitimate reason), whether committed against an individual, an association or a company.[46] The Act amended the 1881 Act on the press in three important ways. First, incitement to discrimination, hatred or violence against a person or a group of persons on grounds of origin or because of belonging or not belonging to a given ethnic group, nation, race or religion was made an offence, punishable by up to one year's imprisonment and/or a fine of FF 2,000-30,000 (Article 24 of the 1881 Act as amended). Second, the scope of the old law was extended by inclusion of the words "or not belonging" and "ethnic group or nation". Third, the right to bring an action, whether criminal or civil, was extended to any association dedicated to opposing racism which had been in legal existence for at least five years. This grant of standing to private associations is a distinctive feature of the French legal system. In 1990, a new law made it a criminal offence to contest the Nazi genocide of the Jews.

The first case brought in the courts under the 1972 Act was against the editor of the news bulletin URSS, published in Paris by the information service of the Soviet Embassy, for an article entitled "school of obscurantism" which contained rabidly anti-Semitic statements, including a rehash of the *Protocols of the Elders of Zion*. Two civil rights associations sued the editor alleging that the article slandered Jews and Zionists and made false statements regarding Zionists beliefs. The editor was convicted of both group libel and racial incitement. He was ordered to pay two fines, to publish the judgment in the paper, and to pay the cost of its publication in six newspapers.

A number of prosecutions have been brought under the anti-incitement and group libel laws, but editors are not prosecuted merely for publishing an article which constitutes group libel or racial incitement unless they share, or may be presumed to share, the guilty intent of the author. Thus, while Robert Faurisson was convicted for two articles he published in *Le Matin* and *Le Monde*, the editors were not prosecuted.[47] In contrast, the editor of an anti-Semitic journal which published an interview with Faurisson was ordered to pay a fine of FF 30,000, damages of FF 20,000 to each of the 11 associations which sued, and the costs of publishing the judgment in four daily newspapers (FF 15,000 each). Faurison received a lighter sentence; he was ordered to pay only a fine of FF 100,000 which was suspended.[48]

---

[45] For a more extensive discussion of laws which prohibit group libel and racial incitement *see* R Errera, "In Defence of Civility: Racial Incitement and Group Libel in French Law," in *Striking a Balance: Hate Speech, Freedom of Expression and Non-Discrimination*, S Coliver (ed.) (London: ARTICLE 19, 1992), 144-58.

[46] Penal Code, Arts. 187(1) and 416.

[47] *LICRA et autres c. Faurrisson*, Paris TGI, 8 July 1981, *Recueil Dalloz* (1982), 59 (note Edelman).

[48] Errera, *supra* note 45, at 155.

21. BLASPHEMY, OBSCENITY AND PROTECTION OF PUBLIC MORALS

There is no prohibition of blasphemy in French law.

Obscenity is one of the grounds on which the Minister of the Interior may restrict the sale and distribution of publications addressed to minors or which, in view of their contents, might pose a danger to them (Act of 1949). This Act was rather widely used until the 1970s, but has not been much used since then in view of the evolution of public mores. Obscenity may also be prosecuted as a crime under Penal Code Article 283, but there have been no such actions for a number of years. In any event, the daily press has not been the target of either of the two obscenity laws.

22. RESTRICTIONS ON ADVERTISING

Advertising of certain products or goods (including tobacco, spirits and pharmaceuticals) is either forbidden or severely regulated in the interests of public safety and health.

Political advertising during election campaigns is regulated by Article 47 *et seq.* and 89 *et seq.* of the Electoral Code; paid political advertisements are forbidden in both the print and broadcasting media during the three months preceding an election (Article 52(1)).

CONCLUSION

Two economic facts have had a substantial impact on the press, namely: (1) the concentration of ownership of the daily press both in Paris and in the rest of the country, and (2) the financial fragility of both dailies and weeklies, caused in part by the loss of advertising income due to the recession. While concentration has limited pluralism in the sense of *numbers* of publications, it has not had a substantial impact on narrowing the range of editorial perspectives or in reducing the quality of serious reporting. The fact is that for the past 20 years the French press has, on the whole, well-informed the public on matters of legitimate public interest; fulfilled its public "watchdog" function; and developed the quality and level of its investigations. Its effectiveness in these areas is illustrated by its role in uncovering the recent blood transfusion scandal and in pursuing the Rainbow Warrior incident in 1985.

Since the basic law on the press has not substantially changed, the improved quality of reporting would appear to have other causes. These include increased competition among dailies, and between them and the public and private broadcasting media; higher expectations of the public; and better training of journalists.

While courts are reluctant to order prior restraints and to discourage legitimate reporting, they are very much aware of the necessity to defend the rights of the individual against press excesses, most particularly invasion of privacy and libel. The defence of good faith to libel charges encourages the press to double-check stories that portray people in a negative light while permitting publication of stories even where facts cannot be confirmed.

There has been no demand, either from the public or the press, for a press council or other non-statutory mechanism of press regulation. This may be due in part to the fact that the legal system provides reasonably prompt, effective and affordable relief; free legal aid is available to anyone who requires legal assistance (and meets a certain low income requirement) in suing the press (*e.g.,* for invasion of privacy, defamation or refusal to publish a reply by right) and court cases are far cheaper than in such countries as the UK and US.

Whether any aspect of the French system of press regulation can serve as a useful model for other countries depends on a variety of contextual factors unrelated directly to press freedom; the crucial first question is to ascertain the values and interests the society is most committed to protecting.

Chapter 5

FREEDOM OF THE PRESS IN GERMANY

Ulrich Karpen

INTRODUCTION

The press is a medium and an actor in the process of forming public opinion in a democracy. Freedom of the press, in addition to being a constitutional right of individuals against the state, is viewed as a guarantor of freedom of speech and informed public debate, and thus as integral to the protection of democracy.[1] This understanding and interpretation of the constitutional guarantee affects the extent and limits of press freedom. The law explicitly protects pluralism of the press by fostering competition and safeguarding collection and dissemination of information, although concerns remain about concentration of press ownership. Press freedom may, however, be limited by the "general laws", including laws on defamation and privacy, but only in cases where individual rights and other pressing social needs outweigh the constitutional interest in protecting freedom of the press.[2]

1. RELEVANT CONSTITUTIONAL PROVISIONS

Paragraphs 1 and 2 of Article 5 of the 1949 Basic Law of the Federal Republic of Germany guarantee the right to freedom of expression in the following terms:

> (1) Everyone shall have the right freely to express and disseminate his opinion by speech, writing and pictures and freely to inform himself from generally accessible sources. Freedom of the press and freedom of reporting by means of broadcasts and films are guaranteed. There shall be no censorship.

> (2) These rights are limited by the provisions of the general laws, the provisions of law for the protection of youth, and by the right to inviolability of personal honour.[3]

---

[1] 7 Federal Constitutional Court (FCC) 198, 208 (Lüth case). *See generally* U Karpen, "Freedom of Expression", in U Karpen (ed.), *The Constitution of the Federal Republic of Germany, Essays on the Basic Rights and Principles of the Basic Law with a Translation of the Basic Law* (Baden-Baden: 1988), pp. 91-106.

[2] For a more extensive discussion (in English) of press law in Germany *see* H Kohl, "Press Law in the Federal Republic of Germany", in P Lahav (ed.), *Press Law in Modern Democracies: A Comparative Study* (1985), pp. 185-228. *See also* discussion of German law in the context of a comparative study in E Barendt, *Freedom of Speech* (Oxford: Clarendon Press, 1987).

[3] Paragraph 3, which is not directly relevant to press freedom, reads: "Art and science, research and teaching shall be free. Freedom of teaching shall not absolve from loyalty to the Constitution."

Article 5 guarantees press freedom in the traditional liberal form by protecting the right of "everyone" including publishers, editors, journalists and readers to freedom from government interference with the right to express and disseminate opinions and to gather information from generally accessible sources. In addition, the second sentence of paragraph 1 grants special institutional guarantees to the mass media.[4] These have been interpreted to include positive government obligations to further media diversity, requiring both an "external plurality" (such as the competition of many newspapers) and an "internal plurality" (diversity in the composition of boards of public broadcasting stations). These special protections are justified on the ground that the media have a "public function" to inform public opinion and act as "public watchdog".[5] This public function must be the responsibility of bodies which are independent of government influence. The special role of the media forms the legitimate basis of privileges, such as the right to refuse to give evidence in court (*see* Section 19, *infra*), and duties, such as the obligation to disseminate only true and accurate information (*see* Section 10.2, *infra*).

The Federal Constitutional Court (FCC) has ruled that Article 5 also guarantees the right of the public to receive information of legitimate public interest,[6] making Germany's protection of this right amongst the strongest in Europe.

Press freedom may be limited by provisions of the "general laws", which are laws that seek to promote a general social value and which may incidentally affect, but are not aimed at curtailing, freedom of expression. General laws which may take precedence over freedom of expression include those which protect youth[7], public morality, personal honour, the rights and reputations of others, national security, and respect for state institutions. Press freedom may also be limited by Article 1 of the Basic Law (protection of human dignity), Article 2 (free development of one's personality), Article 12 (free choice and practice of a profession or occupation) and Article 14 (right to property).

According to Article 19 of the Basic Law, no law or measure may encroach upon the essential content of fundamental freedoms, including freedom of the press. If a law does so, it must, to be valid, explicitly declare its intention to restrict Article 5.[8]

Whoever abuses press or other freedoms in order to combat the free democratic basic order forfeits the right to these freedoms. Forfeiture would occur only in response to acts which the

---

[4] M Löffler, *Presserecht, Kommentar*, 3. Aufl., Band I, Landespressegesetze (München: 1983), Sec. 1, marginal note 83.

[5] 7 FCC 198, *supra* note 1; 42 FCC 170 (1975) (Deutschland-Magazin).

[6] 27 FCC 71 (1969). *See also* Section 8, *supra*.

[7] The laws which protect youth are set forth in the Criminal Code and in a law concerning distribution of printed matter endangering youth of 9 June 1953, Official Gazette of Laws (Offic. Gaz.), 1953, Vol. I, 377.

[8] Basic Law, Article 19(1), second sentence.

FCC determined were intended and likely to undermine democracy or the rule of law. The FCC has never made such a pronouncement and this provision, therefore, is seen as a "dead letter".

German courts do not accept that *any* general law provides a legitimate means for abridging press freedom, but rather balance protection of individual rights and other pressing social needs against the constitutional interest in protecting press freedom.[9] If an individual right or a pressing state interest conflicted with freedom of the press, the courts would *balance* the competing interests. The balancing would take into account the degree to which the increased protection of an individual or state interest might pose a danger of suffocating freedom of the press.

In these circumstances, German courts apply the proportionality principle in a three-part test: they examine whether measures taken to protect an individual right pursuant to a general law which also infringe upon press freedom are: 1) appropriate, 2) necessary and 3) proportionate.[10] At the conclusion of the analysis, any doubts as to which right prevails are to be resolved in favour of press freedom.[11]

2. DISTRIBUTION OF POWERS BETWEEN CENTRAL AND REGIONAL GOVERNMENT

Press law in Germany is primarily *Länder* law. Under Article 70 of the Basic Law, the power to legislate on press matters was given to the *Länder*. The Federal Parliament has only a residual power to legislate on the general legal status of the press (BL, Article 75(2)), which it has never used.

3. ROLE OF THE COURTS

The main guardian of the basic rights set forth in the Basic Law is the *Bundesverfassungsgericht* (BVerfG) or Federal Constitutional Court (FCC), which has the power to declare invalid any statute which is incompatible with those rights. Courts other than the FCC cannot declare laws passed after 1949 unconstitutional, but if a court believes that a law violates a basic right, it must stay proceedings and refer the constitutional question to the FCC. The FCC decides on complaints of unconstitutionality, which may be entered by any person who claims that one of his or her basic rights has been violated by a public authority.[12] Most of the FCC's decisions concerning freedom of the press, of which there

---

[9] *See* 7 FCC 198, *supra* note 1; 30 FCC 173 (1971) (Mephisto); 75 FCC 369 (1987) (Strauss-Karikatur).

[10] U Karpen, *supra* note 1, at 97. *See* discussion of the proportionality principle in Section 18, *infra*.

[11] 82 FCC 236, 260 (1990) (Schuberth).

[12] Basic Law, Article 93(1), No. 4a.

have been hundreds, have arisen from constitutional complaints filed by individuals or press organs. These cases demonstrate that in the area of press freedom (and other areas of human rights as well), the governing law increasingly is being established by case-law rather than code.

4.   STATUS OF INTERNATIONAL HUMAN RIGHTS TREATIES IN NATIONAL LAW

The international obligations accepted by the Federal Republic of Germany have governed the whole of Germany, including the five *Länder* of the former German Democratic Republic, since reunification in 1990, pursuant to Article 23 of the Basic Law.[13]

The Federal Republic ratified the European Convention on Human Rights (ECHR) in 1952, and accepted the right of individual petition to the European Commission of Human Rights under ECHR Article 25. Article 10, guaranteeing the right to freedom of expression, including the right to receive and impart information, plays a growing role as a standard of interpretation in German law. The ECHR has the status of a federal statute in German law. Thus, although a court may not invalidate a federal law on the ground that it violates the ECHR, a breach of the ECHR in all cases will constitute a violation of Article 5 of the Basic Law and as such will be subject to invalidation by the FCC. The ECHR takes precedence over all *Länder* law.

The Federal Republic ratified the ICCPR in 1973. It has the same status in German law as the ECHR.

5.   STATUTORY FRAMEWORK

There are no Federal laws addressed exclusively to the press. All *Länder* have enacted press laws which, while varying in detail, basically follow the same pattern. The laws include some 27 sections, dealing mainly with restatements of the constitutional freedom, qualifications of editors, the right of reply, protection against seizure, right to refuse to give evidence, and criminal responsibility of press personnel. Overall, the press laws impose certain obligations on the press which are not unduly cumbersome and which establish and reinforce several rights. The *Länder* of the former GDR are considering adopting the same or similar press laws but have not yet done so.

---

[13] U Karpen, "The Reunification of Germany - Challenges for Theory and Practice of Legislation", in *Juridisk Tidskrift* (Stockholms Universitet: 3/1991-92), 429-39.

6. REGULATION OF OWNERSHIP

Freedom of the press as a constitutional principle includes pluralism and competition of press organs.[14] Only if people can collect information from different sources are they able to be in a position to participate in democracy. Pluralism of press organs is a vital element of press freedom. The legislature guarantees pluralism by preventing monopolies. Under German law, press pluralism means free access to the press, pluralism in ownership, limits on press concentration, participation of journalists in the editorial process, and liberal rules on the registration and importation of publications.

6.1 Prevention of Press Concentration

From 1950 to 1990, the circulation of daily papers doubled from 10 million to 20.8 million. The circulation of Sunday papers multiplied tenfold to 4 million. The circulation of weekly papers tripled to 1.8 million. In 1991, due to the country's reunification, the circulation of dailies increased to 28 million. Currently, there are four national broadsheet dailies in addition to a daily tabloid, the *Bild-Zeitung*, which has the largest circulation of any daily in Europe (4.8 million in 1991). Editors of these papers place special emphasis on the local editions of their papers, because Germans tend to identify more readily with papers that provide thorough coverage of their immediate vicinity. More than DM 13 billion are spent on newspaper advertising, out of a total DM 24.5 billion spent on all advertising.

Since the mid-1960s, the number of printing houses and editorial units of daily newspapers producing more than one local newspaper has diminished. This trend stabilized in the 1970s. Today there are 159 editorial units producing some 410 dailies (with 1,667 editions varying in local detail).

To better counteract the threats to press freedom posed by concentration of ownership, on 28 June 1976 the legislature amended the Federal Cartel Law of 27 July 1956.[15] Although mergers in other sectors are usually controlled only when the annual turnover of the involved companies exceeds DM 500 million, mergers in the press sector are controlled at the DM 25 million level (which represents a circulation of 60,000 to 70,000 copies). The Federal Cartel Agency may, therefore, control mergers of small and medium sized newspapers, whereas control in other sectors is limited to big business. In case of danger to the free press market, the Federal Cartel Agency may prohibit a merger. However, cross-ownership between print and electronic media is only regulated in some state broadcasting laws (*e.g.*, North-Rhine-Westfalia), and the potential of cross-ownership to compromise media freedom is a matter of current debate. Under the Cartel Law, vertical price-fixing (for instance, regarding the means of editing, printing, data-processing and distribution) is legal, unlike in other market sectors.

---

[14] *See* 12 FCC 261 (1961) (Fernsehurteil); 20 FCC 162, 176 (1966) (Spiegel); *see also* U Karpen, "*Medienrecht*", in Achterberg-Püttner (ed.), *Besonderes Verwaltungsrecht*, Vol. I (1990), 815, 836.

[15] Offic. Gaz., 1976, at 1081.

6.2 Government Subsidies and Concessionary Rates

Under German law, government subsidies to the press are considered to violate press freedom because, to the extent that some publications would receive greater subsidies than others, such subsidies *could* influence the contents or editorial tendency of a paper.[16] However, the government may, and does, grant lower postage rates to newspapers than to other mail.

6.3 Editorial Control

Concentration of ownership poses a particular threat to pluralism of editorial perspective because, under German law, it is the publisher who decides the editorial tendency of the press organ. Accordingly, journalists have taken the initiative to ensure a measure of editorial independence. A few of the more "liberal" papers have accepted editorial understandings, which not only have given staff journalists the right to determine editorial policy independently from the owner but also have given them a voice in the appointment of the editor-in-chief. When there are strong disagreements between publishers and journalists, however, these understandings have generally provided scant protection to journalists. Publishers tend to take control in such circumstances. The number of "editorial understandings" have dropped since their peak in the mid-1970s.

7. REGISTRATION REQUIREMENTS

Freedom of the press, in principle, includes freedom from registration requirements. This is the essence of Section 2 of the *Länder* press laws, which states: "Press activities, including the founding of a publishing house or other establishment, must not be dependent on government authorization." This differs from the private broadcasting sector, where the government justifies licensing on, among other grounds, the scarcity of channels and the public interest in balanced programming.[17]

8. REGULATION OF IMPORT AND EXPORT OF PUBLICATIONS

According to the law of 31 May 1961 on the control of the importation of printed matter with contents relevant under Criminal Law,[18] newspapers and other printed materials may be seized on crossing the border if they are not for sale and if they violate the laws protecting the free democratic order, international relations and the prohibition of pornography. This law illustrates the spirit of the Cold War period and can only be consistent with Article 5 of the Basic Law if applied narrowly. Although the law has not been used for several years, there have been few calls to repeal it.

---

[16] 20 FCC 56; FedAdmCourt, *Die öffentliche Verwaltung* (1969), 392.

[17] *See* Karpen, *"Medienrecht"*, *supra* note 14, at 875.

[18] Offic. Gaz., Vol. I, at 607.

In deciding whether a foreign publication should be confiscated, courts must take into consideration the right of the public to *receive* information, which has constitutional protection from Article 5. In the leading case, the FCC ruled illegal the confiscation of literature imported from the GDR which supported the banned West German Communist Party on the ground that the lower court had not considered the public's interest in informing themselves from this source.[19]

9. MECHANISMS OF PRESS SELF-REGULATION

Section 6 of the *Länder* press laws states that it is primarily the responsibility of the press itself to check the content of all material prior to publication, including its origin and truth. According to Section 21(2) of the press laws this obligation includes the duty to ensure that printed matter does not violate any criminal law.

In 1956, the associations of newspaper publishers and journalists established the German Press Council as an autonomous, non-governmental, incorporated association in order to introduce a measure of press self-regulation.

In 1973, the Council, in cooperation with the associations of publishers and journalists, developed a code of professional ethics. Although the code does not have the strength of binding law, it has become, through interpretation, an element of the general clauses of law as a statement of "public policy" or "ethics". The main principles of the code are respect for truth and personal privacy and honour, rejection of the use of illegal or unfair methods in collecting information, and criticism of insulting reporting of racial, religious or national affiliation.

The Council decides complaints by individuals alleging code violations and, if it finds that a complaint is valid, may issue reprimands which it may require the paper to publish. In 1991, the Press Council dealt with 400 cases. Most of them were handled by good counselling and settlement. In 102 cases, the formal procedure was initiated. In 56 of those cases, the claim was found to be unjustified. In 46 cases, the claim was ruled to be justified; 35 of those cases resulted in a private reprimand and 11 ended with a public reprimand. In all 11 cases, the Council directed the offending papers to publish the reprimand and in all cases the papers complied. In the past, there were arguments that the work of the Press Council was sometimes impeded by boycotts by its constituent groups; however, since the Council was re-established in 1986, its efficiency and effectiveness seem to have improved, as figures show.

---

[19] 27 FCC 71 (1969); *see also* E Barendt, *Freedom of Speech* (Oxford: Clarendon Press, 1987), pp. 111-12.

10. DEFAMATION

10.1 General Considerations

Provisions in German law for protecting press freedom, as well as for protecting individuals against defamation, libel, breach of privacy and encroachment of business reputation, are manifold. Persons seeking protection against breach of individual rights may have difficulties in finding their way through the mass of Federal and *Länder* law and the rich collection of case-law. There are almost no private organizations that assist in initiating criminal or civil actions against the press. Financially needy plaintiffs, however, may obtain legal aid in bringing criminal libel actions.

The right to one's own image, to a fair trial, to privacy, to a business reputation and the right of self-determination as to information and data about oneself ("*informationelles Selbstbestimmungsrecht*") are facets of human dignity protected by Article 1 of the Basic Law and the right to free development of one's personality (self-expression and autonomy) protected by Article 2. In defamation and privacy cases, the court balances these rights against the constitutional guarantees of press freedom and the public's right to information of legitimate public interest.

In addition, the rights to reputation, personal honour and privacy are protected by an array of civil and criminal laws which are both detailed and fragmentary.[20] This situation has prompted calls for improved codification of the law, although not for a change in substantive protections. These efforts have been given additional impetus by the swell of legislative reform necessitated by reunification.

Sections 185 *et seq.* of the Criminal Code prohibit defamation and libel. Pursuant to Sections 823 *et seq.* of the Civil Code, press organs may also be subject to civil actions under tort law for offences defined in the Criminal Code. According to Section 826 of the Civil Code, a published statement which is "immoral" or malicious gives rise to a claim. Business reputation is protected by Sections 14 and 15 of the Law against Unfair Competition of 1909 and by Section 824 of the Civil Code. These provisions establish tort liability for disclosure of false facts which damage a person's credit and business reputation.

10.2 Distinction between Fact and Opinion

The law distinguishes between the expression of an opinion and the making of a factual allegation. The publication of an untrue fact which severely diminishes another's reputation is a crime if the person who published the statement knew it was false or showed malicious disregard for its truth.[21] In a case brought by the author Heinrich Böll for violation of his

---

[20] Privacy interests which can be separated from interests in reputation and honour are discussed in the following section.

[21] Criminal Code, Section 187.

right to free development of personality, the FCC held that the use of inaccurate quotations to vilify him was not protected by Article 5 of the Basic Law.[22]

Under both the civil and criminal law, a plaintiff who accuses a press defendant of defamation or malicious falsehood bears the burden of proving that the press failed to meet its duty to check the facts properly and that this failure was either wilful or negligent. Even if the facts are shown at trial to be wrong, so long as the press defendant was neither negligent nor malicious it is likely to prevail because of the weight given to the public's right to information of public interest.

Courts tend not to give protection to highly offensive expression of opinion concerning private matters. According to Section 192 of the Criminal Code, proof of the truth of a statement is no defence "when the insult arises from the manner in which the assertion was made or disseminated or from the circumstances in which it was made". However, it is a defence if publication of an offensive or insulting statement served a legitimate interest, pursuant to Section 193. Opinions expressed in the context of political debate are subject to particular protection (*see* Section 10.3, *infra*).

Highly insulting expressions of opinion are more likely to be tolerated when made in response to a personal attack. In the *Schmid/Spiegel* case, the FCC held that a person (including a journalist) who makes a provocative statement must accept a "counter attack", even if it is defamatory.[23] *Der Spiegel* had published an article attacking the character and qualifications of a prominent judge. In response, the judge stated that *Der Spiegel* was, in the field of politics, what pornography was in the field of morals. The judge was found immune to libel charges under Article 5, since he had made his offensive statement in the course of protecting his reputation.

10.3   Political Debate

A greater degree of insult will be tolerated when made in the course of political debate against a politician or other public figure than when made against a private person.

In 1976, the FCC reversed a criminal conviction for defamation resulting from the publication of a story about the involvement of two politicians in the 1939 invasion of Poland. The Court based its ruling on considerations that the article contributed to a political debate and that public figures must accept a greater degree of criticism about their public actions than private persons.[24] On the other hand, a ban on news was found to be in accordance with freedom

---

[22] 54 FCC 208 (1980) (Böll).

[23] 12 FCC 113 (1961).

[24] *See* 43 FCC 130 (1976) (Politisches Flugblatt).

of the press when ordered by the government to protect the life of a hostage even though there was a legitimate public interest in the hostage's life.[25]

11. INVASION OF PRIVACY

Several criminal laws provide additional protection of the right to private life protected by Articles 1 and 2 of the Basic Law. Section 201 of the Criminal Code prohibits telephone tapping and the use of bugging devices. Section 202 protects the privacy of correspondence, and Section 203 prohibits the disclosure of information told in confidence to such professionals as lawyers, doctors, psychologists and pharmacists. The Federal Law of Data Protection of 20 December 1990 protects the privacy of personal data files.[26]

There are special protections against unauthorized use of photographs of individuals. According to Section 22 of the Law for the Protection of Copyrights in Art and Photography of 1907, pictures of a person may be published only with his or her consent. Exceptions apply, however, for photographs of public figures and people attending public gatherings. Court decisions have distinguished between "absolute" public figures, such as politicians and sportsmen, and others, such as defendants in criminal trials, who are only of public interest because of their involvement in a particular event. Their pictures may be published only if public interest outweighs other interests (such as rehabilitation of the offender).[27]

12. RIGHT OF REPLY AND/OR CORRECTION

Interests in reputation and privacy are better protected by private civil law than by criminal law. Civil protections include *punitive measures* such as damages beyond actual compensation, as well as *preventive measures* such as injunctive relief (for example, to compel someone to refrain from using illegally obtained information) and destruction of printed matter, and *measures of "repressive protection"* such as declaratory relief (a judicial statement that the defendant committed an illegal action), a right of reply, publication of a correction, publication of a court decision and actual damages.

The right of reply is the only remedy that receives extensive regulation in the *Länder* press laws. Pursuant to Section 11, a newspaper or other periodical publication is obliged to publish a reply by any person who is the subject of an assertion of fact published in the paper so long as the reply does not exceed the length of the text to which objection has been raised, does

---

[25] *See* C Starck, Informationsfreiheit und Nachrichtensperre, Archiv für Presserecht (1978), 171-77. The case concerned Mr Schleyer, the president of the German Employers' Association who was held hostage by terrorists and finally murdered. The Court ruled that, while the Federal government was engaged in negotiations with the terrorists, the papers were prohibited from publishing information about the negotiations.

[26] Offic. Gaz., Vol. I, p. 2959.

[27] 35 FCC 202 (1973) (Lebach). It should be noted that the distinction between absolute and limited public figures is not made in the defamation case-law.

not involve an advertisement and is confined to factual assertions. The injured party must communicate the reply to the responsible editor without delay and at the latest within three months. The reply must be printed, without additions or omissions, in the same type and with the same prominence as the original text. It is not sufficient to publish the reply as a reader's letter. If the paper refuses to publish the reply, a court may order it to do so. For instance, in 1992, a lower court ordered a paper to publish a reply by the Princess of Monaco on the cover page where the offending story had been published.

Even if the paper publishes the reply voluntarily, the offended person may still sue for monetary damages or seek a criminal prosecution, and the paper's publication of a reply will not necessarily reduce the amount of damages awarded or have any other effect on the trial on the merits.

Traditionally, damage awards have been the most common remedy sought by offended parties and, although seeking a right of reply has gained popularity, plaintiffs still seem to prefer to seek monetary damages.

Imposition of remedies against the press for infringement of protected individual rights, including heavy financial awards ("freedom with a big stick"), has not reached levels that discourage the press from fulfilling its role as a "public watchdog". Preventive measures are rarely taken. The number of cases of awards against the press, whether granting a right of reply or damages, is not excessive.

13.   INSULTS TO GOVERNMENT INSTITUTIONS OR OFFICIALS

Among the general laws which limit press freedom are various criminal provisions to protect the Constitution and state organs (Sections 84 *et seq.* of the Criminal Code), government officials (Sections 111 *et seq.*), and public order (Sections 123 *et seq.*). Section 90 prohibits defamation of the Federal President in public by spoken or printed word. Section 90(a) protects the Federal Republic and its symbols (including its colours, flag, insignia and anthem), and Section 90(b) protects the Federal and *Länder* legislatures, governments, constitutional courts and their members against public attacks. Sections 103 and 104 forbid insults to the representatives of foreign states, as well as to foreign flags and national emblems.

In practice, these provisions are of little importance. In recent decisions, the FCC has held that attacks against state symbols, such as against the flag and anthem, even if harsh and satirical, must be tolerated in view of the constitutional protections of freedom of speech, the press and the arts.[28] Similarly, criticisms of Federal policy and politicians, even if sharp and

---

[28] 81 FCC 278, 294 (1990) (Bundesflagge); 81 FCC 298, 306 (1990) (Bundeshymne).

obviously unfair are entitled to protection unless they amount to defamation.[29] Thus, the general law on defamation concerning politicians (*see* Section 10.3, *supra*) has tended to overtake the various specific laws on insult to government officials.

Given the FCC's statements that vigorous criticism of public officials is an acceptable and necessary part of a democracy, it has generally overturned convictions for defamation of government officials.[30] However, in the Frankfurt Airport case, the FCC, by a split vote of four to four, upheld a conviction of a city official for breach of public order for having called (in an ironic manner) for the use of violence in protesting against building a new runway at the Frankfurt Airport.[31] The four judges in the minority held that speech must not be judged as criminal due to its dramatics, use of exaggeration or appeal to emotion. This rule appears not to have impeded either the press or political parties.

14. OFFICIAL SECRECY AND ACCESS TO GOVERNMENT-HELD INFORMATION

Press access to information held by the government, parliament, courts and private parties is a necessary prerequisite to fulfilment of its "public function". This term, used in Section 3 of all *Länder* press laws, describes the press' role in informing the public in a democracy.[32] Section 3 reads: "The Press fulfils a public function in that in matters of public interest it collects and disseminates information, presents commentary and criticism, and otherwise contributes to the formation of public opinion."

The *Länder* press laws provide in Section 4 for a right of access to government information. The same right concerning Federal government information is protected by Article 5 of the Basic Law. The Federal and *Länder* governments may refuse press requests for information only if disclosure would interfere with judicial proceedings; the "rules of secrecy stand in the way"; an overriding public or private interest would be infringed; or the amount of information requested is excessive. The press may apply to the courts for a ruling in the event of a refusal. In some cases, however, public authorities refuse to disclose information even when disclosure would not seem seriously to threaten the interests listed in Section 4.

There is no precise definition of "secret" or even of "the rules of secrecy". Most of these rules are part of statutory law. According to Section 93 of the Criminal Code, "state secrets" are facts, objects or information which are accessible only to a limited number of persons and

---

[29] Federal Penal Court, 19 official collection (BGHSt) 311 (*Neue Volkszeitung*, Communist Party). The court struck down the conviction, primarily because the trial court had not specified the exact statement which it found offensive.

[30] *See* 24 FCC 278, 283 (1968) (Tonjäger); 54 FCC 129, 139 (1980) (Römerberg).

[31] 82 FCC 236, 260 (1990) (Schuberth), *supra* note 11.

[32] 50 FCC 234, 239 (1979) (Kölner Volksblatt).

must be kept secret from foreign powers to avert serious damage for the external security of the Federal Republic. Section 203 of the Criminal Code uses comparable language for secrets concerning private persons.

In addition to these absolute secrets, there are matters and information which have been classified by administrative regulations. Doubts are possible as to whether a fact has been legitimately classified. If the press publishes classified information, the courts will decide whether the information was legitimately classified; journalists will not be punished if the information should not have been made secret. Clearly, governments are not entitled to classify information simply in order to keep it secret from the press.[33]

Press freedom is not a legitimate ground for illegal collection of information.[34] Publication of such information, however, may be excused if the interest in disclosure is strong and outweighs the interest in secrecy.[35] This doctrine of the FCC is reflected in such statutes as Section 93(2) of the Criminal Code which states: "Facts which are in contradiction to the free democratic order or which are kept secret from treaty partners in violation of arms limitation agreements are not state secrets." Moreover, Section 97(b) provides that publication of a genuine secret by one who, however, erroneously, believed that the information was not entitled to be kept secret, is not a crime if the person acted with the intent to stop some supposedly illegal activity.[36]

15.   ACCESS TO AND DISCLOSURE OF COURT DOCUMENTS AND PROCEEDINGS

A very difficult issue concerning press freedom under German law (and one in dynamic development) concerns legal measures to protect the rights of a person involved in a trial. Freedom of the press under Article 5 of the Basic Law includes the right of the press to attend criminal trials, free from arbitrary exclusion.[37] This privilege of access is necessary to enable the press to discharge its special responsibilities. At the same time, the individual deserves protection against show trials and pre-judgment by the press. The law has to safeguard the right to a fair trial and the presumption of innocence.

Filming and taking photographs is legal only until the beginning of the hearing. In the recent case of Honecker, *Staatsratsvorsitzender* of the former GDR (Head of the Council of State)

---

[33] *See* C Starck, *Archiv fur Presserecht* (1978), *supra* note 25, at 177.

[34] 66 FCC 116, 137 (1984) (Wallraf).

[35] 7 FCC, *supra* note 1, at 212; 61 FCC 1, 11 (1982) (Christlich Soziale Union).

[36] *See also* Kohl, *supra* note 2, at 198-99.

[37] *See* 50 FCC 234 (1979), *supra* note 32; *see also* U Karpen, *Der Rechtsstaat des Grundgesetzes* (Baden-Baden: 1992), 101 *et seq.*

the FCC quashed an order of the lower court banning all cameras and ruled that filming and photographing was legal prior to the commencement of the hearing.

According to Section 353(d)(3) of the Criminal Code, it is an offence to publish the bill of indictment or other trial documents.[38] This provision prohibits only verbatim citation; its reach, therefore, is limited. Because of the public's right to information about cases, recording words and taking pictures at hearings is not illegal (although television cameras are not permitted and the presiding judge may prohibit the taking even of still photographs). The *publication* of information about trial proceedings, however, may be illegal under the proportionality principle. The right of the individual to a fair trial and to protection of his or her privacy may be violated by publishing facts about the party's private life or business. If the rights of a person subject to a trial are so infringed, he or she may seek injunctive relief to stop publication. Such relief is provided only on the ground of infringement of individual rights and not, for instance, on the ground of contempt of court.

16. ACCESS TO AND DISCLOSURE OF LEGISLATIVE DOCUMENTS AND PROCEEDINGS

Reporting on parliamentary proceedings is part of the public function of the press. According to Article 42(3) of the Basic Law, "true and accurate reports on the public meetings of the *Bundestag* (Federal Parliament) and of its committees shall not give rise to any liability" on the part of either the speaker in the *Bundestag* or the press. This is particularly important for public investigative committees (Article 44(1) of the Basic Law). Open access is also given to the meetings of municipal councils.

17. COMMERCIAL SECRECY AND ACCESS TO INFORMATION HELD BY PRIVATE PARTIES

In order to fulfil its public function, the press has access privileges to information held by private persons and companies. The privileges of the press, however, are limited by the rights to human dignity and privacy as well as professional and property rights. (*See* Sections 10 and 11, *infra*, on defamation and the right to privacy.) The rights to dignity and privacy prohibit unauthorized collection and use by the press and others of names, telephone communications, personal tape recordings, photographs and similar materials.

The FCC, in the *Mikrozensus* case, developed a "right to one's own data", which is the basis for data protection laws.[39] While data processing in public and private enterprises is subject to regulation, the press is exempt from such regulation. Misuse of personal data by the press, however, may constitute a breach of privacy and thus form the basis for liability under

---

[38] *See* 71 FCC 206, 214 (1985) (Flick-Affaire).

[39] 27 FCC 1, 6 (1969) (Mikrozensus).

Sections 823 *et seq.* of the Civil Code or for a right of reply under Section 11 of the *Länder* press laws.

18.   PRIOR RESTRAINTS

The public prosecutor, upon request of a person alleging libel, slander or invasion of privacy, or in an *ex officio* capacity regarding claims of treason, insults against state organs or threats to state security, may initiate an inquiry and take "immediate measures", including seizure. In some *Länder*, publications which insult the dignity of a national, ethnic or religious group may also be seized without court order (*see* Section 20, *infra*).

When determining whether to uphold an immediate measure, such as an interlocutory order against publication, the FCC considers the likelihood of the measure being upheld on the merits; it then balances the likely impact of refusing an injunction if the applicant is successful on the merits against the negative effects which may occur if the injunction is granted and the applicant is unsuccessful on the merits. In so doing, the court examines first whether the interference with press freedom is *appropriate*. In general, the court considers that restraints on publication may be appropriate to protect state security, confidentiality and other interests listed in Article 10 of the ECHR. Second, the court examines whether the measures to be taken are *necessary* to protect an important state or private interest; such interest must be overriding. Third, the court considers whether the interference is *proportionate* in the sense that the damage to the constitutional freedom must not be disproportionate to the enhancement of the countervailing interest.

19.   PROTECTION OF SOURCES

Sections 13-20 and 24 of the *Länder* press laws deal with protection of the sources of press information, namely, the right to refuse to give testimony and to be exempt from search and seizure except in very limited circumstances. In addition, these privileges are set forth in Sections 383 *et seq.* of the Civil Procedure Code and Sections 53, 97 and 111(m) and (n) of the Criminal Procedure Code.

In civil cases, Section 383 of the Civil Procedure Code acknowledges that when facts are confided to persons, including journalists, because of their profession, these persons are entitled to refuse to give testimony on these facts unless their source consents to disclosure.

In criminal cases, Section 53 of the Criminal Procedure Code authorizes radio and print journalists to refuse to testify concerning the content or source of information given in confidence. In the *Spiegel* case, the FCC affirmed that the right to refuse to give evidence about the source and contents of information is essential to the public function of the press.[40] However, the press' right to refuse to disclose sources may be overridden by other pressing

---

[40] 20 FCC 162 (1966).

considerations. In one case, a reporter was required to answer questions regarding the identity of suspects who had claimed to him that they had been promised sums of money by law enforcement authorities. In that instance, the Court determined that the state interest in exposing corruption by public officials outweighed the interest in protecting the confidentiality of the journalist's sources.[41]

Section 53 does not entitle journalists to withhold photographs or films (and does not expressly apply to television journalists). In a 1980 case,[42] the FCC ruled that a television station had to turn over to the prosecution a tape of a violent demonstration which it had broadcast, and that it might have to turn over additional footage based upon a balancing of the press' interest in the confidentiality of its materials against the need for the film in prosecuting a criminal action and the seriousness of the criminal charge.

Section 97 of the Criminal Procedure Code prohibits searches and seizures of the premises of newspapers or radio stations for material which is entitled to be kept secret, except where the person entitled to exercise the right to testify is under strong suspicion "of being the perpetrator or accomplice of a criminally punishable act".

In the *Spiegel* case, the FCC, by a split decision of 4 votes to 4, upheld the legality of the search of *Spiegel's* offices on the ground that the magazine was suspected of disclosing state secrets in violation of the law on treason. It had published an article criticizing the performance of the German army in NATO manoeuvres and revealing plans, allegedly then contemplated, to equip the army with nuclear weapons. The dissenting four judges reasoned that the press enjoyed greater freedom to publish military secrets than private persons particularly when the supposedly secret information was already available elsewhere, as apparently was the case, and that the lower court had not adequately explored the existence of other options for obtaining the information. The majority rejected these contentions. While it affirmed the importance of press freedom and the presumption against searches of newspaper premises, and noted that the proportionality principle places limits on the permissible scope of searches, it ruled that the search was lawful in the light of credible suspicions of the magazine's criminal behaviour.[43]

Public outrage at the *Spiegel* affair led to the collapse of the coalition government and was a major factor in prompting a total revision of the law of treason as well as in amending the law of disclosure to provide a limited defence of good faith belief that disclosure was necessary to stop unlawful activity.[44]

---

[41] 25 FCC 296 (1969) (Pressezeugnisverweisungsrecht).

[42] 56 FCC 247, 249 (1980) (Demonstrationsphotos).

[43] *See* E Barendt, *supra* note 2, at 76.

[44] *See, e.g.,* Criminal Code Section 97b discussed in Section 14, *supra*; and Kohl, *supra* note 2, at 200.

Seizure of all copies of a publication is legal only if it is subject to confiscation and destruction due to its criminal contents (*see* Section 18, *supra*). For the sake of preservation of evidence, two copies only may be seized.

As a related matter to protection of sources, a person may sell exclusive rights to a story to one newspaper. The breach of this exclusive contract is legal, however, if there are pressing public interests in the information and if the sale would close the only source of information.[45]

20. RESTRICTIONS ON OFFENSIVE LANGUAGE AGAINST IDENTIFIABLE GROUPS

According to Article 3(3) of the Basic Law no one may be prejudiced or favoured because of sex, parentage, race, language, homeland and origin, faith, or religious or political opinions. Sections 130 and 131 of the Criminal Code protect groups of society, in particular different national or "racial" groups, against defamation and violence, and Section 185 protects against libel.[46]

According to Sections 9 and 11 of the Press Council's Press Code of 1973, a journalist's responsibility for tolerance forbids discrimination against a person due to membership of a racial, religious or national group.

21. BLASPHEMY, OBSCENITY AND PROTECTION OF PUBLIC MORALS

Since 1969, blasphemy is no longer a criminal offence under German law. The subject of protection, however, was not God but the religious feelings of people. This subject is now protected by Section 166 of the Criminal Code, which forbids insults to religions or philosophies of life, publicly or by dissemination of publications. Moreover, publications that violate the moral or religious sensitivities of a group are not in accordance with responsibility of the press as set forth in the Press Code of 1973.

Section 184 of the Criminal Code prohibits the offer or sale of all pornographic materials to persons under 18 years of age and bans the publication and sale of such materials by means and in premises to which the young have access. The FCC has upheld the provisions' constitutionality on the ground that the ban was necessary to protect children and also upheld a ban on the supply by mail order of named pornographic magazines.[47] Although Section 184 makes it more difficult for adults to obtain pornographic materials, this inconvenience

---

[45] *See* Supreme Court, *Gewerblicher Rechtsschutz und Urheberrecht* (1968), 209 (Lengede).

[46] The word "racial" has been put in quotes because, when applied to human beings, it has no scientific or other clear meaning. Nonetheless, it is used here because of its traditional and widespread use.

[47] 30 FCC 337 (1971).

is deemed to be outweighed by the difficulty that sales people may have in verifying the ages of their customers.

German Law differentiates between kinds of pornography. Section 184(3) of the Criminal Code prohibits the distribution, offer or advertising of pornography which "depicts violence, abuse of children, or sexual activity with children". Other less objectionable forms of pornography may be freely distributed except to children. Section 5 of the Law of 29 April 1961 on Dissemination of Writings Morally Harmful for Juveniles prohibits advertisements for certain kinds of writings.[48] Each *Land* has considerable discretion in interpreting the pornography laws. The public prosecutor in each region determines whether a particular publication would be banned under either the law to protect youth or the law to protect public decency. As a result, there is a divergence among regions as to the publications which are permitted or banned.

22.   RESTRICTIONS ON ADVERTISING

Advertisements enjoy many of the protections of press freedom.[49] Section 10 of the *Länder* press laws requires that advertisements must be marked as such in newspapers. Paid information in the editorial section of a publication is illegal under the press laws, and the Press Council is of the opinion that public confidence in the public function of the press would be eroded if the *editorial* part of newspapers were to contain advertisements.

Advertising in the guise of information is unfair competition by the editor and the advertiser. However, in every case the line has to be drawn between information and advertisement. The general clause of Section 1 of the Law against Unfair Competition of 1909 permits injunctive relief and claims for damages against acts of unfair competition. Dissemination of false facts about goods, services and customers would qualify as such an act.

Comparative advertising (whereby one product is compared favourably to another named product) in general is illegal. Exceptions are given, however, in cases where there is a serious public interest in information. This is the case, for example, where a product poses health hazards.[50] These provisions are not applicable to official comparative tests of goods. In view of the public interest in the quality of goods which are on the market, in 1964 the Federal Government set up a foundation named *Warentest* to make comparative tests of goods in independent laboratories and publish results. In approving publication of such information,

---

[48]   Offic. Gaz., Vol. I, 497.

[49]   *See* 21 FCC 271 (1967) (*Südkurier*).

[50]   *See* Federal Civil Court, *Gewerblicher Rechtsschutz und Urheberrecht* 350 (1957) (Phylas-Apparate); and 45 (1962) (Betonzusatzmittel).

the courts held that the public interest in objective information outweighs business interests in unhindered competition.[51]

CONCLUSION

Today, concerns about media freedom and freedom of expression generally focus on the electronic media, in particular regarding the issue of public versus private broadcasting. There are discussions concerning the extent to which cross-ownership of print and electronic media will diminish free exchange of differing points of view (that is, press pluralism). The actual and potential loss of advertising income due to such combinations is a threat to the press and public broadcasting.

Some observers are of the opinion that the Federal Cartel Law does not address sufficiently a major modern source of threats to press freedom, namely economic power and press concentration. Although several mergers have been prevented in recent years, it remains to be seen whether this sole instrument to battle monopolies and oligopolies will suffice.

Nearly all governments in the history of the Federal Republic have promised to draft a "Federal Press Framework Law". Indeed, issues related to strikes and lock-outs as well as representation of journalists in the editorial process need regulation. These are very controversial issues, however, and consensus has not yet been achieved concerning them. As a consequence, case-law of the Federal Labour Court is prevailing in this field.

Because the laws which affect press freedom are scattered throughout different codes and law reports, questions arise concerning the *efficiency* of this complicated system. Indeed, the system's complication and the unification of Germany in 1990 have fostered calls to improve the law, especially regarding defamation and protection of privacy. Although German journalists seem to be less aggressive in investigating stories than their colleagues in some other countries, amendments of the law seem inevitable in this area because of the public's concern about media abuses (however well justified). The liberal times, when the best media policy was considered to be no media policy, are over.

Law reform concerning press freedoms is accomplished more and more by the courts rather than the legislatures, and codification is becoming more difficult. This trend is promoted by the speed of technical and legal administrative developments.

Currently, German press law (particularly protection of personality) is complicated not only for the above-noted reasons but also because of the Federal-*Länder* allocation of responsibilities established in the Basic Law. It may be necessary or at least appropriate to grant more powers to the Federal government in light of the trend to harmonize media law in the European Community.

---

[51] *See* 65 Federal Civil Court 325 (Warentest).

On the whole, the German press (especially the national press) well serves its public function of contributing to the formation of public opinion on matters of public interest and acting as "public watchdog". For instance, the national press played a role in exposing the illegal trade in weapons to "regions of tension" like the Middle East and, in the famous *Spiegel* case,[52] the press contributed to the long-term military security of the country by exposing deficiencies in defence policies of Germany as well as NATO. The regional press on the whole has not been as energetic as the national press in uncovering wrongdoing and corruption; controversies, especially those involving major political figures, are not "good business".

In conclusion, freedom of the press as a key element of democracy enjoys solid protection in German law. The general laws and the *Länder* press laws impose certain obligations on the press that are not unduly cumbersome in daily business. Although they establish certain rules that theoretically could infringe on the free exchange of ideas, in practice these rules have not resulted in suppression of press freedom. Other rules have been established which obviously further the constitutional guarantee of free expression. The FCC, while taking into consideration the particular facts of each case, has tended to favour press freedom and the public's right to information, especially concerning political and other matters of legitimate public interest, over other social and individual interests (such as the rights to reputation and privacy), so long as the press has not acted with negligence or malice.

---

[52] 20 FCC 162 (1966), *supra* note 40.

Chapter 6

PRESS LAW IN THE NETHERLANDS

Francine van Lenthe and Ineke Boerefijn

INTRODUCTION

Freedom of the press in the Netherlands enjoys a high degree of respect. Dutch constitutional traditions, the integration of international free expression standards into Dutch law, the attitudes of the courts and governmental authorities as well as a system of self-regulation, headed by the Press Council, all contribute to the maintenance of a free press. The law on defamation and privacy both provide that the press is to be given greater latitude regarding public figures and matters of legitimate public interest and, in fact, public figures rarely are successful in defamation and privacy actions. In any event, damage awards are generally modest, and the prevailing view among the press is that the law on defamation and privacy does not have a chilling effect on reporting.

The Act on Public Access to Information is premised upon the basic rule that government documents should be accessible. The Act established a process for reviewing requests for such information, including official secrets. A consultative body of public prosecutors, the police and the press was created to address concerns about access to information in criminal cases as well as to provide an avenue for the press to lodge complaints concerning police behaviour. The Ombudsman also plays a part in protecting press freedom.

1. RELEVANT CONSTITUTIONAL PROVISIONS

The Constitution of the Netherlands has protected freedom of expression since 1815. Article 7 of the current Dutch Constitution reads as follows:

> 1. No one shall require prior permission to publish thoughts or opinions through the press, without prejudice to the responsibility of every person under the law.

> 2. Rules concerning radio and television shall be laid down by Act of Parliament. There shall be no prior supervision of the content of a radio or television broadcast.

> 3. No one shall be required to submit thoughts or opinions for prior approval in order to disseminate them by means other than those mentioned in the preceding paragraphs, without prejudice to the responsibility of every person under the law. The holding of performances open to persons younger than sixteen years of age may be regulated by Act of Parliament in order to protect good morals.

4. The preceding paragraphs do not apply to commercial advertising.[1]

As the Dutch government stated in its 1988 report under Article 40 of the International Covenant on Civil and Political Rights (ICCPR), it is generally accepted that "the freedom to publish thoughts or opinions also entails the right to disseminate such thoughts and opinions so that others are acquainted with them. The right of dissemination may be restricted by lower authorities in the matter of the time, place and manner of dissemination, but such restrictions may not go so far as to render any independent means of dissemination virtually unusable."[2]

The right to seek, receive and impart information is not explicitly mentioned in Article 7 of the Constitution; however, Article 110 states:

> In the exercise of their duties government bodies shall observe the right of public access to information in accordance with rules to be prescribed by Act of Parliament.[3]

Thus, the Netherlands is one of the few countries to constitutionally enshrine the government's duty to make information available to the public.

2. DISTRIBUTION OF POWERS BETWEEN CENTRAL AND REGIONAL GOVERNMENT

The Netherlands is a unitary state.

3. ROLE OF THE COURTS

As in the United Kingdom, the authority of Parliament is supreme. According to Article 120 of the Constitution: "The constitutionality of Acts of Parliament and treaties shall not be reviewed by the courts." Such assessment is the sole prerogative of the Parliament. The courts nonetheless act as guardians of constitutional rights by reviewing national and local government actions and by ensuring observance of those rights in disputes between individuals.

---

[1] All quotations in this Chapter from the Dutch Constitution are from the English version published by the Ministry of Home Affairs, Oct. 1989.

[2] CCPR/C/42/Add.6 (1 Aug. 1988), 27-29.

[3] Authors' note: While the official translation of Article 110 uses the phrase "the right of public access to information", the original Dutch text uses the term "*openbaarheid*", which is perhaps better understood as "the duty of public bodies to observe openness". See Section 14.1 *infra*, for a discussion of the government's duty to make public certain information under the Act on Public Access to Information.

4.   STATUS OF INTERNATIONAL HUMAN RIGHTS TREATIES IN NATIONAL LAW

The Netherlands ratified the European Convention on Human Rights (ECHR) in 1954[4] and the ICCPR and its First Optional Protocol in 1978.[5]

Article 93 of the Constitution provides that ratified international agreements and "resolutions of international institutions" that may be binding on all persons are part of domestic law, and Article 94 provides that "statutory regulations" (that is, laws, regulations, decrees, or parts thereof), which conflict with such instruments are inapplicable. These provisions give international human rights instruments a powerful legal status in domestic law.

The courts are competent to test national law against the directly applicable provisions of international instruments.[6] Article 10 of the ECHR and Article 19 of the ICCPR, which guarantee the right to freedom of expression, contain directly applicable rights that, therefore, must be applied by the Dutch courts.

5.   STATUTORY FRAMEWORK

The Netherlands does not have a single, comprehensive press act. Provisions affecting the press can be found in the former Dutch Civil Code, the present Civil Code, the Criminal Code, the *Wet Openbaarheid van Bestuur* (Act on Public Access to Information), and the Media Act, insofar as it concerns financial support of newspapers.

6.   REGULATION OF OWNERSHIP

6.1   Ownership Trends

Since the early 1960s, there has been a tendency towards press concentration. The *Nederlandse Dagblad Unie* (Dutch Daily Newspaper Union) was set up as a holding company in 1964, and in the middle of 1968 the *Perscombinatie* (Press Combination) was founded to establish commercial cooperation between *De Volkskrant* and *het Parool. Trouw* joined them in 1974. As a result of this trend, the five largest newspapers account for approximately 70

---

[4] Dutch text published in Netherlands Treaties Series 1951-154.

[5] Dutch text published in Netherlands Treaties Series 1978-177. The ICCPR ratification included a reservation to Article 20 stating that it would be particularly difficult to formulate a statutory prohibition against war propaganda without interfering excessively with freedom of expression, a question which the Dutch courts would not be competent to answer. CCPR/C/10/Add.3, 16 March 1981, p. 27. Otherwise, the substantive provisions of the ECHR and the ICCPR are part of Dutch law.

[6] *See* Supreme Court, 4 May 1984, *Netherlands Jurisprudence* 1985, 510 (in a child custody case, Civil Cold Article 1:161(1) was ruled invalid because it conflicted with ECHR Article 8's right to respect for private and family life).

per cent of the total circulation.[7] Concentration has also affected regional papers. In many Dutch regions only one newspaper exists that publishes substantial regional information.[8]

6.2   Control of Ownership

The *Wet Economische Mededinging* (Act on Economic Competition) sets forth general rules on the abuse of ownership power.[9] There is no specific law regulating press ownership, and the issue of whether one is needed is presently under debate. At issue is whether concentration of publishing houses benefits "press pluralism" (that is, the existence of a large number of editorial viewpoints), because the extended financial base provided by concentrated entities can both support papers that lose money and support new publishing initiatives.

The government favours ownership regulations that promote press pluralism.[10] The *Bedrijfsfonds voor de Pers* (Press Fund, discussed below) and the *Mediaraad* (Media Council, an advisory body of media experts appointed by the government) have both proposed regulations addressing ownership of daily newspapers and news magazines. Both propositions would require permission by the Minister of Justice prior to a merger if their market share reached a certain level. The government so far has rejected both proposals, but deliberations continue. Regulations that would prohibit mergers resulting in an excessive market share by a single owner would not infringe the Constitution.[11]

Other instruments are also available to curb the influence of concentrated ownership on editorial policy. Various collective labour agreements contain an obligation to introduce an "editorial statute". Most newspapers have such agreements, and their editorial statutes ensure editorial independence from the owners of the publication.

6.3   Government Support

Promoting press pluralism is the main objective of the Dutch government's policy toward the press. Before 1967, the press received aid from the government, such as favourable rail and postal rates and exemption from sales taxes. In 1967, the government decided to subsidize the press in order to compensate it for advertising revenue lost to radio and television stations, which were allowed to accept commercial advertising that year. In 1970, these subsidies were continued only for daily and other newspapers and news magazines, because of their importance for freedom of communication in a democratic society. In 1971, a fund was set

---

[7] F W Grosheide, *Hoofdstukken mediarecht* (Alphen aan den Rijn Samsom HD Tjeenk Willink, 1991), 34.

[8] A J Nieuwenhuis, *Persvrijheid en persbeleid* (Amsterdam: Otto Cramwinckel Uitgeverij, 1991), 110-169.

[9] *Wet Economische Mededinging*, Act of 28 June 1956; as amended on 15 Nov. 1989.

[10] *See* F W Grosheide, *supra* note 7, at 36-42.

[11] *See* A J Nieuwenhuis, *supra* note 8, at 143; J M de Meij, "Persfusies en persvrijheid" in 64 *Nederlands Juristen Blad* 177-82 (1989).

up for the press financed by the *Stichting Etherreclame* (Radio and Television Advertising Association).[12] This fund, established under Article 133 of the Media Act, was intended to be temporary. The recent Bill on Commercial Radio and Television proposes to abolish this kind of aid, primarily because newspapers now may advertise through the broadcast media to increase circulation.[13]

Since the 1960s, a system of specific and temporary aid was developed to keep papers with a special character alive. In 1974, the *Bedrijfsfonds voor de Pers* (Press Fund) was established to provide such aid to newspapers and news magazines in financial trouble. The Press Fund also may support the establishment of new daily newspapers. It received legal basis in the Media Act of 1 January 1988.[14] The Act provides two important requirements for financial support: 1) papers are obliged to have an editorial statute;[15] and 2) papers have to be offered for sale.[16]

It has been argued that subsidizing the press presents a danger of distorting competition. Defenders of the Press Fund, however, maintain that by making the aid temporary, the Press Fund ensures that it only supports publications that are financially viable. They also maintain that there is a demonstrable need for new publications, while start-up capital is in short supply, and new technologies demand hugh capital expenditures with risks that are too large to attract the necessary investors.[17]

Final responsibility for the Press Fund's activities rests with the Minister of Welfare, Health and Cultural Affairs, who decides on the amount available to the Fund and who appoints the Fund's board members. The government also may issue regulations affecting the Fund through Orders in Council.[18]

---

[12] F W Grosheide, *supra* note 7, at 32.

[13] *See* A J Nieuwenhuis, *supra* note 8, at 110-69.

[14] Section 123 of the Netherlands Media Act states: "There shall be a Press Fund (*Bedrijfsfonds voor de Pers*) with the aim of maintaining and promoting the diversity of the press, insofar as it plays an important role in providing information and forming opinions...". (All quotations in this Chapter from the Media Act are from the English version published by the Netherlands Broadcasting Corporation.)

[15] Article 129(2c).

[16] Article 129(2f).

[17] J H J van den Heuvel, "Mediabeleid in de interventiestaat" in *Massamedia & Staatsrecht* (Zwolle: W E J Tjeenk Willink, 1988), 77-89.

[18] A J Nieuwenhuis, *supra* note 8, at 110-69.

7.   REGISTRATION REQUIREMENTS

There are no registration requirements other than company law requirements applicable to all corporate entities.

8.   REGULATION OF IMPORT AND EXPORT OF PUBLICATIONS

There are no regulations affecting import and export of publications.

9.   MECHANISMS OF PRESS SELF-REGULATION

Dutch journalists do not have a written code of conduct. In the beginning of the 1970s such a code was drafted but never was adopted. Press associations, however, consider themselves morally bound by the Code of Ethics of the International Federation of Journalists.

9.1   The Press Council

An independent Press Council was created in 1960, in response to public calls for government regulation to protect individuals against journalistic excesses. The Council provides a simple procedure, without the high costs or publicity which usually accompanies lawsuits. The decisions of the Press Council, however, are not binding, and the Council cannot impose heavy sanctions. Individuals may turn to the ordinary courts for that purpose.

The force of the Council's judgments derives from the general consensus of its members, which include the most important coordinating organizations in the mass-media: *Nederlandse Vereniging van Journalisten* (the Dutch Association of Journalists); *Genootschap van Hoofdredacteuren* (the Association of Editors); the broadcasting companies; and the publishing-houses.[19] Publication of its judgment in the trade journal *De Journalist* is the only significant sanction available to the Council. The newspaper concerned is also asked to publish the Council's decision or, at least to, mention the case, but it is not obliged to do so.[20]

The Council consists of 16 members, eight of whom are journalists. The remaining members are media experts but not journalists. The Council's Chairperson and Secretary must be lawyers. The Chairperson selects the members of a reviewing panel and serves as its chair. Reviewing panels consist of a minimum of three and a maximum of five members, decide by simple majority, and hold public sessions (unless the Chairperson decides otherwise in the interest of the case, the plaintiff or other persons concerned). Witnesses and experts may be

---

[19] W van der Putten, "De verbreding van de grondslag van de Raad voor de Journalistiek", in 32 *Ars Aequi* 127 (1983).

[20] F Kuitenbrouwer, "De Raad voor de Journalistiek en vijfentwintig jaar regels van de kunst", in 61 *Nederlands Juristen Blad* 1017-23 (1986).

heard. The Council observes secrecy during its deliberations on complaints, until a decision is reached. The Council must issue its decision within eight weeks, unless a more thorough investigation is needed.

The Council only considers complaints from persons or organizations directly or indirectly mentioned in the challenged publication. The complaint must concern journalistic behaviour (the acts or failures of a journalist in exercising his or her duty) and is lodged against journalists rather than publications or editors, unless the complaint concerns an editorial comment. The Council has to judge "whether the boundaries of that which is socially acceptable have been exceeded, in view of the demands of journalistic responsibility" and will take into account the context of the publication.[21] Importantly, the Press Council not only applies existing regulations but also develops new standards through its decisions, which are analogous to a body of "case-law".[22]

Journalists are not obliged to participate in an investigation by the Press Council, but the statute of the Dutch Association of Journalists, which represents approximately 60 per cent of Dutch journalists, contains this obligation for its members. If the Council believes that the interests of a non-appearing journalist cannot be safeguarded sufficiently, it withholds judgment. The main responsibility for a publication rests with the journalist who has written the article. The chief editor bears final responsibility for the editorial contents of a newspaper.

9.2   The Consultative Body

In 1980, a consultative body of public prosecutors, the police and the press was created to minimize and mediate conflicts between the press on the one hand and the police and the judicial authorities on the other. The Ministers of Justice and Home Affairs drafted guidelines on relations between the press and the police, which enumerate the rights of the press and limitations permitted on the grounds of public order and non-disturbance of criminal investigations. Journalists may lodge complaints against the police with the consultative body.[23]

---

[21] Article 3, Paragraph 1, Statutes of the Council. *See* M P Galama-Kuipers, "Raad voor de Journalistiek en Fair Play", in *Tuchtrecht en Fair Play* (Zwolle: W E J Tjeenk Willink, 1984). 197-214.

[22] *See* F Kuitenbrouwer, "Grenzen en mogelijkheden van de Raad voor de Journalistiek", in *Grenzen en Mogelijkheden* (Nijmegen: Ars Aequi Libri, 1984), 248-63.

[23] H J M Boukema, *Recht voor journalisten* (Zwolle: Tjeenk Willink, 1984), 36-39.

10. DEFAMATION

10.1 General Considerations

Under Section 261(2) of the Criminal Code, a person who publishes a deliberate assault against someone's honour or reputation is guilty of libel and may be sentenced to prison for up to one year or may be fined a maximum of 10,000 guilders (US$5,800). Journalists are rarely charged with criminal defamation. Such a charge may only be brought by a private party filing a complaint with the prosecutor, who then has the discretion to dismiss frivolous complaints. Under Criminal Code Section 261(3), journalists do not need to prove the truth of their accusations; it is sufficient that they assumed the accuracy of their statements in good faith and that they made them in the public's interest.

In practice, journalists must comply with stricter good faith requirements as accusations become more serious. If a journalist knows that there is a considerable chance that an accusation is untrue, he or she should refrain from publication. The increasing risk that the injured party will suffer damages as a result of publication is sufficient to consider it unlawful due to lack of good faith.[24]

Defamation qualifies as a tort under the new Civil Code, which came into force in January 1992. Civil Code Article 6:162 holds a person liable in tort for unlawful actions, while the substantive elements of defamation and libel are provided by Criminal Code Section 261 *et seq.* Legal actions based on tort may be brought against both natural and legal persons. Section 6.3.2. of the new Civil Code deals, amongst other matters, with offenses committed in the exercise of a profession. Even though the new Civil Code is now in force, jurisprudence based on the former Civil Code Articles 1408-16 remains of great importance.

Although an injured party may claim damages as before, the new Code introduced important changes. The requirements for making a claim for immaterial damages are easier to meet.[25] It is no longer necessary to prove that the defendant had the intention to offend (*id.*). In addition, the court can now decide, on demand of the injured party, to order publication of the judgment.[26]

It is recognized that the press acts as a "public watchdog", and as such has a duty to expose abuses. At the same time, citizens may not be exposed to rash imputations. The court, therefore, takes into account all circumstances relevant to the case, for example whether: 1) the statements caused unnecessary harm; 2) a less harmful alternative existed to reveal the

---

[24] Supreme Court 27 Jan. 1984, *Rechtspraak van de Week* 1984, 36.

[25] Article 6:106.

[26] Articles 6:162 and 6:106. *See* F W Grosheide, *supra* note 7, at 133.

abuse; 3) the information would have been made public without press involvement; and 4) the public interest demand publication.[27]

In a lawsuit based on defamation, the injured party can claim the following: 1) compensation for just and reasonable material damages; 2) compensation for immaterial damages; 3) a court declaration that the publication is illegal and offensive; 4) a prohibition to repeat the information; and 5) publication of the judgment or of a correction. Damage awards are moderate; there is not a tradition of high awards nor a trend in that direction. The plaintiff may ask that the defendant be ordered to abstain from comments when publishing the correction or judgment. The courts have to be reserved in granting such a request, however, because this could infringe the right to freedom of expression.[28] On the whole, Dutch defamation law does not appear to have a substantial "chilling effect" on the press.

10.2   Public Figure-Private Person Distinction

Public figures, including politicians, are often expected to accept more criticism than private persons. They are, however, protected against rash accusations. The concept of "public figure" is applied by both the courts and the Press Council, but no agreement has yet been reached on the exact boundaries of this concept. Courts are especially cautious in dealing with the notion of public figure.

11.   INVASION OF PRIVACY

The right to privacy is guaranteed by Article 10 of the Constitution. While protection of privacy interest against government intrusion is well established the parameter of the right *vis-a-vis* another private individual remains unsettled. The Dutch Supreme Court ruled in 1989 that the right to freedom of speech provides no justification for an infringement of privacy.[29] The right to privacy, however, is not absolute. The court takes all circumstances of the case into account in a privacy action, and the journalist may show that the publication was reasonable.

Privacy is also protected by Article 6:162 of the Civil Code and invasion of privacy is a tort.

Aggressive ways of gathering information may be curbed by Articles 139a and 426 bis of the Criminal Code. These articles penalize the tapping of phone calls and the following of persons

---

[27] Under the former Civil Code, courts took into account the following factors: 1) the nature of the published information and the seriousness of the harm to the injured party; 2) the gravity of the abuse, in light of public interest; and 3) the extent the story was supported by the available factual material. Courts also took into account the pressure under which the daily press works in determining standards accuracy. These factors undoubtedly will continue to influence decisions under the new Code.

[28] F W Grosheide, *supra* note 7, at 125-132.

[29] Supreme Court, 4 March 1988, *Netherlands Jurisprudence* 1989, 361.

against their will. These articles may serve as a guideline in a civil suit to judge whether certain ways of collecting information constitute an infringement of the right to privacy.[30]

11.1 Public Figures

The courts have stated that "persons with some public renown" must accept greater infringements on their privacy than private persons, and that the more important a public figure and the information to be exposed, the greater is the degree of acceptable scrutiny.[31] The private life of a public figure, however, is not to be sacrificed completely.[32] The extent to which a person voluntarily cooperates with a journalist is considered when a court examines an alleged infringement, but lack of consent to publish does not automatically lead to finding illegal behaviour. Courts are competent only to judge whether there is a "pressing social need" to protect a person against this degree of infringement of privacy. A court may decide on the importance of the facts concerned.[33] While there is still much uncertainty in this field, the courts generally prefer to give greater weight to the press' role as public-watchdog.[34]

In one well known case a photographer from a gossip magazine followed the children of Princess Irene everywhere and took pictures constantly. The Supreme Court noted that on the one hand the children had to accept that they were of legitimate interest to the public, and on the other hand that they personally had not done anything to draw attention to themselves and that the gossip magazine was not interested in any serious issues. The court stressed the importance of balancing competing interests and issued a declaration finding that the children's privacy interests had indeed been violated, but declined to order the magazine to pay any damages.[35]

11.2 Suspects and Victims

According to Press Council rulings, it is a good journalistic custom to protect the privacy of criminal suspects.[36] Under these rulings a suspect's age, profession, and residential area may

---

[30] G A I Schuijt, *infra* note 31, at 91, 94-95.

[31] *See* Supreme Court, 4 March 1988, *Netherlands Jurisprudence* 1989, 361.

[32] W F Korthals Altes, "Valt schending van privacy te rectificeren?", in *Rectificatie* (Amsterdam: Otto Cramwinckel Uitgeverij, 1989), 57.

[33] G A I Schuijt, "Hinderlijk volgen ofwel: Hoge bomen vangen veel wind" in *Recht in de Kijker, Jonge Balie Congres 1990* (Zwolle: W E J Tjeenk Willink, 1990), 92.

[34] J A Peters, *Het primaat van de vrijheid van meningsuiting; vergelijkende aspecten "Nederland/Amerika"* (Nijmegen: Ars Aequi Libri - Rechten van de Mens - 4, 1981), 82-91.

[35] *See supra* note 31.

[36] See *infra* Section 15.1, for a brief discussion of press self-regulation concerning criminal investigations.

be mentioned, but (with certain exceptions) the press should only use the initials of a suspect's surname and non-recognizable photographs or drawings.[37] The policy on initials is not a binding rule, and the matter of mentioning names of suspects is still rather controversial among journalists.[38] The police and judicial authorities themselves withhold certain data concerning a suspect, which sometimes leads to conflicts with the press.

12. RIGHT OF REPLY AND/OR CORRECTION

Dutch law does not contain a statutory right of reply to insulting or offensive opinions. A judge is authorized to order the publication of a reply in order to limit the harm done. Publication of the reply by the editorial staff does not deprive the injured party of the right of correction. A refusal to publish a reply can in itself constitute the basis for a tort action.

As of January 1992, Articles 6:162 and 6:167 of the Civil Code, in conjunction with Article 289 of the Code on Legal Action (which provides for summary actions), regulate the right of correction for the printed press as well as radio and television. Civil Code Article 167(2) provides for a correction even where an "unjust or misleading publication" is not unlawful under the defamation provisions of the Criminal Code due to the good faith actions of the journalist.[39]

Only *"facts"* can be subject to correction; rectification of opinions which are considered insulting or false cannot be requested. Requests for correction are usually accompanied by further claims, such as a prohibition of future publication or an amount of money to compensate for damages. The court decides how the correction shall be run and in what way costs shall be allocated.

13. INSULTS TO GOVERNMENT INSTITUTIONS OR OFFICIALS

Articles 111 and 112 of the Criminal Code penalize the "deliberate insult" of the King or other members of the Royal Family. Article 113 prohibits imparting such information. Article 118 forbids insulting behaviour toward the head of a friendly nation or ambassadors of such nations, while that person is staying in the Netherlands in an official capacity. Article 119 prohibits dissemination of publications of this nature. There have been no recent cases concerning the press under any of these charges.

---

[37] *See* M P Galama-Kuipers, "Raad voor de Journalistiek en Fair Play", in *Tuchtrecht en Fair Play* (Zwolle: W E J Tjeenik Willink, 1984), 197-214.

[38] F Kuitenbrouwer, "Grenzen en mogelijkheden van de Raad voor de Journalistiek", in *Grenzen en mogelijkheden* (Nijmegen: Ars Aequi Libri, 1984), 248-63.

[39] *See* G A I Schuijt, "Rechtzetting in het recht", in *Rectificatie* (Amsterdam: Otto Cramwinckel Uitgeverij, 1989), 16-20.

14. OFFICIAL SECRECY AND ACCESS TO GOVERNMENT-HELD INFORMATION

14.1 Access to and Disclosure of Government-Held Information

The Act and Decrees on Public Access to Information[40] regulate the state's obligation to provide for a passive[41] and active[42] transfer of information. Information is actively provided when it is "in the interest of a just and democratic government". The Act is based on Article 110 of the Constitution, which imposes a duty on the government to provide certain information.[43]

The objective of the Act on Public Access to Information is to achieve a balance between publicity and other interests which play a role in government decision-making. The basic rule is that documents are of a public nature and should be accessible to everyone, except in explicitly stated circumstances, mentioned in Articles 10 and 11 of the Act.

Article 10(1) contains absolute grounds of exception: danger to the unity of the Crown, state security, and the protection of information held by private parties imparted confidentially to the government. Requests for this kind of information may be refused without weighing the interests concerned.

Article 10(2) contains relative grounds of exemption, including amongst others: the foreign relations of the Netherlands; the economic and financial interests of the State and other public bodies; the investigation and prosecution of crimes and the protection of privacy. Whether this information should be disclosed depends on weighing the interests concerned. Proof of a definite interest in the request for information is not required but may be of importance in evaluating the request.[44] Article 15 states that an appeal against a rejection or grant of the petition based on the Act can be lodged with the Legal Division of the Council of State.

Pursuant to Article 11 there is no duty to disclose regulations meant for "internal consideration", and a document is "internal" if it includes personal views on policy matters.[45] Specific acts and regulations take precedence over the Act, which is considered general in

---

[40] Act on Public Access to Information, Staatsblad 1991, 703. This Act entered into force on 1 May 1992 and replaced the former Act on Public Access to Information of 9 Nov. 1978.

[41] Article 3.

[42] Article 8.

[43] J M de Meij, "Uitgangspunten voor een openbaarheidswet", in *Recht op openbaarheid van bestuur, Tegenspraak cahier 12* (Antwerpen: Kluwer Rechtswetenschappen, 1991), 24-29. *See supra* note 3 and accompanying text for the language of Article 110.

[44] J M de Meij, "Uitzonderingen op het openbaarheidsbeginsel van de WOB", in 34 *Ars Aequi* 35-43 (1985).

[45] *See* Legal Division of the Council of State, 23 April 1981. *Administratiefrechtelijke Beslissingen* 1981, 403.

nature. When a specific act or regulation is contrary to the Act, the case must be interpreted in conformity with the standards of the Act to the extent possible.[46]

14.2   Official Secrets

Articles 98 *et seq.* of the Criminal Code penalize the disclosure of official secrets (that is, data for which secrecy is ordered in the interest of the State or its allies). The Minister of Home Affairs drafted internal regulations that provide a strict procedure for determining what may be considered state secrets. First, the officials who may decide what is a state secret is limited. Second, each ministry, in consultation with the Minister of Home Affairs, must draw up lists of data which are secret. These lists generally provide for a maximum period of validity. The courts may decide whether an official secret is at stake. The courts are authorized to declare Article 98 applicable irrespective of how the data are classified. Conversely, the fact that certain data are marked "secret" is not in itself sufficient proof that data must remain secret.[47]

15.   ACCESS TO AND DISCLOSURE OF COURT DOCUMENTS AND PROCEEDINGS

15.1   General Disclosure Considerations

The public nature of court sessions forms an important feature of a democratic society. In the Netherlands, this recognition takes precedence over convenience in the administration of justice. It is also important to note the applicability in Dutch law of the European Court's jurisprudence, based on Article 6 of the ECHR, which no longer permits general exceptions to the public nature of court sessions. An exception can only be made on grounds of the merits of the case concerned. Exceptions may also be made in cases concerning children or family life.

The public nature of criminal proceedings is limited, however, to the trial and the judgment.[48] The Netherlands does not have a general rule which prohibits the press from writing about pending trials. Witnesses, experts and public opinion may be influenced by publications, and journalists generally take this into account when reporting on pending trials. In summary proceedings, it is possible to ask the court for a prohibition against publication. The courts are generally reluctant to issue such a prohibition, because this might lead to prior censorship, which is forbidden by Dutch law.

---

[46] *See generally* J M de Meij, "Uitzonderingen op het openbaarheidsbeginsel van de WOB", in 34 *Ars Aequi* 35-43 (1985).

[47] Supreme Court, 14 May 1974, *Netherlands Jurisprudence* 1974, 468.

[48] Article 121 of the Constitution; Code of Criminal Procedure, Articles 362 and 500f; Code on Legal Action, Article 18.

In general, the police appear to be willing to inform the press of investigative activities.[49] As a matter of press self-regulation, a *perspauze* (press interval) during which the press can be obliged not to reveal certain information, may be employed in the criminal investigation stage.[50]

15.2   Role of the Ombudsman

Since January 1982, anyone may request the National Ombudsman to investigate the way the government has acted towards a person, natural or legal. The Ombudsman is appointed by the Lower Chamber of Parliament and annually submits a public report on its activities. As a result of a number of reports published by the Ombudsman, the Minister of Justice has drawn up a draft regulation on providing information to the press in criminal cases during the pre-trial stage.

The Ombudsman has stated that it is necessary to inform the litigants when a decision is taken to inform third parties about pre-trial matters. The information disseminated must be limited to undisputed facts and may not include conclusions on criminal behaviour. If the Public Prosecutor decides to inform third parties, the suspect's privacy must be respected, so long as the suspect does not seek publicity.[51]

16.   ACCESS TO AND DISCLOSURE OF LEGISLATIVE DOCUMENTS AND PROCEEDINGS

Article 25a of the Act on the Council of State states that bills and draft Orders in Council are not made public until the Council of State has given its advice. It often happens in practice, however, that the government body itself decides to publicize the documents at an earlier stage. It is not a criminal offence for the press to report on or publish a legislative document before it is publicly released unless it otherwise would be an offence to do so (for example, publishing official secrets).

---

[49] *See* Section 11.1 *supra*, for a more detailed discussion of disclosure of information concerning criminal suspects.

[50] *See* U van de Pol, *Openbaar terecht* (Arnhem: Gouda Quint bv, 1986), 635-46.

[51] R A Vecht, "Informatieverstrekking aan de media vanwege justitie en politie", in *Recht in de kijker; Jonge Balie Congres* (Zwolle: W E J Tjeenk Willink, 1990) 165-81.

17. COMMERCIAL SECRECY AND ACCESS TO INFORMATION HELD BY PRIVATE PARTIES

Companies are required to supply information to various governmental bodies. Such bodies, however, are often obliged to observe secrecy. In determining whether a company has the right to keep a certain fact secret, the interests of the company concerned and the general interest have to be considered. The national legislature has provided guidelines on this question, and the chairman of the Legal Division of the Council of State ruled in a provisional judgment that the Act on Economic Competition permits secrecy concerning certain information.[52]

The Dutch legal system does not contain an obligation for companies to provide citizens with environmental information concerning their operations. Environmental information provided to the government is seldom accessible by citizens. Citizens can obtain certain information during licensing procedures; however, this information often does not give a clear understanding of actual or total environmental damage.

18. PRIOR RESTRAINTS

Under Article 7 of the Constitution, prior restraints against publication of thoughts or opinions are never allowed. The time, place and manner of distribution may be restricted in the public's interest (amongst other bases).[53]

19. PROTECTION OF SOURCES

Deliberations on granting journalists the right of non-disclosure of sources are continuing in the Netherlands. Currently, journalists are obliged to make certain information public. Sources have to remain verifiable, and often an argument is advanced for review by an independent court. The right to freedom of expression does not prevent such requirements.[54]

The jurisprudence of the early 1980s favoured the right of non-disclosure. The Court of Zwolle, while not granting the right, left open the possibility by stating "*in this case* no exception is concerned in which the interests of the gathering of news prevail over those of finding the truth in criminal proceedings".[55] The Press Council maintains that journalists are

---

[52] L Timmerman, "Het aan ondernemingen toekomende recht op geheimhouding", in *Tot Vermaak van Slagter, feestbundel* (Deventer: Kluwer, 1988), 315-20.

[53] *See* Section 1 *supra*, for a discussion of constitutional provisions and the Dutch government's statement in this regard in its 1988 report under the ICCPR.

[54] *See* J B M Vranken, "De journalist gemuilkorfd?", in 51 *Nederlands Juristen Blad* 1015-20 (1976).

[55] Court Zwolle, 4 March 1985, *Netherlands Jurisprudence* 1985, 490.

entitled to withhold information provided they can prove they exercised prudence in their use of sources.[56]

20. RESTRICTIONS ON OFFENSIVE LANGUAGE AGAINST IDENTIFIABLE GROUPS

Article 1 of the Constitution provides that "all people shall be treated equally in equal circumstances. Discrimination on the grounds of religion, belief, political opinion, race or sex or on any other grounds whatsoever shall not be permitted." In addition, the Netherlands ratified the International Convention on the Elimination of All Forms of Racial Discrimination in 1971 and the ICCPR in 1978.[57] Because the Netherlands does not have a comprehensive anti-discrimination act, international non-discrimination provisions are frequently invoked before the courts. In addition, Articles 137(c) through 137(e) and 429*quater* of the Criminal Code, and Article 6:162 of the Civil Code are of importance in this area.

Freedom of expression may be limited if the provisions on prohibition of discrimination are violated.[58] An expression is considered to be insulting within the meaning of the Criminal Code if it is distressing and affects the honour and reputation of the person concerned. The essence of Article 137(c) of the Criminal Code is that the individual is insulted because he or she belongs to a distinct group. In order to determine whether a phrase is insulting, the court looks at the context of the language or images. It considers the text as a whole, title and illustrations included. It is the nature of the expression itself which is crucial *not* the actual effect or the intention of the publisher.[59]

21. BLASPHEMY, OBSCENITY AND PROTECTION OF PUBLIC MORALS

Article 147 of the Criminal Code prohibits blasphemy against any religion in public, orally or in writing. Articles 239-54 of the Criminal Code address crimes against public decency, such as dissemination of pornographic pictures. No cases under these provisions have been brought against the press in recent history.

---

[56] J Doomen, *Opinies over journalistiek gedrag. De uitspraken van de Raad voor de Journalistiek 1960-1987* (Arnhem: Gouda Quint bv, 1987), 112.

[57] *See* Section 4 *supra*, for a discussion of the status of international human rights instruments in Dutch law.

[58] For a discussion of the treatment of hate speech under Dutch law, see I Boerefijn, "Incitement to National, Racial and Religious Hatred: Legislation and Practice in the Netherlands", in S Coliver (ed.) *Striking a Balance: Hate Speech, Freedom of Expression and Non-Discrimination* (London: ARTICLE 19, 1992), 201-07.

[59] *See* Supreme Court 18 October 1988, *Netherlands Jurisprudence* 1989, 476.

22. RESTRICTIONS ON ADVERTISING

Article 7(4) of the Constitution states that commercial advertising is not accorded freedom of expression. The term "commercial advertising" encompasses commercial purposes in the widest sense, involving offers to sell goods or services. Article 1(2) of the Media Act states that the terms "commercials" and "advertising" are not deemed to include raising support for or encouraging favourable attitudes towards institutions of an academic, scientific, cultural, spiritual, religious, political or charitable nature, insofar as such actions do not relate to the purchase or use of a particular commercially available product or service.

22.1 Political Advertising

The right to freedom of speech is pre-eminent when considering political advertisements. Limits to political advertising largely concern election periods. The courts usually limit inquiries to whether a political advertisement is defamatory or misleading. Moreover, the courts apply the rule contained in both Article 10 of the ECHR and Article 19 of the ICCPR, requiring any limitation on the freedom of expression to be necessary in a democratic society.

The Code on the Advertising System, Articles 1-6, contain provisions stating that: 1) paid political advertisements may not be anonymous; 2) that they have to conform with the truth and with general standards of decency and good taste; 3) they may not harm the reliability of the advertising system; and 4) there has to be a clear partition between the advertising and editorial part of a paper. The advertising system allows a type of collective refusal of advertisements. The *Codecommissie* (Code Commission) may recommend withholding further publication of offensive political advertisements. Accordingly, publishers associated with the *Nederlandse Dagblad Unie* (Dutch Daily Newspaper Union) or the *Nederlandse Organisatie van Tijdschriftuitgevers* (Dutch Organization for Publishers of Periodicals) are obliged to refuse publication of the advertisement concerned. This action is justified by the right of the newspaper publisher to decide what will be published in advertising columns.

According to Dutch law, a refusal to publish a political advertisement is generally not considered unjust. With regard to a collective refusal, however, an abuse of power may cause a tort action, based on Article 6:162 of the Civil Code. The Court of Amsterdam ruled that the standards concerning the refusal to publish certain advertisements have to be applied with great restraint to advertisements which only propagate ideas. The court ruled that the general public interest must be weighed against exercising freedom of expression and that the political picture in that case could only have been rejected if it was considered extremely tasteless or indecent by an overwhelming majority of the Dutch population, and publication would make the magazine abhorrent.[60]

---

[60] *See* Court Amsterdam, 30 Oct. 1980, *Netherlands Jurisprudence* 1981, 422.

22.2 Alcohol and Tobacco Advertising

The government limits alcohol and tobacco advertisements under its duty to protect public health. Linking the use of alcohol and sports is prohibited. Linking alcohol with health, children, or maturity is also prohibited. These provisions extend to non-alcoholic beverages which are generally used in combination with spirits. No tobacco commercials are permitted on radio or television, according to Article 50 of the *Omroepwet* (Code on the Broadcasting System).

CONCLUSION

In the Netherlands, the courts and the Press Council constantly strive to balance between the journalistic profession and the protection of rights and freedoms of others. Journalists can freely exercise their profession within the limits prescribed by law. These limitations, which are laid down in the Criminal and Civil Codes, are of a general character and not specifically designed for journalists. By the nature of their work, journalists are expected to take the necessary care in publishing facts. In judging whether they have taken such care, the pressure under which they work is taken into account. Publications affecting the private life require extra care, though in the case of public figures, a greater degree of intrusion is tolerated. Still, publications regarding such persons may not go so far as to deprive them entirely of a private life.

Journalists sometimes raise the criticism that they have limited access to information. This holds for government information as well as information from the police. Regarding government information, the Act on Public Access to Information contains a number of far-reaching restrictions, which on the whole justify the press' criticism. As far as information held by the police is concerned, the Minister of Justice has proposed a draft regulation on providing information to the press during the pre-trial stage of criminal investigations. The fact that the proposal resulted from reports of the Ombudsman indicates that the press' complaints in this area have considerable merit.

Control of the press is self-regulated to a significant extent. Journalists consider themselves bound by the Code of Ethics of the International Federation of Journalists. The Press Council actively seeks to advance the standards of the journalistic profession and provides a mechanism by which citizens may seek redress for journalistic abuses, thus reducing the need for government regulation. Only in exceptional cases are the courts seized with matters involving the press. For these reasons, court decisions addressing press freedom are not numerous, which may be seen as a tribute to the professional judgement of Dutch journalists.

Chapter 7

PRESS LAW IN NORWAY

Steingrim Wolland

INTRODUCTION

Freedom of the press in Norway first received constitutional protection in 1814. Press freedoms are an indispensable part of Norwegian democracy. There is not only a relatively high level of freedom from interference concerning what to print, but also a well-established right of access to information, which is essential for the press in safeguarding the public's interest against government wrongdoing. The press enjoys some recognition of its right to protect its sources of information, and the Norwegian government provides subsidies to promote pluralism amongst the press. Also important is a strong tradition of self-regulation involving adherence to an ethical code implemented by the Press Council.

This is not to say that there are no shortcomings. There is no clear statutory framework addressing press freedoms; indeed, legal provisions are spread amongst numerous laws. The Supreme Court has not played a vigorous role in advancing freedom of expression, while the law of defamation and protection of privacy has been extended in ways that threaten press freedom.

On the whole, however, the press enjoys a very strong position. There is a great variety of editorial viewpoints and ardent journalistic and editorial independence.

1. RELEVANT CONSTITUTIONAL PROVISIONS

Article 100 of the Norwegian Constitution of 1814 guarantees freedom of the printed press, in what, for its time, was remarkably powerful protection. Article 100 states:

> There shall be liberty of the press. No person may be punished for any writing, whatever its contents may be, which he has caused to be printed or published, unless he wilfully and manifestly has either himself shown or incited others to disobedience to the laws, contempt of religion, morality or the constitutional powers, or resistance to their orders, or has made false and defamatory accusations against anyone. Everyone shall be free to speak his mind frankly on the administration of the State or on any other subject whatsoever.[1]

Over the years, several statutes and court interpretations narrowed the range of freedom of expression, especially in the area of defamation. Today, a person may be punished for

---

[1] All quotations from the Constitution in this Chapter are from *The Constitution of the Kingdom of Norway*, produced for the Royal Norwegian Ministry of Foreign Affairs by NORINFORM (May 1989).

accusations which are true or which the person reasonably believed to be true. The Constitution has not served to restrain the legislature or the courts in this area.

The Constitution does not explicitly guarantee the right to receive information, and it is highly uncertain whether such a guarantee will be provided by the Supreme Court's interpretations. A decision by Tromsø City Court[2] stated that freedom of information had no legal protection in Norway. This is a debatable contention, given that Norway has ratified the International Covenant on Civil and Political Rights (ICCPR) and the European Convention on Human Rights (ECHR); nonetheless, it illustrates the vulnerable position of freedom of information in Norwegian law.

Today the constitutional protection of "liberty of the press" is regarded as a general prohibition of prior censorship. Nevertheless, the Court of Enforcement may suspend a publication if it is likely that it contains offensive information, such as, defamatory statements. This prohibition on publishing may later be made permanent.[3]

2. DISTRIBUTION OF POWERS BETWEEN CENTRAL AND REGIONAL GOVERNMENT

Norway is a unitary rather than a federal state. All powers relevant to the press are exercised by the central government.

3. ROLE OF THE COURTS

Norway does not have a separate constitutional court. The Constitution is interpreted by the regular courts, and the Supreme Court is the final arbiter of disputes.[4]

Far from having extended protection for freedom of expression, the Norwegian Supreme Court has contributed to what today is recognized as a certain "constitutional custom", which in some cases has led to an interpretation of Article 100 of the Constitution which is narrower than its actual language would suggest.

---

[2] 21 Aug. 1986.

[3] *See* Section 18 *infra* for a discussion of prior restraints.

[4] Articles 88 and 90 of the Constitution.

4. STATUS OF INTERNATIONAL HUMAN RIGHTS TREATIES IN NATIONAL LAW

Norway ratified the ECHR in 1952 and the ICCPR and its First Optional Protocol in 1972. Norway has ratified a considerable number of international human rights conventions and is noted for its strong commitment to human rights. These conventions, however, are not incorporated into national law. They may be raised before the courts as part of legal argument and have been noted in court decisions, but Norwegian courts are not empowered to base their decisions directly on such instruments.

Norwegian law is "presumed to be in accordance with" ratified international conventions and, in theory, if there is any doubt that a Norwegian legal rule is not in harmony with the corresponding international rule, the courts must interpret the pertinent Norwegian rule so as to be "in harmony" with the convention. This is because of Norway's so-called "dualist system" (whereby domestic law and applicable international standards exist side-by-side and function *as if* such standards were part of or incorporated into domestic law). While a number of international human rights standards have been embraced in this manner by the courts, free expression standards under Article 10 of the ECHR and Article 19 of the ICCPR to date have not been incorporated into Norwegian court decisions.

5. STATUTORY FRAMEWORK

Norway does not have a comprehensive press act. Various provisions of the Penal Code, discussed below, affect the press in significant ways. Penal Code Chapter 23, for example, concerns offences against personal honour. Chapter 43, on misdemeanours in printed matter, holds the editor responsible for the contents of periodicals. Numerous other laws with provisions that effect press freedom include the Act on Public Access to Documents, the Act on Court Proceedings, and the Act on Marketing.

6. REGULATION OF OWNERSHIP

6.1 Ownership Provisions

There are approximately 200 newspapers in Norway which publish more than once a week, including over 60 dailies (six of which have a national circulation). In addition, there are approximately 2,000 periodicals. While there are no major newspaper publishing chains as in some countries, three companies dominate the newspaper market (Schibsted, Orkla, and A-pressen, a newspaper group owned by the labour movement). A number of major newspapers are controlled by political parties or tendencies. The rest are privately owned.

There are no special legal regulations concerning ownership of the printed press. The right of newspaper proprietors to own broadcasting media is limited, although broadcast media owners may purchase a newspaper. In practice, however, this loophole is not used due to economic factors limiting the profitability of both the press and the broadcast media.

There is no specific restriction on foreign ownership of the printed press, but the Act on Purchasing of Waterfalls, Mines and Real Estate, of 17 December 1917, establishes that foreigners need the government's permission to buy real estate. Most publishing companies have real estate, and permission is therefore required and usually granted as a routine matter.

6.2   Press Subsidies

While just three companies dominate the newspaper market nationally, there is strong competition in most localities. In order to ensure a wide variety of editorial viewpoints as well as local perspectives, the government provides subsidies, in the form of direct payments, to newspapers in difficult market positions. Any paper that publishes at least twice a week and is not the largest in the area where it publishes is entitled to receive a subsidy, the amount of which is based upon the paper's circulation. A paper which makes a profit will lose its subsidy if it pays the profit to its owners but not if it ploughs the profit back into the company.

Financially troubled newspapers must apply annually for subsidy, which is conditioned on a paper's editor-in-chief having complete editorial independence. This support is crucial to a great number of Norway's newspapers. Many of them would not survive financially without it. Subsidies have helped promote pluralism amongst the press and limited the negative effects of press concentration experienced in a significant number of other countries.

In addition, the Norwegian government provides indirect subsidies to the press through reduced postal rates and, more importantly, by exempting publications from Value Added Tax (VAT).

7.   REGISTRATION REQUIREMENTS

There are no registration requirements.

8.   REGULATION OF IMPORT AND EXPORT OF PUBLICATIONS

There are no regulations concerning import or export of printed materials.

9. MECHANISMS OF PRESS SELF-REGULATION

9.1 The Press Council

Since 1936, the newspapers have had a voluntary Press Council. The Press Council (PFU) consists of four persons from the press and three from the public. The members are appointed by the board of The Norwegian Press Association (NP), which is an organization founded by the national union of journalists (NJ), the editors association (NR), and the publishers association (NAL). The PFU is highly respected amongst the press.

The PFU hears complaints against virtually all publications that traditionally fall within the term "press". Individuals, organizations and public authorities may file complaints with the PFU. The Secretary-General of the Press Association, who is not a member of the PFU, may also raise matters on his or her own initiative. Complaints must be filed within three months of the date of the offending article's publication.

It is not necessary for the complainant to first take up the matter with the concerned editor. The actual complaint may be presented quite informally. In fact, it need not be written or very specific. Supporting documentation is not required. The PFU will assist an individual to sufficiently develop his or her complaint so that the PFU may give it meaningful consideration. The PFU also will usually contact the concerned editor and attempt to assist the parties to reach an informal resolution of the complaint.

The PFU will not consider a complaint if legal action has been commenced or if the complainant states an intention to take such action. The PFU, however, does not require that the right to legal action be waived. As a consequence, complainants may turn to the courts if they are not satisfied with the PFU's decisions.

The PFU always makes a statement about the article or behaviour that is the subject of a complaint. If the PFU determines that there was a press abuse, it issues a "damning" statement, which should be printed in a conspicuous place in the concerned publication and, as of 1992, should also carry the PFU's logo. The PFU, however, does not have any enforcement power, which would be in conflict with the *Redaktørplakaten* (discussed below).

9.2 The *Redaktørplakaten*

The *Redaktørplakaten*, or Editors' Code, specifies the rights and duties of editors. It plays a fundamental role in guaranteeing editorial independence. It was signed by both the editors' and the publishers' associations in 1953 and revised in 1973. Since the *Redaktørplakaten* has been valid and respected for many years, most courts recognize it as a statement of custom under the common law. Editorial independence is also a part of the Norwegian Press Association's Code of Ethics and of the journalists' tariff-agreement.

Under the *Redaktørplakaten* as well as Section 436 of the Penal Code, the editor-in-chief has the sole and unlimited power to decide what to publish. The publisher has no legal right to make decisions concerning the content of the paper. In 1987, when the publisher of

Morgenbladet changed the front page of the newspaper, all the editorial staff resigned. Later that year, the publisher of *Midhordaland* ordered the technical staff to remove an article about him and his family business from the next day's edition; the editor and the journalist resigned immediately and started a newspaper across the street. *Midhordaland* went bankrupt, and the new paper is still flourishing. These incidents illustrate that journalists and editors are fervent about their editorial independence, and that genuine editorial autonomy can effectively limit owners' attempts to restrict information and views from reaching the public.

10.   DEFAMATION

Norwegian legislation provides for criminal as well civil causes of action for defamation (including libel) and infringement of the right to privacy. There is practically no difference between the two actions. The elements for establishing the charge of libel for both criminal and civil actions are provided by Section 247 of the Penal Code.

Under Section 247, the plaintiff's only burden is to prove that the statement was actually made and that its nature was "likely to harm" his or her reputation. Whether it did or not is irrelevant. The defendant then has the burden of proving the truth of the allegation. Truth, however, is not an absolute defence. A statement proven to be true is punishable under Section 249(2) of the Penal Code if the court finds that it was made "without respectable reasons" or was otherwise improper "because of its form or the manner in which it [was] made, or for other reasons".[5] This allocation of burdens heavily favours defamation plaintiffs. Civil damage awards in defamation cases alleging serious harm typically fall in the range of 50,000 to 150,000 kroners (approximately US$8,000 to US$24,000).

Criminal charges for defamation are rare. The plaintiff may initiate a private criminal case by simply claiming criminal penalties against the defendant in the complaint. Penalties in criminal defamation cases include fines and possible imprisonment. Fines generally are even more modest than in civil cases, approximately 1,000 to 20,000 kroners (US$160 to $3,200). The last time a person was imprisoned for defamation was 1933. With such modest penalties, a criminal action against the press has no practical value.

Norwegian press organizations claim that the defamation laws have a negative impact on investigative journalism and reporting on matters of legitimate public interest. In February 1992, the Editors Association advanced a proposal to change the defamation law. The most important point recommended was to increase emphasis on the public interest aspect of expression in order to extend the privilege of reporting statements from public authorities. The proposal also recommended that proper and immediate corrections of an erroneous statement should preclude a civil action or at least reduce the amount of damages.

---

[5] *See, e.g., Frantzen* (11 Sept. 1987). In this case, the Supreme Court granted a libel judgment against a newspaper even though the article in question did not contain untrue allegations. The large letters in the headline stating "Tax collector Franzen gets double pay", plus his photograph, were considered by the Court to be sufficient grounds for it ruling.

10.1   Politician/Private Person Distinction

Politicians are required to suffer a greater degree of criticism concerning political issues than are private persons. The same may apply to other public figures regarding their work or position, but this is very uncertain. There is no "public figure" doctrine in Norwegian jurisprudence and, as noted above, even the public interest doctrine is only partly accepted in Norwegian law.

10.2   Fact-Opinion Distinction

No distinction *per se* is made between fact and opinion in Norwegian law. Generally, more leeway is afforded to editorial pronouncements than news coverage. If a statement contains both an opinion and a factual allegation, attention is primarily focused on the latter. Moreover, a higher degree of tolerance is granted to criticism of political, religious or cultural matters than of other subjects.

11.   INVASION OF PRIVACY

The right to privacy is protected under Section 390 of the Penal Code, which provides that anyone who unlawfully violates the right to privacy by giving information to the public about personal or domestic matters, is subject to fines or imprisonment of up to three months. Section 390 also provides that publications violating its prohibition may be confiscated. Suits under Section 390 are rare; no confiscations have taken place under the section, and fines have been modest, approximately 10,000 kroners.

The Privacy Act of 1978[6] regulates, amongst other things, the use of personal files in the government and private sectors. The Act requires that newspapers obtain a licence to maintain electronic "clipping files" (an archive accessible by subject, including names of persons). The *Datatilsynet* (Data Inspectorate) set a requirement that certain types of information, when more than seven years old, may be available only to newspaper employees and not to other members of the public.

In addition, Section 15 of the Act on Rights in Photographic Pictures requires a person's permission prior to publication of his or her photograph. Section 15 recognizes a public interest exception, amongst others, which usually makes gaining permission unnecessary for the press.

In *Filmdommen*, a 1952 judgment, the Supreme Court blocked distribution of a film on the grounds that the plaintiff, who was not identified in the film, was protected by a non-statutory right to privacy.[7] The article did not discuss the relevance of Article 100 of the Constitution.

---

[6] Act No. 48 of 9 June 1978.

[7] *See Filmdommen*, Rt. 1952, at 1217.

While not directed at the press, the ruling indicates a laxness in the Court's attitude towards freedom of expression. Courts still recognize the non-statutory right to privacy set forth in *Filmdommen* even though the Supreme Court stated that the contents and scope of this right are uncertain and even though Norway ratified the ECHR six months later, Art. 10(2) of which requires any exception from the right to expression to be "prescribed by law". The courts have continued to find the scope of the right to be unclear.[8]

12.   RIGHT OF REPLY AND/OR CORRECTION

Section 430 of the Penal Code gives anyone who is directly concerned a right to correct a factual statement if a request is made within one year of publication. If the editor refuses to publish the correction, he or she could be ordered by the courts to publish, under the threat of unlimited fines. Section 430, however, has not been used to impose fines for the last 40 years. When a complaint against an editor is upheld, Section 430a requires the editor to publish the court's judgment in a "prominent place".

In addition to the legal right of correction, the Norwegian Press Association's Code of Ethics affords a right of reply to persons who "have been made subject to attacks". In practice, the Code of Ethics is used to provide replies to critical opinions, whereas the legal right of correction is used to obtain replies to factual information only. The Code also calls for publication of an apology should incorrect information be mistakenly published. There are no powers to enforce the Code of Ethics, but virtually all publications respect the Press Council's decisions regarding the right to reply.

Publication of a correction, reply or apology does not preclude a civil action but may affect the amount of damages awarded.

13.   INSULTS TO GOVERNMENT INSTITUTIONS OR OFFICIALS

The Penal Code contains several sections to protect different aspects of the reputation of state institutions, and the authorities may initiate civil actions or public criminal prosecutions to enforce these provisions. Under Section 130 of the Penal Code, any person who "against his better judgment ... gives a misleading account of the circumstances under which or the way in which [any public authority] has acted, or is accessory thereto" is liable to fines or imprisonment of up to one year. If the intention is "to harm the general reputation of the authority", a penalty for gross negligence is applicable as well. Although these rules have not been used for many years, they also have not been repealed.

---

[8] *See, e.g.*, the *Lindberg* case, *Sarpsborg namsrett*, 2 March 1989 (discussed at Section 18 *infra*).

14. OFFICIAL SECRECY AND ACCESS TO GOVERNMENT-HELD INFORMATION

All administrative documents are in principle public, unless a statutory exception applies. Anyone may demand access to such documents. Even if the document may be excepted from disclosure pursuant to provisions of the Act on Public Access to Documents, the administrative agency concerned must consider whether the document nevertheless should be disclosed. The Act, thus, is very useful to the press and plays an essential role in advancing its ability to scrutinize the activity of public authorities as well as, to some degree, private parties, since their official correspondence with the authorities may be accessible.

Pursuant to Sections 4, 5, and 6 of the Act, the pertinent administrative agency may decide that access shall be granted at a later date or that the documents are excepted from access because they concern internal agency matters, they contain information subject to statutory obligations of secrecy (for example, military secrets and personal matters), or because of a number of other specified reasons less relevant to the press.

Any request for access must be decided without undue delay. If the agency refuses the request, it must refer to the provision upon which the refusal is made. It must also provide information on the right to appeal its determination.

The public and press appear generally satisfied with this law, although problems arise concerning the way in which public officials implement the provisions. Officials regularly cause delays, even after they have been ordered by a court to disclose the documents.

The Public Access Act does not apply retroactively. However, by statute, all documents older than 30 years are to be declassified unless a longer embargo is specifically mentioned. Moreover, the Ministry of Justice's Security Instruction of June 1990 contains a general provision granting members of the public the right to request that old documents be reviewed for declassification. The Council for Declassification was established to monitor the declassification procedures and to implement standards of practice for classifying and declassifying documents.

There is no law establishing a duty of confidentiality owed to the government. A newspaper that publishes "secret" information received from a government employee may only be prosecuted if the information itself is of a character that is illegal to publish (for example, threatening national security or infringing the right to privacy). The law does not explicitly permit disclosure of information of legitimate public interest, but the public interest principle is likely to be taken into consideration both by prosecutors when deciding whether to file charges as well as by courts when formulating their decisions.

The cumulative effect of various secrecy provisions has raised a measure of concern. In addition to provisions commonly found in other countries, the courts accept the so-called "combination" or "mosaic" principle which may hold a person liable not for collecting any single piece of illegal information but for collecting many items of legal information which, when pieced together intrude into the protected zone of secrecy.[9] While this rule does not pose an immediate problem for the "mainstream" press, it sets a worrisome precedent.

15. ACCESS TO AND DISCLOSURE OF COURT DOCUMENTS AND PROCEEDINGS

The press and the public in general have a right to attend court trials. The court may, however, decide to close the courtroom to the public or to prohibit the press from referring to the court proceedings in certain circumstances. Section 126 of the Penal Code provides that a judge may bar the public from a trial if the right to privacy of a participant outweighs the public's right of access. This provision applies to cases involving criminal defendants under 18 years of age and to family law cases, such as child custody proceedings. Section 130 of the Act on Court Proceedings also grants the judge discretion in such situations.

In addition, there is a general prohibition on taking photographs of a criminal defendant on his or her way to and from the court or in the courtroom. In cases concerning serious criminal matters, and in other cases of public interest, the courts nevertheless regularly give permission to take pictures. Recording for radio and television is technically prohibited, but this is also allowed in most cases upon request.

The *Riksadvokaten* (Director General of Public Prosecutions) publicly stated on 11 October 1992 that he intends to seek huge fines (up to millions of kroners) against newspaper companies that publish "leaked" information from police sources or from trials where the court has ordered a prohibition on reporting. This action could be taken under new laws, Penal Code Sections 48a and 48b, which allow fines against companies for actions taken by someone on their behalf. These sections were introduced mainly to increase companies' responsibility regarding pollution. This proposed new application of the law is deeply troubling to the press. The *Riksadvokaten* may not succeed in his attempt, but this development provides a clear example of how fragile freedom of expression is and how creative the authorities can be in seeking to impose new restrictions.

The broad common law concept of "contempt of court" does not exist in Norwegian law. Judges have powers to impose order in the face of improper behaviour inside the courtroom, but they may not imprison journalists for conduct outside the court.

---

[9] *See, e.g.*, the *Listesaken* case (1974) at 1492 (journalists fined for gathering list of intelligence agency employees); the *Loran C* case (1982) at 436 (researchers fined for gathering information about Norwegian NATO base). In contrast, German courts have not applied the "mosaic" theory since the *Spiegel* case in 1966. (*See* the chapter by Ulrich Karpen, *supra*, and H Kohl, "Press Law in the Federal Republic of Germany", in P Lahav (ed.), *Press Law in Modern Democracies: A Comparative Study* (1985), at 201.

16. ACCESS TO AND DISCLOSURE OF LEGISLATIVE DOCUMENTS AND PROCEEDINGS

There is no legislation in Norway directly relevant to the question of access to legislative documents and proceedings. The press has access to legislative proceedings and also may publish legislative documents which it obtains, even before the documents are made publicly available. Should such documents contain "secret" information, the press may not be prosecuted unless the information is illegal to publish on independent legal grounds, as is the case with government-held information.

17. COMMERCIAL SECRECY AND ACCESS TO INFORMATION HELD BY PRIVATE PARTIES

There is no law directly relevant to "whistleblowers". In practice, whistleblowers are not likely to risk a public charge but are not protected from civil liability or job loss. If the whistleblowing is considered by the employer to be a disloyal act, the employee would most likely lose his or her job and could be liable for damages. This may be the case even if the disclosure of confidential information revealed illegality. The legal status of such situations, however, is uncertain.

Under Section 49 of the Pollution Act, upon request from governmental authorities, everyone is obligated to provide information about conditions that may cause pollution. This is applicable regardless of any duty to private parties to protect secrecy. The contamination authorities have the right of access to any property and the right to unhindered scrutiny of properties that may cause pollution or where pollution may occur. Companies are also required to hold official meetings about operations that could entail pollution problems. Such information, once provided to the authorities, would in most cases become publicly accessible.

18. PRIOR RESTRAINTS

Article 100 of the Norwegian Constitution is generally understood to be an absolute prohibition against prior censorship of printed matters. Anyone may nevertheless apply to the Court of Attachment for an interlocutory injunction on publishing a magazine, newspaper, film, book or similar material. An order to restrain publication may be issued if publication would seriously harm the plaintiff's interests. In practice, such orders are only given if the plaintiff can show that the publication carries defamatory information. Such orders are not frequently granted and are only of practical value to plaintiffs concerned with materials such as books and films rather than newspapers, because there is rarely an opportunity to anticipate the content of news stories.

In the *Lindberg* case,[10] the Court of Attachment first gave an order to restrain Lindberg's publication of his films, a report he (as a Sealing Inspector for the Ministry of Fisheries) had

---

[10] *Sarpsborg namsrett*, 2 March 1989.

made for the Ministry, and a photograph of sealers (the plaintiffs). The preliminary injunction was effective until the City Court determined that the materials were defamatory and ordered a permanent prohibition on publishing the materials, which was later upheld by the Supreme Court.

19.   PROTECTION OF SOURCES

Journalists and editors have a qualified right not to answer questions concerning the identity of their sources. The court may, nevertheless, order the editor or journalist to disclose a source if the court finds that it is of particular importance to have this information. The court must take into consideration the conflicting interests, the character of the case and the need for the information. If the information sought by learning the identity of the news source can otherwise be obtained, it is extremely unlikely that a court would order the source revealed.

In its January 1992 decision in the *Edderkopp* case,[11] the Supreme Court declared that: "In some cases ... the more important the violated interest is, the more important it will be to protect the sources." The case involved two journalists who had written a book entitled *Edderkopp* (Spider), about the activities of a Norwegian furniture manufacturer who had secretly taped his telephone conversations with noted politicians. Various passages in the book discussed connections between the Labour Party and the Norwegian intelligence agency. A Parliamentary oversight body sought the source of this information in order to determine whether it had been wrongfully provided by an agency employee. The authors refused to reveal their sources, and the body attempted to obtain a court order compelling them to do so. The court refused the application. The Supreme Court, in upholding the lower court, ruled that the authors had a right to protect their sources. The press welcomed the decision which is likely to have a significant influence on this area of the law.

In this century, in spite of the law and legal practice, journalists and editors have rarely revealed their sources after a court order to do so. They are fined moderate amounts for this practice. For instance, an editor recently was fined NK 20,000 (US$ 3,200). Imprisonment has not been used for at least several decades. Editors and journalists still risk imprisonment and large fines, including continuing fines, but this has not been a substantial threat.

20.   RESTRICTIONS ON OFFENSIVE LANGUAGE AGAINST IDENTIFIABLE GROUPS

Under Penal Code Section 135a, a person is liable for fines or imprisonment of up to two years if he or she, by any utterance or other communication disseminated among the public, threatens or subjects to hatred or contempt a person or group because of their religion, creed, race, skin colour or national or ethnic origin. The same penalties apply to offensive conduct towards persons or groups because of their homosexual status, lifestyle or inclination.

---

[11] Rt. 1992, at 39.

The Norwegian Press Association's Code of Ethics contains a provision that requires the press "always to respect a person's identity, privacy, race, nationality or religious belief", and "never to draw attention to personal peculiarities when this is irrelevant to the matter". The Code has contained a similar provision for many years without raising problems. Press organizations nevertheless argued strongly against introducing Section 135a in 1970 and against its amendment concerning homosexuals in 1981.

The press argued that penalizing expression is not the way to fight opinions in a democracy. With or without Section 135a, "hate speech" has not been a particular problem in Norway. Breaches of the Code's provision on this point are very rare, and only three cases concerning Section 135a of the Penal Code are known since 1970. Two of these cases concerned letters to the editor, and both resulted in acquittals. The third was not relevant to the present topic.

21.   BLASPHEMY, OBSCENITY AND PROTECTION OF PUBLIC MORALS

Under Section 142 of the Penal Code, any person who "publicly insults or in an offensive manner shows contempt for any religious creed ... or for the doctrines or worship of any religious community lawfully existing here" is subject to fines or imprisonment of up to six months. This section has not been applied by the courts since an author, Arnulf Øverland, was acquitted in 1936. Several muslim leaders brought a lawsuit against the Norwegian publisher of "Satanic Verses" but withdrew it, probably because they recognized that they had virtually no chance of winning the case.

There is no general protection of public morals in Norwegian law. Penal Code Section 211 prohibits indecent or obscene behaviour in public and publication of pornographic material. This section has not been applied to the daily press.

22.   RESTRICTIONS ON ADVERTISING

Alcohol and tobacco advertising is forbidden. This includes advertising any product that carries the same label as a tobacco brand (for example, Camel Boots).

Advertising that conflicts with the principle of equality of the sexes is prohibited under Section 1 of the Act on Marketing. Section 1 states:

> An advertiser and anyone who creates advertising matter shall ensure that the advertisement does not conflict with the inherent parity between the sexes and that it does not imply any derogatory judgment of either sex or portray a woman or a man in an offensive manner.

Section 1 has not caused any problems for the daily press.

The *Forbrukerombudet* (Consumers Ombudsman) supervises marketing and may forbid marketing which conflicts with the law. The *Forbrukerombudet's* decision may be appealed to the Marketing Council, which makes the final decision.[12]

CONCLUSION

The Norwegian press enjoys a relatively high degree of freedom. The right of access to government documents is well established, as is the right of the press and public to attend court proceedings and meetings of national and local government authorities. The print media operate free from government control over what to publish and how to run their businesses. The press on the whole respects the ethical standards enunciated in the Norwegian Press Association's Code of Ethics, including those regarding libel and invasion of privacy. In addition, the right of correction set forth in the Penal Code and right of reply recognized in the Code of Ethics provide the public with speedy and often adequate remedies.

However, several aspects of the situation give cause for concern. It is often said that, as in Sweden and Denmark, the connections between the press and the establishment are too close. On the other hand, a significant tendency has developed over the last 20 to 30 years whereby newspapers act more independently, including from political parties and organizations. Editorial independence has surely increased over the last decades.

During the same period, newspapers have changed character in their layout and by carrying articles about the private lives of private persons as well as about celebrities and persons in power. These developments have fostered criticism of the press for invasion of privacy, inaccuracy and defamation and have led, since the 1950s, to stronger protections for privacy and "personality". The threat of abuse posed by electronic surveillance equipment and "data-registrars" has undoubtedly contributed to this process. All of these factors have fostered increased public demands for more "protection laws" and more vigorous prosecutions of the press, which may translate into more restrictions on freedom of information and expression.

Virtually every year, one or more government ministries propose new bills that threaten to reduce freedom of expression in one way or another. In spite of the fact that they are meant to promote "the best interests" of the public and may be supported by a majority, they are a cause for concern. For the most part, these proposals do not attempt to restrict the essential core of press freedom but, nonetheless, as Justice Brandeis of the United States once said: "Liberty dies by inches." The number of such limitations are numerous, and the sum of them could have an undesirable effect.

The press is particularly worried about the defamation laws. There is no doubt about their strong chilling effect on journalism, particularly regarding allegations of economic wrongdoing (rather than political criticisms). The press associations claim that the courts do

---

[12] Advertising for political or religious views on radio or television is prohibited. The provisions concerning broadcast advertising are more detailed and regulate advertising more extensively than for the press. These provisions include restrictions on form, quantity, content, and placing of commercials.

not sufficiently emphasize the public interest aspects of cases, and the associations have asked for several changes in the law to assist the press' "public watchdog" function.

A strength of the Norwegian press is the wide variety of newspapers and magazines. There are approximately 200 newspapers and 350 to 400 scientific, non-fiction and professional magazines. These numbers ensure a considerable diversity of editorial views. In addition, the editorial autonomy within every newspaper is protected by the *Redaktørplakaten* (Editor's Code) and the contractual structure which reinforces it. With this background, it is hard to imagine that a Springer or a Murdoch could achieve the same level of editorial influence in the Norwegian press as they have in other countries.

Chapter 8

FREEDOM OF THE PRESS IN SPAIN

Blanca Rodriguez Ruiz

INTRODUCTION

In Spain, freedom of the press is treated as an aspect of freedom of expression and freedom of information, which are protected, respectively, by Articles 20.1.(a) and (d) of the Constitution of 1978. Freedom of expression has been a key political issue in modern Spanish history. It was included as a fundamental right in most of the former constitutions[1], but respect for freedom of expression has often been interrupted by political authorities and dictatorships, most recently during Franco's regime, under whose laws this freedom was only faintly protected.[2] Since adoption of the 1978 Constitution, Spain has enjoyed fundamental rights and freedoms comparable to those in other democratic countries. Freedom of information, as distinct from freedom of expression, was recognized for the first time by the 1978 Constitution.

1.   RELEVANT CONSTITUTIONAL PROVISIONS

Article 20 of the Constitution of 1978 reads, in relevant part, as follows:

1.   The following rights shall be recognized and protected:

   a) the right to express freely and to disseminate thoughts, ideas and opinions orally, in writing or by any other means of reproduction;
   ...
   d) the right to receive and communicate accurate information by any means of dissemination. The right to invoke the conscience clause and that of professional confidentiality shall be governed by statute.

2.   The exercise of these rights may not be restricted by any prior censorship.
   ...

4.   These freedoms shall be limited by respect for the rights secured in this Title, by the provisions of the implementing

---

[1] *See* Const. 1837, Art. 2; Const. 1845, Art. 2; Const. 1856 (not promulgated), Art. 3; Const. 1869, Art. 17; Const. 1876, Art. 13; Const. 1931, Art. 34.

[2] Article 12 of "*Fuero de los Españoles*".

laws and in particular by the rights to honour, to privacy, to control the use of one's image and to protect youth and children.

Article 20 belongs to the second chapter of Title I of the Constitution which concerns "fundamental rights and freedoms". The fundamental character of rights and freedoms listed in the second chapter is confirmed by Article 53.1 of the Constitution which specifies that they are binding on all public powers.[3]

Article 53.2 provides certain procedural advantages for the judicial protection of rights and freedoms recognized in Articles 14 to 29. First, when one of those rights is violated, their judicial protection may be obtained by way of a preferential and speedy procedure called the "ordinary recourse *de amparo*" (similar to habeas corpus).[4] Second, appeal to the Constitutional Court for the protection of those rights is possible by way of a "constitutional recourse *de amparo*". Direct appeal to the Constitutional Court, however, is only possible concerning allegations of violations caused by a non-legislative act of the central or of a regional Parliament (Art. 42 of the Ordinary Law (L.O.) 2/79 of 3 October). In all other cases (namely, alleged violations by the government or miscarriages of justice), the constitutional recourse *de amparo* is permitted only after the suitable ordinary procedures have been exhausted (*id.*, Arts. 43.1 and 44.1).

The relevance of the liberties recognized in Article 20.1 has been stressed by the Constitutional Court. With free speech at their core, these liberties stand as cornerstones of informed public opinion. They are, thus, basic conditions for effective political pluralism which, together with justice, liberty and equality are considered "superior values" in Spain's democratic state (Article 1.1 of the Constitution).[5]

Although the point of reference of Article 20 is the protection of the freedoms of expression and information, the structure and wording of the article suggest that the freedoms it recognizes are independent of one another. The Constitutional Court has repeatedly confirmed the independent vitality of freedom of expression (Art. 20.1(a)) and freedom of information (Art. 20.1(d)).[6]

---

[3]   Article 55.1 of the Constitution permits the suspension of the freedoms of expression and information recognized by Article 20.1.(a) and (d) when states of emergency or siege are lawfully declared according to Article 116 of the Constitution.

[4] L.0. 62/78 of 26 Dec.

[5] *See* STC (*Sentencia del Tribunal Constitucional* [Decision of the Constitutional Court]) 6/81, 17 March, F.Jco. (*Fundamento Jurídico*) 3; STC 12/82, 31 March, F.Jco. 3; STC 104/86, 17 July, F.Jco. 5; STC 6/88, 21 January, F.Jco. 5; 107/88, 8 June, F.Jco. 2.

[6] *See, e.g.,* SSTC (*Sentencias del Tribunal Constitucional* [Decisions of the Constitutional Court]) 6/81 and 107/88, *supra* note 5; STC 105/83, 23 Nov., F.Jco. 11.

Freedom of expression protects the communication of "thoughts, ideas and opinions, broad concepts within which beliefs and value judgements may also be included".[7] Freedom of information protects the communication of "facts, or more particularly ... facts that may be considered newsworthy ... and true".[8] The basic distinction consistently applied by the Constitutional Court, therefore, is that freedom of expression refers to opinions, whereas freedom of information refers to facts.[9] Despite its theoretical clarity, a borderline between freedom of expression and freedom of information does not always prove easy to draw in actual cases since the communication of facts or news items also frequently includes value judgements. As a consequence, the above-mentioned criterion has been given a certain flexibility. Whenever facts and opinions appear intermingled in the transmission of information, account must be taken of which predominates.[10] Accordingly, freedom of information may be claimed only where facts lie at the core of the information transmitted. Free expression may be claimed where comments on facts outweigh their actual informative content.

The protected area of free expression is wide. Its only limit is the use of "undoubtedly defamatory statements, not related to the ideas or opinions expressed, and unnecessary to their expression".[11] Freedom of information, on the other hand, is more severely limited. It only covers the communication of facts which prove newsworthy and accurate.[12] The newsworthy requirement (that information must focus on facts of certain public importance) was introduced by the Constitutional Court because the final aim of Article 20.1.(d) is to promote the genuine participation of citizens in public life.[13]

The requirement that information must focus on accurate facts is contained in Article 20.1.(d) itself. The Constitutional Court's interpretation of Article 20.1.(d) loosened the strict terms of this requirement. According to the Court, the requirement of accuracy does not exclude from constitutional protection information which might turn out to be incorrect, or the truth of which has not been ascertained. Rather, accuracy imposes on the journalist the duty to act with due diligence in gathering information and to check any news which he or she intends

---

[7] STC 6/88, *supra* note 5 (author's translation).

[8] *Id.* (author's translation).

[9] Compare the ruling of the European Court of Human Rights that a person or publication accused of having made a defamatory value judgment cannot be required to prove its truth, because value judgments are not susceptible of being proven true or false. *Lingens v. Austria*, Judgment of 8 July 1986, Series A no. 103, paras. 44-46.

[10] STC 6/88, *supra* note 5.

[11] STC 105/90, June 6, F.Jco. 4.

[12] For a more thorough analysis, see STC 105/83, note 6 *supra*. *See also* STC 6/88, note 5 *supra*.

[13] SSTC 105/83, *supra* note 6; 6/88, *supra* note 5.

to publish against other data or sources which might confirm or improve the accuracy of the information transmitted, so that public opinion is not misled.[14]

Articles 20.1.(a) and (d) provide protection only against acts of interference by public authorities; they impose no direct duties on private individuals and contain no right against private interference with freedom of expression or information.[15] Moreover, consistent with their status as freedoms in the traditional sense, they do not impose any obligations on public authorities to take positive measures to promote their exercise.[16]

While all persons are entitled to the rights to freedom of expression and information,[17] the media are accorded special protection in recognition of their important role in informing public opinion.[18]

2. DISTRIBUTION OF POWERS BETWEEN CENTRAL AND REGIONAL GOVERNMENT

Articles 148 and 149 of the Constitution are the basis for the distribution of powers between the State and its Autonomous Communities. Article 148 lists the powers that regions may exercise; Article 149 lists the powers of the central state. Two provisions of Article 149 are particularly relevant. Article 149.1 states:

> The State holds exclusive competence over the following matters:
>
> 1) The regulation of the basic conditions which guarantee the equality of all Spaniards in the exercise of their rights and fulfilment of their constitutional duties.
> . . . .
> 27) Basic norms of the system of press, radio and television and, in general, of the other means of social communication, without prejudice to the competence of the Autonomous Communities for the development and execution of such basic norms.

The State, therefore, plays the most important role in the regulation of freedom of expression and information. It is for the State to set out the "basic norms" concerning these regulations, that is, to set out "those general criteria for the regulation of a juridical area that must be

---

[14] *See, e.g.,* SSTC 6/88, *supra* note 5; 171/90, 12 Nov., F.Jco. 8.

[15] *See, e.g.,* STC 673/85, 9 Oct., F.Jco. 3; STC 129/89, 17 July, F.Jco. 3; STC 77/82, 20 Dec., F.Jco. 1.

[16] SSTC 12/82, *supra* note 5; 77/82, *supra* note 15.

[17] STC 6/81, *supra* note 5.

[18] STC 165/87, 27 Oct., F.Jco. 10.

common to the whole of the State".[19] Nevertheless, within this framework Autonomous Communities assume certain powers of an administrative nature (*e.g.,* concerning radio frequencies) or even of a rule-making nature (*e.g.,* concerning the control of the regional public television channels).[20]

The Constitutional Court may ultimately rule on the scope of the powers of both the State and the Autonomous Communities.

3.   ROLE OF THE COURTS

The Constitutional Court is the only organ authorized to decide the constitutionality of Spanish laws. Rules concerning the structure and functioning of the Court are contained in Title IX of the Constitution, developed by organic law, specifically by L.O. 2/79 of 3 October.

Two of the competencies of the Constitutional Court are particularly important for the protection of fundamental rights (*see* Article 161 of the Constitution). First, the Court may decide appeals of *amparo* against the violation of certain fundamental rights contained in Articles 14 to 29 of the Constitution in cases where these rights are inadequately protected by ordinary courts.[21]

Second, the Constitutional Court has exclusive competence to review the constitutionality of laws and regulations having the force of law that were passed after the Constitution came into force. This power may be exercised in two different ways: 1) in an abstract way, following a so-called *recurso de inconstitucionalidad* (recourse of unconstitutionality) against a published law;[22] or 2) in a substantive-concrete manner, that is by way of an answer to a *cuestión de inconstitucionalidad* (incidental question of unconstitutionality) raised by an ordinary judge who has doubts about the constitutionality of a particular legal provision relevant to the case at trial.[23] In both cases, the decision of the Constitutional Court takes the form of a ruling, the scope of which is final and binding on all.[24]

---

[19] STC 25/83, 7 April, F.J.4.

[20] *See the* Autonomy Statutes of Andalucía, Art. 16; Cataluña, Art. 16; Galicia, Art. 34; País Vasco, Art. 19; Madrid, Art. 31; Baleares, Art. 15; and Aragón, Art. 37.

[21] L.O. 2/79, Arts. 41-58.

[22] Art. 161.1.(a) of the Constitution; L.O. 2/79, Arts. 31, *et seq.*

[23] Art. 163 of the Constitution; L.O. 2/79, Arts. 35, *et seq.*

[24] Art. 164 of the Constitution; L.O. 2/79, Art. 38.

The Constitutional Court does not need to decide on the constitutionality of laws promulgated before the Constitution came into effect. In case of a conflict with the Constitution, these laws must be considered abrogated and must be ignored by ordinary courts.[25] However, if an ordinary court has doubts about the constitutionality of a pre-Constitutional law it may raise a *cuestión de inconstitucionalidad* to the Constitutional Court. Ordinary courts may not address questions to the Constitutional Court concerning regulations not having the force of law, but must not enforce such regulations if they consider them to be unconstitutional. Only administrative courts may make abstract decisions on the constitutionality of regulations, and may declare them "void with general effects".

4. STATUS OF INTERNATIONAL HUMAN RIGHTS TREATIES IN NATIONAL LAW

Spain ratified the International Covenant on Civil and Political Rights (ICCPR) in 1977, its First Optional Protocol in 1985, and the European Convention on Human Rights (ECHR) in 1979. Spain accepted the direct recourse of individuals to the European Commission of Human Rights under Article 25 of the ECHR.[26]

Two provisions of the Constitution refer to the status of international human rights in domestic law. Article 10.2 states:

> The norms relative to basic rights and liberties which are recognized by the Constitution shall be interpreted in conformity with the Universal Declaration of Human Rights and the international treaties and agreements on those matters ratified by Spain.

Article 96.1 states:

> Validly concluded international treaties once officially published in Spain shall constitute part of the internal [legal] order . . . .[27]

As a result of these two articles, human rights recognized in international conventions ratified by Spain play a double role in the Spanish juridical system. First, they belong to domestic law and must accordingly be directly applied by national courts. Thus, domestic courts *must* follow interpretations, when directly relevant, of authoritative international bodies which implement treaties to which Spain is a party, such as the European Court of Human Rights,[28] so long as such interpretations do not narrow the scope of a right as recognized in the

---

[25] The Third Abrogative Disposition of the Constitution; *see, e.g.,* STC 4/81, 2 Feb., F.Jco. 1.

[26] Declaration of 15 Oct. 1985.

[27] *See also* Art. 1.5 of the Civil Code.

[28] *See, e.g.,* SSTC 6/88, *supra* note 5; 106/88, 8 May, F.Jco.3; 114/84, 29 Nov., F.Jco. 3.

Constitution.[29] Second, domestic courts should use the interpretations of non-authoritative bodies, such as the European Commission of Human Rights and the UN Human Rights Committee as interpretative guides in applying domestic law. Thus, the Constitutional Court explicitly followed the European Commission's interpretation of Article 10 of the ECHR in the absence of an interpretation by the European Court.[30]

5. STATUTORY FRAMEWORK

Freedom of expression and information, as fundamental freedoms, may only be regulated by organic laws. Organic laws, according to Article 81 of the Constitution, require an absolute majority of Congress for their approval, modification or repeal, as opposed to ordinary laws which require only a simple majority. The most significant organic law which restricts freedom of expression and information is L.O. 2/84 of 26 January 1984 concerning the right to correction (discussed below in Section 12).

6. REGULATION OF OWNERSHIP

Government-controlled papers ceased to exist in 1982 as a result of L.O. 11/82 of 3 April which authorized the privatization of the property of the public body which controlled public newspapers. Ownership of publishing enterprises now is directly regulated by Article 38 of the Constitution, according to which "Free enterprise within the framework of a market economy is recognized . . . .." As a result there are no laws which regulate ownership of the press by Spanish citizens or companies.[31]

Foreign ownership of publishing enterprises, however, is subject to the provisions of the *R. Decreto Legislativo* (R. D-Leg.) 1265/86, 27 June, on foreign investment in Spain. This act, which has the force of law, was adopted after Spain became a member of the European Community and reflects a strong commitment to free markets. The R. D-Leg. applies to all foreign persons, whether juridical or natural, and to Spanish persons resident abroad (Article 1.1). It describes the three different types of foreign investment which are allowed and which are sometimes subject to prior administrative verification of their nature and real value (Articles 5-14). Any type of foreign investment not regulated by the R. D-Leg must be

---

[29] *See* Art. 17 of the ECHR for a similar non-limitation principle. The "non-limitation" principle is implicitly assumed in the decisions of the Constitutional Court. *See* SSTC 19/83, 14 March, F.Jco. 2; 30/86, 21 Feb., F.Jco. 4; 40/87, 3 April, F.Jco. 2; 196/87, 17 Dec., F.Jco. 7.

[30] STC 53/85, 16 April, F.Jco. 6.

[31] Chap. 3 of the Law of the Press 14/66, 18 March, which formerly regulated press ownership, was repealed by Law 29/84, 2 Aug.; this gap has since remained unfilled.

authorized by the administration (Article 15). In no case is there a limit to the maximum percentage of a company or of the market that a foreign investor may own.[32]

7.   REGISTRATION REQUIREMENTS

Obligatory registration of publications is regulated by a decree enacted on 23 December 1957. It requires that publications be registered with the *Depósito Legal* (Legal Depository), which works both at the provincial and central level (Article 12). Publishers are obliged to register publications at the respective provincial office of the *Depósito Legal*, which must send copies of all registrations to the central office in Madrid (Article 3).

The publisher must apply for its registration number, which will be given automatically (Article 4 (a)). These requirements must be followed by publications including periodicals. Accordingly, each periodical must be registered, although only one registration number is needed for each journal (Article 5). The registration number must be included in each published issue (Article 10).

Registration requirements do not amount to a control on the content of publications. They merely keep account of the number of the publications in existence and of certain other formal details (Article 6). Thus registration is not a form of prior censorship (which is banned by Article 20.2 of the Constitution, *see* Section 18, *infra*).

8.   REGULATION OF IMPORT AND EXPORT OF PUBLICATIONS

The *Dirección General* (General Directions) of Customs and Special Taxes of the Ministry of Economy provides the only existing rules regarding import and export of publications.[33] These regulations do not impose any restriction on import or export of publications.

9.   MECHANISMS OF PRESS SELF-REGULATION

The Spanish press has no self-regulatory bodies.

---

[32] The above-mentioned freedom of investment does not apply to the broadcast media. Chapter 8 of R. D-Leg. 1265/86 refers to sectors of the economy in which, according to Arts. 56.1 and 223.1 of the Treaty of Rome, Spain may limit foreign investment. Radio and television are among these sectors. For instance, regarding private commercial television, no more than 25 per cent of the shareholders of one company may be foreign (Article 19).

[33] *See* Regulations of 21 June 1989 and 20 Oct. 1988 (regarding procedural steps for the international trade of publications).

10. DEFAMATION

According to Article 18.1 of the Constitution: "Everyone is entitled to the protection of his honour, his personal and family privacy and his own image." Moreover, according to Article 81:

> The rights recognized by Article 18 enjoy the same protection as the freedoms included in Article 20. Their judicial protection is laid down by the principles of preference and speed, and guaranteed by the possibility of an appeal *de amparo* [Constitution, Article 53.2]. Moreover, Article 18.1 must be directly developed through organic laws.

10.1 Criminal and Civil Law Provisions

The rights contained in Article 18.1 are also protected by criminal and civil laws. Defamation (Criminal Code, Articles 457 *et seq.*) and false accusation of a criminal offence (Criminal Code, Article 453 *et seq.*) traditionally have been sanctioned as crimes against honour.

In the field of civil law, L.O. 1/82 of 5 May regulates the "civil protection of the rights to honour". Although in some instances this law is wider than the relevant criminal provisions, the objects of both civil and criminal protection overlap substantially. This circumstance accounts for inevitable conflicts of jurisdiction between civil and criminal procedure. In this respect, Article 1.2 of L.O. 1/82 states that criminal procedure must be pursued whenever the facts challenged may be qualified as criminal.

The Supreme Court, however, has softened the absolute terms of Article 1.2. Applying Articles 111-112 of the Law of Criminal Procedure, the Supreme Court stated that the criminal action *must* be pursued only when a public prosecution is at stake; in all other cases civil actions may be undertaken, although this extinguishes the possibility of subsequent recourse to criminal courts.[34]

Plaintiffs generally prefer civil trials to criminal trials because they provide a more flexible alternative to criminal trials. As an example, under civil procedures plaintiffs do not bear the burden of proof whereas in criminal procedures they must overcome the presumption of the defendant's innocence. Moreover, in criminal procedures, plaintiffs must prove that the defendant had the requisite criminal intent, which can be difficult in light of the fact that most media defendants claim that their chief intent was to communicate information or opinions of public interest.

The courts of first instance determine the amount of damages to be awarded to a successful plaintiff and the amounts vary considerably depending on a variety of factors. The amount is to take into consideration the actual material damage caused by the defamation (or invasion

---

[34] *See* STS, 1a. Sala, 23 Feb. 1989. Most common crimes are subject to public prosecution; some crimes, in particular defamation and sexual crimes, may only be initiated and pursued with the consent of the victim or the victim's representatives and thus are subject to private prosecution.

of privacy, *see* Section 11, *infra*); the economic benefit the defendant received by publishing the defamation; and the more nebulous concept of moral damages. Awards generally range from some 100,000 to, in very rare cases, 20 million pesetas (US$ 800 to 160,000). It must also be taken into account that Article 65 of the Law on the Press, dating from 1966, establishes the joint responsibility of the author, the publisher, the editor, the printer, the importer (if any) and the distributor of the publication. Although Article 65 establishes an unusually broad net of responsibility, the Constitutional Court has affirmed that it remains in force.

The government recently proposed a new crime of defamation as a result of a widespread sense of "social defencelessness" against abuses of the press. The proposed crime would penalize the publication of information by the media which does not meet the standard for accuracy set by the Constitutional Court (namely, that either a statement must be true or else the journalist must have acted with due diligence in gathering and checking the information, *see* Section 1 *supra*). The proposal has been heavily criticized owing to the high penalties it would impose, including suspension of the right to work as a journalist.

10.2   Conflict of Rights Considerations

As noted in Article 20.4 of the Constitution, the rights recognized in Article 18.1 limit the rights to freedom of expression and information guaranteed by Article 20.1 (*see* Section 1, *supra*, for text of Article 20). Conflicts between the exercise of these rights and freedoms are thus likely to arise. The Constitutional Court has provided guidelines for the solution of such constitutional conflicts. The cornerstone of its doctrine is the higher status enjoyed by the freedoms recognized in Article 20.1, owing to their contribution in forming public opinion.[35]

10.3   Public Interest and Political Figures

The extent to which public opinion is involved is thus the central question to be decided in each case. To this end, certain points must be measured and balanced: 1) whether opinions or facts have been communicated by means of the media which would therefore contribute to the free formation of public opinion;[36] 2) whether the opinion or information communicated is of public relevance, taking account of the public character of the persons and the facts involved;[37] 3) whether opinions (freedom of expression) have been expressed

---

[35] STC 104/86, *supra* note 5.

[36] STC 165/87, *supra* note 18.

[37] STC 171/90, *supra* note 14.

strictly within the sphere of public interest;[38] and 4) whether facts (freedom of information) are accurate.[39]

The Constitutional Court ruled in a 1990 case that information or opinions involving politicians are considered of public character, and thus relevant to the free formation of public opinion. As a consequence, politicians are required to submit to a greater invasion of their honour and privacy for the sake of the protection of freedom of expression and information.[40] Moreover, because of the media's special role, criticisms published by the media are entitled to increased protection.

11.   INVASION OF PRIVACY

Privacy, like honour, is protected by Article 18.1 of the Constitution, as well as by criminal and civil laws. The following aspects of privacy are protected by provisions of the Criminal Code: the secrecy of private papers is protected by Articles 191, 192 and 497); the confidentiality of personal secrets known through fiduciary relations is protected by Article 498; and the interception of telephone conversations is prohibited by Articles 192 bis and 497 bis. In the civil law field, L.O. 1/82 of 5 May protects the rights to privacy and one's own image. The right to privacy is treated in all substantial respects in the same way as the right to honour and privacy. (*See* Section 10 *supra*).

12.   RIGHT OF REPLY AND/OR CORRECTION

Every person alluded to in published information which he or she considers incorrect and damaging has the right to have a correction published, pursuant to L.O. 2/84 of 26 January. The right involves the immediate publication by the same journal, radio or T.V. station of a version of the disputed information as corrected by the complainant, without additional comments by the media organ concerned, and with the same prominence as was given to the original version (Article 3). If the paper does not publish the correction voluntarily, there may be a brief trial on the appropriateness of the correction (Articles 2 and 4, respectively).

The publication of a corrected version is not an admission that the original information was wrong. The affected media entity may, in a separate piece of news, confirm its version of the facts. Accepting the truth of the correction is not necessary for its voluntary publication, nor must the truth be fully ascertained in the judicial decision of a case of correction. The truth of the different versions of the facts concerned may be decided by a civil or a criminal action

---

[38] *Id.*

[39] *Id.* at F.Jco.8.

[40] STC 105/90, *supra* note 11.

for defamation or violation of privacy, actions which are not precluded by the publication of a correction (Article 6).[41]

13. INSULTS TO GOVERNMENT INSTITUTIONS OR OFFICIALS

Various provisions of the criminal code penalize the use of offensive language against state institutions and government officials. False accusation of a criminal offence, defamation and serious threats are more serious crimes if they are addressed against the Head of State (Article 147), the Regents, the Government, the General Council of the Judiciary, the Constitutional Court, the Supreme Court, the Regional Governments (Article 161), the Military (Article 242), or against ministers or public authorities when they are acting in their official capacities (Articles 240-241, 244).

It is settled constitutional doctrine that respect for their dignity and prestige was a legitimate limitation to freedom of expression and information.[42] However, the evaluation of this scope of this limitation by the Constitutional Court has changed over time. In a 1985 case, the Constitutional Court stated that the transmission of both news and opinions was absolutely limited by the protection of national security, which could be endangered by offences against democratic institutions.[43] The Court abandoned this doctrine in 1989, announcing that the reputation of public institutions constituted a weaker limitation on freedom of speech or information than the honour or privacy of individuals.[44] The Court extended the new doctrine in STC 105/90 of 6 June, holding that government officials and politicians are required to submit to a greater invasion of their honour and privacy than are private individuals.

The King also must tolerate a measure of insult. In 1987 the Constitutional Court invalidated a six years' prison sentence given to a journalist (pursuant to Article 147) for having insulted the Crown and the King in a newspaper article.[45] The Court ruled that the sentence violated Articles 16 (guaranteeing freedom of ideology) and Article 20.1(a) and (d) of the Constitution. The Court stayed execution of the sentence pending the case's final resolution (as it commonly does in such cases) with the result that the journalist never spent a day a jail.

No treason or sedition charges have been used against the press since democracy was re-established in Spain. Other limitations to Article 20 of the Constitution, however, have been laid down in the name of national security, in particular, in the case of support for terrorism

---

[41] STC 168/86, 22 Dec., F.Jco. 4, 5.

[42] SSTC 51/85, F.Jco. 10; 105/90, F.Jco.2, 8; *see also* ATC 297/90, 16 July, F.Jco.3.

[43] STC 51/85, 10 April.

[44] STC 51/89, 22 Feb., F.Jco. 2.

[45] STC 20/90, 15 Feb.

(Criminal Code, Article 268). The Constitutional Court has made clear that Article 268 only limits the freedom to express opinions showing solidarity with terrorism, and does not limit the freedom of the press to publish facts related to terrorism.[46] Thus the Court invalidated the conviction of the editor of *Eguin* who had published a statement sent by the Basque separatist group ETA. Although the statement advocated support for terrorism the journal, merely by publishing the statement without comment, could not be found to have done so.

14. OFFICIAL SECRECY AND ACCESS TO GOVERNMENT-HELD INFORMATION

As a necessary counterpart to freedom of information, the principle of public access to the activities of public authorities is at the core of democratic societies. Under certain circumstances, however, exceptions to this principle are permissible. Threats to national security, to the adequate administration of justice, or to an individual's right to privacy or honour are the most common grounds for the withdrawal of information from the public domain. The general rule and its exceptions are discussed in the following sections.

The Spanish Constitution does not expressly state that governmental and administrative acts should be public. Yet, this is a necessary step to fulfil the duties of responsibility and non-arbitrariness that the Constitution imposes on the administration (Article 9.3). In this respect, Article 105 states:

> The law shall regulate:...
> b) Access by the citizens to the administrative archives and registers except where it affects the security and defence of the State, the investigation of crimes and the privacy of persons.

No law has yet been enacted pursuant to Article 105.

The exceptions to public access to acts and documents of the administration are regulated by Law 9/68 of 5 April, as modified by Law 48/78 of 7 October on official secrets. It defines "classified matters" (including issues, acts, documents, information, data and objects) as matters about which general knowledge might be damaging or threatening to the security and defence of the State (Article 2). Matters may be classified as either "secret" or "reserved", according to the level of protection required (Article 3), and such classifications may be made only by means of a formal act of the Council of Ministers or the "*junta de Jefes del Estado Mayor*" in their respective (civil and military) areas of competence (Articles 10.1 and 4). In order to inform the public of their character, classified matters must be labelled as such by an annotation (Article 10.3).

---

[46] STC 159/86, 16 Dec.

The administrative classification of a matter as secret or reserved may be judicially challenged by individuals under Law 48/78.[47] Individuals may claim that an allegedly unlawful classification restricts their freedom of information under Article 20. They may thus pursue their claims through a speedy and preferential procedure before the ordinary courts, and from there to the Constitutional Court via a recourse *de amparo*.

The classification of a matter as secret or reserved implies that access to it is limited to persons duly authorized, who must not divulge their knowledge. Unauthorized persons are not only subject to a restriction on their freedom of information, but also must inform public authorities when they come across such matters (Article 9.1). This also applies to the media. The media, however, must be explicitly informed of the classified character of a certain matter, if they are considered likely to gain knowledge of it (Article 9.2). The Criminal Code prescribes certain penalties should the above-mentioned duties not be met. In this regard, paragraphs (a) to (d) of its Article 135 bis penalize the acts of obtaining, revealing, falsifying and reproducing official secrets. Both the civil servant who divulges classified information and the media organ which publishes it are subject to special penalties.

15. ACCESS TO AND DISCLOSURE OF COURT DOCUMENTS AND PROCEEDINGS

Article 120.1 of the Constitution establishes that: "Judicial proceedings shall be public, with the exceptions provided for by the laws on procedure."

The principle of public access to judicial proceedings is considered to be a precondition for fair trials. It is thus an essential aspect of justice, which is amongst the "superior values" of the Spanish legal order under Article 1.1 of the Constitution. The Constitution also approaches the principle of the publicity of judicial proceedings from the point of view of the individual. First, it recognizes an individual's right to a public trial (Article 24.2) as among those fundamental rights with strong constitutional protection. Second, it recognizes the openness of judicial trials as a particular aspect of freedom of information.

The requirement of openness and publicity is subject to exceptions (set forth in the Law of Criminal Procedure), provided they are duly justified and submitted to strict interpretation. In the first place, pre-trial procedures and pre-trial evidence, the *sumario*, have a secret character *vis-à-vis* third parties (Article 301). This legal provision is a means to ensure the secure prosecution of the crime at stake. This provision does not imply that access to matters connected with the *sumario* may not be gained by different means, and that the knowledge so obtained may not be divulged. Only direct access to the particular acts and documents which themselves constitute the *sumario* is prohibited.[48] In other words, the secrecy of the *sumario* is a formal, not a material limitation to freedom of information.

---

[47] Art. 48.1, Law 17 July 1958, "*de Procedimiento Administrativo*" (Law of Administrative Procedures).

[48] STC 13/85, 31 Jan., F.Jco. 3.

Reasons of morality or of public order may also justify the exclusion of the public from a trial (Article 680). Apart from cases in which these reasons apply, the Constitutional Court has stated that proceedings must be as accessible as possible to the public and the media. Due to their informative role, the mass media should be the last to be excluded if trial attendance is restricted owing to security problems or space limitations.[49]

16. ACCESS TO AND DISCLOSURE OF LEGISLATIVE DOCUMENTS AND PROCEEDINGS

Public access to parliamentary debates should be the rule in a democratic society. Article 80 of the Constitution states:

> The plenary sessions of the Chambers shall be public except when there is an agreement against it in each Chamber, an agreement which must be arrived at by an absolute majority or in agreement with the Regulations.

The regulations of the Congress and Senate specify the scope of the publicity of parliamentary debates.[50] It is noteworthy that they allow journalists to be present during the debates of both congressional and senatorial commissions. The freedom of individuals to receive information is the basis for this provision.

Commentators have noted that the lack of secrecy of such debates may result in a lack of spontaneity and even render the debates meaningless, because the members of such commissions may be concerned about their public image.[51] It must be pointed out, however, that the commissions' debates do not always need to be open to the public. The regulations of both the Congress and Senate provide that certain parliamentary commission sessions must be secret. This is the case with Congressional Commissions concerning the "*Estatuto de los Diputados*" (Status of the Members of Congress), congressional investigatory commissions, and Senatorial Commissions dealing with irregularities, procedures for waiving *suplicatorios* (parliamentary privileges) and personal questions affecting the senators. The regulations of both the Congress and Senate also state that any commission may decide to hold its sessions in secret by an absolute majority decision on any grounds, such as threats to the independence of the debates.

Matters dealt with in congressional investigatory commissions are secret, as are any subsequent parliamentary debates concerning such matters. This secrecy applies as an automatic rule, without having to justify the need for secrecy on any grounds, such as concern

---

[49] STC 30/82, 1 June, F.Jco. 4.

[50] *Reglamento del Congreso de los Diputados* (Rt.C.D), 10 Feb. 1982, Arts. 63-64; *Reglamento del Senado* (Rt.Sen), 26 May 1982, Arts. 72-75.

[51] M Carrillo, *Los Límites a la libertad de prensa en la Constitución Española de 1978* (*The Limits of Freedom of the Press in the Spanish Constitution of 1978*) (PPU, Barcelona 1987).

for national security. As a result, areas of social and political importance can be absolutely and uncritically withdrawn from public knowledge, in disregard of the right to freedom of information.

17. COMMERCIAL SECRECY AND ACCESS TO INFORMATION HELD BY PRIVATE PARTIES

The exercise of freedom of expression and information by employees in their labour relationships must take into account that labour contracts do not imply a transitory loss or an unjustified relaxation of fundamental rights or public freedoms. Employees' freedoms of expression and information continue to be protected in the same terms and within the same limits as all citizens.[52] Certain duties of loyalty and good faith towards the employer do exist, transgression of which is cause for a fair dismissal.[53] These limits, however, do not apply automatically; the freedoms of expression and information must be balanced against a worker's labour duties in the same terms and according to the same criteria as against the rights to honour and privacy.[54]

Following these criteria, employees may exercise their freedom to convey information provided the information is accurate. In cases when loyalty or good faith is at stake (for example when it concerns a "whistleblower's" disclosure of company wrongdoings), attention must be paid to the public relevance of the information disclosed and to the means by which it was disclosed.[55] The right to express one's opinions freely outweighs any contractual duty in so far as matters of public importance are concerned.[56]

No provision in Spanish law obliges private companies to disclose environmental information to interested groups of citizens. Environmental laws only oblige private companies to undergo administrative control.[57] Nevertheless, citizens may have indirect access to such information. On the basis of Article 105(b) of the Constitution they may consult the administrative files containing information about private companies' environmental behaviour.

---

[52] STC 88/85, 19 July, F.Jco. 2.

[53] Art. 54.1.2.(d), Law 8/80, 10 March, Law on the Status of Workers.

[54] *See* SSTC 88/85, *supra* note 52, F.Jco. at 3; 126/90, 5 July, F.Jco 4, 5. *See also supra* Sections 10 and 11.

[55] STC 120/83, 15 Dec., F.Jco.4.

[56] STC 88/85, *supra* note 52, F.Jco. at 3.

[57] *See, e.g.,* Arts. 67 *et seq.*, of the Decree 833/75, 6 Feb., on the protection of the atmospheric environment; Title V of the R.Decree 849/86, 11 April, on public waters; Chapter XIV of the law 25/64, 29 April, on Nuclear Power.

18.   PRIOR RESTRAINTS

Censorship, defined as any pre-publication restriction on the elaboration or dissemination of intellectual work, is forbidden in all circumstances pursuant to Article 20.2 of the Constitution (set forth in Section 1 *supra*). As a consequence, no prior restraint is allowed that "implies a judgement on the piece of work according to some abstract and restrictive values, in such a way that a *placet* [sign of approval] is conceded to publications that conform to those values or is otherwise denied".[58]

Article 4 of the Law of the Press 14/66 offers the possibility of consulting the government adminstration before publication. This voluntary consultancy is available to anyone who could be held responsible for the publication. Administrative approval of a text presented for consultancy, given explicitly or through silence, frees the consulting party of any responsibility for the text's publication. Disapproving administrative answers, however, do not amount to censorship, nor do they imply any responsibility if the text is published. They are merely indications that such responsibility might arise.

19.   PROTECTION OF SOURCES

The second sentence of Article 20.1.(d) of the Constitution states: "The right to invoke the conscience clause and that of professional confidentiality shall be governed by statute." This provision has not yet been directly developed by the legislature.

The only ordinary regulation on the subject states: "Journalists have the duty to maintain their professional secrecy, except for cases of obligatory cooperation with administration of justice, for the sake of the common good." This provision is found in the General Principles of the Journalists' Profession, which are listed as an annex to the Statute of the Journalists Profession (Decree 744/67, 13 April, paragraph 5). These General Principles, which do not have the force of law, were adopted under Franco's regime and today are of little practical importance since for the most part they have been superseded by laws enacted after the Constitution.

The above-stated general principle on the duty to maintain professional secrecy is clearly insufficient. First, it does not conceive of professional secrecy as a right of journalists, but as a duty imposed on them. Second, indications as to the scope and limits of professional secrecy are imprecise. The question as to what are "cases of obligatory cooperation with justice" and what must be understood by "common good" remain open, and to be solved in each judicial case involving the professional secrecy of journalists. The Constitutional Court has not yet ruled on the subject.

---

[58] SSTC 52/83, F.Jco 5; 13/85, F.Jco. 1 (author's translation).

20. RESTRICTIONS ON OFFENSIVE LANGUAGE AGAINST IDENTIFIABLE GROUPS

No statutory provision is devoted to protecting particular groups or minorities from verbal attack. Protection is only granted to individuals. Individuals, however, may claim that their right to honour is violated if offensive language is used against the group to which they belong. The media are not subject to particular rules in this respect. Most organs of the mass media, however, seem to be respectful of minorities and generally condemn any act of social discrimination towards minorities.

21. BLASPHEMY, OBSCENITY AND PROTECTION OF PUBLIC MORALS

Since 1978 the Spanish Criminal Code has undergone numerous reforms.[59] As a result of one of them, crimes against public morality such as blasphemy and public scandal were repealed.[60] No new laws concerning blasphemy have been adopted, while new and more narrowly defined crimes replaced public scandal, under the heading "crimes of sexual exhibitionism and provocation".[61] Within this framework, Article 432 condemns "whoever by any means would diffuse, sell or exhibit pornographic material to people under sixteen or mentally handicapped".[62] Article 432 is justified on the grounds that it protects children and youth, which is in harmony with Article 20.4 of the Constitution (set forth in Section 1, *supra*).

Article 432 is the only basis to restrain the freedom of expression or information of the press on moral grounds since the recent repeal of Article 566.5 which made it a misdemeanour to commit less severe publishing offences against morality, "good customs" and public decency.[63]

Article 432 only penalizes the publication of material whose pornographic character can be proven. Cases may thus arise where a balance must be struck between the mere transmission of objective information and the publication of pornography. Such a balance should, in principle, follow the general criteria proposed by the Constitutional Court, analyzed in previous sections.

---

[59] The basic text follows the Code of 1973, Decree 3096/73, 14 Sept.

[60] Previously regulated in arts. 239 and 431 respectively, both repealed by L.O. 5/88, 9 June.

[61] Criminal Code, Book II, Title IX, Ch. II.

[62] Author's translation.

[63] L.O. 3/89, 21 June.

22.   RESTRICTIONS ON ADVERTISING

Organic Law 5/85 of 19 June on the regulation of general elections prohibits political advertising outside periods of election campaigns (Article 53). During election campaigns, paid political advertising in newspapers and other private publications and on private radio stations are permitted (Article 58.1-2). Paid political advertisements are prohibited on TV and public radio, where political parties are granted free time for their political propaganda, the length of which varies according to the number of votes each party obtained in the previous elections of the same kind (Article 60). Organic law L.O. 2/1988 of 3 May, states that private television is subject to the same rules as the public media and thus cannot accept payment for political advertisements.

Television advertising of tobacco and drinks containing more than 20 per cent alcohol is prohibited.[64]

CONCLUSION

It is important to recall certain basic points concerning the legal position of the Spanish media. Restrictions on the activities of the media stem from the confrontation of the freedoms of expression and information, as protected by Article 20 of the Constitution, with other constitutional rights or values. In such confrontations the ruling principle is the preferential treatment granted by courts to those freedoms. At the formal level, the position of the different organs of the media varies. Radio and television channels are thoroughly regulated[65], on the ground that usable frequencies are of limited supply. The printed press, on the other hand, is subject to minimal regulation. The existing Law on the Press, dating from 1966, has for the most part been repealed by the Constitution and by subsequent legal texts. This means that few actual regulations remain. The press must only comply with registration requirements. More fundamentally, the freedom of the press is a particularly important aspect of the freedoms of expression and information, since it guarantees a large degree of dissemination of opinions and facts and, therefore, the free formation of public opinion.

---

[64] Article 8.5 of the General Law of Publicity (L.O. 34/1988, 11 Nov.).

[65] *See* Law 4/80, 10 Jan.; Law 46/83, 26 Dec. (on the third television channel); Law 10/88, 3 May (on private television).

Chapter 9

FREEDOM OF THE PRESS IN SWEDEN

Hans-Gunnar Axberger

INTRODUCTION

Freedom of expression is a cornerstone of Swedish democracy, and freedom of the press receives strong constitutional protection. The first Freedom of the Press Act, adopted in 1766, was at the time unique. For that reason it is often said that Sweden was the first country in the world to enjoy constitutional protection of free speech; it is less often mentioned that this freedom was withdrawn in 1772 as a result of a *coup d'état*. The next Freedom of the Press Act was enacted in 1812, and there has been one in force ever since. This does not mean, however, that full press freedom has prevailed since 1812. During the nineteenth century administrative procedures were often used against newspapers. Today's Freedom of the Press Act, based on the 1812 Act, dates from 1949.

1.   RELEVANT CONSTITUTIONAL PROVISIONS

Sweden's Constitution includes the 1974 Instrument of Government (IG), the Freedom of the Press Act (FPA) of 1949 and the Freedom of Speech Act of 1991.

Chapter 2, Article 1 of the IG guarantees to all citizens "in their relations with the public administration" freedom to express opinions and to receive and communicate information, in the following terms:

> 1. freedom of expression: the freedom to communicate information and to express ideas, opinions and emotions, whether orally, in writing, in pictorial representations, or in any other way;

> 2. freedom of information: the freedom to obtain and receive information and otherwise acquaint oneself with the utterances of others . . . .[1]

Article 1 also specifically delegates issues relating to press freedom to the FPA. Article 2 of the IG provides that "All citizens shall be protected in their relations with the public administration against all coercion to divulge an opinion in any political, religious, cultural or other similar connection." Article 20 extends the full range of free expression rights to foreigners on Swedish soil.

---

[1] Quotations from the IG and the FPA are from *The Constitution of Sweden 1989* (Stockholm, 1990), published by the Swedish Riksdag.

Rights protected by the IG may be restricted only to achieve a purpose acceptable in a democratic society (Chapter 2, Article 12). Rights to freedom of expression and information may be restricted only to protect national security and the integrity of the individual, to ensure public safety and order, to facilitate the prevention and prosecution of crime, and where particularly important reasons so warrant (Article 13). In cases relating to freedom of expression and information, the authorities must take account of the importance of maintaining the widest possible freedoms in political, religious, professional, scientific and cultural matters (Article 13). However, the wording of the IG's provisions is vague and cannot be considered to offer a firm protection of free speech.

The FPA, a detailed piece of legislation, is the most important document concerning press freedom. Because the FPA is part of the Constitution, even small alterations in the legal protection of press freedom must be passed twice by Parliament, in identical bills, separated by a general election. The voters, therefore, will always have a chance to influence proposed changes.

Chapter 1, Article 1 of the FPA (as amended) sets forth its basic premise:

> Freedom of the press means the right of every Swedish subject, without prior hindrance by any central administrative authority or other public body, to publish any written matter, and not to be prosecuted thereafter on grounds of the contents of such publication other than before a court of law, or to be punished therefore in any case other than a case in which the content is in contravention of an express provision of law, enacted to preserve public order without suppressing information to the public.

The FPA only concerns printed matter but in practice has served as a guideline for the treatment of freedom of speech generally. Despite this, beginning in the 1960s, demand for formal constitutional protection of the rights of all media steadily increased. In 1974, some provisions concerning freedom of speech were integrated into the IG and in 1991 Parliament adopted the Freedom of Speech Act (FSA) as a constitutional document. The FSA covers, *inter alia*, radio, television, films and videos. Although based on the same principles as the FPA, it does not give the same strong protection in all cases. For example, censorship of films is allowed.

The FPA constitutes a firm legal protection, and has been strictly applied by the courts. In contrast, the vague language of the IG has resulted in its having little impact in expanding protections of media freedom.[2]

---

[2] A well known illustration is provided by the Radio Nova case. Claus Nydahl, the operator of the community radio station, was indicted for breaking a law prohibiting the broadcasting of commercials on community radio. Mr Nydahl argued, *inter alia*, that the legislation in question was not compatible with the IG. The courts paid little attention to that claim.

2. DISTRIBUTION OF POWERS BETWEEN CENTRAL AND REGIONAL GOVERNMENT

Sweden is a constitutional monarchy and a unitary system. All powers relevant to the press are exercised by the central government.

3. ROLE OF THE COURTS

The Swedish legal system is based on civil law principles. The most important sources of law are written statutes, interpreted with the aid of the preparatory works of Parliament, parliamentary committees and other bodies involved in the process of drafting and adopting legislation. The courts pay great attention to these preparatory works.

Rulings of the Supreme Court and the Supreme Administrative Court constitute precedents. The activity of these courts is best described as complementary to the legislative work of Parliament. Certain areas of the law have clearly been influenced by case-law, but in general Swedish courts hesitate to issue rulings that express independent legal opinions. Judges in Sweden on the whole take the view that if the law in a certain area is unsatisfactory, it is the role of Parliament to change it.

In Sweden, there is no separate constitutional court. However, according to the Constitution, the courts at every level have the power not to apply a statute which they find to be "manifestly unconstitutional". Such rulings have no effect on the validity of the statute in question as such; their only effect is to disallow application of the statute in the specific case. Not even the Supreme Court and the Supreme Administrative Court have the right to declare an unconstitutional statute invalid. It should be stressed that Swedish courts, including the supreme courts, only rarely decline to apply a statute as unconstitutional.

In addition to the Supreme Court, there are six courts of appeal and 97 district courts (courts of first instance in both civil and criminal cases). There is also a system of administrative courts which decide such matters as child custody, withdrawal of driving licences and tax questions.

4. STATUS OF INTERNATIONAL HUMAN RIGHTS TREATIES IN NATIONAL LAW

The Swedish government ratified the International Covenant on Civil and Political Rights (ICCPR) and its First Optional Protocol in 1971. It also ratified the European Convention on Human Rights (ECHR) and accepted the obligation to permit individuals to file complaints with the European Commission on Human Rights.

Although there is a lively debate about the legal relevance of international human rights treaties in Swedish law, the prevailing view is that such treaties do not have the status of domestic law within Sweden. When a conflict arises, domestic law overrides international treaty law.

Again, the Radio Nova case provides an apt illustration. The Court of Appeal stated that it was questionable whether the provision in the Local Radio Act which forbids the broadcast of advertisements was compatible with the European Convention and, furthermore, that Swedish law should, *when possible*, be applied to comply with the Convention's requirements. However, the Court concluded that the Local Radio Act was unambiguous on this point and thus ruled that the Convention's requirements could not be applied. The Supreme Court declined to hear the appeal.

There has been much discussion about integrating the European Convention into domestic law, especially since Sweden's application for membership in the EC, and many experts are of the opinion that in due course the Convention will be made directly applicable.

5.   STATUTORY FRAMEWORK

The FPA is the main law which affects the press (*see* Section 1 *supra*).

6.   REGULATION OF OWNERSHIP

There are no restrictions on newspaper ownership. Neither is cross-ownership of newspapers and broadcasting stations prohibited, although a proposed private radio act includes a limitation on the right of newspaper companies to own private radio stations.

Sweden is a country of many newspapers, and Swedes are among the highest purchasers per capita of daily papers in the world. The number of papers is, however, decreasing and will probably continue to decrease. At the moment, there are some 130 dailies (for a population of close to 9 million).[3] While papers frequently close down and merge, virtually no new ones are started.

Swedish newspapers are by tradition political in the sense that they have an explicitly declared political orientation. (Of the 10 largest newspapers, only two are social-democratic; the rest are liberal, conservative and of other political persuasions). A newspaper's political orientation is in principle relevant only to its editorial line. The distinction between "news" and "views" is considered very important. Many Swedish newspapers actually have double editorships: one editor-in-chief for the editorial pages and one for the remaining parts of the newspaper. The result is that, while a paper may carry a very distinct political view on its editorial pages, most papers cover the news with objectivity.

---

[3] The largest morning paper, *Dagens Nyheter*, has a circulation of approximately 400,000 copies, and the largest evening paper, *Expressen*, has a circulation of almost 600,000. Both belong to the Bonnier-group, the largest newspaper group in Sweden, which controls close to 30 per cent of the Swedish newspaper market.

Newspapers are becoming less political for a number of reasons, the most important of which is financial. Nearly half of the Swedish population vote socialist. The large, politically non-socialist newspapers are not satisfied with selling newspapers only to the other half. To achieve as large a market share as possible, a newspaper must maintain political independence in its news coverage. The socialist newspapers maintained their party-political profile longer than other newspapers. They have had continuing economic problems. (The largest social-democratic newspaper group went bankrupt in 1992.)

Sweden has a system of government subsidies for newspapers intended to promote pluralism. The largest subsidies are given to "second-newspapers", that is, newspapers that are second in circulation in the regions they cover. The purpose is to compensate them for lower advertising revenues. The subsidies constitute only about 3 per cent of the total annual turnover in the newspaper business, but for individual papers which receive subsidies, they constitute the difference between financial life and death. For example, two large dailies, *Arbetet* (social-democratic) and *Svenska Dagbladet* (conservative), receive huge sums without which they could not survive financially.

The subsidy system is under debate. Some say it contravenes the principles of freedom of the press and prevents necessary rationalization and market adaptation. Others say it is necessary to achieve the pluralism which is the aim of press freedom. In any case, subsidies are likely to decrease in the near future due to constraints on state funding.

7.   REGISTRATION REQUIREMENTS

Chapter 5 of the FPA contains provisions which require the owner of a publication to register the name of the person who is legally responsible for the publication's contents. The purpose of these provisions is not to control newspapers but to establish responsibility, and in practice they are not enforced. However, an owner who does not comply with them will be held personally responsible if the publication is taken to court.

According to the FPA (Chapter 1, Article 2), the government must not impose any content-based obstacles to the establishment and distribution of a newspaper or any other kind of printed matter. Obstacles not based on content are not forbidden, however. Thus, for instance, tax provisions that apply in the same way to all newspapers do not breach the FPA.

8.   REGULATION OF IMPORT AND EXPORT OF PUBLICATIONS

There are no content-related restrictions on import and export of newspapers.

9. MECHANISMS OF PRESS SELF-REGULATION

The tradition of press self-regulation in Sweden is old and well-developed. In 1916, a Press Council was established, the first in Europe, to function as a tribunal for reviewing the practices of the press. In the 1960s, in response to increasing criticism of press behaviour and calls for tightening of the FPA, the three dominant organizations in the newspaper business -- the Newspaper Publishers Association, the Union of Journalists and the National Press Club -- volunteered a number of professional reforms. The most important of these were lay representation on the Press Council and the creation of the post of Press Ombudsman for the General Public (whose role is to represent "the man in the street"). The Council now has six members: three representatives of the public, including a judge, usually a member of one of the Supreme Courts, who serves as chair; and three representatives of the industry, including one representative of each of the constitutive organizations. The Press Council system operates on a voluntary basis and is financed entirely by the press industry and the Union of Journalists.

The Press Council and Ombudsman seek to encourage compliance with a Code of Ethics. The main aim of the Code is to protect the privacy of private individuals. At the same time, the Code allows wide latitude in the reporting of information about public figures, even about matters touching on their private lives. While the Code protects the anonymity of "ordinary criminals", the Press Council would be unlikely to uphold the complaint of a politician.

The task of the Press Ombudsman is to mediate between the public and the press, and to help individuals protect their privacy and their reputations by ordering the publication of corrections and rejoinders. An individual can file a complaint with the Press Ombudsman. The Ombudsman investigates the case and, if he or she considers it to be well-founded, asks the responsible editor to reply. The process is in writing; there are no oral hearings. The Ombudsman renders a decision based upon the information and arguments received. If he finds that there has been a minor breach of the Code, he can issue a censuring opinion. If he finds that the grievance is of a more serious nature, he files a complaint with the Press Council which then adjudicates the claim. If he rejects the complaint, the complainant may still file the complaint with the Council, although in practice the Council rarely changes the Ombudsman's decision.

If the Council censures a newspaper, the paper is obliged to publish the opinion and pay an administrative fee as a kind of fine. The fee amounts to approximately US$4,000, and is paid to the Council to help finance its operation. Only papers belonging to the Publishers' Association and its affiliated organizations are legally bound to publish the opinion and pay the fee. Most papers are in fact members, and those which are not generally also respect the system. Some smaller magazines do not accept the system for reasons of principle. Others, among them some semi-pornographic magazines, ignore it. In neither case is their lack of compliance regarded as a problem, since virtually all of the newspapers abide by and support the system.

Government authorities, companies and organizations are entitled to complain to the Press Ombudsman, but their complaints must be limited to errors of fact, and the only remedy to which they are entitled is a right of reply. Institutional complainants are given the opportunity to make only limited use of the press complaints system because of the view that institutions, being more influential, have other ways of making their opinions known.

A complainant does not waive his or her legal rights by filing a complaint with the Ombudsman. As a result, a censuring opinion by the Council may be used in any subsequent lawsuit. Courts on occasion support their judgments with arguments drawn from the ethical principles and the Council's opinion. Such recourse to the courts tends to undermine the Press Council system because the newspapers object to submitting themselves to, and financing, a system of voluntary self-regulation when the results of that system may be used against them in court. However, recourse to the courts following a Press Council opinion is rare and, on the whole, the Press Council system has worked well in keeping the number of lawsuits low and in safeguarding the protections of press freedom set forth in the FPA.

The Press Council system is generally respected by both the press and the public. Certain Council decisions may be hotly debated, but this is to be expected and moreover is viewed as beneficial; self-regulation promotes discussion of press ethics which in turn is likely to enhance journalism's ethical standards.

10.   DEFAMATION

The FPA specifies two forms of defamation: libel and affront. The latter primarily concerns personal "face to face" insults, and is rarely the basis of complaints against the press. Libel is by far the most frequent ground for legal action against the media (although libel actions are not themselves very common).

A responsible editor of a newspaper can be found guilty for libel if the paper described a person as criminal, blameworthy in his way of life or in some other way likely to expose that person to the contempt of others. Truth is not an absolute defence. However, if the libellous statement was justifiable with regard to the circumstances *and* the statement was true or the paper had reasonable grounds to believe it to be true, there is no criminal or civil liability.

10.1   Opinions

Opinions or value judgements about a person can never be libellous. If formulated in a very insulting way, they may be judged an affront (although there are few cases to illustrate this). If an opinion is based on implicitly expressed facts, it may thereby constitute a libel.

10.2   Defences: Truth, Public Interest and Public Figures

The key issue in many libel actions is whether the publication was "justifiable". A publication is justifiable when the public interest of the information (not to be confused with the interest of the public, *i.e.,* general curiosity) overrides the interest in protecting the person concerned. For example, it would be considered justifiable to publish information about a minor tax fraud committed by a politician, whereas it would be considered unjustifiable to publish the same information concerning a person with no public record.

Public figures can also be protected by this rule. In a recent case, allegations that former tennis star Björn Borg took drugs and was a "cocaine addict" were considered unjustifiable, whether true or not. The court considered that the allegations were made in a gossip-like way by his former girlfriend with whom Borg was involved in a legal battle regarding the custody of their son. If the accusations had been produced in another context, the court could very well have found them justifiable and allowed the paper to produce evidence of truth, which the court in this case did not allow.

If truth is allowed as a defence, the responsible editor bears the burden of proof.It is enough to prove that the responsible editor had reasonable grounds to believe that the information was truthful.

10.3   Criminal and Civil Actions

Both criminal and civil actions may be brought under the law of libel, and criminal actions may be brought by either public or private prosecution. Public prosecutions are rare and must be conducted by the Chancellor of Justice. Normally, public prosecutions are only brought when the injured party is a civil servant in his capacity as such. For example, the Chancellor has prosecuted cases where police officers were libelled in the line of duty. Individuals normally sue jointly for criminal liability and civil damages. The legal requirements for winning a libel action are the same under criminal and civil law, although the procedure varies slightly depending on the kind of action taken.

One of the most controversial public prosecutions of recent years was brought on behalf of members of several Swedish hockey and other sports teams against *Expressen*, the largest circulation evening newspaper. The Justice Chancellor charged the paper with having printed false reports that several team members had received payments in order to lose certain matches, and that virtually all members of certain teams were aware of the match-rigging. He justified the public prosecution on the ground that the athletes were heroes to a lot of fans and thus were like public servants. The jury exonerated *Expressen*, concluding that it was not guilty of any wrongdoing. Many people believed that the Justice Chancellor had overstepped his powers by pursuing the case. The fact that he lost, and that he received such widespread criticism is certain to make the Chancellor more cautious in bringing public prosecutions in the future; to that extent the case stands as a confirmation of press freedom.

10.4   Institutions

Companies, organizations and government authorities have no rights under the law of libel. "Economic libel" or other defamation of collective entities is not penalized under the FPA, neither can it constitute a ground for civil action. As a result, the press enjoys great freedom in scrutinizing and criticizing government, business corporations, unions and other institutions.

10.5   Penalties and Damages

Sweden has a special system regarding legal responsibility for the contents of a newspaper. Only one person, the "responsible editor" designated by the owner, may be held liable, and that person is held strictly liable for all publications whether or not he or she has actually read them. The system is considered to have at least two advantages; it ensures that one person (with resources) can always be held liable, and it provides security for all others involved in the process, from sources to distributors. In cases of grave abuses of press freedom, persons other than the responsible editor may be prosecuted (*see* Section 14 *infra*).

No responsible editor has as yet served time in jail as a result of a suit under the present libel law, which was enacted in 1965. If convicted, a responsible editor is normally ordered to pay a fine as well as damages to the plaintiff. The amount of damages awarded in Sweden is low. Punitive damages do not exist. A typical libel judgement would result in damages in the neighbourhood of US$3,000. One of the highest sums awarded was in the previously mentioned Björn Borg case, where the court awarded a sum equivalent to US$12,000 (an extremely low figure compared with sums awarded by British and US juries).

10.6   Impact on Reporting

Because it is very difficult for a plaintiff to win a libel suit against a newspaper, it cannot be said that libel law has had a negative impact on reporting. Swedish journalists generally are more concerned about criticism from the Press Ombudsman and Council than the less frequently manifested risk of receiving a libel conviction.

11.   INVASION OF PRIVACY

Privacy is not explicitly protected in the FPA. Indirectly, defamation gives some protection. Stories about private matters are often likely to expose the person in question to the contempt of others and are rarely deemed to be justifiable. However, there is no protection against publication of photographs of people in private situations, for example, pictures of a well-known person taking a swim in the nude. In such circumstances there is no cause of action under Swedish law.

On the other hand, privacy is well protected under the Code of Ethics, although many question whether the Code provides adequate remedies for aggrieved individuals. For instance, the Press Council has no power to award damages to a successful complainant.

12.   RIGHT OF REPLY AND/OR CORRECTION

There is no legal right of reply. The FPA only states that when a reply or correction has been published, this should be taken into consideration by the court in libel cases.

Whereas the *law* does not provide a right of reply, it is a major principle of Swedish press ethics that any person criticized in a news story should be given space to publish a correction, reply or rejoinder. The story itself should include a statement by the criticized person but, if it does not, the person has the right, under the Code of Ethics, to have a reply published as soon as possible. The right of reply is primarily intended for news reporting and has less direct relevance concerning reviews, signed columns and editorials. In practice, most newspapers extend the right of reply also to these sections of the paper.

Swedish newspapers have, over the last decades, gradually become more generous in granting space for replies and rejoinders, a development encouraged by the Press Ombudsman and Council. There is a general sense that, by being generous with space for people with dissenting views, a paper enlarges the scope of its own journalistic freedom.

A great deal of the Ombudsman's work is devoted to mediation in cases where a newspaper has not been willing to publish a reply, or the complainant is unwilling to accept press practice concerning the reply's length or form. The large majority of these complaints are settled amicably.

Although companies, government authorities and organizations in general occupy a weak position *vis-à-vis* the press under both the FPA and the Code of Ethics, they do have a right of reply under the Code. A newspaper which does not publish a correction or a reply from a company concerning errors of fact in a previous publication breaches the Code.

There are no formal rules regarding the placement of a reply, its length or its form. It should be placed where it can easily be seen, and it should have a headline which draws attention to the fact that the paper is correcting something published previously. It does not have to be long; in fact, a short reply is said to attract more readers than a long one, and therefore to be more effective.

The Swedish voluntary system for corrections, replies and rejoinders based on ethical standards works well. It is increasingly respected by all kinds of newspapers and magazines. Even the journalistically more aggressive evening papers tend to be generous with replies; they are a time- and money-saving way to settle disputes. A legally enforceable right of reply would probably be more rigid and would certainly cool the generally positive attitude among Swedish journalists towards the corresponding press-ethical procedure.

13. INSULTS TO GOVERNMENT INSTITUTIONS OR OFFICIALS

There is no criminal law protecting government institutions from insults or libellous statements. The last remnant of such legislation disappeared in the mid-1970s when a provision which prohibited the "belying of state authority" was abolished on the ground that, in a democratic society, government institutions should be open and responsive to all criticism, even when based on lies. Although government officials enjoy protection under the law of libel, actions on their behalf are rarely brought.

The FPA contains a few provisions to be applied in times of war or great unrest which permit far-reaching limitations on press freedom.[4]

14. OFFICIAL SECRECY AND ACCESS TO GOVERNMENT-HELD INFORMATION

14.1 Access to Government-held Information

Laws regarding freedom of information are set forth in Chapter 2 of the FPA, known as the Principle of Public Access to Official Records. This part of the Constitution, which has roots in the Constitution of 1766, is considered one of the most important foundations of Swedish democracy. The core of the principle is that all documents are public if there is not an explicit statute which regulates otherwise. This presumption of openness is a distinctive feature of the Swedish legal and political systems; it may be the strongest statement of government transparency in Europe.

Under the Act any Swedish citizen, not just the press, may go to a state or municipal agency and ask to be shown any documents in the files, whether or not the document concerns the requesting party. Authorities are legally required to comply and even to supply copies of the document if requested. Authorities are generally not allowed to ask the applicant for identification or inquire about the reason for the request. Requests should be answered within a day unless special reasons are given.

Chapter 2 of the Act lists seven areas in which government information may be withheld and delegates to Parliament the right to pass legislation limiting public access to information in these areas. Parliament enacted a new Secrecy Act in 1980, which delineates permissible exceptions to the general rule of accessibility. Areas subject to government secrecy include information relating to national security, foreign policy and foreign affairs, criminal investigations and the personal integrity (privacy) or financial circumstances of individuals.

Anyone refused a public document is entitled to a written statement of the legal authority for the refusal, and must also be told about the right to appeal, ultimately to the Supreme Administrative Court. Courts take a strictly formal view in these matters and often rule in

---

[4] *See* FPA, Ch. 7, Arts. 4 and 5.

favour of applicants from the public. In practice, if access to a certain document is refused, a request for a statement of reasons often results in the authority's change of attitude.

The Principle of Public Access to Official Records is supervised by the Justice (or Parliamentary) Ombudsman who is appointed by Parliament. Complaints against public officials who do not comply with the Act (for example, by failing to answer a request within a day without giving reasons) often lead to action by the Ombudsman. As a result, the principle is well known and generally respected both in state and municipal institutions, despite the fact that it involves a fair amount of extra work for civil servants.

Even though the system works well there are, in Sweden as in every other country, efforts made to bury sensitive matters to prevent public scrutiny. One example concerns the so-called "Bofors Affair". During the 1980s, press reports alleged that Bofors, Sweden's largest arms manufacturer, had obtained a contract with the Indian government through the payment of bribes. At the request of the Indian government the Swedish government instructed the National Audit Bureau to undertake an investigation. A report containing the investigation's findings was completed and, though it found that monetary commissions had been paid to unidentified individuals, it concluded that no Swedish laws had been violated. Citing Sweden's bank secrecy laws, the government withheld sections of the report from the public. In October 1989 an Indian newspaper printed extracts from the unpublished portions of the report which appeared to confirm that large illegal payments had been made to anonymous Swiss bank accounts. Under pressure, the Swedish government finally released the full report in May 1990.

14.2   Disclosure of Secret Information

While government employees may be prosecuted for disclosing secret information in violation of the Secrecy Act, in practice they are virtually immune from prosecution for disclosures made to the press, except in limited circumstances such as where disclosure would endanger national security.[5] This special privilege is called "messenger freedom". The freedom arises from the strong protection afforded to the confidentiality of journalists' sources (*see* Section 20 *infra*). Thus, if a government employee discloses information to the press which is in breach of the Secrecy Act, neither the employee nor the responsible editor will be prosecuted so long as the information does not endanger national security or other substantial governmental interests.

If the disclosure does endanger national security, not only may the source and the responsible editor be prosecuted (and the responsible editor may be compelled to name the source if he is unknown), but also other press people responsible for the story may be prosecuted.[6] There have been few prosecutions; the most recent significant case was the conviction for espionage, in the mid-1970s, of a member of the Investigation Bureau and two journalists for disclosing secret information about the Bureau (*see* Section 18 *infra*).

---

[5] *See* FPA Ch. 7, Art. 3, para. 1; and Secrecy Act, Ch. 16, Art. 1.

[6] *See* Ch. 7, Art. 1.

15. ACCESS TO AND DISCLOSURE OF COURT DOCUMENTS AND PROCEEDINGS

Swedish justice is generally open to the public and the media, although cameras are not permitted in the courtroom. There are no equivalents in Swedish law to such offences as contempt of court or to such measures as gag orders.

However, the Code of Ethics adopted by the press provides that defendants in criminal cases should not be identified unless identification would be in the public interest. Also, media coverage of trials is not as extensive in Sweden as in many other countries.

There is a risk that the absence of explicit legal limitation in this area could endanger the defendant's right to a fair trial. So far, this has not been seen as a major problem, probably because criminal cases in Sweden are tried by professional judges who are more resistant to media influence than jurors.

16. ACCESS TO AND DISCLOSURE OF LEGISLATIVE DOCUMENTS AND PROCEEDINGS

Access to legislative proceedings and to Parliament in general is provided by the Principle of Public Access to Official Records (*see* in Section 14 *supra*). Whereas general sessions of Parliament are open to the public, parliamentary committee sessions are not. Committees can withhold documents from the public while they are at work, but must open their files when they present their proposals. Parliament can only withhold information protected by the Secrecy Act.

There are no restrictions, such as contempt of Parliament, on reporting about Parliamentary matters.

17. COMMERCIAL SECRECY AND ACCESS TO INFORMATION HELD BY PRIVATE PARTIES

While the Principle of Public Access to Official Records has a long tradition and may provide a presumption in favour of access to documents held by government authorities unparalleled in the world, there is no corresponding legislation concerning documents held by private parties, companies, unions and other associations. This area of the law is essentially governed by private agreements between the parties concerned or by civil legislation, such as labour laws.

There is no legislation aimed at protecting "whistleblowers" in the private sector. Private sector whistleblowers are protected by the FPA to the extent that, if they gave information to the press anonymously or on condition that their identities not be revealed, the newspaper is forbidden to disclose the source. Nonetheless, there is no legislation to discourage a private employer from conducting an investigation of its own employees in an effort to discover the "leak".

In 1988 the government proposed a Trade Secrets Act. The proposal was controversial. Among other things, the draft statute specified criminal sanctions for employees who reveal secrets about their employers. The proposal even envisaged sanctions for whistleblowers who disclose information about employer actions which they believe to be contrary to the public interest. The stated goal of the proposal was to protect companies from illegal competition, but many critics saw it as a way to silence employees and diminish their rights to protest against working conditions, environmental pollution or illegal acts by companies. As a result of protests the proposal was amended to allow serious or illegal misdeeds to be revealed, but the main thrust remained intact and was passed into law by Parliament in 1989.

The most famous whistleblower in Sweden in recent years is civil engineer Ingvar Bratt. When Bratt worked for the arms manufacturer Bofors he leaked documents to the media about illegal arms sales to India. Bratt became a symbol of resistance to the proposed Trade Secrets Act, which became widely known as "Lex Bratt". Experts disagree as to whether Bratt would have been convicted under the new act had it been in force when he "blew the whistle". Although the new statute has not yet been applied against a whistleblower, it may have had a certain chilling effect.

In 1990 a legislative committee proposed that the FPA's constitutional protection of public sector whistleblowers be extended to those in the private sector, and that private employers be prohibited from making inquiries regarding sources of publicity. The proposal was rejected as going too far in establishing media rights at the expense of the rights of private parties.

18. PRIOR RESTRAINTS

Article 2 of Chapter 1 of the FPA states:

> No publication shall be subject to scrutiny before printing, nor shall the printing thereof be prohibited.

> Furthermore, no central administrative authority or other public body shall be permitted on grounds of the content of a publication to take any action not authorized under this Act to prevent the printing or publication of the material, or its circulation among the public.

The Constitution contains no exception whatsoever to the ban on pre-publication censorship. There are no orders in Swedish law corresponding to gag orders or similar restraints.

A case from the early 1970s regarding disclosure of information about the security services provides a clear illustration of the prohibition of prior restraints. A member of the Investigation Bureau (IB), a secret part of the security services, disclosed information about the IB to two journalists who, in the spring of 1973, published a series of articles in a magazine. One of the journalists then published a book in September 1973 entitled, in English, *IB and the Threat to Our Security*. The IB agent and the two journalists were charged with espionage, convicted and sentenced to prison (from nine months to one year). No attempt was ever made to restrain the publication of either the articles or the book, nor could any such attempt have been successful.

19.   PROTECTION OF SOURCES

Chapter 3, Article 1 of the FPA explicitly prohibits the investigation or disclosure of a journalist's sources, with certain limited exceptions. A journalist who reveals his or her source without consent is subject to criminal liability.[7] While there have been no prosecutions in recent years there have been a few incidents which have generated public debate. The constitutional protection of sources includes state and municipal employees, who are thus free to give information to the press without fear of legal repercussions or intimidation.

The FPA prohibits any government official from making any kind of inquiry concerning media sources which is not explicitly allowed in the FPA.[8] Normally, the police can only make investigations into a newspaper's source when they have reasonable grounds to believe that the source committed treason, espionage, or other similar crimes referred to in Chapter 7, Article 3 of the FPA. Moreover, since the responsible editor alone is responsible for all crimes committed in publishing the newspaper (*see* Section 8 *supra*), the police have no grounds for conducting searches to discover the identity of a source or of the journalist who wrote a particular article. It should be noted that most breaches of the Secrecy Act cannot be punished under the FPA (*see* Section 14 *supra*).

The responsible editor may be compelled by a court order to disclose the identity of a source which would otherwise be entitled to confidentiality in criminal cases where the published information could jeopardize state security or in which freedom of the press (including libel) is not the central issue and the court finds that the disclosure of a source is justified by an overriding public or private interest.[9] Such an overriding interest includes, for example, the interest of an accused person in obtaining information which he alleges would prove the falsity of accusations made against him and the interest of the police in obtaining evidence about crime.

The protection of news sources under the Swedish Constitution is very strong. Public officials and persons representing other powerful institutions rarely try to challenge this well guarded and traditionally deep-rooted concept, which is considered to be a part of "messenger freedom" (described in Section 14 *supra*). In 1988, a court ordered a reporter working for *Dagens Nyheter*, the largest morning paper, to reveal *when* certain conversations with a *known*

---

[7] *See* FPA, Ch. 3, Art. 5.

[8] *See* Ch 3, Arts. 4-5.

[9] *See* FPA, Ch. 3, Art. 3.

source had taken place. Outraged journalists argued that this was unconstitutional, and the Chancellor of Justice, who was prosecuting the case, eventually withdrew his question. The case illustrates the media's commitment to protecting the confidentiality of their sources.

20. RESTRICTIONS ON OFFENSIVE LANGUAGE AGAINST IDENTIFIABLE GROUPS

The FPA prohibits the expression of threats against, or contempt for, a population group "with allusion to its race, skin colour, national or ethnic origin, or religious faith".[10] This provision is rarely used against the mainstream press, but has been used quite often against materials published by extreme right wing groups. Opponents of this criminalization argue that it might prevent necessary openness with regard to public opinion concerning immigration and the acceptance of refugees. As yet, this has not been widely viewed as a significant freedom of speech concern.

Last year, the Chancellor of Justice prosecuted under this provision an editor who had published a letter to the editor expressing racist opinions. His defence was that views held by the readers must be allowed to surface, or otherwise they could not be debated and refuted. The Chancellor's decision was criticized by many, and the editor was acquitted by the jury.

21. BLASPHEMY, OBSCENITY AND PROTECTION OF PUBLIC MORALS

There are only two provisions in the FPA concerning obscenity, pornography or public morals: one prohibits publication of child pornography, and the other, publication of pictorial depictions of sexual violence (Chap. 7, Art. 4, paras. 12 and 13). Certain circumstances, such as artistic merit, may justify publication.

Depictions of violence may be prosecuted only when extreme in character. Although there are probably many representations of this kind on the video market, few cases are actually brought to court. The provision is of little importance for printed matter, although an editor of a comic-strip was once prosecuted under this section, and acquitted by the jury.

Previous laws regarding public morality and pornography were abolished in the 1970s. Blasphemy laws were abolished long ago.

---

[10] *See* FPA, Ch. 7, Art 4, para. 11.

22.   RESTRICTIONS ON ADVERTISING

The FPA provides that advertising for tobacco and alcohol may be restricted.[11] Although all other advertising, in theory, is protected, the courts have imposed a few restrictions on commercial speech. These restrictions apply only to what the courts call "pure commercial speech" and not to political or ideological advertising.

CONCLUSION

What is striking about Sweden's long-standing constitutional protection of press freedom is that it is matched by a tradition of respect for press freedom among the public (illustrated by widespread public criticism of certain public prosecutions) and the judiciary (as shown by acquittals of papers in a number of borderline cases).

Similarly, the press has demonstrated responsibility and a commitment to its standards of professional ethics: most of the papers, and all of the major ones, comply with the decisions of the voluntary Press Council system; the papers are generous in voluntarily granting space for replies (often pursuant to the mediation of the Press Ombudsman or the decisions of the Press Council); and the press is vigilant in protesting when its integrity is threatened (such as when the Chancellor of Justice sought to compel a journalist to reveal information about his source).

Thus, perhaps because of this respect for press freedom and acceptance of press responsibility, no doubt fostered by a liberal press law, Sweden's press law is in fact little used. Few actions are filed for libel, and relatively even fewer are filed by public officials. Damages and criminal penalties are low. The government does not try to compel disclosure of journalists' sources except under extraordinary circumstances, in part because the law strongly protects the source's anonymity and partly because the system of liability -- which makes a single designated editor responsible for all breaches of law -- means that the authorities have less justification for trying to ascertain the source or author of a story.

As in most countries of Europe, the number of newspapers is declining. However, Sweden has been able to maintain competition in most markets by a system of substantial subsidies to "second papers", namely, papers which have the second highest circulation in a region.

The Swedish press could be described as fairly docile in exercising its legally broad freedom. One reason might be that it stays within the sometimes narrow limits of the press' Code of Ethics, rather than using all the freedom provided by the FPA. In this respect, it could be argued that self-regulation has equalled self-censorship. However, many alternative reasons for the quiescence of the press may be found. It is important to stress that, nonetheless, press-ethical standards have served to support anything but docile journalism concerning politics, government and big business.

---

[11] *See* FPA Ch. 1, Art. 9:1.

Chapter 10

PRESS LAW IN THE UNITED KINGDOM

Andrew Nicol and Caroline Bowman

INTRODUCTION

The United Kingdom has no written constitution and hence no fundamental guarantees for freedom of speech. Neither is there a comprehensive press law setting out rights and restrictions on the media. Freedom of speech is a negative concept. The law abounds with restrictions imposed either by Parliament or by case-law. The "freedom" to speak only exists outside these limitations.

The doctrine of parliamentary supremacy means that the courts have no power to overrule statute. Until recently, this proposition could be stated in absolute terms. However, European Community law must now be given priority over even Parliamentary legislation. In at least *one* instance (importation of indecent material), legislation restrictive of freedom of expression cannot be fully implemented because of European controls.[1]

1. RELEVANT CONSTITUTIONAL PROVISIONS

While the UK has no written constitution, the courts often refer to constitutional principles, including freedom of speech and freedom of the press. One of the explanations given for not enshrining these rights in a written constitution is the doctrine that everyone is free to do anything subject only to the provisions of law and that a written bill of rights is accordingly unnecessary.[2] While administrative and judicial actions may be challenged as contrary to these constitutional freedoms, it is undeniable that they are not accorded the same status as they are in other European countries which have entrenched bills of rights.

2. DISTRIBUTION OF POWERS BETWEEN CENTRAL AND REGIONAL GOVERNMENT

England, Wales, Scotland and Northern Ireland make up the United Kingdom. Parliament enacts legislation which may apply to the whole of the UK or just particular parts of it. England and Wales have a single legal system. Northern Ireland and Scotland each has its own legal system and court structure. Scotland retains its own separate tradition of common law and a separate court system. For all three jurisdictions the Judicial Committee of the

---

[1] *See* Section 8 *infra*.

[2] *See, e.g., Attorney-General v. Guardian Newspapers (No.2)* [1990] 1 AC 109, per Lord Goff of Cieveley at 283.

House of Lords is the highest appellate court in most cases. The Channel Islands and the Isle of Man have their own legal systems, courts and legislatures.

Northern Ireland has been governed directly from Westminster since 1972. Specific anti-terrorist legislation relating only to Northern Ireland additionally restricts freedom of expression within and relating to the province. For example, in Northern Ireland there is a statutory prohibition on collecting information which is likely to be of use to terrorists.[3] Both civil and criminal appeals from Northern Ireland are ultimately heard by the House of Lords.

Unless specifically stated, this summary sets out only the law and legal structure of England and Wales.

3. ROLE OF THE COURTS

England and Wales is a common law jurisdiction. Although based on the fiction that judges merely declare the unchanging law, the common law offers considerable power to the judiciary to be innovative in areas unregulated by statute.

Judicial review is the principal method of challenging the actions and decisions of public bodies which infringe freedom of expression. An application must be made to the High Court and will be heard by one of a special panel of judges. The Court reviews the actions or decisions for errors of law. So, for instance, they may be quashed if the decision maker has acted irrationally or beyond his powers, has taken into consideration irrelevant matters or has failed to consider relevant matters. This supervisory function is much narrower than the powers of a court hearing an appeal on facts as well as law. There is no constitutional court, and no court has the power to declare acts of Parliament illegal unless they conflict with EC law.

3.1 Civil Actions

Civil actions for defamation and breach of confidence are brought in the High Court or County Court. Most civil cases are heard by a single professional judge. However, in defamation cases, either party can insist on trial by judge and jury unless there are a large number of documents or the case involves scientific or local investigation which cannot conveniently be carried out by a jury.[4]

In civil cases there is a right of appeal from the High Court or County Court to the Court of Appeal. A further appeal to the House of Lords is dependent on either the House of Lords or the Court of Appeal granting leave and for this the case must raise a point of law of importance. Appeals are usually heard by five Law Lords.

---

[3] Emergency Provisions (Northern Ireland) Act 1978 s.22.

[4] Supreme Court Act 1981, s.69.

3.2   Criminal Cases

Criminal offences involving the media (such as breaches of national security, collecting information of use to terrorists, criminal libel, obscenity, incitement to racial hatred, blasphemy, sedition, and incitement to disaffection) can be tried in the Crown Court before a judge and jury. Criminal convictions in a Crown Court can be appealed to the Court of Appeal. Convictions in a magistrates' court can be appealed to the Crown Court for a rehearing of the whole case or to the High Court on a point of law. There can likewise be a further appeal on a point of law from the Crown Court to the High Court. In very limited circumstances there may be a further appeal from the High Court or the Court of Appeal to the House of Lords.

All criminal charges (including contempt of court) must be proved "beyond reasonable doubt".

Prosecutions for criminal offences can be brought by the state (referred to as the Crown), or (as a general rule) by private persons. Private prosecutions can be taken over by the Crown which will then have discretion to discontinue the proceedings. However, most media offences can only be prosecuted with the consent of senior law officers (usually the Attorney-General, who is a minister in the government and its most senior law officer) who must be satisfied that this would be in the public interest.

Media defendants are also partly protected against criminal libel proceedings because of the requirement that the prosecution must be authorized by a High Court judge. Libel is usually a civil matter and criminal prosecutions are extremely rare.

Apart from the other penalties which a court may impose, defendants who are found guilty can be ordered to pay all or part of the prosecution's costs. These can be considerable. However, the criminal courts (unlike civil courts) must take account of the ability of the defendant to pay. The prosecution can be ordered to pay the costs of a defendant who is acquitted. Again, the criminal courts have flexible powers and will not invariably make an order of this kind in favour of an acquitted defendant.

4.   STATUS OF INTERNATIONAL HUMAN RIGHTS TREATIES IN NATIONAL LAW

The United Kingdom is a party to the European Convention on Human Rights (ECHR) and accepted the right of individual petition in 1966. Applications to the European Commission and Court of Human Rights have succeeded in striking down several aspects of UK law incompatible with freedom of expression. The UK is also a party to the International Covenant on Civil and Political Rights (ICCPR), although it has not ratified its First Optional Protocol. (As a consequence individuals may not file complaints against the UK with the UN Human Rights Committee.)

Even when ratified, treaties do not become part of the law of the UK until they have been made law by Parliament.[5] However, they may, and some judges have said that they should, be consulted as aids in interpreting ambiguous statutes, unsettled common law and judicial discretion.[6] If the terms of a statute, enacted after the UK's accession to a relevant treaty, are ambiguous and are "reasonably capable" of being construed so as to be consistent with the treaty, then they should be interpreted in this way.[7] On the other hand, if the terms of a statute "are clear and unambiguous they must be given effect to, whether or not they carry out Her Majesty's treaty obligations".[8] Moreover, simply because Parliament has conferred broad powers and wide discretion on a Minister or an administrative or executive body does not mean that the empowering legislation is vague; on the contrary, "to presume that [discretion] must be exercised within Convention limits would be to go far beyond the resolution of an ambiguity".[9]

An appellate court recently ruled that common law, where it is uncertain, should be interpreted to be consistent with international human rights treaties, including the ECHR and the ICCPR, even though unincorporated into national law.[10] An appeal against that judgment is pending before the House of Lords and is likely to be decided by early 1993.

5. STATUTORY FRAMEWORK

There is no unified press or media law. In general the press operate under restrictions which apply to the population at large. Laws of libel, contempt, official secrets etc. are of particular importance to the media, but they are not part of a discrete code applying exclusively to them. There are some provisions which do affect just the media. These are scattered throughout the civil and criminal law, as discussed below.

---

[5] *R. v. Chief Immigration Officer, Ex parte Salamat Bibi* [1976] 1 W.L.R. 979.

[6] E.g., *R. v. Home Secretary, Ex parte Brind* [1991] 1 A.C. 696, at 747-48, 749-50, and at 760-61; *Attorney-General v. Guardian* [1987] 1 WLR 1248, at 1307; *Derbyshire County Council v. Times Newspapers Ltd.* [1992] 3 All ER 65 (CA).

[7] *Garland v. British Rail* [1983] 2 AC 751, Lord Diplock at 771.

[8] *Salomon v. Commissioners of Customs & Excise* [1967] 2 QB 116, at 143.

[9] *R. v. Secretary of State, Ex parte Brind* [1991] 1 AC 696, at 747.

[10] *Derbyshire County Council v. Times Newspapers Ltd.*, *supra* note 6.

6.   REGULATION OF OWNERSHIP

Ownership of UK newspapers is concentrated in only a few hands. Seventy per cent of national daily newspapers are published by four multinational companies which also publish 80 per cent of Sunday newspapers. Regional newspapers are largely controlled by four groups.

The Secretary of State for Trade has powers to limit future concentration of the press by referring proposed newspaper mergers to the Monopolies and Mergers Commission.[11] The Commission is required to report on "whether the transfer in question may be expected to operate against the public interest taking into account all matters which appear in the circumstances to be relevant and, in particular, the need for accurate presentation of news and free expression of opinion". Acquisitions which will give a proprietor control of newspaper circulation amounting to more than 500,000 copies per day require the consent of the Secretary of State, which he may not give until he has received a report on the proposed merger from the Commission. However, if a newspaper is not "economic as a going concern" there is no need for a Commission report. The minister may agree to the transfer if the "case is one of urgency". If the intention is to close the newspaper or to absorb it under a rival title, he must give his consent without a report.

Legislation has proved ineffectual due to the passive attitude of ministers and the Commission and, in particular, because ministers have not examined with sufficient vigour the claim of the prospective proprietors that a newspaper is "not a going concern". The minister's refusal to refer a case to the Commission is theoretically open to legal challenge. In practice, however, the risk of legal costs has discouraged journalists from taking this course.

The Commission has been reluctant to accept the proposition that an assessment of the public interest should involve consideration of the public's interest in being able to choose among a variety of different editorial opinions. Hence, the Commission has refused to consider a proprietor's future political plans for a newspaper. The powers of the Commission are further limited by the fact that there is no presumption against the concentration of ownership: the Commission can only recommend against an acquisition if it can be proved that the merger is not in the public interest.

The Broadcasting Act 1990 contains complex provisions designed to restrict cross-media ownership. Detailed as they are, they have not prevented Rupert Murdoch's companies from owning BSkyB as well as a string of national newspapers.

---

[11] Fair Trading Act 1973, ss.57-62.

7. REGISTRATION REQUIREMENTS

Newspapers are required to register their titles and the names, occupations, places of business and places of residence of their proprietors.[12] There is no discretion to refuse registration which is intended as a source of information as to the paper's owners rather than a means of censorship.

8. REGULATION OF IMPORT AND EXPORT OF PUBLICATIONS

The importation of obscene articles is prohibited. The domestic legislation also prohibits "indecent" imports. However, the European Court of Justice has held that this second category was a restraint on trade under Article 30 of the EEC's Treaty of Rome and not justified on public morality grounds under Article 36.[13]

9. MECHANISMS OF PRESS SELF-REGULATION

A Press Council was originally established in 1953 to remove the spectre of restrictive statutory regulation. It was a voluntary body staffed by media representatives and exercised the dual and, to some observers, contradictory role of protecting freedom of expression and dealing with complaints from the public. Public confidence dissolved due to the Council's lack of sanctions and inconsistent rulings. Additional public dissatisfaction resulted from the adjudication procedure which was only open to complainants who abandoned their rights to sue for libel through the courts.

9.1 Press Complaints Commission

A revised Press Complaints Commission (PCC) was established in 1991. This body was not given the role of championing freedom of the press but only that of protecting the public. A new Code of Practice set out standards on accuracy, fairness, privacy, chequebook journalism, race, financial journalism and protection of sources. The Commission is constituted by six lay members and nine press members, and is funded by the newspaper industry. Adjudications are conducted through written submissions.

Proponents hoped that the existence of a new and comprehensive Code of Practice would produce clearer adjudications. However, the new Commission retains many of the shortcomings of the Press Council. It has no power to enforce judgments or even to ensure their publication. The Code of Practice itself contains uncertainties which tabloid editors have used to justify invasion of privacy. The PCC does not investigate breaches of the Code of its own accord but waits until it receives a complaint.

---

[12] Newspaper Libel and Registration Act 1881

[13] *Conegate Ltd. v. Customs and Excise Commissioners* [1987] QB 254.

The press was galvanized into accepting the voluntary PCC because of the threat of statutory regulation. A report in 1990 by David Calcutt into the law of privacy envisaged a publicly funded statutory tribunal with power to take evidence on oath, order public corrections and apologies and award compensation. Despite the ill-defined ethical guidelines contained in the Code of Practice the report also envisaged that the tribunal would have power to grant injunctions in circumstances where a breach of the Code of Practice was proven. The report rejected the recommendation that a civil law on privacy be adopted to provide damages where privacy has been invaded without justification.

At the time of writing David Calcutt has been asked to produce a sequel to his report. There is pressure for further remedies for invasion of privacy. The old dilemmas of how to do this without trespassing on the "proper" objects of press inquiry (or even to define what is meant by "proper") remain.

9.2   Press Ombudsmen

A further consequence of the first Calcutt report was the voluntary appointment of ombudsmen to consider readers' complaints by most of the national papers. So far the evidence suggests that ombudsmen have only a limited influence.

9.3   "D" Notice Committee

The "D" Notice committee consists of representatives of the media and armed services. Its ostensible purpose is to help the media to identify subjects whose public discussion truly would be damaging. However, the Committee's clearance provides no bar against prosecution. The Committee is not highly regarded because the government tends to use it to stifle discussion which is politically embarrassing rather than harmful to some wider national interest. It is an entirely voluntary system and many media organizations take a principled position that they will have nothing to do with it.

10.   DEFAMATION

A statement is defamatory if it brings the plaintiff into hatred, ridicule or contempt. In the nineteenth century language (whose flavour still lingers in libel law), the statement must lower the plaintiff in the estimation of right-thinking people generally. A jury decides whether a statement is defamatory unless a judge rules initially that a statement is incapable of being defamatory. The jury are asked to look at the effect of the published words as "ordinary readers". The motive of the author is irrelevant. Apparently harmless statements can be defamatory by innuendo to those in possession of extra information. The plaintiff must prove to the jury that readers of the statement were likely to know of the extra facts which make it defamatory.

The plaintiff must also show that the statement refers to him or her. This is easy if the plaintiff is named. However, anonymity will not protect the media if some readers will be able to infer that the plaintiff is the object of the statement. It is no defence that the readers guess wrong. The intention of the defendant is immaterial if the inference is a reasonable one.

In libel actions, as in all civil cases, the plaintiff must establish his or her case on a balance of probabilities, that is, he or she must show that it is more likely than not that all the ingredients of the action existed. If the defendant puts forward a positive defence this must also be proved on the same balance of probabilities.

10.1   Defences

There are three main positive defences: truth (or "justification"), fair comment, and privilege.

Truth is a complete defence. Except where certain old criminal convictions have been published, it is not necessary to show that a true statement was also in the public interest. "Old" for these purposes depends on the sentence imposed. The difficulty with the defence is not legal, but practical. Assembling admissible evidence sufficient to persuade a jury that a serious defamatory statement is true can be very hard, especially if the source of the statement insists on anonymity. However, the publisher does have the benefit of the usual pre-trial civil procedures including "discovery". This is a compulsory exchange of all documents in the possession of the parties which relate to the dispute between them. Documents must be included whether they help or harm the party producing them. A libel plaintiff as a practical matter must also be willing to face cross-examination.

"Fair comment" is an important buttress of free speech. Comment can be defended even if the defendant cannot prove that it is true. This makes the boundary between "fact" and "comment" all-important. In most cases the issue is decided by the jury although the judge can decide against a defendant if the statement is not capable of being considered a comment. There are additional requirements. The defendant's comment must be based on a factual foundation. Those facts must be true and must be either set out in the publication itself or referred to with sufficient clarity. Alternatively, the comment must be based on a privileged report (see below) which accompanies the defamatory statement. The defendant does not have to show that the comment follows as a matter of logic from the factual foundation (if it did, the defence of truth would apply), but it is enough if an honest person could base the comment on that foundation. If all these conditions are satisfied, the defendant will have a good defence to a libel action unless the plaintiff can show that the defendant was inspired by some improper motive or "malice".

"Privilege" arises from the law's recognition that, on particular occasions, it is important for there to be open communication even if this openness is achieved at the cost of damage to reputations. Fair and accurate reports of court proceedings published in a newspaper as soon as possible after the event in question enjoy "absolute privilege", *i.e.,* a complete defence against suit. Other reports enjoy qualified privilege, *i.e.,* a defence against suit unless it is proved that the reports were made with "malice" in the same sense that word is used in the context of fair comment.[14] Reports of proceedings in Parliament, for example and newspaper

---

[14] Defamation Act 1952, s.7.

reports on a wide (but carefully specified) range of public events all enjoy qualified privilege; in some circumstances this privilege is conditional on publication of a statement in reply on request. Relevant replies refuting defamatory statements are privileged.

The exact limits of privilege are still being explored, but the courts have so far resisted a wider defence for reports concerning the lives of public figures. Neither have they recognized a more general privilege in publishing information of vital public interest which is believed to be true.

There is a defence of innocent defamation[15], but it is extremely restricted in scope and procedural complications deprive it of practically any utility.

Authors, editors, sources of information, printers, proprietors and distributors can all be sued for libel. Repetition of a libel provides a new cause of action. Journalists are not liable if defamatory statements are added without consent to their articles.

Any identifiable living individual can sue. However, since legal aid is not available for libel actions, which are notorious for their expense, only the wealthy or well-patronized can in practice afford to seek redress for injury to their reputations. Companies can sue if their business reputations are affected. Local authorities and other public bodies cannot bring actions for criticism of government or administrative conduct unless it has caused financial loss.[16] Trade Unions cannot sue.[17] English law does not recognize the concept of "group libel".

10.2 Damages and Costs

Damages in libel actions are decided by juries with very little control exercised by judges. The awards are unpredictable. Recent awards include £500,000 to novelist and politician, Jeffrey Archer, as recompense for the wrongful suggestion that he had sex with a prostitute.

In addition to awards for injury to reputation and feelings, punitive damages can be awarded against defendants who deliberately set out to defame another in order to make a profit. These damages are also set by a jury.

In extreme cases the Court of Appeal can overturn jury awards, but a great deal of latitude is allowed before an award is characterized as "extreme". Even though the Court of Appeal can now substitute its own decision as to damages rather than ordering a new trial, it is still very rare for awards to be overturned.

---

[15] Defamation Act 1952, s.4.

[16] *Derbyshire County Council v. Times Newspapers Ltd.* [1992] 3 All E. R. 65 CA

[17] *EETPU v. Times* [1980] 3 WLR 98.

Damages are only part of the gamble which most libel actions become. Costs are very high. The normal rule is that the successful party's costs are ordered to be paid by the loser. This is subject to an important qualification designed to encourage out-of-court settlements. A defendant may pay into a court bank account the sum which he would be willing to pay in damages. If the plaintiff accepts the offer, the action comes to an end and the plaintiff's costs will be paid by the Defendant. If the plaintiff thinks that the sum is too low and continues with the case to trial, the payment into court is kept secret from both the judge and the jury. If the plaintiff is successful, but is awarded no more than the money paid into court, he will only be recompensed for his costs up to the date of the payment in. After that date, the plaintiff will have to pay the defendant's costs. The theory is that the plaintiff could have achieved all that he eventually won by accepting the payment in. The costs after that time were wasted and he should pay them. Since the costs at the end of the case (particularly of the trial itself) are often the most expensive, this system does indeed produce many last minute settlements from litigants who cannot afford to stake so much money on the unpredictable decision of a jury.

10.3   Malicious Falsehood and Conspiracy to Injure

Two other common law actions survive which are distinct from libel, but which may arise in similar circumstances. The first is malicious falsehood. Like defamation, this concerns the publication of words which cause harm. The harm may, but need not, be to reputation. The action was originally intended as a remedy for harmful accusations about a trader's goods or title to property. A plaintiff relying on malicious falsehood faces three additional hurdles beyond those facing a libel plaintiff. He or she must prove: that the words are untrue (in libel the burden is on the defendant to show that they are true); that they were published maliciously (a libel plaintiff has this task only in rebuttal of a defence of fair comment or qualified privilege); and (except in limited circumstances) that the words caused financial loss (in libel, compensation is not dependent on proof of financial loss).

The other action akin to libel is conspiracy to injure, which requires proof of an agreement that has injury of the plaintiff as its dominant purpose.

These actions continue to be of use to those whose reputations are damaged because it may be possible to obtain legal aid whereas, save in exceptional cases, there is no legal aid to defend or to bring libel actions. Furthermore, injunctions may be more easily obtained.

10.4   Criminal Libel

Criminal libel is a virtually extinct yet dangerous common law offence. Truth is not a defence unless the jury is satisfied that publication is for the public benefit. The defendant's intention in publishing a statement is irrelevant. The criminal action does not preclude a civil action for damages. The press have the limited protection that the permission of a High Court judge must be obtained for the prosecution. For this to be given there must be an exceptionally strong *prima facie* case, a very serious libel, and the public interest must require institution of criminal proceedings.[18]

11. INVASION OF PRIVACY

See discussion in Section 9.1 *supra*.

12. RIGHT OF REPLY AND/OR CORRECTION

As already noted, the statutory defence of qualified privilege to a defamation action is sometimes dependent on publication of a reasonable reply at the request of the person defamed. The code of practice which is "enforced" by the Press Complaints Commission requires newspapers to give a fair opportunity for reply to inaccuracies when reasonably called for. However, if this opportunity is not given, the only recourse is a complaint to the PCC which will publish its own adjudications but which cannot compel a recalcitrant editor to do likewise. The Broadcasting Complaints Commission hears complaints of unfair treatment against broadcasters. It does have a statutory power to require the broadcaster to publish its findings[19].

13. INSULTS TO GOVERNMENT OFFICIALS OR INSTITUTIONS

Although the offence of seditious libel was used extensively in the past to silence radical protest, it is now most unlikely to be used against journalists. No prosecution has been brought since 1947. Analysis of the offence since 1945 has defined sedition as speech intended to stir up tumult and disorder for the purpose of disturbing constitutional authority.[20]

There are no equivalent laws in England making it a crime to insult the Head of State or the flag. In the past intemperate criticism of the judiciary has been punished by a form of contempt known as "scandalising the court". It is now virtually obsolescent in the UK.[21]

---

[18] Law of Libel Amendment Act 1888, s.8.

[19] Broadcasting Act 1990 s.146

[20] *R. v. Bow Street Magistrates' Court ex parte Choudhary* [1991] 1 All ER 306

[21] *Secretary of State for Defence v Guardian Newspapers Ltd.* [1985] AC 339, 347

14. OFFICIAL SECRECY AND ACCESS TO GOVERNMENT-HELD INFORMATION

The UK has no Freedom of Information Act. Government decision-making is shrouded in secrecy.

14.1 Official Secrets Act

The Official Secrets Act 1989 uses the criminal law to guard against the disclosure of state secrets. The main disclosure offences all carry the right to jury trial and a maximum penalty of two years' imprisonment.[22] None of the offences provide for a defence of public interest or "moral duty"; even where damage must be proved courts are unlikely to rule that evidence may be introduced to show that any damage was reduced by the public interest in disclosure unless the damage was thereby reduced to zero.

Members or past members of the security or intelligence services can be prosecuted for the unauthorized revelation of any information whether truly secret or not, relating to security or intelligence.[23] It is not necessary to prove that the state has been harmed.

Other crown servants, contractors and employees of various private corporations and regulatory bodies may be prosecuted for the unauthorized disclosure of information concerning security or intelligence[24], defence[25] or international relations.[26] For these offences the prosecution must prove that damage to the work of the security and intelligence services has occurred or is likely to occur. Additionally the Act penalizes the disclosure of information which would be likely to result in the commission of a criminal offence.[27] This last offence does not require proof of damage. A defendant can avoid conviction by proof that he or she did not know or have reason to believe that the information concerned security, defence, international relations or crime.

Anyone not employed by the government commits an offence if they publish without authority information originating from a Crown servant or contractor which they know is protected by the Official Secrets Act.[28] The prosecution must prove that the "outsider" had

---

[22] Official Secrets Act 1989, s.10(1).

[23] *Id.* s.1(1).

[24] *Id.* s.1(3)

[25] *Id.* s.2.

[26] *Id.* s.3.

[27] *Id.* s.4.

[28] *Id.* s.5.

reason to believe that publication would be damaging to the security services or to the interests of the UK. Unless the offence involves information relating to crime, the prosecution must also prove that damage to the work of the defence, security and intelligence services has occurred or is likely to occur.[29]

Despite the breadth of the language of the Official Secrets Acts prosecutions are rare. It is rarer still for the media to be charged with one of these offences. Understanding the role of the jury is crucial to appreciating why this is so. Well-publicized acquittals are extremely embarrassing for the government and a trial in any case will often lead to a great deal of further publicity. Moreover, approval of the Attorney-General (or in some cases the Director of Public Prosecutions) is required to initiate a prosecution. While this gives uncertain protection, taken with the right to jury trial and a public consciousness which is generally sceptical of the need for official secrecy, the official secrets legislation is not as inhibiting for the media as it might appear.

14.2   Duty of Confidentiality and "Whistleblowers"

On appointment, civil servants undertake an absolute duty of confidentiality. Breach of this duty may lead to dismissal and prosecution. No legislation exists to protect "whistleblowers". The government regularly silences unauthorized disclosures by applying for injunctions for breach of confidence. In cases involving the government an injunction for breach of confidence will be granted only if the government can show that the public interest (*e.g.*, national security) requires a restraining order. Hence, the English government ultimately failed to have an injunction upheld against the serialization of *Spycatcher*.[30] This book, which chronicled Peter Wright's experiences in the UK security services, had already been widely published abroad, so that further publication in the UK would have made no difference to national security.

14.3   Deportation of Foreign Journalists

Foreign reporters who investigate UK security matters risk deportation. A US journalist who wrote about signals intelligence in the 1970s was deported on "public good" grounds. No further official explanation was given.[31]

14.4   Classification of Documents

Government records are only released to the public after 30 years. Many categories of records are withheld for 50-100 years or even more for no obvious reason. The difficulties in obtaining government documents in the United Kingdom have led some British journalists to

---

[29] *Id.* s.5(3).

[30] *Attorney-General v. Guardian Newspapers (No.2)* [1988] 3 All ER 545.

[31] *R. v. Secretary of State for the Home Office ex parte Hosenball* [1977] 3 All ER 452.

use the United States Freedom of Information Act in order to obtain information relating to the UK.

14.5   Access to Local Government Information

Rights of access to local government information are greater than to information held by the national government. Council and committee meetings are open to the press and public unless certain categories of statutorily exempt information are to be discussed in which case the council must state in advance the reason for secrecy.[32] The press and public also have a right to inspect a wide range of local authority documents.

Access to local government information is important for environmentalists. Authorities are required to keep public records of waste disposal licences, some information on noise levels and compulsorily obtained information on air pollution[33]. New legislation will provide for public registers concerning hazardous substances.[34] Since 1985 water authorities have been obliged to keep public registers concerning pollution matters.[35] Local authorities also hold registers of planning applications and under-used land in public ownership.

EEC law forces the pace on environmental disclosure in the UK. The Directive of 7/6/90 requires public authorities to make available information relating to the environment.[36] Commercial and industrial confidences, unfinished documents and data, and internal communications can be withheld.

Despite the access of the press to such information, local reporting is often of poor quality. Partly this is because most local council policy decisions are taken at closed meetings of the majority political party. Partly it is the result of the highly centralized nature of the British state which leads journalists to focus scrutiny upon central government. Partly it is because investigative reporting takes time and money which local papers are often unwilling to commit. Central government remains obdurately resistant to the idea that it should set its own house in order by parallel legislation providing for access to information at central level.

---

[32] Local Government Act 1972, s.100(A)(5).

[33] Control of Pollution Act 1974, ss. 6, 64 and 82(3)(d); Control of Atmospheric Pollution (Research and Publicity) Regulations 1977, Reg. 6.

[34] Planning (Hazardous Substances) Act 1990, s.28.

[35] Control of Pollution Act 1974 ss.41 and 42; see now Water Act 1989 s.117 and Control of Pollution (Registers) Regulations 1989. SI 1989 No 1160.

[36] 90/313/EEC, OJ No. L 158, 23.6.1990, p.59.

15. ACCESS TO AND DISCLOSURE OF COURT DOCUMENTS AND PROCEEDINGS

15.1 Open Justice and Exceptions Thereto

Although open justice is a fundamental principle of English law, there are a number of statutory qualifications to this principle. Official secrets trials, for instance, may be held in private if publication of the evidence would be prejudicial to national security. In the absence of a statutory power, the press and public must be admitted unless "the administration of justice would be rendered impracticable by their presence".[37] Even when *some* limitation on this normal principle is justified, it should be kept to a minimum. So, for instance, if disorder breaks out in court the public can be excluded; but journalists who take no part in the disruption would be allowed to stay.[38]

Courts must sit in private in cases involving mental patients, guardianship and adoption proceedings. Courts may sit in private in other cases involving children, families, confidential information or national security. The public but not the press are excluded at juvenile criminal proceedings.[39]

The usual rule is that hearings heard in public may be reported in the media. This is an important principle that gives real meaning to the concept of "open justice". However, there are a number of exceptions. Statutes forbid reporting the evidence and argument in certain hearings preliminary to criminal trials unless the defendant consents to publication.[40] Victims of sexual offences may not be named without their consent unless the court rules that reporting is necessary to avoid prejudice to the defence or is otherwise in the public interest.[41] If the court is permitted by some other power to receive evidence (for instance, to persuade blackmail victims to give evidence in private), then it may also prohibit reporting of that evidence.[42] The court may also postpone reporting if this is necessary to avoid a serious risk of prejudice to the case which it is trying to some other pending or imminent case.[43]

---

[37] *Scott v. Scott* [1913] AC 417.

[38] *R. v. Denbigh Justices ex parte Williams and Evans* [1974] 2 All ER 1052.

[39] Children and Young Persons Act 1933, s.47.

[40] Magistrates Courts Act 1980, s.8. Criminal Justice Act 1987, s.11.

[41] Sexual Offences (Amendment) Act 1976, s.4; Sexual Offences (Amendment) Act 1992.

[42] Contempt of Court Act 1981, s.11.

[43] Contempt of Court Act 1981 s.4(2)

The press has learnt that if this increasing tendency to restrict reporting is to be curbed, they have to take a more active role. This can take a number of forms. At its simplest it can involve sending a lawyer to argue before the judge who imposed the order that it was wrong and should be set aside. This is simple, quick and cheap. The press are not a party in a formal sense to the criminal proceedings, but the courts have recently confirmed that they have the right to make these representations.[44]

A second alternative is to seek judicial review of the order. This is appropriate where the judge made some legal error. The merits cannot be re-examined unless the order was so wrong that it can be described as irrational.

A third course is restricted to orders made in Crown Court trials. These orders may be appealed by the press to the Court of Appeal.[45] The introduction of this remedy is a good example of the effect of the European Convention on Human Rights since it followed a friendly settlement of a case brought by a journalist against the UK at a time when there were no means for the press to challenge postponement orders.[46]

15.2 Contempt of Court

One of the aims of the criminal law of contempt is to punish and prevent trial by newspaper. It is the only major criminal offence which carries no right to a jury trial. The offence can be punished by an unlimited fine and up to two years' imprisonment.[47] Prosecutions are usually instigated by the Attorney-General, but occasionally the judge will act on his or her own initiative.

The English law of contempt has been developed by the courts. In 1977, however, a case brought by the *Sunday Times* newspaper before the European Court of Human Rights forced the enactment of the Contempt of Court Act 1981.[48] Parents of thalidomide victims launched legal proceedings designed to prove the negligence of the company which had manufactured this drug. The UK courts prevented the Sunday Times from criticizing the drug company's handling of the claim during a lengthy pre-trial settlement period because its article pre-judged issues which the trial judge would have to decide if the case did not settle.[49] The

---

[44] *R. v. Clerkenwell Stipendiary Magistrates ex parte the Telegraph plc and others* (October 1992); *R. v. Beck ex parte Daily Telegraph* [1991] 94 Cr App R 376.

[45] Criminal Justice Act 1988, s.159.

[46] *Hodgson v. UK* (No.11553/85) and *Channel 4 v. UK* (No.11658/85) decision on admissibility 9th March 1987.

[47] Contempt of Court Act 1981, s.14(1).

[48] *See Sunday Times v. United Kingdom*, Judgment of 26 April 1979, Series A no. 30.

[49] *Attorney-General v. Times Newspaper Limited* [1974] AC 273.

European Court of Human Rights held that the UK ruling was an interference with freedom of expression and was not justified by a pressing social need.

The Contempt of Court Act 1981 reformulated the offence which is now committed if a publication "creates a substantial risk that the course of justice in particular proceedings will be seriously impeded or prejudiced".[50] Proceedings must be sanctioned by the Attorney-General. The risk of prejudice amounting to contempt is greatest when reporting criminal trials decided by a jury. Because most civil cases are tried by judges alone, comment is unlikely to result in contempt proceedings. Recently the House of Lords ruled that it was extremely unlikely that a professional judge and even less likely that an appellate judge would be influenced by anything he might read about a case.[51]

Contempt of court of the type so far considered can only be committed whilst a case is "sub judice" or, in the statutory language, "active".[52] In criminal cases a matter is active from the moment that a suspect has been charged or arrested, or a warrant for arrest issued until the convicted defendant has been sentenced or until any appeal is decided.[53] Civil proceedings become active when a case is formally declared ready for trial or when a hearing date has been fixed, and remain active until the action is disposed of, discontinued or finally decided on appeal.[54]

Publication of matters concerning a court case which are of general public interest are not to be treated as contempt of court "if the risk of impediment or prejudice is merely incidental to the discussion".[55] This defence will not apply if the prosecution proves bad faith, such as a deliberate attempt to prejudice proceedings. The defence was given by a wide interpretation by the House of Lords.[56] During the criminal trial of a doctor charged with allowing a deformed baby to die, a national newspaper published an article attacking this allegedly widespread practice. The House of Lords dismissed the contempt charge, stating that bona fide discussion of controversial matters of public importance could not be prevented merely because of the existence of contemporaneous legal proceedings and any prejudice was incidental to that discussion.

---

[50] Contempt of Court Act 1981, s.2(1).

[51] *Re Lonhro plc and Observer Ltd.* [1989] 2 All ER 1100.

[52] Contempt of Court Act 1981, s.2(3).

[53] Contempt of Court Act 1981, Schedule 1, paras. 4 and 5.

[54] *Id.* paras 12 and 13.

[55] Contempt of Court Act 1981, s. 5.

[56] *Attorney-General v. English* [1982] 2 All ER 903, at 919.

15.3   Common Law Contempts

Despite the Contempt of Court Act 1981, common law contempt offences still survive. Deliberate contempt consists in publishing material designed to prejudice imminent criminal proceedings. The offence is dangerous since prosecution does not require the Attorney-General's permission, public interest and innocent distribution defences do not exist and the prosecution only has to prove a real risk of prejudice, not a substantial risk of serious prejudice. A defence of honest mistake does exist.

The Sun newspaper was found guilty of deliberate contempt after it agreed to fund a private prosecution brought by a mother who alleged her child had been raped by a well-known medical doctor.[57] The newspaper had previously concluded an agreement with the mother that she would provide exclusive interviews and pictures. *The Sun* then launched an attack on the named doctor and declared his guilt.

Common law contempt can also be used to punish the disclosure of information which a court has ordered others not to publish. The courts invented this species of contempt when various UK newspapers published parts of Peter Wright's *Spycatcher* memoirs of life in the United Kingdom secret services after other papers had been ordered not to do so.

It is an offence to publish details of jury deliberations.[58] The offence does not prevent the publication of jurors' views on matters which take place outside the jury room. The offence has prevented research into the effectiveness of jury trials. In November 1992 a newspaper and its editor were fined a total of £60,000 for publishing research into how well a jury had been able to understand a long and complicated fraud trial which lawyers (without research) had said was beyond the comprehension of non-lawyers.

Scandalizing the court is an arcane common law contempt and consists of vilification of the judiciary. It has not been used in the UK for 50 years.

16.   ACCESS TO AND DISCLOSURE OF LEGISLATIVE DOCUMENTS AND PROCEEDINGS

The Bill of Rights 1688 states that "the freedom of speech and debates of proceedings in Parliament ought not be impeached or questioned in any court or place outside Parliament". Hence Members of the House of Commons and the House of Lords are guaranteed immunity against court proceedings concerning statements in Parliament, Parliamentary committees, or Parliamentary reports. Such statements are privileged when repeated by the press. MPs' statements outside Parliament are not privileged. This rule has been used in the past to protect publication of potentially libellous allegations or to reveal information classified under the Official Secrets Act.

---

[57] *Attorney-General v. News Group Newspapers* [1988] 2 All ER 906.

[58] *Id.* s.8.

Whilst MPs' statements are protected from court proceedings, Parliament itself can impose disciplinary sanctions. The Speaker of the House disallows discussion of certain topics.

The Houses of Parliament have the power to punish members or outsiders for Contempt of Parliament. This is an ill-defined offence expressed as directly or indirectly impeding either House in the performance of its functions including bringing the House into contempt. Publications which "bring the House into odium, contempt or ridicule or lower its authority" can constitute contempt.

Both Houses possess power to imprison or to banish members or outsiders from their precincts. The House of Lords has power to fine. Trial for contempt of Parliament involves a total lack of procedural guidelines, judgment by a partial tribunal and no right of appeal to the courts. In the past the powers have been used against newspapers which criticized the conduct of MPs. The offences have fallen into disuse and no-one has been imprisoned since 1880. If they were to be revived and any serious punishment imposed, it is doubtful whether they would withstand scrutiny by the European Court of Human Rights.

17.   COMMERCIAL SECRECY AND ACCESS TO INFORMATION HELD BY PRIVATE PARTIES

Bribing employees to provide information about their work is a criminal offence.[59] The offence stipulates that the payment must be made corruptly, but a corrupt motive is presumed until the contrary is shown. If payment was necessary to expose public wrongdoing it might be argued that the payment was not "corrupt". Disclosure of confidential information (whether corrupt or not) can be prevented by injunction under the law of contract or breach of confidence. If information is not expressly protected in a contract, the courts will imply a term that confidential information will not be used to the detriment of the employer.[60]

A public interest defence applies to breaches of confidence, and may apply to breach of contract. This defence has now been extended beyond cases where the information revealed wrongdoing to cases where there is a serious and legitimate public interest in publication of the information which outweighs the usual public interest in preserving confidences.[61] However, this doctrine does not necessarily justify disclosure to the general public. When a national newspaper attempted to publish material illegally obtained from telephone tapping which allegedly revealed misconduct by a jockey, it was held that the newspaper was not

---

[59] Prevention of Corruption Act 1906.

[60] *Faccenda Chicken v. Fowler* [1987] Ch 117 (CA).

[61] *Attorney-General v. Guardian Newspaper* (No 2) [1988] 3 All ER 545; *Lion Laboratories v. Evans* [1985] QB 526.

justified in publishing the material although it would have been justified in disclosing the material to the police or to the jockey's professional body.[62]

No specific law protects whistleblowers from reprisals. However, if an employer dismisses an employee for revealing information not protected contractually or by the doctrine of breach of confidence, or if the employer uses another pretext in order to dismiss in connection with information revealed, it may be possible to claim that the dismissal is unreasonable and hence unfair according to the normal principles of UK employment law.

18.   PRIOR RESTRAINT

Historically "prior restraint" referred to licensing requirements. Licensing of broadcasters and other electronic media is still the norm, but it is virtually non-existent for the print media. However, the term has come to be applied as well to the prevention of publication of particular articles, books or programmes by court order. The absence of prior restraint ought to be a hallmark of free speech. The phrase "publish and be dammed" captures the idea that the public should be free to be informed even if the publisher must pay the price in damages if the publication infringes a private right or in punishment if the publication is a crime.

Unfortunately, the principle has been much eroded. The rule survives in defamation actions where an interim injunction will not be granted if the defendant indicates that the action will be defended on the basis of justification or fair comment.[63] The same attitude does not prevail in cases concerning breach of confidence or breach of copyright. The courts argue that publication pending trial in these cases can irreparably prejudice a plaintiff and are very willing to grant an interim injunction to preserve the status quo pending a full court hearing.

Publication of confidences owed to the government will only be restrained permanently at trial if the government proves that the public interest will be harmed.[64] The government in *Spycatcher* obtained an interim injunction by simply presenting an "arguable" case, but it is doubtful whether the government would try again to enjoin publication of some other book that was selling millions of copies around the world.

In the *Spycatcher* hearing before the European Court of Human Rights, the Court was asked to declare that the English interim injunction test was itself in breach of Article 10 of the Convention. This the Court refused to do although it accepted that the "dangers inherent in prior restraint are such that they call for the most careful scrutiny on the part of the Court".[65]

---

[62] *Francome v. Mirror Group Newspapers* [1984] 2 All ER 408.

[63] *Bonnard v. Perryman* [1891] 2 Ch 269.

[64] *Attorney-General v. Guardian Newspapers* (No 2) [1988] 3 All ER 545.

[65] *Observer and Guardian v. United Kingdom*, Judgment of 26 Nov. 1991, Series A no. 216, para. 60.

19. PROTECTION OF SOURCES

19.1 Contempt of Court Act

Section 10 of the Contempt of Court Act 1981 provides that no court may require an author or journalist to disclose the source of published information "unless it is established to the satisfaction of the court that it is necessary in the interests of justice or national security or for the prevention of disorder or crime". Judges must perform a balancing exercise and weigh the public interest in disclosure of the source for one of the specified purposes against the journalist's undertaking of confidence.

Of the grounds justifying an order to compel disclosure, "the interests of justice" is the widest and most amorphous. Judicial faith in the importance of protecting sources is very limited. In 1980 during a large scale steel strike, Granada TV obtained secret documents from the nationally owned British Steel Corporation concerning the Corporation's massive losses. In confirming an order that Granada had to disclose its source, one member of the House of Lords remarked "This case does not touch on the freedom of the press even at the periphery."[66] Only one member of the House of Lords thought that protecting sources was democratically important. This case was decided before the 1981 Act, but the "interests of justice" exception to Section 10 makes it doubtful that the result would be any different now.

National security is another ground on which journalists can be required to break their source's confidence.[67] The mere assertion by the government that national security was endangered would not be accepted unless there was evidence to support its case. But the courts are extremely wary of rejecting the government's claim of national security interests. Prevention of crime also justifies a disclosure order. Case-law has defined this category broadly. An order may be made to enable prosecution for an offence which has already been committed, or to assist in the prevention of future crime.[68]

An order to disclose a source is less likely where there is a legitimate public interest in the information and is more likely where the information has been obtained illegally.[69] Despite the presumption against disclosure, it is worryingly easy to persuade a court that one of the exceptions in Section 10 is satisfied.

The penalty for refusal to comply with an order is an unlimited fine or committal to prison for up to two years. It is not contempt to destroy or dispose of incriminating material before an order is made.

---

[66] *British Steel Corporation v. Granada Television* [1982] AC 1096.

[67] *Secretary of State for Defence v. Guardian Newspapers* [1985] AC 339.

[68] *Re an Inquiry under the Company Securities (Insider Dealing) Act 1985* [1988] 1 All ER 203.

[69] *X v. Morgan Grampian Publishers Ltd and Others* [1990] 2 All ER 1.

19.2 Prevention of Terrorism (Temporary Provisions) Act ("PTA") 1989

Legislation even more draconian than the Contempt of Court Act exists in relation to Northern Ireland. The PTA 1989 creates a positive duty to tell the police any information that might be of material assistance in preventing an act of terrorism or in apprehending, prosecuting or convicting someone suspected of terrorism in connection with the affairs of Northern Ireland.[70] No prosecutions have yet been brought using this provision. However, when the BBC filmed an IRA roadblock in 1980 the Attorney-General threatened that similar media conduct would lead to prosecution. After the murder of two army corporals at a Republican funeral in 1988, the threat of prosecution was also used to force the media to hand over film of the events leading to the murder.

Besides direct criminal sanctions, the PTA 1989 also provides for compulsory disclosure of journalistic material. Non-compliance can result in the institution of criminal proceedings for contempt of court.

Police officers are given power to apply to a local Crown Court judge for the production of material which there are reasonable grounds to believe will be of substantial value to a terrorist investigation.[71] In making the order the judge is required to consider whether disclosure is in the public interest, the need for disclosure to the investigation, and the circumstances under which the person holds the material. The power was recently used for the first time against Channel 4 TV and Box Productions, an independent production company, which together were responsible for the making of a documentary in which an anonymous source accused the Royal Ulster Constabulary of conspiring with loyalist paramilitary groups to assassinate certain individuals. The RUC denied the allegations. The Director of Public Prosecutions applied to the High Court to commit the two companies for contempt. The High Court ruled that it had no power to set aside an order, simply to decide if the order had been broken and, if it had, to set the punishment for contempt.[72] Channel 4 and Box Productions were fined £75,000. The Court indicated that future contempt proceedings under this Act are likely to be dealt with more severely. This judgment adds to the already grave practical hazards of reporting allegations of misconduct in Northern Ireland by sources who refuse to be identified.

19.3 Police Questioning

Outside Northern Ireland, journalists and the public generally are not required to answer police questions in criminal investigations. The exceptions include compulsory inquisitions

---

[70] Prevention of Terrorism (Temporary Provisions) Act 1989, s.18.

[71] *Id.* Schedule 7, para 5.

[72] *Director of Public Prosecutions v. Channel 4 Television Co Ltd and another* (1992), *The Independent,* 5 Aug.

into spying specially authorized under the Official Secrets Act 1911 as well as investigations into large scale financial misconduct and "insider dealing".[73]

Since 1984 police have possessed extensive powers for seizing unpublished journalistic material such as film and photographs in order to further criminal prosecutions.[74] The police need to show that there are reasonable grounds for believing that a serious offence has been committed, that the material is likely to be of substantial value to the investigation and that the public interest requires the order to be made. The press regularly resist such orders by arguing that they operate against the public interest since they make the task of reporting dangerous situations more hazardous. Courts have not accepted this argument.[75] In more limited circumstances, notably relating to Official Secrets Acts prosecutions, the police can be granted warrants to search for and seize journalistic material held "in confidence".

20. RESTRICTIONS ON OFFENSIVE LANGUAGE AGAINST IDENTIFIABLE GROUPS

It is an offence to use threatening, abusive or insulting words or behaviour with the intention of stirring up racial hatred or in circumstances where racial hatred is likely to be stirred up.[76] Similarly it is an offence to publish such material.[77] This legislation does not extend to stirring up religious hatred, except in Northern Ireland.

Prosecutions can only be brought with the consent of the Attorney-General. Acquittals of racists in past cases may explain to some extent why the legislation is scarcely ever used. There were two prosecutions in 1988, one in 1989 and one in 1990.

The rarely-used common law offence of seditious libel can be committed by "promoting ill-will and hostility between different classes of Her Majesty's subjects". Opponents of Salman Rushdie's *The Satanic Verses* attempted to revive this offence in order to prosecute the author and publisher for incitement to religious hatred. The prosecution was stopped because the offence must necessarily involve incitement to violence against the State. The book did not do this.[78]

---

[73] Official Secrets Act 1911, s.1; Financial Services Act 1986, s.177; Criminal Justice Act 1987, s.2.

[74] Police and Criminal Evidence Act 1984, Schedule 1.

[75] *Chief Constable of Avon and Somerset v. Bristol United Press* (1986), *The Independent*, 4 Nov.; *R v. Crown Court at Bristol ex parte Bristol Press Agency Ltd* (1987) Criminal Law Review 329; *Wyrko v. Newspaper Publishing Plc* (1988), *The Independent*, 27 May.

[76] Public Order Act 1986, s.18.

[77] *Id.* s.19.

[78] *R. v. Bow Street Magistrates ex parte Choudhury* [1991] 1 All ER 306.

The PCC's Code of Practice contains voluntary guidelines aimed at preventing stereotyping and discrimination as follows:

(i)   The Press should avoid prejudicial or pejorative reference to a person's race, colour, religion, sex or sexual orientation or to any physical or mental illness or handicap.

(ii)   It should avoid publishing details of a person's race, colour religion, sex, or sexual orientation unless these are directly relevant to the story

21.   BLASPHEMY, OBSCENITY AND PROTECTION OF PUBLIC MORALS

Offences regarding obscenity are created by the Obscene Publications Act 1959. It is a criminal offence to publish or to possess an obscene article for publication for gain.[79] The maximum penalty on conviction in the Crown Court is three years imprisonment or an unlimited fine. Additionally the Act provides for non-criminal forfeiture proceedings.[80]

Under the Act, an article shall be deemed to be obscene if its effect, taken as a whole, is "such as to tend to deprave and corrupt persons who are likely, in all the circumstances, to read, see or hear the matter contained or embodied in it". The item must have a tendency to corrupt or deprave a significant proportion of the readership. The words "deprave and corrupt" have a strong meaning, not applying to material which is merely shocking or disgusting.[81] The Act provides a defence for a publication which can be shown to be "for the public good on the ground that it is in the interests of science, literature, art or learning, or of other objects of general concern".[82] Much more stringent controls apply to sexual material which portrays children.[83]

In practice, most recent prosecutions have been directed at hard-core pornography and publications which encourage the use of drugs.[84] Depiction of non-sexual violence may also result in prosecution.[85]

---

[79] Obscene Publications Act 1959, s.l.

[80] *Id.* s.3.

[81] *R. v. Martin Secker & Warburg Ltd* [1954] 2 All ER 683.

[82] Obscene Publications Act 1959, s.4.

[83] Indecency with Children Act 1960 s.1(1); Protection of Children Act 1978.

[84] *Calder v. Powell* [1965] 1 QB 509 at p.515; *R. v. Skirving* [1985] QB 819.

[85] *DPP v. A & B Chewing Gum* [1968] 1 QB 119; *R v. Calder & Boyars Ltd* [1969] 1 QB 151.

There is no ban as such on the trade in goods which portray adults and are merely "indecent". There are, though, prohibitions on the public display of material which may offend the sensibilities of the public.[86] It is a criminal offence to distribute indecent material through the postal system. Prosecutions can be brought against erotic magazines distributed in this way.[87]

Blasphemy is an anachronistic common law criminal offence. It protects the Anglican faith against exposure to "vilification, ridicule, or indecency". The intention of the publisher is irrelevant. The Law Commission and high ranking members of the Anglican Church have recommended the abolition of the offence.[88] Since 1922 only one prosecution has taken place: the publisher and author of a poem which metaphorically attributed homosexual acts to Christ were convicted of this offence.[89]

The opponents of *"Satanic Verses"* also tried to prosecute for blasphemy, but failed because the book did not attack the Anglican faith.[90]

22.   RESTRICTIONS ON ADVERTISING

The Advertising Standards Authority (ASA) is a private body set up by the advertising industry. It monitors a code of practice in order to ensure that advertisements are "legal, decent, honest, and truthful". The effectiveness of this body is based on the fact that newspapers will refuse to carry advertisements which are held to fail the ASA Code of Practice.

Political advertising concerning general party policies is unrestricted. Advertising concerning particular candidates during an election campaign must be authorized by the candidate or his or her agent. It is an offence to issue any other advertisement for the purpose of procuring a candidate's election.[91]

---

[86] *R. v. Stanley* [1965] 1 All ER 1035, at 1038.

[87] Post Office Act 1953, s.11.

[88] Law Commission, Working Paper No 79 p.32.

[89] *Whitehouse v. Lemon* (1978) 67 Cr App R 70.

[90] *R. v. Bow Street Magistrates ex parte Choudhury* [1991] 1 All E.R. 306.

[91] Representation of the People Act 1983, ss.75(1)(b) and 75(5).

Chapter 11

PRESS LAW IN THE UNITED STATES

Nadine Strossen[1]

INTRODUCTION

The United States enjoys one of the freest presses in the world, operating relatively unconstrained by legal or other pressures. As a result, a leading authority concluded, "[J]ournalists in the United States are [justly] celebrated for outspoken reporting and critical commentary about those in power. The American press enjoys a glorious tradition, full of important stories unearthed and told effectively despite repeated efforts to stifle independent, iconoclastic journalism."[2]

This generally high level of press freedom is subject to certain significant limitations, however, as a result of both legal norms and other factors, including economic pressures. Both types of constraints were evident, for example, during the Persian Gulf conflict in 1990-91. The Defense Department imposed stringent restrictions on press access to information about the conflict and its ability to publish that information.[3] Moreover, many media critics maintain that the mainstream press engaged in still more extensive self-censorship about the conflict, thus exposing the United States public to an unduly narrow range of information and views.[4]

Throughout the twentieth century, there has been a steadily decreasing number of daily newspapers and an increasing concentration of ownership of such papers.[5] This reduction in the number of press voices may well lead to a reduction in the diversity of views and perspectives they express. Moreover, newspaper publishers are susceptible to pressure from

---

[1] The author and ARTICLE 19 thank Carl Kaplan, Columbia University law student and ARTICLE 19 summer intern, for his assistance in researching and drafting this chapter. They also thank Kate Martin, Director of the Center for National Security Studies; William Mills, New York Law School (NYLS) Associate Librarian; Catherine Siemann, Assistant to the American Civil Liberties Union President; and NYLS students Caroline Gargione, Susan Henner, Jonathan Reiss, Karen Shelton, and Carl Wistreich.

[2] A Soifer, "Freedom of the Press in the United States", in P Lahav (ed.) *Press Law in Modern Democracies: A Comparative Study* (1985), 97.

[3] *See* J R MacArthur, *Second Front: Censorship and Propaganda in the Gulf War* (1992).

[4] *See* M Linfield, "Hear No Evil, See No Evil, Speak No Evil: The Press and the Persian Gulf War", *Beverly Hills Bar J.* (Sum. 1991), 142.

[5] The number of newspapers has dropped from a high of 2,600 in 1909 to 1,611 in 1990. Only about 37 cities have two or more daily papers under separate ownership. Ellerbee, "Another Dead Paper, Another Voice Gone", *The Houston Chronicle*, Star Edition (5 Jan. 1991), 5.

advertisers and from the public to at times restrain editorial expression in order to promote commercial interests.[6]

1. RELEVANT CONSTITUTIONAL PROVISIONS

Because the United States has a national or "federal" government, as well as 50 states with their own governments, the relevant constitutional provisions are found in both the United States Constitution and the state constitutions.

The most important constitutional provision is in the First Amendment to the United States Constitution: "Congress shall make no law . . . abridging the freedom of speech, or of the press . . . .." In addition, the Fourteenth Amendment to the United States Constitution, which prohibits state governments from denying "due process of law", has been interpreted as "incorporating" the First Amendment, thus obligating state and local governments to respect freedom of speech and of the press.[7] Finally, every state government has its own constitution, each containing a counterpart to the free expression guarantees of the United States Constitution.

The First Amendment is phrased as a negative restraint on government rather than as an affirmative right of individuals. This phrasing reflects a particular perspective of those who drafted and adopted these provisions, which continues to influence their juridical interpretation: namely, a suspicion of government, and a view that a "free market-place of ideas" -- similar to a free economic market-place -- would be most effectively secured by governmental non-interference, rather than by governmental intervention.

1.1 Scope of the First Amendment

In one important respect, the First Amendment has been interpreted more narrowly than its plain language would indicate: while it expressly permits "*no*" law abridging freedom of speech or press, it has not been so strictly interpreted. Still, to justify any restriction on speech, the government bears a heavy burden of proof. It must show that such a restriction is necessary to promote an interest of "compelling" importance, such as national security or personal privacy. At least in principle, expression may generally be restricted only to avert a "clear and present danger" of some great harm that it would directly and immediately cause. Throughout United States history, though, courts have on occasion relaxed this standard in certain contexts, especially when national security concerns have been implicated.

In another significant respect, the First Amendment has been interpreted more expansively than its actual terms. Although the Amendment expressly refers only to statutory law, it has been construed to apply to any governmental action, including measures adopted by executive,

---

[6] *See* H E Goodwin, *Groping for Ethics in Journalism* (2d ed. 1987), 37.

[7] *Gitlow v. New York*, 268 U.S. 652, 666 (1925).

judicial, and administrative officials.[8] While the Amendment thus limits *all* government action, it is important to note that it limits *only* government action; it does not secure press freedom from non-governmental constraints.[9] However, the Supreme Court has ruled that when a private party invokes judicial machinery to pursue a libel action, that constitutes governmental action sufficient to trigger First Amendment protections.[10]

The First Amendment has been construed more broadly than its literal terms in a second important respect: although it expressly refers only to rights of speech and press, it has been interpreted as implicitly guaranteeing the right to *receive* information and ideas, not only the right to impart them.[11]

The most central interpretational debate regarding the First Amendment concerns the scope of the crucial term "speech". On the one hand, that term has been construed more broadly than its literal meaning, as extending to many forms of expressive conduct: for example, carrying signs and marching in a demonstration, burning a United States flag, and wearing certain clothing or insignia. On the other hand, certain words, although literally constituting "speech", are deemed to be either completely outside the First Amendment's protection, or entitled only to a reduced level of protection. Although the historic trend generally has been to expand the range of speech subject to First Amendment protection, "obscenity" is still completely unprotected, and "commercial" speech is less protected than the political speech that is said to be central to the First Amendment's values.

1.2 "Press" vs. "Speech"

Because the First Amendment guarantees not only "freedom of speech" but also "freedom of the press", some have argued that the institutional press is entitled to special constitutional protections. The courts, however, have treated the two clauses as affording one uniform standard of protection, regardless of the speaker's identity.[12] Accordingly, individuals and the press enjoy the same high standard of protection of their free expression rights. Moreover, all publications enjoy the same degree of constitutional protection. As stated by the Court, "The Constitution specifically selected the press, which includes not only newspapers, books and magazines, but also humble leaflets and circulars, to play an important role in the discussion of public affairs."[13]

---

[8] *See, e.g., New York Times Co. v. Sullivan*, 376 U.S. 254 (1964).

[9] *See* L Tribe, *American Constitutional Law* (2d ed. 1988), Ch. 18, 1688 ff.

[10] *See, e.g., New York Times v. Sullivan, supra* note 8.

[11] *See* Tribe, *supra* note 9, Ch. 12, 944-55.

[12] *See, e.g.,* G Gunther, *Constitutional Law* (12th ed. 1991), 1457-58.

[13] *Mills v. Alabama*, 384 U.S. 214, 219 (1966).

2. DISTRIBUTION OF POWERS BETWEEN CENTRAL AND REGIONAL GOVERNMENT

The United States Constitution, as well as treaties and federal statutes (which are of equal status under US law), are the "supreme" law of the land, thus pre-empting any inconsistent state laws. State constitutions and laws, however, are allowed to deviate from the Constitution by providing *more* rights. The United States Constitution, as interpreted by the United States Supreme Court, can put a floor *beneath* individual rights; that is, a level below which no federal or state government official or body may sink. The Supreme Court's interpretation of the Constitution, however, does not impose a ceiling *over* individual rights. State governments, therefore, may recognize more rights than required by the Supreme Court's pronouncements on the Constitution.

Many state constitutional counterparts of the First Amendment contain more expansive language protecting free expression. Moreover, even identical state constitutional language may be interpreted more broadly than the Supreme Court has interpreted the First Amendment.[14]

3. ROLE OF THE COURTS

Because the United States is a common law jurisdiction, the courts have significant power in developing the common law, as well as in interpreting statutes and constitutions. While various courts have limited jurisdictions in terms of the matters they may adjudicate, all courts are bound by the Constitutions of the United States and of the state in which they are located. Therefore, any court must refuse to enforce any law in a manner that is inconsistent with a constitutional provision. All courts have the power to interpret and enforce constitutional commands in cases properly before them; there are no specialized "constitutional courts" to which such issues must be referred.

There is a hierarchy of courts in terms of the binding or precedential effect their constitutional rulings will have on future decisions by other courts. The United States Supreme Court is the final interpreter of the United States Constitution, and the highest court of each state is the ultimate interpreter of that state's constitution. The only way these interpretations can be altered is by either a subsequent decision of the same court or a constitutional amendment.

---

[14] *See City of Mesquite v. Aladdin's Castle, Inc.*, 455 U.S. 283, 293 (1982).

4.   STATUS OF INTERNATIONAL HUMAN RIGHTS TREATIES IN NATIONAL LAW

The United States has taken an isolationist stance toward public international law, including international human rights law. The United States has ratified very few international human rights treaties; it has made substantial reservations to those it has ratified; and it has taken the position that ratified treaties are not "self-executing" (that is, they are not enforceable in United States courts unless Congress passes specific legislation implementing their provisions).

The most significant treaty that the United States has ratified, in terms of its free expression provisions, is the International Covenant on Civil and Political Rights (ICCPR). In ratifying this treaty in 1992, however, the United States entered a declaration that the treaty is not self-executing and also made a reservation to Article 20 (which prohibits war propaganda and hate speech), declaring that the United States would abide by the more speech-protective standards of United States law in this area.

Many United States courts have recognized the principle that customary international norms (that is, those that are widely accepted by the community of nations) can be binding in the United States without United States ratification of any instrument expressly setting them forth.[15] Few courts, however, have been willing to actually implement this principle, because of their expressed concern for preserving both United States national sovereignty and the power of democratically elected government officials, whose decisions could potentially be invalidated if deemed inconsistent with customary international law norms.

United States legal scholars have argued that, at the very least, customary international human rights norms should be used to interpret ambiguous terms in the United States Constitution and statutes.[16] The current Supreme Court, however, has evinced hostility even to this limited domestic role for international law.[17]

5.   STATUTORY FRAMEWORK

The United States has no comprehensive statutory framework governing the press. Particular federal and state statutes, however, affect various aspects of the press's operations.

---

[15] *See* J Paust, "On Human Rights: The Use of Human Rights Precepts in US History and the Right to an Effective Remedy in Domestic Courts", 10 *Mich. J. Int'l L.* 543 (1989).

[16] *See, e.g.,* N Strossen, "Recent US and International Judicial Protection of Individual Rights: A Comparative Legal Process Analysis and Proposed Synthesis", 41 *Hastings L.J.* 805, 824-42 (1990).

[17] *See Stanford v. Kentucky*, 492 U.S. 361, 369 n. 1 (1989) (customary international norms regarding death penalty irrelevant to determining whether it is "cruel and unusual" under the United States Constitution).

6. REGULATION OF OWNERSHIP

While the press is subject to general ownership regulations, such as the antitrust laws and state corporate laws,[18] the First Amendment has been interpreted as sheltering the press from any special regulations directed specifically at the press. As stated above (in Section 1), the Amendment has been viewed as securing the press's right to be free from government constraints, including constraints on ownership, and has not been construed to afford any affirmative rights, such as the right of the public to a diversity of editorial perspectives.

Unlike the print media, the electronic media have been subject to special regulations, including of ownership. The asserted rationale for this distinction is the public ownership and scarcity of the airwaves.[19] The print media are indirectly affected by the ownership restrictions on the electronic media, since these include a prohibition on the "cross-ownership", by a single owner, of TV stations and newspapers in the same city or market.[20]

7. REGISTRATION REQUIREMENTS

The notion of governmental registration of publications is anathema to the First Amendment, which has always been viewed as prohibiting any system of prior restraints on publication.

8. REGULATION OF IMPORT AND EXPORT OF PUBLICATIONS

In 1988, the United States economic embargo laws were amended to make clear that they could not restrict the import or export of informational materials. Restrictions may, however, be imposed on the export of classified information under the espionage laws, and on the export of "technical data" under the Export Administration Act of 1979. In 1985, though, Congress affirmed the right of scientists and scholars to communicate research findings freely.[21]

9. MECHANISMS OF PRESS SELF-REGULATION

Consistent with the First Amendment's guarantee of press autonomy from government regulation, there are no press councils in the United States with governmental authority to adjudicate disputes or enforce standards. Although press self-regulation would not violate the First Amendment, there are no significant self-regulation mechanisms. Industry-wide codes

---

[18] *Associated Press v. US*, 326 U.S. 1 (1945).

[19] *See Red Lion Broadcasting Co. v. F.C.C.*, 395 U.S. 367 (1969).

[20] 47 CFR 73.3555(c) (1991).

[21] 50 U.S.C. App. Sec. 2402(12).

of ethics adopted by national journalists' organizations are essentially unenforceable "statements of ideals and aspirations".[22] Individual news organizations may adopt more detailed codes of conduct, but they too lack the force of law.

There has been a recent trend toward adopting internal monitoring procedures. Many major newspapers have hired "house critics" or "ombudsmen", whose findings are sometimes published. Many major papers also have introduced "Op-Ed pages", containing opinion pieces by non-staff members. Corrections or retractions are now more openly displayed. Most newspapers publish letters to the editor.

External monitoring is also provided through major weekly news magazines, as well as specialized journalism reviews, which comment on news coverage in the daily press.[23]

10. DEFAMATION

10.1 Public Officials and/or Matters of Public Interest

In its landmark 1964 decision, *New York Times Co. v. Sullivan*,[24] the Supreme Court "constitutionalized" the law of defamation, recognizing that defamation actions could unduly inhibit free expression. The Court declared that it was considering the case against "the background of a profound national commitment to the principle that debate on public issues should be uninhibited, robust and wide open".[25] It recognized that some erroneous statements are inevitable in such a free debate and, therefore, that they "must be protected if the freedoms of expression are to have the 'breathing space' that they need to survive".[26] In other words, the legal system must avoid any deterrent or "chilling" effect on speech.

Sullivan held that public officials could not recover damages for defamation regarding their official conduct unless they proved that the defamatory statements were both false and made with what the Court termed "actual malice". The latter is a term of art that has nothing to do with "malice" in the ordinary sense of "ill will". Rather, it consists of "knowledge that [the defamatory statement] was false or . . . reckless disregard of whether it was false or not".[27]

---

[22] Goodwin, *supra* note 6, at 352.

[23] Soifer, *supra* note 2, at 116-17.

[24] 376 U.S. 254 (1964). Sullivan was a public official whose duties included supervising the Montgomery, Alabama Police Department. He alleged that the *Times* had libelled him by printing an advertisement, paid for by a civil right organization, stating that the Montgomery police had intentionally harassed Martin Luther King, Jr and his followers, and that Dr King had been arrested seven times when in fact he had been arrested only four times.

[25] *Id.* at 270.

[26] *Id.* at 271-72.

[27] *Id.* at 279-80.

Sullivan's significant impact in promoting press freedom was recently extolled by Professor Ronald Dworkin. He stated:

> [This] decision freed the American press to play a more confident role in protecting democracy than the press plays anywhere else in the world .... The *Sullivan* rule has made the American press much less cautious in criticizing public officials than journalists tend to be in Britain, for example, where public figures commonly sue newspapers and often win large verdicts against them. It is doubtful whether the Watergate investigation, or similar exposés, would have been possible if the Court had not adopted something like the *Sullivan* rule.[28]

Since *Sullivan*, the Court has developed constitutional standards governing various aspects of defamation, seeking an approach that respects not only First Amendment values, but also the countervailing individual reputational interests that are likewise of constitutional dimension. The Court has recognized that the protection accorded to such interests by defamation actions "reflects . . . our basic concept of the dignity and worth of every human being -- a concept at the root of any decent system of ordered liberty . . .".[29]

Some of the particular rules concerning defamation that the Court has crafted reflect deeply divided opinions and, hence, are believed by commentators to be relatively unstable.[30] The basic *Sullivan* principle, though, remains firmly entrenched: that all defamation standards must avoid any chilling impact on expression regarding matters of public concern.

10.2 Public Figures

The Supreme Court has extended *Sullivan's* "actual malice" *scienter* requirement to cases involving "public figures",[31] which it has defined as either those who "occupy positions of such . . . influence that they are deemed public figures for all purposes", or those who "have thrust themselves to the forefront of particular public controversies in order to influence the resolution of the issues involved" and, thus, are public figures for purposes of those specific controversies.[32] Like public officials, the Court reasoned, public figures invite the comment

---

[28] R Dworkin, "The Coming Battles over Free Speech," *The New York Review of Books* (11 June 1992), 55, 64.

[29] *Gertz v. Robert Welch, Inc.*, 418 U.S. 323, 341 (1974).

[30] *See, e.g.*, Tribe, *supra* note 9, at 344-45.

[31] *Curtis Publishing Co v. Butts* and *Associated Press, Inc. v. Walker*, 388 U.S. 130 (1967).

[32] *Gertz, supra* note 29, 418 U.S. at 345.

to which they are exposed and have access to the media to counteract false statements.[33] The Court has found that a university football coach and a prominent retired army general were public figures,[34] but that a wealthy socialite who held some press conferences during her divorce was not a public figure for purposes of evaluating a story that her divorce was precipitated in part by adultery.[35]

10.3 Civil Actions by Private Persons

In *Gertz v. Robert Welch, Inc.,*[36] the Supreme Court held that private plaintiffs could recover damages for actual injuries caused by defamation (including intangible injuries, such as mental anguish) merely by showing negligence. Although this burden of proof is lower than that borne by public figures, it is still higher than under the common law, which requires no showing of fault. Moreover, where the defamation relates to a matter of public concern, *Gertz* held that even a private plaintiff cannot recover presumed or punitive damages without meeting *Sullivan's* actual malice requirement.[37]

Any defamation plaintiff also has the burden of proving the challenged statement's falsity, at least when it relates to a matter of public concern.[38]

10.4 Criminal Actions

Shortly after its *Sullivan* decision, the Supreme Court ruled that, to pass constitutional muster, a criminal libel statute could apply only to statements that: 1) satisfied *Sullivan's* strict actual malice requirement; *and* 2) were likely to cause an imminent breach of the peace.[39] In fact, long before *Sullivan*, criminal libel laws had lapsed into disuse precisely because they are inconsistent with free expression.[40]

---

[33] *Id.*

[34] *Curtis Publishing* and *Associated Press*, note 31 *supra.*

[35] *Time, Inc. v. Firestone*, 424 U.S. 448 (1976).

[36] *Gertz, supra* note 29, 418 U.S. 323 (1974).

[37] *Id.* at 348-50.

[38] *Philadelphia Newspapers, Inc. v. Hepps*, 475 U.S. 767 (1986).

[39] *Garrison v. Louisiana*, 379 U.S. 64, 70, 74 (1964).

[40] *See* D M Gillmor, *Power, Publicity and the Abuse of Libel Law* (1992), 61-62.

10.5 Actual Impact of Defamation Standards[41]

Sullivan was expected to cause considerable declines both in the number of defamation cases filed and in their success rate. These anticipated decreases, however, have not in fact materialized, as documented by the Libel Defense Resource Center (LDRC), an information clearinghouse organized by media groups to monitor defamation litigation. LDRC has shown that, notwithstanding the strict *scienter* requirements that public persons must meet to prevail in defamation cases, their success rate and damage awards have been comparable to those of defamation plaintiffs generally.[42] Available data indicate that both the loss rates and the damage awards faced by defamation defendants significantly exceed the corresponding figures for United States civil litigation defendants generally.[43]

As burdensome as post-*Sullivan* defamation damage awards have been, they still constitute only a fraction of the total expenses incurred in defending defamation actions, which also include attorneys' fees and costs.[44] In the US civil litigation system, the prevailing party almost never has a right to collect these expenses from the unsuccessful party. In addition, defamation defendants must divert substantial time from their primary, journalistic pursuits. For all of these reasons, media defendants are inevitably economic losers (and, thus, losers in terms of free press concerns), even if they ultimately emerge from the litigation as *legal* victors.

Ironically, the fact that defending against defamation actions by public persons has become so time-consuming, expensive, and intrusive into editorial processes results from the very *scienter* requirement that *Sullivan* crafted in an attempt to minimize the burdens of defending against such actions. Before *Sullivan*, the media had successfully contended that such materials as reporters' notes and drafts were privileged and not subject to discovery. As the Supreme Court ruled in 1979, however, the "actual malice" standard elevates such materials to central relevance.[45] Recent surveys of reporters, editors, and media lawyers have confirmed that the ongoing burdens of defamation litigation have chilled the press's vigour and openness.[46]

---

[41] For a more thorough discussion of the issues addressed in this section, see N Strossen, "A Defence of the Aspirations -- But Not the Achievements -- of the US Rules Limiting Defamation Actions by Public Officials or Public Figures", 15 *Melbourne University Law Review* 419 (1986).

[42] *See* LDRC Bulletin, *Trial Results, Damage Awards and Appeals, 1980-89 and 1990-91: The "Chilling Effect"*, Special Issue B (31 July 1992).

[43] *See* Blum, "Verdict Trends Remain Elusive", *The National Law Journal* (29 Jan. 1990), at S1.

[44] *See* Guzda, "Dealing With Libel Suits", *Editor & Publisher* (11 May 1985), 16.

[45] *Herbert v. Lando*, 441 U.S. 153 (1979).

[46] *See* Massing, "The Libel Chill: How Cold is it Out There?", 1985 *Col. Journ. Rev.* 31.

Although the precise post-*Sullivan* rules currently in effect have not fully achieved the vision of press freedom that inspired this landmark decision, *Sullivan's* ongoing importance should not be overlooked. As Professor Ronald Dworkin has written:

> It does not detract from the achievement [of Justice Brennan, who authored the Court's opinion in *Sullivan*] that the intellectual premises of his argument must now be expanded .... *Sullivan* was a crucial battle in the defense of our first freedom. But now we have new battles to fight.[47]

11. INVASION OF PRIVACY

While the Constitution contains no express guarantee of "privacy" in a comprehensive sense, the Supreme Court consistently has interpreted various specific constitutional provisions, as well as the overall philosophy and history reflected in the Constitution, as giving rise to some such right (although the Justices have disagreed vigorously as to its precise contours).[48] The most often quoted definition of the implied constitutional privacy right was formulated by Justice Louis Brandeis: "the right to be let alone -- the most comprehensive of rights and the right most valued by civilized men".[49] A more recent, unanimous Supreme Court opinion described this right as embracing both an "interest in avoiding disclosure of personal matters" and an "interest in independence in making certain kinds of important decisions".[50]

Consistent with the concept of privacy as an "interest in avoiding disclosure of personal matters," the Supreme Court has acknowledged the government's power to limit the collection or dissemination of information about an individual. The Court has recognized four aspects of this type of privacy: 1) the right not to be put in a "false light" by the publication of true facts; 2) the right not to have one's name or likeness "appropriated" for commercial purposes; 3) the "right of publicity" on the part of a person whose name has a commercial value; and 4) the right to avoid the publicizing of "private details".[51] Nevertheless, measures protecting these privacy interests may not abridge the press's right to convey, and the public's right to receive, information about matters of public concern. While the Court has issued several rulings making particular accommodations between First Amendment rights and competing privacy claims of the foregoing types, it has not provided any bright-line rules for making such accommodations in future cases.

---

[47] Dworkin, *supra* note 28, at 64.

[48] *See* Tribe, *supra* note 9, at Chap. 15, 1302ff.

[49] *Olmstead v. United States*, 277 U.S. 438, 478 (1928) (dissenting opinion), overruled by *Katz v. United States*, 389 U.S. 347 (1967).

[50] *Whalen v. Roe*, 429 U.S. 589, 599-600 (1977).

[51] *See Zacchini v. Scripps-Howard Broadcasting Co.*, 433 U.S. 562, 571-72 & nn. 7&8 (1977).

In "false light" cases, a plaintiff claims to have been placed into the public's view in a misleading manner that would be highly offensive to a reasonable person. The Court held in *Time, Inc. v. Hill*[52] that public officials and public figures must meet *Sullivan's* strict *scienter* requirement of "actual malice" in such cases.[53] In cases centering upon publication of "private details", a plaintiff claims damages for the accurate publication of highly personal facts that are of no legitimate interest to the public. The Court has not addressed the extent to which the First Amendment's protection of debate on matters of public interest limits such claims, nor has it discussed whether truth would be an adequate defence. Certainly, it would be more difficult for public officials and public figures, in contrast with private persons, to establish that a personal fact was of no legitimate public interest.[54]

12. RIGHT OF REPLY AND/OR CORRECTION

Far from guaranteeing an individual who has been criticized in the press a right of reply, to the contrary, the First Amendment bars statutes that purport to grant any such right. The Supreme Court so held in *Miami Herald Publishing Co. v. Tornillo*.[55] The law at issue required a newspaper to print the reply of any political candidate who had been criticized in the newspaper's editorial pages. The law's proponents had argued that, in light of the concentration of newspaper ownership, such a measure was necessary to ensure that a variety of viewpoints reached the public. The Court, though, struck down the law as an unwarranted interference with the publishers' editorial decision-making. Under the First Amendment, it ruled, government may no more *mandate* publication of certain material than it may *prohibit* publication of certain material. The Court further noted that the law might well not serve its intended purpose of increasing the range of published viewpoints; by imposing a penalty for printing certain material, it would likely deter newspapers from printing such material.

The statute struck down in *Tornillo* did not require any showing that the material to which the reply was directed was false or defamatory. Accordingly, as two Justices noted in *Tornillo*, the Supreme Court's ruling "implies no view upon the constitutionality of ... statutes

---

[52] 385 U.S. 374 (1967).

[53] The Supreme Court later ruled in *Gertz, supra* note 29, 418 U.S. 323 (1974), that a plaintiff who is neither a public official nor a public figure need not meet *Sullivan's* strict *scienter* requirement in defamation actions. The Court declined to consider whether its decision reached situations where the story's potential damage was not apparent to the publisher, as might be the case in "false light" actions. The effect of *Gertz* on "false light" cases has not been resolved by subsequent Supreme Court decisions. *Cantrell v. Forest City Publishing Co.*, 419 U.S. 245 (1974), held that the Constitution permits "false light" privacy cases where the publication is inaccurate and causes mental anguish, but it left open the question of whether the plaintiff in such cases must prove knowing or reckless falsehood.

[54] In *Cox Broadcasting Corp. v. Cohn*, 420 U.S. 469 (1975), the Supreme Court ruled that the publication of a juvenile rape victim's name contained in publicly available court records was protected expression. *Accord Florida Star v. B.J.F.*, 491 U.S. 524 (1989). The Court stressed that its decision did not address publication of private facts that are not publicly available. Thus, the states have latitude to permit such suits.

[55] 418 U.S. 241 (1974).

affording plaintiffs able to prove defamatory falsehoods ... [an] action to require publication of a retraction ...".[56]

The remedy of retraction, as a substitute for the damages now available in defamation actions, is supported by many libel law experts.[57] They have advocated a new form of action that would determine only the truth or falsity of any allegedly defamatory statement and, by way of remedy, would assure correction or retraction. This alternative approach should be advantageous from the perspective of both plaintiffs and defendants. Empirical evidence shows that most libel plaintiffs are mainly interested in correcting false statements rather than in money damages.[58] The media would be relieved from the enormous damage awards and the intensive probing into editorial processes that defamation actions now entail. Currently, the publication of a retraction or a reply does not foreclose a libel action for damages, although such steps may be part of pre-judgment settlements and can reduce damage awards.

13.   INSULTS TO GOVERNMENT INSTITUTIONS OR OFFICIALS

Imposing liability upon an individual for insulting the government is anathematic to United States law and, indeed, to the United States concept of a democratic government. In the words of one of the United States's "Founding Fathers", James Madison: "The censorial power is in the people over the government, and not in the government over the people."[59] This rejection of the common law crime of seditious libel motivated the Supreme Court's ruling in *New York Times Co. v. Sullivan*,[60] which was intended to sharply limit defamation actions by public officials.

Likewise, although early in the twentieth century the Court upheld convictions for "subversive advocacy" (that is, advocating ideas that might ultimately undermine United States interests), those cases were definitively rejected in 1969 by *Brandenburg v. Ohio*.[61] Since then, expression may be punished because of its potential for prompting illegal or violent conduct by those who hear it only if it was intended to *and* likely *imminently* to incite such conduct.

---

[56]   *Id.* at 258.

[57]   *See, e.g.*, M Franklin, "Declaratory Judgment Alternative to Current Libel Law", 74 *Calif. L. Rev.* 809 (1986).

[58]   *See* R Bezanson, G Cranberg & J Soloski, *Libel Law and the Press: Myth and Reality* (1987).

[59]   4 Annals of Cong. 934 (1794).

[60]   *Supra* note 24, 376 U.S. 254 (1964).

[61]   395 U.S. 444 (1969).

The rejection of any form of seditious libel also coloured the Supreme Court's two widely-discussed flag-burning decisions, in 1989 and 1990, in which the Court held that the First Amendment protects the right to defile the United States flag to express political protest.[62]

14. OFFICIAL SECRECY AND ACCESS TO GOVERNMENT-HELD INFORMATION

14.1 Constitutional Standards

While the Supreme Court has not held that the First Amendment contains an implicit guarantee of access to government-held information, it has held that the Amendment limits government's power to withhold certain types of information. As Professor Tribe has observed, "[t]hese limits are especially strict when the information is produced or released in a forum (such as a trial) that, by its nature or by express constitutional command, is open to the public...".[63] Conversely, within "restricted governmental environments", such as prisons[64] and battlegrounds,[65] the press has been denied access to information.

The government may impose certain limits on access to and disclosure of information on national security grounds. Because of the US law's particular abhorrence of prior restraints on publication, the Court consistently has invalidated attempts to *bar* publication of material that is said to jeopardize national security. In contrast, it has upheld other types of government measures that *punish* the publication of such material.[66]

14.2 Statutory Standards

Although the Constitution does not guarantee a general right of access to government-held information, many federal and state laws enacted over the past two decades grant such access.

---

[62] *United States v. Eichman*, 496 U.S. 310 (1990); *Texas v. Johnson*, 491 U.S. 397 (1989).

[63] Tribe, note 9 *supra*, at 955.

[64] *See Houchins v. KQED, Inc.*, 438 U.S. 1 (1978); *Saxbe v. Washington Post Co.*, 417 U.S. 843 (1974); *Pell v. Procunier*, 417 U.S. 817 (1974).

[65] *See generally* Cassell, "Restrictions on Press Coverage of Access, Grenada and Off-the-Record Wars", 73 *Georgetown L.J.* 931 (1985).

[66] *See Haig v. Agee*, 453 U.S. 280 (1981) (upholding government's power to revoke passport of a former agent of the Central Intelligence Agency (CIA) on the ground that his disclosures of sensitive information threatened national security); *Snepp v. United States*, 444 U.S. 507 (1980) (holding that former CIA agent breached his employment contract when he failed to submit for pre-publication review a book containing information about the CIA that he had learned through his work, even though the government conceded that it divulged no classified information).

The federal Freedom of Information Act[67] requires disclosure of government information upon request, with certain exceptions, including properly classified information, private information about individuals, and law enforcement information. The federal "Government in the Sunshine Act"[68] also made more government information subject to public disclosure by requiring more public meetings. Although journalists and scholars have received much valuable information under these statutes, they still criticize the statutes' numerous exceptions.[69]

14.3 Standards Regarding Disclosure of Classified Secrets

Government employees are prohibited from disclosing classified information as a condition of their employment and may be dismissed for doing so. A federal statute specifically criminalizes the disclosure by government employees of the names of intelligence agents, when done with reason to believe that such disclosure would impede the United States' foreign intelligence activities.[70] It is not clear whether government employees may constitutionally be prosecuted, under general laws prohibiting espionage or theft of government property, for disclosing other classified information to the press.

Only one statute expressly makes it a crime for the press to publish classified information; the Intelligence Identities Act[71] makes publication of the names of intelligence agents a crime only when there is a pattern of such publication and reason to believe that it would impair United States foreign intelligence activities. Although some statutes criminalizing espionage and theft of government property might be interpreted as extending to the press (they do not do so explicitly), no court has thus interpreted them.

14.4 Whistleblowers[72]

A federal statute protects federal employees who "blow the whistle" on government wrongdoing by disclosing information confidentially to members of Congress and to the Inspector General of the relevant agency. Statutory protection does not extend to public disclosures.[73] However, the Supreme Court has held that the First Amendment protects

---

[67]   5 U.S. Code Sec. 552.

[68] This act is codified in scattered sections of titles 5 and 39 of the U.S. Code.

[69]   *See* Soifer, *supra* note 2, at 105-07.

[70]   Intelligence Identities Act, 50 U.S. C. sec. 421.

[71]   50 U.S.C. Sec. 421.

[72] *See also* Section 17.1 *infra.*

[73]   5 U.S.C. Sec. 2302.

government employees' speech about matters of public concern[74] in circumstances where the free speech interests outweigh the government's interest in promoting an efficient workforce.[75]

15. ACCESS TO AND DISCLOSURE OF COURT DOCUMENTS AND PROCEEDINGS

15.1 Access to Court Proceedings

The press has access to judicial proceedings that are open to the public. Those proceedings from which the public may be excluded may also be closed to the press. Even when certain proceedings are generally open, the press and public may still be excluded from them when necessary to promote a countervailing compelling purpose. For example, the Supreme Court has held that the press and the public have a right to attend criminal trials unless, in a particular situation, there is a compelling interest that could be served only through limiting such attendance.[76] Such a compelling interest could include protecting certain crime victims from further trauma and encouraging witnesses to come forward and testify truthfully.[77] Although the Court has not expressly addressed the issue, it probably would find that the press and public have the same presumptive right to attend civil trials as they have to attend criminal trials.[78]

15.2 Contempt of Court Concerning Trial-Related Information

Contempt citations issued in response to a particular statement violate the First Amendment unless the punished statement was an "imminent threat to the administration of justice".[79] Under this strict test, virtually nothing said outside the courtroom is constitutionally punishable as contempt.[80]

---

[74] *See Connick v. Myers*, 461 U.S. 138 (1983).

[75] *See Pickering v. Board of Education*, 391 U.S. 563 (1968).

[76] *Richmond Newspapers, Inc. v. Virginia*, 448 U.S. 555 (1980).

[77] *See Globe Newspapers Co. v. Superior Court*, 457 U.S. 596 (1982) (invalidating state law requiring judges to exclude press and public from courtroom during testimony of *all* victims of certain sex crimes, but leaving open possibility that court could constitutionally issue exclusion orders in particular cases).

[78] *See Richmond Newspapers*, 448 U.S. at 579 n. 15.

[79] *Eaton v. City of Tulsa*, 415 U.S. 697, 698 (1974).

[80] *See Bridges v. California*, 314 U.S. 252 (1941) (overturning contempt citation based on union leader's public release of telegram he had sent Secretary of Labor predicting massive strike if state court issued certain ruling in labor dispute); R McCloskey, *The Modern Supreme Court* (1972), 15 (if this threat to cripple economy of entire West Coast did not present clear and present danger, then almost nothing would meet this standard).

When a court issues an order prohibiting in advance certain statements regarding a judicial proceeding, enforceable through contempt citations, the United States law's general aversion to prior restraints comes into play. Therefore, such judicial "gag orders" are even more vulnerable to First Amendment challenge than are after-the-statement contempt citations.

In *Nebraska Press Association v. Stuart*,[81] the Supreme Court unanimously invalidated a court order prohibiting the press from publishing confessions by a murder defendant, as well as other facts "strongly implicative" of him. The order had been designed to avoid interference with the defendant's constitutional right to a fair trial. The Court ruled, however, that before the government could suppress press commentary on evidentiary matters, it must first show that no other procedures could assure the empanelling of a jury that would base a verdict solely on the evidence presented in court. Because the Court has consistently found that alternative procedures (including extensive questioning of jurors regarding their awareness of the potentially prejudicial information and jury sequestration) have guaranteed a fair trial despite prejudicial publicity, the *Nebraska Press* ruling has been described as "a virtual bar to prior restraints on reporting of news about crime".[82]

One alternative to prohibitions on the press, for purposes of assuring a fair trial, is the imposition of restraining orders on the parties and their attorneys to limit their comments about the case. Such "silence orders" against attorneys will more readily withstand First Amendment scrutiny than "gag orders" against the press, because journalists (in contrast with attorneys for the litigants) are independent of the proceedings. Orders silencing attorneys will be upheld if they avert "a substantial likelihood of material prejudice to a fair trial".[83]

16. ACCESS TO AND DISCLOSURE OF LEGISLATIVE DOCUMENTS AND PROCEEDINGS

Congress has an implied contempt power that "rests upon the right of self-preservation, that is, the right to prevent acts which ... inherently obstruct ... the discharge of legislative duty ...".[84] Congress apparently has used this power only to punish the refusal to provide evidence it has demanded.[85] It has not used this power to punish the disclosure of confidential information.

---

[81]   427 U.S. 539 (1976).

[82]   Tribe, *supra* note 9, at 858-59.

[83]   *Gentile v. State Bar of Nevada*, 111 S. Ct. 2720 (1991).

[84]   *Marshall v. Gordon*, 243 U.S. 521, 542 (1917).

[85]   *See* J Hamilton, *The Power to Probe: A Study of Congressional Investigations* (New York: Random House, 1976).

Congress's reluctance to use its contempt power in a manner that would chill press freedom is illustrated by the unsuccessful effort, in 1991, to compel two reporters to divulge how they learned of Anita Hill's confidential allegations to the Senate Judiciary Committee that then-Supreme Court nominee Clarence Thomas had sexually harassed her. Precisely because of the potential chilling effect on the media, the Chairman of the Senate Rules Committee rejected the request of the Senate's independent counsel to force the journalists to disclose information about these leaks.[86]

17.   COMMERCIAL SECRECY AND ACCESS TO INFORMATION HELD BY PRIVATE PARTIES

In terms of protecting employee speech from employer regulation, the First Amendment assists only public employees. Nonetheless, there is not necessarily a sharp distinction between the rights of public and private employees to disclose information of public concern that was obtained through their employment because statutes and judicial decisions afford some protection to private employees who disclose work-related information of public concern.

17.1   Whistleblowers[87]

Three major federal statutes protect certain private employees who "blow the whistle" on their employers' wrongdoing.[88] In addition, most states have statutes protecting some whistleblowers employed by the government, the private sector, or both. Also, despite the common law doctrine that employers may terminate employees "at will", a majority of state courts have created a public policy exception to this doctrine, to protect certain whistleblowers from retaliation.[89]

The press may not be penalized for publishing confidential information about a company, so long as it did not act unlawfully in obtaining the information.

17.2   Environmental Information

Many federal environmental statutes require companies to file with the government information about chemical discharges into the air and water. These filings are then generally available to the press under the Freedom of Information Act. In addition, states are beginning

---

[86]   S Gerstel, "Special Counsel Refused Permission to Go After Reporters in Leak Inquiry", United Press International (March 25, 1992).

[87]   *See also* Section 14.4 *supra*.

[88]   The Energy Reorganization Act, 41 U.S.C. Secs. 5801-91; The Mine Safety and Health Act, 30 U.S.C. Sec. 815*ff.* The Occupational Safety and Health Act, 19 U.S.C. sec. 657*ff.*

[89]   *See, e.g., Sabine Pilot Service v. Hauck,* 687 S.W.2d 733 (Tex. 1985).

to pass "right to know" laws which provide broader public access to information about the manufacture and storage of hazardous substances, including the amount and composition of such substances at particular locations.

18.   PRIOR RESTRAINTS

Prior restraint is especially antithetical to First Amendment values. Given the absence of any registration or licensing requirements, prior restraint in the United States generally takes the form of a court injunction. Such an injunction is subject to a strong presumption of unconstitutionality, which may be overcome only upon showing the following three circumstances: 1) that the publication would pose a clear threat of immediate and irreparable damage to a "near sacred" right;[90] 2) that the prior restraint would be effective; and 3) that no other measures, less restrictive of free expression, would be effective.[91]

The First Amendment's virtually absolute prohibition of prior restraints was first enunciated in *Near v. Minnesota*,[92] which invalidated a state statute permitting the enjoining of any "malicious, scandalous and defamatory ... periodical". The Court has indicated that exceptions to *Near*'s ban on prior restraints should be tolerated only in extraordinary circumstances and only concerning an exceedingly narrow range of publications: "when a nation is at war", information that amounts to "actual obstruction to its recruiting service or the publication of the sailing dates of transports or the number and location of troops"[93]; "incitements to acts of violence and the overthrow by force of orderly government"[94]; and statements that pose a clear and imminent threat to a defendant's fair trial rights where those rights cannot be safeguarded by less onerous means.[95]

The most important case invalidating a pre-publication restraint that was sought on national security grounds is the *"Pentagon Papers case"*.[96] The Court refused to enjoin two major newspapers (*The New York Times* and *The Washington Post*) from publishing a classified study on United States policy-making in connection with the Vietnam War, which they had obtained through an unauthorized leak from a former government employee. The war was ongoing and the United States argued that the publication would prolong it. Although a

---

[90] *Matter of Providence Journal Co.*, 820 F.2d 1342, 1351 (1st Cir. 1986).

[91] *Nebraska Press Association v. Stuart*, 427 U.S. 539, 565-66 (1976).

[92]   283 U.S. 697 (1931).

[93] *Id.* at 716.

[94] *Id.*

[95] *See Nebraska Press, supra* note 91; *Cable News Network v. Noriega and United States*, 111 S.Ct. 451 (1990).

[96] *New York Times Co. v. United States*, 403 U.S. 713 (1971).

majority of the Justices believed that the publication might well undermine national security interests, they concluded that the government had not carried its heavy burden of proving that such harm would *certainly* occur. In contrast with its bar on prior restraint, the Court did not bar the government from prosecuting either the newspapers that published the Pentagon Papers or their source; the government did prosecute the source, but its case was dismissed because of prosecutorial misconduct.[97]

Only one United States court has ever upheld a prior restraint on publication on a national security rationale. In *United States v. Progressive, Inc.*,[98] a federal trial court stopped a magazine from publishing an article that described how the H-bomb was built. The information in the article was not classified. The trial judge acknowledged that issuing an injunction in this case constituted a radical departure from nearly two centuries of United States law, but nevertheless did so because of the unique dangers associated with nuclear proliferation. No appellate court had the opportunity to review this much-criticized ruling[99] because, before the appeal was heard, the information in the article was published elsewhere, thus making the case moot.

19.   PROTECTION OF SOURCES

19.1   Constitutional Standards

Branzburg v. Hayes[100] is the Supreme Court's only ruling which addresses the claim that the First Amendment encompasses a journalist's qualified privilege to refuse to divulge the names of confidential sources to government investigators, in order to maintain the free flow of information to journalists.[101] The Court addressed only a narrow aspect of the asserted privilege. Specifically, it held that journalists could be compelled to appear and testify before grand juries investigating criminal cases. It did not decide the scope of a reporter's privilege, if any, regarding testimony in administrative hearings, legislative hearings, and civil suits.

Branzburg cited several reasons for rejecting the asserted privilege in the grand jury context: that the press had not shown that the privilege was necessary to maintain its information-gathering processes; that the public interest in the investigation and prosecution of crimes

---

[97]   *See* J E Nowak, R D Rotunda, *Constitutional Law* (4th ed. 1991), Sec. 16.17, at 977.

[98]   467 F. Supp. 990 (W.D. Wis. 1979).

[99]   *See, e.g.*, L Powe, "The H-Bomb Injunction", 61 *U. Colo. L. Rev.* 55 (1990); E Knoll, "National Security: The Ultimate Threat to the First Amendment", 66 *Minn. L. Rev.* 161 (1981).

[100]   408 U.S. 665 (1972).

[101]   For another Court decision concerning journalists' promises of confidentiality, see *Cohen v. Cowles Media Co.*, 111 S.Ct. 2513, 115 L.Ed.2d 586 (1991) (First Amendment does not bar states from enforcing reporter's promise to protect source's confidentiality through breach of promise action against newspaper that identifies source despite promise).

outweighs the interest in the availability of sources for providing additional information in the future; and that making case-by-case determinations of whether the privilege had been overcome would be very difficult.

It is possible that, when information is sought for purposes other than criminal investigations, the Court would hold that the public interest in obtaining the information is sufficiently reduced to warrant the recognition of a constitutional privilege. Lower federal courts have so held.[102]

While *Branzburg* required reporters to testify before grand jury proceedings that were conducted in good faith, it did recognize that the First Amendment forbids grand juries from harassing the press through grand jury subpoenas issued in bad faith.[103] For any additional protections, the Court invited Congress and state legislatures to pass whatever statutes they might deem prudent.

19.2   Statutory Standards: "Shield Laws"

Although no federal law yet provides a statutory journalists' privilege, United States Department of Justice guidelines recognize a qualified privilege as a matter of prosecutorial policy.[104] Moreover, more than half the states have enacted "shield laws",[105] providing journalists with an absolute or qualified privilege not to disclose information they received in confidence. The courts of additional states have found such a privilege in the common law or in their respective state constitutions. These state law privileges vary in the degree of protection provided, depending both on the relevant statutory language and the judicial interpretations.[106]

The incarceration of journalists for refusing to disclose information is viewed as "un-American". Courts rarely compel disclosure,[107] and even more rarely enforce disclosure

---

[102]   *See, e.g., Democratic Nat'l Committee v. McCord,* 356 F. Supp. 1394 (D.D.C. 1973) (party seeking discovery was required to show that information requested was central to its claim and that alternative sources had been exhausted).

[103]   408 U.S. at 707.

[104]   28 C.F.R. Sec. 50.10 (1986). *See United States v. Blanton,* 534 F. Supp. 295, 297 (S.D. Fla. 1982) (holding guidelines to be binding on Justice Department).

[105]   *See* R Eclavea, "Privilege of Newsgatherer Against Disclosure of Confidential Sources of Information", 99 A.L.R. 3d 37 (1980).

[106]   *See* P Marcus, "The Reporter's Privilege: An Analysis of the Common Law, Branzburg v. Hayes, and Recent Statutory Developments", 25 *Ariz. L. Rev.* 815 (1984).

[107]   Cases in which reporters are ordered to produce information are reported in *Media Law Reporter* and *News Media and the Law.*

orders through imprisonment.[108] Accordingly, United States journalists do not readily reveal information sought by either prosecutors or civil litigants.[109]

20. RESTRICTIONS ON OFFENSIVE LANGUAGE AGAINST IDENTIFIABLE GROUPS

The Supreme Court has long interpreted the First Amendment as protecting "hate speech" except in very narrow circumstances,[110] not applicable to newspaper publications.[111] In June 1992, the Court unanimously reaffirmed that even vicious racist expression may not be singled out for punishment merely because the community is offended by its message.[112]

In contrast to the absence of governmental controls on offensive speech, many journalists and editors voluntarily pursue practices designed to avoid offending racial and other minority groups, and to counter stereotypes about them. These practices include using appropriately respectful language, hiring staff members from diverse groups, issuing apologies for offensive language or stereotypes, and including columns specifically addressed to certain groups. Such practices reflect the widespread debate in the United States about the press' role regarding prejudice.[113]

---

[108] *See* T Jacobs, "The Chilling Effect in Press Cases: Judicial Thumb on the Scales", 15 *Harv. C.R.-C.L. L. Rev.* 684, 703 (1988).

[109] *See* T Moran, "The Unloved, Over-Privileged Press", *The Legal Times* (6 May 1991), 23.

[110] For a more extensive discussion, *see* N Strossen, "Balancing the Rights to Freedom of Expression and Equality: A Civil Liberties Approach to Hate Speech on Campus", in S Coliver (ed.), *Striking a Balance: Hate Speech, Freedom of Expression and Non-Discrimination* (London: ARTICLE 19, 1992), 295-312.

[111] *See Cohen v. California*, 403 U.S. 15, 21 (1971) (government may prohibit speech to protect hearers' sensibilities only when "substantial privacy interests are being invaded in an essentially intolerable manner"); *Brandenburg v. Ohio*, 395 U.S. 444, 447 (1969)(government may prohibit speech to avert violent or unlawful conduct by those who hear it only when the speaker intends to, and is likely to, cause *imminent incitement* of such conduct).

[112] *See R.A.V. v. City of St. Paul*, 112 S.Ct. 2538 (1992) (burning a cross on black family's property in middle of night, while punishable under other laws, could not be punished under law banning "fighting words" that arouse anger on basis of race, color, creed, religion, or gender).

[113] *See, e.g.,* M Gartner, "Political Correctness and News Don't Mix", *USA Today* (11 March 1992), 11A; N Strossen, "Thoughts on the Controversy Over Politically Correct Speech", 46 *SMU Law Review* 119-44 (1992).

21. BLASPHEMY, OBSCENITY AND PROTECTION OF PUBLIC MORALS

The concept of blasphemy is antithetical to the First Amendment, which prohibits punishing any expression merely because of community disagreement with, or offence at, the idea it conveys.[114] Similarly, no expression in the press may be proscribed merely because it is deemed offensive to prevailing views of morality.[115] Rather, any expression alleged to undermine public morals may be restricted only if it constitutes a "clear and present danger" of causing some tangible harm. It is hard to imagine any publication that would satisfy this exacting standard.

"Obscenity" is a narrow subset of sexually explicit expression that the Supreme Court has ruled to be wholly unprotected by the First Amendment. An "obscene" work must (1) "appeal[ ] to the prurient interest" in sex, (2) describe sexual conduct "in a patently offensive way", and, (3) "taken as a whole, lack[ ] serious literary, artistic, political, or scientific value".[116] The first two criteria are judged from the perspective of "the average person applying contemporary community standards".[117] However, the third criterion, concerning the work's value, is judged from the perspective of a "reasonable person", and thus does not turn on the degree of local acceptance the work has won.[118] Although publications containing only words and no pictures may in theory be obscene,[119] in fact, it is extremely hard to show that predominantly verbal works meet the foregoing three-part test. Accordingly, newspapers are not prosecuted under obscenity statutes.

The Court has permitted certain additional restrictions on sexually explicit material, beyond the subset of such material considered "obscenity". These limitations are designed to advance the "compelling interest" in protecting children from sexual exploitation. Accordingly, a state may prevent non-obscene sexually explicit material from being distributed to children,[120]

---

[114] *See* L W Levy, *Treason Against God* (1981), 307, 333, 338.

[115] *See generally Kingsley International Pictures Corp. v. Regents*, 360 U.S. 684 (1959) (state may not deny license to film on ground that it presents "acts of sexual immorality ... as desirable"); *Joseph Burstyn, Inc. v. Wilson*, 343 U.S. 495 (1952) (state may not ban motion pictures on ground that they are "sacrilegious").

[116] *Miller v. California*, 413 U.S. 15, 24 (1973).

[117] *Id.* at 24.

[118] *Pope v. Illinois*, 481 U.S. 497, 501 n.3 (1987).

[119] *Kaplan v. California*, 413 U.S. 115 (1973).

[120] *Ginsberg v. New York*, 390 U.S. 629 (1968).

and it may also prohibit any distribution[121] or possession[122] of non-obscene material that depicts children engaging in sexual conduct.

22.   RESTRICTIONS ON ADVERTISING

Consistent with the First Amendment's special protection of speech concerning public affairs, regulations of political advertising are presumptively unconstitutional, and could be upheld only if shown to be necessary to promote some compelling public interest. As always, this stringent standard is difficult to satisfy.[123]

While the Supreme Court has strongly protected political speech by commercial entities, such as corporations,[124] it has accorded only weaker protection to "commercial speech", which it has defined as speech that advertises a product or service for profit or for another business purpose. While commercial speech currently receives less protection than political speech, it still receives far more protection under modern Supreme Court jurisprudence than it did until the early 1970s, when it was deemed wholly beyond the First Amendment pale.[125] First Amendment analysis of commercial speech regulations now entails two steps. First, the court must determine whether the expression is truthful, non-misleading, and concerns a lawful commercial activity. If not, it may be freely regulated; if so, it may be regulated only if the regulation directly advances a substantial government interest without unnecessarily restricting speech.[126]

The Court's modern commercial advertising cases reflect the view that the consuming public has a protected interest in the free flow of accurate information concerning lawful activity. Consequently, the advertising of potentially harmful but nonetheless legal products, such as alcohol and tobacco, is as protected as that of any other lawful product. While the states have broad constitutional authority to regulate the liquor industry, including its advertising,[127] there are currently no federal restrictions on advertisements of alcohol in the print media. The

---

[121]   *New York v. Ferber*, 485 U.S. 747 (1982).

[122]   *Osborne v. Ohio*, 495 U.S. 103 (1990).

[123]   *See, e.g., Brown v. Hartlage*, 456 U.S. 45 (1982) (invalidating state's corrupt practices act as applied to candidate who promised voters that if elected he would lower his salary, when that salary was fixed by law).

[124]   *See, e.g., First National Bank v. Bellotti*, 435 U.S. 765 (1978).

[125]   *See Valentine v. Chrestensen*, 316 U.S. 52 (1942).

[126]   *See Central Hudson Gas & Electric Corp. v. Public Service Comm'n*, 447 U.S. 557 (1980).

[127]   *See* U.S. Constitution, Am. XXI.

only federal restriction on tobacco advertisements is a requirement that they bear a health warning prescribed by the United States Surgeon General.[128]

CONCLUSION

As a leading authority recently concluded: "The American press undoubtedly performs an influential role and sometimes serves as a check on government."[129] The vigour with which it pursues these functions ebbs and flows, however, depending upon public attitudes and the political climate, which the press both faces and helps to create. Commercial considerations inevitably play their part, too, for it remains an open question how fearless, enterprising and responsible an increasingly concentrated press buffeted by advertising losses can afford to be. Nevertheless, overall, the American press is "unusually, perhaps uniquely, forceful and untrammelled".[130]

---

[128]   15 U.S.C. Sec. 1333.

[129]   Soifer, *supra* note 2, at 97.

[130]   *Id*. at 117.

Chapter 12

PRESS FREEDOM UNDER THE EUROPEAN CONVENTION ON HUMAN RIGHTS

Sandra Coliver

INTRODUCTION

The Council of Europe has developed a considerable body of law, jurisprudence and standards regarding press freedom and access to information. The primary statement of law is set forth in Article 10 of the European Convention on Human Rights (ECHR). The impact of Article 10 on press freedom and related rights has been authoritatively construed by the European Court of Human Rights ("the Court") in a dozen or so decisions, and has been further elaborated by non-binding reports of the European Commission of Human Rights ("the Commission"). The Commission decides the admissibility of applications, reports on the facts, and offers its opinion as to the relevant law. Additional guidance, particularly concerning press pluralism and access to information, is provided by recommendations of the Committee of Ministers and the Parliamentary Assembly.[1]

Article 10 also has implications for the law of the European Community (EC). The institutions of the EC have declared that they are bound to consider the ECHR in the exercise of their powers,[2] and the European Court of Justice has consistently held that fundamental human rights, especially as set forth in the ECHR, are "enshrined in the general principles of Community law".[3]

The judgments of the European Court of Human Rights are legally binding only on the countries which are party to the ECHR (currently numbering 25).[4] Nonetheless, the ECHR

---

[1] The Committee of Ministers, the political and executive arm of the Council of Europe, is composed of one representative, usually the Minister for Foreign Affairs, of each of the member states. The Parliamentary Assembly, which submits recommendations to the Committee of Ministers, is composed of representatives appointed or elected by the parliaments of the member states.

[2] *See* the Preamble to the Single European Act (OJ 1987, L 1); and Article F of Title I of the Maastricht Treaty on European Union [1992] 1 CMLR 719.

[3] *See*, *e.g.*, *SPUC v. Grogan and Others*, Case C-159/90 [1991] 3 CMLR 849, in particular the opinion of Advocate General Van Gerven at paras. 30-31.

[4] As of 15 Jan. 1993 the 25 parties to the ECHR were: Austria, Belgium, Bulgaria, Cyprus, Denmark, Finland, France, Germany, Greece, Hungary, Iceland, Ireland, Italy, Liechtenstein, Luxembourg, Malta, Netherlands, Norway, San Marino, Spain, Sweden, Portugal, Switzerland, Turkey and the United Kingdom. Poland is the only member of the Council of Europe which is not a party to the ECHR. Until its dissolution on 31 Dec. 1992, the Czech and Slovak Federal Republic was a member of the Council of Europe as well as a party to the ECHR, but the Council decided that the newly-formed Czech and Slovak republics, which currently have observer status, must apply for membership and may not automatically assume the CSFR's seat and treaty obligations.

has considerable influence outside Europe in that its provisions are consulted in construing similar provisions of the International Covenant on Civil and Political Rights (ICCPR);[5] the American Convention on Human Rights;[6] and national constitutions and laws.[7]

This chapter discusses the obligations relevant to press freedom imposed by the ECHR. It also notes the obligations set forth in Article 19 of the ICCPR, which are generally deemed to be similar to, though not as extensively or authoritatively interpreted as, those mandated by Article 10 of the ECHR. The chapter begins with a summary of general principles relevant to the interpretation of the ECHR, and then proceeds with an examination of various aspects of press freedom following the analytical framework of the country chapters.

1. GENERAL PRINCIPLES

Paragraph 1 of Article 10 states that "Everyone has the right to freedom of expression. This right shall include freedom to hold opinions and to receive and impart information and ideas without interference by public authority and regardless of frontiers." But, pursuant to paragraph 2, the exercise of those freedoms "may be subject to such formalities, conditions, restrictions or penalties as are prescribed by law and are necessary in a democratic society" in order to protect various public and private interests.[8]

The Court has stressed that, in evaluating a particular restriction, it is faced "not with a choice between two conflicting principles but with a principle of freedom of expression that is subject to a number of exceptions which must be narrowly interpreted".[9] The respondent State must establish that any restriction: (1) is "prescribed by law", (2) has a legitimate aim (namely, one of those enumerated in paragraph 2), and (3) is "necessary in a democratic society" to promote that aim.[10]

---

[5] *See* D McGoldrick, *The Human Rights Committee* (Oxford: Clarendon Press, 1991).

[6] *Stephen Schmidt* case, Inter-American Court of Human Rights, Advisory Opinion OC-5/85 of 13 Nov. 1985.

[7] *E.g., DPP v. Mootoocarpen*, Supreme Court of Mauritius, Judgment of 21 Dec. 1988, in (1989) Law Reports of the Commonwealth (Const.), 768, citing *The Sunday Times* case, *infra* note 9. *See* A Lester, "Freedom of Expression" in R Macdonald, F Matcher and H Petzold (eds), *The European System for the Protection of Human Rights* (The Hague, 1993).

[8] *See* Appendix B for the full text of Art. 10.

[9] *The Sunday Times v. the UK*, Judgment of 26 April 1979, Series A no. 30, para 65.

[10] *The Observer and Guardian v. the UK* (*Spycatcher* case), Judgment of 26 Nov. 1991, Series A no. 216, para. 59(a); *The Sunday Times (II)*, Judgment of 26 Nov. 1991, Series A no. 217 (companion *Spycatcher* case).

To be "prescribed by law" a restriction must be "adequately accessible" and foreseeable, that is, "formulated with sufficient precision to enable the citizen to regulate his conduct".[11] The restriction however, does not have to be codified; it is sufficient if it is part of the common law.

In order to have a legitimate aim, a restriction must be in furtherance of, and genuinely aimed at protecting, one of the permissible grounds set forth in Article 10(2).

To be "necessary" a restriction does not have to be "indispensable" but it must be more than merely "reasonable" or "desirable". A "pressing social need" must be demonstrated, the restriction must be proportionate to the legitimate aim pursued, and the reasons given to justify the restriction must be relevant and sufficient.[12] To assess whether an interference is justified by "sufficient" reasons, the Court must consider any public interest aspect of the case.[13] Where the information subject to restriction involves a matter of "undisputed public concern", the information may be restricted only if it appeared "absolutely certain" that its dissemination would have the adverse consequences legitimately feared by the State.[14]

The breadth of a restriction is also relevant. An absolute restriction, for instance a prohibition on disclosure of all information concerning all pending cases, is unacceptable; a court may approve an interference with freedom of expression only once it is "satisfied that the interference was necessary having regard to the facts and circumstances prevailing in the specific case before it."[15] The practice of other contracting states is another factor to consider in assessing a restriction's necessity.[16]

The contracting states have a certain margin of appreciation in determining the necessity of a restriction, but this margin "goes hand in hand with a European supervision".[17] This supervision must be strict and is not limited to ascertaining whether the state has exercised its discretion reasonably, carefully and in good faith; rather, the necessity for any restriction "must be convincingly established".[18] The scope of the margin of appreciation varies

---

[11] *Sunday Times* case, *supra* note 9 at para 49.

[12] *Handyside v. the UK*, Judgment of 7 Dec. 1976, Series A no. 24, paras. 48-50; *Sunday Times, id.* at para. 62.

[13] *Sunday Times* case, *supra* note 9 at para. 63.

[14] *Id.* at paras. 65-66.

[15] *Spycatcher* case, *supra* note 10 at para. 65. *See also Open Door Counselling, Well Woman Centre and Others v. Ireland*, Judgment of 29 Oct. 1992, Series A no. 246.

[16] *E.g., Marckx v. Belgium*, Judgment of 13 June 1979, Series A no. 32; *Dudgeon v. UK*, Judgment of 22 Oct. 1981, Series A no. 45.

[17] *Sunday Times* case, *supra* note 9 at para. 59.

[18] *Spycatcher* case, *supra* note 10 at para. 59(c).

according to the aim at issue. For example, protection of morals is accorded a wide margin because national authorities are considered to be in a better position than the Convention organs to assess the need for the interference.[19] An aim which is more objective in nature, such as maintaining the authority of the judiciary, is accorded a narrower margin of appreciation.[20]

2. SPECIAL ROLE OF THE PRESS IN A DEMOCRATIC SOCIETY

The European Court has consistently emphasized "the pre-eminent role of the press in a State governed by the rule of law".[21] Enhanced privileges (as well as special duties) for the press are necessary in order to enable the press to perform its dual role of "purveyor of information and 'public watchdog'."[22] While the press must not overstep the bounds set forth in Article 10(2) of the ECHR, it is "incumbent" on the press "to impart information and ideas on matters of public interest".[23] "Not only does the press have the task of imparting such information and ideas: the public also has a right to receive them."[24] In emphasizing that the press' role includes the communication of ideas and opinions, the Court has expressly rejected the contention that "the task of the press [is] to impart information, the interpretation of which ha[s] to be left primarily to the reader".[25]

Information or ideas concerning matters of public interest,[26] or communicated in the context of a political debate or about a politician are to be afforded special protection.[27] In the words of the Court:

---

[19] *See, e.g, Müller v. Switzerland*, Judgment of 24 May 1988, Series A no. 133, paras 33-35.

[20] *Handyside* case, *supra* note 12 at para. 48; *Sunday Times* case, *supra* note 9 at paras. 79-81.

[21] *See, e.g., Castells v. Spain*, Judgment of 23 April 1992, Series A no. 236 at para. 43; *Thorgeirson v. Iceland*, Judgment of 25 June 1992, Series A no 239, para. 63.

[22] *Lingens v. Austria*, Judgment of 8 July 1986, Series A no. 103, para. 42; *Spycatcher* case, *supra* note 10 at para. 59.

[23] *Sunday Times* case, *supra* note 9 at para. 65; *Spycatcher* case, *supra* note 10 at para. 59(b).

[24] *Id.*

[25] *Lingens* case, *supra* note 22 at para. 45.

[26] *Sunday Times* case, *supra* note 9 at para. 65 (information about the health risks of legal drugs); *Barfod v. Denmark*, Judgment of 22 Feb. 1989, Series A no. 149 (opinion concerning a court's lack of impartiality).

[27] *Lingens* case, *supra* note 22 at para. 42; *Oberschlick v. Austria*, Judgment of 23 May 1991, Series A no. 204, paras. 57-61.

Freedom of the press affords the public one of the best means of discovering and forming an opinion of the ideas and attitudes of their political leaders. In particular, it gives politicians the opportunity to reflect and comment on the preoccupations of public opinion; it thus enables everyone to participate in the free political debate which is at the very core of the concept of a democratic society.[28]

Penalties against the press for publishing information and opinions concerning matters of public interest are intolerable except in the narrowest of circumstances because of their likelihood to "deter journalists from contributing to public discussion of issues affecting the life of the community".[29]

In five of the six cases in which the applicant was a journalist or a newspaper, the Court stressed the special role of the press in ruling a restriction on press freedom to be incompatible with Article 10 of the ECHR.[30] Moreover, the Court also stressed the press' important role in several cases in which the applicant, though not a member of the press, had published an article in the press. For instance, in the *Barthold* case, the Court expressly criticized measures which restrict people from communicating information to the press on the ground that they are liable to hamper the press in the performance of its special task.[31]

The Court has frequently reaffirmed the principle, first stated in the *Handyside* case, that Article 10 protects publication of information and ideas which are offensive or shocking as well as information which is not controversial:

> Freedom of expression, as secured in paragraph 1 of Article 10 constitutes one of the essential foundations of a democratic society and one of the basic conditions for its progress ... . Subject to paragraph 2, it is applicable not only to 'information' or 'ideas' that are favourably received or regarded as inoffensive or as a matter of indifference, but also to those that offend, shock or disturb. Such are the demands of pluralism, tolerance and broadmindedness without which there is no 'democratic society'.[32]

---

[28] *Castells* case, *supra* note 21 at para. 43.

[29] *Lingens* case, *supra* note 22 at para. 44.

[30] The five press cases in which the Court ruled a restriction incompatible with Article 10 are *Lingens*, *Oberschlick*, *Spycatcher*, *Sunday Times*, and *Thorgeirson* (*infra* note 60). The one press case in which the Court upheld a restriction is *Markt Intern*, (*infra* note 35), which involved commercial speech.

[31] *Barthold v. FRG*, Judgment of 25 March 1985, Series A no. 90, para. 58. *See also Castells* case, *supra* note 21 at para. 43.

[32] *Handyside* case, *supra* note 12 at para. 49; *Lingens* case, *supra* note 22 at para. 41.

Not only matters of burning public interest are entitled to protection; also deserving are mundane pieces of information such as radio and television programme schedules[33]; artistic expression[34]; and commercial speech[35].

3.   REGULATION OF OWNERSHIP

Article 10 of the ECHR limits the guarantee of freedom of expression to freedom from "interference by public authority". There is no corresponding provision in Article 19 of the ICCPR. Article 19's drafting history reveals that such language was discussed but ultimately rejected following the expression of concern by a number of delegations that control of the media by private groups could jeopardize press freedom as much as state interference.[36] As stated by the Human Rights Committee (HRC) in its only General Comment on Article 19:

> [B]ecause of the development of modern mass media, effective measures are necessary to prevent such control of the media as would interfere with the right of everyone to freedom of expression in a way that is not provided for in paragraph 3 [of Article 19]."[37]

The European Court and Commission have ruled that various articles of the ECHR impose positive obligations on member states to take action and not merely to refrain from interference.[38] Concerning press freedom, the Commission has stated that the right to information and opinions might raise an issue "where a State fails in its duty to protect against excessive press concentrations".[39]

In a 1974 resolution, the Committee of Ministers recommended that member states examine the introduction of public aid to the press, including subsidies for various categories of

---

[33] *Geillustreerde Pers v. the Netherlands*, Commission Report of 6 July 1976, 8 D&R 5 (1976), App. No. 5178/71.

[34] *Müller* case, *supra* note 19.

[35] *Markt Intern Verlag GmbH v. Federal Republic of Germany*, Judgment of 20 Nov. 1989, Series A no. 165.

[36] *See* UN Doc. A/500, para. 35. *See also* G Malinverni, "Freedom of Information in the European Convention on Human Rights and in the International Covenant on Civil and Political Rights", 4 *Human Rights Law Journal* (1983), 443, 451; D McGoldrick, *supra* note 5, 459-79.

[37] Adopted by the HRC at its 461st meeting on 27 July 1983, UN Doc. A/38/40, 109.

[38] *See Marckx* case, *supra* note 16 ("there may be positive obligations inherent in an effective respect for family life" under Article 8); *Plattform Ärzte für das Leben v. Austria*, Judgment of 21 June 1988, Series A no. 139 (Article 11, regarding the right to peaceful assembly, obliges the state to take measures to protect protesters from counter-demonstrators, although the obligation is to take reasonable measures and does not include the obligation to succeed).

[39] *Geillustreerde Pers* case, *supra* note 33.

newspapers.[40] In 1978, the Parliamentary Assembly of the Council of Europe called for the enactment of national laws restricting press monopolies and concentrations, recognized the likely need of public subsidies to ensure financial viability of newspapers, and recommended that any form of selective aid should be administered only by an independent body.[41]

The Committee of Ministers declared in 1982 that:

> states have the duty to guard against infringements of the freedom of expression and information and should adopt policies designed to foster as much as possible a variety of media and a plurality of information sources, thereby allowing a plurality of ideas and opinions.[42]

Support for the interpretation that Article 10 imposes positive obligations may also be found in the final report on the ECHR of the Sevilla-colloquium of 1985:

> 5. The notion 'necessary in a democratic society', as such, is not only fundamental in the supervision of the duty of the public authorities not to damage or interfere in the exercise of the right to freedom of expression and information, but also implies the obligation of States Parties to ensure plurality and to correct inequalities.

The Committee of Ministers and the Parliamentary Assembly have continued to urge states to take positive measures to promote press pluralism while at the same time "taking" care not to influence the content of press coverage or to link government aid in any way to editorial policy.[43]

4.   REGISTRATION REQUIREMENTS

Licensing requirements, by which government approval is necessary before a new entity may begin publishing, although not expressly prohibited by the ECHR are widely held to be prohibited implicitly. Neither the Court nor the Commission has ever ruled on an application challenging a licensing requirement, reflecting the virtual demise of the requirement throughout the member states of the Council of Europe. The American Convention on Human Rights, in Article 13(2), expressly prohibits all "prior censorship". In contrast, registration requirements, which require registration of the names and addresses of those legally

---

[40] Resolution (74)43.

[41] Recommendation 834 (1978).

[42] Committee of Ministers, Declaration on the Freedom of Expression and Information, 29 April 1982.

[43] *See generally* D Voorhoof, "From Government Regulation to Market Regulation: The Press in a New Environment", (University of Ghent, Dec. 1992).

responsible for a publication, are permitted under the ECHR and are present in several European countries.

5. REGULATION OF IMPORT AND EXPORT OF PUBLICATIONS

Both Article 10 of the ECHR and Article 19 of the ICCPR guarantee the free flow of information and ideas "regardless of frontiers". These words prohibit export or import controls which would place restrictions on the circulation of information and ideas beyond those applied by the general law.

6. DEFAMATION[44]

The discretion of governments and courts throughout Europe regarding the law of defamation has been limited in significant ways by the European Court over the last half dozen years. In the landmark *Lingens* case, the European Court established the rule that "the limits of acceptable criticism are ... wider as regards a politician as such than as regards a private individual."[45] Politicians must tolerate this greater degree of criticism because:

> Freedom of the press affords the public one of the best means of discovering and forming an opinion of the ideas and attitudes of political leaders. More generally, freedom of political debate is at the very core of the concept of a democratic society ... .

The applicant, an Austrian journalist, had been convicted under Article 111 of the Criminal Code for publishing two articles strongly criticizing then Chancellor Kreisky for supporting a politician who had served as an SS officer. The Austrian court conceded that the article did not contain any false statements but found that Mr Lingens could not prove that his opinions were "true", a necessary step in establishing his innocence of criminal libel. Mr Lingens was fined and the relevant issues of the publication were confiscated.

The European Court ruled unanimously that: (1) "the limits of acceptable criticism are wider as regards a politician as such than as regards a private individual"[46], and (2) the requirement that an accused must prove the truth of an allegedly defamatory opinion infringes his or her right to impart ideas, within the meaning of Article 10, as well as the public's right to receive ideas. As stated by the Court:

---

[44] The following analysis is drawn from an article by the author first published in the *Interights Bulletin*, Vol. 7, Issue 1 (1992).

[45] *Lingens* case, *supra* note 22 at para. 42.

[46] *Id.*

[A] careful distinction needs to be made between facts and value-judgements. The existence of facts can be demonstrated, whereas the truth of value-judgements is not susceptible of proof.[47]

The Court elaborated on its *Lingens* ruling in *Oberschlick v. Austria.*[48] Mr Oberschlick, an Austrian journalist, had been convicted and fined for publishing a criminal complaint he and others had filed against the leader of the Austrian Liberal Party in which they accused him of incitement to national hatred and also of activities on behalf of the aims of the National Socialist Party (NSDAP). The complaint referred to statements made by the politician in which he urged that family allowances of Austrian women should be increased by 50 per cent in order to discourage them from seeking abortions for financial reasons, while allowances paid to immigrant mothers should be reduced by 50 per cent. The complaint alleged that this proposal was "entirely consistent with and corresponded to the philosophy and aims of the NSDAP", a criminal offence under Austria's Prohibition Act.[49] The trial court convicted Mr Oberschlick of defamation, ordered him to pay a fine and damages to the politician, and ordered the seizure of all issues of the offending publication. According to the court, the politician's statements "did not yet amount to a National socialist attitude or to a criminal offence" and thus Mr Oberschlick had not established the truth of his allegations. The court further concluded that Mr Oberschlick had "disregarded the standards of fair journalism by ... insinuating motives which [the politician] had not himself expressed".[50]

The European Court reiterated its *Lingens* holding that a libel defendant must not be required to prove the truth of his or her opinions. The Court considered that the published complaint stated facts followed by a value judgement, and that the requirement that a journalist prove the truth of a value judgement is impossible and "itself an infringement on freedom of expression".[51]

In reiterating the second prong of the *Lingens* holding that politicians must tolerate a higher level of criticism concerning their public actions than private citizens, the Court added an additional reason for the different level of scrutiny: "The [politician] inevitably and knowingly lays himself open to close scrutiny of his every word and deed by both journalists and the public at large, and he must display a greater degree of tolerance, especially when he himself makes public statements that are susceptible of criticism."[52]

---

[47] *Id.* at para. 46.

[48] *Oberschlick* case, *supra* note 27.

[49] *Id.* at para. 13.

[50] *Id.* at para. 16.

[51] *Id.* at para. 63.

[52] *Id.* at para. 59.

What is particularly striking about the decision is the Court's willingness to treat the allegation that the politician's views "corresponded to the philosophy and aims of the NSDAP" as a statement of opinion. Only one dissenting judge viewed the allegation as an erroneous statement of fact.[53] The majority recognized that the allegation was provocative, but reasoned that "[a] politician who expresses himself in such terms exposes himself to a strong reaction on the part of journalists and the public."[54] In other words, an inflammatory statement may justify a more provocative response than the same ideas expressed in more measured terms.

In a third case against Austria, *Schwabe v. Austria*, the Court again criticized the Austrian courts for requiring a person accused of defamation to prove the truth of a value judgement.[55] Mr Schwabe had issued a press release, thereafter published in a newspaper, in which he called attention to an 18-year-old criminal conviction of the Vice-President of the Carinthian Government for a traffic accident while driving under the influence of alcohol in which one person had been killed. Mr Schwabe made the statement in the context of arguing that the Head of the Carinthian Government was applying a double standard in calling for the resignation of a mayor recently convicted of drunk driving, while remaining silent about the Vice-President's accident while driving under the influence of alcohol; Mr Schwabe suggested that both politicians were unfit for office.

Mr Schwabe was convicted of defamation on the ground that his comparison of the culpability of the two politicians suggested a falsehood; namely, that the Vice-President had been convicted of drunk driving when in fact he had been convicted only of negligent homicide (although his blood alcohol content had been sufficiently high to justify a drunk-driving conviction). Mr Schwabe was also convicted of the crime of reproach, for having mentioned a conviction for which the sentence had already been served.

The European Court ruled that Mr Schwabe's convictions violated Article 10 because it was evident from his press release that he had not meant to imply a falsehood but rather had made a value judgement in good faith that the two convictions were morally comparable. In other words, as in *Oberschlick*, where a value judgement is based on facts (here, a comparison between two driving accidents; in *Oberschlick*, a comparison between a politician's statement and the aims of the NSDAP), it should not be considered defamatory so long as the facts are reasonably accurate and told in good faith, and the value judgement is not intended to imply a falsehood, even if a false implication is possible.[56]

---

[53] Two other judges dissented on the ground that publication in the form of a criminal complaint could create the impression that a criminal action had actually been initiated by a public prosecutor.

[54] *Oberschlick* case, *supra* note 27 at para. 61.

[55] *Schwabe v. Austria*, Judgment of 28 Aug. 1992, Series A no. 242-B.

[56] *Id.* at para 34.

In addition, the Court ruled that Mr Schwabe's conviction for reproach was inappropriate because certain criminal convictions (including negligent homicide) could be relevant factors in assessing a politician's fitness to exercise political functions.[57]

In the *Castells* case, the Court added an additional aspect to the protection of political speech. Not only is criticism of politicians and governments to be accorded special protection (*see* also Section 9, below), additional protection is due when the criticism is voiced by an elected representative, especially if a member of the opposition. Thus, in ruling that a conviction of an opposition Member of Parliament violated Article 10, the Court concluded that:

> "While freedom of expression is important for everybody, it is especially so for an elected representative of the people. ... Accordingly, interferences with the freedom of expression of an opposition Member of Parliament, like the applicant, call for the closest scrutiny on the part of the Court."[58]

The decision is important for the additional reason that it establishes the principle that when a defamation is based in part on an allegation of fact, the defendant must be permitted to try to prove its truth. The Spanish court had refused to permit Mr Castells to try to establish the truth of his claim that the government had acted unlawfully by intentionally failing to investigate the murders of people accused of belonging to the Basque separatist movement. While the Court recognized that Mr Castells' article included statements of opinion as well as fact, and that some of his accusations were serious, it attached decisive importance to the fact that the courts had precluded him from offering any evidence as to the truth of his assertions. The Court ruled that the article had to be considered as a whole, and that Mr Castells was entitled to try to establish the truth of his factual assertions as well as his good faith.[59]

The question of whether matters of public interest other than politics are entitled to the same high degree of protection was decided in the affirmative by the Court in the *Thorgeirson* case.[60] The Court rejected the Government's contention that political discussion should be treated differently from discussion of other matters of legitimate public concern.[61]

Mr Thorgeirson had published two articles about police brutality in which he called for a new and more effective system of investigating accusations against the police. He was convicted and fined for defaming police officers on the grounds that some of his statements constituted "insults" and "vituperation" (for example, calling police officers "brutes in uniform") and that

---

[57] *Id.* at para. 32.

[58] *Castells* case, *supra* note 21 at para. 42.

[59] *Id.* at para. 47.

[60] *Thorgeirson* case, *supra* note 21.

[61] *Id.* at para. 64.

other allegations were untrue (such as that police officers had committed numerous serious acts of physical assault on people who had become disabled as a result and, in particular, that a paralyzed man Mr Thorgeirson had seen in a hospital had been the victim of police brutality).

Other relevant factors were that no police officers were expressly named, the articles bore on a matter of serious public concern and, in the Court's opinion, Mr Thorgeirson's primary purpose in publishing the article had been to promote reform and not to disparage the police.

In addition to clearly extending the *Lingens* holdings to all matters of public concern, the judgment is noteworthy for its finding that the articles had an adequate factual basis. The Court noted that many of the statements reflected public opinion or were based on "rumours", "stories" or the statements of others, and concluded that it would therefore be unreasonable to require Mr Thorgeirson to establish the factual basis for those statements. In fact, the government had provided substantial evidence at trial of the falsity of one of Mr Thorgeirson's most sensational claims by producing as a witness a man who appeared to be the paralyzed man (mentioned in his article) who testified that he had been beaten by someone he knew and not the police. Mr Thorgeirson's only response was that, although he did not remember faces very well, he did not think that the witness was the same man.

In light of these facts, the *Thorgeirson* judgment appears to stand for the principle that a speaker or publisher is protected so long as his claims are based upon public opinion, do not disparage specific named individuals and/or are primarily intended to promote a positive aim such as institutional reform. The publisher must provide some evidence to support his good faith in believing public opinion (in this case, a police officer recently had been convicted for brutality), but the burden appears to be light.

The one defamation case in which the Court did not find a violation of Article 10 is *Barfod v. Denmark*.[62] Mr Barfod, a journalist, was convicted of criminal libel for writing an article in which he criticized a judgment of a three-person high court in favour of a local civil service agency on the ground that the two lay judges were both employed by the agency and thus should have been disqualified. In particular, he wrote that the lay judges "did their duty", clearly suggesting that they had been influenced by improper factors in reaching their decision. The European Commission ruled, by 14 votes to one, that even that claim was protected on the ground that "the functioning of the judiciary weighed more heavily than the interest of the two lay judges in being protected against criticism of the kind expressed in the applicant's article."[63] The Court disagreed, ruling that, while criticism of the composition of the Court was protected, Mr Barfod's claim "was a serious accusation which [was] likely to lower [the judges] in public esteem".

The *Barfod* case was decided in 1989 and might well be decided differently today in light of *Castells* and *Thorgeirson*. To the extent that a distinction based on substance may be

---

[62] *Barfod* case, *supra* note 26.

[63] *Id.* at para. 31.

discerned, *Barfod* may stand for the proposition that the scope of acceptable criticism concerning judicial officers is narrower than concerning politicians, executive officials and law enforcement personnel, and also is narrower when directed at named individuals rather than at an institution generally.

The above cases establish a number of principles which national courts are to consider in assessing defamation claims: (1) the important role of the press in informing public opinion on matters of public interest and in acting as a public watchdog requires that the press be accorded particular latitude when commenting on matters of political or other public interest; (2) elected representatives, especially opposition members, are also entitled to special latitude; (3) the limits of acceptable criticism are wider concerning political figures and governments than concerning private individuals, and in general are wider when no named individuals are specifically criticized; (4) judicial officers do not seem to have to tolerate the same degree of scrutiny as other government agents; (5) a defendant must not be required to prove the truth of value judgements, statements which reflect public opinion or allegations based on rumours or the statements of others; (6) in assessing whether reproach of a person for having committed a crime for which he or she has already served a sentence, courts must consider the public interest in being reminded about the conviction; an automatic penalty for reproach violates Article 10; and (7) a claim for defamation is weaker if the allegedly defamatory statement was made in response to a statement which itself was provocative or inflammatory.

7.   INVASION OF PRIVACY

Article 8(1) of the ECHR guarantees to everyone the "right to respect for his private and family life, his home and his correspondence." Article 8(2) permits the right to be subject to restriction by public authority when necessary to protect various private and public interests. The list differs from the list of interests in Article 10(2) in that it includes "the economic well-being of the country" and does not include "territorial integrity", "preventing the disclosure of information received in confidence", or "maintaining the authority and impartiality of the judiciary". None of the cases decided under Article 8 have concerned the extent to which the press may intrude into private life.

Decisions of the Commission have established that disclosure to, or improper discovery by, third persons of facts relating to an individual's physical condition, health or personality violate the right to privacy, but may be justified in the interest of preventing crime.[64] Similarly, the placing of intimate photographs in evidence at trial, and the keeping of records, including documents, photographs and fingerprints relating to past criminal activity, may violate Article 8 but may also be justifiable in the interests of preventing crime and protecting public order.[65]

---

[64] *Van Oosterwijck v. Belgium*, App. No. 7654/77, Report of 1 March 1979.

[65] *X v. Federal Republic of Germany*, App. No. 5339/72, CD 43, 156; *X v. Federal Republic of Germany*, App. No. 1307/61, CD 9, 53.

It does not appear that the European Convention requires contracting states to adopt laws to protect privacy interests. In 1986 the Commission ruled inadmissible an application claiming that the absence of a law protecting privacy in the UK was a breach of Article 8.

8.   RIGHT OF REPLY AND/OR CORRECTION

Some legal scholars have argued that the right of reply should be regarded as implicitly guaranteed by Article 10(2) in light of its express protection of "the reputation and rights of others". However, that is a difficult argument to sustain, and the fact that the Committee of Ministers has urged states parties to recognize the right suggests that the right is not already guaranteed.[66]

9.   INSULTS TO GOVERNMENT INSTITUTIONS OR OFFICIALS

The Court has not yet gone so far as to prohibit all punishment for insults to the government, its institutions or symbols. However, in *Castells v. Spain*, a chamber of the Court, by six votes to one, made clear that governments are required to tolerate an even greater degree of scrutiny than politicians, and may prohibit criticism of themselves only in the narrowest of circumstances, such as when the country is torn by national unrest or terrorist attacks, and the criticism is likely to promote further unrest or violence.[67]

In 1979, Mr Castells, a senator who represented Herri Batasuna, a Basque separatist coalition, published in a weekly magazine an article condemning murders and attacks committed by armed groups against Basque citizens. In particular, he accused the government of failing to investigate any of the crimes and of actually supporting and instigating the attacks. He was convicted for insulting the government and sentenced to imprisonment and disqualification from public office for one year. (The penalties were suspended by the Constitutional Court and never actually imposed.) The government contended that Mr Castells had insulted a democratic government in order to destabilize it during a particularly critical time when groups of various political persuasions were resorting to violence. In addition to establishing precedents concerning defamation generally (*see, supra,* Section 6), the Court ruled:

> "The limits of permissible criticism are wider with regard to the Government than in relation to a private citizen, or even a politician. In a democratic system the actions or omissions of the Government must be subject to the close scrutiny not only of the legislative and judicial authorities but also of the press and public opinion."[68]

---

[66] *See* G Malinverni, *supra* note 36 at 448 (citing Resolution 26/1974 of the Committee of Ministers).

[67] *Castells* case, *supra* note 21.

[68] *Id.* at para. 46.

10. OFFICIAL SECRECY AND ACCESS TO GOVERNMENT HELD INFORMATION

The right to receive information "basically prohibits a Government from restricting a person from receiving information that others may wish or may be willing to impart to him."[69] The state's obligation not to interfere with the communication of information is particularly strong where the information is of vital concern to the recipient's private or family life. Thus, the Court has held that Article 8 of the Convention (which guarantees the right to private and family life) imposes an affirmative obligation on governments to ensure that individuals are able to seek review of denials of requests for confidential government records of vital interest to their private or family life from an authority independent of the agency which refused the request.[70]

In the *Gaskin* case, the Court decided that an individual who had been in government care as a foster child had a vital interest in files about his childhood development and history. It also noted that both individuals and the government have an interest in maintaining the confidentiality of documents provided in confidence (the government's interest arising from its need to encourage the flow of confidential information). The Court concluded that the applicant had a right of access to information held by the government of vital personal interest, and that the UK had violated Article 8 by failing to establish an authority independent of the agency which held the information to decide on requests for information. However, the Court found no violation of Article 10, making clear that the right under discussion gives rise to a presumption of access only to information vital to an individual's private life.

In the *Leander* case, the Court considered a request from a person who had been denied a post of some sensitivity with the Swedish government based on information kept in a secret police register which the government refused to disclose on national security grounds. The Court, in ruling that the government's denial was compatible with the ECHR, nonetheless did state that the government's margin of appreciation in matters of national security was not without bounds:

> [I]n view of the risk that a system of secret surveillance for the protection of national security poses of undermining or even destroying democracy on the ground of defending it, the Court must be satisfied that there exist adequate and effective guarantees against abuse.

The European Court has thus ruled that the right to receive information does not entail a general presumption of access to information held by the government, although a limited presumption, such as to information of general public interest, is by no means precluded. Moreover, although there is no binding case-law establishing a general presumption, the

---

[69] *Leander v. Sweden*, Judgment of 26 March 1987, Series A no. 116, para. 74.

[70] *Gaskin v. UK*, Judgment of 7 July 1989, Series A no. 160.

Committee of Ministers adopted a recommendation and declaration calling on member states to recognize such a presumption. The Recommendation on the Access to Information Held by Public Authorities, adopted in 1981, urges member states to grant "[e]veryone within [their] jurisdiction ... the right to obtain, on request, information held by the public authorities other than legislative and judicial authorities ..., subject only to such limitations and restrictions as are necessary in a democratic society for the protection of legitimate public ... or private interests".[71] It is further recommended that the right should include the right to a decision within a reasonable time, a statement of reasons for any refusal, and a right to seek a review of any denial.

The Committee of Ministers followed the above Recommendation with a Declaration of the intent of the member states to pursue "an open information policy in the public sector ... in order to enhance the individual's ability to freely discuss political, social, economic and cultural matters.[72]

There is no ECHR case-law on the right of access to environmental information. As discussed in the chapter on EC law, the Council Directive on the Freedom of Access to Information on the Environment calls on member states to ensure access to environmental information held by public authorities, subject to various exceptions. The ECHR is consistent with the Directive; arguably Article 6 of the ECHR, guaranteeing a right to a fair hearing by an independent tribunal in determination of "civil rights and obligations", may require judicial review of refusals of environmental and other information in certain circumstances.[73]

11. ACCESS TO AND DISCLOSURE OF COURT DOCUMENTS AND PROCEEDINGS

Access to court documents and proceedings may legitimately be regulated under Article 10(2) of the ECHR in order to protect "the rights ... of others" or to maintain "the authority and impartiality of the judiciary".

The chief "right of others" which may be implicated by questions of access is the right set forth in Article 6 of the ECHR of any person charged with a criminal offence or involved in proceedings to determine his or her civil rights and obligations "to a fair and public hearing within a reasonable time by an independent and impartial tribunal established by law." While all judgments are to be made public, Article 6 provides that:

---

[71] Rec. No. R(81)19, adopted by the Committee of Ministers on 25 Nov. 1981 at the 340th meeting of the Ministers' Deputies.

[72] Adopted on 29 April 1982 at the Committee's 70th session.

[73] *See* S Weber, "Environmental Information and the European Convention on Human Rights", 12 *Human Rights Law Journal* (May 1991) 177, 184.

"the press and public may be excluded from all or part of the trial in the interest of morals, public order or national security in a democratic society, where the interests of juveniles or the protection of the private life of the parties so require, or to the extent strictly necessary in the opinion of the court in special circumstances where publicity would prejudice the interests of justice."

The rationale for public hearings is two-fold, First, as stated by the Commission, "the public nature of the proceedings helps to ensure a fair trial by protecting the litigant against arbitrary decisions".[74] Second, "[c]ombined with the public pronouncement of the judgment, the public nature of the hearings serves to ensure that the public is duly informed, notably by the press, and that the legal process is publicly observable. It should consequently contribute to ensuring confidence in the administration of justice."[75] Thus, the public arguably has a right, independent of the parties, to attend hearings, and moreover, the press arguably could invoke this passage to support a claim for standing to raise the right of public access. On the other hand, in several cases the Court has approved closures of hearings based only on the consent of the parties, thus suggesting that the public interest in access may not be very strong.[76]

The second interest which national courts legitimately may seek to protect by limiting disclosure of information about court proceedings is the interest in maintaining the authority and impartiality of the judiciary. The European Court has stressed that, in assessing claims based on this ground, national courts must accord due weight to the countervailing public interest in receiving information about matters of public concern, and that decisions of national courts are entitled to only a narrow margin of appreciation.[77]

In the *Weber* case,[78] the Court considered a challenge to a conviction and fine under a Swiss criminal law which made it an offence to make public "any documents or information about a judicial investigation" until the investigation had been "finally completed". Franz Weber, a journalist and well-known ecologist, sued the author of a letter to the editor for defamation. Dissatisfied with the judge's conduct of the investigation, Weber held a press conference in which he announced that he had filed the action, that the judge had ordered him to produce certain documents, and that he had partially complied. One year later, he held a second press conference in which he reiterated the information previously disclosed and further announced that he had lodged a complaint against the investigating judge. Weber was convicted of

[74] *Axen* case, Report of 14 Dec. 1981, B.57.

[75] *Id.*

[76] *See, e.g., Le Compte, Van Leuven and De Meyere* case, Judgment of 23 June 1981, para. 43. *See also* P van Dijk and G J H van Hoof, *Theory and Practice of the European Convention on Human Rights* (Kluwer, 2d ed., 1990), 325-28.

[77] *The Sunday Times* case, *supra* note 9 at para. 59.

[78] *Weber v. Switzerland*, Judgment of 22 May 1990, Series A no. 177.

disclosing confidential information and his conviction was affirmed. The Swiss courts conceded that he had previously disclosed the information but ruled that he nonetheless continued to have a duty not to republish the information.

The European Court noted three relevant factors in ruling that the conviction was not necessary to safeguard a legitimate interest and thus violated Article 10. First, though not of decisive importance, the public had an interest in the case because of Weber's notoriety and his claim that the investigation had been unfair. Second, the Court ruled that the Swiss government had no legitimate interest in maintaining the confidentiality of information which had been previously disclosed.[79] Third, the press conference could not have placed pressure on the investigating judge because, by that time, the judge had already decided to commit the letter-writer to trial and thus had virtually completed the investigation.[80]

Similarly, in the *Spycatcher* case, the European Court ruled that the UK government had no interest in suppressing publication of the book *Spycatcher* once it had been published outside the country.[81]

In *The Sunday Times* case[82], Times Newspapers was enjoined from publishing an article critical of the testing and marketing practices of the UK manufacturer and marketer of thalidomide, a drug which had caused severe deformities in children of women who had taken the drug during pregnancy. The UK's House of Lords held that the injunction was necessary to preserve the integrity of the judicial process because, although trial proceedings had been suspended, the parties were engaged in protracted settlement negotiations which could be affected by the article's publication. The Court concluded that the injunction violated Article 10 on the grounds that the thalidomide disaster was a matter of undisputed public interest, publication would not substantially distort the settlement process and legal proceedings might not recommence. In so ruling, the Court pronounced as follows:

> There is general recognition of the fact that the courts cannot operate in a vacuum. Whilst they are the forum for the settlement of disputes, this does not mean that there can be no prior discussion of disputes elsewhere, be it in specialised journals, in the general press or amongst the public at large. Furthermore, whilst the mass media must not overstep the bounds imposed in the interests of the proper administration of justice, it is incumbent on them to impart information and ideas concerning matters that come before the courts just as in other areas of public interest.[83]

---

[79] *Id.* at para. 51.

[80] *Id.* at para. 52.

[81] *See Spycatcher* case, *supra* note 10, *also* discussion in Section 10.

[82] *Sunday Times* case, *supra* note 9.

[83] *Id.* at para. 64.

In addition, the Court disapproved of the adoption by some members of the House of Lords of an absolute rule (similar to that applied by the Swiss courts in *Weber*) that no information concerning a pending case could ever lawfully be disclosed.[84] The Court reiterated the importance of evaluating the necessity of a restriction based upon the particular facts of a case.

12. PRIOR RESTRAINTS

Article 10 does not prohibit the imposition of all prior restraints on publication. Nonetheless, the European Court, in the *Spycatcher* case, emphasized that "the dangers inherent in prior restraints are such that they call for the most careful scrutiny on the part of the Court" and that this is especially so as far as the press is concerned, because "news is a perishable commodity and to delay its publication, even for a short period, may well deprive it of all its value and interest."[85]

In that case, the UK courts had issued and upheld various injunctions which prohibited newspapers from publishing excerpts of the book *Spycatcher*, the memoirs of a former high-ranking intelligence officer, even after it had been published in the United States and other countries. (The banning of the book itself was not challenged.) The UK government claimed that the injunctions were necessary for national security reasons to preserve the confidence of other governments in the secrecy of information held by the intelligence services, to enforce the duty of confidentiality owed by Crown servants, and to safeguard the rights of the Attorney-General pending final determination of the injunction's lawfulness by the House of Lords (*see* Section 11, *supra*). The Court ruled that, once the information had been published elsewhere, the interest of the press and public in imparting and receiving information outweighed the government's interests.[86] However, the Court also ruled that, prior to publication elsewhere, the injunctions came within the government's margin of appreciation.

13. RESTRICTIONS ON OFFENSIVE LANGUAGE AGAINST IDENTIFIABLE GROUPS

In the *Jersild* case, a journalist was convicted and fined for broadcasting a television interview with members of a white supremacist youth gang, even though the Danish court accepted that he had not endorsed the views and was motivated by an interest in informing the public about the existence of violent racism in Denmark. After the journalist filed an application with the European Commission, the Danish law was amended so as to exclude liability for journalists

---

[84] *Id.* at para. 65.

[85] *Spycatcher* case, *supra* note 10 at para. 60.

[86] *Id.*, at para. 65.

unless, by publishing racist ideas, they intended to "threaten, insult or degrade" people. The Commission ruled the application admissible, but has yet to rule on the merits.[87]

The Commission has declared all other applications which challenged convictions for racist, fascist or revisionist statements or activities inadmissible on the ground that the convictions were manifestly consistent with the ECHR. For example, one application challenged an Italian law which made it a criminal offence to "engage in intrigue aimed at reconstituting a fascist party".[88] A second application was filed by a leader of a white supremacist political party in the Netherlands who had been convicted, sentenced to two weeks' imprisonment and had his named removed from the electoral lists for publicly stating that it was time to make guest workers leave the country.[89]

The Human Rights Committee similarly has ruled inadmissible applications challenging convictions for racist or fascist speech, on the grounds that the convictions were consistent with the ICCPR's Article 19, Article 20 (prohibiting "any advocacy of national, racial or religious hatred"), and Article 5 (denying "any right to engage in any activity ... aimed at the destruction of any of the rights and freedoms" set forth in the ICCPR).[90]

14.   BLASPHEMY, OBSCENITY AND PROTECTION OF PUBLIC MORALS

In the *Handyside* case the Court reviewed the conviction under the Obscene Publications Act of the publishers of *The Little Red Schoolbook*, which encouraged its readers to take a liberal attitude towards sexual activity and drug use.[91] The Court, while articulating strong endorsements of the importance of the right to freedom of expression, nonetheless found that the prohibition on sales fell within the UK's margin of appreciation. The Court accorded considerable weight to the fact that the *Schoolbook* was aimed at children, and noted that the failure of authorities in other European countries to ban the book did not limit the UK's discretion to do so.

In the *Müller* case, the Court made clear that governments may prohibit the sale of obscene material to youths under 18 or their display in such manner that youths could have access to

---

[87] Application No. 15890/89, decision on admissibility issued 8 Sept. 1992.

[88] *X v. Italy*, Application No. 6741/74.

[89] *Glimmerveen v. Netherlands*, Application Nos. D 8348/78 and 8406/78. *See also X v. Federal Republic of Germany*, Application No. 92351/81; *T v. Belgium*, Application No. 9777/82; *Felderer v. Sweden*, Application No. 11001/84.

[90] *M A v. Italy*, Application No. 117/81; *J.R.T. and the W.G. Party v. Canada*, Application No. 104/1981.

[91] *Handyside* case, *supra* note 12.

them.[92] In that case, the Court upheld an obscenity conviction and fine for painting and displaying sexually explicit paintings at an exhibition open to the public including children.

Although the European Court has not ruled on the issue, the ECHR appears to permit the crime of blasphemous libel, and further appears to tolerate blasphemy statutes which protect only one religion. In two cases, the Commission ruled inadmissible applications challenging the UK's common law crime of blasphemous libel which makes it an offence to publish material that produces shock or resentment among Christians even in the absence of any intent to shock. In the *Gay News* case, the applicant, a respected writer, had been convicted for publishing a poem in a magazine with a predominantly gay readership which depicted Christ as a homosexual.[93] In the *Choudhury* case, the applicants were Muslims who had sought to have Salman Rushdie prosecuted for writing *The Satanic Verses*.[94] The UK courts refused to prosecute him on the ground that the blasphemy statute protects only the Christian religion; the Commission, in ruling the application inadmissible, explained that the UK's failure to provide a cause of action for Muslims did not violate the UK's obligation not to discriminate in the protection of rights recognized under the ECHR.

While most of the decisions of the Court or Commission which have considered restrictions on expression based on public morals have upheld the restrictions, the Court has made clear that a state's discretion in the field of protection of morals is not unfettered. In the *Open Door Counselling* case, the Court recently rejected Ireland's claim that the prohibition on information about where to obtain legal abortions outside of Ireland was necessary to protect public morals.[95]

15.   RESTRICTIONS ON ADVERTISING

Information of a commercial nature is protected under Article 10 although the Court will grant governments a wider margin of appreciation to restrict commercial speech than other forms of expression. The Court, in the *Markt Intern* case, examined restrictions on information of a commercial nature found by the German courts to constitute unfair competition and thus to injure the reputation or rights of others.[96] *Markt Intern*, a consumer magazine, had published an accurate account of a chemist's dissatisfaction with a mail-order firm. The German courts ruled that the story created a false impression and thus constituted unfair competition. A bare majority of the European Court (by a vote of 10 to 9) upheld the

---

[92] *Müller* case, *supra* note 19.

[93] 5 EHRR 123 (1983).

[94] Application No. 17439/90.

[95] *Open Door Counselling* case, *supra* note 15 at para. 67.

[96] *Markt Intern* case, *supra* note 35 at para. 33.

court's order and rejected arguments urging a greater measure of protection for commercial speech.

In a second case, the Court ruled that a statement should not be treated as commercial speech if its primary purpose is to inform the public about a topic of legitimate public interest.[97] In that case, the German courts had issued and upheld an injunction against a veterinary surgeon on the ground that information he had given to a journalist concerning his own practice in the course of urging the need for more comprehensive veterinary night services violated the prohibition on advertising by members of the "liberal professions". The Court concluded that the publicity Dr Barthold may have received was secondary to "the nature of the issue being put to the public at large" and that the German courts' prohibition of any statement that might have a slight advertising effect was likely to discourage "members of the liberal professions from contributing to public debate on topics affecting the life of the community" and "to hamper the press in the performance of its task of purveyor of information and public watchdog."[98]

16. CONCLUSION

Whatever complaints may legitimately be levelled against the European Court and Commission in general regarding their interpretation of freedom of expression and the wide margin of appreciation they are willing to accord national courts,[99] they undeniably have established several solid precedents protective of press freedom. They have consistently stressed the vital role of the press to serve as a "public watchdog" and to communicate information and ideas about matters of public interest; and in five of six cases decided by the Court which were filed by journalists or newspapers (all except *Markt Intern*, concerning commercial speech), restrictions on press freedom were found to be incompatible with Article 10.

In particular, the Court has ruled that: (1) a person must not be required to prove the truth of a value judgment, and may not be found guilty of defamation merely for expressing an opinion about a matter of public interest unless based on false facts, made in bad faith or expressed in a particularly insulting manner; (2) a wider ambit of criticism is permissible concerning politicians, governments and government institutions than private individuals; (3) neither national security nor the duty of confidentiality can justify the suppression of information which has already been published elsewhere; (4) the right to receive information of legitimate public concern takes precedence over the interest in the confidentiality of legal proceedings which have been indefinitely suspended; (5) prior restraints, especially against the press, are to be subjected to the most careful scrutiny; and (6) a statement which both

---

[97] *Barthold* case, *supra* note 31 at para. 58.

[98] *Id.*

[99] *See* A Lester, *supra* note 7, text accompanying nn. 121-22.

informs about matters of public interest and advertises a product or service is entitled to full Article 10 protection so long as its primary purpose is not commercial.

Other organs of the Council have also taken steps to promote press freedom. The Committee of Ministers and the Parliamentary Assembly have both declared that member states have a positive duty to promote press pluralism, and have called on them to take affirmative measures such as adoption of laws restricting concentration of media ownership. They also have encouraged states to pursue "an open information policy in the public sector".

The Court's jurisprudence concerning press freedom has developed slowly, and many issues have not begun to be addressed. A number of cases are pending which raise press issues, including the confidentiality of journalists' sources and the requirements of media pluralism. It may be hoped that the Court and Commission will admit and decide these and future cases consistent with their strong, principled statements in support of the press's pre-eminent role in a democratic society.

Chapter 13

EUROPEAN COMMUNITY LAW WHICH AFFECTS THE PRESS

Nigel Cooper

INTRODUCTION

The European Communities do not provide a comprehensive legislative framework governing the press.[1] Community law is primarily concerned with the economic regulation of the press and the press' role in the economies of the member states. Specific examples of that regulation are discussed in the following sections and concern, for example, the advertising of tobacco, alcohol and medicine (Section 8); measures which restrict or distort competition within the Community (Section 5); classification and protection of information relating to Community activities (Section 6.1.); access to environmental information (Section 6.2.); and protection of data files (Section 6.3.). Moreover, Community law has incorporated aspects of human rights law as one of its fundamental principles. In tandem with the principle of the free movement of goods and services and the freedom of establishment (Sections 3 and 4), this has extended the relevance of Community law to questions of press regulation and practice.

1. BASIC STRUCTURE OF THE COMMUNITIES

A brief introduction to the structure and legal regime established by the Communities is useful in order to understand those provisions of Community law which have an impact on the press.[2] The competence of the Communities and their institutions is established by the constitutive treaties.[3] Although these treaties were originally aimed at harmonizing the economic policies of the member states, the Communities have increasingly become the fora for political cooperation as well.

---

[1] This chapter focuses on the European Economic Community ("EEC") rather than on the European Coal and Steel Community ("ECSC") or the European Atomic Energy Community ("Euratom"), which are limited in their application to particular sectors of industry. The following abbreviations will be used throughout this chapter: OJ for the Official Journal of the European Communities; ECR for the European Court Reports; CMLR for the Common Market Law Reports.

[2] For detailed commentary on Community law *see* Vaughan, *Law of the European Communities* (Butterworths) and Kapetyn & Verloren van Themat, *The Law of the European Communities* (2nd. ed.).

[3] The ECSC Treaty; the EEC Treaty (the "Treaty of Rome"); the Euratom Treaty; the Treaty on Certain Institutions Common to the European Communities; the Merger Treaty; the two Budgetary Treaties; the three Accession Treaties; the Single European Act; and (if and when ratified by the member states) the Treaty on European Union.

1.1.   The Constitutional Framework

Twelve states are currently members of the European Communities: Belgium, Denmark, France, Germany, Greece, Ireland, Italy, Luxembourg, the Netherlands, Portugal, Spain and the United Kingdom.

The treaties establishing the Communities do not enumerate specific human rights. The Communities do, however, regard fundamental rights as a general principle of Community law and policy. The primary objective of the EEC is to establish a common market among the member states and to harmonize the economic policies of the member states. The freedom of movement for goods, persons, services and capital are essential to this economic convergence.

1.2.   The Institutional Framework of the European Economic Community

There are five primary EEC institutions: the Commission, the Council of Ministers, the Parliament, the Court of Justice and the Court of First Instance. The primary legislative organ of the EEC is the Council of Ministers, comprising ministerial representatives of the member states. The Commission acts as the executive to the Council, drafting proposals for legislation for the Council and passing subordinate legislation in those areas where the Council has delegated authority to the Commission. The Commission plays the primary role in ensuring the implementation of Community legislation by the member states, and also exercises an investigative and judicial power over member states and individuals alike in certain policy areas (namely, competition and external trade relations).

Although there are plans to extend the legislative powers of the Parliament, it is at present substantially an advisory body which must be consulted by the Council in the process of promulgating primary legislation. Since 1979, its members have been elected by the various national electorates. The Parliament is the institution which has concerned itself most with the issues of press freedom, press self-regulation and concentration of press ownership.

The Court of Justice was established as the original judicial organ for the enforcement and interpretation of Community law. It acts as arbiter in disputes between member states, between the institutions and between member states and the institutions. It is also an appeal tribunal for individuals challenging the decisions of the institutions and, further, acts as an interpretative body for questions of Community law referred by the courts of the member states.

Since 15 November 1989, the Court of Justice has been supported by the Court of First Instance. The Court of First Instance has taken over first instance jurisdiction from the Court of Justice in certain defined areas of Community law. Perhaps its most important area of competence concerns appeals from decisions of the Commission in competition cases. Proceedings before the courts are public unless the court decides otherwise for serious reasons, and judgments are given in open court.

The institutions discussed above are supported by a number of advisory and consultative bodies. In addition, there is a growing number of bodies of specialized competence, such as the European Bank for Reconstruction and Development.

1.3 The Sources of EEC Law

The sources of Community law can be divided into the following groups:

1) constitutive treaties of the Communities;
2) subsidiary conventions;
3) Community acts;
4) general principles of law;
5) agreements with non-EEC countries.

The sources particularly relevant to the press are the Constitutive Treaties of the EEC, Community acts, and agreements with third countries.

Community acts are the legislative and administrative measures of the Community institutions. Within the EEC, the Council and the Commission can adopt five different kinds of acts: regulations, directives, decisions, recommendations and opinions. Recommendations and opinions are not binding, but they are useful as an expression of policy or the current thinking of the institution concerned. Regulations are general legislative instruments and have binding force in all member states of the Community without any further action by the member states. Directives are also general in their scope, but they set forth only the objectives to be achieved and the framework for those objectives. It is left to the member states to implement directives through their own binding national measures. Decisions are binding, but are only addressed to limited categories of persons.

Although the Parliament has no autonomous legislative power, it can express its opinions either in the course of the legislative process or by way of separate non-binding resolutions.

The general principles of Community law are drawn from the Community treaties and from the national legal systems of the member states. These general principles are of particular importance in examining the relationship between the press and Community law.

2. COMMUNITY LAW AND NATIONAL LAW

Community law is supreme over conflicting domestic legislation. National courts must give effect to applicable Community law and must accord it supremacy over any conflicting domestic legislation.

The supremacy of Community law has been established and upheld by the Court of Justice since the early years of the Communities and is now accepted by the courts of all member states. More recently, there have been a number of important decisions from the Court specifying the extent of that supremacy.

In the recent case of *Frankovitch v. Italian Republic*,[4] the Court of Justice ruled that the obligations of member states under Community law require them to provide a remedy to individuals for loss caused by a breach by the member state of its obligations under Community law. In an earlier case, *The Queen v. Secretary of State for Transport, ex parte Factortame*,[5] the Court required the High Court of England and Wales to grant interim injunctive relief, pending final hearing, against the United Kingdom government in order to prevent a national law which was potentially contrary to Community law from coming into force. The novelty of the decision was two-fold. Firstly, no such relief was available to an individual against the government as a matter of purely domestic law. Secondly, the decision emphasized that such relief was to be available to individuals not only in situations where it was certain that national measures were subject to Community law, but also in situations where the application of Community law was uncertain.

3. THE STATUS OF INTERNATIONAL HUMAN RIGHTS LAW WITHIN THE COMMUNITY

The three political institutions of the Community (the Commission, the Council and the Parliament) have declared their commitment to fundamental rights in a joint declaration.[6] By this declaration the institutions stressed the importance they attach to fundamental rights as drawn, *inter alia*, from the constitutions of the member states and international conventions such as the European Convention on Human Rights (ECHR). The institutions have further pledged to respect those rights in the exercise of their powers,[7] although no specific list of rights has been enumerated. This expression of political will is reiterated in the Maastricht Treaty on European Union.[8]

The most effective protection of fundamental rights under Community law is through the jurisprudence of the European Court of Justice. It has consistently held that fundamental human rights are "enshrined in the general principles of Community law and protected by the

---

[4] Joined Cases C-6/90 and C-9/90, judgment of 19 Nov. 1991, reported in *The Times*, 20 Nov. 1991.

[5] Case 213/89, ECR 2433.

[6] Joint Declaration by the European Parliament, the Council and the Commission, 5 April 1977, OJ 1977, C 103/1.

[7] The preamble to the Single European Act (OJ 1987, L 1), for example, provides: "Determined to work together to promote democracy on the basis of the fundamental rights recognized in the constitutions and laws of the Member States, in the Convention for the Protection of Human Rights and Fundamental Freedoms and the European Social Charter, notably freedom, equality and social justice ... ."

[8] [1992] 1 CMLR 719. The common provisions of the Treaty acknowledge that the Union: "shall respect fundamental rights, as guaranteed by the European Convention for the Protection of Human Rights and Fundamental Freedoms signed in Rome on 4 November 1950 and as they result from the constitutional traditions common to the member-States, as general principles of Community law. [Article F.]"

Courts".[9] In defining the Community concept of fundamental rights, the Court looks both to the national legal systems of the member states and to international treaties.[10] Paramount among the international treaties relied on by the Court of Justice is the ECHR, but the Court may also turn to texts such as the International Covenant on Civil and Political Rights (ICCPR). The case law of the Court has firmly established Article 10 of the ECHR, guaranteeing the right to freedom of expression and information, as a fundamental right within Community law.

From the jurisprudence of the Court it is now clear that the Community concept of fundamental rights, including the Convention, can be used against the Community itself to challenge measures which conflict with those rights. This challenge may be laid against (1) directly applicable measures of Community law and (2) national measures implementing Community legislation.

It was originally considered that the fundamental rights under Community law could not be used to challenge the national law of the member states.[11] This position has now been qualified. National law falling within the field of application of Community legislation must comply with the fundamental rights. Where the national legislation lies outside the scope of Community law, however, the principle of fundamental rights cannot be used to attack the national legislation. It is not yet clear just how widely the Court of Justice or national courts will interpret the notion of national legislation falling within the scope of Community law. Nevertheless, recent authority has emphasized that member states must respect fundamental rights, including those set forth in the ECHR, when they seek to rely on issues of public policy or public interest as grounds for justifying national legislation that derogates from the principles of Community law.[12] Discussion of the way in which fundamental rights may be used to challenge national restrictions on the press is continued in the next section.

---

[9] *E.g.*, Case 29/69, *Stauder v. City of Ulm*, [1969] ECR 419, para. 7.

[10] Case 4/73, *Nold v. E.C. Commission*, [1974] ECR 491. At para. 13 the Court stated:

> "[F]undamental rights form an integral part of the general principles of law, the observance of which [the Court] ensures.
>
> In safeguarding these rights, the Court is bound to draw inspiration from constitutional traditions common to the member-States, and it cannot therefore uphold measures which are incompatible with fundamental rights recognized and protected by the Constitutions of those States.
>
> Similarly, international treaties for the protection of human rights on which the member-States have collaborated, or of which they are signatories, can supply guidelines which should be followed within the framework of Community law."

[11] *See, e.g.*, joined cases 60 - 61/84, *Cinéthèque S.A. v. Fédération Nationale des Cinémas Français*, [1986] 1 CMLR 365.

[12] Case C-260/89, *Elliniki Radiophonia Tiléorassi - Anonimi Etairia v. Dimotiki Etairia Pliroforissis*, judgment of 18 June 1991 (unreported); Case C-159/90, *S.P.U.C. v. Grogan*, [1991] 3 CMLR 849, in particular the opinion of Advocate General Van Gerven at paragraphs 30-31.

4.   PRESS REGULATION AND THE PRINCIPLES OF FREEDOM OF MOVEMENT

Underlying the steps to establish the common market are the principles of free movement of goods, persons, services and capital. The principles of free movement of goods and services, together with that part of the principle of free movement of persons embodied in the freedom of establishment (that is, the freedom to establish businesses), all have an effect on the legislative and administrative controls a member state may impose on the press functioning in its territory and on those from other member states seeking to provide press services within its territory.

The principle of free movement of goods is embodied in Articles 30 to 36 of the EEC Treaty. In essence, the principle prevents member states from introducing or maintaining any quantitative restrictions (or measures having equivalent effect) on the import or export of goods in free circulation within the Community. The member states may only derogate from this principle on the grounds provided in Article 36,[13] and then only if such derogations do not constitute arbitrary discrimination or a disguised restriction on trade between member states.

A distinction must be made between the free movement of services and the freedom of establishment. The former concerns (1) the right to provide services from one member state across the border in another member state and (2) the right of citizens to move across borders to receive services. The latter protects the right of a person from one member state to establish a business in another member state. The rules governing the free movement of services are set out in the EEC Treaty Articles 59 to 66; the rules governing the freedom of establishment are set out in Articles 52 to 58. These rules do not apply to activities concerned with the exercise of official authority nor do they apply to provisions providing for the special treatment of foreign nationals on grounds of public policy, public security or public health.

The Court of Justice has made it clear that the principles of free movement of goods and services and the freedom of establishment are applicable to both broadcasting and press services.[14] The principle of free movement of goods may be affected when restrictions on press or broadcasting services create, as an ancillary consequence, restrictions on the cross-frontier movement of goods (such as the necessary equipment to transmit programmes or produce newspapers).

The principles of free movement are primarily aimed at breaking down the overt and covert barriers to trade between member states. Provided that the legislation or administrative

---

[13] The grounds are: public morality; public policy; public security; the protection of health and life of humans, animals or plants; the protection of national treasures possessing artistic, historic or archaeological value; and the protection of industrial or commercial property.

[14] *See, e.g.*, Case 18/84, *Commission v. France*, [1986] 1 CMLR 605. The Court of Justice held that tax concessions granted by France to newspaper publishers for publications printed in France were contrary to EEC Treaty Article 30, on the grounds that they encouraged the publishers to have their newspapers and publications printed in France rather than in other member states and were likely to restrict the import of publications from abroad.

measures being challenged can be shown to act as such barriers, the principles may also offer a means of protecting the fundamental rights and freedoms of the press. The impact on the press of the principles of free movement may be examined from two angles: the ownership or control of press undertakings and the free flow of information.

4.1   Freedom of Movement and Regulation of Ownership

While there is no decision of the Court of Justice on point, it is certain that Community law would not accept state control of ownership of the printed press similar to that allowed for broadcasting.[15] The Commission and the Parliament have already expressed their support for policies encouraging the diversity of ownership of media organizations (*see infra* Section 5).

Community law restrains member states from imposing restrictions on the ownership of any enterprises, including press companies, by nationals of other member states which are stricter than those it imposes on its own nationals. Such a restriction would constitute a *prima facie* breach of the prohibition on discrimination set out in Article 7 of the EEC Treaty as well as of the rules on freedom of establishment set out in Article 52. While there have not been any cases brought concerning ownership of press companies, the Court of Justice has ruled that limitations imposed by the British government on foreign ownership of British-registered fishing vessels were contrary to Community law.[16] A member state might seek to uphold restrictions on the ownership of press companies as being a matter of public policy or security under Article 56. However, the burden would rest with the member state to justify both the need for the restriction and that such restriction was a proportionate means of achieving those needs. Such justification would probably be difficult to establish.

4.2   Regulation of the Free Flow of Information

In relation to the free flow of information, the principles of free movement act as a restraint on national measures to limit publication of the press or access to information. Any such measure must be justified by a member state on the grounds of public policy, public security or public health if the free movement of persons or services is affected or, on the wider grounds of exemption set out in EEC Treaty Article 36, if the free movement of goods is affected. Such justifications must be compatible with the fundamental rights of individuals.

---

[15] In the field of broadcasting, Community law does not prohibit member states from granting exclusive rights within their territory for the transmission and distribution of television and wireless programmes to one or several enterprises where the reasons for such grant are based on public interest grounds of a non-economic nature. The principles of free movement, however, do prohibit enterprises holding such rights from discriminating between programmes originating within the member state and programmes originating outside the member state concerned. The reasoning of the Court of Justice on the control of broadcasting organizations is set out *inter alia*, in Case 260/89, *Elliniki Radiophonia Tiléorassi-Anonimi Etairia v. Dimotiki Etairia Plirioforissis*, judgment of 18 June 1991 (unreported), and Case 155/73, *Saatchi* [1974] ECR 409. In *Saatchi*, Advocate General Reischl set out some of the grounds on which the control of broadcasting organizations may be considered a matter of public interest: "Television is without doubt a means of mass-communication of great cultural and educational significance, an instrument which, on account of the intensity of its effect, is particularly capable of influencing public opinion." [1974] ECR at 443.

[16] Case 221/89, *Reg. v. Secretary of State for Transport ex parte Factortame Limited* [1992] QB 680, 3 WLR 288.

Although briefly stated, this broad statement of principle is often difficult to apply, particularly when there are competing fundamental rights.

In *GB-Inno-BM v. Confederation du Commerce Luxembourgeois Asbl*,[17] the Court of Justice considered the compatibility of Luxembourg's legislation restricting the advertising of sales-promotion literature with the principles of free movement of goods. The Luxembourg law governing unfair competition provided that sales offers involving a temporary price reduction could not state the duration of the offer or refer to previous prices. The literature in question consisted of pamphlets published on behalf of a Belgian supermarket and distributed in both Belgium and Luxembourg. Although the pamphlets complied with Belgian law, they did not comply with Luxembourg's law. Injunctive proceedings were brought against the supermarket in Luxembourg. Answering a request for a preliminary ruling from the *Cour de Cassation* of Luxembourg, the European Court of Justice affirmed that restrictions in one member state on the distribution of advertising lawful in another member state are contrary to the principle of free movement of goods, unless those restrictions can be justified, *inter alia*, by reasons of consumer protection or the fairness of commercial transactions. The Court went on to find that the provision of information to consumers was an important element in consumer protection and that, consequently, national legislation which denied the consumer access to such information could not be justified on the ground of consumer protection.

The issue of access to information and the right to publish information arose in more controversial circumstances in *Society for the Protection of Unborn Children Ireland Ltd. (S.P.U.C.) v. Grogan*.[18] S.P.U.C. brought proceedings in Ireland against the officers of three student associations which published monthly bulletins for its members containing information about the availability of medical termination of pregnancy in the United Kingdom and the means of contacting clinics there where abortions were carried out lawfully. S.P.U.C. wrote to the student associations requesting an undertaking that they cease including such information in their publications on the ground that doing so breached the right to life enshrined in Article 40.3 of the Irish Constitution. When no undertakings were forthcoming, S.P.U.C. began injunctive proceedings against the associations, represented by their respective officers, to restrain publication of the information. The associations argued that the restrictions on the provision of information imposed by the Irish Constitution as interpreted by the Supreme Court were, among other things, contrary to the rules on the free movement of services embodied in the EEC Treaty. The case obviously raised sensitive political issues and a conflict between freedom of expression, including the right to receive and impart information, and Ireland's recognition of the right to life of the unborn. These issues were brought before the Court of Justice on a preliminary ruling from the Irish Supreme Court.

Both the Court of Justice and Advocate General Van Gerven emphasized the dual nature of the free movement of services (namely, the right to provide and the right to receive services and, ancillary to that, the right to provide information or to receive information about such services). The Court, no doubt mindful of the political sensitivity of its decision, restricted

---

[17] Case C-362/88, [1991] 2 CMLR 801.

[18] Case C-159/90, [1991] 3 CMLR 849.

its judgment to an examination of the impact of the injunction restraining publication on the student associations and did not examine the impact on the women seeking abortion information and services. The Court held that, as a matter of fact, the distribution of information was not carried on in cooperation with or on behalf of the economic operators concerned, namely the clinics providing the abortion services. On the contrary the Court found:

> "the information constitutes a manifestation of freedom of expression and of the freedom to impart and receive information which is independent of the economic activity carried on by clinics established in other member States."[19]

On this basis, the Court held that the proceedings in question did not raise an issue of the free movement of services and did not fall within the scope of Community law. Therefore, the Court, in contrast to the thorough and thought-provoking analysis of Advocate General Van Gerven, did not examine the compatibility of the restriction on communication with the principle of fundamental rights.

The judgment of the Court emphasizes the fact that the principles embodied in the ECHR do not, on their own, form a part of Community law which can be invoked against member states in all circumstances. The fundamental rights only come into play to control national measures which fall within the field of application of Community law. Secondly, in giving its judgment the Court concentrated on the right to distribute the information. No real consideration was given to the nature of the right of a "consumer" to receive information. The question which must therefore be asked is whether the right under Community law is limited to the receipt of information from a source acting on behalf of a service provider. The Court has also left open the issues of (1) whether clinics themselves have the right to distribute such information, and (2) the rights of the press to accept advertisements from such clinics for payment of a fee.[20] If and when these latter questions involving commercial transactions come before the Court, the Court will be forced to examine the impact under Community law of the principle of fundamental rights and the conflict between the rights of a foetus and the right to receive and impart information.

Despite the final decision, the *Grogan* case highlights: (a) the potential for using the principles of free movement in support of attempts to exercise fundamental rights, including the right to freedom of expression; and (b) the use of fundamental rights in conjunction with the principle of proportionality to check the justifications member states may advance for derogating from the principles of free movement.

---

[19] *Id.* at para. 25.

[20] The European Court of Human Rights in its Oct. 1992 decision in *Open Door Counselling, Dublin Well Woman Centre and Others v. Ireland* ruled that under Art. 10 of the ECHR women have the right to receive information about where and how to obtain lawful abortions outside Ireland. Judgment of 29 Oct. 1992, Series A no. 246.

5.   EEC COMPETITION POLICY AFFECTING THE MEDIA

The rules for the enforcement of EEC competition policy apply to the press as they do to any other economic sector. Articles 85 and 86 of the EEC Treaty prohibit behaviour which has the effect of restricting or distorting competition within the common market so as to affect trade between member states. Article 85 applies to agreements or concerted practices between businesses and to decisions of associations of businesses. Any agreement or decision falling foul of Article 85 is automatically void unless it qualifies for an exemption from the Commission. Article 86 controls the unilateral conduct of businesses which have a dominant position within the common market and prohibits conduct which is abusive of that position.

Although Articles 85 and 86 do not affect the regulation of the press by government,[21] they do apply to the behaviour of the press organizations amongst themselves. For example, in *German Television Stations,*[22] the Commission intervened to require amendments to agreements between various German television stations and the American film company Metro-Goldwyn-Mayer/United Artists Entertainment Co. to provide access for the German television stations to the American company film libraries.

More recently, the Commission was requested to review an agreement between a French racing pictures company, Pari Mutuel International (PMI), and a German sports publisher, Deutscher Sportverlag Kurt Stoof. The agreement granted the German firm exclusive rights to relay French race news and pictures owned by PMI to betting shops in West Germany and Austria. Although the Commission originally refused to grant an exemption in the agreement under EEC Treaty Article 85(3), it has indicated a favourable attitude to a modified agreement.[23]

In a series of cases, *RTE, BBC and ITV v. Commission,*[24] the Court of Justice was asked to consider the right of television companies to restrict access to their weekly programme schedules. The three plaintiffs had all been found liable by the Commission for infringing EEC Treaty Article 86, by refusing to grant licences for the publication of their advance weekly programme listings to publishers of magazines other than their own affiliated publishing operation. The Court upheld the Commission's decision.

---

[21] EEC Treaty Articles 92 to 94, however, prohibit member states from granting aid in any form to businesses, except in limited circumstances, which distorts or threatens to distort competition by favouring those businesses. The state aid regime extends to state subsidy of the press. *See* Case 18/84, *Commission v. France*, [1986] 1 CMLR 605 (regarding tax concessions to French newspapers).

[22] OJ, 1989 L 284/36; on appeal, case T168/89 *MGM/UA v. Commission*.

[23] European Report no. 1799, 30 Sept. 1992, [1992] 5 CMLR 600.

[24] Cases 69/89, 70/89, and 76/89, [1991] 4 CMLR, 586, 669 and 745.

The control of mergers and takeovers with a Community dimension is governed by Regulation 4064/89.[25] The Regulation requires notification to and approval by the Commission of all mergers and takeovers that fall within the thresholds set by the regulation. Presently, the Regulation provides that a concentration will have a Community dimension if the aggregate turnover of all businesses involved is more than ECU 5,000 million (US$ 3,447 million) and the aggregate Community-wide turnover of at least two of the concerned businesses is more than ECU 250 million (US$ 172 million). The limits will not apply if each of the concerned businesses achieves more than two-thirds of its aggregate Community-wide turnover within one member state. The Commission is pressing for the thresholds to be lowered. The Regulation currently applies to the press although this could change if specific legislation concerning media concentration is adopted. Under the Regulation, the Commission is given sole jurisdiction to take decisions concerning concentrations with a Community dimension to the exclusion of the competent authorities of the member states. No member state may apply national competition legislation to a concentration with a Community dimension. Member states are entitled, however, to take appropriate steps to protect their legitimate interests, including the plurality of the media.[26] There do not seem to have been any Commission decisions either prohibiting or approving a press or cross-media merger.

A report of the European Parliament has called for specific provisions preventing concentration of media ownership and guaranteeing diversity of opinions and pluralism.[27] The Commission is considering the issue but, as of the end of 1992, had not published any proposals for such provisions. The Commission currently takes the view that it and the member states have ample power to control media concentrations under Regulation 4064/89.

6.   ACCESS TO CLASSIFIED INFORMATION AND DATA PROTECTION

The Commission has advanced specific proposals for legislative measures to harmonize national laws in the fields of classified information and data protection. The principles of free movement discussed in Section 4 above are relevant when considering the question of access to information more generally. There is no harmonizing legislation governing the question of access to information held by national governments or their institutions. Indeed, it is arguable that such a topic falls outside the competence of the Community. The Parliament's Fayot/Schinzel Report, however, calls on the Commission to develop a proposed directive, similar to the US Freedom of Information Act, which would guarantee journalists access to information from the Community and national authorities.[28]

---

[25] OJ 1989, L 257/14.

[26] Article 21 of the Regulation.

[27] *See Fayot/Schinzel Report* on media concentration and diversity of opinion of 27 April 1992 (Doc. EN/RR/207249), debated on 9 July 1992.

[28] *Id.* The Report also asks that the proposed directive address protection of journalists' sources and "whistleblowers".

6.1   Classified Information

At present there is no general measure governing the classification and protection of information relating to Community activities transmitted between one institution or member state and another.

Only the Euratom Treaty makes specific provision for the classification and protection of information. This is a consequence of political sensitivity attached to nuclear research. The framework provisions of Article 24 of Euratom are enhanced by Regulation 3 (Euratom) of 31 July 1958, which created a category of classified information known as Euratom Classified Information ("ECI") and established a four-tiered system of classification: Eura-Top Secret, Eura-Secret, Eura-Confidential and Eura-Restricted.[29] The Regulation also sets forth the criteria for access to the various levels of information, including a system of authorization and screening. There is no public interest defence for unauthorized disclosures. Disclosure of classified information also might be subject to applicable national criminal law. However, Regulation 3 does not provide any specific penalties for unauthorized disclosures.

6.2   Environmental Information

More recently the Single European Act strengthened the EEC Treaty with regard to environmental policy. Included among the measures to implement that policy was a Council Directive on the Freedom of Access to Information on the Environment.[30] The objective of the directive is to "ensure freedom of access to, and dissemination of information on, the environment held by public authorities and to set out the basic terms and conditions on which such information should be made available."[31] Under this objective, all member states have an obligation to ensure that public authorities are required to make available information relating to the environment to any natural or legal person without that person having to prove an interest.

The potential impact of the directive is weakened by the wide-ranging exemption clauses. Article 3 permits member states to refuse requests which affect: (1) the confidentiality of the proceedings of public authorities, international relations or national defence; (2) public security; (3) matters which are, or have been, *sub judice,* or are under enquiry (including disciplinary enquiries), or which are the subject of preliminary investigation proceedings; (4) commercial and industrial confidentiality, including intellectual property; (5) the confidentiality of personal data and/or files; (6) material supplied by a third party without that party being under an obligation to do so; and (7) material the disclosure of which would make it more likely that the environment to which such material related would be damaged. Nevertheless, the directive has considerable force in that it (a) imposes a requirement on

---

[29] OJ 1958, at 406; English text published in *Encyclopaedia of Community Law,* (Sweet and Maxwell) at C6 - 003.

[30] OJ 1990, L 158/56.

[31] Article 1.

public authorities to respond to requests for information within two month, and (b) creates a legal duty on member states to supply information or to give reasons for any refusal.

Apart from the measures discussed in this sub-section and *supra* in Section 6.1, the Commission has proposed a Council Regulation governing grading, storage, distribution and access to classified information connected with EEC or Euratom activities.[32] The proposed regulation is similar to Regulation 3. The proposal provides for the establishment of a three-tiered system of security grading for EEC classified information and for disciplinary action against any Community employee who fails to comply with the regulation's requirements, although the nature of such action is unspecified. Disciplinary action by member states against public servants and persons or firms under contract is left to the state concerned. As presently drafted, the proposed regulation does not allow employees of the institutions the defence that disclosure was justified in the public interest. Amendments to the proposed regulation are expected before it is passed.

6.3   Data Protection

The growth in the transfer of information between states has led the Commission to propose harmonization of national laws on the protection of data. In the context of freedom of the press, the most significant of the proposed measures is a proposal for a Council Directive Concerning the Protection of Individuals in Relation to the Processing of Personal Data.[33] The measure is intended to ensure the protection of individuals' privacy regarding processing of personal data contained in data files. To this extent, the objectives of the proposal provide protection for the rights guaranteed by Article 8 of the ECHR.

The proposal covers data files in the public and private sectors, which are either automatically processed or held in a structured and accessible, organized collection. It does not apply to files held by non-profit bodies as part of their legitimate aims if those files relate to members who have consented to be included. The proposal sets out the criteria under which public and private sector institutions are entitled to hold files on people. In addition, private sector institutions may only hold files with the consent of the individual concerned or in accordance with the terms of the proposed directive.[34]

With regard to data held by the private sector, a person has the right *inter alia*: (a) to oppose for legitimate reasons the processing of personal data; (b) to know of the existence of a file and its main purposes; (c) to obtain at reasonable intervals and without excessive delay confirmation of the existence of a file and copies of the data in an intelligible form.

---

[32] OJ 1992, C 72/15.

[33] OJ 1990, C 277/3.

[34] Article 8. The alternatives to consent are: (a) the data is collected and maintained under a contract, or in the context of a quasi-contractual relationship of trust with the person who is the subject of the data, and the maintenance of the data file is necessary for the accomplishment of the contract or quasi-contract; or (b) the data comes from sources generally accessible to the public and their processing is intended solely for correspondence purposes; or (c) the controller of the file is pursuing a legitimate interest which overrides the interest of the data subject.

As drafted, the proposal allows member states to permit the press and audiovisual media exemption from some of its requirements when this is necessary to reconcile the rights of data subjects with the rules governing the freedom of information. It is, however, for member states to decide the nature and extent of exceptions in the first instance. If the proposal becomes legislation in its present form without the inclusion of suitable exceptions, it would impose stringent restrictions on the investigative powers of the press and on the right of journalists to maintain the confidentiality of their sources.

7.   RIGHT OF REPLY

There is no EEC legislation dictating situations when newspapers are bound to give a right of reply. In the field of broadcasting, the Community has, however, acknowledged the importance of the right of reply in its Directive on television broadcasting activities.[35] Article 23 of the Directive requires all member states to ensure that, whatever the other legal remedies available, any person whose legitimate interests have been damaged by an assertion of incorrect facts in a television programme has a right of reply or equivalent remedy.

8.   THE REGULATION OF ADVERTISING

Various EEC measures govern the harmonization of the legal regimes within the member states concerning misleading advertising and the advertising of particular products such as foodstuffs,[36] and medicinal products for human use.[37]

The Directive on Television Broadcasting prohibits televised advertisements for cigarettes, tobacco products, medicinal products and treatment available only on prescription, and limits the advertisement of alcoholic beverages. In addition, television advertisements must not prejudice respect for human dignity, include any discrimination on grounds of race, sex or nationality, be offensive to religious or political beliefs, or encourage behaviour prejudicial to health, safety, or the protection of the environment.

---

[35] Council Directive on the Coordination of Certain Provisions Laid Down by Law, Regulation or Administrative Action in Member States Concerning the Pursuit of Television Broadcasting Activities, OJ 1989, L 298/23.

[36] Council Directive on the Approximation of the Laws of the Member States Relating to the Labelling, Presentation and Advertising of Foodstuffs for Sale to the Ultimate Consumer, OJ 1979, L 33 /1 amended OJ 1989, L 186/17.

[37] Council Directive on the Advertising of Medicinal Products for Human Use, OJ 1992, L 113/13.

Specific reference to advertising in the press is contained in a draft proposal on tobacco product advertising.[38] The proposal at present is for a directive which would require member states to introduce legislation which would, amongst other measures: (a) prohibit all advertising for tobacco products in publications mainly intended for persons under the age of 18; and (b) require the inclusion of a certain specific health warning in any advertisement in the press or any bill or poster for cigarettes, and of a general health warning for other tobacco products.

None of the directives or proposals discussed above provides specific penalties or methods of enforcement.

---

[38] Proposal for a Council Directive on the Advertising of Tobacco Products in the Press and by Means of Bills and Posters; OJ 1989, C 124/5, amended OJ 1990, C 116/7.

Chapter 14

COMPARATIVE ANALYSIS OF PRESS LAW
IN EUROPEAN AND OTHER DEMOCRACIES

Sandra Coliver

INTRODUCTION

The European Court of Human Rights has declared that press freedom requires particular protection so as to enable the press "to play its vital role of 'public watchdog'" and "to impart information and ideas on matters of public interest".[1] What becomes clear in reading the country chapters in this collection is that press law plays but one part, and surely not the most important, in determining the degree to which the press carries out these twin functions. Other crucial factors include cultural, historical and market influences.

Culture influences the public's attitude towards the press, the degree to which the public values strong investigative reporting, and the extent of its outrage over reporting which intrudes into private matters. While actions for defamation and invasion of privacy undeniably can harm the financial health of papers, the potential impact on a paper's reputation can be at least as important a deterrent. In some countries, an accusation of defamation, or of withholding evidence which could assist the police in their investigations, may significantly harm a paper's reputation and its circulation; in others, the public may be more inclined to accept the occasional lawsuit as the price for vigorous investigative reporting. In some countries the press views its role as working in partnership with the government to promote the policies and personalities for which the public has voted, while in other countries even the mainstream press believes that good government requires constant vigilance.

In some countries, the popular press manifests a commitment to high journalistic standards and respects the decisions of the voluntary press council; in others, commitment to accepted professional standards is less prevalent. Market influences clearly play a significant role: in some countries competition for sales and concentration of ownership have resulted in the lowering of general journalistic standards and/or reduction in the diversity of opinions expressed, while in others, especially where editors have more independence from their publishers, market concentration may not have as strong an influence.

In Spain, the historical proximity of dictatorship has led to stronger protection for the reputation of democratic institutions; in several countries concern over support for revisionist, fascist or terrorist ideologies has led to tougher restraints on the advocacy of those ideas.

---

[1] *The Sunday Times v. UK*, Judgment of 26 April 1979, Series A no. 30, para. 65; *Lingens v. Austria*, Judgment of 8 July 1986, Series A no. 103, para. 42.

The interplay of different cultural, historical and market influences and interactions makes it impossible to identify any one system of press law as a model for other countries in the abstract. Nonetheless, the role of law should not be discounted. Laws are both a product of and a formative influence on cultural, political and market dynamics; a law that has worked well in one country may indeed work well in others, especially if other relevant influences are also taken into account.

This chapter sets forth the prevailing patterns concerning, as well as minority approaches to, the different aspects of press freedom examined in the country chapters. Throughout, countries which follow an identified pattern are noted in parentheses; these lists of countries are not comprehensive but rather are included to assist the reader who might wish to consult a country chapter for greater detail. Because this chapter is not intended to stand alone, it includes few footnotes; substantiation of any point may be found in the referenced country chapters.

The aim of this chapter is two-fold. First, the patterns, as well as unusual variants, may suggest legislative models suitable for adaptation to other countries. Second, to the extent that a practice is common among all or virtually all of the European countries studied, that practice may provide compelling evidence of an evolving interpretation of Article 10 of the European Convention on Human Rights (discussed at greater length in this chapter's conclusion).

1.   CONSTITUTIONAL PROVISIONS

The only two countries of the eleven studied that do not have an explicit guarantee of freedom of expression entrenched in a written constitution are the United Kingdom and Australia. While lawyers in both the UK and Australia contend that the freedom is guaranteed in their *unwritten* constitutions, it nonetheless becomes apparent that in a number of areas protection of freedom of expression in general and press freedom in particular lags behind protection in countries with written constitutions.

Of the nine countries that have express constitutional protection, all except Spain include express protection of the press, and the Spanish courts have construed an implied protection. In at least two countries (Germany, Spain) the press is deemed to have greater rights than others to collect and publish information (as well as certain responsibilities). These rights arise from the press' special role in contributing to the formation of public opinion and serving as public watchdog. In some countries, the government has a positive duty to promote press freedom and pluralism (in addition to the traditional liberal duty to refrain from interference), either by explicit statement in the Constitution (Netherlands, Sweden) or else by judicial interpretation (France, Germany). The Constitution of Sweden offers the most explicit protection of press freedom.

Three countries include in their constitutions express protection of the right of the public to receive information of legitimate public interest (Netherlands, Spain, Sweden), and the courts of another three countries have interpreted their constitutions to include such a guarantee

(France, Germany, US). The Constitution of the Netherlands provides that "government bodies shall observe the right of public access to information" (Article 110). The Constitution of Sweden guarantees to all citizens "in their relations with the public administration ... the freedom to obtain and receive information and otherwise acquaint oneself with the utterances of others".[2]

2. DISTRIBUTION OF POWERS BETWEEN CENTRAL AND REGIONAL GOVERNMENT

Australia, Austria, Canada, Germany and the United States are federal systems. In Australia, Canada and the US, the primary laws affecting the press, including defamation and privacy, are state laws (although in Canada and the US, all state laws must comply with basic principles set forth in the federal constitutions). In Austria, the federal government exercises all powers relevant to the press. In Germany, federal law largely controls defamation and invasion of privacy actions; other issues are primarily regulated by the states. There is some sentiment within Germany that press powers should be concentrated in the federal government in order to minimize complexities due to shared jurisdiction, particularly in light of the trend towards harmonization of media law in the European Community.

The Netherlands, Norway and Sweden all have unitary systems of government. Although France, Spain and the UK have (relatively weak) regional systems, all powers relevant to the press are exercised by the central government.

3. ROLE OF THE COURTS

Six countries have courts that can declare statutes to be unconstitutional and thus invalid (Austria, Canada, France, Germany, Spain and the US). Four of these (Austria, France, Germany and Spain) have separate constitutional courts. The constitutional courts of Austria and France may only rule on constitutional issues in the abstract; the courts of Spain and Germany may also decide appeals involving constitutional issues. The lower courts of Austria, Germany and Spain may stay proceedings and refer a question to the constitutional court if they believe that a statute is invalid. The lower courts in Austria have been applying constitutional principles at least since the early 1980s. France's *Conseil constitutionnel* may declare a statute unconstitutional only when a statute passed by Parliament and not yet promulgated is referred to it by one of various government or legislative authorities; courts may not refer constitutional questions to it.

In the US and Canada, all courts are bound to apply the constitution and to disregard laws that they deem to be unconstitutional (with the proviso that in Canada, the provinces are entitled to derogate from certain constitutional provisions). The federal Supreme Courts of

---

[2] Chapter 2, Article 1 of the Instrument of Government, elaborated in the Freedom of the Press Act, Chapter 2.

both countries are the final arbiters concerning compliance with the federal constitutions, and the state supreme courts are the final interpreters of their state constitutions.

Although Norway and Sweden have no separate constitutional court, the courts at every level have the power not to apply a statute that they find to be unconstitutional (with Supreme Courts in each country resolving conflicts), and to apply the constitution in disputes involving government or private action. Nonetheless, Swedish courts rarely decline to enforce a statute, and the Norwegian Supreme Court has construed the constitutional guarantee of freedom of expression narrowly.

In Australia, the Netherlands and the UK, parliamentary supremacy is strongly respected. The courts, however, may invalidate acts of public bodies as unconstitutional and may ensure observance of constitutional (or fundamental) rights in disputes between individuals.

Because of the obvious constitutional importance of press freedom, the governing law, even in many civil law systems, is increasingly being established by case-law rather than by statute.

4.   STATUS OF HUMAN RIGHTS TREATIES IN NATIONAL COURTS

All countries discussed in this study are parties to the International Covenant on Civil and Political Rights (ICCPR), and all countries save Germany, the US and the UK are also parties to its First Optional Protocol (which entitles individuals to file complaints against the country with the UN Human Rights Committee). All eight European countries are parties to the European Convention on Human Rights (ECHR) and have accepted the right of individual petition as well as the jurisdiction of the Court. All except Austria, Norway and Sweden are also members of the European Communities (EC) and parties to the EC Treaty of Rome, which is binding within domestic legal systems without any further legislative action. Neither of the two countries in the inter-American system (Canada and the US) has ratified the American Convention on Human Rights. Although all countries are parties to the ECHR and/or the ICCPR, the status of these treaties in domestic law differs considerably.[3]

In Spain and the Netherlands, duly ratified treaties are immediately enforceable by the courts, without further legislative action. In Spain, domestic courts must follow treaty interpretations, when directly relevant, of authoritative international bodies (such as the European Court of Human Rights), so long as such interpretations do not narrow the scope of a constitutional right. Moreover, courts are to apply the interpretations of non-authoritative bodies (such as the European Commission on Human Rights and the UN Human Rights Committee) as interpretative guides in applying domestic law. In the Netherlands, treaty provisions pre-empt conflicting statutes, and all courts may refuse to apply a statute that is inconsistent with a treaty provision.

---

[3] This study does not discuss the status of customary international law in domestic courts because customary norms on freedom of expression are broad and do not impose standards more demanding than those recognized in the domestic laws of the countries studied.

In France and the US, provisions of ratified treaties are immediately enforceable by the courts without legislative incorporation if they are deemed to be self-executing (i.e., that they impose obligations which are specific, mandatory and capable of implementation without further legislative action). However, the two countries follow dramatically different approaches. In France, there is a presumption in favour of a treaty being self-executing, and Article 10 of the ECHR is directly applied by the courts. Moreover, self-executing treaty provisions, like treaty provisions in Dutch law, take precedence over all statutes, even if enacted later in time, and all courts are empowered to construe and apply treaties. Since courts (other than the *Conseil constitutionnel*) are not empowered to set aside statutes as contrary to the Constitution, the result is that treaties enjoy a stronger protection than the Constitution *vis-a-vis* conflicting statutes. In the US, in contrast, courts have been reluctant to find human rights provisions of treaties to be self-executing, and the US declared when it ratified the ICCPR that it did not consider any of its provisions to be self-executing.

In most countries (Australia, Austria, Canada, Germany, Norway, Sweden, UK), the legislature must expressly incorporate or otherwise endorse a treaty before it may be applied by the courts. Germany's parliament has approved the ECHR and the ICCPR, and Austria's parliament has incorporated the ECHR. In Austria, the ECHR has constitutional status and in Germany it has the status of a federal statute.

The UK, Sweden and Norway have not incorporated either the ECHR or the ICCPR, and Canada and Australia have not expressly incorporated the ICCPR (although a number of the provisions of Canada's Charter of Rights and Freedoms are modelled on those of the ICCPR and the ECHR[4]). Nonetheless, the courts of all five countries have held that national law should be construed, whenever possible, to be consistent with international standards, and that a statute should pre-empt a treaty provision only when there is a clear conflict between the two. Despite the similarity of their doctrines in law, in practice the courts of Australia, Canada, Sweden and Norway have been more receptive to the international standards than the courts of the UK. Nonetheless, the UK's House of Lords recently declared that "it was appropriate" for the Court of Appeal "to have regard to" the ECHR in construing an ambiguous aspect of the common law in light of the fact that "the law of England was uncertain upon the issue lying at the heart of the case".[5]

5. STATUTORY FRAMEWORK

Only two of the countries, Austria and Sweden, have a single press law which contains most major provisions applicable to the press (Sweden's law being of constitutional status). While Germany has a number of federal laws which affect the press, each *Land* has a single press law, all of which broadly follow the same pattern. France has a number of laws which apply

---

[4] *See* A Bayefsky and J Fitzpatrick, "International Human Rights Law in United States Courts: A Comparative Perspective", 14 *Mich. J. of Int'l L.* 1, 48 (1992).

[5] *Derbyshire County Council v. Times Newspapers Ltd.*, Judgment of 18 Feb. 1993 (per Lord Keith of Kinkel), approving [1992] 3 All ER 65 (CA).

only or primarily to the press, but which are scattered throughout various codes. Seven countries have no single press law and few or no laws which apply exclusively to the press (Australia, Canada, Netherlands, Norway, Spain, UK, US). In many of the countries, press reformers have been calling for consolidation and rationalization of the laws, and such an undertaking is well under way in France. The fact that Sweden and Germany offer among the strongest protection of press freedom demonstrates that the presence of a unified press law does not, by itself, bode ill for the press.

6.   REGULATION OF OWNERSHIP

Nearly all of the countries studied have been experiencing a dramatic increase in the concentration of ownership of the press, and a number, most notably Australia and Austria, have also suffered a process of "newspaper dying" (a significant drop in the number of titles being published with the consequence that many regions are served by only a single paper). The governments of the various countries have reacted to these trends in different ways.

France and Germany adopted strict laws (France in 1986 and Germany in 1976) prohibiting transactions that would lead to high levels of ownership concentration. France also requires publications to publish information concerning their ownership in every issue. The effectiveness of these laws has been limited, however, owing in part to their failure to regulate cross-media ownership.

The UK's Monopolies and Mergers Commission reviews mergers of newspapers, but in practice its power to prevent a merger is quite limited. Australia and Austria were (as of the end of 1992) considering recommendations to regulate mergers and take-overs of press companies, while Canada's federal government has declined to act on recommendations to limit ownership to a certain market share.

The remaining five countries (the Netherlands, Norway, Spain, Sweden and the US) do not specifically regulate ownership of the press, although they may subject the press to anti-trust and corporate laws to varying degrees. Ownership is not more concentrated in these countries than in those which regulate ownership more closely, suggesting that other factors play a more significant role.

Five countries (Australia, Canada, Norway, the UK and the US) restrict or limit cross-ownership of different types of media (i.e., newspapers, television, radio). However, such regulations are not uniformly implemented and in some countries (e.g., the UK) have not proved effective in practice. Austria is currently considering an amendment to its anti-trust law that would prohibit media cross-ownership.

Several countries (Australia, Canada, France and Spain) regulate the acquisition by foreigners of shares in press companies. In Australia and Canada, foreigners must pass governmental review but are seldom prohibited from acquiring shares. In Spain, regulation is largely administrative in character and does not involve limits on percentage of foreign ownership. German companies own substantial shares in major Austrian publications, and Rupert

Murdoch, now of US citizenship, exercises a substantial influence in the UK's tabloid market. France imposes the tightest controls on foreign investment; since 1984, foreigners have been barred from owning or acquiring more than 20 per cent of a press enterprise (which may well violate EC Law).

Five countries (Austria, France, the Netherlands, Norway and Sweden) provide government subsidies to certain newspapers experiencing financial difficulties in order to preserve diversity. Some of the subsidy systems were established following the rise in popularity of television and radio and the corresponding substantial reduction in advertising revenue available to the press. Press subsidies tend to be controversial, with some arguing that they prevent necessary rationalization and market adaptation while others maintain that they are necessary to achieve pluralism. The Netherlands and Norway condition the granting of subsidies on protection of the editorial independence of journalists. The Dutch system is interesting in that most kinds of subsidies may be only temporary, to assist papers "with a special character" to start publishing or to survive a difficult period. Subsidies are generally thought to be successful in Sweden, where they are given only to the second strongest paper in each market.

Germany does not subsidize newspapers owing to a concern that, to the extent that some publications would receive greater subsidies than others, subsidies could influence editorial tendency. Austria has addressed this problem by granting the same amount to *all* newspapers which apply.

Most countries provide indirect subsidies by granting concessions on taxes and/or postal or telephone rates (e.g., Austria, France, Germany, Norway, Sweden, US). These indirect subsidies are for the most part not controversial and are seen as important supports for the press.

In light of the fact that concentration of ownership is a reality of press life, mechanisms for protecting editorial independence *vis-à-vis* publishers may be at least as important as controls on ownership concentration. In Germany, the Netherlands, Norway, and Sweden journalists have taken concrete steps to protect their editorial independence. Many of Germany's more "liberal" papers have accepted editorial understandings giving staff journalists a voice in editorial policy as well as in the selection of the editor-in-chief, although the understandings offer scant protection when strong disagreements arise. Dutch journalists have had "editorial statutes" included in their collective labour agreements. In Sweden, where most papers, at least until recently, were owned by political parties, many papers have two editors-in-chief: one for the editorial page, and one for the rest of the paper.

Norwegian editors have achieved a particularly effective protection of their independence, the *Redaktørplakaten* (Editors' Code), drafted in 1953 and revised in 1973. Under this Code, recognized by the courts as a statement of custom under the common law, the editor-in-chief has the sole and unlimited power to decide what to publish. Publishers who have tampered with editorial decisions have found themselves without an editorial staff; in one case a paper went bankrupt when its staff quit following the publisher's order to remove an article about his family business. The strength of journalistic support for the Code and for editorial autonomy has tended to reduce the potentially negative impacts of ownership concentration.

7.   REGISTRATION REQUIREMENTS

None of the countries studied requires any form of government approval to launch a newspaper or periodical. In fact, in Austria, papers and periodicals are exempt from having to get a trading licence, required of such businesses as book publishers and printers.

A few countries (France, Spain, UK) impose registration requirements, but the authorities have no power to refuse registration. The requirements were never used as mechanisms of censorship in France, and have not been so used for at least several decades in the UK and since the Franco period in Spain. In France, prior to the launching of any daily or periodical, a declaration must be filed with the State Prosecutor's office indicating the title and names and addresses of the publisher and printer. In Spain, the publisher must obtain a registration number, which is given automatically. In Sweden, the publisher must register the name of the person who is legally responsible for the publication's contents; the requirement is not enforced but an owner who does not register will be personally liable for any offences committed by the publication.

Several countries require papers to include the names and addresses of their publishers and printers (Australia, Austria). Most require that at least one copy of each issue of a paper or periodical be deposited with the national library or other depository. In France, copies must be deposited with various local authorities, including the State Prosecutor's office or town hall.

8.   REGULATION OF IMPORT AND EXPORT OF PUBLICATIONS

None of the countries studied impose restrictions on the export of publications. The French Government positively promotes the circulation of French publications abroad by granting small financial incentives.

The laws governing import of publications range from extremely liberal (Austria, Netherlands, Norway, Spain, Sweden and the US, where even embargo laws do not apply to informational material) to restrictive (France). Australia, Canada and the UK regulate the import of printed material involving obscenity, violence, the promotion of terrorism and prostitution.

The laws of France and Germany continue to reflect a cold war spirit. Germany still prohibits the import of publications, even if not brought into the country for sale, which might threaten the "free democratic order", although the prohibition is narrowly applied. In France, any writing in a foreign language or "of a foreign origin", even if published in France by a French company, may be banned. The law was widely used until the late 1970s to ban the import of communist publications, and still is used against extreme forms of pornography and anti-

Semitism. It has also been used at the request of some African and Middle-Eastern governments to ban opposition newspapers published in or outside of France. During the Gulf War, two Arabic-language papers were banned. The law is archaic and seems clearly to violate Article 10 of the ECHR.

9.   MECHANISMS OF PRESS SELF-REGULATION

9.1   Press Councils and Ombudsmen

Eight of the countries studied have some system of voluntary press self-regulation. Six of the eight European countries have press councils (Austria, Germany, Netherlands, Norway, Sweden, UK), as does Australia. While there is no Canadian national press council, five of the provinces have their own councils, and four provinces have a regional council. (The following discussion focuses on the seven countries that have national press councils.)

All seven of the national councils have authority to hear and decide cases of individual complaints against the press. A few also promote press freedom by contributing to public policy debates and making representations to their governments (e.g, Australia and Austria). While the former British Press Council (replaced in 1991 by the Press Complaints Commission) was widely criticized for exercising these dual functions, even critics of the Australian Press Council have not complained about, and see no conflict between, its dual roles.

In addition to a press council, Sweden has a Press Ombudsman, and the Executive Secretary of the Australian Press Council serves a role similar to that of ombudsman. Both attempt to mediate disputes before they are submitted to the more formal procedure of the councils.

The national press councils and ombudsman all were established jointly by publishers, journalists and other press associations. Most were established in response to increasing calls by the public for statutory regulation in the face of perceived journalistic excesses.

All of the press councils are financed by their constituent press associations. The Swedish Press Council supplements its finances by fining offending papers up to the equivalent of approximately US$ 4,000 per violation.

The effectiveness of a press council in promoting responsible reportage while safeguarding essential press freedoms may be judged by three primary factors: (1) the degree to which the ethical guidelines forming the basis of its decisions adequately balance the protection necessary for the press to perform its special functions against various governmental and individual interests; (2) the consistency and forcefulness with which the council applies the standards; and (3) the degree to which newspapers comply with the council's decisions.

9.1.1   Content of press codes

Most of the seven national press councils have elaborated press codes which they use to guide their decisions. All of the codes address most or all of the following issues:

> (1) honesty and fairness; duty to seek the views of the subject of any critical reportage in advance of publication; duty to correct factual errors; duty not to falsify pictures or to use them in a misleading fashion;

> (2) duty to provide an opportunity to reply to critical opinions as well as to critical factual reportage;

> (3) appearance as well as reality of objectivity; some codes prohibit members of the press from receiving gifts;

> (4) respect for privacy;

> (5) duty to distinguish between facts and opinion;

> (6) duty not to discriminate or to inflame hatred on such grounds as race, nationality, religion, or gender; some codes call on the press to refrain from mentioning the race, religion or nationality of the subjects of news stories unless relevant to the story; some call for coverage which promotes tolerance;

> (7) duty not to use dishonest means to obtain information;

> (8) duty not to endanger people;

> (9) general standards of decency and taste;

> (10) duty not to divulge confidential sources;

> (11) duty not to prejudge the guilt of an accused and to publish the dismissal of charges against or acquittal of anyone about whom the paper previously had reported that charges had been filed or that a trial had commenced.

9.1.2   Membership

All of the councils, except the Austrian and German ones, include public members who do not have press backgrounds (Australia: 7 of 21 members; Netherlands: 8 of 16; Norway: 3 of 7; Sweden: 3 of 6). The absence of public representatives is one of the chief factors cited for lack of public awareness of the work of the Austrian Press Council, as well as for its ineffectiveness.

Three of the councils are chaired by lawyers (Netherlands, Sweden and Australia).

9.1.3   Mechanisms

Most press councils permit complaints to be filed only by people who are directly or indirectly mentioned or affected by an article. The Austrian Press Council is unique in that it permits anyone to file a complaint, not only persons who are directly injured by an article. The Norwegian Press Council authorizes the Secretary-General of the Press Association (who is not a member of the Press Council) to file complaints on his own initiative.

Most press councils hold oral hearings at which the parties may present evidence; the Swedish and British press councils base their decisions only on written proceedings.

Most press councils try to discourage complainants from also taking their complaints to the courts on the ground that the press complaints process then becomes redundant and the press will be inclined to disregard it. In Sweden, dissatisfied complainants do on occasion file lawsuits, and courts on occasion support their judgments with arguments drawn from the Council's opinion and ethical principles; papers are particularly unhappy when the results of a voluntary process are used against them in court, but in practice the number of such cases is small. The Australian Press Council actually requires complainants to sign a declaration that they will not go to court if dissatisfied; it reports that the waiver requirement works well, that few complainants are discouraged by it and that none has challenged it in the courts.

For most councils, the chief sanction is the obligation of an offending paper to publish any negative findings; the chief impetus for a paper to publish a negative finding is the desire to remain a member of the association or council in good standing and to impress the public that it plays by the rules. The Netherlands Press Council publishes decisions in the major journalists' trade journal, and also asks (but does not oblige) the offending papers to publish or summarize its decisions. The Australian Press Council only obliges papers to publish summaries rather than full decisions.

9.1.4   Effectiveness

The Swedish, Norwegian and Dutch press councils are among the most effective. All include non-press members, and the Swedish and Dutch councils have lawyers as chairs which may serve to improve the consistency of their judgments as well as to assist in promoting the clarification of standards through the development of a body of "case-law." All have worked reasonably well in keeping the number of lawsuits against the press low and in safeguarding press freedoms. In particular, all have proved reasonably satisfactory to the press and public in safeguarding the privacy of private individuals while permitting scrutiny and criticism of politicians and public officials.

Probably the two most important factors accounting for the councils' success is the respect of the major papers for their decisions and the confidence of the public. (In contrast, the Austrian Press Council's authority is seriously undermined by the refusal of the most powerful Austrian newspaper to comply with, or publish, its rulings.) Major papers, in turn, seem to respect the councils' decisions where there are strong publishers' associations which actively support the councils. The public's respect appears to flow from the papers' compliance with decisions as well as from the participation of public members on the councils.

The Australian Press Council has done much to enhance the responsibility of the press, but its record demonstrates the constraints caused by lukewarm support from publishers and laws which make it fairly easy, even for public officials, to win libel lawsuits against the press.

The value of an effective press council is that it provides a process which is quicker and less expensive than a court hearing for the resolution of complaints against the press. On the other hand, some critics counter that press councils contribute little to protecting press freedom or countervailing individual interests (such as in privacy or reputation) owing to the weakness of their sanctions. This argument may be more persuasive in countries, such as France, where taking cases to court is a viable option for the average person owing to the fact that the process is relatively simple, speedy and inexpensive (or where plaintiffs in libel and privacy actions may qualify for legal aid).

9.2 Other Mechanisms of Self-Regulation

In some countries (e.g, Canada, US and UK), papers have appointed their own ombudsmen, often journalism professors, to consider readers' complaints and make recommendations to the editors. In the UK, they seem to have only limited influence.

The inclusion of Letters to the Editor and "Op-Ed pages" (containing opinion pieces by non-staff members) is an increasingly popular mechanism for publishing alternative views and criticisms of reportage and editorial policies.

10. DEFAMATION

10.1 Constitutional Protection

The constitutions of Germany, the US and Sweden all offer a measure of constitutional protection for the right to personal reputation. The protection is explicit in Germany's Constitution; and Sweden's Freedom of the Press Act (which is part of the Constitution) offers a measure of protection in its prohibition of defamation. The US Supreme Court has construed the US Constitution to offer implicit protection. Owing to the fundamental importance in these countries of the rights of the press to impart, and of the public to receive, information and opinions, the constitutional status of the right to reputation has, however, not resulted in the favouring of plaintiffs in defamation actions.

10.2 Statutory Provisions

Most countries studied provide statutory protection for the right to reputation and/or personal honour. In the majority of countries, defamation is both a criminal offence and a civil tort. In some countries where criminal actions previously were more common, there has been a trend towards greater use of civil law (e.g., Austria). In others, civil actions have for a long time been more common (Australia, Canada, Netherlands, Norway). In the US, criminal defamation laws lapsed into disuse by the 1950s (and would today be found unconstitutional unless limited to statements that were likely to cause an imminent breach of the peace. In the UK, criminal libel remains part of the common law, although virtually unused in recent years. In France, Germany and Sweden, civil and criminal actions may take place before the same court at the same time. If convicted, a defendant may be ordered to pay a criminal fine to the state as well as civil damages to the injured party.

In some countries, criminal actions may be brought by public as well as private prosecution. In Sweden, public prosecutions are rare and normally are brought only when the alleged defamation was directed against a civil servant in his or her capacity as such.

10.3   Defamation based on Allegation of Fact

In a number of countries, truth is a complete defence to a defamation based on an allegation of fact (Austria, Germany, UK, US). In Germany, the plaintiff bears the burden of proving that damaging facts were untrue. Similarly, in the US, the plaintiff must prove the statement's falsity, at least when it relates to a matter of public concern (*see* Section 10.7, *infra*). In Austria, the plaintiff in a civil action must prove falsity, though not in a criminal action. In Austria and the UK, truth is not a defence, although public interest is, concerning one type of statement; namely, reproach of a person for having committed a criminal offence in respect of which the sentence has already been served or suspended.

In France, truth is a defence, except when the facts are older than ten years; when they infringe upon privacy; or when they relate to an offence which has been pardoned, which is older than the time-limit set in the statute of limitations or which involves a person who has been rehabilitated. The defendant bears the burden of proving truth, as does the defendant in the UK. The drawback of requiring the press to prove truth is that responsible journalists often rely on sources who insist on remaining confidential, thus making proof virtually impossible.

Even if the facts are wrong, in many countries a press defendant will not be found guilty unless it failed to meet its duty to check the facts properly (Austria, France, Germany, Netherlands, US). Moreover, in Germany the plaintiff must prove that the failure was wilful or negligent; and in the US the plaintiff, if a public figure, must prove that the failure was knowing or reckless. In France, the defendant bears the burden of proving good faith; while there appears to be a presumption of bad faith, this may be countered by the right and duty to inform, which is similar to a public interest defence. In practice, however, the courts have been inclined not to give the benefit of the doubt to the press. In Austria and the Netherlands, the press defendant bears the burden of proving good faith and public interest; in the Netherlands, journalists are expected to demonstrate a higher standard of good faith concerning more serious allegations.

Norway is one of the few countries in which the defendant is required to prove truth *and* something more; the defendant must also prove that the allegation was "made for respectable reasons" and was not "improper because of its form or the manner in which it was made".

The Norwegian press is strongly critical of the absence of a public interest defence, which has discouraged investigative reporting especially into corporate wrongdoing.

In Sweden, the responsible editor must prove that publication was justifiable (that is, that the public interest in the information outweighed the interest in protecting the person concerned) and that the information was true *or* published in good faith. Thus, for example, publication of information about a minor tax fraud committed by a politician would be justifiable, whereas publication of similar information about a private person would not be.

Several countries recognize a defence of privilege for fair and accurate reports of court proceedings, parliamentary sessions, and various public events usually specified by statute (Australia, UK).

10.4   Defamation based on Critical Opinion

In the US, there is no cause of action in the absence of a false statement of fact. Similarly in Sweden, value judgements can never be libellous, although when formulated in an exceptionally insulting way, they have on rare occasion been judged an affront (a special form of defamation).

In other countries, truth is no defence if the insult arises from the manner in which a statement was made or disseminated or from the circumstances in which it was made (Austria, Germany, Norway). In a few countries, courts tend to treat statements which primarily involve value judgments but have a factual basis, for instance obvious hyperbole, as factual statements requiring proof of truth or journalistic care.

In several countries, public interest is a defence to insulting opinions (Austria, Germany). Opinions in the context of political debate, especially when made against a politician or other public figure, are subject to particular protection (Austria, France, Germany). Moreover, insulting expressions of opinion are more likely to be tolerated when made in response to a personal attack (Germany).

In Australia, Canada and the UK, "fair comment" is a defence if it is based, in good faith, on a factual foundation that is true and is set out either in the publication itself or else referred to with sufficient clarity.

10.5   Public Officials, Public Figures and other Plaintiffs

In several countries, plaintiffs who are public officials, politicians and/or other public figures are required to meet a higher standard of proof either *de facto* (France, Netherlands, Norway) or in law (US) for both false facts and critical opinions. Several countries use the concept of "public figure" although the parameters of the category are often not well defined (Netherlands). In France, the relevant category is defined as "persons performing a public function" which includes ministers, members of Parliament, civil servants and any public agent or person performing a public duty, even on a temporary basis (such as a juror or a witness); in practice, political leaders who do not fall into one of the specified categories also are held to a higher standard.

The most developed elaboration of the "public figure" doctrine may be found in US case-law, which defines "public figures" as either those who "occupy positions of such ... influence that they are deemed public figures for all purposes", or those who "have thrust themselves to the forefront of particular public controversies in order to influence the resolution of the issues involved" and thus are public figures for purposes of those specific controversies only.[6] Like public officials, public figures invite the comment to which they are exposed and have access to the media to counteract false statements.

The Swedish law is unusual in that companies, organizations and government authorities have no right to initiate libel actions. As a result, the press enjoys great freedom in scrutinizing and criticizing government, businesses and other institutions. The press, however, has a professional/ethical obligation under the voluntary Press Code to grant institutions a right of reply to factual statements made about them.

10.6   Costs of Suit

In most countries, the costs of bringing a lawsuit are sufficiently high to discourage all but the well-to-do. (e.g., Australia, Austria, UK, US). One result is that, even in countries where public figures may carry a heavier burden of proof, the vast bulk of cases are nonetheless initiated by public figures. In such countries, the defamation laws (and, where they exist, the privacy laws) primarily serve to protect the rich and/or powerful. This situation is addressed in a few countries (France, Germany) by the granting of legal aid to defamation plaintiffs upon a modest showing of the merit of their claim. In Australia, although legal aid is not available for defamation or malicious falsehood (which requires the plaintiff to prove both falsity and malice), government ministers have on occasion had their costs underwritten by the government. In the UK, legal aid is available for malicious falsehood.

10.7   Penalties and Damages

In most countries, the primary difference between criminal and civil actions concerns the remedies available. In some, while a plaintiff in a criminal action may be entitled to claim compensation for non-material damage (such as pain and suffering), the amount that may be awarded is usually limited by statute (Austria).

By contrast, in some countries a plaintiff in a civil action may be able to recover only for actual damage (such as loss of business) but the amount generally is not limited by statute (Austria). In other countries (Netherlands), plaintiffs can recover for immaterial damages as well. In most European countries, damages, while higher than criminal fines, are relatively modest, even in cases involving major public figures (for example, France: US$ 8-20,000; Norway: US$ 8-24,000; Sweden: US$ 3-12,000). For instance, the tennis star Bjorn Borg received only US$ 12,000 in his successful libel action against one of Sweden's leading

---

[6] *Gertz v. Robert Welch, Inc.*, 418 U.S. 323, 341 (1974).

papers. In Austria, damages may reach as high as AS 1 million [US$ 90,000]; in Australia, A$ 100,000 [US$ 70,000]; in Canada, up to C$ 135,000, but usually under C$ 30,000; and in Spain, 100,000 to, very rarely, 20 million pesetas [US$ 800 to 160,000]. Awards are highest in the UK, where they often reach hundreds of thousands of pounds [up to US$ 800,000], and in the US, where successful plaintiffs have been awarded millions of dollars. The highest award in the UK, £1.5 million [US$ 2.4 million] to Lord Aldington, has been challenged in an application to the European Commission on Human Rights.

In most civil law countries, plaintiffs can also receive non-monetary relief, such as a right of reply, retraction, correction, publication of a court judgment or prohibition of further publication. (*See also* Section 12 *infra* on the right of reply.) While the laws of some countries permit imprisonment for defamation for periods of up to one year, in no country has anyone been imprisoned for defamation in recent memory.

In Sweden, only one person, the "responsible editor" designated by the owner, may be held liable, and is held strictly liable whether or not he or she has read the offensive publication. The arrangement has at least two advantages: (1) it ensures that one person with resources can always be held liable, and (2) it provides security for all others involved in the publication process. By contrast, in the UK, journalists and even distributors and printers may be sued. Warnings in January 1993 from Prime Minister John Major's solicitors that they would file writs stopped some distribution chains from stocking a magazine which discussed rumours that the Prime Minister had had an affair.

10.8 Chilling Effect of Defamation Laws

Despite the powerful US case-law which makes it difficult for public figures to win defamation actions, public figures bring defamation actions, and win, at approximately the same rate as other plaintiffs. Moreover, as burdensome as are the awards, they are generally dwarfed by the enormous costs of defending these actions, and the successful party (as in virtually all civil actions) cannot recover costs. Thus, win or lose, press defendants inevitably are economic losers, and surveys show that the possibility of defamation actions constitutes a substantial disincentive to the coverage of certain kinds of stories, especially by small and medium-sized papers. The possibility of defamation actions similarly exerts a strong chilling effect in Australia and the UK, where costs and awards are also high. In contrast, in countries such as the Netherlands and Sweden, where most defamation complaints are handled by press councils, few go to the courts, and damages are low, the press does not complain that defamation actions negatively affects its activities. This pattern seems to suggest that high costs associated with defending defamation actions may be more of a deterrent to investigative reporting than laws which favour plaintiffs.

Proponents of libel law reform in the US urge the creation of a new defamation action limited to determining the truth or falsity of any allegedly defamatory statement and for which remedies would be limited to publication of a correction or reply. The proposed law would avoid constitutional problems by requiring the paper to consent to being sued for the limited, rather than a full-blown, defamation action (*see* Section 12 *infra*, on the right of reply).

11.   PRIVACY

11.1 Constitutional Protection

A few countries expressly protect the right to privacy in their constitutions (Germany, Netherlands). Sweden's constitutional document protects privacy indirectly via its prohibition of defamation.

Although France's *Conseil constitutionnel* has not yet decided any cases concerning privacy, it is arguable that the right to privacy has acquired constitutional status, in part owing to its recognition as one of the fundamental principles of the Republic and in part owing to the incorporation into French law of the ECHR and the ICCPR and Political Rights.

The US Supreme Court has interpreted various constitutional provisions as giving rise to a right to privacy. Although the Justices have disagreed vigorously as to its precise contours, in a unanimous opinion they did agree that it embraces both an "interest in avoiding disclosure of personal matters" and an "interest in independence in making certain kinds of important decisions".[7] The Court has recognized four aspects of the privacy interest in avoiding disclosure of personal matters: (1) the right not to be put in a "false light" by the publication of true facts; (2) the right not to have one's likeness "appropriated" for commercial purposes; (3) the "right of publicity" on the part of a person whose name has commercial value; and (4) the right to avoid the publicizing of "private details" of no legitimate public interest.[8]

11.2 Statutory and Other Provisions

Most countries prohibit telephone tapping and the use of bugging devices (e.g., Germany, Netherlands). Most protect the privacy of correspondence (Germany), and information told in confidence to professionals such as lawyers and doctors. Many protect the privacy of personal data files (Germany, Norway). Some countries require newspapers to obtain a licence to maintain electronic "clipping files" on individuals (eg. Norway). A few countries prohibit the unauthorized collection of personal data by the press as well as private individuals (Germany).

Whereas most countries prohibit the unauthorized use of photographs of individuals (Austria, Germany, Norway), most also recognize exceptions for photographs of public figures and people attending public gatherings (e.g., Austria, Germany, Netherlands, Norway). German courts have distinguished between "absolute" public figures, such as politicians and sports personalities, and others, such as defendants in criminal trials, who are only of public interest because of their involvement in a particular event. The "public figure" doctrine in Austria has not yet been accepted in defamation law, although some experts speculate that it may eventually be accepted.

---

[7] *Whalen v. Roe*, 429 U.S. 589, 599-600 (1977).

[8] *Zacchini v. Scripps-Howard Broadcasting Co.*, 433 U.S. 562, 571-72 & nn. 7&8 (1977).

Some countries provide a separate cause of action for the publication of information concerning a person's private life in such a way as to be degrading (Austria, France, Norway). Austria permits publication if there is any "connection with public life". In France, invasion of privacy is a tort only (and not also a criminal offence as is defamation); neither truth, nor good faith, nor the public interest provides a defence.

Under Swedish law, privacy receives scant protection, and there is no cause of action even for the publication of photographs of people in private situations, such as swimming in the nude. On the other hand, the privacy of private persons is well protected under the Code of Ethics applied by the Press Council and Ombudsman, although some critics complain that the Council does not constitute an adequate alternative to legal action since there is no opportunity for compensation.

12.   RIGHT OF REPLY

Of the seven civil law countries studied, all save Sweden offer some form of a legal right of reply or correction (Austria, France, Germany, Netherlands, Norway, Spain). In most of these countries, a person who is the subject of factual allegations which cast him or her in a negative light is entitled to respond without having to demonstrate that, for example, the story was false or defamatory (Germany, Netherlands, Norway, Spain). In others, the right may be triggered by critical opinions as well as factual allegations (France).

In Norway, while the legal right of reply is reserved for replies to factual information, the Code of Ethics affords a right of reply to persons who "have been made subject of an attack". The Code also calls for publication of an apology for publication of inaccurate information. Virtually all papers respect the Press Council's decisions regarding replies.

The Austrian law was amended in 1981 to permit a paper (or other mass media organ) to refuse to publish an untrue reply. While this was considered to be a substantial reform, the complicated procedural rules for establishing truth have been criticized. A paper which refuses to publish a reply that is later determined by the courts to be legitimate may be required to pay a sizeable fine.

In the majority of countries, the reply may be no longer than the original story, and the paper is obliged to give it equal prominence; generally it is not sufficient to publish the reply as a reader's letter. In most countries, additional requirements are imposed, such as that the reply may not involve an advertisement, must be confined to factual assertions, and/or must not be libellous, otherwise unlawful, or insulting to the integrity of the journalist.

An injured person is generally required to communicate the reply to the editor without delay; most countries also impose an absolute time limit for submitting a reply of between several months (Germany) and one year (Norway).

In most countries that recognize a right of reply, the offended party may seek a court order if the paper refuses to publish it (France, Germany, Norway, Spain). In France, there is an accelerated judicial procedure for actions, which is even swifter during election campaigns.

In most countries, publication of a reply will not affect other available actions or remedies, and does not amount to an admission of wrongdoing (France, Germany, Spain). In some countries, publication may reduce the amount of damages awarded (Germany, Norway).

In Sweden, there is no legal right of reply. However, courts in libel cases are directed to take into consideration the publication of a reply or a correction. Moreover, it is a well-respected principle of Swedish press ethics that any person or institution criticized in a news story should be allowed to comment, preferably in the story itself, or else in a reply given equal prominence to the original story. In practice, this principle is applied to opinion pieces as well. Short replies are encouraged on the ground that they are more effective. Papers tend to be generous in printing replies; this appears to be due, in large measure, to the fact that the remedy is voluntary and flexible.

None of the common law jurisdictions studied provide for a legally enforceable right of reply. The US Supreme Court has ruled unconstitutional laws that require a right of reply. Proponents of legally enforceable rights of reply, especially for candidates during election campaigns, have argued that the right is necessary to ensure the dissemination of a variety of views especially in light of the concentration of newspaper ownership. The Supreme Court noted a possible counter-danger; namely, that papers would refrain from publishing controversial stories.

There is no legal right of reply or correction in Australia, Canada or the UK. The Code of Practice applied by the UK Press Complaints Commission (PCC) requires papers to give a fair opportunity for reply to inaccuracies when reasonably called for. However, if this opportunity is not provided, the only recourse is to the PCC which can publish a negative adjudication but cannot compel an unwilling paper to do likewise; the decisions of the PCC cannot be enforced by the courts.

13.   INSULTS TO GOVERNMENT INSTITUTIONS OR OFFICIALS

A number of civil law countries still have laws on the books that make it a crime to insult the national government; its members or symbols (including its colours, the flag, and the anthem); the Monarch or Head of Government; the legislature, the courts, the army, and their members; and/or the representatives of foreign states (Austria, France, Germany, Netherlands, Norway, Spain). However, in all of the countries (except Spain), such laws are no longer used, and insults are punishable only if they are unlawful under the normal defamation laws. Germany's Constitutional Court has ruled that the use of such laws to restrict speech beyond the limits of defamation law would be unconstitutional. Spain, the country to have most recently emerged from fascism, appears increasingly tolerant of insults even against the King.

In Sweden, the last law protecting government institutions from insults was abolished in the mid-1970s on the ground that, in a democratic society, government institutions should be open and responsive to all criticism, even when based on lies. In the US, Supreme Court case-law has made clear that all criticism of or insults to the government or any of its institutions or symbols (including the flag) must be tolerated.

A few countries have laws limiting the press' freedom to express opinions that reflect support for terrorism. These countries recognize that the constitutional protection of press freedom precludes restraints on publication of facts about terrorist groups, including statements issued by terrorist organizations themselves, so long as they are not editorially endorsed by a paper. For example, in Spain, the Constitutional Court in a 1986 decision reversed the conviction of an editor who had published a statement by the Basque separatist organization ETA.

In the US, Canada and the UK, common law crimes such as seditious libel or advocacy (*i.e.*, advocacy of ideas that might undermine the interests of the state) have either fallen into disuse (Canada, UK) or been ruled unconstitutional (US). The laws that have superseded them prohibit advocacy only when it is likely to incite public disorder. Expression may be punished because of its potential to undermine US national interests only if it was *intended* and likely *imminently* to incite violent or otherwise illegal conduct.

14. ACCESS TO GOVERNMENT HELD INFORMATION

14.1 Right of Access

Of the countries studied, Austria, the Netherlands and Sweden provide an express constitutional right of access to information held by the government. Both Sweden and Austria follow the principle that all documents are public unless a statute expressly permits exceptions. In Austria, the principle is elaborated in the federal and *Länder* Freedom of Information Acts. Even when a request appears to touch on one of the excepted areas, the authorities must nonetheless weigh the interest in disclosure against the interest in secrecy. Swedish authorities are compelled to deal with requests within one day or else provide reasons for the delay. Under Dutch law, the authorities may reject, without weighing competing interests, a request for information which could endanger the unity of the Crown, state security or the protection of information held by private parties imparted to the government in confidence.

In the US and Germany, a constitutional right of access is implied in the provisions guaranteeing freedom of expression and press freedom. In the US the right belongs to every individual (as elaborated in the Freedom of Information Act). In contrast, in Germany only the media have the right of access; their right to federal government information is premised on the second sentence of Article 5(1) of the Constitution (guaranteeing press freedom), and their right to *Land* government information arises from the different *Länder* press laws.

The Spanish Constitution implicitly recognizes the right of public access to government documents, except where access would affect the security and defence of the State, the investigation of crimes or the privacy of persons. "Classified matters" are defined by statute.

Although Norway's Constitution does not guarantee a right of access, documents are deemed public subject to statutory exceptions. The Act on Public Access to Documents compels the authorities to consider access to exempt documents without delay; however, in practice authorities often engage in delay, sometimes even following issuance of a court order.

In France, a 1978 act created the right of everyone to have access to public documents subject to certain enumerated exceptions.

The UK is the only country that does not have general legislation on access to government information and the only country where there is a presumption in favour of government secrecy.

14.2   Exceptions to Access

In all of the countries studied, government authorities are entitled to withhold information which could affect national security or defence. In most of the countries, information is also entitled to exemption if disclosure would impair international relations, law enforcement, public safety, personal privacy or commercial secrecy.

Although Swedish law provides for considerable access to most government documents, in practice the authorities have been known to withhold information that could be embarrassing to them and journalists tend not to be vigorous in their pursuit of government-held information. The best known example of this tendency was the Bofors affair. After journalists alleged that Bofors, Sweden's largest arms manufacturer, had obtained a contract with the Indian government through the payment of bribes, the government conducted an investigation and produced a report, portions of which it refused to make public. Only after publication by an Indian paper of some of the most damaging information did the government make the full report public.

In several countries (Australia, Netherlands, UK), there is no right of access to internal government working papers, whether or not relating to one of the exempt topics.

14.3   Right of Appeal Against Refusal of Information

In most countries, refusal of information is subject to administrative review either by a body specifically constituted to oversee compliance with the disclosure laws (Australia, Canada, France, Sweden) or else by a general administrative body (Germany, Netherlands). Decisions of these bodies may then be appealed to the courts. The availability of administrative review by a specially constituted body is useful in that it can facilitate speedier attention to complaints, although administrative delay is a problem that plagues virtually all of the systems studied.

In France, a special commission, the *Commission d'acces aux documents administratifs* (CADA) examines complaints and difficulties concerning access. Most problems are resolved at this level. An applicant dissatisfied with CADA's decision may seek review by an administrative court. In Sweden, a Justice Ombudsman, appointed by the Parliament, supervises disclosure and tries to resolve disputes. Australia allows appeals to an ombudsman or an administrative appeals tribunal, and Canada allows appeals to a special commissioner. However, only the Australian tribunal can order disclosure; the ombudsman and commissioner are limited to recommendations. In the US, an appeal may be made to the head of the agency which denied the request.

A number of countries require that the reasons for any refusal be given in writing and that the applicant be informed of the right to appeal (Australia, Norway, Sweden). In Sweden, a request for a written statement often leads to production of the requested documents.

14.4   Penalties for Disclosure of Official Secrets

Austria, Sweden and the US provide the strongest protection to the press for publication of government secrets. In Austria and Sweden, journalists and editors are not subject to prosecution for publishing official secrets, unless the disclosure risked severe damage to national defence or international relations. Moreover, in Sweden, journalists cannot be compelled to reveal the source of a government leak unless disclosure severely endangered national security; the journalist's right to refuse in turn provides considerable protection for public sector employees who "blow the whistle" on government misconduct. In the US, the press may not be prosecuted for publishing virtually any secret information; the only publication that will subject the press to liability is disclosure of the names of intelligence agents, when there is a pattern of such publication and when publication is likely to impair intelligence activities. (However, a somewhat broader category of information may be subject to prior restraint. *See* Section 18 *infra*.)

In several countries (Australia, Germany and Norway), the fact that disclosure serves the public interest provides a defence for publication of information collected by illegal means, and also provides a defence to any government employee who leaked the information. However, in Germany there is no defence for publication of anything that is classified as absolutely secret.

Even in countries that do not punish the press for publishing information, any civil servant who leaks information is generally liable for breach of confidentiality and may be subject to criminal or civil liability or dismissal (Austria, Australia, US). In some countries there is no law establishing a duty of confidentiality owed to the government (Norway).

In France, the UK and Canada, it is a crime to publish secret defence information, and there is no public interest defence for the press or the employee who supplied the information.

15. ACCESS TO AND DISCLOSURE OF COURT DOCUMENTS AND PROCEEDINGS

In all eleven countries, the principle of open trials is respected, and in most it receives constitutional protection. Nonetheless, all recognize certain exceptions either in law or practice. Most countries permit trials, or parts of trials, to be closed in order to protect the rights of the litigants (and, especially, to protect the fair trial rights of criminal defendants), fundamental privacy interests of the witnesses, national security interests, and/or the interests of juveniles. In some countries, trials involving family matters and children are presumptively closed. Several countries have special rules regarding rape cases, including exclusion of the public at the request of the victim and bans on the publication of the victim's name or identifying characteristics (e.g., France). In the UK, cases involving mental patients, guardianship and adoption proceedings must be private, and other cases involving children, families, confidential information or national security may be private.

The courts in several countries (Austria, Sweden, the US) tend heavily to favour the interest in openness, and will not punish publication of confidential court information (unless the information was secret for independent reasons). In contrast, Norway's Director General of Public Prosecutions announced in October 1992 an intention to seek large fines (up to the equivalent of hundreds of thousands of US dollars) for publication of confidential information leaked from police sources or non-public court proceedings. Where cases are tried by a judge rather than a jury, concerns about prejudging guilt and impairing fair trial rights generally are greatly reduced.

Pre-trial proceedings, unlike trials, are closed in many civil law countries. In the Netherlands, an ombudsman appointed by the Parliament drafts statements about undisputed facts concerning pre-trial criminal investigations which may be published with the consent of the parties.

In the common law countries, the presumption of openness extends to pre-trial proceedings, although it is not as strong as the presumption of trial openness. In the US most pre-trial proceedings are open, and the press may publish anything disclosed in open court or which is part of the public record. In contrast, in the UK it is a contempt of court to publish any information or opinions which create a substantial risk of prejudice to the course of justice while a case is *sub judice* or "active" (in a criminal case, from the moment that a suspect has been charged or arrested until decision of any appeal). The risk of prejudice is deemed greatest in criminal trials decided by jury, and smallest in cases tried by a professional judge or on appeal. The law of contempt has been liberalized as a result of the 1979 judgment of the European Court of Human Rights in the *Sunday Times* case (concerning a lawsuit against a thalidomide manufacturer). Since then, publication of matters concerning a pending court case which are of general public interest will be treated as contempt of court only "if the risk of impediment or prejudice is merely incidental to the discussion". The *Spycatcher* case established that contempt of court may extend to information that a court has ordered others not to publish.

The press may also be punished for publishing information that may tend to impair public confidence in judicial proceedings, including the substance of jury deliberations following pronouncement of a verdict (Australia, France, UK) and groundless allegations of judicial bias (Australia, UK). In November 1992, a UK newspaper and its editor were fined the equivalent of US$ 90,000 for publishing research into how well a jury had been able to understand a long and complicated fraud trial which lawyers (without research) had used to illustrate their argument that lay juries are incapable of deciding complex fraud cases.

In the UK, the standing of the press to contest an order closing a hearing or prohibiting publication was recently confirmed; in Australia the question remains unsettled. In both countries, an order, once made, is subject to judicial review but in general can be vacated only if "irrational". As a result of a friendly settlement of a case filed with the European Commission of Human Rights, the British press is entitled to appeal orders made in Crown Court trials.

In Austria, although criminal investigations and criminal proceedings are confidential, publication of confidential information has not been an offence since 1981; even some members of the press believe that as a result the media have often exceeded the limits of legitimate reporting by conducting "trials by press". A proposal has been made to forbid the publication of the names of criminal suspects except where the person's identity would be of public interest. In a few countries, publication of a suspect's name, while not prohibited by law, is prohibited by a voluntary press code (Sweden). An interesting approach has been initiated in France by a 1993 law which permits courts to order the press to publish a rectification whenever a suspect's presumption of innocence has been violated by the reporting of confidential information.

While most countries prohibit the taking of pictures during trials, a few allow pictures and films of trial participants on their way to and from the courtroom (Germany, Norway, UK, United States).

Owing to the press' special duty to inform, in several countries representatives of the mass media are the last to be excluded from court proceedings for reasons of security or space limitations (Spain).

16. ACCESS TO AND DISCLOSURE OF LEGISLATIVE DOCUMENTS AND PROCEEDINGS

Parliamentary sessions are generally public in all of the countries studied. In Austria, Germany and Sweden, openness is mandated by the constitution. Exceptions are permitted in narrowly drawn circumstances, such as when classified information is to be discussed. Spain's Constitution provides that plenary sessions of the Congress and Senate shall be public but may be closed by majority vote of each chamber.

In a few countries, there is also a presumption of access to sessions of parliamentary committees. In Germany, this presumption is included in the Basic Law, Article 42(3) of which provides: "True and accurate reports on the public meetings of the Federal Parliament and of its committees shall not give rise to any liability" on the part of either the Parliamentary speaker or the press. This is particularly important regarding public investigative committees (Article 44(1)). For similar reasons, the media in Austria may attend investigative committees even though the public generally is excluded from other parliamentary committees. In France, certain permanent and select committees of the National Assembly and Senate conduct their hearings in public.

In several countries, parliamentary committees are presumptively closed and neither the press nor the public may have access to their proceedings or to their documents (Austria, Netherlands, Spain, Sweden). In Sweden, committees must open their files when they present their proposals. Nonetheless, in most countries, there is no penalty for disclosure by the press of committee or other non-public documents unless the documents were entitled to secrecy for some other substantive reason (Austria, Germany, Netherlands, Norway). In France, publication of non-public matters is an offence, although there are no recent cases.

In most countries, all statements made during a parliamentary session are absolutely privileged (that is, they cannot form the basis of an offence) and good faith reporting about statements made during public sessions are also privileged. For instance, in the UK, MPs may not even be prosecuted for intentionally disclosing secret information during public sessions, and the press may not be punished for republishing the information; however, MPs may be subject to parliamentary discipline.

In the common law jurisdictions of the UK, the US, Canada and Australia, a person may be held in contempt of Parliament (or Congress), and fined or imprisoned, for directly or indirectly impeding Parliament in performing its functions, such as by (in the UK) bringing either House "into odium, contempt or ridicule". The offences have fallen into disuse and, even in the UK, no one has been imprisoned this century. In the US, the contempt power, which has been used only to punish the refusal to provide requested evidence, has rarely been exercised against the press.

17. COMMERCIAL SECRECY AND ACCESS TO INFORMATION HELD BY PRIVATE PERSONS

In a number of countries, employees are obliged by statute (Austria, France, Netherlands, Spain, Sweden) or common law (UK, Australia, Canada) not to disclose the business secrets of their employers. In several countries, however, this obligation does not prevent the disclosure of information about illegal actions (Austria) or other wrongdoing (Spain, Sweden). For instance, in Spain, the freedoms of expression and information must be balanced against an employee's duty of confidentiality, and will outweigh any duty of loyalty in so far as matters of public importance are concerned.

Most countries do not protect whistleblowers (employees who disclose information about their employer's wrongdoing) from termination or discipline, even if their disclosures were in the public interest and/or were not unlawful (Austria, France, Norway, Sweden). Sweden's approach of open access to government information and protection of public sector whistleblowers contrasts markedly with its restrictive approach to information held by the private sector. Private whistleblowers are protected by the constitution to the extent that journalists may not divulge their identity if given information in confidence; however, there is no legislation to discourage employers from conducting their own investigations and disciplining those they conclude are the source of "leaks".

In some countries, even though employees may be punished for disclosure, the press may not be prosecuted for publication (Norway, Spain, Sweden). In a few countries, the press may be punished as well (France).

Increasingly, companies are being required to make public information relevant to environmental protection. In Norway, companies are required to supply considerable information about waste disposal to the government, and such information is generally available to the public. In Spain, citizens have access to some environmental information. People in the UK can obtain information on hazardous substances, pollution and waste disposal from local government authorities. A few European countries are considering expanding disclosure requirements in keeping with the European Communities Council Directive on the Freedom of Access to Information about the Environment (*see* Chapter 13 *infra*). In contrast, environmental information required to be provided to the Dutch government is seldom accessible to citizens.

18.   PRIOR RESTRAINTS

In all of the countries studied, prior restraints on publication of printed matter are prohibited, and in many of the countries the prohibition is of constitutional magnitude (Austria, Germany, Norway, Spain, Sweden, US). While licensing requirements and administrative censorship are absolutely barred, in most countries the police and/or prosecutors are empowered to seize printed matter without prior judicial order in exceptional circumstances (and must then promptly seek judicial authorization). The grounds for seizure and the showing required to sustain a prior restraint vary considerably.

The phrase "publish and be damned" captures the idea that the publisher should be free to communicate and the public should be free to be informed even if the publisher must pay the price in damages or criminal punishment. Nonetheless, the principle has been limited in practice in all countries save Sweden and the US.

The Swedish Constitution admits no exceptions whatsoever to the ban on pre-publication censorship, and no form of prior censorship has been upheld in recent memory. A case from the early 1970s illustrates the absolute nature of the prohibition. A member of the Investigation Bureau (IB), a secret part of the security services, disclosed information about the IB to two journalists who published a series of articles in a magazine and later in a book which was translated into English. The IB agent and the two journalists were convicted of espionage and sentenced to prison for terms of up to one year. No attempt was ever made to restrain publication of the articles or the book, nor could any such attempt have succeeded.

In the US, restraints on publication may be ordered in a truncated hearing but can overcome the heavy presumption of unconstitutionality only if it can be shown that: 1) publication would pose a clear threat of immediate and irreparable harm to a "near sacred" right; 2) the restraint would be effective; and 3) no other measures less restrictive of free expression would be effective. The Supreme Court has indicated that it might uphold a prior restraint on information about troop movements during time of war, direct incitements to violence or the forceful overthrow of government, or statements that pose a clear and imminent threat to a defendant's fair trial rights. The Supreme Court has never upheld a restraint on national security grounds; in rare cases, courts have upheld temporary bans on information that directly threatened a criminal defendant's rights. In addition, the process for reviewing an injunction against the press is expedited; for example, the entire controversy in 1990 regarding CNN's tapes of Manuel Noriega's telephone conversations with his defence lawyer, including a Supreme Court hearing and numerous lower court appearances, lasted less than three months.

In Norway, the Constitution is widely understood to prohibit all prior censorship of printed matter. Nonetheless, courts may and do order preliminary injunctions which may be extended into permanent injunctions to protect such interests as reputation. Thus in a 1989 case a court ordered an immediate restraint on publication, and the Supreme Court upheld a permanent injunction, to stop publication of a defamatory film and report about several seal hunters.

In France, the most common ground for seizure is the protection of core privacy interests. The reluctance to uphold seizures on other grounds is illustrated by a 1992 case in which a court refused to suppress a tape recording of a conversation, intercepted by a CNN reporter, between a recently convicted criminal and his lawyer, despite the threats to his privacy, rights before the courts, and professional secrecy. On rare occasions materials are seized or posters are covered or destroyed on grounds of public morals. Authorities have also seized foreign-language publications (*see* Section 8 *supra*) and publications likely to incite hatred against a national, religious, racial or ethnic group (*see* Section 20 *infra*).

In Germany, a court will uphold an "immediate measure" only if it concludes that the seizure was *appropriate*, that is, for a legitimate purpose, *necessary* to promote that purpose, and *proportionate*. In Austria, a publication may be seized and confiscated if there is a concrete suspicion that it violates a criminal law (including libel). Confiscation in libel cases is rare, however, because it may be avoided by the paper's publication of a statement announcing the libel action.

A Spanish law provides a mechanism whereby the press may consult the authorities in advance of publication; administrative approval of a text presented for consultancy frees the consulting party of any responsibility *vis-à-vis* the government (though not private parties) for the text's publication.

In the UK, publications can be restrained in advance of trial and permanently on grounds of breach of confidence, copyright and defamation (so long as justification or fair comment is not alleged as a defence). Prior restraints on publication of government confidences can be obtained merely by presentation of an "arguable" case that the public interest will be harmed. Moreover, prior restraints even against newspapers are not handled on an expedited basis; the book *Spycatcher* (the memoirs of a high-ranking member of the security services) and newspaper extracts from it were banned for 29 months until the House of Lords ruled that further censorship would be futile.

The law of Australia and Canada resembles the UK law, although Australia's highest court, in ruling that embarrassment of the government in its international relations was not a sufficient ground for an injunction, made clear that it was not as sympathetic as the British courts to restraints on information about the government.

19. PROTECTION OF SOURCES

Of the countries studied, Austria, France, Germany and Sweden afford the strongest legal protection to the confidentiality of sources and other information communicated in confidence to journalists. This protection is premised on the assessment that society is better served by encouraging people to disclose matters of public interest to the press, even when the information may include evidence of their own wrongdoing, than by identifying and possibly convicting a particular wrongdoer. Journalists rarely divulge information that would compromise sources, courts rarely compel disclosure, and even more rarely do courts enforce a disclosure order through imprisonment.

Journalists in Germany, Spain and Sweden are among the professionals required to observe professional secrecy (unless their source consents to disclosure). In Germany, professional secrecy only applies in civil cases. In criminal cases in both Germany and Sweden, journalists may be compelled to testify concerning the content or source of confidential information when a countervailing interest is of overriding importance, such as the state's interest in exposing corruption or prosecuting crime. In Austria and France, the law provides that any journalist called as a witness has the right to refuse to answer questions concerning the source of confidential information gathered in the course of his or her journalistic activities; in Austria, the journalist (and any other press personnel) may also refuse to testify about the contents of confidential information.

The US Supreme Court has not defined the parameters of a journalist's privilege although it did rule that journalists may be compelled to testify before criminal grand juries. Lower federal courts have recognized a constitutional privilege to refuse to testify except in criminal cases, and US Department of Justice guidelines also recognize a qualified privilege. More than half the states have enacted "shield laws" providing journalists with absolute or qualified privileges, and courts in other states have found such privileges in the common law or in their state constitutions. The interest of criminal defendants in obtaining evidence which could assist their defence is considered the strongest countervailing interest, followed by the government's interest in obtaining evidence of serious criminal activity.

In Norway, journalists do not enjoy such strong protection in law and may be compelled to testify if the court finds that the information sought is of particular importance. Nonetheless, journalists rarely reveal their sources, and none has been imprisoned in the last few decades, though newspaper editors have occasionally been fined modest amounts (the equivalent of about US$ 3,000). In 1992, Norway's Supreme Court signalled that a journalist's right to protect a source increases with the public interest in the information revealed; it thus refused to compel disclosure of a source who had given information about connections between the Labour Party and the intelligence agency even though the authorities believed that the source was an agency employee who had acted unlawfully in leaking the information.

In the UK, journalists have a limited statutory right to protect sources, but judicial faith in the importance of protecting sources is limited. For instance, in one 1980 case, a TV station was compelled to reveal its source of information about mismanagement and government intervention at the nationally-owned British Steel Corporation, despite considerable interest in its poor performance. One member of the highest court went so far as to remark that "[t]his case does not touch on the freedom of the Press even at its periphery"; only one Lord Justice was of the opinion that protecting sources was important in a democracy. The courts have continued to compel journalists to reveal sources, and at least one case, involving a source who leaked a commercial secret, has been filed with the European Commission on Human Rights.[9]

In Australia and Canada, journalists have no statutory protection and have been fined and imprisoned for refusing to disclose sources. In Canada, one journalist was imprisoned recently (although he might not have been jailed but for his refusal even to be sworn as a witness); in Australia, a journalist was jailed for 14 days in 1992 for refusing to reveal the source of a story about a court case.

Photographs and films receive less protection in most countries than confidential information, and journalists have been compelled to turn them over where authorities have established a good faith belief that the pictures could assist in the identification of suspects.

Newspaper offices in several countries (Canada, Germany, UK) may be searched only with a court order, and only upon a showing that information is relevant and unavailable from a reasonable, alternative source. Nonetheless, in 1992, the Toronto police served warrants on nine media outlets to obtain film and negatives of a riot. All of the affected media chose to co-operate although some were considering legal action as of the end of 1992. In Austria, a media enterprise can be subjected to surveillance only on the strength of a court order in the context of an investigation of a crime which carries a sentence of at least ten years.

In a number of countries, the protection of confidential sources applies to government employees, thus providing protection for whistleblowers who reveal information about government wrongdoing (*see* Section 14.4 *supra*).

---

[9] *Goodwin v. UK*, Application No. 17488/90 (decision on admissibility pending).

20. RESTRICTIONS ON OFFENSIVE LANGUAGE AGAINST IDENTIFIABLE GROUPS

Voluntary codes of press associations in several countries call on papers not to promote contempt for people on the basis of, or make gratuitous mention of, the race, ethnicity, national origin, skin colour and/or religion of individuals or groups (Australia, Austria, Germany, Norway, UK). Responding to readers' complaints about reporting that promotes negative stereotypes is a major function of the ombudsmen that many papers in a number of countries now employ (*see* Section 9 *supra*).

Several countries have laws prohibiting racist speech, propaganda, and/or promotion or expression of hatred or contempt for individuals or groups on grounds of race, religion, skin colour or national or ethnic origin. Norway has extended those grounds to include homosexual status, lifestyle or inclination. A few countries have special laws aimed at stopping the spread of national socialist ideology. Most of these laws exempt fair reports of public acts and statements of others so long as it is clear that the publication does not endorse the speaker's sentiments. As a result, these laws are rarely used against the mainstream press. For instance, although Robert Faurisson, a much-publicized racist and anti-Semite, was convicted for two articles he published in *Le Matin* and *Le Monde*, the editors were not prosecuted. In contrast the editor of an anti-Semitic journal which published an interview with Faurisson was convicted and ordered to pay fines and damages of more than FF 300,000 (US$ 60,000, while Faurisson himself received only a suspended fine of FF 100,000).

A few countries permit prosecution of editors for publishing the racist statements of others even where they do not endorse those views (Norway, Sweden). The Swedish law, which prohibits the mere expression of contempt for a population group, while used primarily against materials published by extremist groups has been used on occasion against the mainstream press. In 1991, the Chancellor of Justice prosecuted an editor for having published a letter to the editor which expressed racist opinions. His defence was that views held by the readers should be allowed to surface so that they could be debated and refuted. The Chancellor's decision to prosecute (a step usually taken only to defend the rights of public officials) was widely criticized, and the editor was acquitted by the jury.

In Norway, only three prosecutions for hate speech have been reported since 1970: two concerned letters to the editor, which resulted in acquittals, and the third involved facts that make it irrelevant to the present discussion. The leading Norwegian press organizations, while firmly supporting the prohibition in the voluntary press code of reporting that fans intolerance and hatred, argued strongly against adoption, and then for repeal, of the criminal law. They argued that making the expression of opinions criminal was not the way to fight opinions in a democracy, especially one such as Norway where racist speech has not been a widespread problem.

21.   BLASPHEMY, OBSCENITY AND PROTECTION OF PUBLIC MORALS

In most countries, it is a criminal offence to publish certain kinds of pornographic, obscene and/or other materials which offend public morality. Canada has an unusual law which prohibits the publication in court reports of any "indecent medical, surgical or physiological details ... calculated to injure public morals". Portrayals of non-sexual violence may be prosecuted in the UK. These restrictions, at least in recent years, have been of scant importance for all but a small portion of the specialized press.

In several countries, the sale of pornography to children under 18 years is prohibited or restricted. German law prohibits the sale of all pornographic materials to persons under 18, and bans the sale of all pornography by means and in premises to which the young have access. Certain named pornographic magazines may not be supplied by mail in Germany, and all indecent material is banned from postal delivery in the UK. In Sweden only child pornography and graphic depictions of sexual violence may be prohibited on grounds of public morals, and artistic merit may constitute an exception. An editor of a comic strip prosecuted under this section was acquitted by a jury.

In the common law countries, the determination of what constitutes an obscene publication is based upon community standards. However, in the US, the issue as to whether the matter "taken as a whole, lacks serious literary, artistic, political or scientific value" is to be judged from the perspective of a "reasonable person", and thus does not depend on the degree of local acceptance achieved by the work.

The crime of blasphemous libel remains on the books in Canada, the Netherlands and the UK, but has been used in recent years only in the UK. The UK law is distinctive in that it protects only the Anglican religion. In Canada the offence is statutory and requires a showing that the blasphemy could lead to a disturbance of the peace.

A few other countries punish a related crime of ridicule to persons, beliefs or institutions associated with a religion recognized in the country, but in recent years the laws have not been used (or in some countries only rarely) against the press (Austria, Germany, Norway). In Norway, several Muslim religious leaders withdrew a lawsuit against the Norwegian publisher of *The Satanic Verses* shortly after filing it, probably because they recognized that they had virtually no chance of success. In Austria, at least one film was banned on grounds of blasphemy (and an application challenging the ban was ruled admissible by the European Commission on Human Rights in 1991).

22. RESTRICTIONS ON ADVERTISING

All countries distinguish between ordinary commercial speech and political advertising.

22.1 Political Advertising

In some countries (Germany, Spain), political advertising is restricted except during declared campaign periods. Other countries (France, UK) impose restrictions only during campaign periods. In France during the three months preceding an election, paid political advertisements are forbidden in both the print and broadcasting media, and the content of unpaid advertisements is regulated. In 1984 the Canadian Supreme Court struck down as unconstitutional sections of the election law which prohibited anyone other than candidates and registered parties from paying for political advertisements during election campaigns. As a result corporations and other private parties are entitled to advertise their views on political issues. In the UK, it is an offence to issue an advertisement during an election campaign in support of a particular candidate without that candidate's authorization.

The Dutch courts generally will enquire only whether a political advertisement is defamatory or misleading. However, a Dutch voluntary code provides additional standards, requiring that political advertisements be clearly marked as such and may not be anonymous, untruthful, below the general standards of good taste, or published in the editorial part of a paper. A Code Commission recommends whether or not political advertisements should be published, and publishers associated with the two leading publishers' associations have agreed to follow the Commission's recommendations. Although refusal to publish a political advertisement is generally not unlawful, collective refusal pursuant to a Commission recommendation may constitute a tort; in one case a court ruled that refusal to publish a political advertisement that included a picture was justifiable only if the picture would be considered extremely tasteless or indecent by an overwhelming majority of the Dutch population.

In the US, any regulation of political advertising, including by commercial entities such as corporations, is presumptively unconstitutional and would have to satisfy a heavy burden to be permitted.

22.2 Commercial Advertising

In several countries, commercial advertisements (those whose primary purpose it to promote a product or service for profit or other business interest) receive constitutional protection, although to a lesser degree than press freedom and other forms of expression (Austria, Germany, Sweden, US); in a few, commercial speech receives no constitutional protection (Canada, Netherlands).

Most countries restrict or prohibit the advertising of alcohol and/or tobacco products for reasons of public health (Austria, Canada, Netherlands, Norway, Spain, Sweden), and some also regulate advertisements for pharmaceutical products (France). In Austria the ban applies only to radio and TV broadcasting. In the Netherlands linking the use of alcohol with sports, health, children, or maturity is prohibited, and tobacco advertisements are banned from radio and TV. Canada bans all tobacco advertising but permits alcohol advertisements. In the US, while the states have broad authority to regulate tobacco and alcohol advertising, there currently are no federal restrictions on alcohol advertising in the print media and the only requirement concerning tobacco advertisements is that they bear a health warning prescribed by the US Surgeon General.

Paid advertisements must be marked as such in Germany, and are entirely prohibited in the editorial sections of papers.

In the UK, the advertising industry established a private Advertising Standards Authority which monitors a code of practice to ensure that advertisements are "legal, decent, honest and truthful". Most newspapers refuse to carry advertisements which the Authority considers to fall below code standards.

Several countries require advertisements not to be misleading or untrue (Canada, Germany, US). Norwegian law bans advertisements which "imply any derogatory judgment of either sex or portray a woman or a man in an offensive manner". A consumers' ombudsman supervises marketing and may forbid advertisements that conflict with the law; decisions may be appealed to a Marketing Council.

Comparative advertising (stating that the advertised brand is better than other named products) was banned for several years in Austria until the European Court of Human Rights ruled that commercial speech is entitled to some protection. Austria now permits such advertisements so long as they are neither misleading, deprecating, insulting nor offensive. Germany generally prohibits comparative advertising except when there is a serious public interest in the information, such as concerning hazardous products. The government established an independent foundation to carry out comparative tests, the results of which may be published. In Canada, comparative advertising may constitute libel.

Several countries prohibit or regulate advertising by members of certain professions, although the Austrian Constitutional Court declared restrictions on advertising by lawyers and tax consultants to be unconstitutional.

CONCLUSION

The common practice of states contributes to the development of international law in two ways. First, to the extent that the practice is followed out of a sense of legal obligation, it may give rise to a norm of customary international or regional law binding on all countries which do not expressly dissent from its development.[10] Second, to the extent that a practice is common among states which are party to a treaty containing a provision relevant to the practice, the existence of a common practice may contribute to the development of an

---

[10] North Sea Continental Shelf Cases (*FRG v. Denmark; FRG v. Netherlands*), 1969 I.C.J. 3, 44; I. Brownlie, *Principles of Public International Law* (3rd ed. 1979), 6-7.

authoritative interpretation of the treaty provision.[11] For example, in the *Marckx* case, the European Court of Human Rights, after invoking the principle that the Convention must be interpreted in the light of present day conditions, ruled that legitimate and illegitimate children were legally to be treated the same for purposes of inheritance.[12] In 1981 the Court ruled that, based upon evolving practice, a Northern Ireland law which criminalized homosexual practices between consenting male adults fell foul of the ECHR's right to respect for private life.[13] Recently, the Court, in ruling Ireland's ban on the provision of information about where to obtain lawful abortions outside the country observed that "[l]imitations on information concerning activities which ... have been and continue to be tolerated by [other] national authorities, call for careful scrutiny by the Convention institutions as to their conformity with the tenets of a democratic society."[14]

Seven practices, described below, have achieved widespread acceptance among the countries studied and, accordingly, provide compelling evidence of the way in which the ECHR is likely to be interpreted by the European Court and Commission.

1. None of the countries studied require any form of government approval to launch a newspaper or periodical; in all, freedom from licensing requirements and other forms of government approval is considered a vital aspect of press freedom.

2. None of the countries impose restrictions on the export of publications. In Europe, only Germany and France impose content-based restrictions on the import of publications. In Germany, the restrictions are rarely applied; in France, restrictions are applied from time to time against writings in a foreign language or "of a foreign origin". The laws are archaic and, if challenged, would likely be found to violate Article 10 of the ECHR.

3. In none of the countries studied has anyone in recent memory been imprisoned for defamation or for insults to the government, its institutions or its symbols (in the absence of a substantial threat to public order). Moreover, while laws penalizing insults to the government or its members remain on the books in a number of countries, the courts of virtually all the countries have reasoned that the laws do not impose any restraints greater than the normal defamation laws. It is thus likely that the European Court would find a prison sentence for insult to the government or defamation disproportionate to the legitimate aims pursued.

---

[11] P Mahoney, "Judicial Activism and Judicial Self-Restraint in the European Court of Human Rights", 11 *Human Rights Law Journal* (1990) 57, 73-74.

[12] *Marckx v. Belgium*, Judgment of 13 June 1979, Series A no. 31.

[13] *Dudgeon v. United Kingdom*, Judgment of 22 Oct. 1981, Series A no. 45, at para. 60.

[14] *Open Door Counselling Ltd. and Well Woman Centre Ltd. v. Ireland*, Judgment of 29 Oct. 1992, Series A no. 246, at para. 72.

4. All of the European countries save the UK recognize a right of access to information held by the government except when disclosure would threaten one of several enumerated values (virtually all of which are also included in Article 10(2) of the ECHR).

5. Parliamentary sessions are presumptively open in all of the countries studied and may be closed only in narrowly-drawn circumstances. While the offence of contempt of Parliament continues to exist in the common law jurisdictions, it does not appear that any member of the press has been excluded from an open legislative session in recent years for insulting or offensive reporting.

6. In all of the European countries studied except the UK and France, it is a defence to the publication of secret government information that disclosure was in the public interest. This practice, in light of the powerful right of the public under Article 10 of the ECHR to information of legitimate public interest, may well require recognition of a public interest defence to disclosure of government secrets.

7. All of the European countries studied, except the UK and Norway, recognize the right of journalists to protect their confidential sources especially concerning information of public interest (including serious crime and official corruption). In Norway the right appears to be consistently recognized in practice. The relevant French law recently was amended to bring it into conformity with the common practice.

The above practices have achieved such consensus among the countries studied that, assuming the trends hold true throughout most of the other member states of the Council of Europe,[15] it reasonably may be maintained that the norms illustrated by the practices have entered into European law either as part of customary regional law or else as evolving interpretations of Article 10 of the ECHR.

---

[15] Arguably, the practice of the newly-admitted Central European states, during the first years of their membership, will not be as important as the practice of long-standing members in establishing consistent state practice.

APPENDIX A: LIST OF NATIONAL LAWS

AUSTRALIA

Constitutional Provisions: None

Anti-Discrimination Act 1977 (NSW), Section 20C
Broadcasting Services Act 1992 (Cth), Sections 59-61
Crimes Act 1914 (Cth), Sections 24A, 24D, 79
Criminal Code 1899 (Qld), Sections 365 -389
Defamation Act 1901 (NSW), Section 6
Defamation Act 1974 (NSW), Section 15
Federal Copyright Act Section 201
Freedom of Information Act 1982 (Cth), Article 24
Privacy Act 1988 (Cth), Parts III-V

AUSTRIA

Constitutional Provisions:
    Basic Law of 21.12.1867, Article 13

Broadcasting Act 1974, Sections 1-33
Civil Code 1811, Article 1330
Criminal Code, Sections 111, 112, 115, 188, 218, 219, 220, 255, 283, 297
Media Act 1981, Articles 24, 25, 41, 43
Periodical Promotion Act 1984, Sections 1-12
Press Promotion Act 1985, Sections 1-10
State *(Länder)* Freedom of Information Acts

CANADA

Constitutional Provisions:
    Canadian Charter of Rights and Freedoms, Constitution Act 1982, Section 2

Access to Information Act, Section 74
Criminal Code, Sections 9, 10, 163-169, 296, 318, 319,
Official Secrets Act 1939, Sections 4, 14
Privacy Act 1985
Uniform Defamation Act 1978, Section 11

FRANCE

Constitutional Provisions:
>   Constitution of 1958, Preamble, Articles 16, 54, 55

Access to Information Act 1978
Act of 1881, as amended in 1972 (Press Law), Articles 7, 10, 12-14, 24, 26, 29, 31, 35, 38, 39, 41
Act of 1986, Press Ownership, Article 11
Civil Code, Article 9
Code of Criminal Procedure, Articles 40, 283, 306
Penal Code, Articles 74, 76, 78, 148, 209, 378

GERMANY

Constitutional Provisions:
>   Basic Law of the Federal Republic of Germany of 1949, Articles 1, 2, 5, 19, 42, 44

Civil Code, Sections 241-246, 819-831
Civil Procedure Act, Sections 383-395
Criminal Code, Sections 84-100, 106, 109, 123, 129-132, 164, 166, 184-210, 353,
Criminal Procedure Act, Sections 94-112
State (*Länder*) Press Laws, Sections 1-27

THE NETHERLANDS

Constitutional Provisions:
>   The Constitution of the Kingdom of the Netherlands, Articles 1, 7, 10, 93, 94, 110, 120

Netherlands Media Act, Sections 1, 127, 129, 130, 133
Act on Public Access To Information, Articles 3, 8, 10, 11
Criminal Code, Articles 4, 98, 111-113, 118, 119, 131, 132, 137, 139a, 147, 239-254, 261, 262, 266, 267, 426
Code of Criminal Procedure, Article 362
Civil Code, Articles 6:106, 6:162, 6:167
Code of Civil Procedure, Article 18

NORWAY

Constitutional Provisions:
Constitution of the Kingdom of Norway 1814, Article 100

Act on Court Proceedings, Section 130
Act on Public Access to Documents, Sections 4-6
Penal Code, Sections 122-147, 189-216, 246-257, 390, 391, 428-436
Privacy Act 1978

SPAIN

Constitutional Provisions:
Constitution of 1978, Articles 10, 18, 20, 53, 80, 96, 105, 120, 148,149, 161, 163, 164

Civil Code, Article 1
Criminal Code, Articles 147, 161, 191, 192, 240-242, 244, 268, 432, 453-457, 497
Code of Criminal Procedure, Articles 111, 112, 301, 680
Law 14/66 18 March, Press Law, Article 3
Law 9/68, as modified by L. 48/78, Official Secrets, Articles 2-4, 9, 10
Law 10/88, 3 May, Private Television, Articles 1, 2, 19
Law 34/88, 11 Nov., Publicity, Article 8
L.O. 1/82, 5 May, Civil Protection of the Right to Honour, Personal and Family Privacy and
 Identity, Articles 1, 2, 3, 4, 6
L.O. 2/84, 26 January, Right of Reply and Correction, Articles 2-4, 6
Statute of the Journalists Profession

SWEDEN

Constitutional Provisions:
Freedom of Press Act 1949, Chapters 1-7, 16
Instrument of Government, Chapert 2, Articles 1, 20
Freedom of Speech Act 1991

Secrecy Act 1980, Chapter 2
Trade Secrets Act 1989

UNITED KINGDOM

Constitutional Provisions: None

Contempt of Court Act 1981, Sections 2, 5, 11, 14; Schedule 1, paras 4, 5, 12 and 13
Criminal Justice Act 1988, Section 159
Defamation Act 1952, Sections 4 and 7
Law of Libel Amendment Act 1888, Section 8
Obscene Publications Act 1959, Sections 1, 3 and 4
Official Secrets Act 1989, Sections 1-5(3) and 10(1)
Police and Criminal Evidence Act 1984, Schedule 1
Public Order Act 1986, Sections 18-19
Prevention of Terrorism (Temporary Provisions) Act 1989, Section 18

UNITED STATES

Constitutional Provisions:
    First Amendment to the United States Constitution

Freedom of Information Act, 5 U.S.Code Section 522
Government in the Sunshine Act, 5 U.S.Code, Sections 551-553, 556-558, 2901-2903, 3341, and 3343
Intelligence Identities Act, 50 U.S. Code Section 421
State Laws on Defamation and Privacy
State "Shield" Laws on Protection of Confidential Sources

APPENDIX B: PROVISIONS OF INTERNATIONAL TREATIES AND INSTRUMENTS

UNIVERSAL DECLARATION OF HUMAN RIGHTS
Adopted and proclaimed by General Assembly resolution 217 A (III) of 10 December 1948.

Article 19

Everyone has the right to freedom of opinion and expression; this right includes freedom to hold opinions without interference and to seek, receive and impart information and ideas through any media and regardless of frontiers.

Article 29

...
2.   In the exercise of his rights and freedoms, everyone shall be subject only to such limitations as are determined by law solely for the purpose of securing due recognition and respect for the rights and freedoms of others and of meeting the just requirements of morality, public order and the general welfare in a democratic society.

3.   These rights and freedoms may in no case be exercised contrary to the purposes and principles of the United Nations.

INTERNATIONAL COVENANT ON CIVIL AND POLITICAL RIGHTS
Adopted and opened for signature, ratification and accession by General Assembly resolution 2200 A (XXI) of 16 December 1966. Entered into force 23 March 1976.

Article 19

1.   Everyone shall have the right to hold opinions without interference.

2.   Everyone shall have the right to freedom of expression; this right shall include freedom to seek, receive and impart information and ideas of all kinds, regardless of frontiers, either orally, in writing or in print, in the form of art, or through any other media of his choice.

3.   The exercise of the rights provided for in paragraph 2 of this article carries with it special duties and responsibilities. It may therefore be subject to certain restrictions, but these shall only be such as are provided by law and are necessary:

(a) For respect of the rights or reputations of others;

(b) For the protection of national security or of public order (*ordre public*), or of public health or morals.

Article 20

1. Any propaganda for war shall be prohibited by law.

2. Any advocacy of national, racial or religious hatred that constitutes incitement to discrimination, hostility or violence shall be prohibited by law.

OPTIONAL PROTOCOL TO THE INTERNATIONAL CONVENANT ON CIVIL AND POLITICAL RIGHTS

Article 1

A State Party to the Covenant that becomes a party to the present Protocal recognizes the competence of the Committee to receive and consider communications from individuals subject to its jurisdiction who claim to be victims of a violation by that State Party of any of the rights set forth in the Covenant. No communication shall be received by the Committee if it concerns a State Party to the Covenant which is not a party to the present Protocol.

AMERICAN CONVENTION ON HUMAN RIGHTS
Adopted by the OAS on 22 November 1969. Entered into force 18 July 1978.

Article 13: Freedom of Thought and Expression

1. Everyone has the right to freedom of thought and expression. This right includes freedom to seek, receive, and impart information and ideas of all kinds, regardless of frontiers, either orally, in writing, in print, in the form of art, or through any other medium of one's choice.

2. The exercise of the right provided for in the foregoing paragraph shall not be subject to prior censorship but shall be subject to subsequent imposition of liability, which shall be expressly established by law to the extent necessary in order to ensure:
    (a) respect for the rights or reputations of others; or
    (b) the protection of national security, public order, or public health or morals.

3.   The right of expression may not be restricted by indirect methods or means, such as the abuse of government or private controls over newsprint, radio broadcasting frequencies, or equipment used in the dissemination of information, or by any other means tending to impede the communication and circulation of ideas and opinions.

4.   Notwithstanding the provisions of paragraph 2 above, public entertainments may be subject by law to prior censorship for the sole purpose of regulating access to them for the moral protection of childhood and adolescence.

5.   Any propaganda for war and any advocacy of national, racial, or religious hatred that constitute incitements to lawless violence or to any other similar illegal action against any person or group of persons on any grounds including those of race, colour, religion, language, or national origin shall be considered as offences punishable by law.

Article 14: Right of Reply

1.   Anyone injured by inaccurate or offensive statements or ideas disseminated to the public in general by a legally regulated medium of communication has the right to reply or to make a correction using the same communications outlet, under such conditions as the law may establish.

2.   The correction or reply shall not in any case remit other legal liabilities that may have been incurred.

3.   For the effective protection of honor and reputation, every publisher and every newspaper, motion picture, radio, and television company, shall have a person responsible who is not protected by immunities or special privileges.

EUROPEAN CONVENTION ON HUMAN RIGHTS
(Convention for the Protection of Human Rights and Fundamental Freedoms)
Signed by Contracting States of the Council of Europe on 4 November 1950. Entered into force 3 September 1953.

Article 10

1.   Everyone has the right to freedom of expression. This right shall include freedom to hold opinions and to receive and impart information and ideas without interference by public authority and regardless of frontiers. This article shall not prevent States from requiring the licensing of broadcasting, television or cinema enterprises.

2.   The exercise of these freedoms, since it carries with it duties and responsibilities, may be subject to such formalities, conditions, restrictions or penalties as are prescribed by law and are necessary in a democratic society, in the interests of national security, territorial integrity or public safety, for the prevention of disorder or crime, for the protection of health or morals, for the protection of the reputation or rights of others, for preventing the disclosure of information received in confidence, or for maintaining the authority and impartiality of the judiciary.

Article 17

Nothing in this Convention may be interpreted as implying for any State, group or person any right to engage in any activity or perform any act aimed at the destruction of any of the rights and freedoms set forth herein or at their limitation to a greater extent than is provided for in the Convention.

Article 25

1.   The Commission may receive petitions addressed to the Secretary-General of the Council of Europe from any person, non-governmental organization or group of individuals claiming to be the victim of a violation by one of the High Contracting Parties of the rights set forth in this Convention, provided that the High Contracting Party against which the complaint has been lodged has declared that it recognizes the competence of the Commission to receive such petitions. Those of the High Contracting Parties who have made such a declaration undertake not to hinder in any way the effective exercise of this right.

Article 46

1.   Any of the High Contracting Parties may at any time declare that it recognizes as compulsory *ipso facto* and without special agreement the jurisdiction of the Court in all matters concerning the interpretation and application of the present Convention.

TREATY ESTABLISHING THE EUROPEAN ECONOMIC COMMUNITY
("Treaty of Rome")

Article 7

Within the scope of application of this Treaty, and without prejudice to any special provisions contained therein, any discrimination on grounds of nationality shall be prohibited.

The Council may, on a proposal from the Commission and in cooperation with the European Parliament, adopt by a qualified majority, rules designed to prohibit such discriminiation.

Article 30

Quantitative restrictions on imports and all measures having equivalent effect shall, without prejudice to the following provisions, be prohibited between Member States.

Article 34

1. Quantitative restrictions on exports, and all measures having equivalent effect, shall be prohibited between Member States.

2. Member States shall, by the end of the first stage at the latest, abolish all quantitative restrictions on exports and any measures having equivalent effect which are in existence when this Treaty enters into force.

Article 36

The provisions of Articles 30 to 34 shall not preclude prohibitions or restrictions on imports, exports or goods in transit justified on grounds of public morality, public policy or public security; the protection of health and life of humans, animals or plants; the protection of national treasures possessing artistic, historic or achaeological value; or the protection of industrial and commercial property. Such prohibitions or restrictions shall not, however, constitute a means of arbitrary discrimination or a disguised restriction on trade between Member States.

Article 52

Within the framework of the provisions set out below, restrictions on the freedom of establishment of nationals of a Member State in the territory of another Member State shall be abolished by progressive stages in the course of the transitional period. Such progressive abolition shall also apply to restrictions on the setting up of agencies, branches or subsidiaries by nationals of any Member State established in the territory territory of any Member State.

Freedom of establishment shall include the right to take up and pursue activities as self-employed persons and to set up and manage undertakings, in particular companies or firms within the meaning of the second paragraph of Article 58, under the conditions laid down for its own nationals by the law of the country where such establishment is effected, subject to the provisions of the Chapter relating to capital.

Article 59

Within the framework of the provisions set out below, restrictions on freedom to provide services within the Community shall be progressively abolished during the transitional period in respect of nationals of Member States who are established in a State of the Community other than that of the person for whom the services are intended.

The Council may, acting by a qualified majority on a proposal from the Commission, extend the provisions of the Chapter to nationals of a third country who provide services and who are established within the Community.

Article 85

1. The following shall be prohibited as incompatible with the common market: all agreements between undertakings, decisions by association of undertakings and concerted practices which may affect trade between Member States and which have as their object or effect the prevention, restriction or distortion of competition within the common market, and in particular those which:

    (a) directly or indirectly fix purchase or selling prices or any other trading conditions;

    (b) limit or control production, markets, technical development, or investment;

    (c) share markets or sources of supply;

    (d) apply dissimilar conditions to equivalent transactions with other trading parties, thereby placing them at a competitive disadvantage;

    (e) make the conclusion of contracts subject to acceptance by the other parties of supplementary obligations which, by their nature or according to commercial usage, have no connection with the subject of such contracts.

2. Any agreements or decisions prohibited pursuant to this Article shall be automatically void.

Article 86

Any abuse by one or more undertakings of a dominiant position within the common market or in a substantial part of it shall be prohibited as incompatible with the common market in so far as it may affect trade between Member States.

Such abuse may, in particular, consist in :

(a) directly, or indirectly, imposing unfair purchase or selling prices or other unfair trading conditions;

(b) limiting production, markets or technical development to the prejudice of consumers;

(c) applying dissimilar conditions to equivalent transactions with other trading parties, thereby placing them at a competitive disadvantage;

(d) making the conclusion of contracts subject to acceptance by the other parties of supplementary obligations which, by their nature or according to commercial usage, have no connection with the subject of such contracts.

THE EUROPEAN COMMUNITIES COUNCIL DIRECTIVE ON THE FREEDOM OF ACCESS TO INFORMATION ON THE ENVIRONMENT
7 June 1990 (90/313/EEC)

Preamble

...

Whereas access to information on the environment held by public authorities will improve environmental protection;

Whereas the disparities between the laws in force in the Members States concerning access to information on the environment held by public authorities can create inequality within the Community as regards access to information and/or as regards conditions of competition;

Whereas it is necessary to guarantee to any natural or legal person throughout the Community free access to available information on the environment in written, visual, aural or data-base form held by public authorities, concerning the state of the environment, activities or measures adversely affecting, or likely so to affect the environment, and those designed to protect it;

...

Article 1

The object of this Directive is to ensure freedom of access to, and dissemination of, information on the environment held by public authorities and to set out the basic terms and conditions on which such information should be made available.

Article 3

1. Save as provided in this Article, Member States shall ensure that public authorities are required to make available information relating to the environment to any natural or legal person at his request and without his having to prove an interest.

    Member States shall define the practical arrangements under which such information is effectively made available.

2. Member States may provide for a request for such information to be refused where it affects:
    - the confidentiality of the proceedings of public authorities, international relations and national defence,
    - public security,
    - matters which are, or have been, *sub judice,* or under enquiry (including disciplinary enquiries), or which are the subject of preliminary investigation proceedings,
    - commercial and industrial confidentiality, including intellectual property,
    - the confidentiality of personal data and/or files,
    - material supplied by a third party without that party being under a legal obligation to do so,
    - material, the disclosure of which would make it more likely that the environment to which such material related would be damaged.
    Information held by public authorities shall be supplied in part where it is possible to separate out information on items concerning the interests referred to above.

3. A request for information may be refused where it would involve the supply of unfinished documents or data or internal communications, or where the request is manifestly unreasonable or formulated in too general a manner.

4. A public authority shall respond to a person requesting information as soon as possible and at the latest within two months. The reasons for a refusal to provide information requested must be given.

Article 4

A person who considers that his request for information has been unreasonably refused or ignored, or has been inadequately answered by a public authority, may seek a judicial or administrative review of the decision in accordance with the relevant national legal system.

Article 6

Member States shall take the necessary steps to ensure that information relating to the environment held by bodies with public responsibilities for the environment and under the control of public authorities is made available on the same terms and conditions as those set out in Articles 3, 4 and 5 either via the competent public authority or directly by the body itself.

Article 7

Member States shall take the necessary steps to provide general information to the public on the state of environment by such means as the periodic publication of descriptive reports.

COUNCIL OF EUROPE RECOMMENDATION NO. R (81) 19 OF THE COMMITTEE OF MINISTERS TO MEMBER STATES ON THE ACCESS TO INFORMATION HELD BY PUBLIC AUTHORITIES
(Adopted by the Committee of Ministers on 25 November 1981 at the 340th meeting of the Ministers' Deputies)

Considering the importance for the public in a democratic society of adequate information on public issues:

Recommends the governments of member states to be guided in their law and practice by the principles appended to this recommendation.

Appendix to Recommendation No. R (81) 19

I   Everyone within the jurisdiction of a member state shall have the right to obtain, on request, information held by the public authorities other than legislative bodies and judicial authorities.

II   Effective and appropriate means shall be provided to ensure access to information.

III   Access to information shall not be refused on the ground that the requesting person has not a specific interest in the matter.

IV   Access to information shall be provided on the basis of equality.

V   The foregoing principles shall apply subject only to such limitations and restrictions as are necessary in a democratic society for the protection of legitimate public interests (such as national security, public safety, public order, the economic well-being of the country, the prevention of crime, or for preventing the disclosure of information received in confidence), and for the protection of privacy and other legitimate private interests, having, however, due regard to the specific interest of an individual in information held by the public authorities which concerns him personally.

VI   Any request for information shall be decided upon within a reasonable time.

VII A public authority refusing access to information shall give the reasons on which the refusal is based, according to law or practice.

VIII Any refusal of information shall be subject to review on request.

NOTES ON EDITORS

Sandra Coliver is Law Programme Director of ARTICLE 19. She received her law degree from the University of California (Berkeley), practised criminal, constitutional and international law for several years, taught international law and international human rights courses as US law schools, and currently serves on the Board of the US Section of Amnesty International. She has co-authored briefs to the European Court of Human Rights and has written several articles on freedom of expression and other aspects of human rights law.

Patrick Merloe is Special Legal Counsel to ARTICLE 19 and a lawyer with the San Francisco law firm of Heller, Ehrman, White & McAuliffe. He has taught international human rights law at the University of San Francisco. He completed graduate studies in public policy analysis at the Institute for Policy Studies in Washington, D.C. and received his law degree from the University of Pennsylvania Law School (1986). He is *pro bono* counsel to the International Human Rights Law Group and to the Lawyers Committee for Human Rights and has written on human rights and private international law.

Ann Naughton, senior staff member and Programme Coordinator at ARTICLE 19, has worked with the organization since its launch in 1986. She has taken a central role in the commissioning and editing of many of ARTICLE 19's reports as well as providing background research.

NOTES ON CONTRIBUTORS

Hans-Gunnar Axberger is an Assistant Professor of Criminal Law at the University of Stockholm and a practising lawyer with a Stockholm law firm. From 1990-1992, he served as Sweden's Press Ombudsman for the General Public and as such was responsible for the system of press self-regulation. He has written widely in both popular and academic journals on media issues.

Jan Bauer is a writer and journalist. She served as Executive Director of the Canadian Centre of International PEN from 1986 to 1992 and was International PEN's representative to the United Nations Commission on Human Rights in 1990 and 1991. She is ARTICLE 19's representative in Canada and a member of the Executive Committee of the Network on International Human Rights, a cooperative of nearly 60 Canadian NGOs working on issues of human rights and international development.

Walter Berka is Professor of Administrative Law at the Johannes-Kepler University of Linz. Previously he was an Assistant Professor of Constitutional and Administrative Law at the University of Salzburg. His areas of specialization are human rights and media issues.

Ineke Boerefijn graduated in international law from the University of Utrecht in 1985, and has been a legal researcher at the Netherlands Institute of Human Rights (SIM), Utrecht since 1986. She is a former chairperson of the Dutch section of the International Commission of Jurists. She recently co-authored an analysis of the Netherlands Media Act.

Nigel Cooper is a barrister practising in London. He was called to the Bar of England and Wales in 1987 and did post-graduate studies in European Communities Law at the Europa Institute of the University of Amsterdam. He spent five months with the legal service of the Commission of the European Communities as a *stagiaire* (intern). He was a contributor to the chapter on European Community Law in the latest edition of *Coping & Skone-James on Copyright*.

Frances D'Souza has been the Director of ARTICLE 19 since July 1989. Previously she was a lecturer in race and culture at the London School of Economics, founding Director of the Relief and Development Institute and, for several years, Editor of the *International Journal of Disaster Studies and Practice*. She has conducted research work in Africa, Asia, the Middle East and South Pacific.

Roger Errera is a member of the Conseil d'Etat, France's highest court of administrative law, and a member of the Board of Governors of the Ecole nationale de la magistrature (at which most French judges are trained). He was a Visiting Professor of French Law at University College, London (1983-84) and British Council Senior Research Fellow at the Institute of Advanced Legal Studies (1987-88). He serves on the editorial committee of *Public Law* and has published numerous articles and studies on EC law, judicial review, privacy and press law.

David Flint is Chair of the Australian Press Council and Chair of the Executive Council of the World Association of Press Councils. He is a Professor of Law and currently is Dean of Law at the University of Technology, Sydney. He has written books and numerous articles on media law and international economic law.

Ulrich Karpen, Dr. jur., is Professor of Constitutional and Administrative Law at the University of Hamburg and at Freiburg. He has been a Visiting Professor at Asmidale (Australia), Guatemala City and Southampton. He is a Member of the Hamburg State Parliament, and Chairman of the German Association of Legislation and the European Association of Legislation. He has written widely, including in English, on freedom of expression, German constitutional law and higher education, and has edited a leading text on Germany's Basic Law.

Andrew Nicol is a barrister in London whose specializations include media law and immigration. He was educated at Cambridge, studied at Harvard and Berkeley as a Harkness Fellow, worked for the State of California and a solicitors' firm in Sydney, Australia, and taught law at the London School of Economics for ten years. He is the co-author of *Media Law*, a 600+ page compendium of UK media law, and has written a number of articles on the topic.

Blanca Rodriguez Ruiz graduated in law at the University of Seville in 1989. She is presently a Ph.D. candidate at the European University Institute, Florence, Italy. Her area of study is media law and her concentration is on telecommunications rights.

Nadine Strossen was elected President of the American Civil Liberties Union in January 1991, which she had served as general counsel since 1986. She is the first woman, and the youngest person, to serve as ACLU President. Since 1989 she has been Professor of Law at New York Law School, and has written, lectured and practised extensively in the areas of constitutional law, civil liberties and international human rights. She received her law degree from Harvard in 1975.

Francine van Lenthe graduated in international law from Utrecht University in 1991. Her final essay concerned freedom of expression, including press freedom in the United Kingdom, the Netherlands and South Africa. Since 1991, she has been a legal researcher at the Netherlands Institute on Human Rights (SIM).

Steingrim Wolland graduated in law from the University of Oslo in 1985. He is a practising lawyer in Oslo and has been a legal advisor to Norwegian press organizations since 1987. He has written widely on media issues in popular and academic journals and recently co-authored a book on press ethics, media legislation and freedom of expression.

ARTICLE 19
The International Centre Against Censorship

ARTICLE 19 takes its name and purpose from Article 19 of the Universal Declaration of Human Rights which states:

> *Everyone has the right to freedom of opinion and expression; this right includes freedom to hold opinions without interference and to seek, receive and impart information and ideas through any media and regardless of frontiers.*

ARTICLE 19, the International Centre Against Censorship, works impartially and systematically to identify and oppose censorship world-wide. We believe that freedom of expression and information is a fundamental human right without which all other rights, including the right to life, cannot be protected. ARTICLE 19 defends this right when it is threatened, opposes government practices which violate it and exposes censorship.

ARTICLE 19's programme of research, publication, campaigning and legal intervention addresses censorship in its many forms. We work on behalf of victims of censorship: individuals who are physically attacked, killed, unjustly imprisoned, banned, restricted in their movements or dismissed from their jobs; publications which are censored or banned; media outlets which are closed, suspended or threatened with closure; organizations, including political groups or trade unions, which are harassed, suppressed or silenced.

ARTICLE 19 monitors individual countries' compliance with international standards protecting freedom of expression; prepares reports for inter-governmental organizations such as the United Nations Human Rights Commission and Committee; and files legal interventions on behalf of individuals with the European Court of Human Rights, other international bodies and national courts.

ARTICLE 19 has established a growing international network of concerned individuals and organizations who promote awareness of censorship issues and take action on individual cases. Members of ARTICLE 19 around the world help to protect and defend victims of censorship by mobilizing public opinion, calling on governments to respect freedom of information and expression, and promoting improved national and international standards to protect these freedoms.

ARTICLE 19 is a registered charity in the UK (Charity No. 327421) and is entirely dependent on donations.

If you would like more information about ARTICLE 19 or if you wish to join the campaign against censorship, please contact:

ARTICLE 19
Lancaster House, 33 Islington High Street
London N1 9LH
Tel. 071 278 9292   Fax. 071 713 1356

Executive Director: Frances D'Souza

ARTICLE 19

INTERNATIONAL CENTRE AGAINST CENSORSHIP

Publications List

July 1994

Recent Publications

Forging War: The Media in Serbia, Croatia and Bosnia-Hercegovina (May 1994) 288pp., £9.99/$15.00

Freedom of Expression Handbook: International and Comparative Law, Standards and Procedures (August 1993) 322pp., £12.00/$20.00 (**SPECIAL OFFER:** £4 off price, excluding postage, if purchased with **Press Law and Practice**)

Press Law and Practice: A Comparative Study of Press Freedom in European and Other Democracies (April 1993) 320pp., £12.00/$20.00

Urgent Business: Hong Kong, Freedom of Expression and 1997 (Joint Report with the Hong Kong Journalists Association, January 1993) 96pp., £6.00/$12.00

Freedom of Expression in Hong Kong: 1994 Annual Report (Joint Report with the Hong Kong Journalists Association, June 1994) 32pp., £3.00/$6.00

Cry for Change: Israeli Censorship in the Occupied Territories (October 1992) 51pp., £3.00/$6.00

Striking a Balance: Hate Speech, Freedom of Expression and Non-Discrimination (May 1992) 432pp., £9.95/$18.00

Fiction, Fact and the *Fatwa*: A Chronology of Censorship - Revised (Prepared on behalf of the International Committee for the Defence of Salman Rushdie and his Publishers, London, November 1992) 94pp., £6.00/$12.00

State of Fear: Censorship in Burma (December 1991) 120pp., £3.95/$8.00

Truth from Below: The Emergent Press in Africa (October 1991) 91pp., £3.95/$8.00

Silent Kingdom: Freedom of Expression in Saudi Arabia (October 1991) English and Arabic editions available 57pp., £3.00/$6.00

Information Freedom and Censorship: The ARTICLE 19 World Report 1991(London and Chicago: Library Association, April 1991) 471pp., £22.50/$39.00

Starving in Silence: A Report on Famine and Censorship (April 1990) 146pp., £3.95/$8.00

The Crime of Blasphemy - Why it Should be Abolished (International Committee for the Defence of Salman Rushdie and his Publishers, London April 1989) 22pp., £3.95/$8.00

Censorship News Free for first copy (£1.00/$2.00 for each additional copy)

Bulletin

The ARTICLE 19 Newsletter, published 3 times per year. The Bulletin is available for an annual subscription of £15/$25 which includes membership.

Submissions and Interventions Free of charge unless otherwise indicated

Comments on Preliminary Draft Principles Concerning Journalistic Freedom and Human Rights: Submission to the Council of Europe Steering Committee on Mass Media (March 1994)

Press Freedom Concerns in Norway: Submission to the UN Human Rights Committee (November 1993)

Statement to CSCE Human Dimension Seminar on Free Media, Warsaw (November 1993)

Blasphemy and Film Censorship: Third Party Intervention filed with the European Court of Human Rights in *Otto-Preminger-Institut v. Austria* (jointly with Interights, October 1993)

Submission in Response to the UK Government Consultative Paper on Invasion of Privacy (October 1993)

Submission to the Government of Malawi on Guidelines for Media Coverage of Elections (October 1993) 24pp., £2.00/$4.00

Broadcasting Monopolies: Third Party Intervention filed with the European Court of Human Rights in *Radio Melody v. Austria* (Jointly with Interights, May 1993)

The Right to Abortion Information - *amicus curiae* brief submitted to the European Court of Human Rights in *Open Door Counselling and Dublin Well Woman Centre v. Ireland* (November 1991) 18pp., £3.00/$6.00

Prior Restraint and National Security - *amicus curiae* brief submitted to the European Court of Human Rights in the *Spycatcher* case (July 1991) 41pp., £3.00/$6.00

Ordering Information

Please add the following to your payment for postage and packing:

UK and EC countries - Orders under £25/US$40 add 20% of total; orders over £25, add 10%.
Overseas - add 50% of total for airmail; 20% for surface mail.

*** Only payment in UK £ sterling or US dollars can be accepted ***

Subscriptions

* An annual subscription to **all ARTICLE 19 publications** is available at a cost including postage of £75 (UK) or £85/US$130 (Overseas).

* An annual subscription to the **Censorship News** series only (8-10 reports annually) is available for £12/US$18 per year, including postage.

All publications are available from:

ARTICLE 19
The International Centre Against Censorship
33 Islington High Street, London N1 9LH, United Kingdom
Tel: (071) 278 9292 Fax: (071) 713 1356

ABOUT THIS BOOK

Exams are about much more than just repeating memorised facts, so we have planned this book to make your revision as **active and effective as possible**.

How?

- by showing you exactly what examiners are looking for (Coursework Guidance)

- by breaking down the content into manageable chunks (Revision Sessions)

- by testing your understanding at every step of the way (Check Yourself Questions)

- by providing extra information to help you aim for the very top grade (A* Extras)

- by listing the most likely exam questions for each topic (Question Spotters)

- by giving you invaluable examiner's guidance about exam technique (Exam Practice)

COURSEWORK GUIDANCE

- The first section of the book contains lots of information on what examiners are looking for in order to award high marks for a coursework assignment. There's also plenty of help with planning and presentation. Important words are highlighted in yellow.

REVISION SESSION 1

Revision Sessions

- Each topic that you need to revise for your exam is divided into a number of **short revision sessions**. You should be able to read through each of these in no more than 30 minutes. That is the maximum amount of time that you should spend on revising without taking a short break.

- Ask your teacher for a copy of your own exam board's **GCSE Design and Technology: Food Technology** specification. Tick off on the Contents list each of the revision sessions that you need to cover. It will probably be most of them.

CHECK YOURSELF QUESTIONS

- At the end of each revision session there are some Check Yourself Questions. By trying these questions, you will immediately find out whether you have understood and remembered what you have read in the revision session. **Answers** are at the back of the book, along with **extra hints and guidance**.

- If you manage to answer all the Check Yourself Questions for a session correctly, then you can confidently tick off this topic in the box provided in the Contents list. If not, you will need to tick the 'Revise again' box to remind yourself to return to this topic later in your revision programme.

A* EXTRA

These boxes contain some **extra information** which you need to learn if you are aiming to achieve the **very top grade**. If you have the chance to use these additional facts in your exam, it could make the difference between a good answer and a very good answer.

QUESTION SPOTTER

It's obviously important to revise the facts, but it's also helpful to know how you might need to **use** this information in your exam.

The authors, who have been involved with examining for many years, know the sorts of questions that are most likely to be asked on each topic. They have put together these Question Spotter boxes so that they can help you to **focus your revision**.

Exam Practice

- These give you help with **answering exam questions well**. There are students' answers to some questions, with examiner's hints highlighting **how to achieve full marks**.

- There are also questions for you to try, with answers given at the back of the book for you to check your own answers against.

- There is a **complete exam paper** with student's answers, so that you can get a feel for what a complete paper looks like. The examiner's comments show **how to achieve the highest marks**.

Three final tips

1 Work as consistently as you can during your GCSE Design and Technology: Food technology course. Plan your coursework project carefully. Remember that it accounts for 60% of your mark.

2 Plan your revision carefully and focus on the areas you find hard. The Check Yourself questions in this book will help you to do this.

3 Try to do some exam questions as though you were in the actual exam. Time yourself and don't cheat by looking at the answers until you've really had a good go at working out the answers.

ABOUT YOUR GCSE FOOD TECHNOLOGY COURSE

GCSE specifications

All the Exam Board specifications have to meet the requirements of National Curriculum Design and Technology. This means that they are all quite similar. This book has been written to support all the GCSE Food Technology specifications and provides help and guidance for both the written exam and coursework.

Coursework and written exam

Your final GCSE grade is made up of the marks that you have gained for your coursework and your exam. Your coursework makes up 60% of your final GCSE grade and your exam 40%.

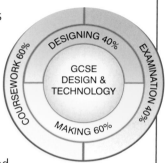

The key to getting a good grade in Design and Technology: Food Technology is to plan your coursework well, to finish it on time and to achieve a high standard. Section I of this book gives you lots of guidance on how coursework is assessed and how to gain high marks.

What is assessed?

In GCSE Design and Technology: Food Technology, you have to develop your knowledge and understanding of materials and components, design techniques, systems and control, and industrial practices. All these areas are covered in this book.

You then have to apply this knowledge through the skills of designing and making.

Designing is about knowledge and understanding combined with the design and communication skills needed to design products for a specific purpose.

Making is about the knowledge and understanding of materials, techniques, processes and equipment in order to make quality products for a specific purpose.

In GCSE Design and Technology: Food Technology, you are assessed on your ability to 'design' and your ability to 'make' and this applies to both your coursework and your written exam. The marks are allocated like this:

> **Designing – 40% of the total marks**
>
> **Making – 60% of the total marks**

Foundation and Higher tier papers

Your coursework is not tiered but in the written exam you will be entered for either the Foundation or the Higher tier. The Foundation tier allows you to obtain grades from G to C. The Higher tier allows you to obtain grades from D to A*.

There is no difference in the specification content for both tiers. Your teacher will have marked your coursework before your exam entry is finalised. This means your school will have a good idea about which is the most appropriate exam tier to enter you for.

SECTION 1:
COURSEWORK GUIDANCE

SESSION 1 ■ Research ■

¶●¶ What is research?

■ At all stages of your coursework project you will need to seek the sort of information that will help you to develop your ideas and also increase your knowledge about how food products are planned and made. In order to collect this information you will need to carry out **research**.

■ At the beginning of a project you will not always know exactly what information you are going to need later on but as you work through the project you will probably discover that you need to find out more about various aspects of food technology. Research can take place at any point in your project and you should do your research as and when it is needed, rather than trying to do all of it at the start.

■ You will need to research information for some or all of the following reasons:

- To develop some ideas for your own product(s).

- To find out about types of products which are already on sale.

- To test products.

- To see what information packaging labels provide.

- To find out what ingredients are used.

- To find out how food products are made.

- To understand how good quality food products are made safely.

- To find out about processing and storage methods.

¶●¶ Analysing your design brief

■ All projects begin with a **design brief**. This describes the particular problem you are facing or outlines the need for a new food product or products. Design briefs are written to allow you a wide range of responses. They are the initial stimulus for research and ideas.

■ You may be given one design brief by your teacher or you may be given several different briefs and asked to choose one. Once you decide on a brief, you need to analyse it carefully. There will be certain key words in it and it is important that you identify these. Examples of key words include:

special diet   main meal   baked product   cook chill   frozen

children   low cost   low fat   high energy   snack

alternative protein   interesting   well flavoured   sweet

- You need to pick out the key words and any other points which you think are important to the brief. This is called **analysing the brief**.

- Analysis can be presented in a variety of ways. Examples include spider diagrams, lists, brainstorming sessions, charts, and simple notes.

- Your analysis needs to make your own interpretation of the brief quite clear. There is no right or wrong answer. You must proceed with the rest of your project in the light of your own personal interpretation of the brief you have been given.

- Figure 1.1 gives an example of the analysis of a design brief. Here a spider diagram has been used to demonstrate how you can quickly pick out the important key words from a brief to highlight which research you need to begin with.

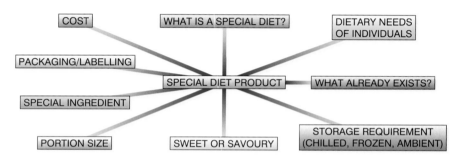

Figure 1.1 *A spider diagram*

🍽 Initial research

- To begin with you should only collect information on the topics you have identified during your analysis of the design brief.

- For this particular design brief, you would initially need to collect information on special diets, such as:
  - diets for **diabetics**
  - **low-fat** diets
  - diets for **coeliacs**
  - **slimming** diets
  - diets for **vegetarians**
  - diets for **babies**.

- Students usually tend to collect and present too much information at this early stage. Only collect information which is *relevant*. For example, for this particular design brief you would only need to find out what people with a special diet are able to eat, not the medical details of the person and the diet.

- Now look at Figure 1.2 on page 3 and then read the examiner's comments on it on page 4.

Figure 1.2 *Looking at special diets*

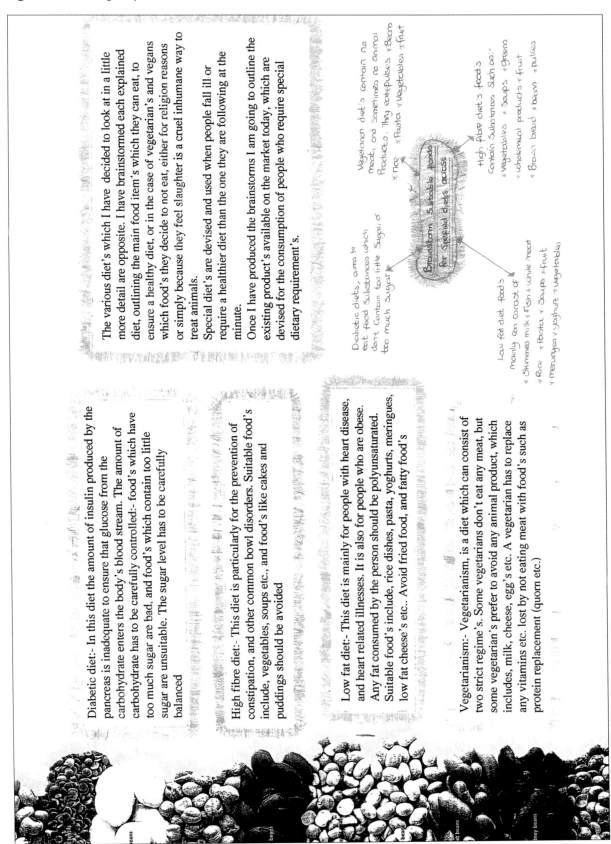

The various diet's which I have decided to look at in a little more detail are opposite. I have brainstormed each explained diet, outlining the main food item's which they can eat, to ensure a healthy diet, or in the case of vegetarian's and vegans which food's they decide to not eat, either for religion reasons or simply because they feel slaughter is a cruel inhumane way to treat animals.

Special diet's are devised and used when people fall ill or require a healthier diet than the one they are following at the minute.

Once I have produced the brainstorms I am going to outline the existing product's available on the market today, which are devised for the consumption of people who require special dietary requirement's.

Diabetic diet:- In this diet the amount of insulin produced by the pancreas is inadequate to ensure that glucose from the carbohydrate enters the body's blood stream. The amount of carbohydrate has to be carefully controlled:- food's which have too much sugar are bad, and food's which contain too little sugar are unsuitable. The sugar level has to be carefully balanced

High fibre diet:- This diet is particularly for the prevention of constipation, and other common bowl disorders. Suitable food's include, vegetables, soups etc., and food's like cakes and puddings should be avoided

Low fat diet:- This diet is mainly for people with heart disease, and heart related illnesses. It is also for people who are obese. Any fat consumed by the person should be polyunsaturated. Suitable food's include, rice dishes, pasta, yoghurts, meringues, low fat cheese's etc.. Avoid fried food, and fatty food's

Vegetarianism:- Vegetarianism, is a diet which can consist of two strict regime's. Some vegetarians don't eat any meat, but some vegetarian's prefer to avoid any animal product, which includes, milk, cheese, egg's etc. A vegetarian has to replace any vitamins etc. lost by not eating meat with food's such as protein replacement (quorn etc.)

Vegetarian diet's contain no meat, and sometimes no animal Products. They eat:- pulses + Beans *rice *Pasta *vegetables *fruit

Brainstorm Suitable foods for Special diets across

High fibre diet's foods contain Substances such as:- *vegetables * Soups *greens *wholemeal products *fruit *Brown bread *beans *pulses

Diabetic diets, aims to eat food Substances which don't Contain too little Sugar, or too much sugar

Low fat diet foods mainly can consist of *Skimmed milk *Fish & white meat *Rice *Pasta * Soups *fruit *meringues *yoghurt *vegetables

Examiner's comments on 1.2

Good Points

- The student has chosen to look at four different diets.
- A lot of information on each of the diets has obviously been researched by the student but this has been summarised well.
- The summary is in the student's own words and is not a direct copy from books or other sources.
- Only the main facts about specific diets have been given.
- Reference is made to nutritional requirements.
- Some ideas for products are given.
- The information is written in such a way as to help the reader to what the student is thinking.

Areas for Improvement

The brainstorm diagram at the bottom right-hand corner is very relevant. It needs to be easier to read. The colours used do not make the diagram stand out clearly enough.

- Based on this initial information, you would then choose one of the special diets to study in detail. You would need to ask yourself what additional information is needed. Remember that it is the diet, not the medical condition, that you will be concerned with. For example, if you decided to choose to study a diabetic diet you would need to:

  - Find out:
    - what a diabetic can and cannot eat
    - the quantities required
    - about products already available
    - if there is a gap in the market for a particular type of product.

  - Design a questionnaire for diabetic people.

  - Compare specialist diabetic products with similar non-diabetic products. (Think here about cost, value for money, sensory characteristics, nutritional value, etc.)

  - Carry out some blind tasting, e.g. digestive biscuits versus diabetic digestive biscuits.

- All of this is **initial research**. Further research would probably be needed later when you have chosen a particular product to develop.

🍽 Questionnaires

- Part of your initial research may involve obtaining information from consumers about existing products. You will need to design a questionnaire that will help you to extract specific information from people. The questions need to be clear and easy both to understand and to answer. It should also be easy for you to collate the results from the questionnaire. You should be able to use these results to generate ideas for products.

- The questionnaire in Figure 1.3 was designed as part of the initial research for a design brief to 'design and make a pasta sauce snack which can be reheated in a microwave cooker'.

- Look at Figure 1.3 on page 5 and then read the examiner's comments on it on page 6.

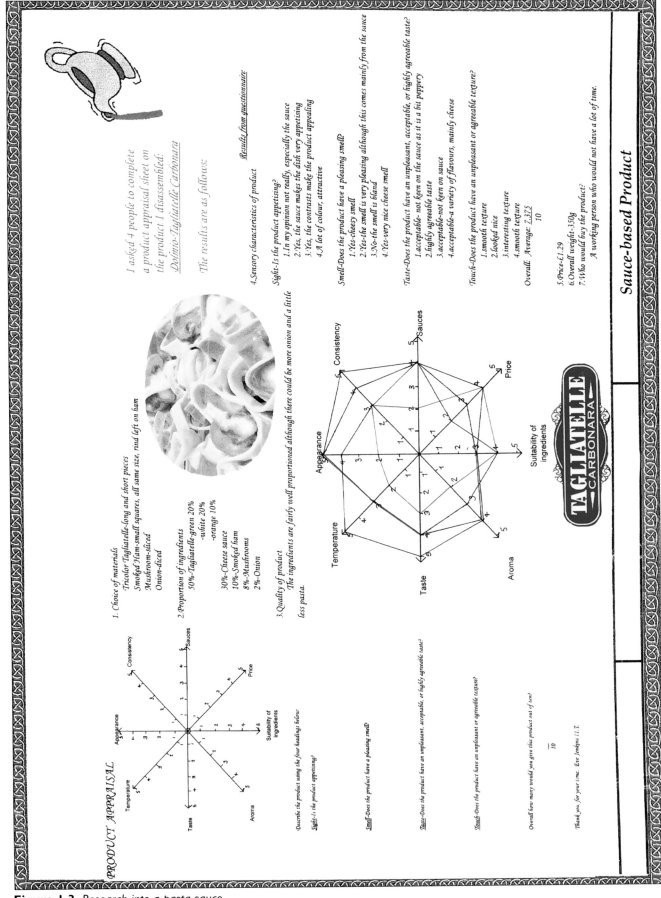

PRODUCT APPRAISAL

Describe the product using the four headings below:

Sight–*Is the product appetising?*

Smell–*Does the product have a pleasing smell?*

Taste–*Does the product have an unpleasant, acceptable, or highly agreeable taste?*

Touch–*Does the product have an unpleasant or agreeable texture?*

Overall how many would you give this product out of ten?

$\overline{\quad\quad}$
10

Thank you for your time. Eve Jenkins 11.I.

I asked 4 people to complete a product appraisal sheet on the product 1 disassembled: *Dolmio–Tagliatelle Carbonara*

The results are as follows:

Results from questionnaire

4.Sensory characteristics of product

Sight–*Is the product appetising?*
1.In my opinion not really, especially the sauce
2.Yes, the sauce makes the dish very appetising
3.Yes, the contrasts make the product appealing
4.A lot of colour, attractive

Smell–*Does the product have a pleasing smell?*
1.Yes-cheesy smell
2.Yes-the smell is very pleasing although this comes mainly from the sauce
3.No-the smell is bland
4.Yes-very nice cheese smell

Taste–*Does the product have an unpleasant, acceptable, or highly agreeable taste?*
1.acceptable- not keen on the sauce as it is a bit peppery
2.highly agreeable taste
3.acceptable-not keen on sauce
4.acceptable-a variety of flavours, mainly cheese

Touch–*Does the product have an unpleasant or agreeable texture?*
1.smooth texture
2.looked nice
3.interesting texture
4.smooth texture

Overall: *Average:* $\dfrac{7.375}{10}$

5.Price-£1.29
6.Overall weight-350g
7.Who would buy the product?
A working person who would not have a lot of time.

1. Choice of materials
Tricolor Tagliatelle-long and short pieces
Smoked Ham-small squares, all same size, rind left on ham
Mushroom-sliced
Onion-diced

2.Proportion of ingredients
50%-Tagliatelle-green 20%
                    -white 20%
                    -orange 10%

30%-Cheese sauce
10%-Smoked ham
8%-Mushrooms
2%-Onion

3.Quality of product
The ingredients are fairly well proportioned although there could be more onion and a little less pasta.

Sauce-based Product

Examiner's comments on 1.3

Good Points

- The student has designed a star profile to use for consumer testing of the tagliatelle. The different points which the student wants consumers to comment upon have been clearly thought out.
- The results from the sensory testing are clear.
- The product profile diagrams show the results from the four testers and the differences can be picked out easily.
- The actual disassembly activity which the student has carried out has produced some useful facts about the tagliatelle in terms of ingredients and percentages.

Areas for Improvement

- The student does not comment sufficiently on how the results from the disassembly and the sensory testing will be used to develop ideas for a new product.

- There is no reference to the nutritional information given on the product packaging and whether nutritional value could be improved.

🍽 Analysing initial research

- All initial research needs to be analysed to help you to produce design criteria, design ideas and specifications. Look at the analysis in Figure 1.4 below and then read the examiner's comments on it.

SHOP SURVEY

- This helped me to see what type of cook-chill products are already on the market. With this I am able to see the variety, so when I make my product it gives me an idea of what to do.
- It also shows the price range of the products that are on the market. So I am able to price my products in the same range as the other products, but still make a profit at the same time.
- The packaging has to be bright and eye-catching to make it stand out from the other products. It also has to give the correct information for the product, so that the buyer can see it straight away.
- The size of the product would depend on who you were going to sell to.

QUESTIONNAIRE

- This has helped me a lot as it tells me what other people would like to see on the market. From this I can see which would be the most popular.
- I have also found out what price range they would prefer. With this I can see what price range would be best to suit my products.
- Also what size portions they would prefer to buy, so that I know what would be best to sell my product.

CONCLUSIONS TESTING SESSION

- Here I am able to try the products that are already on the market. So with this I can see what types are already being sold.
- Knowing what is on the market already and being able to try them out, this helps me to know what type of thing I want to make with my product.
- When trying the product you know that it has to taste really nice for the customer to buy it again. Also that the product has to look really good too.

LETTERS

- This has helped me a lot with my research as it shows me what the manufacturers have put on the market.
- From the products that the manufacturers have sent me, it shows me the variety that they produce. So with this I can see which products would be the best to produce.
- Also from the information I have been given I am told the different ranges of meals. So I can produce things from soups to desserts.

Figure 1.4 *Analysis of initial research*

- The student has looked back at all the research that has been done and has very quickly and simply pulled together the main points from each section of the research.
- Some specific points are identified which will enable the student to produce useful and relevant design ideas.

Areas for Improvement

- The points are very general; e.g. that the questionnaire gives information about the price range which people would prefer. However, the student does not state what the price range is. When the student eventually produces the product specification it should be possible to trace the chosen price back to the research and, in particular, the analysis of the research.

- After completing the analysis of your initial research you should begin to get ideas for a new product or products. It is very likely, however, that you will still need additional information at other stages in your project work.

- For the pasta sauce snack design brief, further research might be needed at the following stages:

  - **design ideas stage** – you might need to research recipes and methods for products and find pictures to illustrate your ideas.

  - **development stage** – you might need information on different methods and times for cooking pasta, the characteristics of particular ingredients and their function, e.g. herbs and spices, different methods of sauce making, e.g. white and others. (Look at Session 5, page 29.)

MANUFACTURING STAGE

- When you begin to think about developing your product in large quantities, you might need information on:

  - industrial case studies

  - manufacturing specifications

  - production methods

  - hazard analysis critical control points (HACCP)

  - packaging and labelling requirements.

- Look at Session 8 on Industrial Practice (page 53) which shows how further research is needed into the packaging and labelling requirements of a product.

⦿ How much research should you do?

- There is no rule about how much research is needed in a project. However, you must remember that:

  - projects have to be completed within a certain number of hours

  - research is only one part of the process

  - if you spend too long on research it will limit the time you can spend on other aspects and your grade is likely to be affected.

¡●¡ How to present your research

■ When you have collected and sorted all your information you need to think about how you are going to present it. The presentation of each sheet of research needs to be planned. Always arrange the information on the page before you actually type it out or stick it down. This takes time but will be well worth it. Think about the order in which you are arranging your information. Make sure the page is clear and that you have shown why and how this information is of use. Use a mixture of words and pictures.

■ The following list gives some ideas to get you started:

- Written summaries, giving the main points, are much better than very long accounts.
- Produce your own work, not long sections copied from textbooks.
- Use:
  - lists
  - bullet points
  - pictures, labels, diagrams, drawings, sketches, photographs (good use of scissors, paper trimmers, guillotines and appropriate glue will be rewarded).
- Include clear labelling for pictures, diagrams and drawings. (A picture of a ready-made bought lasagne tells someone very little other than that it looks very appealing.) Labels should refer to colour, texture, shape, size, consistency, weight, and how the product is assembled and finished, e.g. layers, toppings, decoration, techniques used, etc.
- Include only one sample of a completed questionnaire. Produce your collated results as graphs.
- Write up your conclusions from the results of the questionnaire.
- Summarise the main points from letters and interviews. (It is not necessary to include entire letters and replies as they are often of very little use.)
- Include nutritional information from packages, together with some comments.
- Attach information from manufacturers only if it is relevant.
- If you are fortunate enough to receive information from a manufacturer, it is likely that they will send their standard information pack, not a pack made up specially for you. This pack will probably contain only a very small amount of relevant information. You need to cut out useful information and attach it to your design sheet with a brief description of what it says and how it is of use.
- The same applies to information which comes from CD-ROMs and the Internet.
- Produce computer printouts from CD-ROMs and the Internet.

CHECK YOURSELF QUESTIONS

Q1 Look carefully at all the information you have collected while doing your research. Based on what you have learned in this session, which information can you really use and which is not needed?

Q2 Does all the information need to be presented at the beginning of your project work or would it be better to leave some information until later?

Q3 How are you going to present the information on your sheets of A3 or A4 paper?

Q4 Have you labelled each picture, diagram, sketch, photograph or drawing to show why you are using these examples?

Q5 Will the questions you have written for your questionnaire(s) produce the answers you want and will you be able to collate the results and draw conclusions?

Q6 Can the examiner understand what you are thinking by reading your research sheets?

Q7 Have you arranged the information on each sheet so that there are few gaps?

Q8 Have you written a short conclusion to the research, summarising what you have found out and how you are going to use the information?

COMMENTS

Q1 It is a good idea to obtain a research folder to hold all the information you collect.

When you are at the point of presenting your initial research you need to sort and group the research information from your folder. Think about:
- How each piece of information relates to the design brief you have been given.
- How you will use the information.
- The quantity of information or whether you could you reduce it by giving a summary or a list of important points?

Q2 As you sort the information try to organise it into sections. For example, pictures of products could be used to identify particular characteristics of existing products or as examples of design ideas. Recipes could be used for design ideas or to give some knowledge of a particular process at the development stage.

Q3 A3 or A4 sheets of paper can be used to present your research. A4 sheets are easy to carry and store but A3 sheets allow you to put a lot more information on each page so that the whole page almost tells a story. You need to plan each sheet, either by dividing the page into sections or by placing information on the page before sticking it down. You need to cut and stick using sharp scissors or a paper trimmer. Use the right type of glue, arrange the information in order and ask someone else to give you their opinion before finally sticking everything into place or producing a final piece of writing. (This is where your teacher can be very useful!)

Q4 Labels, pictures and diagrams add interest to project work and can be a simple way of providing information but they are of little use on their own. For this reason you need to make sure that you have labelled or given a brief description of every picture, package, diagram, photograph, etc.

Q5 Think about what information you want a questionnaire to produce and how you are going to collate the results. If you ask very open questions, such as, 'What products do you buy?', you are likely to get a vast range of replies which will tell you very little. It is better to ask, 'Which of these products would you buy?', then give a list.

Q6 Ask another student, your parent or a teacher to read your research sheets and briefly outline to you what they have understood from them.

Q7 Often candidates do not use the space on their paper very well. There should be very little space left on each page – but this does not simply mean using big print, large pictures and wide borders!

Q8 The most important part of research is being able to give a brief summary or analysis of it. From this a very clear way forward should be obvious to both you and the examiner.

Remember that a project is assessed on quality not quantity!

SESSION 2 ■ General design criteria ■

¶●¶ What are design criteria?

■ Whenever a new product is made, regardless of what it is made from, the designer of the product produces a specification for his or her new idea and a maker then uses this specification to produce the exact product that the designer had in mind.

■ With most materials, like wood, plastic and textiles, it is possible to produce an exact specification quite early in the design process because the materials can be cut, joined, shaped and finished in similar ways. For example, a specification for a storage container might look like this:

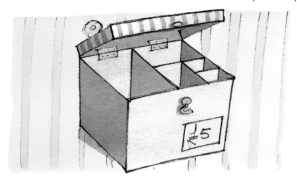

square box with rigid sides, 50 cm x 50 cm
hinged lid
two fasteners to attach lid to base
decoration on lid
compartments inside to divide box into sections
able to be attached to a wall
easy to open
unit cost £5.

This specification would enable the product to be made in any type of wood, metal, plastic or textile.

■ Food, however, is made up of hundreds of individual materials which all behave very differently. The way food materials are shaped, formed and finished depends on how they have been combined (mixed together) and whether they have been cooked or not. It would be impossible to give the same detailed specification for a range of baked products because the specification for a product like a ginger biscuit, for example, would be very different from that for a sponge cake. However, it would be possible to give some common general points. These points are called the **general design criteria** or **general specification** and it is important that you produce these general points for your product ideas *after* you have completed your initial research.

¶●¶ How to produce design criteria

■ First, look back at your design brief and your analysis. You need to make a list of the main points you identified when you analysed the brief you were given. You should reread your research, particularly the analysis of it. You need to home in on particular points that emerge.

■ For example, if you were asked to produce some ideas for new products for school lunches, your analysis might have brought out the following points:

sweet and savoury

hand-held   hot and cold   nutritious

high energy   low cost   appeal for a teenage market

■ Your early research might also have produced other information, e.g.:

a need for multi-cultural products   low fat dishes   more fruit and vegetables within products

smaller portions at lower costs   one-pot takeaway products   different foods in summer and winter

cold desserts   more pasta   more interesting flavours   cheaper dishes   more sweet products

■ You will see from this list that a whole range of school lunch products could fit your criteria. These points are still very general, however, which is why this stage is called general design criteria.

? CHECK YOURSELF QUESTIONS

Q1 Have you identified all the points in your design brief?

Q2 Has the research you have done provided you with relevant information for a new product or products?

Q3 Does your list of points enable you to produce ideas for lots of different products?

COMMENTS

Q1 Look back at the design brief which you were given by your teacher. Select the information from your analysis which relates to the actual food product(s) that you think the brief is asking about.

Q2 Look at all the research you have done. What sort of things have you found out about the types of products which could be developed. For example:
  • If you carried out a questionnaire, what types of products did people want?
  • If you looked at the product ranges which are available in the supermarket, are there any gaps?
  • If you tested existing products by carrying out some sensory evaluation, what points were emerging?
  • Were the products too high in additives? If so, one of the general points for your criteria would be to produce a low-additive product.

  • If the sensory evaluation said that all products seemed very salty, then a general point would be to reduce the salt.
  • If you examined products and checked the weight and nutritional value, you might conclude that the portion size for teenagers needs to be increased to provide more energy value and protein. You might say in your general specification that a product gives 'high energy value' or provides one third of a teenager's protein requirements.

Q3 Look at the list of criteria you have made. Are all the points general enough for you to produce a whole range of very different design ideas?the page into sections or by placing information on the page before sticking it down. You need to cut and stick using sharp scissors or a paper trimmer. Use the right type of glue, arrange the information in order and ask someone else to give you their opinion before finally sticking everything into place or producing a final piece of writing. (This is where your teacher can be very useful!)

SESSION 3 ■ Design ideas ■

🍽 What are design ideas?

■ Design ideas are suggestions for food products that you can draw up when you have:

- studied and analysed the design brief
- produced conclusions from your initial research
- decided upon some general criteria for your product.

■ At this point a whole range of possible ideas will come to mind. You will need to present them all and then do some extra evaluation to find out which of your ideas will be most suitable for further development.

🍽 How to find design ideas

1 Look back at your research.

- What products did people prefer when you asked them?

- Did you find any particular gaps in the market?

- Were there any particular groups of people for whom there was a shortage of products?

- Was there a need to consider a particular price range?

- Was there a particular nutritional need?

2 Look in magazines and books. Do any of the pictures or recipes seem appropriate?

3 What types of product have you made before in school? Would any of these be appropriate?

4 Did the design brief indicate that your product should have certain ingredients or mixtures in it? For example, you may have been asked to design a pasta sauce snack, in which case you have been given some very specific information to influence your ideas.

5 Did the design brief indicate that you could consider a wide range of products? For example, you may have been asked to design a product to be included in the menu for the school canteen. In this case you can produce a whole range of very different ideas, both sweet and savoury, using a wide range of ingredients and mixtures.

🍽 How to present design ideas

■ Whenever you present information in your design folder, you must make sure that whoever is reading it will understand:

- what you mean
- why you have included the information
- what made you use the information
- how you intend using the information.

- There are many different ways of presenting design ideas. Look at the examples given in this chapter and see how many of them would be suitable for you to use.

SKETCHES, DRAWINGS AND DIAGRAMS
- Look at Figure 3.1 and read the examiner's comments on it on page 14. This example relates to a design brief for a new range of decorated cakes.

Figure 3.1
Initial ideas

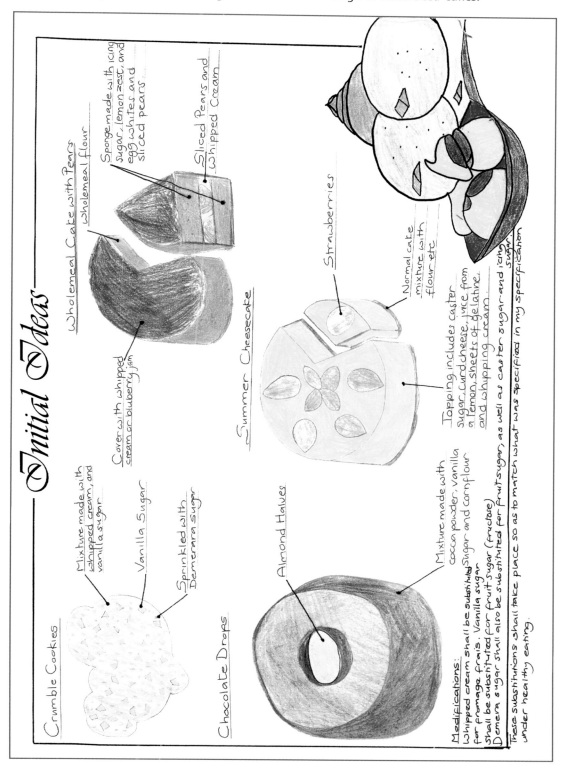

Initial Ideas

Wholemeal Cake with Pears
wholemeal flour
Sponge made with icing sugar, lemon zest, and egg whites and sliced pears.
Sliced Pears and Whipped Cream
Cover with whipped cream or blueberry jam

Summer Cheesecake
Strawberries
Normal cate mixture with flour etc.
Topping includes caster sugar, curd cheese, juice from a lemon, sheets of gelatine and whipping cream.

Crumble Cookies
Mixture made with whipped cream, and vanilla sugar.
Vanilla Sugar
Sprinkled with Demerara sugar

Chocolate Drops
Almond Halves
Mixture made with cocoa powder, vanilla sugar and cornflour.

Modifications:
Whipped cream shall be substituted for fromage frais. Vanilla sugar shall be substituted for fruit sugar (fructose). Demerara sugar shall also be substituted for fruit sugar, as well as caster sugar and icing sugar. These substitutions shall take place so as to match what was specified in my specification under healthy eating.

Examiner's comments on 3.1

Good Points

- Sketches are used to put across new ideas for decorated cakes.
- It is perfectly acceptable for the sketches to be rough ideas and not accurate in size and shape.
- The sketches clearly show various ways in which cakes can be made, shaped, cut, filled, flavoured and decorated.
- Labels on the sketches give additional information which the sketch itself might not make clear.
- Comments link these ideas with previous points in a specification.
- Additional ideas for alterations and improvements are included.
- Colour adds interest to the ideas.
- Design ideas are communicated clearly.

Areas for Improvement

- Alternative shapes could have been suggested.
- Notes and labels could have commented upon any problems which might arise from trying to produce complex shapes.
- Some reference to the different types of base mixtures could have been made.
- Possible problems with substituting ingredients might have been given.

RECIPES FOR SUITABLE PRODUCTS

■ Look at Figure 3.2 and then read the examiner's comments on it below. These ideas relate to a design brief for a low-cost frozen meal product.

Examiner's comments on 3.2

Good Points

- Existing recipes are used as the basis for ideas.
- Only a basic recipe is given and not the method.
- Reasons for selecting the recipes have been included.
- Reasons link back to initial research and use information about different target groups, storage methods, cost, nutritional value and alternative ingredients.
- Four concise ideas have been presented on one page and clearly convey the thought process of the student to the reader.
- Some alternative ideas for ingredients are given to meet design criteria that have already been identified.

Areas for Improvement

- More adaptations for each recipe idea could have been given.
- Some brief outline ideas for future development could have been included. These might have referred to carrying out investigations into the suitability of the product for freezing.
- Possible development for a whole range of products could be added.
- A clear indication should be given of whether or not the ideas are to be made and sensory tested.
- The use of nutritional analysis for each recipe could have led to the production of a model of the idea.

Figure 3.2
Design ideas

7) Pancakes with grated carrot and sweetcorn

100g plain flour
1/4 tsp salt
1 egg
300ml semi-skimmed milk
2 large carrots
200g sweetcorn (canned)

Reasons for choice

This dish is really simple and because of the nature of the ingredients it will also be quite cheap. I think my target audience would enjoy this as pancakes are normally served as a "fun food". The pancake batter contains milk which would give the children protein and calcium. The carrot and sweetcorn would provide vitamin A.

8) Turkey stew

450g skinless turkey breast
350g potatoes
1 large onion
2 carrots
1 tbsp olive oil
1 tsp dried thyme
1.2litres chicken stock
150g curried sweetcorn
150g frozen peas

Reasons for choice

This dish uses turkey which is different from normal "everyday" meats and it is also a cheaper alternative to others. It has a nice variety of vegetables and would be very filling. I think this dish would provide my target group with beneficial nutrients and I believe it would freeze well.

9) Quiche lorraine

350g shortcrust pastry
1 tsp olive oil
1 large onion
4 rashers lean back bacon
3 eggs
75ml semi-skimmed milk
200ml low fat creme fraiche

Reasons for choice

This dish would be good as I would be able to show off some of my skills, such as in pastry making. It contains ingredients which would appeal to my target audience and ones which I think would react well to freezing and re-heating. Although it would provide the child with a lot of protein and calcium there may be too much fat from the pastry and cheese. I'm also not sure whether this dish would end up being low cost!

10) Baked potatoes with tuna

4 large potatoes
50g butter
300g tinned tuna in brine
100g tinned sweetcorn
50ml natural yoghurt

Reasons for choice

Potatoes can be bought very cheaply, thus this dish could be very low cost, as only a small quantity of topping would be needed on the potato. The potato would provide the diner with a burst of carbohydrate which is good for energy. The tuna would provide protein and the sweetcorn gives vitamin C. Instead of using mayonnaise to mix the topping, natural yoghurt offers a low cost, low fat alternative.

- Put together a montage of pictures from books or magazines, showing products or ingredients which depict colour, eye appeal, shape, size, texture, quality, flavour.

- Show the results of nutritional analysis of a recipe. This is a way of modelling an idea without actually making it. It is a good way of checking to see if a product meets the nutritional requirement of the brief or of your own design criteria.

■ You must always ensure that your design ideas are fully explained. You can do this by:

- labelling diagrams and pictures

- listing the main ingredients

- describing/listing the particular characteristics or features of the product

- commenting on each idea

- relating ideas back to aspects of your research or the design criteria which you have produced

- using sensory testing to evaluate some of the ideas which you have actually had a go at making

- producing a summary of the sensory characteristics of each product.

Evaluating all your design ideas

■ You need to consider all the ideas you have presented because you will need to select the most suitable one or ones. You cannot decide to select an idea just because: you like it; it is the cheapest; your family would buy it; you are good at making this type of product.

■ You must evaluate it in terms of:

- Does it fit the brief?

- Does it match the findings from your research?

- Does it meet your general specification?

- Does it fit the nutritional profile?

- Can it be stored according to the requirement of the brief?

- Does it have the correct sensory characteristics, e.g. taste, texture?

- Can it be developed in a variety of ways, e.g:
  - Can it be produced in different shapes and sizes?
  - Can taste, texture, flavours be changed?
  - Can different ingredients and components be used?

■ You will need to reach your conclusions by: looking back at what you said and produced in the earlier parts of your project; testing your ideas; carrying out sensory evaluation.

■ Look at Figure 3.3 on page 18 and then read the examiner's comments below. This gives you some guidelines for evaluating your own design ideas and presenting your conclusions. This evaluation of design ideas relates to the production of a low-cost frozen meal product.

Examiner's comments on 3.3

Good Points

- Each design idea has been evaluated against the original design brief.
- Reference is made to findings from research which relate to target consumer groups and their possible nutritional needs.
- It is clear that any ideas which did not match the brief or research findings have been discarded.
- The student is not deviating from the requirements of the original brief.
- Evaluation refers to storage methods and their suitability. This is important because the product has to be frozen.
- Ideas for development are also indicated.
- The evaluation makes a direct link back to the brief, the research and the design criteria which have already been carried out.
- The route for future development is clear.

Areas for Improvement

- More specific reference to the nutritional content of each product would have been useful as this could be matched more closely to the target group needs. Development could then have used this information.
- Possible changes to the recipes could have been more detailed and linked to sensory characteristics.

Conclusions of Design Ideas

After completing my original design ideas and looking at these I have decided the three appropriate dishes to take further would be:

Potato and Sausage Bake

Cottage Pie

Potato and Carrot Casserole

I shall make these, freezing and reheating them as the design brief states. They should be low cost so I shall cost the ingredients and this will therefore enable me to work out the cost per portion. I will also look at how well the dishes fulfil the nutritional requirements of my target group.

Potato and Sausage Bake

I shall trial the potato and sausage bake because, as I stated in the design ideas, the dish would provide a change from the usual children's meals. I don't think that this dish contains any ingredients which would be too over-powering for children yet it isn't just bland and uninspired.

I think that this dish will be able to fulfil the design brief, as the main ingredient is potato which is one of Britain's staple foods, therefore it is plentiful, readily available and cheap. I think that the dish would end up not being too expensive and I think that it would freeze and reheat well. Also, I could make it up into a range easily, for example by using a different type of sausage or replacing the sausage with other products such as beefburger or chicken.

Cottage Pie

I shall trial this dish because I think that it would be popular with my target group. Again I am using traditional ingredients, which, if proportioned properly, will be low cost as, like my other chosen ideas, it uses potato. I think, also, that this dish could be made into a range by using different bases. It contains carbohydrate as well as protein and so would enable a parent to have a complete meal quickly. Frozen vegetables or tomato could be added as a serving suggestion to provide vitamin C.

Potato and Carrot Casserole

I decided to trial this dish because I think that it is different from the type of frozen meals on the market at the moment. I think that children would enjoy it as it doesn't use any ingredients which they may dislike. I think that it doesn't really use any expensive ingredients so the final dish will be low-cost. It does not contain any ingredients which may not freeze well. I believe that there is a lot of scope to make this dish into a range, perhaps using a different type of vegetable or by adding a meat alternative or using different toppings.

I have decided to make the cottage pie first.

Figure 3.3 *Conclusions of design ideas*

CHECK YOURSELF QUESTIONS

Q1 Have you read all the information you have put into your design folder?

Which parts of the brief and the research will you need to use to produce relevant design ideas?

Q2 Look back at your design criteria/general specification and make sure each idea matches this.

Q3 Have you made your design ideas clear?

Do you need to add any labels or comments to your ideas?

Have you presented your ideas in different forms – pictures, sketches, recipes?

Q4 Which design ideas would you actually want to make? What would be the purpose of making them?

Q5 Would someone who has not been working with you in the classroom know what you were thinking about?

Q6 Have you looked at each idea and thought about how you could evaluate it to meet the needs of the brief and research?

How did you decide on your best idea?

COMMENTS

Q1 You need to read what you have written to remind yourself of the main points about the project. The whole purpose of being given a design brief and carrying out research is to produce information which can be used to stimulate design ideas. Often students spend a lot of time on their research but then never look back at it or use it. Look back at Session 1 on research (page 2) to remind you!

Q2 Anyone who is making a product needs to be given a set of rules about what it should look or taste like. Look at the design criteria you produced and, on rough paper, write down a list of products that immediately come into your mind which would fit those criteria. Look in recipe books for other ideas.

Q3 What is going to be the best way of presenting your ideas? You might like to use several different ones. Writing is not always the best way. Can you find pictures from magazines, packets and leaflets to which you can add your own labels and comments about size, shape, ingredients and possible changes and adaptations? Sketches and drawings add interest, particularly if you can use colour,

Clipart, etc. You do not need to be the best artist in the world. You are not going to be assessed on your artistic ability but on the way in which you can convey your ideas to someone else. Often these sketches do not just give ideas but also give you the chance to show where you can make changes.

Q4 When carrying out a food technology project there is the opportunity to make some products at the design ideas stage. This enables your making skills to be assessed further and gives you the chance to carry out some sensory testing. Sensory characteristics cannot be defined in a picture and without actually making a product you cannot make changes for improvement.

Q5 Ask someone else to look at your design ideas. Get them to list and describe the ideas you have produced and to comment on the particular characteristics of each one.

Q6 Make a list of the points each idea will be evaluated against. You must make it clear why you rejected some and kept others. Always produce a detailed summary of your findings.

SESSION 4 ▮ Specifications ▮

▶ What is a product specification?

■ When you have evaluated your design ideas and chosen the most suitable idea for further development, you will need to produce a **product specification**. If your design brief asks you to design and make more than one product, you will need a product specification for each product that you are going to develop.

■ Even though you are carrying out your project work in school, you are actually working in a similar way to a professional food technologist employed in a real test kitchen in the food industry. Food technologists design product specifications and then use ingredients and methods to make a '**product prototype**' which matches each specification. A prototype is a model from which copies can be made.

■ A product specification does not cover very general points like the design brief. Instead, it describes **very specific characteristics** which a product must have. At this stage it would be too general to say, 'The product must have an edible container.' Instead, you would need to say, for example, 'It must have a pastry container.'

▶ How to design a product specification

■ The following list gives some examples of specific characteristics that might be found in a product specification:

  • indication of portion size, e.g. an individual serving

  • approximate sale cost, e.g. 'Would sell for £1.50'

  • type of outcome, e.g. pastry product, pasta product, filling encased in pastry, vegetables

  • served in sauce, filled and covered cake, protein mixed with spicy sauce

  • approximate energy value, e.g. number of calories to be generated

  • storage conditions, e.g. to be sold chilled or frozen

  • serving requirements if appropriate, e.g. suitable for serving hot or cold

  • cooking/reheating requirements, e.g. suitable for traditional and microwave cooking

  • specific sensory properties, e.g. crispy topping, variety of colours, soft filling and crisp base

  • other nutritional requirements, e.g. percentage of protein, vitamin C content, iron content

  • healthy option product, e.g. low in sugar, high in fibre, low in fat

  • specific target group, e.g. suitable for children

  • type of product, e.g. savoury main meal, sweet, snack.

- Look at Figure 4.1 and read the examiner's comments on it. This design specification relates to the production of a low-cost frozen meal product.

Figure 4.1
Design specification

Design Specification

I am now at a stage where I can make my design criteria more specific.
- My dish will be based on potatoes.
- It will contain a variety of different vegetables.
- It will be suitable to add other ingredients to, in order to make a range.
- It will be suitable for freezing.
- It will be suitable for reheating.
- It will cost no more than 20p per portion at the ingredient stage.
- It will contain nutrients suitable for children aged between 6 and 10.
- It will weigh around 175 g for a one child portion.
- It should have good sensory qualities such as flavour, texture, colour and so forth.
- It will be packaged in material suitable for the method of reheating.
- It will be able to go on sale at a local retail outlet.

I shall take these points into account when making my dish.

Examiner's comments on 4.1

Good Points
- Specific ingredients are identified.
- Points which were in the original design brief have been covered. For example, the brief said the product had to be frozen.
- The target consumer group is referred to, i.e. children.
- Research has been done on cost and portion size.
- As the product will be part of a range of dishes the specification provides the basic information and states that it will be possible to add other ingredients.
- No decision has been made as to the method of reheating but in the specification this is stated as a distinct requirement for both the product and the packaging.

- General reference has been made to sensory qualities.
- There is sufficient flexibility in the specification to allow a good range of development work to take place and enough specific points are made to enable evaluation to take place as the product develops.

Areas for Improvement
- Some additional information on the main nutrient needs of children could have been included.
- Sensory qualities could have been more specific. For example, as the product is for children it could have said 'colourful, crunchy textures'.
- It is not clear if the product is an individual child's portion or a family-size product. This would make some difference at the development stage.

▐◉▌ What is a manufacturing specification?

■ In the food industry, when the food technologist has completed the development work the **final prototype** is ready for manufacturing in large quantities. To enable the prototype to be copied exactly the food technologist will have to provide the food manufacturer with a **manufacturing specification**. This gives the precise details that the manufacturer will need in order to produce an exact replica of the prototype.

■ To say that a product should have a 'pastry case' would be too vague for the manufacturer. The food technologist needs to tell the manufacturer about the type of pastry to use, the ingredients that should be in the pastry, the thickness to which the pastry should be rolled, the exact shape and size of the pastry case, i.e. its dimensions and measurements, and the sensory characteristics of the pastry, e.g. 'crisp short texture, baked to a light golden colour, free from fatty taste, crumbly when broken'. In addition to written details the manufacturer is often provided with a labelled diagram.

▐◉▌ How to design a manufacturing specification

■ The following list gives you some ideas of what to include in a manufacturing specification:

- specific dimensions (with a sketch), i.e. weight, size, shape

- specific qualities of ingredients, e.g. percentage of fat in meat, size of glacé cherries

- names of ingredients with weights and proportions to use, e.g. '200g butter, 450g flaked haddock'

- specific tolerances, e.g. thickness of pastry, viscosity (runniness) of sauce

- the size to which ingredients must be cut, e.g. the exact shape and size of pieces of fruit and vegetables, the nozzle size for mincing meat, the slicing grade for carrots, the grating size for cheese

- types of cooking methods and cooking temperatures with critical control points (see Session 7 page 41 and Revision Session 10 page 143).

- cooling times and methods

- finishing techniques, e.g. 'Brush with whole egg glaze before baking', 'Fill centre of cake with fresh whipped cream to a thickness of 2cm', 'Decorate with six slices of tomato and one teaspoonful of mixed herbs before cooking', 'Cover surface of biscuit with white rolled ' icing to a thickness of 0.5cm'

- specific details of packaging requirements, e.g. 'micowavable dish with sealed film covering in crushproof sleeve'

- wording for the label which will provide information for the consumer about ingredients, nutrition, the name of the product, storage and cooking/reheating instructions, shelf life, etc.

■ Sometimes a photograph is used to help a manufacturer to meet the specification. This would normally still need additional written information but is useful in large-scale catering where a meal is being assembled on a plate from bought components.

■ Look at Figure 4.2 and read the examiner's comments on it on page 24.

Figure 4.2
Manufacturer's specification

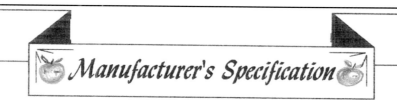

In order to have my final dish manufactured correctly commercially I have come up with the following points for the manufacturer(s):

- The potatoes and carrots will be grated so that they result in strips 1.5 cm × 0.5 cm.

- The leeks will be sliced so that they are 0.5 cm thick and 2 cm in diameter. They will be sliced in half across the diameter if above 2 cm in diameter.

- The Cheddar cheese will be grated so that it results in strips 0.5 cm × 1.5 cm.

- The quantity of each ingredient will be multiplied by a common factor for large scale production. This factor will depend on demand for the product.

- The filling will be packaged in low density polythene containers 15 cm × 12 cm × 7 cm.

- The filling will be in the containers to a depth of 6 cm.

- 50 mls of sauce will be added to the base. The sauce will be spread so that it is 1 cm from the edge of the dish at all times.

- The dishes will be cooked in the oven (before topping) for 20 mins at a temperature of 180°C.

- The "breadcrumbs" will be finely made with margarine and plain flour. They will have no lumps and each crumb will be approximately 2 mm in diameter.

- 6.4 g of the topping will be put onto each dish. It will be spread evenly over the dish ensuring it goes to the edge.

- The dish will be recooked for a further 10 mins in the oven.

- The dish will undergo a rapid chill to 1°C within 1.5 hrs.

- The dish will then be blast frozen to −30°C in a space of 6 hrs.

- The dish will then be heat sealed with low density polythene.

- The dish will then be packaged in card boxes.

Examiner's comments on 4.2

Good Points

- Very detailed information is given.
- Measurements, weights and sizes are very specific. The size of individual ingredients is important to ensure consistency between the end products.
- The candidate has given the depths, coating methods and weight of topping which will ensure quality and consistency in large-scale production.
- Cooking temperatures and times are given.
- Cooling, chilling and freezing times and temperatures are given.
- There is information on the type of packaging and the method of sealing.

Areas for Improvement

- There is little reference to specific ingredients and the production methods which the manufacturer should use. For example, the quantity for sauce is given but not the ingredients or method.
- No indication is given of the thickness of the sauce.
- No order/instructions for assembling the product are given.
- No labelled diagram of the finished product is provided.
- No nutritional information is given for the label.

CHECK YOURSELF QUESTIONS

Q1 Look at the design idea which you have chosen to develop. List the characteristics of the product or the characteristics which you want it to have.

Q2 Will it be possible to change ingredients, methods, shapes, sizes, flavours to achieve the product specification?

Q3 Have you really provided exact information on your manufacturing specification?

Q4 Could the information you have given about the product enable anyone, anywhere, to produce the same outcome?

COMMENTS

Q1 When looking at a recipe, a picture or a sketch some of the characteristics will seem very obvious. For example, 'coated with sauce, crisp brown top, enclosed in pastry, covered in cheese' etc. Other characteristics are not so obvious, e.g. 'high in vitamin C, provides 450 calories, spicy flavour'.

Q2 When you make your final product you do not have to get it right first time. When you look at 'development' in the next session you will see how important it is to change, adapt and amend parts of your product to meet the specification.

Q3 It is important that you give exact measurements, shapes, quantities and details about methods. For example, you need to say, 'Roll biscuit dough to a thickness of 1 cm, cut into circles measuring 6 cm in diameter.'

Q4 This is the ultimate check on a manufacturing specification.

SESSION 5 ■ Development ■

¶●¶ What is development?

■ **Development** is the stage in the design process where changes are made to an idea to enable it to meet the requirements of the design brief, the information which has been gathered during research and, most important, the product specification. Development is the process used to ensure that the product will:

- • be of good quality
- • be good to look at, and enjoyable and safe to eat
- • provide value for money
- • meet the appropriate nutritional profile.

■ Development should form one of the larger sections of your project work. It is also a section in which you can show a good range of making skills.

■ The majority of development work usually takes place when the final product idea has been chosen but it is possible to include some development work at the design ideas stage before a final idea is selected. Development is all about **changing**, **testing**, or **modifying** all or part of a product until a desired outcome, which meets the product specification, is achieved.

¶●¶ Ideas for development work

■ You need to record development work in your design folder. Long sections of writing are not needed. Here you will find some ideas for development work and different ways of recording it in your design folder.

INVESTIGATIONS

■ You need to state what you are doing, why you are doing it and what you have found. The easiest way to do this is to write it up in a similar way to a science experiment.

■ You must always remember to show how you are using the results of your investigation. This is where the examiner will be able to give you credit.

■ It would be possible to carry out a simple investigation, e.g. to find out which is the most suitable type of pastry for a product. Small quantities of ingredients would be used to make small samples. Results presented in a chart would record your findings.

TESTING

■ A chart recording the findings of any test is the quickest, simplest and most meaningful way of presenting information relating to testing. You must make sure that the information is clear and must know how you will use the results.

USING DIFFERENT INGREDIENTS AND METHODS

- If you are beginning your development work from an existing idea or recipe, there is good opportunity for you to change or substitute ingredients and methods. The use of different vegetables, fruits, flavourings, sauces, fillings, flour, fat, spices or herbs can completely change an idea. These ingredients can be evaluated in terms of their effect on the sensory characteristics of the product or on its nutritional value.

- Changing the methods for making products will also produce different outcomes. When making pastry, for example, the use of different methods and ingredients will significantly alter the final texture, appearance, taste and nutritional composition. Bases for pizza can be made by a variety of methods. The texture, flavour and keeping qualities of cakes depend upon the methods used in making them.

- Development gives you the opportunity to try out such changes and **evaluation** enables you to make appropriate decisions. Simple notes, charts or diagrams with comments are adequate ways of recording your results.

- Look at Figure 5.1 opposite and read the examiner's comments on it.

LOOKING AT SIZE, SHAPE AND CONSISTENCY

- At the development stage it is possible to try out different sizes of a product, in terms of both weight and volume. These can then be evaluated against the nutritional requirements. For example, in the case of individual hand-held products, such as biscuits, cakes and pastries, appearance will influence size.

- **Consistency** relates to the thickness or thinness of a liquid or mixture. Different consistencies are required for different functions. Some liquids are needed to bind, coat or moisten other ingredients. For example, the softness of a cake mixture will influence the texture of the cake.

- Storage methods and times will dictate the consistency required. You can carry out some testing to find out the effects of freezing, chilling and reheating on different consistencies. For example, if a sauce product is to be made for the freezer, the sauce needs to be made thinner than if the product was to be consumed immediately. The reason for this is that freezing causes starchy liquids to thicken up.

- It is possible to write up these activities as investigations or experiments.

Adaptations to the Ingredients

The following changes were made to the recipe for the Italian Pasta Soup to improve the overall appearance/texture/taste etc. of the product :-

Original recipe	Final recipe	Reasons for change
75g butter	75g low fat margarine	less fat
1 onion	1 onion	
400g chopped tomatoes	400g chopped tomatoes	
100ml semi-skimmed milk	200ml semi-skimmed milk	to make the soup thinner
100ml water	200ml water	thinner soup
10g tomato puree	25g tomato puree	improve colour
100g pasta shells	75g macaroni	pasta shells were too bulky
40g sweet corn	40g sweet corn	
Italian herbs(as desired)	Italian herbs(as desired)	
Mixed herbs(as desired)	Mixed herbs(as desired)	

75g butter- 75g low fat margarine
This change was made to reduce the amount of fat present in the soup.It would work just as well and wouldn't really affect the flavour.

100ml semi-skimmed milk- 200ml semi-skimmed milk
This change was made as the soup was far too thick.The milk serves as a binder but also as a liquid thinner.

100ml water- 200ml water
This change was also made to thin out the soup.

10g tomato puree- 25g tomato puree
This change was made to improve the colour of the soup and also to make the flavour just that little bit stronger.

100g pasta shells- 75g macaroni
I made this change because the pasta shells were too bulky to be served in a take-away container and using macaroni also helps the overall look of the soup as it is smaller. You don't need as much macaroni either.

Examiner's comments on 5.1

Good Points

- The aims of the development are given, i.e. 'to improve the overall appearance/taste/texture'.
- Details of changes to the original recipe are provided.
- Reasons for changes are given.
- A knowledge of the nutritional effects of changing ingredients is shown, i.e. the use of low-fat margarine.
- A knowledge of the effects of adding different or extra ingredients is shown and linked to the use of the ingredient, i.e. milk is used as a thinner.
- Development is linked to the original brief and uses earlier observations, e.g. 'The soup is to be sold in a carton therefore the size of the pasta is very important and also the quantity.'

Areas for Improvement

- Evaluation of the development should be included on the same page if possible.
- The results of sensory evaluation could have been included.

Figure 5.1 *Adaptations to ingredients*

CHANGING SENSORY CHARACTERISTICS

■ This is perhaps the most common form of development and, unfortunately, students often see this as the only type of development which they need to carry out. However, it is a very important part of product development and needs to be done to meet the sensory characteristics which the product specification has outlined.

■ Changes to taste, texture or appearance can be done throughout the development process, with fine modifications made to the very final product. **Sensory characteristics** will be achieved by the: use of seasoning, herbs, spices; addition of different ingredients to alter both flavour and texture; use of different production methods; addition of fillings, toppings, decorations.

■ A table showing the ingredient or method, together with the resultant effect, is a good recording strategy, especially when combined with a conclusion.

APPLYING DIFFERENT FINISHING TECHNIQUES

■ The application of a glaze, nuts and seeds, icings, grated cheese, sliced fruits or vegetables, piped cream or potato, spices or herbs to products will affect appearance, taste and texture.

DEMONSTRATING KNOWLEDGE OF FOOD MATERIALS AND PROCESSING

■ The ability to understand scientific principles and their application to food production is an essential part of development work. Look at Figure 5.2 and then read the examiner's comments on it.

Examiner's comments on 5.2

Good Points

• The student understands the effects that mixing and cooking will have on the choice of ingredients for the two parts of the product.
• The specification states that the product will contain crunchy vegetables and the composition and cooking of vegetables achieves this.
• The candidate demonstrates the necessary knowledge and understanding of the effects of cooking on potato to achieve the desired result.
• A very clear explanation of gelatinisation is shown for sauce making.
• The candidate explains how the required consistency of sauce is achieved and how ratios and proportions affect the degree of gelatinisation
• Clear understanding of making techniques are also given and can be applied to faults which might occur in a mixture.

Areas for Improvement

• Some actual testing of different vegetables could have been added, particularly for obtaining the best results in terms of cooking methods, the size of individual pieces and critical time controls in cooking.

Scientific Principles

I have decided to discuss the scientific principles behind my dish. This shall enable me to see exactly what happens during cooking.

During cooking potatoes go through a process of gelatinisation. The starch molecules in the potato take up water and swell as the following diagram shows:

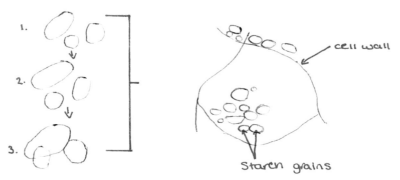

Potatoes need to be cooked long enough for complete gelatinisation of starch otherwise they will have an uncooked taste and texture.

My dish is primarily based on vegetables. Changes occurring in the texture of vegetables during cooking are due to the softening of the cellulose and the gelatinisation of the starch. Overcooking makes the vegetables soft and 'mushy'. The vegetables should be cooked only until tender but firm. This means that some of the crispness of the raw vegetable is retained. The cooking time of vegetables is determined by the amount of cellulose the vegetable contains, e.g. carrots require a longer cooking time than green vegetables.

If overcooked, some flavour can be lost from the vegetables. This is due to the loss of volatile acids in cooking. To combat this I only cooked my vegetables as long as absolutely necessary and did not use more liquid that required.

In my final dish I have a sauce. The sauce was made using the roux method. As in all sauce making gelatinisation occurred. This process thickens a liquid such as a sauce. When starch is mixed with a liquid the granules are suspended in the liquid. As the mixture is heated the liquid begins to penetrate the starch granules causing them to soften. The granules swell to about five times their normal size until they nearly touch each other. This makes the liquid thick and we say that a gel has been formed. The degree of gelatinisation is affected by the proportion and type of starch, the temperature of the liquid and the effect of other ingredients.

The process of gelatinisation is important in all starch thickened liquids, if this process is not correctly done the mixture may be unpleasant, be of the wrong consistency or may become lumpy. Lumps will form in a starch thickened mixture if:
- Dry starch is mixed with warm or hot liquid. On immediate contact with dry starch the hot liquid will gelatinise the outer starch granules. These granules act as a barrier and the liquid is unable to penetrate to the remaining uncooked starch inside.
- The mixture is not stirred whilst heated. The starch granules will not remain in suspension unless the mixture is stirred. They simply settle in groups at the bottom of the saucepan. The starch granules in contact with the liquid gelatinise and prevent the liquid from penetrating the remaining starch.

Figure 5.2 *Scientific principles*

DESIGNATED TOLERANCES, RATIOS AND PROPORTIONS

- The manufacturing specification will need to contain very accurate information about these three factors. Development gives you the chance to try out such things as different thicknesses of dough for pastry, biscuits, scones or bread, different viscosity of sauces, icings or fillings, different sizes of fruits or vegetables, pieces of meat or fish.

- The results of your investigations will provide you with a good quality product and the information that is needed for manufacturing it. This could be presented by giving the base recipe with amendments noted in an adjacent column, showing where and how modifications were made.

CARRYING OUT FURTHER RESEARCH

- Session 1 pointed out that research can be done at any stage in a project. Often, when students reach the development stage, they realise that they still need some specific information on types of ingredient or processes which it was not possible for them to know about at the beginning of the project.

- Look at Figure 5.3 opposite and read then the examiner's comments on it.

Examiner's comments on 5.3

Good Points
- A need for some knowledge of sauce making has been identified by the student.
- A sauce product has been specified in the design brief, therefore the student has found it necessary to discover how sauces can be used in products.
- Different methods for making sauces have been researched.
- Thickening agents have been identified.
- Some scientific understanding is demonstrated, which the student will apply later during making.
- Sources of information are given.

Areas for Improvement
- The need for the information has been related to the design brief but a more specific need may become apparent as a result of the student's design ideas. This should be shown.
- The student must show clearly how this information is to be used.

THE NUTRITIONAL PROFILE

- The product specification will show the nutritional profile that is required. The only way to match the product to the specification is to carry out some **nutritional analysis**.

- By producing a series of computer printout summaries as you carry out changes, you will be able to see how your product is matching up to the specification. Changing ingredients or quantities of ingredients will have a significant effect on the product's nutritional value.

SAUCES RESEARCH

— I referred to cookery and recipe books to obtain information on making all types of sauces.

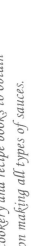

A SAUCE is a thickened, flavoured liquid added to a food or dish for any of the following reasons:

1 To enhance the flavour of the food which it accompanies.

2 To provide a contrasting flavour to an otherwise mildly-flavoured food, e.g. cheese sauce with cauliflower.

3 To provide a contrasting texture to particular solid foods, e.g. poultry or fish.

4 To bind ingredients together for dishes such as fish cakes or croquettes.

5 To add colour to a dish, e.g. jam sauce with a steamed sponge pudding.

6 To contribute to the nutritional value of a dish.

7 To reduce the richness of some foods, e.g. orange sauce with roast duck, apple sauce with roast pork.

8 To add interest and variety to a meal.

ROUX SAUCES

A roux is sometimes used as a method of thickening a sauce with the starch contained in flour. (See Cornflour.)

Method

Melt approximately 12g fat in a pan and add to it the same amount of flour. Stir until well mixed and heat gently for one minute. During this time the starch granules will begin to soften and the starch will start to cook. The fat and flour mixture form the roux which is the basis of a sauce using approximately 275ml of liquid. Examples: white, cheese, mushroom, onion, and parsley sauces.

CORNFLOUR

Cornflour may be used to thicken sweet sauces such as chocolate, lemon, and butterscotch. It contains starch the granules of which, when mixed with cold water and heated to 60°C, begin to absorb the water and swell. On heating further to 85°C they will swell to five times their normal size and thicken the liquid. If heating continues, some of the granules will rupture, releasing starch which will form a gel with the water. On cooling, the gel will set, and the sauce will become solid.

THICKENINGS FOR SAUCES
Starch, in flour, cornflour, arrowroot, etc.
Protein, from eggs.
Emulsification of oil and water.
Puried vegetables or fruits.

SAUCES should be carefully flavoured and should be *tasted* before serving, so that adjustments can be made. A badly flavoured sauce can ruin an otherwise perfectly good dish.

It is important to stir a sauce continuously while it is cooking to prevent it sticking to the bottom of the pan or becoming lumpy.

Consistencies of sauces

Pouring - A pouring sauce, at boiling point, should just glaze the back of a wooden spoon, and should flow freely when poured.

Coating - A coating sauce, at boiling point, should coat the back of a wooden spoon, and should be used as soon as it is ready, to ensure even coating over the food.

Binding - A binding sauce or panada should be thick enough to bind dry ingredients together, so that they can be handled easily to be formed into rissoles, cakes, etc.

A SAUCE can be served as;

a coating for vegetables, meat, or fish

part of a meal

an accompaniment.

PUREES

Cooked or raw fruit or vegetables can be pureed to produce a smooth sauce, by rubbing them through a sieve or by liquidizing.
Examples: apple sauce and tomato sauce.

EGG PROTEIN
The coagulation temperature of a yolk is 70°C.
When egg is used to thicken a sauce it should be added to other ingredients while they are cool and then gently heated to reach this temperature. Once the sauce is thickened, it should be cooled rapidly to stop the coagulation.
Example: egg custard sauce.

All sauces should be free from lumps and should not be overcooked, as this may spoil their flavour.

EMULSIFICATION OF FAT

If oil and water are thoroughly mixed, they become an emulsion. To prevent seperation, egg yolk, which contains the emulsifier lecithin, may be added. This is the method used to thicken and stabilize the oil and water (in the vinegar) of a mayonnaise.

Sauce-based Product

Figure 5.3 Sauces research

COSTING
- Costing is often a major priority in a product specification. Costing tables will show the effects of changing ingredients and quantities but changing ingredients to reduce cost can be detrimental to the successful making of the product. You need to comment on this.

CHECK YOURSELF QUESTIONS

Q1 Are there distinct parts to your product idea?

Q2 Could you make changes or give alternatives for each part?

Q3 Think about the different types of development that you could carry out.

Q4 Have you carried out nutritional analysis? How are you using the results?

Q5 Are you satisfied with the final product? Does it need fine tuning?

Q6 Do your design sheets show everything that you have done? Will the reader understand?

Q7 Have you made sure that your knowledge about food and the effects of mixing, shaping, cooking and storing is evident?

COMMENTS

Q1 Look carefully at the idea for your product. Is it possible to divide the product into separate parts, such as flan case and filling, pasta and sauce, cheesecake base, topping and glaze, pasty and filling, pizza base and topping?

Q2 Once you have identified the different parts of the product, brainstorm ideas for changes. These could include changes to ingredients, methods, shapes, sizes, finishes, storage methods, flavours, textures.

Q3 For each idea give some details about the development. For example, if you are making small cakes, one idea could be to carry out an investigation into the use of different fats to meet certain dietary needs and preferences. You should produce a list of possible fats and the methods to be used. Some thought also needs to be given to the method of recording the results and how the results are to be used.

Q4 Part of your specification might have made some reference to nutritional requirements. One way to check the effects of making changes to a recipe is to carry out computer analysis of the changed recipe. The printout of the results is good evidence to put in your design folder, with comments of your own.

Q5 You will eventually make a final product. Look at it, taste it and ask other people to do the same. Are any small, simple changes needed to improve it?

Q6 Make sure all the work you have done has been recorded in your folder. It is very important that the evidence is clear and the detail shows the changes that you have made.

Q7 You will be given credit if you can show that you understand the effects of mixing foods and how the changes which take place during cooking and processing affect the final result.

🍽 What is evaluation?

■ Evaluation is all about **making judgements**. It is a very important part of designing and making and should be done at all stages of the design process so that you will be able to make the right decisions for the next step in the process.

■ Evaluation is a way of looking back at what you have already found out and using this information to help you produce criteria and ideas and eventually to make a food product which fits the design brief.

■ Evaluation does not just happen at the end of a project. It is the process which enables you to find ideas and adapt and improve a product.

TYPES OF EVALUATION

- looking at and tasting existing products

- reading and summarising relevant points from various sources of information

- considering ideas in the light of consumer preferences

- matching ideas to criteria

- testing products against a specification

- testing products for particular sensory characteristics – sensory evaluation

- carrying out nutritional analysis

- making judgements about the suitability of particular ingredients or methods

- judging the effects of different methods of storage or processing on ingredients, mixtures or complete products

- looking at different packaging materials and judging which would be the most suitable for your product

- making a final evaluation against the original design brief.

🍽 When and where should you carry out evaluation?

THE INITIAL RESEARCH

1 You should examine and taste existing products to assess what is good or not so good and if an alternative or better product could be made.

2 At the initial research stage you should also evaluate the information you have collected and draw together points from questionnaires.

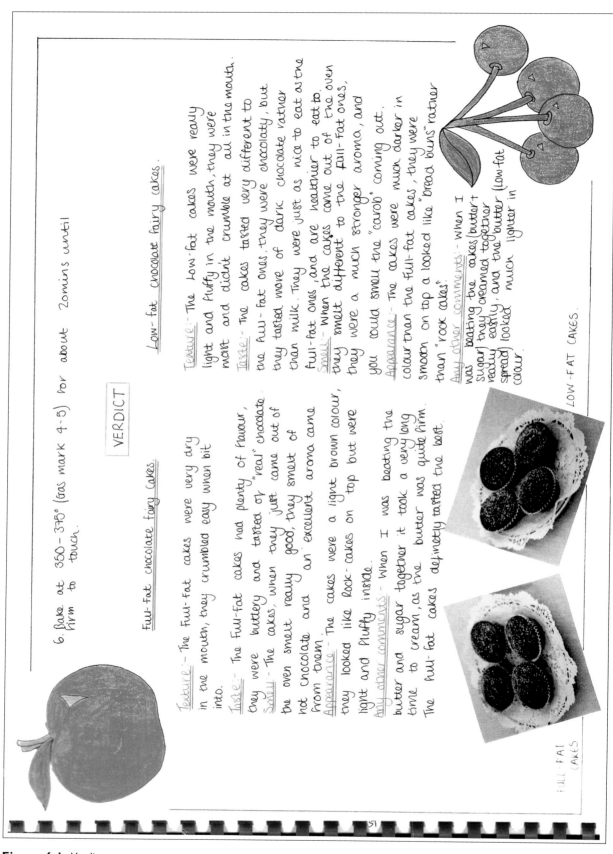

6. Bake at 350 – 375° (Gas mark 4-5) for about 20mins until firm to touch.

VERDICT

Full-fat chocolate fairy cakes.

Texture:- The full-fat cakes were very dry in the mouth, they crumbled easy when bit into.

Taste:- The full-fat cakes had plenty of flavour, they were buttery and tasted of "real" chocolate.

Smell:- The cakes, when they just came out of the oven smelt really good, they smelt of hot chocolate and an excellent aroma came from them.

Appearance:- The cakes were a light brown colour, they looked like rock-cakes on top but were light and fluffy inside.

Any other comments:- When I was beating the butter and sugar together it took a very long time to cream, as the butter was quite firm. The full-fat cakes definitely tasted the best.

Low-fat chocolate fairy cakes.

Texture:- The low-fat cakes were really light and fluffy in the mouth, they were moist and didn't crumble at all in the mouth.

Taste:- The cakes tasted very different to the full-fat ones, they were chocolaty, but they tasted more of dark chocolate rather than milk. They were just as nice to eat as the full-fat ones, and are heavier to eat to.

Smell:- When the cakes came out of the oven they smelt different to the full-fat ones, they were a much stronger aroma, and you could smell the "carob" coming out.

Appearance:- The cakes were much darker in colour than the full-fat cakes, they were smooth on top & looked like "bread buns" rather than "rock cakes".

Any other comments:- When I was beating the cakes (butter + sugar) they creamed together really easily, and the butter (low-fat spread) looked much lighter in colour.

FULL-FAT CAKES

LOW-FAT CAKES

51

Figure 6.1 *Verdict*

THE DESIGN IDEAS STAGE

1 You should look carefully at the ideas you have produced and select the most appropriate ones which match your design criteria and the requirements of the design brief. You should choose the most promising idea and think about how this idea could be developed. (Look back at Session 3, page 11.)

2 You should carry out **sensory testing** (see Revision Session 16, pages 198–202).

THE DEVELOPMENT STAGE

1 You should evaluate and compare similar products which you have made but where you have changed one or more ingredients. Look at Figure 6.1 and then read the examiner's comments on it.
This work is related to a brief which asks for the production of a healthy option cake.

2 At this stage you should also test the products which you make against the product specification.

3 You also need to test parts of the product that you are making. Look at Figure 6.2 (page 36) and then read the examiner's comments on it. Here the student has carried out some development work on part of the product.

Examiner's comments on 6.1

Good Points

- Specific sensory characteristics are identified.
- Useful comparisons are made of characteristics between full fat and low fat.
- Some observations are made about the appearance of the product at different stages of making.

Areas for Improvement

- No clear objectives for the comparison are given.
- No conclusion is made about the results.
- No comments are made which show the candidate's knowledge and understanding of food, i.e. the fact that low-fat spread results are different because of their water content.
- No reasons are given for the different characteristics of the two cakes.
- The photographs need annotating and specific comments should be made about the size and shape of different products.
- No indication is given as to how these results will be used or how and why further testing might be needed.

Evaluation Toppings

In my third development I decided to trial different toppings for my chosen dish, potato and carrot casserole. I didn't use my chosen sauce in this testing because I didn't want anything to detract from the focus of this development: toppings.

I decided to trial the following toppings:

Plain crumble topping: This is a topping made simply from flour and margarine. It is made by rubbing the margarine into the flour until it resembles breadcrumbs. It will be relatively cheap and won't alter my nutritional structure much.

Cheese topping: This topping is made from actual breadcrumbs mixed with cheese and put on the top of the dish. This will also be low cost and won't drastically affect the nutritional values.

Onion topping: This is the same as the cheese topping yet with chopped onion instead of cheese.

Toast topping: This is bread toasted and then put on the dish. It too is cheap and won't alter the nutrients much.

Crisp and breadcrumb topping: This is simply breadcrumbs with crumbled crisps. It will be reasonably cheap and, like all the other toppings, I don't think it will alter the nutritional analysis greatly.

Overall my toppings went well and I was able to complete them well within the time allowed.

The toppings didn't add large costs onto the original cost of the casserole:

1. Plain crumble topping = 3p for 320g worth of potato casserole (which is two portions). This increases the overall cost of the product to 15p per portion.

2. Cheese topping = 5p for 320g worth of casserole. This increases the overall cost of the product to 16p per portion. I may not need to use extra cheese, as before putting the topping on, I put additional cheese onto it, so I could use this cheese in the topping instead.

3. Onion topping = 3p for 320g worth of casserole. This increases the overall cost of the product to 15p per portion.

4. Toast topping = 2p for 320g worth of casserole. This increases the overall cost of the product to 14.5p per portion.

5. Crisp topping = 25p for 320g of casserole. This increases the overall cost of the product to 25p per portion.

Evaluation Toppings

As you can see, the most expensive topping is the crisp one and the least expensive is the toast topping.

All the dishes turned well, the only problem I faced was that the toast burnt, but I was able to rectify this using a fresh piece of bread. In large scale production this is a potential problem.

All the toppings looked very appetising, they added to the appearance and presentation of the dishes. When tasting all the different toppings, they were all delicious. They were crunchy which added to the texture and mouthfeel of the casserole and, I believe, improved it.

I didn't do an ordinary sensory evaluation as I thought it would be better to ask my target group which topping they preferred. As you can see, the favourite was the crumble topping, which I would agree with, as once the dishes cooled down, the crisp and toast toppings went a little soggy. I think that with all the cheese already present in the dish, the cheese topping produced an over-powering taste, as did the onion one. I feel this would be particularly true for my target group.

After freezing and reheating there were no major changes in the consistency, taste, flavour, etc. of the dishes. They all reacted reasonably well. The toast and crisp toppings became even soggier in the microwave, in fact all the toppings weren't as crisp as they were prior to reheating. This is due to the absorption of liquid when in the freezer. I think that to combat this I would state that the dish should either be reheated in the oven or reheated in the microwave and then crisped under the grill. This would improve the texture of the topping.

I decided not to do a nutritional analysis for this development as the toppings were added in such small quantities the nutritional structure of the dish wouldn't be altered too much.

Examiner's comments on 6.2

Good Points

- A good range of alternative or possible toppings is explored.
- Some reference is made to the effect on nutritional value of adding a topping.
- Costing is considered.
- Comments are made about the sensory effects of adding toppings.
- Using a target group for evaluation is a very good strategy.
- The need for some testing of storage methods has been noted.
- The student demonstrates good knowledge and understanding of processing methods, i.e. the effects of freezing and microwaving.
- The student understands why and when nutritional analysis is required.
- It is very clear how the student is going to use the results of their development work.

Figure 6.2 *Evaluation of toppings*

Evaluation - Final Product

For my final practical I decided to put all my developments together in order to see exactly how successful my dish would be. I wanted to see how all my ideas combined together so I used my chosen topping, sauce and vegetable shape.

The dish was finished within the time allowed, and I completed it without any major problems. I tried to complete my work tidily and hygienically.

Overall I found that I was able to show a range of skills, such as vegetable preparation and sauce making. Perhaps the most complex part of the dish was making the "Béchamel" sauce, as one has to be careful to make sure that it does not go lumpy! The scientific principles behind sauce making are explained later.

I found that the dish worked well with all the developments together. Previously the dish had been a little bland and hadn't allowed me to incorporate many of my skills. This dish has improved that greatly.

The final product looked very appealing as the crispy topping made it look very appetising and it added more interest. The sauce moistened the dish and the topping added a crispy texture, which creates a better mouthfeel as it contrasts with the texture of the vegetables.

After freezing I found that the dish reacted well. From my previous trials I knew that I had to have a thinner consistency of sauce, so that it didn't become too thick after reheating. I also knew that it would be better to reheat the dish in the oven or in the microwave and then "crisp-up" the topping under the grill. I found this dish is suitable for freezing and reheating.

After reheating my dish I carried out a sensory evaluation to assess the acceptability of my final idea. I asked five people to complete my evaluation. As you can see it was pretty popular, although as some of the comments suggest, I should have perhaps added more salt, which I realised at the time of making my dish. I was also pleased to see that the marks for texture and mouthfeel increased as these are where the problems were in my previous trials of the dish.

The dish was obviously improved in the opinion of the tasters.

Overall my dish has worked out reasonably cheaply. The total dish costs 90p for six portions which means that it costs 15p per portion; this is satisfactory because my design brief states that it should be a low cost dish.

I did a nutritional analysis of my final product in order to see how all the developments affected the nutritional content. This dish isn't seriously lacking in any nutrients. I would have expected the dish to be higher in carbohydrates as these are found in starchy foods such as potato, however this isn't the case. It is high in protein; this is due to the high presence of dairy products like milk and cheese. Vegetables also contain protein. I could advertise this dish as 'protein and calcium rich.' This may create extra custom as many parents are concerned that children don't have enough calcium, as a lack of it may result in conditions such as osteoporosis, in later life.

Figure 6.3 *Evaluation of the final product*

4   You also need to test the effects of different temperatures and storage methods on parts or all of your product.

■   Finally, you need to evaluate your end product against the product specification and the design brief. Look at Figure 6.3 on page 37 and then read the examiner's comments on it below. This final evaluation refers to a brief which asked for a range of low-cost meals for the freezer.

¶◉¶ Summary of evaluation

■   You must always have clear objectives for your evaluation. In other words, you must be very sure of what it is you want to find out.

■   When you write up your evaluation you must make it clear what you have found out, how successful you have been, and what is right and what is wrong.

■   You must make it clear how you are going to use the information gathered from your evaluation.

■   Your evaluation should guide you towards the next step in your work.

■   The end product which you make will be the result of ideas which you have changed and modified. The final product may be very different from your first ideas. This will be the result of evaluation.

■   For further help on evaluation see Revision Session 16 on Sensory Analysis (page 195).

Examiner's comments on 6.3

Good Points
• All development work has been included in the final evaluation.
• Clear objectives are given for the final evaluation.
• Some evaluation of the student's own personal achievement and progression is included.
• Previous development work and testing are referred to and the student's own knowledge is made clear.
• Points which were outlined in the original brief have been looked at.
• Nutritional analysis results have been used and relate to the consumer group needs.

Areas for Improvement
• Some reference could have been made to the value of the research which was done and how existing products were used.
• A short comment relating the final result to the product specification would be useful.
• A statement saying how this information would be used in a manufacturing context could be added.

? CHECK YOURSELF QUESTIONS

Q1 Look back at the research which you carried out at the beginning and at various other stages in your project. Have you evaluated all the information you collected?

Q2 How did the information help you produce design criteria?

Q3 After producing your design ideas did you really check that the idea or ideas which you decided to develop actually matched the design criteria and the design brief?

Q4 When you began to carry out the development of your chosen product or products did you make it clear how you were using the results of any tests or investigations? Could this be clearly seen both in your design folder and in the making activities which followed?

Q5 Did you have clear objectives for your sensory evaluation? Were the results meaningful and were you able to carry out some modification to your product as a result?

Q6 Did you make checks as you went along and implement modifications or improvements as a result?

Q7 Have you included a final evaluation at the end of your project?

COMMENTS

Q1 Session 1, on research, tells you to collect, sort, sift and present information. Look at the final research which you presented and also at the examples of other students' work shown in Session 1. Make sure that you have collected and presented the main points from your research which you then used in your design criteria and ideas.

Q2 You can produce a whole range of design ideas. Each one can be quite different. However, you must make sure that the design ideas fit the brief and the design criteria which you have drawn up. An idea which you like but which does not fit cannot be given credit.

Q3 Each time you carry out testing or investigations you will collect results. These results are very important because they will have an effect on the next activity you do. However, testing is not an activity which you should include unless there is a real reason for doing it. You must make sure that any tests or investigations are written up in your folder work and that any conclusions which lead to changing ingredients, methods or quantities are incorporated in the making activities which follow.

Q4 Most students really like doing sensory evaluation but often they are not quite sure why it is being done. In other words, they have not given enough thought to the objectives and purpose of the sensory evaluation.

Q5 Often the people used as tasters are not given sufficient guidance. When this happens results can be of little use in changing or improving a product. Inappropriate words may be used, e.g. 'good', 'nice', 'like', 'dislike'. Make sure you receive information which enables you to modify your product.

Q6 Always write up your evaluations as you go along so that they appear in the appropriate section of the folder. This is the only way to make it clear how you are using evaluation to guide the next stage in the process.

Q7 A final evaluation is very important at the end of the project. This uses all the observations you have made throughout the project but also comments on how the final product meets the original brief, where ideas have been developed, how problems have been overcome, and on the success of the end result.

Systems and control

🍽 What are systems and control?

■ A **food-making system** can be broken down into the several different parts which make up a food production method and result in a finished food product. The system ensures that the final product:
- fulfils the purpose for which it was intended
- is of good quality
- is safe to eat
- is cost effective to make
- is suitable for manufacture in large quantities
- has made the most efficient use of people and equipment.

■ **Control** is the range of checks and procedures which are built into the system to ensure that it works as it should.

■ All systems are based on the same model: **input – process – output**.

■ **Input** is everything that goes into the food system: ingredients, effort, time, money.

■ **Process** is what happens to everything that goes into the system: weighing, mixing, shaping, forming, cooking, cooling, finishing, checking.

■ **Output** is the end product and any by-products: the food product, its packaging and labelling, plus any leftover waste materials or recyclable materials.

■ Systems and control are very important in food production because they:

- ensure a good quality product is made. This includes:
  - nutritional content
  - sensory characteristics
  - weight and size
  - meeting a specific need
  - value for money

- ensure a food product is safe to eat

- enable large quantities of products to be made to a consistent standard

- maintain cost effectiveness

- meet legislation requirements

- reduce waste

- increase the speed at which products are made

- reduce the time spent on repetitive, tedious tasks

- control complex processes

- reduce the risk of human error.

THE IMPORTANCE OF FEEDBACK

■ **Feedback** means keeping a check on what is happening. It provides information or evidence which is collected as the system operates. Feedback is given at various points in the system. It is very important because it tells you if you need to make changes in order for the system to work better.

- Weighing scales provide feedback about exact quantities.

- Weighing and measuring parts of a food product as it is made ensure consistency in such things as thickness of dough, weight of bread loaves, viscosity of sauce.

- Checks on oven temperatures ensure accurate cooking temperatures and times.

- Visual checks ensure the appropriate colour and quality of products at both the input and the process stages.

- Sensory testing gives feedback about flavour and texture.

- Computer systems provide feedback through the use of sensors such as a metal detector or a temperature gauge.

HAZARD ANALYSIS AND CRITICAL CONTROL POINTS (HACCP)

■ **HACCP** is a system of risk assessment and safety checks (see Revision Session 10, page 143).

■ If your final product were going to be manufactured commercially, the manufacturer would have to design an HACCP procedure for it. As part of your project you will need to design an HACCP procedure for your final product and place it in your design folder. The following points will help you:

- Produce a list of all the stages involved in the production process. This will include every step from the purchase of ingredients to point of sale of the final product. You will find that a **flow chart** is the best way of recording this.

- For each stage that you have named think about any **hazard** which could occur at that point.

- Describe how this hazard could be prevented or eliminated.

- Decide on a specific control point for each stage. For example, during the storage of raw materials cross-contamination of different components or ingredients has to be prevented. A **control point** would be to separate raw and cooked components.

- Show how each control point will be **monitored**. For example, regular monitoring would be used to check that storage areas are clean and storage temperatures are constant. The written HACCP would state that the refrigerator temperature would be monitored by checking every 60 minutes.

- Indicate where and why records of the monitoring procedures will be kept.

Figure 7.1 *Information must be fed back to make sure all parts of the production system are working properly*

PRODUCTION FLOWCHART
WITH HACCP

---INPUT---

STAGE 1 - BEFORE COOKING

INGREDIENTS STORED IN *FREEZER AT -18°C:*
minced lamb

INGREDIENTS STORED IN *REFRIGERATOR AT 5°C:*
semi-skimmed milk
green and red peppers
celery
mushroom
carrot
aubergine
sweetcorn (once tin is open)
tomato puree (once tube is open)
lemon
low fat and strong flavour cheeses
sunflower margarine

ENSURE THAT ALL THE FOLLOWING AREAS ARE CLEAN:
Sink
work surfaces
chopping board
knives
grater
spoons
weighing scales
measuring jug
frying pan
saucepans
bowl

PERSONAL HYGIENE:
Tie hair back
Remove rings and jewellery
Wash hands
Wear an apron

PREPARE INGREDIENTS:
Wash vegetables
Weigh ingredients
Peel and finely chop onion
Chop: peppers
celery
mushroom
aubergine
Grate: carrot
lemon zest
cheeses
Mix Bisto with a little cold water

POSSIBLE HAZARD (Bacterial):
Cover and return prepared vegetables and cheeses to refrigerator until required.

---PROCESSING---

STAGE 2 - LAMB BOLOGNESE SAUCE

Heat lamb gently in a frying pan until slightly brown and fat has run out.

POSSIBLE HAZARD (Burning):
Drain off and dispose of fat carefully.

Add vegetable oil. When it is hot add the onion, peppers, celery, mushroom, carrot, aubergine and sweetcorn. Cook until tender, stirring continuously.

Add chopped tomatoes to the pan and bring back to simmering point.

Add Marmite, herbs, tomato puree, lemon zest, sugar, seasoning and prepared Bisto. Stir.

POSSIBLE HAZARD (Bacterial):
Taste sauce for level of seasoning using a *clean* spoon. If necessary add more salt or pepper. Retaste with a *clean* spoon.

POSSIBLE HAZARD (Bacterial):
Cover and set aside Lamb Bolognese Sauce to cool until required for assembly of product.

STAGE 3 - PASTA

POSSIBLE HAZARD (Scalding):
Put a saucepan of fresh water on the heat to boil ready for cooking the pasta.

When water boils add pasta to the pan.

Cook pasta for 12 mins, stirring occasionally to prevent sticking to the pan.

POSSIBLE HAZARD (Bacterial, and Scalding):
Remove a piece of pasta with a *clean* fork to test it for 'al dente'. Continue cooking if necessary for another minute and test again.

POSSIBLE HAZARD (Scalding):
Drain water from pasta over a sink.

POSSIBLE HAZARD (Bacterial):
Cover and set pasta aside until required for assembly of product.

STAGE 4 - CHEESE SAUCE

Heat margarine gently until melted. Remove pan from heat and stir in flour to form a 'roux' using a *clean* spoon.

Return the 'roux' to the heat and cook gently for about 1 minute so that it does not brown.

POSSIBLE HAZARD (Bacterial):
Remove pan from the heat and gradually blend in the cold milk straight from the refrigerator. Refrigerate unused milk.

Return saucepan to the heat and bring sauce to the boil stirring continuously until it thickens to a pouring consistency. Remove it immediately to stop it thickening any more.

POSSIBLE HAZARD (Bacterial):
Blend in the cheeses including parmesan, salt, white pepper, and mustard using a *clean* spoon.

Reheat just until the cheese has melted, stirring until the sauce is smooth.

POSSIBLE HAZARD (Bacterial):
Using a *clean* spoon, taste the cheese sauce for level of seasoning required. Add more seasoning if necessary. Retaste using another *clean* spoon.

---OUTPUT---

STAGE 5 - ASSEMBLY, PACKAGING, AND FREEZING

Spread pasta evenly over base of microwaveable tray. Spread Bolognese sauce over it leaving some pasta showing around edges. Pour cheese sauce on top leaving some Bolognese sauce uncovered. Garnish with paprika.

POSSIBLE HAZARD (Bacterial):
Cover tray with microwaveable film and an outer sleeve of cardboard.

POSSIBLE HAZARD (Bacterial):
Freeze finished product quickly to a temperature of -18°C and store in a freezer at a constant temperature.

POSSIBLE HAZARD (Bacterial):
Clean all utensils and store carefully. Wash and dry all work surfaces.

Sauce-based Product

Figure 7.2 *Production flowchart*

Examiner's comments on 7.2

Good Points

- Clear steps in the production process are identified.
- Hazards are identified and recorded in colour on the chart, which makes them easy to identify. This would be useful for personnel who have the responsibility of checking during production.
- Some ways of eliminating hazards are given. For example, 'Cover and return prepared vegetables and cheese to refrigerator until required.'
- Some critical control points are given. For example, 'Freeze finished product quickly to a temperature of -18 degrees and store at constant temperature.'
- The layout of the chart is clear.
- The HACCP procedure has been put on one page in the design folder which makes it easier to read and understand.
- The student has also included information on input, process, output, which shows their understanding of systems and control in food technology.

Areas for Improvement

- Some critical control points have been left out. For example, not all temperatures and timings are given.
- Little mention is made as to how the control points are to be monitored, e.g. temperature checking, metal detection, bacterial control.
- No reference is made to any monitoring procedures and how records of checks will be made, kept and used.
- The chart could have been improved by drawing it as a flow diagram with lines, arrows and symbols, i.e. terminator, process, decision symbols.

■ Look at Figure 7.2 and read the examiner's comments on it.

USING THE COMPUTER

■ It is possible to use software to design an HACCP procedure for your product. Investigate the software available in your school. You may find that you can look at an existing HACCP procedure for a product which the software company has produced. Often you can reuse this diagram by removing existing information and substituting information about your own product. This is an effective way of designing HACCP procedures as it saves you time and provides you with a check at each stage of the product development.

🍽 Input, process, output

■ You could produce a table, diagram or chart to show the specific areas of input, process and output within the production system for your product prototype. Look at Figure 7.3 on page 44 and read the examiner's comments on it.

Figure 7.3 *Input, process and output process sheet*

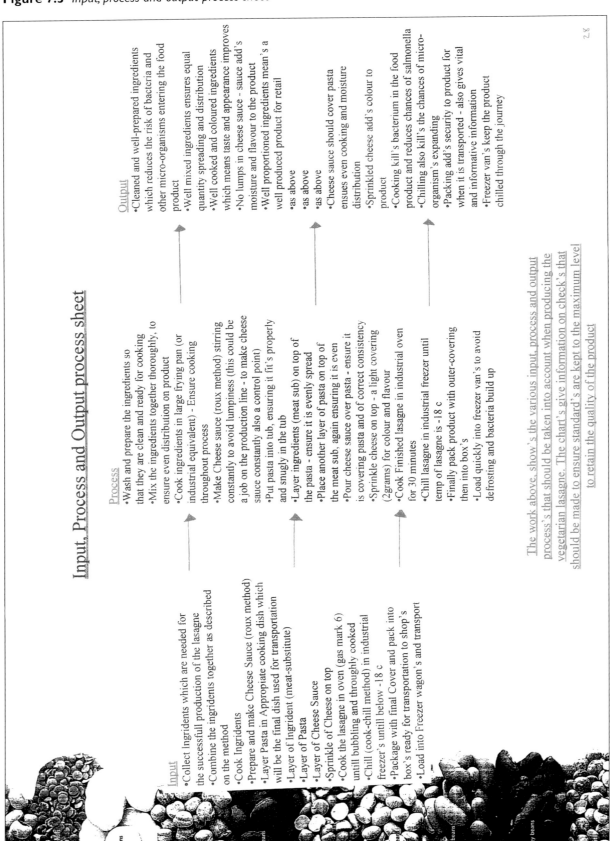

Input, Process and Output process sheet

Input
- Collect Ingredients which are needed for the successfull production of the lasagne
- Combine the ingridents together as described on the method
- Cook Ingridents
- Prepare and make Cheese Sauce (roux method)
- Layer Pasta in Appropiate cooking dish which will be the final dish used for transportation
- Layer of Ingredient (meat-substitute)
- Layer of Pasta
- Layer of Cheese Sauce
- Sprinkle of Cheese on top
- Cook the lasagne in oven (gas mark 6) untill bubbling and throughly cooked
- Chill (cook-chill method) in industrial freezer's untill below -18 c
- Package with final Cover and pack into box's ready for transportation to shop's
- Load into Freezer wagon's and transport

Process
- Wash and prepare the ingredients so that they are clean and ready for cooking
- Mix the ingredients together thoroughly, to ensure even distribution on product
- Cook ingredients in large frying pan (or industrial equivalent) - Ensure cooking throughout process
- Make Cheese sauce (roux method) stirring constantly to avoid lumpiness (this could be a job on the production line - to make cheese sauce constantly also a control point)
- Put pasta into tub, ensuring it fit's properly and snugly in the tub
- Layer ingredients (meat sub) on top of the pasta - ensure it is evenly spread
- Place another layer of pasta on top of the meat sub, again ensuring it is even
- Pour cheese sauce over pasta - ensure it is covering pasta and of correct consistency
- Sprinkle cheese on top - a light covering (2grams) for colour and flavour
- Cook Finished lasagne in industrial oven for 30 minutes
- Chill lasagne in industrial freezer until temp of lasagne is -18 c
- Finally pack product with outer-covering then into box's
- Load quickly into freezer van's to avoid defrosting and bacteria build up

Output
- Cleaned and well-prepared ingredients which reduces the risk of bacteria and other micro-organisms entering the food product
- Well mixed ingredients ensures equal quantity spreading and distribution
- Well cooked and coloured ingredients which means taste and appearance improves
- No lumps in cheese sauce - sauce add's moisture and flavour to the product
- Well proportioned ingredients mean's a well produced product for retail
- as above
- as above
- as above
- Cheese sauce should cover pasta ensues even cooking and moisture distribution
- Sprinkled cheese add's colour to product
- Cooking kill's bacterium in the food product and reduces chances of salmonella
- Chilling also kill's the chances of micro-organism's expanding
- Packing add's security to product for when it is transported - also gives vital and informative information
- Freezer van's keep the product chilled through the journey

The work above, show's the various input, process and output process's that should be taken into account when producing the vegetarian lasagne. The chart's give information on check's that should be made to ensure standard's are kept to the maximum level to retain the quality of the product

Good Points

- A good range of different inputs has been identified by the student and related to all stages in the production process.
- The student has not just considered ingredients.
- The inputs can be tracked through the process stage to the output stage.
- Some reference is made to checks, e.g. control checks for refrigerator temperature, cooking times, etc.

Areas for Improvement

- No specific feedback points are identified.
- No feedback is provided at each stage.
- Action resulting from feedback is therefore not given.

Quality systems

- One of the main aims in the production of a food product is to provide quality. Both **quality control** and **quality assurance** systems are used in industry to ensure a good quality end product.

QUALITY CONTROL

- Quality control is the method used to check and test a product as it is made.

- When your product prototype goes into production, you need to ensure that the following checks are made:
  - quality of ingredients
  - working to designated **tolerances**
  - sizes/thickness/quantities
  - shape
  - texture
  - colour
  - uniformity.

- In your design folder you can show how quality control is achieved by:
  - identifying the stages in the production of your food prototype
  - using the list given above to prompt ideas for checks
  - thinking about how you can carry out checks for quality at each stage
  - describing the checks that you will make
  - showing how you will correct problems after checks have been made.

- A simple chart, table or diagram is the best way of presenting this information. Look at Figure 7.4 on page 47 and read the examiner's comments on it. It shows a simple production sequence for coleslaw.

Manufacturing systems

- A food manufacturer needs to decide which method of production will be most suitable for a food prototype. In your design folder you can discuss the advantages and disadvantages of different methods of production for your particular prototype. You need to know about the different production methods.

- Consider the following production systems:
  - one-off production
  - batch production
  - mass production
  - continuous flow production.

- You can illustrate the production sequence by diagrams, sketches or computer graphics with labels or simple comments (see Figure 7.4).

COMPUTER-AIDED MANUFACTURING SYSTEMS (CAM)

- On your production diagram show where some or all of the following CAM systems would be used:
  - use of sensors to detect weight changes – used for the measurement of ingredients. (The sensors send information back to a central computer which responds and makes changes.)
  - use of flow rate devices for adding liquids or fillings to products
  - use of timing devices for accurate cooking and cooling processes
  - use of temperature sensors for achieving and maintaining constant temperatures for cooking, cooling and storage
  - use of metal detectors (often magnets) to identify the presence of metallic foreign bodies
  - use of sensors to control thickness of dough
  - use of sensors to detect colour changes as a product is cooked.

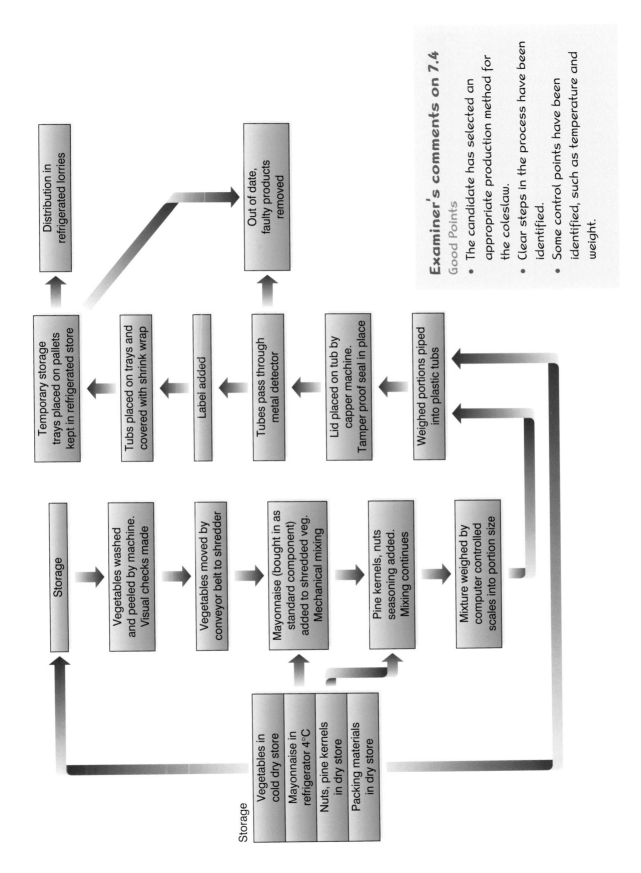

Figure 7.4 *A simple production sequence*

The flow diagram shows the following boxes and connections:

Distribution in refrigerated lorries

Out of date, faulty products removed

Temporary storage trays placed on pallets kept in refrigerated store → Tubs placed on trays and covered with shrink wrap → Label added → Tubes pass through metal detector → Lid placed on tub by capper machine. Tamper proof seal in place → Weighed portions piped into plastic tubs

Storage → Vegetables washed and peeled by machine. Visual checks made → Vegetables moved by conveyor belt to shredder → Mayonnaise (bought in as standard component) added to shredded veg. Mechanical mixing → Pine kernels, nuts seasoning added. Mixing continues → Mixture weighed by computer controlled scales into portion size

Storage
- Vegetables in cold dry store
- Mayonnaise in refrigerator 4°C
- Nuts, pine kernels in dry store
- Packing materials in dry store

Examiner's comments on 7.4

Good Points

- The candidate has selected an appropriate production method for the coleslaw.
- Clear steps in the process have been identified.
- Some control points have been identified, such as temperature and weight.

CHECK YOURSELF QUESTIONS

Q1 Have you decided which method of production would best suit your product prototype?

Q2 Can you separate the different parts of the production process for your product into input, process, output?

Q3 At which points will you get feedback? Make sure you highlight these points.

Q4 Have you included an HACCP procedure for your product prototype? Does it include all the hazards and controls? Have you included specific information on it, e.g. critical temperatures and times?

Q5 How have you planned to make a quality product? If it were to be mass produced, how would you ensure it could be made to a high standard?

Q6 Could parts of the production process be controlled by computers?

COMMENTS

Q1 Read the information in Revision Session 7 on manufacturing processes. What are the advantages and disadvantages of each method? Look at examples of food products which are made by each method. Consider the similarities of your product prototype with these products. Select an appropriate method.

Q2 Working in rough, divide a page into three boxes. Using the headings INPUT, PROCESS, OUTPUT, fit the information about the materials and methods which you are using for making your product into these boxes. Produce a finished, clear diagram which you can include in your design folder.

Q3 Remember that feedback is information which you obtain as a system is working. When you are making your food product you will need to ensure that you have identified the stages where information about your product is provided. Look at your systems diagram and add the points where feedback is essential. This might be related to visual appearance, certain tolerances, sensory characteristics, time, temperature, etc.

Q4 Look back at all the information given on HACCP on page 41. Think about all the different stages in the manufacture of your product, right from the source of ingredients to the point of sale. Does your flow diagram include all these stages? Are there high-risk foods in your product? Have you considered the critical control of these? If you cannot remember specific critical temperatures, do some further research to ensure you include accurate information.

Q5 As you made the prototype you will have worked carefully and accurately to make something which looks and tastes good. Sometimes it is easy to produce a very good quality product as a 'one off' but not as easy if you are making hundreds or thousands of the same product. You must think about how identical-quality products can be made. Every production run must produce identical products. When the consumer buys the products they expect them to look and taste the same each time and the manufacturer's continued sales depend on this.

Q6 Look at the flow diagram which you have produced and at the examples of methods of computer-aided manufacture which were given earlier. Which of these could be used in your product manufacture and where in the process would they be used? For example, metal detection might occur at the storage stage, after mixing, and again when the product has been packaged.

Remember always to include the appropriate symbols on your flow diagram.

■ Industrial practice ■

⦿ Why is industrial practice important?

■ You must make sure that you show evidence of industrial practice in your food technology project. Most of the previous units have included examples of industrial practices which are actually carried out in the food industry. If you have taken notice of them and applied similar practices to your own work then you have already begun to build up your evidence.

⦿ Evaluating existing products

■ This is a common method which is often used in industry by food retailers who are looking for ideas for new products. The food manufacturers buy competitors' products and carry out 'in-house' testing on them.

■ The tests used include **sensory evaluation** and **identification of ingredients**. Judgements are then made about portion size, value for money, etc. When you are doing your own research you will have the opportunity to include this type of industrial practice. Look at Session 1 (page 1), for ideas and methods.

GATHERING INFORMATION

■ Food retailers need to collect a range of information both about food products which already exist and also about ideas for new products. They use many different sources to provide this information, such as **market research**, **taste-testing** in supermarkets and **questionnaires**. Look at Session 1 and decide if a questionnaire would be an appropriate method for you to use.

SENSORY EVALUATION

■ This is used at all stages in food product development. Examining existing products, producing design ideas and developing a **prototype** are all good opportunities to include sensory evaluation.

■ Look at Revision Session 16, on Sensory Analysis (pages 198–202) and decide which methods would be appropriate for you to include in your work. Include a range of different methods if possible.

Figure 8.1 *Taste-testing is often done in supermarkets*

⦿ Using standard components

■ In the food industry manufacturers buy in standard components from other food manufacturers. (Look at Revision Session 5, pages 112 and 113, to check that you understand what a component is.) When you are developing your own prototype you will actually make each part of your product yourself. However, if the prototype is to be manufactured in quantity, the commercial food manufacturer will find it more cost effective to buy in some ready-made parts of the product, e.g. bases for pizzas, stuffing for meat, icing for cakes, pastry cases for savoury flans, etc. You need to identify which parts of your final food product could be bought in ready made. This is a very relevant way to mirror industrial practice.

- The following example shows how you can illustrate the use of standard components in your design folder:

The final result, after carrying out all the development work, is to be a Caribbean Sponge Surprise. The development has shown that this dessert consists of a biscuit base with a layer of exotic fruits on the top covered by a topping of sponge. I have made all the different parts of the product in order to make decisions about size, weight, sensory characteristics, suitable storage methods, effects of storage, packaging and labelling information. However if this prototype were to be manufactured I would suggest that the biscuit base and the exotic fruit filling are bought in as standard components. This would mean that less capital is required for the purchase of equipment and machinery to produce these components of the dessert. The manufacturer would then only need to make the sponge topping and the packaging. A cake manufacturer who already has the plant and machinery for making sponge cakes could manufacture the dessert.

🍽 Developing a prototype

- Within a commercial company in the food industry, there is always a **product development team**. One member of the team is a food technologist who has the knowledge and skills to develop recipes for a wide range of products and who will develop different methods for making these products.

- The **food technologist** will also carry out testing on recipes at the development stage and is later responsible for making the product prototype and supplying the manufacturer with information for the manufacturing specification.

- When you are working on a food technology product, you are working in exactly the same way as a professional food technologist and you will also be responsible for making a **product prototype**. This is another good example of industrial practice but you need to make it clear in your design folder that you know prototype development is an accepted industrial practice. This could be done by writing a paragraph about this topic at the end of the development section. A short piece of text like the one printed on the next page will do the job.

Figure 8.2 *A food technologist will carry out taste-testing on products*

Throughout my development work I have tried to think about all the characteristics that my final product would need to have. I have used different ingredients, quantities and methods to check that the combination of these ingredients will still produce an acceptable product. I have developed and tested products of different shapes, sizes and weights and have carried out nutritional analysis to check that the product is meeting the nutritional profile given in the product specification. I now have exact information about the amounts and types of ingredients which need to be used. The tests which I have carried out have also given me information about suitable storage methods and storage times. I am now in a position to pass my information to the manufacturer for production.

¡●¡ Testing products

- Within any industry making any product, from motor cars to ice cream, testing is a critical part of the process in order to ensure the end product is safe to use, able to do the job for which it was made, is of good quality, works efficiently and meets legislative requirements.

- All the time a food product is being developed, various forms of testing are carried out. Look back at the sessions on Research (page 1), Development (page 25) and Systems and Control (page 40). Identify where you have carried out any kind of testing.

- Will it be clear to someone reading your work that you have deliberately included these aspects of testing to ensure that your product prototype is safe to eat, is of good quality, looks good, tastes good, is stored in an appropriate way, is packaged correctly, and meets food safety legislation?

¡●¡ Carrying out trials

- When a new product is first developed, often relatively small quantities of it are made. These are usually sold in carefully chosen areas of the country as 'trials'. The results from sales, sensory testing carried out in supermarkets, and directly linked market research are all forms of trials for new products.

- You might like to consider how, where and why trials for your product prototype would take place and comment on this in your design folder. You would also need to say what you would expect to happen as a result of the information produced by the trials.

¡●¡ Using standard equipment

- Equipment is a very important tool in product development. As far as food technology is concerned you need to demonstrate the correct use of appropriate equipment in your work, but in terms of industrial practice the type, size and use of equipment is of very great significance. For this reason, you should show the use of equipment in your practical work but not in a normal domestic situation, rather more in line with its use in industry. You should look for opportunities to use equipment when you are

Figure 8.3 *Pastry can be made by hand or by using an electrically operated mixer*

making a food product and choose to use a piece of equipment to overcome problems of human error, to ensure consistency and to save time and labour costs. For example, if pastry were to be rubbed in by hand the following problems could occur:

- Different people have different techniques.

- Judgements about when the mixture has achieved the right consistency vary from person to person.

- Even if one person were to do all the rubbing in, the temperature of their hands might vary and the rubbing in process would then vary in length.

- The process would take a long time.

■ If a piece of equipment were used to do the job:

- The mechanical action is the same each time.

- The process can be timed exactly.

- The equipment can be kept at the same temperature.

- The whole process can be controlled to ensure the pastry crumbs are consistently the same size.

- The process can be done quickly.

¡⊙¡ Packaging

■ The packaging of a food product is one of the things which make a bought product most obviously different from one made at home. The packaging of a food product is an industrial practice and has to meet all **food safety requirements**.

Examiner's comments on 8.4

Good Points

- The student has included information which shows he or she understands about the function of packaging materials.
- These general functions are applied to their own product.
- The student also demonstrates that he or she understand about microwave cooking and the need for certain materials to be avoided.
- A very good point is made about cost. The choice of packaging materials takes account of the fact that the student is making a low-cost product.
- Some reference to food safety is made.
- The shape of the container is linked to the student's chosen method for reheating and specific temperatures are given.

- Overall, the explanation and descriptions about packaging are very clear. They are made very specific to the product which the student has developed and details from the design brief have been taken into consideration.

Areas for Improvement

- A labelled sketch of the packaging used, particularly the dish, would have reduced the amount of writing.
- The illustration used is not appropriate to the product in question and it serves no purpose. In fact, it is misleading and confusing on first glance.

Figure 8.4 *Looking at packaging*

Packaging

Food is packaged for a variety of reasons, one of the most important is protection. Packaging protects the product from dirt and damage. Food needs to be protected from contamination by bacteria. Bacteria carried by flies or present on dirty knives or work surfaces (to name but a few examples) are prevented from getting on to the food. Packaging also prevents contamination from people by such things as touching, sneezing and coughing.

The appropriate packaging helps to increase the time food may be kept in good condition, and allows time for its distribution. Some plastics hold in water vapour, and these are particularly valuable in frozen food cabinets. At cold temperatures food can lose water very quickly, unless this is prevented by the use of waterproof packaging the food can become very dry. This may happen with my dish. Poorly wrapped frozen foods may develop 'freezer burn' and could become very unappetising.

Food can also be packaged for convenience. I am designing a dish for one so my food will be packaged accordingly.

I shall also be able to convey a lot of useful information on the packaging, as shown in my information on labelling.

I think that packaging will help promote my product. I will be able to make the packaging distinct and easily remembered therefore I may end up selling more of my product.

I am packaging my dish in a low density polythene tray. This means that it will be able to be reheated in a microwave. If I put my product in an aluminium tray the microwaves would be reflected and the magnetron would be damaged. This material can also be moulded into my desired shape. Low density polythene is cheap which is important as my design brief states that the dish must be low cost. Another advantage of the ability to mould the plastic is that I shall be able to make the dish shallow enough to be microwaved. If the dish is more than 5cm in depth the microwaves will not be able to penetrate the food deeply enough. This may mean that the food is not reheated evenly and so bacteria may not be killed (food needs to reach an internal temperature of 83°C to ensure that it is safe).

I am going to cover my product with a seal of low density polythene as it can be made into a thin film. It is good too because the heat seal will ensure bacteria aren't allowed into the food. It can also be easily pierced to allow steam to escape during reheating.

I am going to put my product into a cardboard (cellulose) sleeve. I shall coat this with wax in order to prevent the card becoming soggy in the freezer cabinets. On the cardboard I can print vital information and promote the product.

■ The main GCSE Food Technology syllabuses do not ask you to make packaging for your food product. However, you will need to consider the type of packaging which would be suitable for the product you have designed and give reasons for your choice. You need to look at Revision Session 15, on packaging materials (pages 189–193).

■ Look at Figure 8.4 above and read the examiner's coments on it.

LABELLING REQUIREMENTS

■ As a professional food technologist you would need to supply certain information to the packaging department about the food product which you have designed and made as a prototype.

■ Look at Revision Session 14 on Labelling (page 180). Use the information from your final recipe and from the final nutritional analysis which you carried out to produce a list of ingredients and the nutritional information to be printed on the packaging. Some computer software actually allows you to produce nutritional information in the form of a label which looks very similar to the information you see on the packaging of a commercially produced food product.

■ You will also need to produce cooking/reheating and storage instructions and any special claims for the product.

■ This information needs to be a part of your design folder work. Remember that this should be done towards the end of your project when you have made the final product and when you are giving information about its manufacture in large quantities.

■ You can supply the information as narrative or headed paragraphs or actually put it onto a packaging net. This does not need to be to scale. It can be a shape which you think seems appropriate.

Examiner's comments on 8.5

Good Points

• The student demonstrates knowledge and understanding about labelling.
• Some reference is made to information that is required by law and to consumer information.
• The student has taken general information and converted it into information for his/her own food product label.
• Previous information from research and results from tests and development work are incorporated into the label, e.g. a list of ingredients from the recipe used, storage temperatures from research on freezing, and the weight of the product also links with the specification and preparation instructions.
• Some nutritional information is given.
• Special claims are referred to.

Areas for Improvement

• Insufficient attention is given to the nutritional information. Only values per portion are given and not per 100 grams. No protein value is given.
• There is no indication of where on the package the labelling information would be found. A rough sketch showing the positioning of this information would have been useful.
• This student used a software package for the production of the nutritional information. This could have been imported onto a packaging net and would have demonstrated a good use of ICT.
• The student has not made it clear which information is required by law and which is consumer information.

The name and address of the manufacturer needs to be included because they are responsible for the original condition of the food and may need to be contacted if something goes wrong.. I would also put my name and address on it. The place of origin needs to be included in case the customer is likely to be misled, for example, "Cheddar cheese" from New Zealand.

The instructions for use are necessary on the product so that the customers can prepare the food to the best of their ability. This may include how it has to be defrosted and then reheated. It could also include serving suggestions, however these are not vital. My instructions would be as follows:

Take out of cardboard packaging, prick the plastic seal with a fork and put the dish in the microwave for 1½ mins on high power. It can then be served or put under the grill for a couple of minutes to crisp the topping. Alternatively the dish can be heated in the oven for 15 mins at a temperature of 180°C. I would have to include which method I would recommend. The dish has to reach an internal temperature of 83°C so that all bacteria are killed.

Other details that may be useful to the consumer are nutrition labelling, number of servings and serving suggestions. I could also put on a bar code for retailers. This is not only convenient for cashiers but can help the retailer keep stocks high and also see which brands sell the most and so forth.

The nutritional info would appear on the side of my dish →

NUTRITION INFORMATION		Values per portion
Energy	Kcal	355
Fat	g	13
Carbohydrate	g	30
Fibre (NSP)	g	3
Calcium	mg	414
Iron	mg	1
Vitamin C	mg	9

Food labelling is important for many reasons. Many things have to be included by law, for example ingredients and quantity. The labels can also be used to promote and advertise the product. Useful information such as barcodes can also be added. The following is a plan for what I would include on a label for my product.

The name of the product is very important. The brand name means that the product can easily be recognised and chosen by the customer. The name must also include a description of the product, however it mustn't be misleading. If, for example, you have a "strawberry yoghurt", if it is only strawberry flavoured this must be stated. It can only be called "strawberry" or "strawberry flavoured" if the flavour derives from real strawberries. This is very important because if the customer is misled then legal action may be taken against the company.

I would call my dish, "Crisp & Crunchy Potato Casserole". I would describe it as a shredded potato and carrot casserole with a creamy white sauce and crunchy cheese topping. I do not feel that this would mislead the customer in any way.

The net quantity of the food must be included so that the customer can see exactly how much they are paying for. The net weight for my product would be 265g.

The list of ingredients must be included so that the customer can see if they are allergic to any of them or if they don't want to eat any of them. They must appear on the label in descending order of weight and additives must be included on the ingredients list. The following list would be written on my label: Potatoes, semi-skimmed milk, natural yoghurt, carrots, cheddar cheese, leek, wheat flour, onion, margarine, salt and pepper.

Most foods now have to carry a date mark. This is necessary so that retailers can keep their stocks up to date and helps consumers to use food while it is still at its best. This prevents the risk of things like food poisoning. I have made a freezer product so the product will have to be labelled accordingly. In some refrigerators freezer foods may be stored for up to 3 months if three black stars are present. The dish will, however, be best if kept in a freezer where it will be able to last for 3 months, if not longer, at a temperature of -18°C. The British Standard symbol of a white star in front of a 3 star refrigerator symbol denotes this:

As I previously stated, my food is to be stored in a freezer so this information will have to be included on the label. All foods in freezers should be kept at -8°C. They need to be kept at this temperature so that dangerous bacteria can not breed... temperatures... our warmer bacteria find it easier to survive, bacteria can be responsible for making us ill. Also at this low temperature food will remain in a similar state as when it first went into the freezer, as soon as the temperature starts to rise deterioration may start to occur.

Figure 8.5 *What labelling does*

¡●¡ Use of additives

- A wide range of **food additives** are used in the manufacture of food products. See Revision Session 13 on Additives (page 173). Although it is unlikely that your product prototype will contain additives, there may be good reasons for the use of these in products which have to be kept stored for some time without deteriorating. This is known as the shelf life of a product.

- Look at the functions of additives on pages 175–178. Consider the value of using additives in your product if it were to go into commercial production. Would additives give your product better quality, appearance and taste, and would they prolong its shelf life?

- Produce a list of additives which you think might be used in the manufacture of your product and give a reason for using each one. Include this information in the section on manufacturing in your design folder.

? CHECK YOURSELF QUESTIONS

Q1 Make a list of all possible industrial practices outlined in this chapter. Which ones have you already included in your work? Can you use any others?

Q2 Have you provided information on the type of packaging needed for your product?

Q3 Check that you understand about using standard components. Look at Revision Session 15 if you need to.

Q4 Have you produced the information for the nutritional label, the list of ingredients used and the cooking, re-heating and storage information?

COMMENTS

Q1 Read through your folder and write down every example that you think is used in industry. If you have a fairly good list of examples, you are probably providing sufficient evidence.

Q2 Look at the design brief. Did it give information about the storage/cooking method for your product, e.g. cook-chill, microwavable? If so, then this will guide you about the type of packaging required. If there is no direct information in the design brief, has your research identified a specific storage method for the product? Will the packaging need to be moisture-proof or crush-proof, e.g. if the product is for a vending machine then being crush-proof is essential. Think about how the product is to be transported, stored, both in the shop and at home, how a long shelf life can be achieved and how the product is to be cooked and eaten.

Q3 Look at the final product you have made. Can you divide it into separate, distinct parts? Even if you have made all these parts yourself, would or could the manufacturer make them all or might they buy some in already made?

Q4 You need to have carried out some nutritional analysis. This needs to be printed in a format which can be understood by the consumer. Use software which produces a label similar to the ones found on actual packaging. Consider nutritional requirements for the whole product, for a serving, or for 100 grams. A list of ingredients in descending order of quantity needs to be given. This can be done by referring to your final recipe. Provide storage and cooking instructions.

SESSION 9 — Using ICT

❦ Why is ICT important?

- All the food technology projects you work on need to show evidence of your use of ICT (Information Communication Technology). You need to think about how you will use ICT and how you can include different aspects of it in your work. There should be a genuine reason for using ICT, not just because it makes your work look better, although producing a well-presented, high quality design folder is also very important. However, you must not spend more time on using ICT for presentation purposes than you spend on your actual designing and making work.

❦ Evidence in your project work

- The following list gives some ideas of what sort of thing you can use ICT for, although it may not be possible or even practical to include them all.

  - obtaining, handling and presenting information

  - exploring ideas which other people have already produced

  - collecting, collating and presenting data

  - drawing and designing

  - modelling ideas

  - producing high quality results

  - simulating a manufacturing process or industrial practice.

USING WORD PROCESSING/DESK TOP PUBLISHING
- Word processing and desk top publishing can be used to produce neat and well-presented:
  - blocks of written text
  - lists
  - bullet points
  - labels.

- Look at the piece of word-processed coursework in Figure 9.1 on page 58 and then read the examiner's comments on it below.

Examiner's comments on 9.1
Good Points
- The student has summarised all her research information and displayed it on one side of a sheet of A3 paper.
- The use of lists and bullet points and the arrangement of the text, in terms of both size and the style of lettering chosen, enhance the work and make it easy to read.
- The reader's attention is instantly drawn to the most important aspects of the work.

RESEARCH ANALYSIS

Company Research

– Recipes

Many sauces are made with vinegar that helps to form an emulsion with egg. A skin sometimes forms on the sauce once it is left to stand. This can be avoided by lightly dabbing some butter or margarine on the surface, or covering with greaseproof paper. Lots of herbs and spices such as parsley, basil, chives, stem ginger, mint, garlic and tarragon are used in the sauces to add flavour, along with seasoning. All the recipes mix, colour and texture in an effort to appeal to the consumer.

– Development

A flowchart is usually drawn by the supplier showing precisely what happens to the ingredients. The flow process is broken down into stages. A Critical Control Point is the step in the making process where hazards must be controlled. The HACCP system aids safe food production. Freezing should be done quickly, as slow freezing results in large uneven ice crystals which break through the cells on thawing and affect the flavour of the food. Modifications must be made to recipes to ensure that the end product is acceptable.

Research What is already on the market?

There are many products already on the market that are frozen and sauce-based, although very few of these are pasta dishes. The average price of a frozen sauce-based product is 66p per 100g.

Disassembly Research

The product I disassembled: "Dolmio - Tagliatelle Carbonara" had been made to a very high standard and scored an average of 7.4 out of a possible 10 marks. The people I asked to taste the product found its appearance, consistency, taste and temperature satisfactory. The only areas where the product did not receive full marks were, aroma, suitability of ingredients, price and sauces. The product I disassembled was aimed at working people who would not have sufficient time to prepare the product themselves: it was microwaveable and easy to re-heat quickly.

Packaging Research

A package must contain certain labels by law:

List of ingredients
Lot/Batch number
Name of product
Storage instructions
Weight in grams
Price
Instructions for use
Nutritional information,
Use by date or best before date,
Name and address of manufacturer,
Particulars of the place of origin if the name might be misleading
Statement that food has been irradiated or contains irradiated ingredients (if applicable)

Other additional labels may be added:
Serving suggestions,
Customer guarantee

The most common material used for microwaveable and freezable products is a plastic inner tray covered by a thin plastic film, which is pierceable. The outer package displaying the labels is made of cardboard: a cardboard sleeve or a box.

Pasta Research

Costs of types of pasta:

Tagliatelle-26.4p per 100g
Lasagne-24.8p per 100g
Fusilli-13p per 100g
Macaroni-12.8p per 100g
Spaghetti-11p per 100g

Farfelle-10.4p per 100g
Penne rigate-9.8p per 100g
Conchiglie-9.8p per 100g
Penne-5p per 100g

Tagliatelle, although the most expensive at 26.4p per 100g, is the favourite according to my consumer questionnaire. Spaghetti was the second type of pasta preferred by the consumers and has a fairly low price of 11p per 100g. Lasagne the third favourite is almost as expensive as Tagliatelle at 24.8p per 100g. Penne meanwhile, although not a consumer favourite, is only 5p per 100g. The other types of pasta are neither cheap nor consumer favourites and, as such, should no longer be considered for my product. All the types of pasta stated above are ideal for a sauce-based product.

Sauces Research

Sauces should be carefully flavoured and tasted before serving. A sauce can be thickened by starch, egg protein, emulsification or puréeing. A sauce must be stirred continuously while it is cooking to prevent it sticking to the bottom of the pan or becoming lumpy. A roux sauce would be most suitable for a cheese sauce. Cornflour would be most suitable for thickening a tomato or bolognese sauce. A pouring sauce at boiling point should just glaze the back of a wooden spoon, and should flow freely when poured. A coating sauce, at boiling point, should coat the back of a wooden spoon, and should be used as soon as it is ready to ensure even coating over the food.

Consumer Research

Pasta -Tagliatelle was the preferred type of pasta, followed by Spaghetti and Lasagne.
Savoury sauces - Cheese sauce was the favourite followed by tomato and bolognese.
Desserts - Treacle sponge was the preferred dessert, followed by Crème Caramel, Peach Melba, and Lemon Double Delight.
Sweet sauces - Chocolate was the favourite type of sweet sauce, followed by Lemon and Brandy.
Prices - The maximum price people were prepared to pay for a sauce-based product for one person was £1.50.

Healthy Eating Research

Sodium - should be eaten in moderation: no more than 1½ grams per day. Adding large amounts of it to food should be avoided.
Sugar - should be eaten in moderation, and a healthy balanced diet should contain more starchy carbohydrates than sugars.
Vitamins and minerals - are very important and should be eaten as often as possible to avoid deficiencies.
Fibre - both soluble and insoluble, is important. As a nation we do not eat enough of this important substance, as we should be eating around 18g per day. Pasta is a good source of fibre and carbohydrate.
Fat - should be reduced in our diets. For an average woman the consumption of fat per day should not exceed 75g and for an average man no more than 100g.

As a result of my research I should include mostly carbohydrate and fibre in my product and ensure that there are enough vitamins and minerals. A dessert with sauce would be too unhealthy so I shall include a savoury dish with a sauce instead.

Sauce-based Product

Figure 9.1 *This work on research analysis was produced on a word processor*

CHARTS, TABLES AND GRAPHS

- Figures 9.2, 9.3 and 9.4 show how the use of ICT can make information easy to read and will often take up less space than hand-written charts and tables.

Experiment	Control cake	Variaton from control	Comment
1 Soft margarine at room temp	Packet margarine at room temp	Soft margarine at room temp	Sloppy
2 Granulated sugar	Castor sugar	Granulated sugar	Sloppy
3 No additional raising agent	1 × 2.5 ml baking powder	Omit baking powder	Lovely
4 Under-mixed	Beat ingredients together for 2 minutes by hand	Beat ingredients together for ½ minute by hand	Oily
5 Over-mixed	Beat ingredients together for 2 minutes by hand	Beat ingredients together for 10 minutes	White, not firm
6 Electric hand mixer	Standard all in one method by hand	Beat ingredients together using an electric hand mixer	Stodgy and white
7 Low baking temperature	Middle shelf: temp. 160°C	Middle shelf: temp. 140°C	Under cooked and sloppy
8 Low baking temperature	Middle shelf: temp. 160°C	Middle shelf: temp. 220°C	Over cooked

Figure 9.2 *A table used to give details of the all in one creaming method*

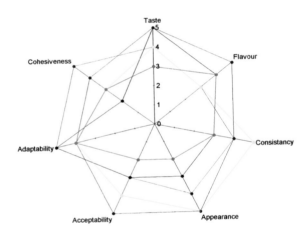

Figure 9.3 *A radar graph used to show the results of a tasting panel*

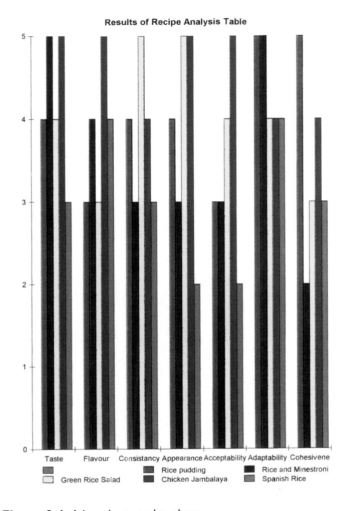

Results of Recipe Analysis Table

Figure 9.4 *A bar chart used to show the results of a recipe analysis table*

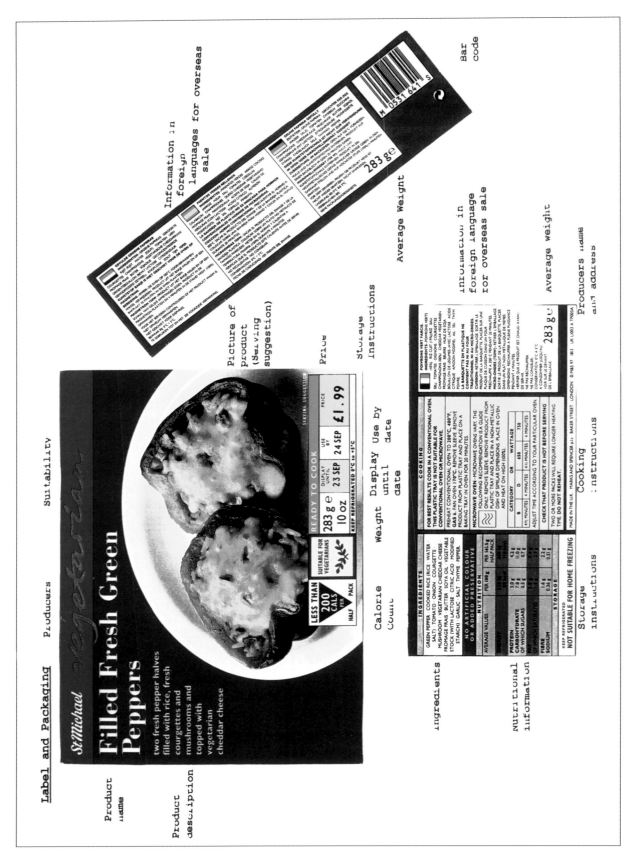

Figure 9.5 *The use of scanning*

ADDING PICTURES TO TEXT
Clipart
- You will find pictures of food ingredients or food products within some software programs, while floppy discs or CD-ROMs also often have such pictures on them. Ask your teacher if your school has access to these resources. You might also find it useful to speak to the teachers who teach information technology. If your school does not have any of these resources, they may be willing to get them for you.

Scanned images
- Look at Figure 9.5 opposite, then read these examiner's comments on it.

Examiner's comments on 9.5

Good Points
- By scanning the packaging the student has been able to add extra information to the image.
- Different parts of the product's packaging have been scanned and the student has also labelled each section to provide additional information.

Digital photographs
- Look at the photos in Figure 9.6, then read these examiner's comments.

Examiner's comments on 9.6

Good Points
- This student has used a digital camera to take photographs of the products she has made.
- The product has been shot from different angles and the results reviewed before printing. These photos show all the products grouped together and also some close-up shots.

Areas for Improvement
- Better use might have been made of the digital camera if the student had added comments about the appearance, shape, smell, taste, texture, etc. of the dishes.
- The student could have used the camera to make comments on the effects of using ingredients which can be seen in the photographs or which are hidden in the mixtures.

Figure 9.6 *The use of digital photography*

- Now look at Figure 9.7 on page 62, which shows a piece of coursework produced using a range of ICT applications, and then read the examiner's comments on it.

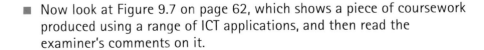

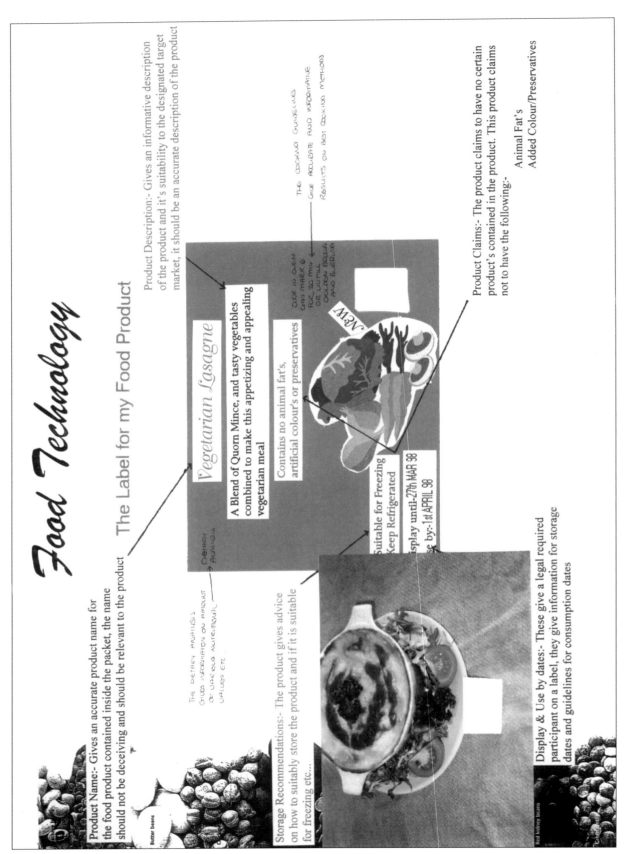

Figure 9.7 *A label for a food product produced by a range of ICT applications*

Good Points

- This student has used a mixture of Clipart, scanned images, digital photographs, word processing and desk top publishing to produce a packaging design for the final product idea. The final idea has been well developed.
- The inclusion of a label provides clear information about the design and also demonstrates that the student understands about the packaging and labelling of foods products.

USING CAD PACKAGES

- You can use CAD packages to produce **drawings** or to use **images** in an interesting way in:

  - spider diagrams

  - product profiles

  - packaging nets

  - food labels

  - design ideas.

DATABASES

- Databases allow the production, collation and presentation of questionnaires and their results. Look at Figure 9.8 on page 64 and then read these examiner's comments on it.

Good Points

- This student has worked out certain clear aims before carrying out his/her questionnaire research and has designed the questions to allow the answers to be collated easily.
- The results, which have been collated using software, give a picture of the main points which need to be taken into account in the development of a vegetarian product.
- By using ICT, the results can be presented in different forms and reduced in size to present them on one sheet. This looks clearer and more accurate than trying to collate and present results by drawing and writing by hand and, of course, it takes less time to produce a professional-looking result.

Questionnaire

My aims with this questionnaire are to find out as many details and requirements of vegetarians as possible. I will gain information about how often they buy convenience foods and the variety. Cost is an important factor as there is no point producing a product which is too expensive for the consumer. I hope to question 10 people from different age ranges to discover their needs and to choose a specific or general age target group.

1) How old are you?
15-20
20-25
25-30
30+

2) How long have you been vegetarian?
1-3yrs
3-6yrs
6-9yrs
Other

3) Why did you decide not to eat meat?
Religion
Health
Animal Welfare
Taste
Environmental
Other

4) Which alternative protein do you mostly eat?
T.V.P
Quorn
Tofu
None

5) How often do you eat ready made meals?
Every day
2-3 times per week
Sometimes
Never

6) What makes you buy a ready made product?
Convenience
Interesting recipes
Cost
Other

7) Do you buy/Would you buy any of the following?
Stuffed Veg.
Pasta dishes
Rice and pulse dishes
Pastry dishes
Dishes with TVP, quorn,tofu

8) How much are you prepared to pay for a ready made meal?
£1
£1.50
£2
More

9) Do you find specific products for this diet expensive and easy to find?
Yes
No

Results

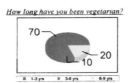

How old are you?

How long have you been vegetarian?

Why did you decide not to eat meat?

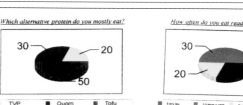

Which alternative protein do you mostly eat?

How often do you eat ready made meals?

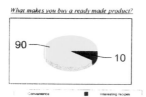

What makes you buy a ready made product?

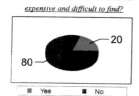

Do you find specific products for this diet expensive and difficult to find?

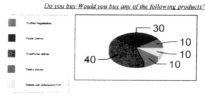

Do you buy/Would you buy any of the following products?

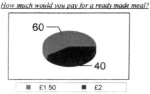

How much would you pay for a ready made meal?

Conclusions

The results from the questionnaire have allowed me to come up with the following conclusions.

Question 1
The majority of vegetarians I asked were teenagers (40%) which demonstrates the current trend of many young people following a meat free diet. The next largest age group was 20-25 which is also made up of young people. There is clearly a generational opinion between choosing to be a vegetarian. The population of those excluding meat from their diet is younger than that of those who eat it.

Question 2
The length of time which people have been vegetarian is between 1 and 3 years. This time span is very short which illustrates the idea that choosing to become a vegetarian may have been influenced by BSE scares, health warnings and food poisoning outbreaks.

Question 3
The vegetarians I asked had excluded meat from their diets for one of three reasons:- health, animal welfare or environmental issues. They considered that the treatment of animals during purposeful breeding for slaughter is inhumane and unjustifiable. medical research has shown that certain health problems could be prevented by eating less or no meat.

Question 4
The most popular alternative protein was shown to be TOFU although the others were also used.

Question 5
Although a high proportion of people buy ready made meals on a regular basis, there is still 30% which never do. This is therefore a challenge for me to design a product which will appeal to them.

Figure 9.8 *A questionnaire about vegetarianism*

USE OF THE INTERNET
■ The Internet can be used to:

- carry out research

- collect information, pictures, data

- visit web sites to research:
  - food manufacturers
  - recipe ideas
  - product ideas
  - information on specific diets/nutritional needs
  - information on ingredients.

MODELLING IDEAS
■ You can use software to carry out **nutritional analysis**. Look at Figure 9.9, then read the examiner's coments on page 66.

Figure 9.9 *Nutritional analysis of a turkey bolognese dish*

Comparison with Dietary Reference Values

Total Energy for this list = 5084 kJ 1215 kcals

% Protein	24
% Fat	32
% Carbohydrate	44

Energy: Current dietary guidelines recommend that a MAXIMUM of 35% of Energy is supplied by fat.
Comparison of your list with the DRVs for a man aged 19–50 years old

		Your Diet	EAR	% of EAR
Energy	(kJ)	5085	10600	48
	(kcals)	1215	2550	48

		Your Diet	RNI	% of RNI
Protein	(g)	72.7	55.5	131
Fibre (NSP)	(g)	7.21	(adults approx. 18 grams/day)	
Sodium (Na)	(mg)	1151	1600	72
Calcium (Ca)	(mg)	990	700	141
Iron (Fe)	(mg)	5.11	8.70	59
Vitamin A	(ug)	1027	700	147
Vitamin B1	(mg)	0.63	1.00	63
Vitamin B2	(mg)	1.06	1.30	81
Niacin	(mg)	21.0	17.0	123
Vitamin C	(mg)	147	40.0	367
Vitamin D	(ug)	6.45	No RNI data for this group	

DRV = Dietary Reference Values. EAR Estimated Average Requirement.
RNI = Reference Nutrient Intake. NSP = Non-starch polysaccharides.

Good Points

- By using nutritional analysis you can model ideas for a product before actually making it. This allows you to see if the product meets the nutritional profile which is asked for in a particular specification. For example, you can check if the protein content is sufficient, if the fat content is too high, and what the overall energy value is.
- This information is essential to a food technologist and also prevents wasting ingredients by making a product which is not nutritionally correct for the target group it is aimed at.

■ You can use **spreadsheets** for costing and scaling up quantities for production, as shown in this table.

Ingredients	1 tray	10 trays	50 trays	100 trays	500 trays	1000 trays
Cooking Chocolate	0.15 kg	1.5 kg	7.5 kg	15 kg	75 kg	150 kg
Caster Sugar	0.1 kg	1 kg	5 kg	10 kg	50 kg	100 kg
Egg	£1.00	£10.00	£50.00	£100.00	£500.00	£1,000.00
Margarine	0.05 kg	0.5 kg	2.5 kg	5 kg	25 kg	50 kg
Desiccated Coconut	0.1 kg	1 kg	5 kg	10 kg	50 kg	100 kg
Self-raising Flour	0.005 kg	0.05 kg	0.25 kg	0.5 kg	2.5 kg	5 kg
Ground Almonds	0.025 kg	0.25 kg	1.25 kg	2.5 kg	12.5 kg	25 kg
Glacé Cherries	0.075 kg	0.75 kg	3.75 kg	7.5 kg	37.5 kg	75 kg

Ingredients	1 tray	10 trays	50 trays	100 trays	500 trays	1000 trays
Cooking Chocolate	£0.74	£7.40	£37.00	£74.00	£370.00	£740.00
Caster Sugar	£0.11	£1.10	£5.50	£11.00	£55.00	£110.00
Egg	£0.08	£0.80	£4.00	£8.00	£40.00	£80.00
Margarine	£0.06	£0.60	£3.00	£6.00	£30.00	£60.00
Coconut	£0.67	£6.70	£33.50	£67.00	£335.00	£670.00
Flour	£0.02	£0.20	£1.00	£2.00	£10.00	£20.00
Ground Almonds	£0.28	£2.80	£14.00	£28.00	£140.00	£280.00
Glacé Cherries	£0.33	£3.30	£16.50	£33.00	£165.00	£330.00
Total	£2.29	£22.90	£114.50	£229.00	£1,145.00	£2,229.00

CONTROL

- Software can be used to **model process flow charts** and **HACCP procedures** which show critical control points and give feedback on the production process. Look at this example.

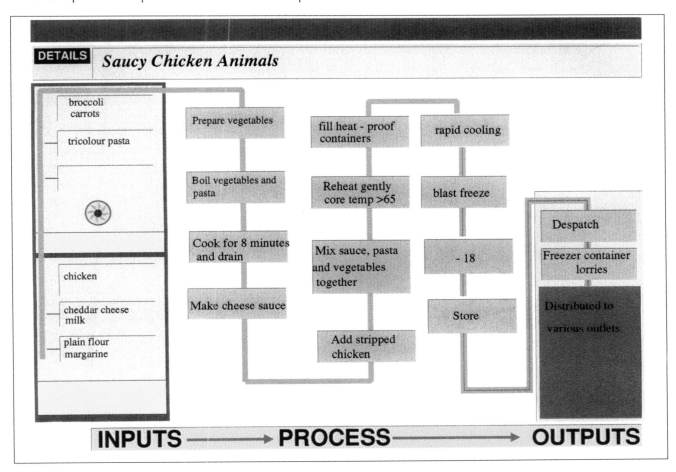

Figure 9.10 *The input, process and output for Saucy Chicken Animals*

Examiner's comments on 9.10

Good Points

- This student has used software to produce a flow diagram which identifies a process, the various stages in the process and the points in the process where specific checks need to be made.
- These checks might be related to quality, time or temperature but are all essential to the safe production of a product.
- In industry this process would also be used to pre-plan the production procedure of all products, identifying where and when hazards could occur and how these could be eliminated.
- By using this type of software this student has produced a clear production plan which is of good quality.
- The use of software programs saves time. The programs also give prompts as they are used which make sure that the users will not omit critical points in the process.

How does the food industry use ICT such as CAD and CAM?

- If your product prototype were to be mass produced, which parts of the production process could be controlled by computer? Look back at Session 7 on Systems and Control (page 40) for ideas.

CHECK YOURSELF QUESTIONS

Q1 Look back through all the work you have presented in your design folder and list the different aspects of ICT which you have used.

Q2 Does your list use a range of different applications or is the use of ICT always the same?

Q3 Does ICT really improve your work? In what ways?

Q4 Could you add any other ICT to your design work?

Q5 Where might commercial food manufacturers use ICT?

Q6 How could ICT be used to make a quality product?

COMMENTS

Q1 Use of ICT has to be planned. As you plan each design sheet or activity, think about how you might use ICT. Before you finally present the work for each section of your project, check that there are no lost opportunities for using ICT.

Q2 Remember that when you use ICT, in addition to improving the appearance of your work, it should have a real purpose. You may decide that all your work will look better if it is computer generated rather than being hand written. This is fine providing that you have time to produce the work and also access to a computer whenever you need it. A project which contains hand-written work but which also includes specific aspects of ICT which were used because they are the most suitable way of presenting information, applying a particular technique or simulating an industrial process, will get just as much credit and often more credit than a project which is all computer generated but only uses a limited range of ICT applications, most of which are for presentation purposes only.

Q3 Look critically at all the ICT work you have included in your design folder. You should be quite convinced that your use of ICT has been the best way of dealing with each particular aspect of the work you have produced.

Q4 Look at the list of ways in which you can include ICT in your work. Examine all the design sheets which you have produced and identify any gaps where you could have added any ICT applications to improve your work.

Q5& 6
Look at the sections of your folder work which relate to industrial practice, systems and control, and manufacturing. Have you included ICT work which reflects these processes, for example CAM applications, HACCP simulations and flow diagrams with control points?

¶◎¶ How important are making skills?

■ While you are carrying out your coursework project you will be assessed on designing and making.

■ In the majority of specifications these two topics are given equal importance but in some specifications 'making' is given more importance and can be worth twice as much as 'designing'. You will see from this, therefore, that making is a very important part of your project work.

■ Many students spend a lot of time producing their design folder and work hard on the designing parts of their project work, often at the expense of the making work. You need to show a wide range of making skills in your project work and you also need to show that you have spent a good proportion of your project time on making.

■ If you make only one food product and use only one or two hours of project time to do this, it would be an insufficient use of your time and would not balance the time spent on making in other materials in your Design and Technology work.

■ You must remember that a making grade is awarded on the basis of the amount of time spent, the quality of the result produced, the knowledge displayed and the demand, in terms of skill, of the making tasks which have been undertaken.

¶◎¶ What is 'making' in food technology?

■ **Making** refers to practical activities which you use to provide information, results and outcomes as part of the process of the development of a food product. You can carry out making at various stages in the design process. If you look back at Session 1 on Research, Session 3 on Design Ideas, and Session 5 on Development, you will see that many examples of making are given.

■ The following list includes examples of making activities:

- evaluating existing products
- comparing products
- sensory analysis
- preparation skills
- cookery skills
- changing ingredients
- altering methods or processes
- using alternative ingredients or substitutes
- mixing
- moulding
- forming
- rolling
- shaping
- manipulative skills
- organisational skills
- using equipment, both hand-held and large electrical equipment
- controlling temperature
- adapting recipes
- applying finishing techniques

Figure 10.1 *Equipment can be used in making*

⫶◉⫶ Providing evidence of making in your project work

■ You need to think of different ways in which you can provide evidence of your making/practical work other than just by making a complete product. On the other hand, you must remember that it is not just the **quantity** of your making which you should show but also the **quality**.

PHOTOGRAPHS

■ These are only useful if the quality and detail of the product or experiment result can be seen clearly.

Figure 10.2 *Mixers can save a lot of time*

■ Photographs of the process can be very informative, e.g. rolled out pastry, chopped vegetables, sauce in a pan, dough being shaped, scones cut out on a baking tray, cream being piped, etc. They can show the examiner the skills which you used and the quality of the work you did. For example, if you show a pastry dough rolled to a regular shape and to an even thickness, this shows that the pastry was well made, of a good consistency and that you could control the rolling out process in terms of keeping both the shape and also the thickness regular.

■ A digital camera can be very useful. You can view the picture before printing and this is a very appropriate use of ICT.

ACTUAL RECIPES

■ Including dozens of recipes and methods is unnecessary and very time consuming. A recipe on its own is not evidence that you have actually made the product.

■ It is much more sensible to refer to a recipe when you are testing a finished product, particularly where you are suggesting improvements, either by using different ingredients or commenting on sensory characteristics. This shows that you have actually made the product.

SENSORY EVALUATION

■ Charts, star diagrams and comments which inform the examiner about specific products are all evidence of making. (See also Session 6 on Evaluation, page 33, and Revision Session 16 on Sensory Analysis, page 195.)

Figure 10.3 *A photograph can show evidence of 'making'.*

RESULTS AND CONCLUSIONS FROM EXPERIMENTS

■ You need to make conclusions from experiments in order to make decisions about ingredients, methods and processes. However, the way you carry out the experiment and the control and procedures which you use are also important evidence for the examiner to assess. This will be proof of your making skills.

■ You should give the **aim** of the experiment, a **brief description** of the method used, the **results** obtained and how you have used these to **draw conclusions**. All of this information should be concise and on the same page. (See also Session 5 on Development and Session 9 on Information Technology.)

EVALUATIONS OF YOUR OWN AND EXISTING PRODUCTS

■ Any activities which relate to the evaluation of products can be counted as making provided that they involve sensory testing and some preparation and cooking skills. You might have the chance to compare products, e.g. to compare a ready-made product with your own version.

⦿ Planning your making activities

■ You will be assessed on your ability to plan your making activities. Time management is a very important part of this. You will need to think and plan carefully both for individual practical lessons and for the overall project.

■ There is no need to include a time plan for every practical that you carry out. In fact, this would be a poor use of project time and would reduce the time left for other, more important aspects of your designing and making work.

■ Students often produce a plan after they have carried out a making activity but this gets no credit. You need to make a plan in advance and then, after completing the making activity, comment on the plan's use and accuracy, adding where and why changes were necessary.

■ Your evidence of good planning could take the following forms:

• a time plan which includes accurate procedures, the dovetailing of tasks and an evaluation. One or two of these are quite sufficient for an examiner to see the process which you have used.

• the breakdown of a product into different parts and suggestions as to how you will make and combine each part. This would be very useful for managing your time in short lessons and for producing a sequence of tasks within the development of a product.

• a flow diagram for a complete product, showing where and how control would be applied. It is likely that this will be appropriate at a later stage of development.

■ You need to include some specific comments about where and why you are including making skills in your project. You could, for example, add these before evaluating a product, or after carrying out an investigation. Remember that you need to show the examiner what you are thinking and why you are carrying out the various making tasks in your project.

? CHECK YOURSELF QUESTIONS

Q1 As you work through your project and begin to look at the different sections of the design process, are there opportunities for making?

Q2 Have you considered looking at existing products and carrying out comparisons as part of your research?

Q3 Can you include some making when you are thinking about design ideas?

Q4 Does your project include experiments and investigations?

Q5 Have you modified existing recipes by changing and substituting ingredients, shapes and sizes?

Q6 Where will an examiner find evidence of your making work?

COMMENTS

Q1 The sections of your project work where there is likely to be some opportunity for making are research, design ideas and development. When you are planning these sections of work always remember that you can include making activities.

Q2 One practice which is used in the food industry is to look at products which already exist within the product range which is being considered. If you include this type of activity in your project work, provided that it involves sensory testing it can be used as evidence of making. It may be that you will need to carry out some preparation and/or cooking of an existing product as part of the testing process.

Q3 Look back at Session 3 on Design Ideas (page 12) and consider ways in which you can adapt existing recipes and products by adding or changing ingredients and methods. To make decisions based on the effects of these changes it would be necessary to make products and then evaluate them.

Q4 You must remember that it is not always necessary to make the whole product and that parts of your chosen idea can be developed. Small quantities of ingredients can be used to set up an experiment or an investigation. This would all be classed as making.

Q5 As a result of experiments, investigations and sensory testing, it may be necessary to change ingredients. Also, after making a product you will need to consider if the shape and size of the product are appropriate. Much time and money is spent on this in the food industry in order to provide a product which is cost effective, meets nutritional requirements, looks attractive and is something entirely new. It may be that a new shape would be the critical selling point for a new food product, or that size is an essential factor if producing a product for a child.

Q6 There are two main ways of providing evidence of making:
- work which you have recorded in your folder
- information which your teacher will give to an examiner about your work, in particular the way in which you have carried out making activities.

Do not spend unnecessary time writing out time plans, recipes and methods. These do not provide evidence that you have actually made something. However, results from tests, experiments, investigations and sensory evaluations give clear evidence of what you have done. Photographs are another good source of evidence but will only show the quality of your work if they are good. Food photography is difficult. You need to use good background colours, close up shots and different angles. A digital camera is an excellent tool because you can view the photo before printing it.

REVISION SESSION I

▬ Food commodities ▬

🍽 What are food commodities?

- Today a vast range of food products are made from a small number of raw foods. These are processed in many different ways to produce products that meet the needs and preferences of consumers everywhere.

- For the food products that you have designed and made you will have used both raw foods, e.g. fruit and vegetables, and processed foods, e.g. flour and sugar. Foods can be classified into two main groups:

  - **primary source** – raw food materials, e.g. milk, fruit, vegetables, wheat grain, sugar beet

  - **secondary source** – processed food materials, e.g. butter, jam, flour, sugar.

- The changes made to raw foods to make them more **edible** are known as **food processing**. Food processing involves changes to **raw materials** which improve:
  - **appearance**
  - **texture**
  - **palatability**
  - **nutritive value**
  - ease of preparation
  - keeping properties.

- Food processing is classified into two main areas:
  - **primary processing**
  - **secondary processing.**

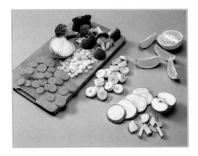

Figure 1.1 *Primary source foods*

Figure 1.2 *Secondary source foods*

🍽 Primary processing

- This involves changing or **converting** the raw food materials into:
  - foods that can be eaten immediately
  - ingredients that can be used to produce other food products.

- It could involve **simple** processes such as:
  - washing salad vegetables, e.g. spring onions, radishes
  - sorting, shelling, peeling vegetables, e.g. potatoes, peas
  - squeezing fruit, e.g. fruit juice
  - chopping, slicing, cutting, e.g. meat, poultry.

- Or it could involve more **complex** processes such as:
  - heat treatment, e.g. pasteurisation of milk
  - milling, rolling, sieving, e.g. cereals such as wheat, corn, rye
  - refining, e.g. sugar beet and sugar cane
  - **extraction** and refining, e.g. vegetable oils.

🍽 Secondary processing

- This involves changing or converting the primary processed foods into other food products. It may involve **combining** one or more food ingredients, e.g.:
  - flour, sugar, butter, eggs to make cakes
  - wheat-durum semolina, water, and sometimes eggs, to make pasta.

- Many different techniques and processes can be used during secondary processing, e.g.:
  - mixing, kneading and proving in bread **manufacture**
  - boiling and crystallisation in sweet manufacture
  - aeration and drying in the manufacture of meringue
  - mixing and extrusion in the manufacture of pasta.

Figure1.3 *Pasta being made in a factory*

- Foods are processed from a primary to a secondary source and then into other food products. Check the chart below for a few more examples and then write out others based on the food materials you have used during your course.

Primary Source Raw Foods	→	Primary Processing converted into	→	Secondary Source Food Ingredients	→	Secondary Processing manufactured into	→	Food Products
olives	→			olive oil	→			salad dressing
sugar cane	→			caster sugar	→			cakes
corn (maize)	→			cornflour	→			sauces
wheat	→			flour	→			pastry
milk	→			cheese	→			pizza

Table 1.1 *Using primary and secondary sources to make food products*

- You will need to understand that raw foods are processed to provide a wide range of food products. During your course you will have studied at least one food **commodity** and you should be able to identify:
  - the food processing stages, i.e. from primary source to secondary source. It is often helpful to draw a flow chart to show these stages
  - the range of food products that can be obtained from a primary source food material.

- Cane sugar and olives are two good examples of this.

Figure1.4 *Different types of sugar*

🍽 Sugar

Refined sugar

- All white sugar is refined and there is no difference between beet and cane sugar.

Unrefined sugar

- The cane sugars to which the term 'raw' or 'unrefined' is applied are generally sugars that have been produced by a simple refining process in the country of origin. As a result they contain some molasses, which affects the texture, aroma, colour and taste.

- The range of secondary source sugar products obtained from the primary source includes: icing sugar, caster sugar, crystal sugar, cube sugar, demerara sugar, granulated sugar, golden granulated sugar, molasses, muscavado sugar, preserving sugar, soft brown sugar, golden syrup, treacle.

Figure 1.5 *Sugar crystals made from refined sugar*

Table 1.2 *Processing sugar cane*

Processing stages
Raw material
– **sugar beet**, a large pale brown root crop similar to the parsnip, has a sugar content of about 17% when it is harvested. It grows in the temperate climate of Europe and North America.
– **sugar cane**, found in the tropical and semi-tropical regions of the world, where it can grow up to five metres in height. The tropics provide the ideal conditions for sugar cane growth. The hot sunny days combined with heavy seasonal rainfall result in the humid conditions that allow sugar cane to thrive.
Sugar beet
▸ The sugar beet is washed and sliced into small pieces known as **cossettes**
▸ The cossettes are sprayed with hot water. Lime and carbon dioxide are added to clean the resulting juice
▸ The brown liquid is filtered
▸ The juice is boiled under vacuum to produce a thick syrup. Crystals start to appear. Tiny sugar crystals called 'seeds' are added to encourage crystallisation
▸ The crystals are separated from the syrup in a **centrifuge**
▸ Pure white sugar is produced and granulated
Sugar cane
▸ The cane is cut into small pieces and shredded
▸ It is crushed between heavy rollers
▸ This is sprayed with hot water. Lime is added to clean the resulting juice
▸ The brown liquid is filtered to produce a thin juice
▸ The juice is boiled under vacuum to form a thick syrup
▸ The crystals (**raw sugar**) and syrup (**molasses**) are separated in a centrifuge
▸ Brown raw sugar crystals are produced
▸ The raw sugar is sent all over the world for refining into pure white sugar

Figure 1.6 *Sugar is used in baking*

- Sugar has several important functions in the manufacture of food products:

  - as a **sweetener** – commonly used to sweeten sweet and some savoury products, e.g. cakes, fruit juice, tomato sauce, baked beans

  - as a **preservative** – it inhibits the growth of micro-organisms (bacteria, yeast and moulds), e.g. in fruit tinned or bottled in sugar syrup. It acts with pectin to form a gel in jams and marmalades.

  - as a **stabiliser** – it helps to maintain consistency and texture, e.g. in frozen/chilled desserts

  - in **aeration** – together with fat, sugar entraps air to aid the rising and aerating of cakes and yeast products

  - in producing **colour** – colour comes from the type of sugar used, e.g. muscavado sugar is dark brown, while caster sugar is white. Colour also comes from **caramelisation**, which happens when the sugar turns brown when heated, e.g. in baked products such as cakes or sweet pastry, or in boiled sugar, e.g. in toffee and caramels

  - in **thickening** – which helps to produce the correct texture in sauces and custards

  - to provide **texture** – it helps to soften gluten and prevents the overdevelopment of gluten in cakes and pastries

  - to retain **moisture** – sugar helps to retain moisture and delays products from drying out and becoming stale.

Olives

Figure 1.7 *Harvesting olives in Italy*

- Olive oil is one of the oldest natural ingredients used as a food. The main areas of cultivation are in Spain, Italy, Greece, Portugal, France, Turkey, Morocco and Tunisia, which together produce 95% of the world's olive harvest. There are several different kinds of olives. Black olives contain most oil.

- A range of secondary source oil products are obtained from the primary source, e.g. olive oil in a wide range of flavours, aromas and colours, such as extra virgin olive oil, virgin olive oil, olive oil.

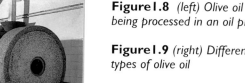

Figure 1.8 *(left) Olive oil being processed in an oil press*

Figure 1.9 *(right) Different types of olive oil*

Harvesting is a labour-intensive process in which the olives are 'combed' onto umbrella-like nets to avoid bruising the fruit.

↓

The olives are transported to processing plants within three days to avoid oxidising and the lowering of the yield of oil.

↙ ↘

Modern Extraction	**Traditional Extraction** – known as 'cold pressing'
↓	↓
Washed four times	Olives are washed once
↓	↓
Crushed into a paste using stainless steel cutters	Crushed to a pulp by stone mills
↓	↓
Resulting oil, water and solids mixed in large stainless steel chamber – heated to 30°C	Pulp spread over synthetic mats which are stacked on top of each other under a hydraulic press
↓	↓
Oil extracted by spinning in a centrifuge	Pressure slowly builds up, squeezing the oil out
↓	↓
Oil separated from the water and solids	Oil separated out from water by spinning in a centrifuge
↓	
Oil filtered, tested, graded, and bottled for sale	

Table 1.3 *Processing stages in making olive oil*

USING OLIVE OIL IN OTHER FOOD PRODUCTS

■ Olive oil has several important functions in the manufacture of many food products:

- to **add flavour** – each variety of olive oil has a distinct characteristic with sensory descriptors such as 'floral', 'nutty', 'hot and peppery', 'grassy'

- it is used to add flavour by pouring/trickling over salad vegetables, potatoes or pasta

- it is used in **marinades** made from a mixture of olive oil/lemon juice/herbs, etc. to **tenderise** or add flavour to meat or fish

- olive oil is stable at high temperatures and is therefore a good **frying** medium e.g. for sauté potatoes or stir fry vegetables

- it adds **moisture** and flavour when used in cakes, bread and pastry

- it is used in **emulsions,** e.g. as a mixture of olive oil/wine vinegar/pepper/salt/garlic/mustard to form a vinaigrette dressing for salads. Also used to **stabilise emulsions**, e.g. mayonnaise

- it has a **natural resistance to rancidity** and will keep unrefrigerated for at least 18 months

- it is a good source of **low saturated fats**.

Figure1.10 *Stir fry vegetables*

Product diversity

■ Many products can be developed from a single food commodity such as wheat, maize, sugar cane or milk. Think of all the products that are made from wheat. This is known as **product diversity**. In the past approximately 13 staple plant foods were used to feed the world's population. These were wheat, corn, rice, potatoes, rye, oats, cassava, sweet potatoes, millet, yams, plantain, teff and taro. Today approximately 50 staple cereals, oilseeds and legumes are used to produce over 20,000 products. Table 1.4 on page 78 shows the range of products that are processed from raw milk.

Figure1.11 *Milk products*

Heat-treated milk	Milk products	Butter	Cream	Cheese	Yogurt
pasteurised ultra-heat treated (UHT) sterilised	skimmed semi-skimmed homogenised dried evaporated condensed	salted unsalted clarified buttermilk	single whipping double clotted creme fraiche soured	soft – no rind, e.g. cottage ripened, soft, e.g. brie semi-hard, e.g. stilton hard cheese, e.g. cheddar very hard, e.g Parmesan	set stirred flavoured or natural Greek style

Table 1.4 *Milk products (from cows, sheep and goats)*

Key Words

These are the key words (highlighted in the text). Tick them if you know what they mean. Otherwise go back and check them again.

primary source
secondary source
edible
raw material
appearance
texture
palatability

nutritive value
primary processing
secondary processing
converting
simple
complex
extraction

combining
manufacture
commodity
harvesting
product diversity

CHECK YOURSELF QUESTIONS

Q1 An important primary source food material is wheat grain. It is milled to produce flour. Briefly describe the two main types of flour that are produced during the primary processing stages.

Q2 White flour is a popular secondary source material. It is used to make many different baked food products. List three types of white flour and give examples of food products they could be used to make.

Q3 Sugar is used in many food products. You will associate sugar with familiar products such as cakes, biscuits, meringues, etc. However, sugar is also added to some food products that you may not immediately think of. Look at the following lists of ingredients.

1 Which food products do you think are made from each list of ingredients?

2 What is the function of the sugar in each of these products?

> Beans, Tomatoes, Water, Sugar, Salt, Modified Cornflour, Spirit Vinegar, Spice Extracts, Herb Extract

> Sugar, Water, Vinegar, Apples, Orange juice (made from concentrate), Apricots, Dried apricots, Modified Cornflour, Dried onions, Mango chutney, Dried onions, Red pepper, Stem ginger, Gherkins, Turmeric, Orange peel, Spice extract, Sultanas, Salt, Carrots, Dates

Answers are on page 227.

Characteristics of food materials

🍴 How do food materials differ?

■ During your course you will have used a wide range of food materials to design and make food products. You need to know and understand the working **characteristics** of the main food materials and what happens when these are combined by different processing methods.

🍴 Eggs

■ Eggs are one of the most useful and versatile food ingredients. They can be used to:

- make a range of egg meals, e.g. scrambled, poached, boiled, omelette

- incorporate their working characteristics in a wide range of food products, e.g. cakes, biscuits, sauces, cold desserts, savoury pastry products.

Composition

■ Eggs have two main parts –the **white** and the **yolk**.

Nutritional components

■ Protein with a high biological value.

■ Vitamins A, D + B$_2$.

■ **Fat** and iron in the egg yolk.

Working characteristics

■ Egg proteins have three main properties:

1 Egg protein **coagulates** when heated and this is used for:

- setting into a firm structure, i.e. liquid to a solid, e.g. scrambled, poached, boiled eggs or baked meringue

- binding – holding dry ingredients together, e.g. burgers, croquettes

- coating/enrobing – holding dry coatings such as breadcrumbs onto a surface and forming a barrier during cooking processes, e.g. fried breaded fish

- thickening – setting a liquid (one medium egg will set 125 ml liquid for egg custard, savoury flan, etc.)

- enriching – thickening a sauce, adding colour and improving the nutritional profile

- glazing – beaten egg or egg and milk is brushed over baked savoury products. As the egg coagulates the surface bakes to a shiny golden brown.

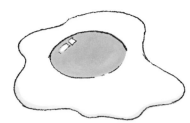

Figure 2.1 *Eggs are a versatile food ingredient*

> QUESTION SPOTTER

Typical exam question on this topic:

▶ Why is it necessary to use eggs in the making of a cake?

Your answer should include the relevant functions of the egg, i.e. aeration, coagulation, binding, enriching, emulsification and how the egg has helped to produce a cake which is well risen, set, light, a good colour, a good flavour and a good texture.

Table 2.1 Temperature range for coagulation of egg protein

	Temperature range °C
egg white	62–70
egg yolk	65–70

2 Egg proteins **stretch** when beaten and hold air in the structure.

- Whisking air into liquid egg white or whole egg creates a foam. Whole egg foam is used in sponge cakes and egg white foam is used to make meringues which, when baked, change to a solid foam. (See Revision Session 3, page 89.)

3 Egg yolk proteins are good **emulsifying agents.**

- Egg yolk contains lecithin, which is an emulsifying agent. Lecithin stabilises **emulsions** of oil and water, e.g. in mayonnaise. (See Revision Session 3, page 89.)

🍽 Milk

Figure 2.2 *Milk is made into a variety of products*

■ Milk is widely available. It is processed to form several milk products. Cows' milk is the main source, with milk from sheep and goats also used for some products. Milk forms the basis of butter, cheese, cream, yogurt and ice cream.

Composition

■ Milk is an emulsion of two liquids, e.g. oil in water. This is visible when the liquids separate and the cream collects (as fat droplets) at the top of a bottle of milk.

Nutritional components

- protein of high biological value

- fat –whole milk 3%, semi-skimmed 1.6%, skimmed 0.1%, Channel Island 5.1%.

- sugar in the form of lactose

- vitamins A and D; a little vitamin B_1, B_2 and C

- calcium and phosphorus

■ Milk provides ideal conditions for the growth of micro-organisms. Most milk sold in the UK is heat treated to destroy harmful bacteria and improve its keeping quality. The main methods of heat treatment include:

- ultra-heat treatment, sterilisation, pasteurised milk, all sold in bottles and cartons

- condensed and evaporated milk, both sold in cans.

■ To find out more about the effect of heat on milk, see Revision Session 12, page 165.

Working characteristics

- Milk is used to give **flavour**, **colour** and **consistency** to sauces, soups, batters, etc.

- In some food products milk **binds** ingredients together.

- It contains the proteins lactalbumin and lactoglobulin, which coagulate when milk is heated. Together they form a skin on the top of boiled milk, custards, sauces and milk puddings. Stirring the milk or milk mixture helps to break up the mass of coagulated proteins.

- To prevent a cream line forming, pasteurised milk can be processed through fine sieves which break the fat globules into very fine droplets which are then dispersed throughout the milk. This is known as **homogenisation**.

¡O¡ Butter

- Butter is a water in oil emulsion made from churned cream. It is a solid, firm fat, sold salted or unsalted. It is used for:

  - **flavouring** –in sauces, desserts, cakes and biscuits etc.

  - **shortening** –it combines with flour to prevent gluten forming so that a short crumbly texture is obtained in shortcrust pastry, shortbread biscuits, etc.

  - **aeration** –when butter is creamed with sugar, air is incorporated to form an air in fat foam. When heated the air acts as a raising agent in creamed cakes and biscuits

  - **extending shelf life** by holding moisture in cakes, scones, etc.

  - **cooking** – used to shallow fry and add flavour, e.g. omelettes.

Figure 2.3 *Different kinds of butter*

¡O¡ Cheese

- There are many different types of cheese, all made by different methods of production and with different types of milk. The main method of cheese production is when a lactic acid starter is added to pasteurised milk. An enzyme rennet is then added to clot the milk and form curds (solids) and whey (liquids). Different moulding and ripening periods then produce a wide range of cheeses. e.g:

  - firm cheeses such as Cheddar, Cheshire, Parmesan, mozzarella, feta, Danish blue, stilton

  - ripened soft cheeses such as brie, camembert

  - other types of cheese, including cream cheese, curd cheese, cottage cheese, Quark.

Figure 2.4 *Different kinds of cheese*

Nutritional components
- This varies with the type of cheese. Firm cheese contains protein, fat, water, vitamins A and D and calcium. Other cheeses may have a different profile. For example, cottage cheese is low in fat; cream cheese is high in fat.

Working characteristics
- Cheese is used to add **flavour**, **texture** and **colour** to sauces, savoury fillings and cold desserts.

- When heated cheese melts, so it is often grated to mix thoroughly with other ingredients. If it is overheated the protein coagulates and squeezes out the fat and water. This is known as **syneresis**. At this stage the cheese can become tough and rubbery.

🍽️ Cream

- Cream is made from the fat content of milk. It is an oil in water emulsion. Cream is available in several forms, e.g. double cream 48% fat; whipping cream 35% fat; single cream; creme fraiche; fromage frais; soured cream.

Working characteristics

- Cream is used to:

  - give **flavour**, **texture** and **volume** to both sweet and savoury products, e.g. chilled desserts, soups, sauces

  - **decorate** sweet products, e.g. cakes or cold desserts, and to garnish starters and soups

  - some cream with a high fat content, e.g. double and whipping cream, can be whisked to incorporate air and form a **foam**. The stable structure of whipped cream is used to decorate cold desserts and to add volume to mixtures such as chocolate mousse.

Figure 2.5 *Different kinds of cream*

🍽️ Yogurt

- Yogurt is made from either cows' or ewes' milk. A culture of lactic acid bacteria is added to whole milk, semi-skimmed or skimmed milk. The proteins coagulate between 37°C to 44°C to set the yogurt. It is then cooled and stored below 5°C.

Working characteristics

- The yogurt can be sold as natural yogurt with no flavouring added. The texture will vary according to the milk used and whether it is set yogurt or stirred yogurt. Yogurt may be flavoured by adding syrup or pieces of fruit or nuts to make whole or real fruit yogurt.

- Yogurt can be used as:

  - a food product to eat for breakfast, a cold dessert or as an accompaniment to puddings and fresh fruit

  - an ingredient in cold desserts or an **alternative to cream**, e.g. in cheesecake

  - a **thickening agent** in sauces, soups, salad dressing and dips

  - an ingredient to add creamy and acidic **flavour** and **texture**, e.g. to casseroles, soups.

Figure 2.6 *Different kinds of yogurt*

🍽️ Meat

- Meat and poultry are the **muscle tissue** of animals and birds. They can be cooked in many ways and used in a wide range of fresh, frozen, cook-chilled and part-prepared food products:

  - **animal meats**: beef, lamb, pork, veal, venison

  - **poultry meat**: chicken, duck, turkey, goose, ostrich

  - **offal**: (internal organs) heart, liver, kidney, ox-tail, tongue.

Composition

■ The **muscle tissue** is made up of long thin muscle fibres. The fibres are held together in bundles by **connective tissue.** There are two types of connective tissue:

- **collagen**, which holds the bundles of muscle fibres together. It is a soluble protein and dissolves to **gelatine** when heated

- **elastin**, which binds the muscle together or to a bone. It is tougher than collagen, insoluble and slightly yellow in colour. It provides elasticity and strength.

Nutritional components

- protein of high biological value

- fat according to type and cut

- iron

- vitamins B_1, thiamin and B_2, riboflavin

Working characteristics

■ Meat is used to make many food products that reflect British or worldwide cuisine. It is made appetising and palatable by preparation and cooking techniques that influence the:

- colour – **myoglobin** is the pigment that causes the colour of raw meat to be red or purplish. When meat is cooked to above 65°C the colour changes from red to brown.

- texture – proteins in the muscle fibres coagulate and the texture of the meat becomes firmer. Overcooking by dry heat methods can make the meat hard and tough.

- moisture – as the muscle fibres become firm and shrink slightly, meat juices are squeezed out. This adds flavour to cooking liquids and gravy.

- flavour and smell – during cooking the fat melts and helps to add moisture and flavour. Some juices evaporate and leave a coating on grilled, fried and roasted meat, Distinct aromas are created, which stimulate digestive juices.

- tenderness – cooking makes meat more tender and digestible. Ways to tenderise meat include:

  - cutting or mincing long muscle fibre meat, e.g. beef stewing steak

  - beating with a meat hammer to separate the fibres

  - scoring across the fibres with a knife

  - marinating in acid-based liquids, e.g. vinegar, lemon juice, to soften the collagen

  - sprinkling with commercial chemical tenderisers, which contain enzymes to break down the proteins in the connective tissue

  - using long slow moist cooking methods, e.g. 75°C to 100°C. The collagen is softened in the cooking liquid and converts to gelatine, which is soluble.

Figure 2.7 *Raw meat and poultry*

QUESTION SPOTTER

Typical exam question on this topic:

▸ If a manufacturer wanted to produce a burger, what type and cut of meat might be used and what cooking instructions would the manufacturer have to put on the packet?

Your answer should include the different types of meat that could be used, e.g. beef, lamb, pork and chicken, with the advantages and disadvantages of using each. The different cuts and sizes of the pieces need to be discussed and linked to the cooking methods which would be used, i.e. grilling, frying, microwave.

Some knowledge of what happens to meat when it is cooked and the tenderness of the meat also needs to be applied to your answer.

Figure 2.8 *Raw fish and shellfish*

🍴 Fish

- Fish can be bought fresh, frozen, canned, smoked or dried. It is caught in the sea or bred on fish farms, e.g. salmon and trout. There are many varieties of fish:

  - **white fish**: halibut, haddock, cod, plaice, whiting, coley

  - **oily fish**: salmon, trout, herring, tuna, sardines, pilchards

  - **shellfish**: lobster, prawns, shrimps, cockles, mussels, oysters.

Composition

- The muscle flesh of fish is made up of bundles of short muscle fibres held together by the connective tissue collagen. Collagen is soluble and, during cooking, converts to gelatine. There is no elastin in fish. Most fish cooks, flakes and tenderises in a short period of time. Overcooking causes the short muscle fibres to fall apart.

Nutritional components

- protein of high biological value

- calcium and phosphorus

- vitamins A and D in the flesh of oily fish.

Working characteristics

- Fish is used to make many food products. It is made appetising by preservation, preparation and cooking techniques that influence:

  - colour – there is very little change in the colour of fish as it cooks

  - texture – proteins in the muscle fibre coagulate and the texture of the fish becomes firmer. When cooked the flesh falls into flakes and a creamy liquid oozes out between the flakes. If overcooked, the flesh becomes dry.

  - moisture – any juices squeezed out can be used in sauces

  - flavour and smell – distinctive aromas develop as fish is cooked or preserved by methods such as smoking

  - tenderness – fish flesh is always tender and only requires short cooking times. It can be cooked by a variety of dry or moist methods. Some fish is eaten raw, e.g. Japanese sashimi and sushi, Scandinavian gravad lax. Some preservation methods cook the fish during processing, e.g. canned salmon, tuna, sardines. Marinating fish also adds flavour and tenderises the muscle fibres, e.g. roll mop herrings served in vinegar.

🍽 Fats and oils

- There are many different types of fats and **oils**. As a general rule, at room temperature fats are solid and oils are liquid.

Figure 2.9 *Solid fats and liquid oils*

Composition

- Fat and oils are formed from glycerol and fatty acids to create triglycerides. The fatty acids are either saturated or unsaturated and the proportions and combination produce a solid fat or liquid oil. **Solid fats** are: butter, ghee, lard, suet, margarine made from blended vegetables or fish oils, low-fat spreads and compound white fats, e.g. Trex.
  Oils are: corn oil, olive oil, sunflower oil, groundnut, and distinctive flavoured oils such as walnut.

- Fat and oil are also visible on some foods, e.g. fat on meat and bacon. They are also present but invisible in foods such as oily fish and processed foods such as cakes, pastry, chocolate, fried foods, crisps, salad dressings.

Nutritional components

- This varies according to the type of fat or oil. For example, butter and margarine contain some saturated fatty acids and vitamins A and D. Lard contains mainly saturated fatty acids, whereas a vegetable oil contains a high proportion of unsaturated fatty acids.

Working characteristics

- There are two main functions of fats and oils in food product development. They are used as an ingredient and as a cooking medium.

1 As ingredients in food products fat and oil are used for:

- **shortening** – coating flour with fat to prevent gluten formation in shortcrust pastry, rubbed-in cakes. (See Revision Session 6, page 121.)

- **emulsions** – oil forms an emulsion with liquids such as vinegar to make salad dressings and mayonnaise. (See Revision Session 3, page 89.)

- **aeration** – fat creamed with sugar holds air. When heated this acts as a raising agent. (See Revision Session 3, page 95.)

- **flavouring** – fats and oils have distinct flavours which improve or develop the aroma and flavour of food products, e.g. olive oil in salad dressings, butter in cakes and icing.

- **plasticity** – by combining fats and oils softer fats have been developed which are sold in plastic tubs, e.g. soft margarine. These are useful for all-in-one cake mixtures and spreading straight from the refrigerator

- **moisture and keeping quality** – fats help to keep food products moist and increase shelf life.

- **sealing** – sealing foods with melted fat to stop them drying out, e.g. a layer of butter on potted meat, paté, potted shrimps.

2 As a cooking medium fats and oils are used for:

- **frying** – the fat or oil increases in temperature, e.g. shallow frying of omelette; deep frying of doughnuts
- **lubrication** – to stop foods sticking to pans and baking trays
- **basting** – spooning fat over roast, grilled and barbecued meats to stop then drying out and to add flavour and colour

Figure 2.10 *Cereal growing*

🍴 Cereals

- Cereals are **cultivated** grasses grown for their nutritious edible seeds known as cereal grains. Cereals can be processed from their primary source into a vast range of secondary source ingredients and food products. (See Revision Session 1.) They are grown all over the world and transported, stored and used creatively in food product development.

Composition

- All cereal grains have the same basic structure but the different types vary in shape, texture, size and colour. Specific uses include:

  - **wheat**: several types of flour, e.g. semolina, breakfast cereals, pasta
  - **maize (corn)**: cornflour, breakfast cereals, popcorn, sweetcorn, corn oil
  - **oats:** rolled oats, oatmeal, breakfast cereals
  - **rice**: long grain (patria, basmati rice), medium grain (arborio-risotto rice), short grain (white pudding rice). Sold in a variety of forms, e.g. easy cook, pre-cooked, boil-in-the-bag, ground, flaked, as breakfast cereals, instant snacks, canned rice puddings.

Figure 2.11 *Different types of rice*

Nutritional components

- all grains contain a high proportion (10–80%) of carbohydrate in the form of starch
- small amounts of protein, fat and water
- NSP (non-starch polysaccharide), i.e. fibre in the bran layer
- B-group vitamins thiamin, niacin, riboflavin in some cereals

Working characteristics

Elasticity

- The protein content in cereals varies. Wheat contains the highest amount of protein and this makes it a very versatile food ingredient. Two proteins, glutenin and **gliadin**, combine with water to form **gluten**. **Gluten** is elastic and will stretch to hold air and gas produced by raising agents. It is an essential component when creating volume in aerated food products. Strong wheat flour is 12–15% protein; weak wheat flour is 7–10% protein. No other cereal has this characteristic.

Gelatinisation
- When milled into wheat flour, cornflour or rice flour cereal grains are insoluble in cold water. When heated the starch grains absorb liquid and swell and soften. Flour granules burst and will then thicken a liquid. Overcooked rice gelatinises and the grains stick together.

🍴 Vegetables and fruit

- Vegetables and fruit are edible plants or parts of plants that are eaten raw or cooked. Many different types and varieties are grown worldwide and many countries import a wide range of fruits and vegetables to supplement out of season demand and to add variety to those grown locally.

Figure 2.12 *A variety of fruits and vegetables*

Composition
- Fruit and vegetables are made up of plant cells containing water, pectin, varying amounts of starch and a cell wall of cellulose. During cooking some softening takes place as a result of absorption of water by the cellulose, starch and pectin. These changes give fruit and vegetables important characteristics which are used in food processing, e.g. gelatinisation and gelling, and also make some fruit and vegetables edible.

- **Enzymic browning** occurs when some fruits are cut, e.g. apples, pears, bananas. (See Revision Session 11, page 151.)

- Fruit and vegetables can be preserved in many different ways.

Nutritional components
- These vary according to the plant or part of the plant used. Fruit and vegetables can contain up to 95% water. They also provide minerals, vitamins, carbohydrate, starch, sugar and protein. Many are important sources of NSP (fibre) and some are major sources of vitamin C.

Working characteristics
- Fruit and vegetables are important food commodities. They are used as:

  - colour, flavour and texture – for example:
    - raw fruit, e.g. fruit salad; decorated fruit gateau; fruit appetisers
    - raw vegetables, e.g. lettuce leaves, coleslaw (cabbage + carrot)
    - cooked fruit, e.g. stewed apples, fruit puddings; fruit sauces
    - cooked vegetables, e.g. stir fried, roasted, casseroled, boiled or microwaved
    - as accompaniments, e.g. pineapple with ham, apple sauce with pork
    - processed, e.g. canned peas, chilled potato salad, dried fruit salad, frozen chipped potatoes, crystallised fruit, tubes and cartons of tomato pureé, jars of chopped garlic.

  - gels – fruit contains pectin, a gum-like substance which is released from the cells of the fruit during cooking. When mixed with acid and sugar, the pectin helps to set mixtures and forms a gel, e.g. in jams, jellies and marmalades. (See Revision Session 3, page 93.)

⚪ Pulses

- Pulses are the ripened and dried seeds of legumes (pod plants). There is an enormous variety, e.g. peas, beans, chick peas, lentils and soya beans.

- They provide a good source of vegetable protein and dietary fibre. As you know, soya beans have a high biological value and are used as a meat analogue called TVP. (See Revision Session 4, page 108.)

- Most dried pulses require soaking before cooking for a long time at a high temperature, particularly dried red kidney beans.

- Pulses are eaten in place of meat by vegetarians. Pulses absorb flavours well and can be used in a wide range of food products.

Figure 2.13 *Dried kidney beans*

Key Words

These are the key words (highlighted in the text). Tick them if you know what they mean. Otherwise go back and check them again.

characteristic	muscle tissue	cultivated
composition	connective tissue	elasticity
fat	collagen	gliadin
coagulate	gelatine	gluten
emulsion	elastin	gelatinisation
flavouring	myoglobin	enzymic browning
shortening	oil	
aeration	plasticity	

CHECK YOURSELF QUESTIONS

Q1 Name three functions of egg in the making of a lemon meringue pie made with rich (sweet) shortcrust pastry.

Q2 Explain why milk will boil over if heated in a saucepan for too long.

Q3 Two different trays of beef have the following cooking instructions printed on the label.

- Tray 1 – Lean Braising Steak – cook (braise) at 180°C/Gas 4 for 2 hours.

- Tray 2 – Thin Cut Rump Steak – cook under a high grill for 4 minutes, turning occasionally.

Explain why the two types of beef need to be cooked in different ways.

Q4 Explain why fish is always tender and requires short cooking times.

Q5 Complete the chart by choosing a fat or oil to use in the following products:

a _____ to cream with sugar in a creamed cake mixture.

b _____ to coat flour in a rubbed-in shortcrust pastry mixture.

c _____ to form an emulsion with vinegar in mayonnaise.

d _____ for easy mixing (plasticity) in an all-in-one cake mixture.

e _____ to deep fry doughnuts or chipped potatoes.

Q6 Explain why the following cereals are used in the food products listed:

a strong wheat flour for breadmaking

b cornflour for custard sauce

c basmati rice for savoury dishes.

Answers are on page 228.

REVISION SESSION 3 — Food processing

🍴 How are food materials used?

■ Most food products are made from food materials combined in ways that determine colour, texture, flavour, shape and volume. The descriptive detail of a particular food product is known as the **product profile**. The **combination** of food materials in varying amounts and by different methods of preparation and processing enables a vast range of food products to be produced.

■ You will need to know and understand:

• the working **characteristics** of ingredients

• the effect of combining different ingredients

• the **interaction** of different foods during preparation, processing and cooking.

🍴 Colloidal structures

■ Processed foods often contain more than one ingredient. When the ingredients are mixed together a **structure** is formed. This is called a **colloidal structure**. A colloidal structure consists of two parts, which are evenly mixed or **dispersed** into one another.

■ The parts may be:

• **liquid**, e.g. vinegar, oil, water, milk

• **solid**, e.g. flour – starch grains of cornflour, arrowroot or wheat flour

• **gas**, e.g. carbon dioxide, air bubbles.

■ You need to know about the four types of colloidal structures: emulsions, **foams** (including solid foam), **gels** and suspensions.

Colloidal Structure	Food Product	Part 1	Dispersed	Part 2
Emulsion	mayonnaise	liquid, e.g. olive oil	in	liquid, e.g. vinegar
Foam	beaten egg white	gas, e.g. air bubbles	in	liquid, e.g. egg white
Solid foam	meringue, pavlova	gas, e.g. air bubbles	in	baked egg white
Gel	jam and jellies	liquid, e.g. water, juice	in	solid, e.g. fruit
Suspension	white sauce	solid, e.g. starch grains	in	liquid, e.g. milk

Table 3.1 *Colloidal structures*

🍴 Emulsions

■ Liquids such as oil and water are said to be 'immiscible', that is they cannot be mixed.

■ When rigorously shaken with water oil breaks into small **droplets** which can be seen in the water, i.e. it forms an **emulsion** of one liquid mixed within another liquid. If left to stand the two parts separate, with the oil floating on top of the water.

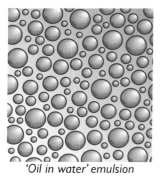

'Oil in water' emulsion

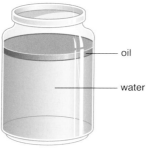

— oil

— water

Two parts separate

Figure 3.1

- Emulsions can be oil in water or water in oil. For example:
  - **oil in water**, e.g. oil beaten into vinegar to make a vinegar dressing – or when if milk is left to stand, the fat in the milk separates into a layer of cream.
  - **water in oil** is fat-free milk beaten into a blend of oil to make margarine.
- To stop the emulsion from separating an extra substance must be added to attract the two parts together. The 'matchmaker' is called an **emulsifying agent**.
- An emulsifying agent is a substance which contains a:
  - 'water-loving' group of **molecules** – **hydrophilic**
  - 'water-hating' group of molecules – **hydrophobic**

  i.e. one part attracts to water and one part attracts to oil to hold the oil and water emulsion together. The emulsifying agent lowers the **surface tension** between the two liquids so that they combine and form a **stable emulsion**.
- Examples of emulsifying agents used in food products include:
  - **lecithin** in egg yolk. Lecithin stabilises mayonnaise and creamed cake mixtures. Lecithin from soya beans is used in large-scale manufacture.
  - **glycerol monostearate (GMS)**, which is used in large-scale manufacture to stabilise foods such as margarine.
- The structure of emulsions is an important characteristic in the manufacture of fats such as butter and margarine. It is also important in the use of fats and oils in food products, e.g. mayonnaise, salad dressings, ice cream, creamed cake mixtures.

Salad dressings

- There are two types of emulsion-based salad dressings.
  - unstable emulsion – vinaigrette or French dressing
  - stable emulsion – mayonnaise.

Unstable emulsion – vinaigrette

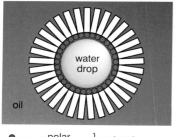

water drop

oil

— polar ⎫ molecule
— non-polar ⎬ of emulsifier

Figure 3.2 *A stable emulsion*

Ingredients	Method of Making
6 tablespoons olive oil 1–2 tablespoons wine vinegar 1 level teaspoon salt 1 crushed clove garlic 1 teaspoon mustard freshly milled black pepper	Put all ingredients in a bowl or screw-topped jar and whisk together or shake until thoroughly combined. Adjust seasoning to taste.

Vinaigrette variations

Herb:	add 2 tablespoons chopped herbs such as parsley, thyme, marjoram.
Garlic:	add 1–2 crushed cloves, 1 tablespoon chopped chives.
Mustard and parsley:	add 1 tablespoon wholegrain mustard, 2 tablespoons chopped parsley.
Blue cheese:	add 25 g finely blended Roquefort cheese, 2 tablespoons single cream.
Sweet and spicy:	add 1 teaspoon mango chutney, 1 teaspoon mild curry paste.

Remember
- The emulsion is unstable and will separate out when left to stand. Shake vigorously to suspend the tiny oil droplets in the vinegar.
- The basic dressing mixture will keep for up to a month as long as you don't add **perishable** ingredients such as herbs.

Stable emulsion – mayonnaise

Ingredients	Method of Making
1 egg yolk 125 ml olive oil 1–2 tablespoons wine vinegar half teaspoon salt freshly milled pepper half teaspoon mustard powder	Put egg yolk, mustard, salt, pepper, 1 teaspoon vinegar in bowl and mix thoroughly. Add oil drop by drop, then in a steady stream, whisking constantly until thick and smooth. Add rest of vinegar drop by drop. Season to taste.

- The egg yolk contains lecithin. This is an emulsifying agent, which helps to hold the olive oil and vinegar (oil and water) together to keep the emulsion stable, i.e. it does not separate out.

Mayonnaise variations

Tartare sauce:	add 5 ml tarragon, 10 ml chopped capers, 10 ml chopped gherkins, 10 ml chopped parsley.
Thousand island:	add 30 ml chopped green olives, 30 ml chopped green pepper, 10 ml chopped parsley, 10 ml tomato purée.
Blue cheese:	add 75 g crumbled blue cheese, 1 crushed garlic clove, 20 ml sour cream.

Function of salad dressing ingredients
- The foundation of a good dressing is the oil. A good choice is olive oil, which has a rich green colour and distinct fruity flavour. Blending stronger-flavoured oils, such as walnut, hazelnut and almond, with blander oils, such as sunflower or groundnut, also produces well-flavoured dressings.

Figure 3.3 *Stable salad dressing, e.g. mayonnaise, and unstable salad dressing, e.g. vinaigrette*

☼ QUESTION SPOTTER

Typical exam question on this topic:
▸ A manufacturer want to produce a marinade to sell with meat kebabs as a barbecue product. Give three ingredients which could be used in the marinade and explain why you have chosen them.

Your answer should refer to the function of a marinade and should include what effects each of the ingredients would have on flavour, tenderisation and cooking of the meat.

Figure 3.4 *A variety of oils and vinegars*

- **Vinegar** is available in all sorts of flavours, e.g. wine, cider, sherry, balsamic, or fruit vinegar. It can be flavoured with fresh herbs such as tarragon, chillies or garlic. In dressings lemon juice can be used along with vinegar to form an acidic contrast to the oil.

- **Other ingredients**, such as salt, mustard and pepper are added for flavour. Product development is obtained by adding one or two ingredients such as spices, herbs, cheese, vegetables, yogurt, cream, etc.

Creamed cake mixture

- Did you know that a creamed cake mixture is an emulsion? (Remember that the recipe for creamed cake is 100 g sugar, 100 g butter/margarine, 2 eggs, 100 g self-raising flour.)

Figure 3.5 *Creamed cake mixture*

Method of Making	Structure
Beat butter/margarine and sugar together. Egg is added gradually and beaten to a smooth consistency.	Air is beaten into the mixture of fat and sugar to form an *air in fat* foam. Watery egg liquid mixes in tiny droplets throughout the mixture to form a *water in oil* emulsion.

Note: If the egg is added cold or all at once the emulsion will not form. The fat becomes solid and looks as if it is floating in the egg. This is an oil in water emulsion, i.e. the cake mixture has '**curdled**'.

🍴 Foams

- A foam is formed when gas is mixed into a liquid, e.g. an egg white foam is gas (air) whisked into liquid (egg white).

- When egg white is whipped, it stretches to hold air bubbles. The large air bubbles break down into very small air bubbles to form a foam. The foam becomes stiffer, white and glossy.

- The stability of an egg white foam is measured by the way it keeps its volume. A **stabiliser** in the egg white foam is the protein **albumen**.

- A foam will not become unstable, i.e. lose air and become soft or runny, if:

  - fat-free equipment is used, i.e. no grease on bowl or beaters

  - no egg yolk is mixed into the white

  - fresh eggs at room temperature are used

  - it is not overbeaten, which causes the protein to overstretch and collapse.

- Examples of foams include beaten egg whites, and food products which are whipped, such as whipped cream, ice cream and cold desserts, e.g. mousse. The foam makes these light, aerated products with a smooth texture.

Figure 3.6 *Two food products made from foams: pavlova (top) and meringue nest*

- Two examples of food products formed from foams are meringue and pavlova.

  - Compare the list of ingredients used in each product:

  - **Meringue** is a solid foam – air is whisked into the egg white foam and baked at a low temperature. The air inside the foam expands to increase the volume of the foam and the protein albumen **coagulates** (sets) to give a solid fine-mesh structure.

  - **Pavlova** – cornflour and vinegar (acetic acid) soften the foam to create a soft marshmallow centre. In some recipes cream of tartar (tartaric acid) is used instead of vinegar.

Meringue	Pavlova
2 egg whites	2 egg whites
100 g caster sugar	100 g caster sugar
	pinch salt
	2 teaspoons cornflour
	1 teaspoon vinegar
	quarter teaspoon vanilla essence

Method of making both
Beat egg whites until stiff.
Half sugar added gradually and whisked in.
Remaining sugar folded in.
For pavlova beat in the cornflour, vinegar, vanilla essence, salt.
Bake at 100°C.

Gels

- A gel is formed when a large amount of liquid is set by a small amount of solid, e.g. jam and marmalade. The products are set but are often soft and elastic.

Setting jam or marmalade

Jam	Marmalade
1.8 kg raspberries	1.4 kg Seville oranges
1.8 kg sugar	3.4 litres water
(liquid is the juice which	2.7 kg sugar
comes from the raspberries)	juice of 2 lemons

- Note the high quantity of liquid compared to the solid parts of the fruit.

- The fruit contains **pectin**, a gum-like substance which is released from the cells of the fruit during cooking. When mixed with acid and sugar the pectin helps to set mixtures and form a gel, e.g.:

  - pectin in raspberries + sugar + acid in raspberries = raspberry jam
  - pectin in Seville oranges + sugar + acid in oranges + lemon juice = orange marmalade.

Figure 3.7 *Making marmalade*

Gelatine

- Gelatine is used to set a variety of cold sweets.

Figure 3.8 *Chocolate mousse*

Chocolate Mousse

200 g plain chocolate	zest and juice of 1 large orange
2 whole eggs	50 ml water
2 egg yolks	10 g powdered gelatine
75g caster sugar	75 ml double cream

- The gelatine is dissolved in warm water and added to the mixture at room temperature. Air is trapped in the whisked cream and egg whites. These two foams are folded into the egg yolk/chocolate creamy mixture to create a high-volume aerated foam mixture. The gelatine sets the foam into a mousse.

¡●¡ Suspension

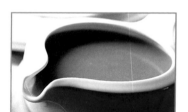

Figure 3.9 *Making white sauce*

- A **suspension** is a solid held in a liquid. The most common example is the starch grains of flour mixed into a liquid to make a sauce or gravy. If left to stand the solids sink to the bottom of the liquid. The mixture has to be stirred to keep the solids evenly mixed in the liquid.

- Examples of suspensions include:
  - white sauce – plain wheat flour in milk
  - gravy – cornflour in vegetable stock
  - glaze – arrowroot in water.

- Details about making sauce are fully explained in Revision Session 6, page 123.

- The solids are held in the liquid when the mixture is heated. The starch grains swell, absorb liquid, burst and thicken the liquid. This process is known as **gelatinisation** (see Revision Session 6, page 124). Custard, gravy and sauces are all examples of suspensions. They are usually served hot. If left to cool the suspension forms an elastic solid, e.g. blancmange.

Figure 3.10 *Gravy*

¡●¡ Aeration

- Many food products have a light, open, airy texture, e.g. bread, cakes, pastries, meringues and desserts such as soufflés.

- Older methods of making bread and cakes produced flat, close-textured products. These **unleavened** products were made by using materials combined in ways that did not **aerate** the mixture. Today products contain raising agents so that a light, open texture is a characteristic of the final product.

RAISING AGENTS

- **Raising agents** are gases that are introduced into a food mixture:
  - during the mixing process
  - in a substance which is added to the mixture.

- The gas is incorporated or released when ingredients are combined. On heating (baking) the minute bubbles of gas enclosed in the mixture expand, causing the mixture to rise.

- The three most common raising agents are **steam**, **air** and **carbon dioxide**. They are frequently used in combination with each other, e.g. in a creamed cake mixture from:
  - steam from liquid (egg/milk/water)
  - air beaten in (creaming butter and sugar)
  - carbon dioxide from chemical raising agents in baking powder or self-raising flour.

Figure 3.11 *The open texture of bread made with a raising agent*

Steam

- Some food products have steam as the main raising agent. These products must contain a high proportion of liquid, e.g. choux pastry, batter used to make Yorkshire pudding.

- For steam to make mixtures rise, two conditions are needed:
  - a large proportion of liquid, e.g. milk/water
  - a high baking temperature of 200°C or above.

- During baking:
  - The liquid content reaches boiling point.
  - The steam forces its way up through the mixture, stretching the mixture and making it rise.
  - The steam escapes and is replaced by air. The mixture bakes and sets into the risen shape.
  - Sometimes steam is trapped inside. It **condenses** on cooling and then the product collapses. This often happens with Yorkshire pudding.

- Steam also combines with:
  - air in pastry, e.g. shortcrust, flaky pastry
  - air and carbon dioxide in bread and cakes.

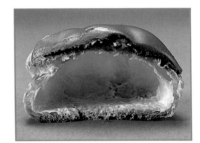

Figure 3.12 *A cross-section of a choux bun*

Air

- Air is the main raising agent in some food products, e.g. whisked sponge cake, soufflé. It is also used in combination with steam and/or carbon dioxide.

- Air is mechanically introduced into mixtures by:
  - **sieving** flour – air is trapped between fine particles, e.g. pastry, cakes, batters

Figure 3.13 *Introducing air into mixtures*

Figure 3.14 *Sieving flour*

Figure 3.15 *Folding puff pastry*

- **rubbing fat into flour** – air is trapped between 'breadcrumbs', e.g. shortbread, scones, shortcrust pastry

- **creaming** fat and sugar – air is beaten in to form an air in fat foam, e.g. cakes, biscuits

- **whisking** egg/sugar or egg white – air is whisked into the egg to form a high-volume foam, e.g. sponge cake, swiss roll, meringue

- **beating** batter – air is beaten in but steam is the main riser, e.g. choux pastry, batters

- **rolling and folding** pastry – air is trapped between the layers of pastry, e.g. flaky, puff, rich, yeast pastries, filo, strudel.

Carbon dioxide

- Carbon dioxide is produced in two ways:

  - **biologically** from yeast cells during the fermentation process of yeast, i.e. biological raising agents

  - **chemically** from the action of bicarbonate of soda with an acid, i.e. chemical raising agents.

Biological raising agents

- Yeasts are micro-organisms (see Revision Session 11, page 151). During the fermentation process the yeast cells feed on sugar and reproduce to produce carbon dioxide.

- Certain factors affect the action of yeast:

Temperature

- The **optimum** temperature range is 25°C–35°C.

- Above 60°C the fermentation process is destroyed.

- Below 25°C the reaction is slowed down.

- Fresh yeast can be frozen without killing the yeast: on defrosting it becomes active again.

Remember that warm temperatures are crucial! Take care to control the temperature of the liquid and the dough.

Moisture

- This is provided from milk/water/egg added to a mixture.

- Dried yeast needs to soak in a liquid to reactivate it. Remember to control the temperature of the liquid.

Food

- During the complex chain reaction of fermentation yeast cells need to feed on sugar to produce carbon dioxide.

- Sugar is added to yeast mixtures. There is also a very small amount in the flour.

Figure 3.16 *Well-risen sliced bread*

Proportion of ingredients

- High proportions of fat and sugar slow down the action of yeast, e.g. in rich yeast dough mixtures. A higher proportion of yeast to flour is needed, e.g. rum baba, Chelsea buns.

Salt

- Too much or too little salt prevents the yeast from working well.

- The correct proportion of salt controls the fermentation process and helps to develop the flavour.

Chemical raising agents

- Carbon dioxide is produced from **chemical reactions**. This can be made to happen in many recipes for baked products, e.g. cakes and scones, by the addition of chemical raising agents.

- Chemical raising agents must be measured accurately. They:

  - are used in small quantities

  - are easy to use and often already combined, e.g. in self-raising flour

  - will produce controlled amounts of carbon dioxide to aerate mixtures evenly.

- The three types of chemical raising agents are: **bicarbonate of soda**, known as sodium bicarbonate; **bicarbonate of soda and acid** (alkali and acid); **baking powder**, or baking powder in self-raising flour.

Figure 3.17 *Chemical raising agents*

Bicarbonate of soda

- This is the simplest type of chemical raising agent.

- When heated in a mixture it produces sodium carbonate (soda), steam and carbon dioxide. The carbon dioxide and steam aerate the mixture. The soda leaves a dark yellow colour (tinge) and gives a sharp alkaline taste to the mixture.

- It is used successfully in recipes which have other strong-flavoured ingredients to disguise this, e.g. parkin, chocolate cake, gingerbread.

Bicarbonate of soda plus acid

- The bicarbonate of soda reacts with the acid to produce carbon dioxide. The acid helps to neutralise the compound and prevents the taste and colour residue left when bicarbonate of soda is used on its own.

- A traditional source of acid is sour milk, which provides a dilute form of lactic acid. This is still used today in scone mixtures. The level of lactic acid cannot be measured, so it is not an accurate method.

- A more controlled method is to use cream of tartar (tartaric acid). When combined with bicarbonate of soda the reaction releases the carbon dioxide slowly, leaving a tasteless salt behind. It is used in drop scones. The ratio is two parts tartaric acid to one part sodium bicarbonate.

Baking powder

- This is a commercial mixture of bicarbonate and acid substances ready mixed in the correct proportions. A **'buffer'** is added in the form of cornflour or rice flour to absorb any moisture and prevent the reaction taking place in the storage container. Several brands of baking powder are available. Each one will have a specific formula but the amount of carbon dioxide is regulated by law.

- Baking powder is very easy and convenient to use as the raising agent is incorporated as a single ingredient.

- Baking powder is added to plain flour to produce self-raising flour, which is an easy and convenient way of incorporating pre-measured raising agents into a mixture.

COMMERCIAL BREAD PRODUCTION

- Bread is a high-volume, well-risen product. To achieve this characteristic texture three particular methods are used commercially to manufacture dough:

  - bulk fermentation process
  - activated dough development
  - Chorleywood bread process.

Bulk fermentation process

- Traditional method

- Combined dough ingredients are left to ferment for up to three hours.

- During fermentation the dough changes from a dense mass into an elastic dough.

- The time needed for this to happen depends on the amount of yeast and the temperature of the dough.

- Large-scale bakers do not have enough time or space for dough to be left this long.

Activated dough development

- A bread improver is added to the dough.

- This speeds up the process so that the dough does not have to be left for long periods of time.

Chorleywood bread process

- The most commonly used method for large-scale production.

- First developed in 1961.

- Flour treatment agents (ascorbic acid – vitamin C) are added.

- The first fermentation stage is replaced by a few minutes of intense **mechanical** mixing of the dough.

- This rapidly stretches the gluten and produces the elasticity needed to hold the expanding carbon dioxide.

- Yeast is still required to produce the carbon dioxide.

￼ Coagulation

Figure 3.18
Heating causes liquid egg yolk and white to coagulate

■ In this process protein foods change their **soluble** structure so that they become insoluble. An example of coagulation occurs when an egg is cooked in boiling water and becomes hard.

■ Coagulation can be caused by heat or strong acids. The structure of the protein is permanently changed. This is called **denaturation**, i.e. the protein coagulates or sets. Examples include:

Heat
■ High temperatures coagulate:

- eggs in baked cakes, biscuits
- gluten protein in bread dough for loaves
- whisked egg white into solid white hard meringue
- egg yolk into a dry solid for hard boiled egg
- milk proteins to form a 'skin' – lactalbumin and lactoglobulin
- meat proteins (collagen and elastin) firm and shrink slightly when grilled, fried, poached, etc.

■ Acids coagulate:

- milk by using a lactic acid starter in the cheese making process
- cream/condensed milk by using lemon juice (acetic acid) in cold sweets.

￼ Setting

■ Some food products are made by **setting** a liquid into a semi-solid or a solid, e.g. custard, jelly, mousse. There are several ways to do this, using:

- gelatine
- pectin
- starch
- egg.

Figure 3.19 *A custard tart is made from a liquid set into a semi-solid or solid*

Gelatine

- The setting agent gelatine is a protein which is extracted from parts of animals. It is available in powder or sheet form, and when dissolved in a small amount of water can be incorporated into mixtures which then set, e.g. ice cream, jellies, cheesecakes, mousse.

- It is colourless and almost tasteless. It can also be used in commercially produced yogurts, pâté and tinned cold meats, e.g. ham and tongue.

- For vegetarian products **agar** is used instead of gelatine. Agar is made from seaweed.

Pectin

- Pectin is a complex carbohydrate present in most fruits. The pectin, a gum-like substance, is released from the cell walls by crushing the fruit and cooking it at a high temperature for a short time.

- Fruit, sugar and water are boiled to form a mixture that will set and form a gel. To obtain a good, clear, well-set jam the fruit should be just ripe and combined with the correct proportion of acid and sugar. The pectin traps the water, sugar and fruit into a gel. The final percentage of sugar is 60%.

- Fruit which has a low pectin content is often used together with high-pectin-content fruit, e.g. in apple and blackberry jam.

Starch

- Starch thickens liquid by the process of **gelatinisation**. See Revision Session 6, pages 123 and 124 for information on:

  - starch-based sauces

  - methods of making sauces

  - thickness and consistency of sauces

  - the function of starch and the process of gelatinisation.

- Starch is used to:

  - thicken sauces, e.g. white sauce, custard

  - produce a gel that sets when cooled, e.g. blancmange.

Egg

- Egg contains a protein which coagulates when heated. Eggs are also used in combination with other ingredients and in some cases the egg is used to coagulate and set a liquid. For example, one medium egg will set 125 ml liquid:

  - savoury flan – 1 egg: 125 ml milk/cream

  - egg custard tart – 2 eggs: 250 ml milk.

Figure 3.20 *Egg is used to bind the mince in a burger mixture*

- During cooking the egg/milk mixture sets to form a firm, springy filling.

- Some factors will affect the coagulation characteristic of eggs, e.g:

  - A firmer set is achieved if extra egg is added to the liquid.

  - A looser set is achieved if a high proportion of sugar is added.

¶●¶ Binding

- Loose or dry ingredients are held together (**bound**) by the addition of liquid, fat or egg. The **binding** ingredient may also have other functions. For example, water is used to bind fat and flour together in pastry and bread mixtures but the water also helps to develop the gluten in flour required for the elastic stretchy dough in bread making.

- Milk forms a suspension when mixed with flour and egg in batters, e.g. pancakes and Yorkshire pudding. It also produces steam, which is the essential raising agent in Yorkshire pudding.

- Egg is used to moisten and bind ingredients together in burgers, rissoles, croquettes and savoury loaf, but when these mixtures are cooked the egg protein coagulates, holding the mixture together.

¶●¶ Bulking

- Sometimes ingredients are added to increase the **bulk** or volume of the finished product. Some of the most common ingredients are:

  - breadcrumbs – used in savoury loaf, nut roast, burgers, stuffing, steamed puddings. Breadcrumbs absorb flavours and liquid to help bind ingredients together.

  - potatoes and other vegetables – e.g. pulses – used in a variety of savoury products, e.g. meat pasties, soup, casseroles. They help to absorb flavour and liquid and add texture and volume.

  - textured vegetable protein (TVP) (see Revision Session 4, page 108). TVP can be reconstituted and added in different ratios to meat-based products. TVP needs to be combined with strong-flavoured ingredients, e.g. chilli, bolognese sauce, curry, cottage pie.

- Non-nutritive substances, e.g. **non–starch polysaccharides**, can be added to foods designed to aid weight reduction.

¶●¶ Finishing

- It is important to make food products look attractive. This can be done by decorating the surface of the product with a **glaze**:

  - **egg** – beaten egg or egg and milk is brushed over the surface of savoury products before baking. The surface bakes a shiny golden brown as the egg coagulates, e.g. vol-au-vonts, sausage rolls, pasties

  - **milk** – brushing the surface of pastry with milk produces a light matt brown colour when baked, e.g. mince pies, scones

  - **sugar** – sprinkling sugar or brushing sugar/water over sweet baked products produces a shiny, sticky, crystalline surface finish. The liquid evaporates and the sugar caramelises to give a very attractive appearance, e.g. to Eccles cakes, yeast buns, and some cakes where the sugar is combined with lemon juice.

Figure 3.21 *A glazed product*

■ Other finishes can be obtained by using:
  • honey to glaze ham and breakfast cereal
  • glaze icing on cakes and biscuits.

🍽 The effect of acids and alkalis

■ Acids and alkalis influence the changes that occur when ingredients are combined. Both acids and alkalis effect the flavour, appearance, texture and nutritional value of food products. They are found in many different foods and should be used carefully and accurately to gain the desired effect.

■ **Acids** increase the concentration of hydrogen ions when added to a water solution (pH 1–6).

■ **Alkalis** take up the hydrogen ions to produce hydroxyl ions in a solution (pH 7–14).

Acids

■ **Citric acid** (lemon juice) is used to:
  • make jam to help pectin form a gel
  • stop enzymatic browning of cut fresh fruit, e.g. dipping sliced banana in lemon juice
  • coagulate the protein caseinogen when cream/condensed milks are used in cold desserts.

■ When acids are cooked with a starch mixture they lessen the thickening power of the starch, e.g. adding lemon juice to a cornflour sauce mixture for lemon meringue pie. The lemon juice must be added after the starch has gelatinised (see Revision Session 6, page 124).

■ **Acetic acid** (vinegar) is used to:
  • preserve a wide variety of foods, e.g. chutney, piccalilli, pickled beetroot, onion, cabbage
  • marinate meat to tenderise it
  • give a sharp acidic flavour to dressings for salad and vegetables.

■ The most traditional vinegar is malt vinegar but wine vinegar, cider vinegar and vinegar flavoured with herbs are becoming popular.

■ **Ascorbic acid** (vitamin C E300) is used to act as a flour treatment agent. It helps to speed up the yeast fermentation process.

■ **Tartaric acid** (cream of tartar) is used to neutralise the reaction of the bicarbonate of soda used as a raising agent to produce carbon dioxide gas in some sweet baked products, e.g. gingerbread.

■ **Lactic acid starter** is used to coagulate milk in cheese making.

■ Acids are used in commercial food manufacture to help preserve foods. Acidic conditions prevent the growth of micro-organisms.

Alkalis

■ Alkalis are used as raising agents, e.g. bicarbonate of soda which produces carbon dioxide when heated.

Key Words

These are the key words (highlighted in the text). Tick them if you know what they mean.
Otherwise go back and check them again.

product profile	droplet	setting	setting
combination	emulsion	pectin	binding
characteristic	emulsifying agent	suspension	bulk
interaction	molecules	gelatinisation	non-starch
structure	hydrophilic	aerate	polysaccharides
colloidal structure	hydrophobic	raising agents	glaze
dispersed	surface tension	steam	finish
liquid	stable	condenses	acids
solid	lecithin	optimum	alkalis
gas	perishable	chemical reaction	
foam	curdled	buffer	
gel	stabiliser	mechanical	
immiscible	coagulate	soluble	

CHECK YOURSELF QUESTIONS

Q1 What is a colloidal structure?

Q2 Describe how an emulsion is made.

Q3 Look at the ingredients list on the label from a bottle of mayonnaise:

> INGREDIENTS: VEGETABLE OIL, WATER, PASTEURISED
> EGG & EGG YOLK, SPIRIT VINEGAR, SALT, SUGAR,
> LEMON JUICE, MUSTARD FLAVOURING , ANTIOXIDANT
> (CALCIUM DISODIUM EDTA), PAPRIKA EXTRACT.

Egg and egg yolk are included in the list. What is the function of egg yolk in the production of mayonnaise?

Q4 A tray of Yorkshire puddings is made correctly but when brought out of the oven they collapse and are wet inside. Suggest a reason for this.

Q5 Yeast is used to aerate bread products. Why then do large-scale manufacturers use the Chorleywood bread process to make bread? Give three reasons in your answer.

Q6 A cake manufacturer is going to use bicarbonate of soda as the raising agent in a range of baked cake products. What advice would you give to him or her on the use of bicarbonate of soda?

Q7 Explain the reason why, when baked in a pastry case, a mixture of 250 ml milk, 2 eggs, 25 g sugar and a pinch of nutmeg sets to form an egg custard tart.

Q8 Meat or vegetable burgers are popular food products for cooking on a barbecue. Why would egg be listed in the ingredients?

Answers are on page 229.

■ Exam questions and student's answers ■

1 Primary source food materials are processed to make secondary source foods that are used to manufacture a wide range of products.

Complete the chart by naming the Primary source food. (4 marks)

Primary Source	Secondary Source	Manufactured Product
Wheat	Flour	Pasta
Sugar Beet	Sugar	Caramel Toffees
Oats	Oatmeal	Biscuits
Milk	Cheese	Pizza

4/4

2 A manufacturer of vegetarian main meals has decided to use myco-protein (Quorn) in their products. Give three advantages for using myco-protein in vegetarian main meal products. (6 marks)

Reason 1 *Myco-protein does not have a strong flavour but it absorbs other flavours. It can be used as a replacement for meat, e.g. in chilli which contains strong spicy flavours.*

Reason 2 *Good nutrition. High in protein, low in fat.*

Reason 3 *It has a texture similar to chicken and it can be bought as mince or pieces so it is similar to meat in appearance.*

5/6

3 Fish can be coated with egg and breadcrumbs before it is cooked.

(a) What is the name given to this manufacturing process? (1 mark)

enrobing

1/1

(b) Explain two reasons for coating the fish with egg and breadcrumbs. (4 marks)

Reason 1 *Egg holds the breadcrumbs onto the fish. When it is cooked the coating gives a crisp crunchy texture.*

Reason 2 *When the egg is cooked it sets and stops fat soaking into the fish, e.g. fried fish.*

4/4

■ How to score full marks ■

1 It is easy to gain maximum marks with recall questions like these. The vast range of food products available to consumers are made from a smaller number of raw foods. Try and become familiar with some of the main food commodities which are processed for food product diversity.

2 Parts of this answer are good and show that the student has a sound understanding of alternative proteins to meat. Reason 2 gives some accurate information but the answer is not developed to explain the advantage of this when manufacturing vegetarian products.

3 The term 'enrobing' is used in the food manufacturing industry to describe coating a product with another ingredient, e.g. biscuits, fish, potato. The rest of the question is about the working characteristics of eggs. Eggs are used in many food products and you need to know and understand the main properties of eggs.

1 A food manufacturer decides to develop a range of savoury cheese flans which will be sold from a chill cabinet. The design team have a basic recipe which they will modify to produce two different cheese flans.

Basic Recipe

Pastry Case	**Filling**
200 g plain flour	250 ml milk
100 g fat	2 eggs
quarter tsp salt	75 g cheese
water to mix	salt and pepper

(a) (i) What type of fat would be suitable to make the pastry?   (1 mark)
    (ii) Give a reason for your choice.   (2 marks)
    (iii) Explain the function of fat in the preparation and cooking of pastry.   (3 marks)
    (iv) Explain the function of eggs in the preparation and cooking of the filling.   (3 marks)

(b) The test kitchen develops the basic filling recipe to extend the product range.
Give details of two fillings that would be suitable for:

    (i) vegetarians
    (ii) a 'value for money' family meal.   (12 marks)

Record your answer in the charts below.
Remember to include all the ingredients for the filling.

Vegetarian Cheese Flan	**Value for Money Family Meal**
Filling	Filling
Quantity Ingredients	Quantity Ingredients
Reasons for Choice	Reasons for Choice

(c) Vegetables can be used in several food products which can be served with a cheese flan.

Choose a vegetable that can be used in the following products.
Give a reason for your choice.

    (i) The vegetable . . . . used in coleslaw.   (1 mark)
        Reason for choice.   (2 marks)
    (ii) The vegetable . . . . used in stir-fry vegetables.   (1 mark)
        Reason for choice.   (2 marks)
    (iii) The vegetable . . . . used in Italian bread.   (1 mark)
        Reason for choice.   (2 marks)

Answers and comments are on page 222.

■ Alternative ingredients ■

Figure 4.1 *Soya beans growing as a crop*

Figure 4.2 *A variety of soya products*

¡O¡ What are alternative ingredients?

■ Food manufacturers need to consider consumer needs when designing new food products. In recent years some consumers have shown an increasing preference for food products which contain an **alternative protein** food, rather than meat.

■ Manufacturers have developed several meat-like products, which are used in commercially manufactured food products as well as being bought by consumers to add to meals made at home. The two terms used to describe this 'new' group of non-meat protein ingredients are:

- **alternative protein foods** – foods used instead of meat to provide necessary protein in the diet

- **meat analogues** – foods that can be used in the same way as meat but which are different in structure.

■ These meat-like products provide the sensory qualities of meat but they are not produced in the same way. They have some similarities but also some definite differences.

■ Meat analogues include:

- **soya bean** products, such as textured vegetable protein (**TVP**) or **tofu**

- **myco–protein** product, such as **Quorn**.

■ There are a variety of reasons why consumers may prefer to eat a wide range of protein foods. Reasons may include:

- more people are becoming **vegetarian**, eating a restricted range of animal proteins or no animal protein at all

- the nutritional profile – plant-based protein foods, e.g. soya beans, have a high protein content but are lower in fat than meat

- there is less waste from plant-based protein

- the overall production costs of plant-based protein may be cheaper than the production costs of animal protein.

Figure 4.3 *This symbol is used to indicate foods suitable for vegetarians*

Vegetarian Groups	Will not eat:	Will eat:
Lacto vegetarian	meat, fish, poultry, eggs	milk or milk products
Lacto ovo vegetarian	meat, fish, poultry	milk or milk products, eggs
Vegan	any animal protein	plant-based protein products

Table 4.1 *Types of vegetarianism*

- Meat analogues make several other important contributions to the manufacture of food products and they are used in the food industry in both meat-based and non-meat-based products as:
  - **meat extenders** – e.g. soya beans can be made into TVP, which is used to replace some of the meat content in meat products to reduce costs
  - **bulking agents** – used to bulk out the meat content and change the product profile of some food products, e.g. to reduce the fat content
  - **shelf life extenders** – added to food products which are stored in a dried or **dehydrated** state and are then reconstituted with a liquid, such as instant savoury snacks, dried soups.

Soya beans

- The soya bean is a **legume** vegetable – a pod-bearing plant from the same plant family as beans and peas.
- It has been used as a protein food in Far Eastern countries for hundreds of years.
- The USA grow 70% of the world crop with many varieties also grown in South East Asia.
- Soya beans come in several sizes and colours, such as yellow, green, black and brown.
- There is a high yield per hectare therefore soya beans are cheaper to produce than many other crops.
- Soya beans have a high protein content, a low starch content, and contain many micronutrients.
- Soya beans were originally grown as an oil seed to produce an important vegetable oil. The soya bean is now also used to make many other food products, such as TVP, soya flour, soya milk, bean curd tofu, soy sauce and the fermented soya bean paste known as miso, which is used in Japanese cooking.
- Raw beans are used to produce fresh bean sprouts for stir fry cooking.

Figure 4.4 *Soya can be used in Bolognese sauce for spaghetti*

Soya flour
- Soya flour does not contain gluten so it can be used by people on a **gluten–free** diet.
- It is combined with wheat flour in bread and cakes to produce a whiter loaf with improved keeping qualities.
- It gives a creamy texture to soups and sauces.

Figure 4.5 *Soya can be used in soya milk*

Soya milk

- Soya milk has a high nutritional value but it does not taste like cows' milk.

- It is used in cooking but may have a slightly bitter flavour unless sugar has been added.

- It is a useful product for people who suffer from lactose intolerance and who therefore cannot eat dairy products.

Other soya products

- **Soya oil** is a useful, high quality, all-purpose oil with little flavour.

- **Soya lecithin** (protein) is used as an **emulsifier** in a wide range of products, e.g. low-fat spreads.

- **Soya concentrates** are used in baby foods where the level and type of protein is important.

Soya textured vegetable protein (TVP)

The main stages of production

- Oil is extracted from hard soya beans by large industrial pressing machines.

- The remaining beans are ground into fat-free soya flour with a high protein content.

- Soya flour and water can be mixed to form a dough.

- Any desired colourings and flavourings can be added.

- Soya dough can be heated and extruded through shaped nozzles to produce a variety of shapes, e.g. chunks, flakes, grains.

- Shapes can be dried (dehydrated) and packaged with a shelf life of about a year.

Characteristics of TVP

- A spongy-textured mass which can be **extruded** to resemble the shape and texture of pieces of meat.

- The flavour is bland but flavourings can be added to give a taste of meat. A wide variety of flavoured TVP products are available.

- TVP is best cooked with distinctive-flavoured foods such as tomatoes, curry spices, garlic and herbs.

Nutritional content of TVP

- It is high in biological protein, containing all the essential amino acids. Methionine and tryptophan are sometimes added during production.

- It is fortified with vitamin B and iron.

- It is low in fat.

- It is low in cholesterol.

- It is high in dietary fibre.

Figure 4.6 *TVP burger*

Uses of TVP

- In the food industry to add bulk, i.e. as a 'meat' extender in very many types of food products, e.g. sausages, burgers, pies and mince-based products such as lasagne, chilli, cottage pie.

- In canned, dried (dehydrated), frozen, chilled ready meals and snack meals.

- Food products made at home. TVP is sold as an individual ingredient. It can be used along with meat, e.g. in a percentage of 50/50 TVP/minced beef, or to replace meat totally in a recipe. Well-flavoured stock flavours the TVP. It requires a shorter cooking time than meat.

⦿ Tofu

- Tofu is also known as soya bean curd. It is an important food in East Asia, China and Japan, where is has been used for thousands of years.

Production

- Soya beans are washed and then soaked in water at a temperature of 25°C for 5–6 hours.

- The beans are ground to a paste and sieved, to produce a milk.

- The milk is boiled then cooled to 50°C and calcium sulphate is added to set (**coagulate**) the milk.

- The solids (curds) are separated (**precipitated**) out.

- The curds are pressed to remove extra liquid and to form blocks of tofu.

Figure 4.7 *Tofu curd and tofu pieces used in a sauce*

Characteristics of tofu

- Tofu is a soft, smooth-textured, semi-solid food.

- It is available in original flavour, smoked or **marinated** forms.

- It is high in protein and low in fat.

- It has very little flavour of its own but it does absorb the flavour of the ingredients it is mixed with, e.g. marinated in dressings.

Uses of tofu

- A wide variety of food products, e.g.:
  - cut into chunks for oriental dishes, stir fry, casseroles, savoury flans, soups, salads
  - grated or chopped to make burgers and roasts.

- Silken tofu is soft and creamy and can be used in dressings, cheesecakes, sauces and dips.

Figure 4.8 *Quorn used in vegetarian moussaka*

🍽 Myco-protein, e.g. Quorn

- Myco-protein is a tiny fungus which is processed in a similar way to yogurt or cheese. It is a relatively new product but is already a popular replacement for meat.

Production

- Myco-protein is produced commercially by **fermentation** in large vats. It grows rapidly under carefully controlled conditions, e.g. temperature, food and pH. Oxygen, nitrogen, glucose and vitamins are added.

- The myco-protein is grown as fine fibres of different lengths depending on the texture required in the final meat analogue.

- It is heat-treated to stop further growth.

- The myco-protein is separated from its liquid in a centrifuge.

- Egg white is added to bind the myco-protein fibres together and to develop the texture.

- Flavours and colours are mixed into the myco-protein.

- It is then processed into shapes – cubed, sliced, shredded or minced to produce a meat analogue.

Characteristics

- After processing the texture is similar to chicken.

- It is high in protein, low in cholesterol, low in fat.

- It contains a small amount of fibre but is higher in fibre than some meats.

- It lacks flavour but absorbs surrounding flavours well and can be processed to taste like chicken, veal or ham..

- It benefits from being marinated before cooking.

- It is available as mince or pieces which have the appearance and texture of lean meat.

- It is sold fresh and stored in a chill cabinet. It can be frozen for up to three months and used straight from the freezer.

- It is unsuitable for **vegans** because it contains egg albumen.

Uses of myco-protein

- Ready meals, e.g. nuggets, fillets, sausages, burgers, grill steaks.

- Meals made at home as an alternative to meat, e.g. kebabs, pies, sauces.

CHECK YOURSELF QUESTIONS

Q1 A selection of milk chocolates filled with soft, flavoured mallow are made from the following ingredients:

INGREDIENTS

SUGAR · DRIED WHOLE MILK · COCOA BUTTER · COCOA MASS · GLUCOSE SYRUP · PECAN NUTS · BUTTEROIL · WALNUTS · DRIED EGG WHITE · DRIED SKIMMED MILK · EMULSIFIER: SOYA LECITHIN · FLAVOURINGS · COFFEE · DRIED ORANGE JUICE · COLOURS: E100, E120, E150(a), E153. E160(c) · ACIDITY REGULATOR: CITRIC ACID.

Why is soya lecithin included in the list?

Q2 A bag of six soft white bread rolls lists the following ingredients on the packet.

INGREDIENTS: Unbleached wheat flour, water, yeast, soya flour, salt, wheat protein, emulsifiers: E471, E472(e), E481; preservative: calcium propionate; flavourings, flour treatment agents: ascorbic acid (vitamin C).

Why is soya flour included in the list?

Q3 A snack meal consists of dehydrated pasta noodles, vegetables and small cubes of flavoured 'beef'. The list of ingredients includes textured vegetable protein.

NO ARTIFICIAL COLOURS OR PRESERVATIVES

NOODLES IN A BEEF & TOMATO FLAVOUR SAUCE MIX WITH TEXTURISED SOYA PIECES, DRIED VEGETABLES AND A SACHET OF TOMATO SAUCE.

Ingredients: Noodles (Wheatflour, Vegetable Oil, Salt), Wheatflour, Beef & Tomato Flavour [Flavourings, Colour (Paprika Extract)], Maltodextrin, Texturised Soya Pieces (produced from genetically modified soya flour), Vegetables (Tomatoes, Carrots, Peas). Sachet: Tomato Sauce.

Give two reasons why textured vegetable protein has been used in this product.

Q4 Which meat analogue would not be suitable for a vegan to eat?

Q5 What is meant by the term 'meat-extender'?

Q6 Packets of dried soya mince can be bought to use in food products made at home. Before use it must be rehydrated by adding one and a half cups of water to one cup of soya mince and simmered for two to three minutes. A tablespoon of oil may be added to the water to enhance the flavour. The rehydrated soya mince can then be used in the following recipe.

RISSOLES
4½ ozs Soya Mince
½ pint water
1 medium onion chopped
1 oz vegetable fat
2 tsp Marmite
Pepper
1 tbs Tomato Ketchup
1-2 level tsp mixed herbs
1 egg, beaten
2 tsp Holbrooks Worcester Sauce

Hydrate Soya Mince with water, seasoning and herbs. Cook onion in the fat until soft and just colouring. Add Soya Mince and brown over the heat until the mixture is firm. Cool a little, and bind with beaten egg. Form into rounds and coat in seasoned flour. Fry in hot oil until browned, turning once.

Give reasons for adding Marmite, tomato ketchup, herbs and Worcestershire sauce to the recipe.

What is the function of the egg?

Q7 Tofu is available in original, smoked or marinated forms. Look at the label from a packet of marinated tofu pieces.

MARINATED TOFU PIECES

Ingredients: Tofu (water, soya beans, calcium sulphate - natural coagulant), marinade (water, soya sauce, salt, fructose, citric acid, spice extracts), vegetable oil.
FREE FROM ARTIFICIAL ADDITIVES

What are the advantages of buying ready-marinated tofu pieces?

Answers are on page 231.

Manufacturing in quantity

How do manufacturers plan their production?

- Food manufacturers need to ensure that all the products they make are of a quality that will be acceptable to the consumer. Manufacturers carefully plan how the different parts of a product can be produced and put together to meet the **design specification**. The design specification includes details about the size, weight, appearance and cost of the product and the number to be made.

- The manufacturer needs to decide:

  - how **quickly** the product needs to be made

  - how **each part** of the product can be made

  - how much each part or process will **cost**

  - how each product will turn out **exactly the same**.

- Manufacturers often find it quicker, cheaper or simpler to 'buy in' **ready–prepared** ingredients or parts to make their food product. These are called **standard components**.

Figure 5.1 *Stock cubes can be used in many different recipes*

Standard components

- A standard component is a **pre-manufactured** or **ready–made ingredient**.
  For example:

  - A manufacturer of novelty cakes may choose to 'buy in' marzipan, ready to roll icing and cake decorations from another supplier.

  - A manufacturer of cook-chill spaghetti bolognese may choose to 'buy in' ready-grated parmesan cheese and ready-chopped herbs from other suppliers.

Figure 5.2 *A decorated novelty cake may use 'bought in' marzipan*

- Standard components are used to maintain **consistency of outcome** in:

  - **size**, e.g. pizza base, sponge flan case, meringue nest

  - **weight**, e.g. sachet of gelatine, canned pie filling

  - **shape**, e.g. cake decoration, pastry case

  - **flavour,** e.g. chopped herbs, stock cubes, dried vegetables

  - **ratio/proportion**, e.g. cake mix, ready-made filo pastry.

- Using standard components helps to:

  - **save time** by reducing the number of manufacturing processes

  - keep the assembly process as **simple** as possible

  - achieve consistent outcomes, i.e. each product is of the **same quality**

  - **reduce the production costs** as little or no skill is required to use them

  - **maintain stock control** because some components have a relatively long shelf life.

- When manufacturers buy in standard components from another supplier they need to check to make sure the standard components will not change the product profile.

  For example, do the standard components:

  - contain additives such as flavour enhancers or artificial colours?

  - contain additional amounts of fat, salt or sugar?

  Or will the standard components:

  - reduce the quality as the flavour, texture and colour may not be as good?

  - increase the overall cost of the product because they are expensive to buy in?

Figure 5.3 *A cook-chill ready meal may use ready-made ingredients*

QUESTION SPOTTER

Typical exam question on this topic:
  - A manufacturer is developing a savoury pasty.

What standard component(s) might the manufacturer buy in and why might this be done?

Your answer should explain what a standard component is and the reasons why a manufacturer would use standard components, e.g. reducing time, reducing cost, less labour involved, less investment in plant and machinery.

KEY WORDS

These are the key words (highlighted in the text). Tick them if you know what they mean. Otherwise go back and check them again.

ready-prepared	consistency	flavour
standard components	size	ratio
pre-manufactured	weight	proportion
ready-made	shape	stock control

CHECK YOURSELF QUESTIONS

Q1 A manufacturer of novelty celebration cakes buys in ready-made marzipan from two different suppliers. Give reasons for this.

Q2 A pie manufacturer decides to develop a new savoury product by adapting a sausage and apple roll. At first the company chooses to buy in ready-made frozen pastry because they are unable to make the necessary quantity of pastry themselves. Give three advantages and three disadvantages of buying in ready-made pastry.

Q3 A pizza manufacturer wins a contract to supply a supermarket with a range of 'traditional Italian pizzas'. To produce the order on a weekly basis the manufacturer decides to buy in some standard components. This will speed up production. List three standard components that the manufacturer could buy in. Give reasons for your choice.

Q4 A cafe prepares, cooks and serves 60 lunches every day. The menu is changed each week. Name two standard components that could be kept in stock to use in a variety of food products on the cafe menu.

Q5 An independent baker makes individual fruit pies in tin foil dishes. Canned pie filling is used instead of fresh fruit. Give reasons for this.

Answers are on page 232.

Measurement, ratio and proportion

🍽 Why *do* you need to measure ingredients?

■ It is important to be **accurate** when:

- weighing and measuring **raw materials (ingredients)** and/or **components**

- working out the ratios and proportions of raw materials and/or components

- selecting and maintaining the correct temperature for cooking or cooling food products.

■ During your course you will have used recipes which are made up of a collection of ingredients, each with a specified weight. Some recipes are known as **traditional recipes** because they can be found written out in early recipe books. These recipes are often referred to as **basic** or **foundation** recipes. These include recipes for biscuits, cakes, pastry, sauces and bread.

■ Today these foundation recipes form the basis of **recipe development** or **product formulation**. They can be adapted or amended to make food products which meet particular consumer needs or preferences, e.g. low-sugar biscuits, fruit-flavoured cakes, enriched bread dough.

🍽 Designated tolerances

■ Recipe development has to be done skilfully because ingredients can only be added or altered to a certain degree before the recipe will no longer produce the desired outcome. Examples of exceeding **designated tolerances**, i.e. not working within limits which have been proved to lead to a successful outcome are:

- a creamed cake mixture containing a large amount of sugar will probably have a crisp top and will sink in the middle

- a savoury scone mixture with too much extra cheese will not rise but will spread out and become flatter.

■ To produce good quality food products you need to:

- understand the importance of combining materials and components in appropriate ratios and proportions to make and shape particular types of food products

- be accurate in weighing and measuring to obtain the desired outcome

- understand that any changes you make to the quantities of an individual ingredient or any addition of one or more different ingredients can affect the structure, shape or texture of the finished product.

Figure 6.1 *Different types of weighing machines*

Figure 6.2 *Spoons used to measure volumes*

Figure 6.3 *Large-scale weighing of spices in the commercial food industry*

Shortbread recipe
Proportion:
150 g flour
100 g butter
Ratio: 3:2:1 (3 parts flour to 2 parts fat to 1 part sugar)
50 g sugar

¡●¡ Weight or volume

- **Measuring** of food ingredients can be done by weight or volume.

Weight

- Weighing is accurate if reliable scales are used.

- Scales may be: spring balance, digital electronic, or balances with loose weights.

- Most foods are sold and weighed in metric **measurements,** i.e. grams and kilograms.

Volume

- Liquid and some solid (granules or powder) ingredients can be measured by volume.

- Volume measuring equipment includes: measuring jugs, funnels, spoons or American cups.

- The units of measurement are fluid ounces or millilitres and litres.

Calibration

- Calibration is the term used for any activities that involve weighing and measuring. It includes any regular checks made to make sure that scales are accurate. Think what would happen in the manufacture of rich tea biscuits (e.g. when 4 tonnes of rich tea mixture are made every hour for 24 hours a day) if inaccurate weights of ingredients were used. There would be a lot of wasted biscuit mixture!

¡●¡ Combining ingredients

Proportion

- Each ingredient has a specific function in a recipe and all ingredients need to be combined in the correct proportions to produce a successful result. Ingredients combined in the same proportion each time should produce the same result.

- For example, the proportions of a foundation recipe for a cake made by the creaming method are:

  100 g self raising flour
  100 g caster sugar
  100 g butter/margarine
  2 eggs

Ratio

- The amount of one ingredient in a recipe in relationship to another ingredient in the same recipe can often be expressed as a number. This is known as the **ratio of ingredients**. The ratio of ingredients for shortbread is shown to the left.

Small-scale prototypes

- In the test kitchen of a commercial food manufacturer basic or foundation recipes will be studied and changes will be made to meet a general **design specification**. The following information will be needed:

  - the **function** of each ingredient
  - the exact ratio and proportion of ingredients
  - accurate weights and measures of ingredients
  - an accurate method of mixing and combining ingredients
  - accurate temperatures for heating or cooking.

- Sample or test recipes are made and the results recorded. Sensory tests are carried out to tell the manufacturer what changes are needed.

The production specification

- The **production specification** contains essential information about a product:

  - types of ingredients
  - ratio and proportion of ingredients
  - finished weight or volume
  - manufacturing processes
  - specific time schedules and temperatures
  - quality control procedures.

- It also contains information relating to packaging, labelling, shelf life, storage requirements and distribution.

SCALING UP

- The **small-scale** recipe has to be scaled up for mass production.

- Scaled-up quantities must be in the same proportion as the **prototype**. This can be worked out by computer.

Small-scale/prototype	Large scale
Egg Custard	**Egg Custard**
Pastry	
200 g flour	100 kg flour
50 g vegetable fat/lard	25 kg shortening
50 g margarine/butter	25 kg margarine
2–3 tablespoons water	15 kg caster sugar
pinch of salt	14 kg whole egg
	dextrose
	salt
Egg Custard Filling	
2 small eggs	10 kg whole egg
50 g caster sugar	7 kg caster sugar
500 ml milk	32 kg whole milk
2–3 drops vanilla essence	vanilla flavour
grated nutmeg	colouring
	grated nutmeg

Table 6.1 *Moving from a small-scale prototype to a large-scale manufactured product*

Figure 6.4 *Large-scale production of sauce*

⚡ A* EXTRA

Use words like 'designated criteria', 'ratio' and 'proportion' when describing the functions of ingredients and the way in which ingredients combine together to produce specific characteristics in a food product (e.g. shortness of pastry, soft crumb texture of cakes, smooth glossy and well-flavoured sauce).

AMENDMENTS REQUIRED FOR LARGE-SCALE PRODUCTION

■ To enable ingredients to be combined and processed successfully by **large-scale** production lines some adjustments may need to be made, such as:

- the use of oil instead of solid fat to increase the **plasticity** of a pastry mixture

- adding glycerine to increase the moisture of a cake mixture

- adding water to create steam as an additional raising agent

- adding dextrose to pastry to give a light brown colour when baked

- the use of additives such as emulsifiers to stabilise a mixture

- adding preservatives to increase shelf life.

■ To carry out recipe development and product formulation successfully you will need to understand:

- foundation recipes

- the **function** of ingredients

- ratio and proportion.

🍽 Biscuits

■ There are many types of biscuit, made from a variety of ingredients. The ingredients are combined using the same methods as for cake making. Two examples are given in Table 6.2.

	Proportion of Ingredients	Ratio	Method	Outcome (Designated Criteria)
Rubbed-in biscuit mixture e.g. shortbread	150 g plain flour 100 g butter 50 g caster sugar	3:2:1 Air trapped during rubbing in	Mix flour and sugar ↓ Rub in butter ↓ Knead well to form smooth paste (Sometimes the sugar is added after rubbing in)	Sweet, short, crumb texture **6.5** *Shortbread*
Creamed biscuit mixture e.g. Viennese fingers	150 g self raising flour 150 g butter/margarine 50 g caster sugar Few drops of vanilla essence	6:6:2 Air trapped during creaming	Cream fat and sugar ↓ Stir in flour and essence	Sweet, rich short texture **6.6** *Viennese fingers*

Table 6.2 *Two methods of making biscuits*

🍽 Cakes

- The main ingredients in cake making are fat, sugar, eggs, flour, a raising agent and often a liquid such as milk or water.

- All ingredients, especially the raising agent if added separately, need to be measured accurately.

- Each ingredient has a specific function in the recipe.

- Additional ingredients, e.g. flavourings, essences, chocolate, coffee, spices, dried fruit, may be added.

- There are four basic cake recipes. Using these four basic recipes, ingredients are added or combined in different ratios to produce different textures and finishes.

THE FUNCTION OF CAKE INGREDIENTS

Flour
- Forms the main structure of cakes.

- Soft flour with a lower gluten content produces a soft, even texture.

Raising agent
- Aerates the mixture to increase the volume.

Fat
- Gives colour and flavour if butter or margarine is used.

- Holds air bubbles produced from mixing or the raising agent to create texture and volume.

- Creates texture according to the ratios used, e.g.:
  - short crumb from the rubbed-in method
  - soft even texture from the creamed method

- Helps to extend shelf life.

Sugar
- Sweetens cake mixtures.

- Develops flavour, e.g. soft brown sugar, or treacle in the melted method .

- Increases the bulk of the mixture.

- When creamed with fat, sugar helps to hold air as an additional raising agent.

Eggs
- Add colour and flavour to all cakes.

- Egg **protein–albumen** holds air when whisked into a foam – this is used as a raising agent in the whisked method.

- Form an emulsion when mixed into fat, e.g. egg beaten into creamed sugar/fat.

- Egg yolk contains **lecithin** which helps to keep the emulsion stable.

Liquid
- Liquids such as milk or water produce steam, which acts as a raising agent.

- Gluten is formed when liquid mixes with protein in the flour.

Table 6.3 *Basic cake making*

Detail	Proportion of Ingredients	Ratio	Method	Outcome (Designated Criteria)
Creamed cake e.g. Victoria sandwich, small buns, Madeira cake **All in one method**	100 g self-raising flour 100 g caster sugar 100 g soft margarine or butter 2 eggs Plus 5 ml baking powder All ingredients mixed together for 2 minutes by hand, mixer or food processor.	Equal quantities Raising agent – self-raising flour (chemical)	Fat + sugar creamed together → Beaten egg added gradually → Fold in flour	Light brown sponge with fine even texture **6.8** *Victoria sandwich cake*
Whisked cake e.g. swiss roll, sponge buns, cake, gateaux, flan case	50 g caster sugar 50 g plain flour 2 eggs (100 g) No fat May go stale quickly	1:1:2 Raising agent – Air Steam from water in eggs	Whisk eggs and sugar until thick and creamy → Fold in flour	Very light sponge Even, soft moist texture **6.9** *Whisked sponge product*
Rubbed-in cake e.g. fruit loaf, cake, rock buns, raspberry buns, scones	200 g plain flour 10 ml baking powder 100 g margarine 100 g caster sugar 2 eggs 30 ml milk Flavouring ingredients 175 g dried fruit or 75 g cherries (half or less fat to flour)	8:4:4:2 cake mixture or 8:4:2:1 scone mixture Raising agent baking powder or self-raising flour (chemical)	Fat rubbed into flour → Add additional ingredients → Bind together with liquid	Well-risen product Rougher surface Open crumb texture **6.10** *Rubbed-in product*
Melted cake e.g. flapjack, parkin, gingerbread cake or biscuits	200 g plain flour 50 g soft brown sugar 100 g margarine 150 g black treacle 50 g golden syrup 125 ml milk 2 eggs 5 ml bicarbonate of soda 100 ml ground ginger 5 ml mixed spice 50 g sultanas (optional) Proportion of syrup/treacle	8:4:2:8 (sugar content is 50 g sugar + 150 g black treacle) Raising agent bicarbonate of soda – chemical Spice masks the flavour and yellow tinge caused from raising agent	Melt fat, treacle, syrup, sugar → Stir into dried ingredients → Add egg/milk	Moist and sticky Soft even texture **6.11** *Melted method product*

🍽 Pastry

- Main ingredients are flour, fat, water and a little salt.

- Richer pastries may include eggs, cheese, sugar, herbs, spices.

- There are several types of pastry, e.g. filo, strudel, hot water crust, suet, shortcrust, choux and flaky.

- Similar ingredients are combined in different ratios by different methods to produce a variety of textures and finishes. (See Table 6.4.)

THE FUNCTION OF INGREDIENTS IN PASTRY

Ingredient	Shortcrust	Flaky
Type of flour	Soft plain flour Low gluten content for short crumb texture	Strong plain flour High gluten content for crisp flaky layers Stretchy dough needed to roll and fold
Fat	Mixture of white fat and butter or margarine Coats the flour granules with fat to reduce the water mixing with gluten	Mixture of white fat and butter/margarine blended together Place in small pieces on the dough to trap air between the layers of dough
Water	Binds rubbed-in fat/flour mixture together Ease of rolling out	Combines with gluten to form stretchy elastic dough Lemon juice (citric acid) added to strengthen the gluten
Salt	Helps develop flavour	Helps develop flavour and strengthen gluten

Table 6.4 *The function of ingredients in shortcrust and flaky pastry*

- **Shortcrust and flaky pastry** contain some similar ingredients, i.e. flour, fat, water and salt. The functions of each of these ingredients is explained in Table 6.4.

- **Choux pastry** contains egg and is made in a very different way. Check yourself if the function of the ingredients is the same in choux pastry. Look at Table 6.5. Cover the right-hand side of the page, give your answer and then check your answer against the table.

Ingredient	Function
Water – boiled to 100°C	Mixes with strong flour to develop gluten Heat causes starch to gelatinise
Flour – strong, plain	Starch cooks in the boiling water, i.e. gelatinisation takes place High gluten content Gluten is strengthened by beating in the eggs Gluten stretches to hold the expanding steam and air Coagulates when baked at high temperature
Fat – butter/margarine	Flavour
Egg	Helps to hold air in the starch mixture Gives a smooth glossy finish to aid piping through a tube or nozzle

Table 6.5 *The function of ingredients in choux pastry*

Table 6.6 *Pastry chart*

	Proportion of Ingredients	Ratio Flour to Fat	Method	Outcome (Designated Criteria)
Shortcrust pastry e.g. pies, pasties, tartlets	200 g plain flour 100 g margarine/white fat pinch of salt 2 tablespoons cold water to mix	2:1 Air trapped during rubbing-in process	Rub fat into flour to look like breadcrumbs → Mix together with cold water	Short crumb, light, crisp texture **6.12** *Products made with shortcrust pastry*
Rich shortcrust pastry e.g. fruit flans and tartlets	**Wholemeal pastry** 100 g wholewheat flour 100 g white flour 200 g plain flour 100 g margarine or butter 50 g caster sugar pinch of salt 1 egg yolk about 1 tablespoon cold water to mix **Cheese pastry** exchange sugar for 150 g dry grated cheese + pinch of cayenne pepper	2:1 Air trapped during rubbing-in process	Rub fat into flour to look like breadcrumbs → Stir in sugar → Mix together with egg and water	Short crumb, sweet, light crisp texture **6.13** *Rich shortcrust pastry product*
Choux pastry e.g. eclairs, profiteroles, cream buns	75 g plain flour 25 g butter or margarine 2 eggs 125 ml water	3:1 Raising agent steam from high water content Air from beating in eggs	Heat water and melt fat in pan → Add flour → Beat in eggs	Light, well risen Crisp texture Hollow inside **6.14** *Choux pastry products*
Flaky pastry e.g. Eccles cakes, sausage rolls, vol-au-vents	200 g plain flour 150 g fat mixture – white fat with butter or margarine pinch of salt 2 teaspoons lemon juice 100 ml cold water (approx.)	4:3 Air trapped between many layers	Rub quarter of fat into flour → Mix together with liquids → Roll and fold adding a quarter of the fat each time	Many layers of crisp flakes **6.15** *Flaky pastry forms many layers in cooking*

🍽 Sauces

- There are several types of sauces, based on different ways of thickening mixtures. Some of the main ones are listed below.

- **Egg-based sauces** – egg coagulates on heating and thickens a liquid. For example, 1 egg will thicken 125 ml milk to be used to make egg custard.

- **Oil/water emulsion sauces** – used for oil and vinegar dressing. Egg yolk stabilises the emulsion used to make mayonnaise.

- **Fruit or vegetable sauces** – fruit or vegetables are cooked and puréed to make and thicken sauces, e.g. raspberry coulis, tomato sauce.

- **Starch-based sauces** – starch from wheatflour, cornflour or arrowroot is used to thicken liquids such as water and stock:
  - wheatflour is used in white sauce and flavoured to make parsley sauce
  - cornflour is used in custard and gravy
  - arrowroot is used in a glaze for fruit flans and gateaux.

Figure 6.16 *A variety of sauces*

STARCH-BASED SAUCES

- Thickening a liquid with starch is a traditional method of making sauces. The ingredients are combined by three different ways:

  - **roux method** – flour is stirred into melted fat. Liquid is then carefully added. This is the best way of making sauces when the liquid is hot

  - **all-in-one method** – uses the same ingredients and proportions as the roux method but all ingredients and cold liquid are mixed together in a pan and then brought to the boil

  - **blended method** – starch is blended with the liquid. No fat is added.

- The proportion of flour/fat to the amount of liquid used determines the consistency (thickness) of the sauce. Traditionally, three thicknesses can be achieved, to pour over, coat or bind ingredients together:

  - **pouring sauce** – white sauce flavoured, e.g. with vanilla or chocolate, and poured over sponge pudding

  - **coating sauce** – white sauce flavoured, e.g. with cheese or parsley, and used to coat fish

  - **binding sauce** – white sauce used as a base, e.g. for cheese soufflé.

QUESTION SPOTTER

Typical exam question on this topic:

▸ A manufacturer has found that a prototype of cheese sauce has the following faults:
- too runny
- raw taste
- some lumps

What might be the reasons for this?

Your answer should include the scientific principles involved in making a sauce, e.g. gelatinisation and functions of the ingredients in the sauce.

	Proportion of Ingredients	**Ratio**	**Method**	**Outcome (Designated Criteria)**
Pouring white sauce	15 g plain flour 15 g fat 250 ml milk	1:1:16	Roux or all-in-one method	Smooth well-flavoured sauce Pours freely in thin flow
Coating white sauce	25 g plain flour 25 g fat 250 ml milk	1:1:10	Roux or all-in-one method	Smooth, well-flavoured sauce Thick enough to coat the back of a spoon and not run off. It is served on cauliflower/fish etc.
Binding white sauce	50 g plain flour 50 g fat 250 ml milk	1:1:5	Roux or all-in-one method	Smooth well-flavoured sauce Very thick to hold other ingredients or bind them together, e.g. egg white in soufflé, dried ingredients in meat loaf

Table 6.7 *Types of sauces*

Gelatinisation occurs in the following way:

▸ Starch grains are mixed into a liquid. Because the starch grains do not dissolve, they are suspended in the liquid. This is called a **suspension**.

▸ Stirring helps to keep the starch grains suspended.

▸ If the liquid is not stirred, the starch grains will join together and form lumps of starch which may not cook correctly.

▸ The mixture is heated and at approximately 60°C the starch grains will absorb the liquid and swell.

▸ As heating continues the starch grains swell even more then break open and release starch, which forms a gel with the liquid. This is known as gelatinisation. The process of gelatinisation is completed at boiling point (100°C).

▸ If the gelatinised starch mixture is cooled, the gel becomes stiffer and will set to form a mould, e.g. in blancmange. This is the same for all starch-based sauces but do remember that cornflour and arrowroot are pure starch while wheatflour contains a high proportion of starch and also some protein.

FUNCTION OF STARCH-BASED SAUCE INGREDIENTS

■ When mixed with a liquid and heated, starch thickens the liquid. This is called **gelatinisation**.

■ When you are designing and making products that require a sauce you must consider anything which may affect the consistency e.g.:

• For a sweet sauce you may add sugar, but large amounts of sugar will soften the starch gel.

• For a sauce made from cornflour, e.g. for a lemon meringue pie, you need to add lemon juice, but too much acid will reduce the thickening ability of the starch.

• To extend the shelf life of a main course pasta dish with a sauce, e.g. vegetable lasagne, you may store the dish in a chill or freezer cabinet but the change in temperature may affect the consistency of the sauce when reheated. An adaptation may need to be made at the recipe development stage.

Figure 6.17 *A range of bread products*

🍽 Bread

■ The main ingredients of bread are flour, yeast, liquid and salt.

■ Additional ingredients can be added, such as sugar, fat, eggs.

• In large-scale bread production flour treatment agents, such as soya flour, ascorbic acid (vitamin C) and emulsifiers, are added.

Table 6.8 *The ingredients of bread*

White Bread – Proportion of Ingredients	Designated Criteria
450 g white strong flour 15 g fresh yeast 25 g fat 5 ml salt 5 ml caster sugar 150 ml warm water	Increased volume Well risen and golden brown Firm outside structure Maybe crisp crust Soft even open texture inside Distinct smell and taste

THE FUNCTION OF BREAD INGREDIENTS

Flour

- Use strong wheat flour with a high gluten content.

- **Gluten** is a protein which, when mixed with a liquid, forms an elastic stretchy dough.

- Gluten stretches to hold the carbon dioxide bubbles produced by yeast.

- During cooking at high temperatures the gluten **coagulates** (sets) to form the structure of the bread.

- Wholemeal flour contains bran and wheatgerm. It absorbs more water than strong white flour and the gluten is often weaker. For best results use half wholemeal flour to half white strong flour in a standard recipe.

Flour treatment agents

- These include soya flour, emulsifiers, ascorbic acid and preservatives.

- They are added to improve the keeping quality of the bread and qualities such as texture.

Yeast

- Yeast is the raising agent used in bread making.

- Three types of yeast are available for use: fresh yeast, dried yeast, easy blend yeast with vitamin C added.

Salt

- Salt is a very important ingredient, used in the ratio of 2% to the weight of the flour.

- Salt provides three functions:
  - it strengthens gluten
  - it controls the action of yeast
  - it develops flavour in the dough.

Liquid

- Usually water is used but in an enriched dough milk, or milk and water, are added for a soft texture.

- Liquid must be lukewarm (25–35°C) to provide warm conditions for yeast fermentation.

- Correct temperature is vital. If the temperature is too hot, it destroys the yeast. If too cold, it slows the action of the yeast.

Sugar

- Small amounts of sugar are added to aid the fermentation process of the yeast.

- Larger amounts of sugar are added to rich yeast doughs, e.g. for hot cross buns or savarin.

Fat

- Fat is usually added to increase the moisture content of bread. It also helps to extend the shelf life of bread products because it prevents the bread going stale too quickly.

Additional nutrients
- In the United Kingdom it is a legal requirement in bread making that for every 100 g of flour there must be a minimum content of iron, calcium and B-vitamins.

KEY WORDS

These are the key words (highlighted in the text). Tick them if you know what they mean. Otherwise go back and check them again.

accurate	volume	production
raw materials	calibration	specification
ingredient	proportion	small-scale
components	ratio	prototype
designated	design	large-scale
tolerances	specification	emulsion
weight	function	gluten
measurement		coagulate

CHECK YOURSELF QUESTIONS

Q1 What type of measuring equipment would a manufacturer choose to install on a new large-scale production line to weigh the filling for fruit pies which are being assembled on the line? Give reasons for the method the manufacturer would choose.

Q2 One recipe for curry sauce contains the following spices: ground coriander, fenugreek seeds, ground cumin, turmeric. These are fried together for two minutes. An experienced chef may guess the right amounts of the spices to add to one small batch of curry sauce. Would a manufacturer who is mass producing hundreds of cartons of cook-chill curry sauce be able to guess the amounts equally as well?

Q3 A cake manufacturing company produces chocolate sponge cakes in three factory units situated in different parts of the country. How would the cake manufacturer know that all the cakes produced were made to the same standard and that consumers would not be able to tell which factory the cakes were made in?

Q4 Work has started in a test kitchen to improve and promote a 'meal for one' pasta and cheese sauce product, which has recently become less popular than it used to be. Suggest three recipe developments that could make the pasta and cheese sauce more popular. The prototypes would be assessed by consumers carrying out sensory analysis.

Q5 A small bakery business makes a batch of white bread dough every day and uses the dough to produce loaves and bread rolls. Fresh yeast, bought in 1-kg blocks, is the amount required in each batch of bread dough. Give three reasons why the baker uses fresh yeast.

Answers are on page 233.

EXAM PRACTICE 2

Exam questions and student's answers

1 A manufacturer of Italian foods buys in processed tomato products to use as standard components. Explain why the manufacturer would use the following processed tomato products in each of the Italian foods.

(a) Tinned Italian chopped tomatoes to use for making minestrone soup. (3 marks)

Saves time preparing the tomatoes because they are washed, skinned and chopped before they go in the tin. The chopped pieces are in tomato juice. Also they add colour, flavour and liquid to the soup. Sometimes they have herbs added. ³/3

(b) Sundried tomatoes to use for making Italian focaccia bread. (3 marks)

These can be bought in packets or in jars of oil. They have a highly concentrated flavour and a rough texture. They are interesting ingredients in the soft bread. ³/3

(c) Tomato pureé to use for making pizza toppings. (3 marks)

This can be bought in tubes or tins. It is thick and concentrated with no solid bits of tomatoes in it. It is a dark red colour. It can be spread on a flat pizza base and no juice will run off. ³/3

2 A cake manufacturer is planning to make a new range of 'Tray Bake' style cakes.

Explain four pieces of information that would be needed in order to plan for production. (8 marks)

(a) *The manufacturer will need to know how many tray bake cakes have to be made, and when they need to be made to meet the orders from shops.*

(b) *The recipe and the type of ingredients.*

(c) *What equipment has the manufacturer got to make the cakes and how many workers are available to operate the equipment.*

(d) *What is the final product to be like. Is it to be sold in a tin foil tray? Or cut and wrapped to be sold as individual pieces.* ⁷/8

3 Give two advantages of each of these two types of manufacturing systems:

(a) Batch production (4 marks)

Advantage 1 - This is used to make more than one product in small quantities e.g. a bakery business makes a batch of bread buns.
Advantage 2 - The equipment can be used for more than one product, e.g. a baker may make a batch of bread dough in the large mixer and then make a batch of pastry using the same mixer. ³/4

(b) Continuous flow production   (4 marks)

Advantage 1 - This produces one specific product all the time. It means that a large quantity of a product can be made to a consistent standard to meet consumer demands.

Advantage 2 - The production line is usually controlled by computers CAM which saves time because the same task e.g. cutting out pastry lids can be done at the same time and quickly.   ⁴/₄

How to score full marks

1 These are good answers to each part of the question. They show that the student has a sound understanding of the materials that are being used as standard components. You should be able to think around the issues and apply knowledge gained from practical lessons when you have made these or similar food products.

All these processed tomato products give authentic Italian flavours, colours and textures. Some of the main advantages are that they save the manufacturer time and labour costs as they are ready prepared and give a consistent quality. They also have a longer shelf life than fresh tomatoes.

2 These are correct answers to the question, which is testing your ability to plan before making a product. Think about the things you need to know before you carry out your own project work and then think about what you would need to know if you were to make large quantities on a regular basis.

Point 2 (b) is not fully explained. It refers to the recipe and the ingredients but it does not explain what the manufacturer would need to be aware of, e.g. do they already use the ingredients? Have they got the correct storage conditions? Is the recipe part of a manufacturing specification?

3 Different manufacturing systems are an important aspect of industrial practice. Explaining what they are and the reasons for choosing a particular system are usually straight forward questions to answer.

This answer contains some good points but you need to be careful to direct your answer to what the question is asking for. In this case the question was asking for the advantages of each system, not just a description of what they are.

1 Popular biscuits for children are large gingerbread shapes. A biscuit manufacturer uses the following recipe for the gingerbread mixture.

Recipe: 350 g plain flour
5 ml (1 tsp) bicarbonate of soda
10 ml (2 tsp) ground ginger
100 g butter/margarine
175 g light brown sugar
60 ml (4 tbsp) golden syrup
1 egg beaten

(a) (i) Name a method for combining the ingredients to make the biscuits.   (1 mark)
(ii) Give a reason for your choice.   (1 mark)

(b) Explain the function of the bicarbonate of soda in this recipe.   (2 marks)

(c) Explain how the manufacturer could get the maximum number of biscuits from the rolled out biscuit mixture and avoid wastage.   (2 marks)

(d) The biscuit manufacturer has asked you to design two ideas for a large shaped gingerbread biscuit to celebrate the Olympic Games. Show how your shaped biscuit would be decorated. The manufacturer has asked you to use no more than three standard components for decoration.

(i) Use notes and sketches to describe your ideas in the spaces below.   (6 marks)

Design Idea 1   Design Idea 2

(ii) Explain in detail the reasons for your choice of three standard components used to decorate your biscuit designs.   (6 marks)

Answers and comments are on page 223.

EXAM PRACTICE 2

■ Manufacturing systems ■

🍽 Different scales of production

■ It is important for you to identify different types of manufacturing processes and the characteristics of different scales of production.

🍽 Individual one-off crafted production

■ This production system is sometimes known as **job production**. It is used when one product is made. It occurs when:

1 The product meets the design specification drawn up from a request or order from an individual customer, e.g. a novelty birthday cake, celebration cake, extra-large pizza. It will involve:

- an individual recipe, method or components being used
- more processes being carried out by hand than by equipment
- special skills from experienced staff
- an individual or unique finished product
- more time to make and finish the product
- the production of high quality goods.

2 The product is a **prototype** made in a **test kitchen** to meet a design specification from a **client** such as a major retail supermarket. It will involve:

- a prototype being presented to the client to see if it meets their requirements
- modifications being made to finalise the design
- the prototype being used as the reference product for the manufacturing specification.

⦿ Batch production

- This production system is used when more than one production is required. Small numbers of identical or similar products are made. For example, each day a small bakery may make batches of Chelsea buns, teacakes, white loaves and wholemeal bread rolls. Each day a butcher may make 20 kg of sausages.

- Some of the reasons and advantages of this system include:

  - Raw materials and components may be purchased in **bulk**.

  - Only a small number of people are involved.

  - Equipment can be used for more than one product, which reduces the 'down time' of machines.

  - Production costs are reduced as more products can be made in the same time it takes to make a '**one-off**' product.

  - Slight adaptations can be made to different **batches** to meet consumer demand or to create consumer interest. For example:
    - Different flavours can be added to batches of pork sausages to make pork and leek, pork and apple, etc.
    - Different colours and decorations can be used for icing small cakes.
    - Different flavours can be added to a sponge cake recipe, e.g. coffee, chocolate, lemon, vanilla, etc.

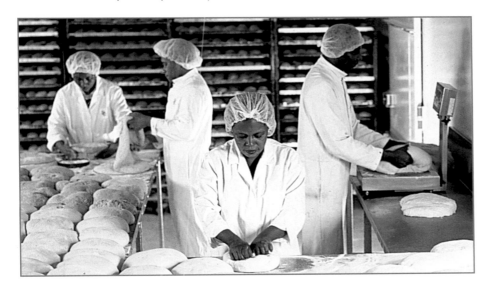

Figure 7.1 *A batch production system*

⦿ Mass production

- **Mass production** is used when large numbers of one product are required, e.g. white sliced loaves, digestive biscuits, potato crisps, tea bags. Some of the advantages of this system include:

  - The manufacturing processes are split into tasks which are sequenced into a production line.

  - At each stage, specialised equipment or line operators carry out the tasks.

- **Large-scale**, specialist equipment is used for processes such as cutting, mixing, moulding, wrapping and packaging. Sometimes special equipment is developed to do a particular process, e.g. to cut lattice pastry tops for pies; to cut and shape chicken for chicken Kiev.

- As it passes from one stage to the next the food product is assembled by means of a series of moving sections, e.g. **conveyor belt,** rollers.

- Food products are produced quickly and efficiently.

- Raw materials and components are purchased in bulk.

- There is a lower ratio of workers to the number of products produced.

- The workers do not have to be highly skilled.

- Parts or all of the production line can be **automated**.

- **Maintenance** routines and checks must be very thorough and regular to avoid a breakdown, which would be very expensive to the company in terms of lost production, i.e. 'down time'.

- The large numbers of food products produced keep the **unit cost** per item low because the production costs are spread over a large volume output.

- After a large run is finished the production line may be adjusted to make another product.

Figure 7.2 *A mass production assembly line*

🍽 Continuous-flow production

- This production system extends mass production by producing one specific product continuously, e.g. 24 hours a day, seven days a week, every year.

- It will involve:

  - the production of a product which is sold in large quantities regularly

  - high investment in equipment and machinery that is used constantly to produce high-volume food products with a low unit cost

  - wasting time if the process is stopped and started several times day.

¡●¡ Automated manufacture

- Production process systems are becoming increasingly automated. The whole production line may be fully automated or large sections of the line may be involved.

- Automated manufacture and the use of computers to control individual machines and the overall system are part of many commercial food industries. You will be expected to know the reasons for automating production and to be able to quote examples of how it is used in the food industry.

- Automated manufacture is often referred to as **CAM (computer–aided manufacture)**. Reasons and examples for using CAM include:

  - It saves time – 'multi-tasks' can be carried out **simultaneously**, e.g. cutting out several pastry pie tops at one time rather than one by one.

  - It increases speed – tasks can be repeated rapidly and **continuously** without any **variations** in quality or level of effort, e.g. cutting and weighing pieces of bread dough, rolling and forming biscuit shapes.

  - It standardises production – the process time can be repeated time after time with **accuracy** and **precision**, e.g. spraying flavouring onto potato crisps or sugar coating onto breakfast cereal.

  - It monitors the production system – by the continual **surveillance** of critical control points, e.g. **designated tolerances** for temperature, pH, moisture content, weight, thickness, etc.

  - It increases the reliability of the finished product – all stages of production are controlled, which reduces the need to 'end test' and reject substandard products, e.g. it ensures evenly baked bread products, an even coating on chocolate biscuits, etc.

  - It increases productivity – there are more products to divide into the overall cost of production. More products mean a lower **unit cost**, e.g. popular, high-demand products cost less, such as white sliced bread, biscuits, etc.

  - It reduces the need for storage – manufacturers are able to work on the 'just in time' system, i.e. nothing is made in advance and put into store. Food products are made only as an order is received. This saves floor space in ambient, chilled or frozen storage facilities. It is used, for example, in batch production of specialist bread products, certain flavours of potato crisps, etc.

  - It increases safety by reducing the need for workers to carry out hazardous tasks, e.g. cutting, mixing processes, etc. (None the less, risk assessment and all health and safety procedures still need to be observed.)

  - **Data handling** can deal with the large amount of information required to set up and monitor complex production schedules, e.g. HACCP schedule, stock control, etc.

Figure 7.3
Computer-aided manufacture

■ When you study a commercial food industry to find out about production process systems you will find that certain key words or terminology are used to describe tasks, systems or processes. Some of the terms you may need to know about are listed below:

- **assembly** – fitting/putting together the parts of a food product, e.g. base with topping for pizza, pastry case, lemon sauce with meringue for lemon meringue pie

- **combining** – joining together different raw materials or components to produce food products with specific qualities, e.g. the ingredients for cakes can be combined by the melting, rubbing-in, creaming or whisking method, each producing a different type of cake

- **enrobing** – coating a product with another ingredient to give it an outer layer, e.g. putting chocolate round a biscuit to make a chocolate bar, breadcrumbs on fish fingers or fillets, etc. Dry coatings, e.g. breadcrumbs, chopped potato skin, are put on after the product has been dipped or sprayed with a liquid

- **extrusion** – a process which forms or shapes food. A soft mixture is extruded (squeezed) under pressure through a specially shaped die into three-dimensional continuous strips. A wire cutter or blade cuts the product into smaller, even-sized pieces which are either dried or cooked, e.g. snacks, pasta, confectionery, breakfast cereals, etc.

- **filling** – (i) putting a measured amount of a sweet or savoury mixture into a case, e.g. fruit in a pastry case with a lid to make a pie, or a quiche-egg mixture into a pastry case
  (ii) injecting mixture into the centre of a food product, e.g. jam in a doughnut, cream in a choux bun

- **forming** – shaping foods by methods which make sure that all products are the same, e.g. cutters for biscuits, gauge rollers for dough, drum moulds for pattern markings on biscuits, moulds for chocolates

- **mixing** – combining materials which interact to produce a desired texture, volume, flavour, etc.

- Try to find examples of food products which have been made by these methods.

- Even though many production processes are automated today there is still a need for these systems to be managed and co-ordinated. The food industry offers career opportunities in a wide range of management, technical and operational fields. You will need to acquire some information about the management structure of a food company and about the type of work involved in each job role.

KEY WORDS

These are the key words (highlighted in the text). Tick them if you know what they mean. Otherwise go back and check them again.

'prototype'	large-scale	continuously
test kitchen	conveyor belt	variation
client	automated	accuracy
bulk	maintenance	precision
'one-off'	unit cost	surveillance
batch	CAM	designated tolerance
mass production	simultaneously	data handling

? CHECK YOURSELF QUESTIONS

Q1 Food products can be manufactured by different types of production systems. What points should a food manufacturer consider when selecting the best method of production?

Q2 A cake shop sells approximately 120 cream cakes each day. Choux pastry is used as the base for some of the cakes. Describe a product range of cakes that could be developed from a batch of choux pastry made in the bakery each day.

Q3 A biscuit manufacturer uses the mass production system to manufacture chocolate-coated digestive biscuits. The manufacturer links the mass production system to a 'just in time' method of production. What is meant by 'just in time' production? Give some reasons why the biscuit manufacturer uses this method.

Q4 'Enrobed' products have become increasingly popular. What does the term 'enrobing' mean? Give some reasons for the increased use of this production method. Include examples in your answer.

Q5 What does CAM mean and how is CAM used in the food industry?

Answers are on page 234.

Quality assurance and quality control

¦●¦ What do these terms mean?

■ It is important that all food products produced by manufacturers are safe to eat. **Consumers** expect a **consistent** standard each time they purchase the same food product so food manufacturers must aim to meet the demands and **expectations** of consumers if they are to remain in business and make a profit.

■ Quality assurance and **quality control procedures** are used in the food industry to set standards which meet consumer demands and expectations. You will need to understand these two systems, how they relate to each other and how they are applied in the food industry.

¦●¦ Quality

■ If you look '**quality**' up in a dictionary, you will find it defined as 'a degree of excellence or character'. It can be used to describe a food product or the level of service a consumer receives. For example, a lamb rogan josh with pilau rice could be described as 'good quality' because:

  • It has been designed and made so that it is very authentic to Indian cuisine.

  • There is a consistent **standard** of the lamb rogan josh each time a batch is made so consumers feel that they receive good quality service from that food company.

■ The level of excellence is determined by the expectations of the consumer. For example, the lamb rogan josh may be described as good quality because it accurately represents the combination of spices expected in an Indian curry. On the other hand, some consumers may think that it is good quality because it has a large number of lamb pieces in the sauce.

■ From this you can see that it is important for the food manufacturer to find out what consumers expect of the products they buy and then to use this information to set quality standards for the food company.

¦●¦ Quality assurance

■ The word 'assurance' means 'a level of guarantee' or 'positive declaration'. Food manufacturers use the term '**quality assurance**' to describe and **guarantee** the total standard of the food products they design, make and sell. The food manufacturer sets **criteria** or **specifications** for all the stages involved in designing and manufacturing a food product. This makes sure that the food product is manufactured to agreed standards, with consistent outcomes guaranteed.

■ The **quality assurance system** will be a series of planned criteria or specifications to cover:

- sourcing of suppliers to provide good quality raw materials or components

- consistent and reliable supplies of raw ingredients and components

- recipe formulation and development to satisfy consumer **preference**

- manufacturing processes and equipment

- methods and types of production

- process control and feedback systems

- suitable food packaging

- accurate food labelling and instructions for the consumer

- storage, temperature and environment control

- distribution and retail (sales)

- consumer aftersales service.

■ By making sure that standards are met in these areas, the manufacturer knows that the consumer will be supplied with food products that are safe to eat and of a reliable standard every time.

▥ Quality control

■ You will recall that quality is defined as 'a degree of excellence'. The term 'control' means a check or restraint.

■ In the food industry quality control is part of the quality assurance system. It involves checking the standards of a food product as it is being designed and made. Quality control checks make sure that the product meets both the design specification and the manufacturing specification.

■ If you refer to Revision Session 10, page 145, you will learn about the control checks that are identified and monitored using the HACCP system of risk assessment. You will learn that if things go wrong at certain stages of production, the food product may not be safe to eat. These stages are known as critical control points. At these points extreme care must be taken to control the standards of production, i.e. they are critical if a safe, reliable outcome is to be achieved.

Figure 8.1 *Quality control includes temperature checks*

■ Quality control checks may include:

- measurement checks of weight or volume
- temperature checks of tolerance limits, e.g. 0–5°C for a chill cabinet
- sensor detectors for finding metal or foreign bodies
- random sampling for microbacterial checks.

▥ Total quality management (TQM)

■ **TQM** is an extension of quality assurance. It is used by manufacturers who aim for, or pledge to make, continuous improvement in their working practice, i.e. they are always trying to make things better.

Figure 8.2 *A process model for quality assurance*

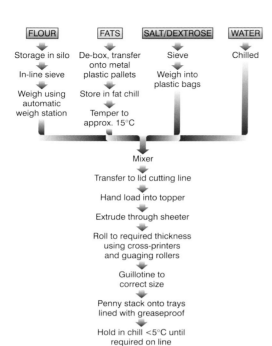

FLOUR
↓
Storage in silo
↓
In-line sieve
↓
Weigh using
automatic
weigh station

FATS
↓
De-box, transfer
onto metal
plastic pallets
↓
Store in fat chill
↓
Temper to
approx. 15°C

SALT/DEXTROSE
↓
Sieve
↓
Weigh into
plastic bags

WATER
↓
Chilled

Mixer
↓
Transfer to lid cutting line
↓
Hand load into topper
↓
Extrude through sheeter
↓
Roll to required thickness
using cross-printers
and guaging rollers
↓
Guillotine to
correct size
↓
Penny stack onto trays
lined with greaseproof
↓
Hold in chill <5°C until
required on line
maximum 24 hours

Figure 8.3 *Production stages in making pastry pie lids*

■ Some food industries now follow established guidelines and standards for delivering quality products and services. These guidelines are set out in British Standard Number BS5750 and also as a European Standard ISO9000 for quality management systems.

■ A food company can gain the BS5750 accreditation certificate by drawing up a policy document which outlines procedures such as:

- contracts and transactions with all suppliers
- contracts and transactions with all clients
- purchase and maintenance routines for equipment and large-scale machinery
- risk assessment documentation to include HACCP
- customer relations and a complaints procedure
- the appraisal and training of the workforce.

KEY WORDS

These are the key words (highlighted in the text). Tick them if you know what they mean. Otherwise go back and check them again.

consumer
consistent
expectation
quality control
procedure
quality
standard

guarantee
quality assurance
criteria
specification
preference
total quality management

CHECK YOURSELF QUESTIONS

Q1 What could a food manufacturer do within a quality assurance system to make sure that only the best and freshest raw materials and components are used?

Q2 How would a research and development team apply quality assurance procedures to the development and formulation of a new food product?

Q3 Why do some food companies use systems such as TQM (total quality management) or British Standard 5750?

Q4 What is meant by the terms quality assurance and quality control?

Answers are on page 236.

Food production systems

🍽 What is a production system?

- Food manufacturers plan carefully the way food products are manufactured in large quantities. This is known as a **production system**. It is a series of interconnected events which work together to manufacture food products efficiently, safely and consistently. To understand industrial food production you will need to know what a system is and to understand how systems are set up and work.

- A system is a **sequence** of activities that work together to make a food product.

- A system has three parts: **input**; **process**; **output**.

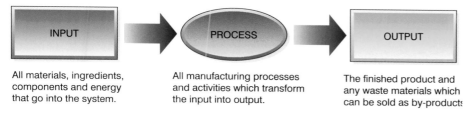

All materials, ingredients, components and energy that go into the system.

All manufacturing processes and activities which transform the input into output.

The finished product and any waste materials which can be sold as by-products

Figure 9.1 *A food production system*

- A system must be **monitored** closely if the processes are to run efficiently and continuously. This is known as **process control**. Process control monitors the system and information is fed back to the controllers of the system to make sure that all processes are being carried out correctly. This is called **feedback**. Process control is sometimes referred to as a **closed loop system**.

- **Continuous monitoring** provides feedback on the performance of all the stages of production. Monitoring, receiving feedback and acting on the information received all increase the efficiency of production.

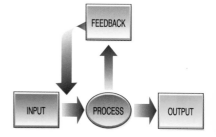

Figure 9.2 *A closed loop system*

- For example, this system will prevent:

  - raw materials and components from being wasted

  - time being wasted while production lines are temporarily closed down to find and fix manufacturing faults

  - faults occurring which cause inconsistency of results in the final product.

- See also Session 7, pages 40 and 41.

- A systems approach is a useful way of managing the complex production of a food product. To set up a new system or to review an existing system a **systems analysis** needs to be undertaken. This involves looking at each part or process and identifying the sequence and connection between them. A **logical order of events** can then be established.

- An analysis of complex situations may lead to the system being broken down into a series of smaller **sub-systems**. The sub-systems then operate alongside the main system, linking in at the appropriate stage of production.

- The total system needs to be carefully monitored and controlled so that information from one part of the complex system is received as feedback in another part. This makes sure that the system runs smoothly.

Figure 9.3 *The use of three sub-systems to make a quiche*

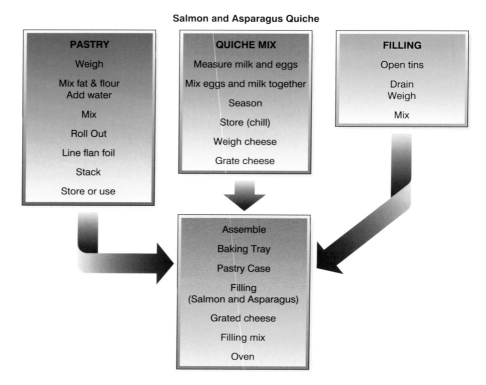

Salmon and Asparagus Quiche

PASTRY	QUICHE MIX	FILLING
Weigh	Measure milk and eggs	Open tins
Mix fat & flour	Mix eggs and milk together	Drain
Add water	Season	Weigh
Mix	Store (chill)	Mix
Roll Out	Weigh cheese	
Line flan foil	Grate cheese	
Stack		
Store or use		

Assemble

Baking Tray

Pastry Case

Filling
(Salmon and Asparagus)

Grated cheese

Filling mix

Oven

- A **flow diagram** is often used to represent the many stages of a food production system and the interconnection of sub-systems. The flow diagram must indicate clearly:

  - the different stages of production in correct sequence

  - a logical order which makes economical use of energy and labour

  - connections with sub-systems

  - control points and feedback systems.

🍽 Process control methods

- You can now understand that control and feedback are important in food production systems. Many manufacturers use computers to operate a control and feedback system. **Data logging systems**, which you may have used in developing your own food products, are part of this control and feedback system process.

- Computers monitor aspects such as:
  - weight, e.g. of an individual ingredient, component or finished product
  - temperature at various stages, e.g. storage, mixing, baking, chilling, freezing
  - moisture content, e.g. during storage of dry ingredients, mixing, heat processing, etc.
  - the pH level – the pH condition of ingredients (i.e. acid, neutral or alkaline) is important to the shelf life and processing of some products
  - flow rates, e.g. the speed at which ingredients are added to the product, such as chocolate coating on biscuits, flavourings sprayed onto potato crisps, etc.
  - the metal detection of pieces of metal that may enter the food product, such as nuts or bolts from pieces of equipment
  - the rate of production, e.g. the speed of a biscuit production line through a tunnel oven or bread through a proving oven
  - the quantity of products, e.g. the total number produced in a specified time, counting the number of products into a packaging system.
- This is known as **computer–integrated manufacture** (CIM).
- The information in the computerised control system is collected by electronic sensors and relayed to the main computer system. Appropriate action is taken in response to the feedback received. Electronic devices include:
  - moisture sensors
  - mechanical switches
  - transducers
  - temperature sensors in temperature probes
  - thermostats
  - weight/volume sensors.
- In the last few years the use of computerised control systems has become more and more sophisticated, with recent developments assisting in the control and monitoring of:
  - the sorting and grading of raw materials, e.g. potatoes for crisps
  - units of weight for a product that is to be packaged
  - colour and shades, e.g. of baked products, breakfast cereals, etc.
  - shapes and decorations, e.g. the position of toppings on cakes and pizzas through the use of digitised visual images stored in the computer
  - the bacterial content of products
  - seals on food packaging, e.g. packets of crisps.

You may find other examples of computerised control systems in the particular commercial food system that you study. You must remember, however, that in some instances control checks are made by the workers operating the production line. They may carry out processes which have not yet been automated, e.g. a visual check of peeled potatoes for blemishes before they are sliced to make potato crisps. The workers may also carry out spot checks at a variety of stages along the production line.

KEY WORDS

These are the key words (highlighted in the text). Tick them if you know what they mean. Otherwise go back and check them again.

sequence	feedback	sub-system
input	closed loop system	flow diagram
process	continuous	computer integrated
output	monitoring	manufacture
monitor	systems analysis	
process control	complex	

? CHECK YOURSELF QUESTIONS

Q1 (i) Temperature control is a critical measurement in food production. With reference to a product flow diagram or to the production system for a product you have designed and made yourself, give three different examples of production stages with a temperature control point.

(ii) Describe how the temperature would be monitored.

Q2 Computer-integrated systems can be used for monitoring the amount of raw materials, components or finished products a company has in stock. This is often called stock control. List some of the advantages of stock control.

Q2 The stages in a food production system can be divided into input, process and output. Explain these three stages by referring to the production of a fruit pie.

Q2 During manufacture a food product moves along a conveyor belt. Products that are overcooked or undercooked are diverted to a waste bin by a control gate.

(i) Draw a flow diagram to describe the system, using the six stages listed below in the correct order:
• chill unit
• packaging unit
• waste bin
• weighing/forming unit
• tunnel oven
• control gate.

(ii) Show how feedback will be used to form a closed loop system.

Answers are on page 236.

REVISION SESSION 10 ▪ Risk assessment ▪

🍽️ What is risk assessment?

- There are many regulations for the food industry, which set out basic requirements to make sure that our food is safe to eat. One of the new requirements of the new Food Safety (General Food Hygiene) Regulations 1995 establishes **risk assessment** as the starting point of food manufacturing management's responsibility for food hygiene and safety standards.

- Risk assessment means making an assessment of any risk to a food product during its production. This involves working out what chances there are of a food product being damaged or made incorrectly.

- Useful definitions include:

  - **risk** – the likelihood of occurrence, i.e. what could happen and when it could happen

  - **assessment** – to form an estimate of something.

- Remember that risk assessment is:

  - thinking about what could happen

  - planning how to prevent it from happening.

🍽️ Hazard analysis and critical control points

- The system of risk assessment in the food industry is referred to as the **hazard analysis** and **critical control point system (HACCP)**.

- This approach is used to **analyse** what *could* go wrong in the production of food and to set up **procedures** and controls to *avoid* any potential problems. HACCP replaced earlier systems which relied heavily on '**end testing**', i.e. inspecting the finished product and rejecting any faulty or damaged ones. Although 'end testing' is a form of control method, it does waste a lot of money, time and ingredients if manufacturers have made food products that they can't sell. It could also mean complaints from customers or local health inspectors if faulty goods slip through the net.

WHAT IS HACCP?
- HACCP is:

  - a method of food safety management

  - an important risk assessment method

  - a procedure whereby the whole food company makes a commitment to quality production.

- HACCP may be part of **TQM (total quality management)**, an important management system used by some companies.

- HACCP involves:
  - identifying stages where hazards may occur
  - assessing the degree of risk involved
  - deciding on stages which are critical to food safety
  - setting standards for each stage and maintaining them
  - checking the critical points
  - taking action to maintain safe limits.
- Some important terms to understand include:
  - hazard – anything that can cause harm to the consumer
  - critical control point (CCP) – a stage where a food safety hazard can be prevented, eliminated or reduced to an acceptable level
  - **control** – setting standards for a system and maintaining them.
- See also Session 7, page 41.

WHY DO WE NEED HACCP?
- Hazards may be:
  - **microbiological**, e.g. salmonella in chicken, listeria in soft cheese. (To discover the conditions for the growth of pathogenic micro-organisms that can cause food poisoning, refer to Revision Session 11.)
  - **physical**, e.g.:
    – glass from bottles, jars, light fixtures
    – metal from machinery, equipment, packaging
    – wood from pallets, boxes
    – insects from plants, open windows
    – personal items, e.g. jewellery, hair, cigarettes
    – packaging faults, e.g. bags not sealed.
  - **chemical**, e.g. agricultural chemicals, cleaning chemicals, paint, oil.
- Hazards can occur at any stage in the food production chain from field to factory to shop to table.

HOW IS HACCP APPLIED IN THE FOOD INDUSTRY?
- A team of people is needed to organise the HACCP system. They will collect and collate data and then act on the information they have gathered. The team needs to:
  - understand food processing
  - be trained in food hygiene
  - have knowledge of microbiology.
- Such a team would usually involve:
  - up to six people

Figure 10.1 *The HACCP team*

- a range of staff, i.e.
  - quality assurance staff
  - an engineer
  - a microbiologist
  - production staff
  - and maybe an external consultant on HACCP.

■ To understand fully how HACCP is applied in the food industry you will need to know the various stages involved in HACCP.

THE STAGES OF HACCP

■ There are seven basic principles in the HACCP system:

1 Hazard analysis

■ Draw up a flow chart of the food production process, from raw materials, processing and storage to consumer use.

■ Identify any potential hazards.

■ Describe ways and options for control of the hazards.

2 Critical control points (CCPs)

■ Identify the critical control points using a **decision tree** (see Figure 10.2).

■ At critical control points hazards must be prevented by the manufacturer taking special care to set up **preventive measures**.

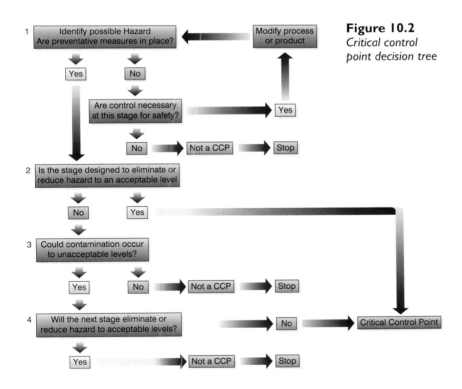

Figure 10.2
Critical control point decision tree

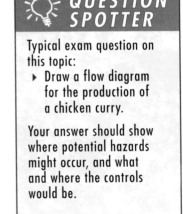

:¤: QUESTION
    SPOTTER

Typical exam question on this topic:
▶ Draw a flow diagram for the production of a chicken curry.

Your answer should show where potential hazards might occur, and what and where the controls would be.

■ CCPs could involve:

• Control of temperature during storing, processing or the storage of the final product to prevent growth of micro-organisms.

- Control of temperature during cooking to give even cooked results.

- Control of time at specific stages, e.g. the proving of bread, the cooking time of products or the setting of chilled desserts.

- Control of weights to give consistent quantities, e.g. raw ingredients, or of portion control to give even-sized products.

- Safety from contamination by unwanted materials, e.g. metal, wood, glass, jewellery.

3 Critical limits

■ To control each CCP target levels need to be set, e.g. the correct temperature range for a cook-chill cabinet is 0–5°C.

■ These targets or **tolerance** levels are called critical limits.

4 Monitoring

■ A monitoring system must be set up for each CCP. This involves:

- measuring or observing stages of the production process

- making sure that the critical limits of each CCP are being met, i.e. everything is under control.

■ Examples of monitoring activities could include:

- digital temperature displays on refrigerator cabinets

- metal detectors on production lines

- pest control units

- wiping temperature probes before and after use

- regular checks by staff, e.g. taking temperature readings every hour.

■ Some information or data is monitored all the time, e.g. temperature or weight. This is known as **continuous monitoring**. All checks must be carefully recorded: time, date, results and the name of the checker.

5 Corrective action

■ If a problem occurs and critical limits are exceeded, e.g. the temperature of a refrigerator rises to 22°C, all staff must know what action to take.

■ Solving the problem is known as **corrective action**. It could include:

- repairing a refrigerator

- training staff in food hygiene

- replacing a machinery part

- sieving an ingredient to detect any unwanted bits.

6 Record keeping

■ Full details of the raw materials, components, the processing and the final product are required. Additional details could include:

- the HACCP plan

- staff training

Figure 10.3 *Using a temperature probe*

- audit details

- temperature logs of cold storage

- cleaning schedules

- maintenance records

- delivery schedules.

■ Records must be made and kept. Computerised record keeping is often used.

7 Verification

■ Set up a system, tests or procedures to check if the HACCP plan is working effectively.

■ Review or modify the HACCP plan according to the findings.

APPLYING HACCP IN THE FOOD INDUSTRY

■ At first the HACCP procedure seems quite complex but it is a straightforward series of events which eliminate health risks.

■ Some points to remember about HACCP include:

- HACCP can be used by any food industry.

- HACCP can be applied to the total production process or to one part of the process.

- The HACCP team will draw a **flow diagram** to show the whole process.

- During the identification of hazards the team may identify all hazards or only one category, e.g. physical, microbiological or chemical.

- If too many hazards are identified, the total production process needs to be redesigned.

- All staff must know and understand the HACCP system that has been put in place.

- Training is essential for all staff.

KEY WORDS

These are the key words (highlighted in the text). Tick them if you know what they mean. Otherwise go back and check them again.

risk assessment	control	corrective action
risk	microbiological	record keeping
hazard analysis	decision tree	verification
critical control point	preventive measure	flow diagram
HACCP	tolerance	
procedure	critical limits	
end testing	monitoring	
TQM (total quality management)	continuous monitoring	

CHECK YOURSELF QUESTIONS

Q1 Critical control points can occur at any stage in the food production process.

(i) What potential hazards could there be in the purchase, delivery and storage of raw materials?

(ii) What control checks would need to be put in place to ensure that raw materials are safe?

Q2 The manufacture of cook-chill chicken curry has the following instructions printed on the label.

Conventional Oven: Remove packaging and pierce film lid. Place directly onto oven shelf in a preheated oven at 190°C, 375°F, Gas Mark 5 for 25 minutes.

Why does the consumer need this information?

Q3 A bread manufacturer receives a complaint from a customer who has found a piece of metal in a loaf of bread. What could be the cause of this?

Q4 HACCP analysis is carried out by a small team. Which personnel would make up the team? Give a reason for your answer.

Q5 One hazard may be contamination of food products caused by the poor personal hygiene standards of food handlers. What control measures could be applied to ensure and maintain high standards of personnel hygiene?

Answers are on page 238.

EXAM PRACTICE 3

Exam questions and student's answers

1 In food production there are usually three stages in the system.

What do the following refer to in the production of a bread product? **(6 marks)**

Give an example in your answer.

INPUT	PROCESS	OUTPUT
These are the raw ingredients that are needed including the wheat grain that has to be turned into flour.	This is the step when the input is turned into the output. It normally includes a mechanical process.	This is the finished product so it will be the actual bread product.
EXAMPLE	EXAMPLE	EXAMPLE
Flour, yeast	Mixing and kneading dough	Sliced bread, bread buns

6/6

2 During the setting up of a food production system it is vital for the manufacturer to test the product at different stages to ensure and maintain quality.

(a) Explain the terms:
   (i) quality assurance
   (ii) quality control **(4 marks)**

Quality assurance is when the quality of a food product is assured by the manufacturer by looking at the quality of all the steps in the production process.
Quality control is the testing of a product as it is made. 3/4

(b) Giving examples, explain the term quality control in relation to a lasagne product. **(5 marks)**

In the case of a lasagne several things would have been checked. These are the quality of the ingredients, the weighing out, the size of the pieces of vegetables, the type and thickness of the sheets of lasagne and the consistency of the sauce. There would be sensory evaluation of the different parts of the product and the final lasagne. 5/5

How to score full marks

1 The question was obviously read carefully because the student has given examples in the answer as she was asked to do.

The box which asks for information about process could have had more information in it, e.g. 'In bread production the process could be milling the wheat, mixing the ingredients together or kneading the dough'. However, the student included this information in the example box and therefore was still given credit.

2 (a) In part (a) the student has shown an understanding of both quality control and assurance but has not given a clear explanation.

(b) In part (b) the answer about the quality control in a lasagne product is good and the student has given at least five different points.

1 HACCP is a standard procedure used in the food industry.

(a) (i) What does HACCP stand for? (2 marks)

(ii) How is it used in the food industry? (2 marks)

2 The flow chart below shows the system which a manufacturer might use to produce a frozen chicken pie.

On the chart show:

(a) Possible hazards that might occur during the production of the pie.

(b) The controls which can be used to prevent these.

(c) Quality control checks which will be carried out during production. (10 marks)

One example is already shown in bold type.

Stages in the production of a frozen chicken pie	Possible Hazards	Controls Used	Quality Control Checks
Collect raw ingredients	**Cross contamination Temperature control**	**Separate storage areas for dry and perishable goods**	**Reputed supplier, visits to supplier, quality standards**
Weigh ingredients			
Mix ingredients for pastry			
Cook chicken			
Make white sauce for chicken filling			
Combine sauce with chicken and cool			
Roll out pastry			
Add filling			
Bake			
Freeze			
Store			

Answers and comments are on pages 223–4.

Food safety and food spoilage

🍽 What causes foods to go bad?

- Fresh foods cannot be stored for very long before changes occur which affect the texture, flavour or colour of the food. For example, it is easy to see the changes in the colour of a banana as it ripens from green to yellow. Eventually it will turn black. Some changes in foods are not as noticeable as this but within short periods of time foods can often undergo changes which make them unfit to eat. This is known as **food spoilage**. It is important for you to know the causes of these changes.

- Many of the changes in food are caused by **micro-organisms** and **enzymes** and you will need to know about their characteristics.

🍽 Changes caused by micro-organisms

- There are three types of micro-organisms:

  - **yeasts**

  - **bacteria**

  - **moulds**.

- Micro-organisms can perform useful functions in the production of food products such as cheese, yogurt, bread, beer and Quorn, but they can also be harmful and cause food spoilage.

- Foods that are unfit to eat are described as **contaminated,** which means that they are infected with micro-organisms and therefore are not safe to eat.

- Some micro-organisms, known as **pathogenic bacteria**, can cause food poisoning, resulting in serious illness or even death.

- Micro-organisms are usually only visible under a microscope. They are found in water, soil, air and rubbish and on animals, humans and equipment. They can be transferred to food by poor hygiene practices, e.g. by humans, flies and rodents. Some foods may already contain micro-organisms, e.g. salmonella in chicken.

YEASTS

- Yeasts are:

  - found in the air, in soil and on the skin of some fruits, e.g. grapes

  - microscopic single-celled fungi which reproduce by budding, i.e. the yeast cell divides into two cells

  - anaerobic, i.e. the cells do not need oxygen to reproduce

  - active in warm, moist conditions with food for growth and reproduction. The optimum temperature is 25–30°C

  - inactive in very cold conditions, i.e. the yeast cells are dormant and will not grow or reproduce

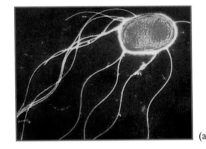
(a)

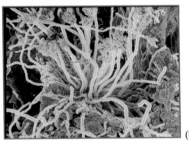
(b)

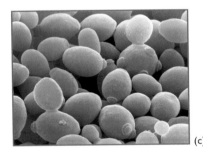
(c)

Figure 11.1 *Bacteria (a), moulds (b) and yeasts (c)*

- destroyed at temperatures of 100°C or over

- able to break down sugars to produce alcohol (ethanol) and carbon dioxide gas. This process is known as **fermentation** and is used to make bread, alcoholic drinks and yeast extract spreads

- responsible for food spoilage in high-sugar foods such as fruit, jam and fruit yogurts.

MOULDS
- Moulds are:

  - fungi which grow as thread-like filaments in food. They can be black, white or blue

  - visible as minute plants which grow on many types of food. The food may be dry, moist, acid, alkaline, or have salt or sugar concentrations

  - able to reproduce by producing spores which travel in the air. The spores settle, germinate and multiply into new growths

  - very productive in moist conditions at 20–30°C. They grow slowly in dry, cold conditions

  - able to produce heat-resistant spores, e.g. clostridium botulism. Very high temperatures are required to destroy these spores, e.g. above 100°C

  - harmful when they produce **mycotoxins**, which are poisonous substances

  - used in food manufacture to produce specific flavours and textures, e.g. the manufacture of blue-veined cheeses such as Danish Blue, Gorgonzola, Stilton. The moulds are injected into the cheese and left to ripen during the maturing stage of cheese production. These moulds are considered harmless.

BACTERIA
- Bacteria are:

  - single-celled organisms found everywhere in air, water, soil and on animals and people

  - microscopic, i.e. they can only be seen under a microscope

  - classified, and those which cause food poisoning are known as pathogenic bacteria, e.g. *Escherichia coli* (*E. coli*) which is infectious and very harmful

  - able to reproduce very rapidly by dividing in two and again in two in minutes – often as quickly as 10–20 minutes. From one bacterium a whole colony of bacteria can develop within 12 hours

  - active in optimum conditions of warmth, moisture, food and oxygen

  - able to grow rapidly in neutral pH conditions (6.8–7.2) Most pathogenic bacteria are unable to grow in acid or alkaline conditions, e.g. beetroot preserved in vinegar

Figure 11.2 *Mould on a slice of bread*

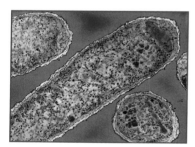

Figure 11.3 *E. coli bacteria seen under a microscope*

- able to form spores that can lie dormant but will germinate when the right conditions occur

- often undetected because the food looks, tastes and smells as it should but the presence of bacteria makes it potentially very dangerous to eat

- most active in the wide temperature range of 5–65°C. The optimum temperature is 37°C, i.e. the human body temperature. During storage, preparation and cooking processes it is very important that food is not kept in this temperature zone for longer than necessary

- used in food manufacture, e.g. in making cheese and yogurt. The lactic acid bacteria cultures used in these products are not harmful.

> Some key terminology you may come across includes:
> **aerobic** – requires oxygen to grow
> **anaerobic** – does not require oxygen to grow
> **binary fission** – reproduces by means of a cell dividing in two again and again.

🍽 Changes caused by enzymes

- Enzymes also cause changes in food. Enzymes are:

  - protein molecules that control chemical reactions in food

  - active at the optimum temperature of 35–50°C

  - inactive at high temperatures

  - most active in neutral conditions around pH7

  - sometimes inactive in acid conditions.

- Enzymes are used in a wide range of manufacturing processes, e.g.:

  - bread and brewing, where enzymes that are present in yeast are active in the fermentation process

  - cheese, where enzymes speed up the ripening stage.

- Enzymes can cause undesirable changes in foods which make them unsightly. This is called 'browning' and is caused by the action of an enzyme called polyphenol oxide in the presence of oxygen. Enzymatic browning can be reduced by:

  - high temperatures, e.g. blanching cut vegetables in boiling water

  - acidic conditions, e.g. dipping cut fruit into lemon juice

  - other methods which are used in commercial food processing.

Figure 11.4 *Enzymatic reaction – the surface of cut fruit goes brown*

🍽 Food risk categories

- Food can be infected with micro-organisms at any stage of its production, from the source of the raw ingredients through to when being served and eaten by the consumer. Everyone involved in the food chain, e.g. farmer, manufacturer, retailer and consumer, must make sure that the food is safe to eat.

- You have learnt that micro-organisms multiply rapidly in conditions which, when combined, offer:

  - warmth
  - moisture
  - food
  - time.

■ Foods can be put into three **risk categories** against micro-organism growth. These three categories are:

1 High-risk foods

■ These are foods which have a high protein and moisture content. They provide ideal conditions for micro-organic growth, e.g.:

- raw meat, fish
- dairy products
- cooked meat and poultry
- shellfish and seafood
- gravies, sauces, stocks, soups and stews
- egg products, e.g. raw egg in chilled desserts and mayonnaise
- cooked rice
- protein-based baby foods.

2 Medium-risk foods

■ These include:

- dried or frozen products containing fish, meat, eggs, vegetables, cereals or dairy ingredients
- fresh sandwiches and meat pies
- fat-based products.

3 Low-risk foods

■ These include:

- high acid-content foods, e.g. pickles and chutney, fruit juice
- high sugar-content foods, e.g. marmalades, jams, fruit packed in syrup
- sugar-based confectionery, e.g. sweets, icing
- unprocessed raw vegetables, e.g. potatoes, carrot
- edible oils and fats.

▌◉▐ Food poisoning

■ Food poisoning is an illness caused by eating contaminated food or water. Thousands of cases of food poisoning occur each year. Food poisoning occurs if food is contaminated by:

- harmful bacteria or other micro-organisms
- **toxic** chemical contamination.

■ It can also develop following an adverse reaction to certain **proteins** or other naturally occurring **constituents** in the food.

■ However, most food poisoning is caused by bacterial contamination which occurs because of some of the following reasons:

- storage of high-risk foods at room temperature

Figure 11.5 *Raw meat is a high-risk food*

Figure 11.6 *Sandwiches are a medium-risk food*

Figure 11.7 *Chutney is a low-risk food*

- poor hygiene routine at any stage of production and serving

- cross-contamination between raw foods and cooked foods, e.g. raw meat to cooked ham

- poor personal hygiene standards of food handlers

- poor preparation and cooking routines, such as:
  - not thawing foods thoroughly
  - not re-heating foods to the correct temperature for long enough
  - not allowing foods to cool before putting them in chill cabinets or freezers
  - keeping 'hot' foods below 63°C
  - under-cooking 'high-risk' foods, e.g. shellfish
  - preparing food too far in advance
  - leaving food on display at room temperature for longer than the maximum safe period of four hours.

■ Some people are more susceptible to food poisoning than others. Extra care must be taken with food products manufactured for babies, pregnant women, elderly people or anyone else with a low resistance to infection.

■ Many types of bacteria cause food poisoning and the incubation periods, symptoms and methods of control vary accordingly. Some of the most common types of food poisoning are listed in Table 11.1 on page 156.

CROSS-CONTAMINATION

■ During food processing micro-organisms can transfer from raw to cooked foods, causing infection. This is known as **cross-contamination**.

- To prevent cross-contamination you must avoid:

- allowing raw and cooked foods to touch each other

- allowing the blood and juices of raw foods to drip onto cooked foods, e.g. during storage in refrigerators

- allowing bacteria to be transferred during handling or preparation, e.g. from hands, work surfaces, equipment.

Bacteria	Symptoms	Period of Incubation and Illness	Found in	Control
Salmonella • Most common form of food poisoning in UK • Optimum temperature for growth 7–45°C • Does not form spores	• High fever, diarrhoea, vomiting, headache, abdominal pains • Frequent but rarely proves fatal	Incubation – 12–36 hours Duration of illness – 1–7 days	• The gut of most animals and birds, particularly chicken • Raw meat, poultry, eggs and raw egg products, sea food, dairy products e.g. cream • Cross contamination from infected food handlers and pets	• Destroyed by heating to temperatures above 70°C • Make sure food is cooked through to high temperature in the centre e.g. foods which have been frozen • Avoid cross contamination • Government warning to avoid the risk of infection from raw egg or uncooked egg products.
Listeria monocytogenes • Common form of food poisoning • At risk – pregnant women, new-born babies, elderly and sick • Does not form spores	• Ranges from mild flu like illness to meningitis, septicaemia, pneumonia • Can cause miscarriage, premature labour or birth of an infected baby	Incubation – no specific time, may be few days to several weeks Duration of illness – no specific time e.g. 1–70 days	• Unpasteurised sheep's and cows' milk, soft cheese, meat-based pate, meat, cooked poultry • Cook-chill ready meals may be a source if they are not heated to the correct temperature for long enough	• Store products below 5°C • Use by date marked on label • Accurate stock rotation • Heat food to be cooked to 100°C e.g. poultry • Make sure food is heated through to the centre
Campylobacter • Most frequent cause of food poisoning in milk • Often known as gastroenteritis • Optimum temperature for growth 30–40°C	• Diarrhoea is the most common symptom • Headache, fever and abdominal pain	Incubation – 1–11 days Duration of illness – 2–7 days but may recur over several weeks	• Meat, poultry, milk, shellfish • Untreated water • Cross contamination from animals • Easily transmitted between humans	• Destroy by heating above 60°C • Avoid cross contamination of raw to cooked foods • Avoid infection from animals or pests
Staphylococcus aureus • Bacteria creates toxins which cause toxic food poisoning • Present in nose, throat and skin of humans	• Mild to severe vomiting • Abdominal pain • Diarrhoea • Low temperature	Incubation – 1–6 hours Duration of illness – 6–24 hours	• High-risk foods e.g. meat, meat products, poultry and poultry products, egg, filling for sandwiches, baked potatoes, salads • Food handlers by infected nose, throat, skin etc.	• High standards personal hygiene • Storage of food below 5°C • Handle food as little as possible • Spores germinate in warm slow cooking methods but do not multiply at high temperatures
Escherichia coli (E coli) 0157 • Several types which cause gastroenteritis in humans • Causes toxic food poisoning which can be fatal i.e. results in death	• Diarrhoea, abdominal pain, vomiting • Bloody diarrhoea • Kidney failure in serious cases	Incubation – 12–24 hours Duration of illness – 1–5 days	• Raw meat and poultry • Unpasteurised milk and dairy products • Untreated water in some countries	• Cook foods thoroughly at a high temperature • Avoid cross contamination from raw to cooked meats • Drink bottled water rather than untreated water • Avoid foods with high water content
Clostridium perfringes • Common form of food poisoning • Optimum temperature 15–50°C • Forms spores which cause toxic food poisoning	• Nausea and diarrhoea • Abdominal pain • Vomiting rare	Incubation – 8–22 hours Duration of illness – 12–24 hours	• Raw meat, poultry • Cooked meat, meat products, gravy	• Bacteria grow fast in optimum temperature range so heat hood rapidly and cook at high temperature • Cool food rapidly and store below 5°C • Spores are not normally killed by high temperatures but will multiply in warm conditions
Colstridium botulium • Rare type of food poisoning • Spores from toxic bacteria which are very poisonous • Majority of cases are fatal	• Difficulty in breathing and swallowing • Double vision, headaches, nausea, vomiting • Paralysis	Incubation – 12–48 hours Duration of illness rapid decline, death within a week or very slow recovery	• Incorrect processing of food or food too low temperature. e.g. faulty canning, vacuum packed foods • Packaged and canned meat, fish, vegetables	• Quality control procedures in processing of canned or packaged foods • Does not multiply in high acid foods. Take care with low acid canned foods • Spores are not destroyed by high temperatures but toxins are
Bacillus cereus • Two forms of food poisoning with the most common caused by toxic bacteria • Forms spores	• Nausea, vomiting, diarrhoea	Incubation – 1–6 hours Duration of illness 6–24 hours	• Cooked rice products • Cereal products • Starchy foods such as potatoes • Grows in soil and can survive milling and processing techniques	• Avoid cooking rice and pasta well in advance and keeping warm – better to cook when required • Cook thoroughly and cool rapidly

Table 11.1 *Common types of food poisoning*

🍽️ Food safety legislation

- Several laws cover the regulations for the preparation, storage and sale of food. You will find it useful if you can identify and understand the main pieces of legislation.

THE FOOD SAFETY ACT 1990

- This Act was introduced to ensure that all food produced in the food industry is safe to eat. The Food Act covers the whole spectrum of food production, manufacture and retail. The Food Safety Act is very detailed and some of the details you need to know about it include:

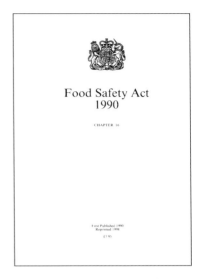

Aims

- To ensure that all food produced or prepared is safe to eat.

- To prevent the sale of food which may be harmful to health by causing food poisoning.

- To prevent the sale of food which is contaminated by pieces of metal, pests, chemicals, antibiotics, etc.

- To make sure that food products actually match the descriptions or claims made about them, i.e. 'the nature, substance or quality' expected by the consumer.

Foods included

- All materials used as a food ingredient, either in or on a food product, e.g. ingredients, additives, water.

- Liquids and ingredients used in drinks.

- Nutrient supplements and slimming aids.

- Food sources, e.g. farms and the growing areas of animals, plants, cereals.

The Act covers:

- All stages of food production, from farm to factory to retail outlet. A retail outlet may be:

  - any type of shop, from a vending machine to a large supermarket

  - eating places such as restaurants, cafes, takeaway outlets, railway buffets, hotels, fast food outlets.

- Everything that comes into contact with the food, e.g. equipment, machinery, storage and transport equipment.

- All people who handle the food at each stage of the food industry.

Enforcement

- The Food Safety Act is enforced by local government officers, i.e.:

  - trading standards officers

  - environmental health officers.

- They have the authority to:

  - enter food premises to investigate a possible offence

  - inspect food to see if it is safe

- take suspect food or food samples away for testing

- condemn unsafe food to stop it from being sold

- give instructions for improvements to unsatisfactory food premises

- close down unfit food premises.

FOOD SAFETY (GENERAL FOOD HYGIENE) REGULATIONS 1995
- These regulations give specific instructions about food hygiene standards in the UK and across the European Union, as set out in the European Food Hygiene Directive (93/94/EEC).

Aims

- To ensure high standards of hygiene in the food industry.

- To ensure that all food and food products are prepared, supplied or sold under hygienic conditions.

Stages covered by the regulations

- These include:

  - preparation

  - processing

  - manufacturing and packaging

  - transportation

  - distribution

  - serving in a commercial eating place or selling in a shop.

Risk assessment

- In addition, the regulations require the food industry to assess the risks involved in food production. This means that there is a requirement to **identify** and **control** food safety risks at each stage of production and the selling of food.

- This is done by:

  - identifying food safety hazards

  - knowing which stages in a food production system are critical to food safety

  - setting up and monitoring safety checks and procedures.

- An example of a risk assessment procedure is HACCP (hazard analysis and critical control points).

- This ensures that an analysis of the system is made and all potential hazards identified. A set of safety rules is then made for each CCP (critical control point) (see Revision Session 10 pages 145 and 147).

- Some of the other important legal requirements for the food industry are set out in the:

  - Health and Safety at Work Act

  - Sale of Goods Act

- Food Safety (Temperature Control) Regulations 1995
- Food Labelling Regulations 1984
- Protective Workwear Act

🍽 Food hygiene training

- An important factor in food safety is developing the knowledge and understanding of all staff involved in food production and serving. These people are known as food handlers and they must all be trained in food hygiene and food safety risks.

- The first level of qualification is the Basic Food Hygiene Certificate. This certificate is awarded by the Chartered Institute of Environmental Health (CIEH). The Basic Food Hygiene course covers topics such as:

  - hygienic food preparation
  - causes of food poisoning
  - prevention of food poisoning
  - food preparation areas
  - personal hygiene
  - food storage
  - waste and pest control.

PERSONAL HYGIENE

- Personal hygiene is vital and all food handlers are expected to:

  - wear clean, protective clothing, e.g. overall, apron, hat, shoes
  - remove all jewellery, e.g. rings, watches, bracelets, earrings and necklaces
  - cover over all cuts and skin grazes with a waterproof dressing, e.g. blue waterproof plaster, often incorporating a metal strip to aid detection along the production line
  - tie back and/or cover their hair with a net, e.g. hat net or beard net
  - take special care with their hands before touching food ingredients, e.g.:
    - wash with anti-bacterial soap and hot water
    - keep fingernails short and scrubbed, with all nail varnish removed
    - dry their hands with a hot air drier or disposable paper towels
    - wear disposable gloves whenever possible for handling food (these gloves are often blue in colour).
  - report any illness to a supervisor, e.g. sickness, diarrhoea, cold, flu – this is a legal requirement
  - follow clean handling rules, such as:
    - do not eat, chew or smoke near food
    - do not transfer bacteria by touching nose, hair or ears when handling food
    - do not taste food with fingers or lick equipment, e.g. spoons.

Figure 11.9 *The Food Safety (Temperature Control) Regulations 1995 (Reproduced under the terms of Crown Copyright Policy Guidance issued by HMSO)*

Figure 11.10 *Food handlers wearing protective clothing*

Figure 11.11 *A commercial food preparation area*

FOOD PREPARATION

■ Food preparation equipment can become infected with micro-organisms and soiled with contaminated food during preparation.

■ Arrangements for keeping food preparation areas and equipment clean and hygienic include:

  • well-designed food preparation areas that give good lighting, ventilation, efficient cleaning and adequate washing facilities

  • regular maintenance of the fixtures and fittings to avoid cracked surfaces, flaking paint, etc. by organising routine repair and painting programmes

  • keeping different work areas for designated tasks, e.g. the separation of preparation areas for high-risk foods, medium-risk foods, low-risk foods and waste products to prevent **cross-contamination**. These areas are often colour coded:
    – **red** for raw meat
    – **blue** for raw fish
    – **green** for fruit and vegetables
    – **yellow** for cooked meat

  • the equipment can also be colour coded and often the food handlers wear coloured neck ties to distinguish their area and the type of food they work with. All of this helps to prevent cross-contamination

  • good facilities for washing and cleaning, e.g. hot water, stainless steel sinks, drainage

  • equipment kept in good condition and appropriately designed for the intended task, e.g. no cracks or chipped or porous surfaces

  • specific equipment used for raw and cooked foods, e.g. chopping boards, bowls and knives may be colour coded

  • efficient waste disposal units and systems, e.g. clean bins, colour-coded bin liners, regular removal of rubbish and waste

  • methods for preventing insect contamination, e.g. food covers, ultra-violet light insect traps, fly screens on windows, control of rodents, etc.

  • separate facilities for staff from each area, e.g. changing areas with washing facilities.

■ Food must continue to be protected during distribution to retail outlets and storage.

STORAGE AND DISTRIBUTION

■ Storage and distribution arrangements for keeping food safe from contamination include:

  • keeping food at a temperature which will prevent the growth of micro-organisms, i.e. well below 5°C in refrigerated delivery vans and lorries, point of sale display cabinets, etc.

Figure 11.12 *A refrigerated food delivery lorry*

- temperature control checks of equipment such as refrigerators, chill cabinets and freezers

- protective packaging for products during transportation and storage.

■ The choice of packaging material is important as it needs to:
  – prevent contamination from micro-organisms, pests, dust, dirt and fumes
  – prevent contamination from the packaging materials, e.g. splinters from wooden pallets, metal staples used to seal boxes, etc. Suitable packaging materials include plastic trays or pallets, shrink-wrap plastic, plastic adhesive tape and first-grade cardboard, i.e. not recycled materials which could be contaminated with toxins or chemicals

- clear labelling with date marking, e.g. 'use-by', 'best before', 'display until'

- well-monitored stock rotation

- clear instructions and symbols for stacking and handling containers to prevent drainage of the contents, e.g. 'store this way up'.

KEY WORDS

These are the key words (highlighted in the text). Tick them if you know what they mean. Otherwise go back and check them again.

food spoilage	moulds	anaerobic
micro-organisms	contaminated	binary fission
enzymes	pathogenic bacteria	risk categories
yeast	fermentation	toxic
bacteria	aerobic	cross-contamination

CHECK YOURSELF QUESTIONS

Q1 Yeast is an ingredient used in the food industry. Name a food product that has yeast as an ingredient. Explain the function of yeast in your chosen product.

Q2 A simple approach within food safety is to describe foods as belonging to a risk category. What is meant by the risk category of foods? Give reasons for this approach.

Q3 The local environmental health officer announces that there has been an increasing number of reported cases of salmonella food poisoning. What factors could have led to this increase in salmonella food poisoning?

Q4 Many people are employed in the food industry, preparing or serving food products. These people are often referred to as food handlers. What has been done to make sure that food handlers understand food hygiene and food safety risks?

Q5 Bananas, apples and pears are sometimes dipped in lemon juice (citric acid) when being prepared for fruit salad. What is the reason for this process?

Answers are on page 239.

REVISION SESSION 12

Temperature and preservation

|⬤| Why does temperature matter?

■ **Temperature** control is critical in food production systems, risk assessment, food safety and food spoilage.

■ Temperature can:

- change the working **characteristics** of a raw food ingredient

- change the physical properties of individual foods and combination of foods

- change the nutritional profile of some foods

- destroy micro-organisms and enzymes to preserve or extend shelf life.

|⬤| Heat transfer

■ The characteristics of certain foods can be altered by the **transfer** of heat to or from the food.

■ When applied to foods **warm**, **high** or **hot temperatures** have the following effects:

- Food is made more **digestible**, e.g. heat softens the cell structure of potatoes.

- Heating improves the appearance, flavour, texture and smell of a wide range of foods, e.g. meat, fish.

- Heating prevents food spoilage as very high temperatures destroy micro-organisms.

- Heating **preserves** or extends shelf life.

- Heating increases the availability of some nutrients.

■ When applied to foods **low temperatures** have the following effects:

- They prevent food spoilage by retarding the growth of micro-organisms.

- They extend shelf life, e.g. chilling between −1°C and 4°C.

- They introduce a greater variety of textures and flavours, e.g. ice-cream, chilled desserts.

■ Milk is a good example of how both high and low temperatures can change the characteristics of a primary source food to create a wide range of different products.

Figure 12.1 *High temperatures*

Figure 12.2 *Low temperatures*

132°C	ultra heat treated (UHT)	shelf life in airtight cartons 6 months
115°C	evaporated	canned
113°C	sterilised	bottled with a shelf life of a few weeks
80°C	condensed	sugar added and canned
72°C	pasteurised semi-skimmed skimmed homogenised	with a cream line and bottled half the fat is removed, bottled all fat removed and bottled fine sieving breaks up the fat into fine droplets. No cream line
43°C	yogurt	lactic acid culture sets the milk
30°C	cheese, creme fraiche, fromage frais	lactic acid starter and enzyme cause milk to clot and form curds and whey
5°C 4°C −1°C	legal storage temperature for chilled foods	
−30°C −30°C	ice cream frozen yogurt	stirred, frozen and stored skimmed milk with yogurt culture

Figure 12.3 *The temperatures used to produce different milk products*

Figure 12.4 *Long-life milk products*

Methods of heat transfer

■ Heat can be transferred in three ways: **conduction**, **convection** and **radiation**. One or more methods may be used together depending on the food concerned and the time and equipment available.

Effects of heat on the properties of food

■ An increase in temperature can cause foods to change. For example, fat softens or melts, protein sets, sugar caramelises, starch thickens liquids, baked products turn brown.

MACRO NUTRIENTS

Fat

■ Solid fats soften at room temperature. This is important for:

- spreading butter or margarine on bread, etc.
- creaming butter or margarine with sugar to incorporate air for a creamed cake mixture.

■ Solid fat or foods which contain a high percentage of fat, such as chocolate, melt to a liquid at high temperatures. This is useful for:

- melted cake or biscuit mixtures, e.g. gingerbread, flapjack
- melted chocolate for chocolate mousse or cake decoration.

- When heated fat or oil can be used for cooking, e.g. shallow frying or deep fat frying. Each fat or oil has an optimum temperature, e.g. butter 140°C; corn oil/lard 220°C. Above this temperature the fat/oil begins to break up. It will produce an **acrid** smoke with a flash point occurring when flames appear.

Protein
- Protein changes when heated. The main change is that protein coagulates. The changes that occur are known as the **denaturation** of protein. (See Revision Session 3, page 99.)

Carbohydrates

Starch
- When mixed with a liquid and heated starch grains (flour) undergo the process of gelatinisation (see Revision Session 6, page 124).

- When baked or toasted the starch in bread, cakes, pastry and biscuits changes to dextrin and turns a light golden brown. This is known as **dextrinisation**.

Sugar
- Sugar dissolves in liquids. A syrup is formed which, when heated, gradually gets thicker, producing various degrees of hardness on cooling, e.g. fudge 116°C; caramel 138°C. The colour changes to shades of brown and the whole process is known as **caramelisation**.

- When heated sugar dry melts and caramelises. It is used to give texture and colour to some cakes and desserts such as creme brulee.

Colour and flavour
- Heating foods that contain a combination of protein and carbohydrate causes reactions which produce brown colours and flavourings. This is characteristic of roasted vegetables and nuts, baked bread and cakes and toasted breakfast cereals. It is often referred to as **non-enzymatic browning** or the **Maillard reaction**. This reaction can also produce unpleasant flavours, e.g. in overcooked crisps or chipped potatoes.

- Heat causes other foods to change colour, e.g.:

  - green vegetables such as broccoli and cabbage change from bright green to dark green.

  - red meat changes to brown as the protein coagulates.

- Heat can change or intensify the flavour of some foods and often produces distinctive smells (aroma) as food cooks, e.g. baked bread, roasted coffee beans.

Figure 12.5 *Bread is heated to make toast*

MICRO NUTRIENTS
- Minerals, e.g. iron and calcium, and fat-soluble vitamins, e.g. A, D, E and K, remain unchanged by cooking temperatures.

- Water-soluble vitamins, e.g. B and C, are usually destroyed by heat and high cooking temperatures.

¡O! Preservation and shelf life

- All around the world various methods of storing food have been developed. Some methods, e.g. smoking and salting, have been used for centuries to preserve locally produced food, while modern methods, e.g. **freezing** and **chilling**, are used to preserve vast quantities of raw and ready-prepared foods for worldwide distribution.

- Many techniques use the principle of temperature to preserve or extend shelf life. High temperatures, low temperatures or temperature in combination with high concentrations of sugar can be used to preserve a wide variety of foods.

HIGH-TEMPERATURE METHODS

Pasteurisation

- Pasteurisation is a method of heat treatment.

- Heat, i.e. high temperatures, destroys pathogenic micro-organisms.

- It extends the storage time of foods for a limited time.

- It is used mainly to heat-treat milk.

- The process of pasteurisation destroys all the pathogenic bacteria by passing the milk through a plate heat exchanger, which heats it to 71°C, holds it at that temperature for 15 seconds then cools it rapidly to 10°C.

Sterilisation

- **Sterilisation** is a method of heat treatment for a longer period of time at higher temperatures.

- Heat destroys nearly all micro-organisms and enzymes.

- It extends the storage period.

- It is a process used for milk and fruit juice.

- The process of sterilisation destroys pathogenic bacteria and heat-resistant spores by heating the milk to 104°C for 40 minutes or 113°C for 15 minutes.

- The combination of high temperatures and time change the flavour and colour of milk to a creamy flavour with a slight caramelisation of the milk sugar content.

- Sterilised food products can be packaged before or after the heat treatment process.

Ultra Heat Treatment (UHT)

- Very high temperatures are used to destroy all bacteria.

- This process is used to extend the storage period for milk.

- Milk is heated to 130–140°C for 1–5 seconds.

- The advantages of this process over the traditional sterilisation process is that there is:
  - little colour change
  - only slight change in taste
  - little loss of nutrient content.

■ UHT milk is sold in airtight cartons and will keep for up to six months.

Irradiation

■ **Irradiation** is a relatively new technology introduced into Great Britain in 1991.

■ It is a method of preservation which is strictly controlled.

Figure 12.6 *Irradiated strawberries (right) last longer*

■ In irradiation X-rays from a radioactive or electron beam are passed through the food. This means that the food has been treated with ionising radiation.

■ This process helps to:

  • stop vegetables sprouting, e.g. potatoes and onions
  • delay fruits from ripening
  • destroy insects and pests that may damage foods, e.g. rice, wheat, spices
  • destroy micro-organisms which may cause food spoilage.

■ All foods preserved by irradiation must be clearly labelled.

■ Some people are concerned are about the process of irradiation. Consumers have asked the following types of questions:

Question   Will the food be radioactive?

Answer   No – there is no evidence to suggest that the food is unsafe.

Question   Are the food factory workers safe?

Answer   Yes, strict safety regulations control the processing of the irradiated food and risk assessment is undertaken.

Question   Is the nutrient content of the food changed during the irradiation process?

Answer   There is no major change to the macro nutrients – carbohydrates, proteins, and fats – or to the mineral content. However, the micro nutrient content of vitamins A, C, E K may be affected.

Canning

Figure 12.7 *A range of canned foods*

■ **Canning** is one of the most widely used methods of preserving a huge range of foods, e.g. fruit, vegetables, meat, fish, soup, sauces.

■ High temperatures, i.e. heat sterilisation, destroy the micro-organisms and enzymes that cause food spoilage.

■ Foods are prepared for canning:
  • fruit and vegetables may be washed, peeled, sliced, chopped
  • meat and fish may be boned, cut, chopped, diced.

■ Foods are often packed into the cans together with a liquid, e.g. water, brine, fruit juice, sugar syrup or a sauce. A space is left at the top of the cans to prevent them distorting in shape during cooking due to an expansion of the liquid.

■ Cans are sealed with a double seam to prevent leakage or the re-entry of bacteria.

- The filled, sealed cans are placed in a retort (a large pressure cooker). They are heat-treated to 121°C. The time span is adjusted according to the filling, e.g.:
  - fruit and vegetables in liquid approximately 10 minutes
  - meat packed solid approximately 15 minutes.

- The type of packaging includes tin plate cans and aluminium cans (see Revision Session 15, page 188).

- Acid foods, e.g. fruit and vegetables such as rhubarb and grapefruit, are often canned in plastic-lined cans to prevent corrosion caused by the reaction of acid with metal.

- Cooked ready meals are often packed in plastic trays or containers. These are known as plastic cans. They are used for ready meals stored at ambient temperatures.

- Accuracy with regard to time and temperature is essential so that:

  - the sterilisation process is complete and harmful spore-forming bacteria will not germinate after processing

  - the food retains its structure and texture, e.g. too high a temperature would overcook and soften fruit.

- After sterilising the cans are sprayed with water or passed through a cooling tank to prevent the contents overcooking.

¡©¡ Low temperatures

- Two familiar but different methods of storing food products at low temperatures are freezing and chilling.

  - Freezing is a method of preservation. It preserves food for between one week and one year. The food often needs to be thawed fully before being cooked.

  - Chilling does not preserve food. It merely extends shelf life by a few days. The foods do not need to be defrosted.

- Remember that a key safety point for both of these methods is that food must be kept in the recommended temperature zone. This temperature must not rise during transportation or storage.

FREEZING
- Over the past 50 years freezing has become the most popular domestic method of food preservation.

- Freezing involves preserving foods at very low temperatures. Recommended temperatures are:
  - minus 18°C for domestic freezers
  - minus 18°C to minus 29°C for commercial freezers.

- At these temperatures the following principles apply:

  - The growth of micro-organisms stops at very low temperatures.

  - Enzyme activity is slowed down.

Figure 12.8 A deep freeze in a supermarket

- Water in the food changes to ice crystals and is not available to promote the growth of micro-organisms.

■ Food must be frozen very quickly so that small ice crystals form in the cells and no damage is caused to the structure of the food. A slow freezing process allows large uneven ice crystals to form, which will later rupture the cells and cause the flavour, texture and nutritional value to change when the food is thawed.

■ Overall there are no changes to the food during storage. The nutritional value of the food is mainly unaffected. In some cases flavours may become weaker or stronger. However you must remember that:

- cell damage can occur in soft fruits e.g. strawberries

- the colloidal structure of some food products, e.g. sauces, can collapse when frozen.

■ Frozen food products must have instructions for storage printed on the packaging to inform consumers on the correct ways of keeping the product in good condition after purchase. A system of star ratings is used on all commercially prepared foods (see Revision Session 14, page 181).

CHILLING

■ This is a method of **extending shelf life** for a short period of time. It has become very popular during the last fifteen years.

■ Chilled foods are **perishable** foods, e.g. prepared salads, fresh pasta, sandwiches, pâtés, pies, which are kept in prime condition for a limited amount of time by storing them at a low temperature between −1°C and 8°C.

■ The low temperature inhibits the growth of micro-organisms. Bacteria are not killed but they will remain dormant.

■ The low temperatures also slow down enzyme activity.

■ The bacterium *Listeria monocytogenes* has become a common form of food poisoning. The main sources of this bacterium are high-risk foods. Because of this it is required by law that chilled foods are stored below 4°C, i.e. in the temperature range of −1°C to 4°C.

■ A cook-chill system is when foods are prepared, cooked and chilled rapidly. This system is used for retail sales and in the catering industry.

■ Chilled foods are always sold from chill cabinets. At home chilled foods and those prepared by the cook-chill process must be kept in a refrigerator.

■ Some advantages of chilling as a method of extending shelf life include:

- Single or a mixture of fresh foods can be kept in prime condition for a longer time, e.g.
  - single raw foods such as meat, fish, salad, vegetables
  - a mixture of fresh foods such as coleslaw, stir fry vegetables.

- A large range of ready prepared foods are available. These require little or no preparation and are convenient for consumers to use.

- Some food products are a mixture of cooked and raw ingredients, e.g. potato salad.

- There is very little change to the flavour, colour, texture or shape if best quality foods are used.

- There is no change to the nutritional content.

- Manufacturers must provide storage instructions including temperature. Consumers should check the temperature of their refrigerator.

COLD STORAGE

- Some foods are held in cold storage in an atmosphere of carbon dioxide gas. This method is often referred to as **controlled atmosphere (CA)** storage. In these conditions the growth of micro-organisms is slowed down. CA is used for storing eggs, apples, pears, root vegetables and meat.

Drying

- **Drying** is the removal of moisture by warmth or high temperature. It is often referred to as **dehydration**. Micro-organisms need moisture to grow and reproduce so without moisture they cannot thrive.

- **Sunlight** – Drying foods in direct sunlight is a very old and traditional method of preserving foods, e.g. fruit and vegetables such as tomatoes, raisins. The moisture evaporates slowly but the foods can become contaminated by bacteria in the air or by the re-entry of bacteria.

- **Oven drying** – Warm ovens are used for this type of preservation, which is suitable for vegetables, herbs, tea and coffee.

- Removing water from food may cause:
  - a concentration of flavours, e.g. in juices, syrups and tomato puree
  - an increase in the concentration of salt and sugar
  - a reduction in the bulk and weight of the food, which often means it is cheaper to handle and transport

- Dried food must be stored in a cool dry place.

- **Rehydration** is when liquid is added to reconstitute the foods. When the foods have absorbed liquid they must be treated in the same way as fresh food because micro-organisms will be able to grow and reproduce again.

- The effects of dehydration may include changes in:
  - colour, e.g. green grapes to brown sultanas
  - texture, e.g. crumbly coffee granules, brittle herbs or peas
  - a shrunken and wrinkly skin, e.g. prunes
  - flavour, e.g. sweeter or saltier fruit and vegetables
  - nutritional profile, e.g. vitamin C or thiamin may be destroyed
  - additives, e.g. anti-caking agents are added to salt and icing sugar to help them flow freely.

Figure 12.9 *A variety of dried fruits*

MECHANICAL DRYING METHODS

- In industry, mechanical drying methods are used. These methods include:

Spray drying

- This method is suitable for foods which may be damaged by excessive heating, e.g. milk, coffee, potato.

Fluidised bed drying

- This can be used to clump-dry particles into granules which dissolve more easily in water, e.g. potato, coffee.

Roller drying

- Used for instant breakfast cereal, mashed potato and baby foods.

Accelerated freeze drying (AFD)

- This is the most modern method of commercial drying. It produces an excellent quality dried product.

- The food is frozen and then the temperature is increased to vaporise the ice, which turns to steam as it dries out the food.

- Advantages of AFD are:
  - the colour, texture and most of the flavour are kept
  - the food does not shrink as much as in other methods
  - the nutritional profile is retained
  - it preserves the food longer than other drying methods
  - it can be used for coffee and complete meals which include meat and fish. Products have an open texture which rehydrates well.

- Disadvantages of AFD include:
  - it is a more costly method of drying
  - AFD foods need to be handled with care as they crumble easily.

OTHER PRESERVATION TECHNIQUES

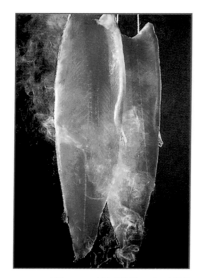

Figure 12.10 *Smoked fish*

- Preservation techniques also include smoking and adding chemicals such as salt, vinegar or sugar. Micro-organisms are unable to grow in strong solutions of vinegar, salt or sugar. For example:

  - **Vinegar** is acetic acid with a low pH of 3.5. The strong acid solution preserves foods such as pickled onions and cabbage because the bacteria cannot survive below pH4.5.

  - **Salt** is used to coat foods such as ham, bacon and fish or it is also used in a solution of salt and water (brine). It reduces the moisture content of the food by **osmosis**. Some foods are canned in brine.

  - **Sugar** in high concentrations prevents bacteria from growing. It is used in jams, marmalade and jellies where the sugar content is 60% of the final product. A strong sugar solution is also used for coating candied and crystallised fruit which dry out by the process of osmosis.

Figure 12.11 *Pickled onions*

- **The critical temperature control points must be strictly kept.**
- Pastry ingredients mixed and kept below 20°C
- Cutting and shaping pie lids and bases below 10°C
- Meat-based filling mixed and stored below 10°C
- Baked in a rotary oven at 195°C
- Very quickly cooled to ambient temperature of approx. 20°C
- Blast chilled in chilling unit at −10°C
- Transported by chilled delivery vans below 5°C
- Stored in chilled cabinets between −1 and 4°C
- Stock used in strict 'use-by-date' order
- To prepare for eating, reheat in centre to 70–75°C

Table 12.1 *The production process for a meat-filled pastry product*

- Modern methods of extending shelf life and preservation include:
  - additives – preservatives are added to foods to extend their shelf life (see Revision Session 13)
  - packaging – **modified atmosphere packaging (MAP); controlled atmosphere packaging (CAP); vacuum packaging** (see Revision Session 15).

Food safety and risk assessment

- Temperature control is a critical measurement in food production. In a food production system the temperature for a particular process will be a **critical control point (CCP)** and vital to the food safety.

- Look at the temperature control points in the production of a meat-filled pastry product (Table 12.1).

KEY WORDS

These are the key words (highlighted in the text). Tick them if you know what they mean. Otherwise go back and check them again.

temperature	dextrinisation	canning
characteristics	caramelisation	extending shelf life
transfer	non-enzymatic	perishable
digestible	browning	drying
preserves	freezing	dehydration
conduction	chilling	rehydration
convection	pasteurisation	accelerated
radiation	sterilisation	freeze drying
acrid	ultra heat treatment	
denaturation	irradiation	

CHECK YOURSELF QUESTIONS

Q1 Why is 'Refrigerate after opening' printed on the product labels of mayonnaise and salad cream?

Q2 Why is it important to monitor the temperature of chill cabinets and freezers?

Q3 Complete a chart to show that foods can be preserved in a number of ways. Use the following headings to show ways of preserving raspberries, tomatoes, fish.

Food   Preservation method   Principle

Q4 Explain three changes which happen to solid fats stored in a refrigerator at 5°C when there is an increase in temperature. Give examples to qualify your answer.

Q5 Irradiation is a new technology used to preserve foods. What are the advantages of irradiation as a method of preservation?

Q6 Chilling is a method of extending the shelf life of certain food products. It has become very popular over the last 15 years. Give three reasons why chilling has increased in popularity.

Answers are on page 240.

EXAM PRACTICE 4

Exam questions and student's answers

1 The safe storage of food is very important. Some food are classified as 'high risk'.

(a) Explain the term 'high-risk' food. (4 marks)

A high-risk food is one which is suitable for the growth of bacteria. These foods are usually moist and high in protein. High-risk foods need to be kept in a refrigerator. 4/4

(b) Give four different examples of 'high-risk' foods. (4 marks)

Cooked meat

Cream

Shellfish, e.g. prawns

Mayonnaise 4/4

2 Many 'high risk' foods can be purchased from chill cabinets.

Explain the 'cook-chill' system. (4 marks)

This is a system which uses the normal methods for the preparation and cooking of food but it is then followed by a very fast chilling process just above freezing point at 3 degrees C. If a product is to be reheated after purchase it should be reheated to a temperature of 70 degrees C. 4/4

How to score full marks

This student has answered questions 1 and 2 very well which seems to be due to good revision. She would have scored full marks.

Questions to try

1 (a) What is the purpose of chilling food? (2 marks)

(b) Why is it so popular? (2 marks)

2 Accurate time and temperature control are essential in the 'cook-chill' system.

(a) What are the critical time and temperature control points? (3 marks)

(b) Explain how you would make sure the temperature of a chill cabinet is kept within the correct temperature range. (5 marks)

Answers and comments are on page 224.

Additives

What are additives?

- **Additives** are substances that are added to foods during manufacturing or processing to improve their keeping properties, flavour, colour, texture, appearance or stability. Additives are used in a huge range of food products today.

- Additives may be:

  - obtained from **natural** sources, e.g. a red colouring made from beetroot juice (E162) is used in making ice cream and liquorice

  - **synthesised** in a laboratory to be *chemically* the same as certain natural materials, such as vanillin, which is found naturally in vanilla pods

  - **manufactured synthetic** compounds which do not occur in nature, such as saccharin (E954), a low-calorie intensive sweetener.

- The use of over 300 additives is **permitted** in the UK. Flavourings are not included in this figure. In the UK over 3000 flavourings are used in many different combinations.

- You will find that consumers prefer food products to contain additives obtained from natural sources. For this reason many manufacturers try to use fewer synthetic additives, e.g. a cake manufacturer may use additives from natural sources and will then advertise the range of cakes as 'Home Style Baking'.

- **Artificial** additives are still used extensively by the food manufacturing industry but the use of these additives is controlled by the following government departments:

  - FAC (Food Advisory Committee)

  - MAFF (Ministry of Agriculture, Fisheries and Food)

  - COT (Committee of Toxicity of Chemicals in Food, Consumer Products and the Environment).

- Specific regulations controlling the use of additives include:

  - The Preservatives in Food Regulations 1974

  - The Sweeteners in Food Regulations 1983

  - The Bread and Flour Regulations 1984

Safety

- Food additives must be safe for consumers to eat.

- Consumer groups constantly pressure food manufacturers to use fewer or no additives in their products.

- Some people have **allergies** (unpleasant reactions) to certain additives, but this is less common now than in the past.

Table 13.1 *Some additives cause allergic reactions*	BEWARE!	MAY BE FOUND IN
	E102 tartrazine can affect some chidren and asthmatics	soft drinks
	E110 sunset yellow can cause a skin rash	biscuits and sweets

- The long-term effects of additives are not known.

- Research must be continually carried out on the safety of food additives.

Quantity

- Legally enforced regulations control the maximum amount of additives that can be safely used in foods.

- Additives should be used in minimum quantities.

- Using large quantities of additives can be expensive for the manufacturer and harmful to consumers' health.

Labelling

- Additives must be shown on food labels in the list of ingredients.

- Additives must be listed in the descending order of the amount used (greatest amount first) and by name or **'E' number**. (See Revision Session 14.)

Figure 13.2 *Additives are shown on food labels*

A COFFEE AND WALNUT CAKE FILLED WITH COFFEE FLAVOUR BUTTERCREAM TOPPED WITH COFFEE FUDGE AND NIBBED WALNUTS
ⓘ **INGREDIENTS:**
Sugar, Vegetable Margarine, (with Emulsifier: Mono- And Di-Glycerides of Fatty Acids, Flavouring), Wheat Flour, Egg, Glucose Syrup, Butter, Walnuts, Dextrose, Sweetened Condensed Milk, Soya Flour, Flavouring, Modified Starch, Whey Solids, Sorbital Syrup, Emulsifier (Mono- And Di- Glycerides of Fatty Acids), Instant Coffee, Dried Egg White, Salt, Preservative (Potassium Sorbate), Sodium Caseinate, Stabiliser (Xanthan Gum).
NOT SUITABLE FOR VEGETARIANS

UNSUITABLE FOR YOUNG CHILDREN WHO CAN CHOKE ON NUTS

🍽 Advantages and disadvantages of using additives

- Why does a food manufacturer use additives? There are several advantages and disadvantages!

Advantages

- To produce a wide range of food products to meet consumer needs, e.g. quick, easy, convenient meals, such as pot noodles, instant whipped desserts, instant potato mash, etc.

- To improve a specific characteristic of a food, e.g. vanilla-flavoured ice cream, orange-flavoured soft centres in chocolates, chocolate and coffee liqueur-flavoured hot chocolate drinks, etc.

- To produce expected qualities in foods, such as colour and flavour, e.g. soft-centred chocolates with pink colouring and strawberry flavouring or green colouring with mint flavouring.

- To produce a product range by using different additives in the basic food, e.g. potato crisps flavoured with salt and vinegar, cheese and onion, smoky bacon, chicken, prawn cocktail, etc.

- To help maintain product consistency in large-scale production, e.g. the use of emulsifiers to stabilise salad cream, anti-foaming agents to reduce foaming in jam, etc.

- To restore original characteristics of a food after processing, e.g. adding colour to processed vegetables.

- To prevent food spoilage, to preserve foods and give them a longer shelf life, e.g. bread.

A* EXTRA

Try to include the specific names of additives. Explain what their function is and how this is important in the specific product which is stated in the question.
Also include advantages and disadvantages of using additives.

DISADVANTAGES

- The disadvantages of using additives include:

  - Additives could be used to disguise inferior ingredients.

  - Some colours and flavourings may not really be necessary.

  - Some people may have an allergy to additives. A problem here is that it is often difficult to find out which additive is causing the allergic reaction. Examples of allergies caused by food additives include asthma attacks, skin rashes, and hyperactivity in children.

- All additives have to be approved by the Government Food Advisory Committee. Long, strict tests are carried out before approval is given. On approval each additive is given a number as a means of identification. If the additive is given an 'E' prefix to the number this means that it is accepted for use throughout the European Union.

Types of food additives and their functions

COLOURS

- **Colours** are added to make foods look attractive. During manufacture and processing colours:

  - replace colour lost during heat treatment, e.g. in canned peas

  - boost colours already in foods, e.g. strawberry yogurt

  - maintain consistency between different batch productions as they are added in precise quantities, e.g. yellow colouring in tinned custard

  - make foods that are normally colourless look attractive, e.g. carbonated drinks.

- It is interesting to note that:

  - caramel (E150) is the most popular colouring used in soft drinks

Figure 13.3 *Food colouring is listed in the ingredients*

ADDITIVES ○ ○ ○ ○ ○ ○ ○ ○ ○ **175** ○ KNOWLEDGE AND UNDERSTANDING

- some colours are artificial, e.g. titanium dioxide (E171) used in sweets

- some colours come from natural sources, e.g. beetroot red (E162), which is used in ice cream and liquorice

- no colours are allowed to be added to baby foods. However, three **micronutrients**, i.e. vitamins that are used in baby foods, do add colour to the food. These are riboflavin (E101), riboflavin-5'-phosphate (E101a) and beta-carotene (E160a).

■ Some consumers believe that the addition of colour additives is not necessary for foods to taste good. Should we therefore cut down on the quantity of food colouring added to food products?

LUXURY SAGE AND ONION STUFFING MIX WITH SULTANAS, ALMONDS AND APPLE - add butter and boiling water
INGREDIENTS: Breadcrumbs (Wheat Flour; Wholemeal Flour; Yeast; Salt; Herbs; Emulsifier: Mono- and Di-Acetyltartaric Esters of Mono- and Di-Glycerides of Fatty Acids), Sultanas (13%), Dried Onion, Flaked Almonds (6%), Dried Apple (2%) (with Preservative: Sulphur Dioxide), Dried Parsley, Salt, Vegetable Oil, Dried Sage, Dried Chives, Black Pepper, Flavouring.

Figure 13.4 *Preservatives are listed on food labels*

INGREDIENTS
WATER, ORANGES, PINEAPPLE JUICE, CITRIC ACID, ACIDITY REGULATOR (TRISODIUM CITRATE), PRESERVATIVES (POTASSIUM SORBATE, SODIUM METABISULPHITE), SWEETENERS (ASPARTAME, SACCHARIN), STABILISER (E466), FLAVOURING, COLOUR (BETA-CAROTENE), CONTAINS A SOURCE OF PHENYLALANINE

DILUTE ONE PART CONCENTRATE WITH AT LEAST 4 PARTS WATER. IT IS IMPORTANT TO ADD EXTRA WATER IF GIVING TO TODDLERS

Figure 13.5 *Intense sweeteners are listed on food labels*

PRESERVATIVES

■ **Preservatives** help to keep food safe for longer than they would normally last. They are added to foods to:

- extend their shelf life, which is of benefit to consumers, e.g. preservatives in salad dressing, concentrated lemon juice, etc.

- prevent the growth of micro-organisms which can cause food spoilage and lead to food poisoning (see Revision Session 11).

- Preservatives are found in:

- many processed foods with a long shelf life

- cured meats, such as bacon, ham, corned beef

- dried fruit, such as sultanas, raisins, etc.

SWEETENERS

■ There are two types of **sweeteners**: intense sweeteners and bulk sweeteners.

■ Intense sweeteners are:

- artificial sweeteners such as aspartame, acesulfame-k, thaumatin and saccharin

- approximately 300 times sweeter than sugar

- low in calories

- used in low-calorie drinks and reduced-sugar products, and are also available as sweetening tablets

- useful for people who want to eat less sugar in their diet.

■ However they:

- lack the bulk that is needed in recipes which normally use cane or beet sugar

- do not have the same characteristics as sugar for cooking

- may leave a bitter aftertaste.

- **Bulk sweeteners** are:
  - hydrogenated glucose syrup, sorbitol (E420) and mannitol
  - similar to sugar in levels of sweetness
  - used in similar amounts to sugar
  - used in sugar-free confectionery and preserves for diabetics.
- However, bulk sweeteners are not absorbed by the body's digestive system or used by it as efficiently as sugar.

EMULSIFIERS AND STABILISERS

- These help to improve the consistency of food during processing and storage.

- **Emulsifiers** and **stabilisers** are:
  - used to help substances such as oil and water to mix together, form an emulsion and stay mixed. Normally, when shaken together, oil and water would separate
  - found in eggs, e.g. lecithin is a natural emulsifier and is used to make mayonnaise, low-fat spreads, salad dressings, etc.
  - important for giving foods a smooth creamy texture
  - used to lengthen the shelf life of baked products
  - also made from locust beans, e.g. xanthan gum which is used to thicken salad cream.

FLAVOURINGS AND FLAVOUR ENHANCERS

- These are used to improve the taste of foods by:
  - adding flavour e.g. vanilla in yogurt or ice cream
  - restoring flavours lost in processing, e.g. acetaldehyde gives an apple flavour.

- **Flavourings** and **flavour enhancers** must meet the requirements of the Food Safety Act 1990 and all other flavouring regulations. They can be classified into three groups:
  - natural, e.g. herbs and spices
  - nature identical, e.g. flavours extracted from natural substances
  - artificial, e.g. substances which are not themselves natural flavours but have the ability to make other flavours stronger, e.g. monosodium glutamate (E621).

- **Monosodium glutamate (MSG):**
  - intensifies the flavours of other foods
  - is used in Chinese recipes and savoury foods

STUTE
DIABETIC
Morello Cherry Extra Jam with sweetener
STUTE is a genuine NO SUGAR ADDED DIABETIC jam with 45% less calories and higher fruit content than ordinary jam.
INGREDIENTS: Sweetener (Sorbitol), Morello Cherries, Gelling Agent (Citrus Pectin), Citric Acid.

Figure 13.6 *Bulk sweeteners are listed on the label*

 INGREDIENTS:
Water, Soya Oil, Pasteurised Egg Yolk, Glucose Syrup, Modified Starch, Vinegar, Salt, Lactic Acid, Preservative (Potassium Sorbate), Stabiliser (Xanthan Gum), Flavourings.

INGREDIENTS:
Spirit Vinegar
Vegetable Oil
Water, Sugar
Mustard, Salt
Egg Yolks
Modified Cornflour
Stabilisers –
Xanthan Gum
and Guar Gum
Colour –
Riboflavin

Figure 13.7 *Emulsifiers are listed on the packaging*

INGREDIENTS
Water, Mushrooms
Dried Skimmed Milk
Vegetable Oil
Modified Cornflour, Salt
Whey Protein
Flavour Enhancer -
Monosodium Glutamate
Flavouring
Yeast extract, Sugar
Stabiliser - Polyphosphates
and Sodim Phosphates
Spice Extract

Figure 13.8 *Mushroom soup ingredients. Some people are allergic to monosodium glutamate.*

- may cause allergies in some people, producing sickness and dizziness. (For this reason some foods are advertised as 'MSG free'.)

ANTIOXIDANTS

- **Antioxidants** are used to:

  - prevent fat in foods combining with oxygen and becoming **rancid**. This process is called **oxidation**. Rancid foods have an unpleasant odour and flavour.

  - slow down enzyme activity in fruit and vegetables which go brown when cut.

- Ascorbic acid (vitamin C) is a natural antioxidant found in fruit. It helps to prevent other fruits going brown. For example, apple/pears/bananas for a fruit salad can be dipped in lemon juice first to prevent them from browning.

- Another natural antioxidant is tocopherol (vitamin E), which is used to increase the shelf life of food products. Sulphur dioxide is also an antioxidant.

- Antioxidants are used in dried soups, preserved meat and fish products, stock cubes, cheese spreads, etc.

ANTI-CAKING AGENTS

- These are used to stop crystals and powders from sticking together and to keep them free flowing. They are found in dried milk, cocoa, salt, etc.

ANTI-FOAMING AGENTS

- These are used to stop large amounts of foam and froth occurring during the making of jam, syrup and fruit juices.

ACIDS, BASES AND BUFFERS

- These are used to control the **acidity** or **alkalinity** of food products. Acids used include: citric acid (E330); acetic acid (E260); tartaric acid (E334).

- There are other categories of additives. Look up the following list and find out what they are used for:

firming agents	packaging gases	gelling agents	raising agents
glazing agents	propellants	humectants	sequesterants
modified starch	thickeners		

KEY WORDS

These are the key words (highlighted in the text). Tick them if you know what they mean. Otherwise go back and check them again.

additives	'E' number	stabilisers
natural	colours	flavourings
permitted	preservatives	flavour enhancers
artificial	sweeteners	antioxidants
allergy	emulsifiers	

CHECK YOURSELF QUESTIONS

Q1 Some foods contain preservatives. What are the advantages to the consumer of these food products?

Q2 The following two pieces of information are printed on a tin of creamed rice pudding.

| No Preservatives | 3 |
| Gluten Free | 3 |

INGREDIENTS

Full Cream Milk, Skimmed Milk, Whey, Rice, Sugar

What does this information tell the consumer?

Q3 A chocolate bar has the following information printed on the label.

Milk Chocolate with Raisins and Almonds

Ingredients: milk chocolate (milk, sugar, cocoa mass, cocoa butter, vegetable fat, emulsifiers: E442 and E476, flavourings), raisins, almonds.

Why are emulsifiers used in the manufacture of chocolate products?

Q4 A tin of low-fat custard has the following information on the label.

INGREDIENTS

Skimmed Milk, Full Cream Milk, Modified Starch, Sugar, Flavouring, Colours: Curcumin, Annatto, Artificial Sweetener: Acesulfame Potassium.

No Artificial Colours ✓

What does this tell the consumer about the colour additives in the custard?

Q5 Dried packet soups contain flavourings and flavour enhancers (E621, E635). Why are these additives used in these food products?

CREAM OF CHICKEN & SWEETCORN SOUP WITH CROUTONS

INGREDIENTS as served (greatest first)

Water, Glucose Syrup, Cornflour, Hydrogenated Vegetable Oil, Sweetcorn, Croutons, Potato Starch, Salt, Chicken, Milk Proteins, Flavourings, Flavour Enhancers (E621, E635), Acidity Regulator (Potassium Phosphates), Emulsifier (E471), Herb and Spice Extracts including Celery, Sage, Black Pepper and Spices.

Q6 Mashed potato can be formed into shapes such as potato waffles which can be served individually grilled or baked. The ingredients of one brand of frozen potato waffles are:

INGREDIENTS

Potato, Vegetable Oil, Starch, Salt, Stabiliser (E464), Pepper, Vitamin C, Mustard.

The stabiliser E464 is included in this list of ingredients. Why has the manufacturer added a stabiliser to the potato waffles?

Answers are on page 242.

Product labelling

🍽 Labelling information required by law

- It is a **legal requirement** to inform customers about the food products they are buying. The Food Labelling Regulations 1996 state the type of information that must be displayed on a food product label. We can look in detail at each of these eight requirements.

🍽 1 Food product name

- The name of the product must clearly tell consumers what the product is, e.g. cornflakes, teabags, etc.

- Sometimes extra words are needed. For example, the word 'jam' would not let you know the type of jam. It would be necessary to use the name of the flavour, e.g. strawberry jam.

- Processed foods must be identified by printing the process in the title, e.g. smoked salmon, roasted peanuts, etc.

Figure 14.1 *Products must be clearly named*

- Differences between similar products must be indicated, e.g. fruit-flavoured yogurt and strawberry yoghurt.

- Well-known foods are allowed to keep traditional names as long as a subtitle is given naming the food product, e.g. 'Chicken Madras – marinated pieces of chicken breast in a spicy tomato sauce with fresh coriander'.

- Some foods are allowed to keep their names even though they are not accurate. For example swiss roll does not come from Switzerland.

- The pictures must not mislead the consumer. For example, raspberry-flavoured instant dessert must not have a picture of raspberries on the label.

🍽 2 List of ingredients

- All ingredients must be listed on the label.

- **Ingredients** are listed in descending order of weight, starting with the largest amount and finishing with the smallest.

- The amount of each ingredient does not have to be given.

- Food additives and water must be included. The name of the additive can be used or else the UK name or the 'E' number. The category name of the additive must be written before each additive or group of additives, e. g. preservatives or flavour enhancers.

Figure 14.2 *The list of ingredients for teacakes*

- Some foods, e.g. unwrapped bread, do not have an ingredient list but information must be displayed at the point of sale if they contain such additives as preservatives and colourings, without giving individual names or 'E' numbers.

⦿❘ 3 Storage conditions

- The **storage instructions** give details of the best conditions in which to keep the food in order to prevent food spoilage.

- Temperature guidelines are important. A temperature range or a symbol may also be given, e.g.:
  - keep refrigerated
  - keep refrigerated max. 5°C
  - store 0°C to +5°C.
  - should be −18°C or colder.
  - suitable for home freezing.

Figure 14.3 *Advice on storing*

Figure 14.4 *The home freezing symbol*

⦿❘ 4 Shelf life

- **Date marking** is used to indicate how long foods should be kept (their **shelf life**). The dates marked on food labels help to ensure the quality of the food and reduce the risk of food poisoning or food spoilage.

- Two ways of date marking include:
  - **'use by'** date
  - **'best before'** date.

'Use by' date

- A 'use by' date is for high-risk foods such as raw and cooked meat, fish, pâté, etc. These highly perishable foods spoil quickly and the 'use by' date is a clear instruction that the food is safe to eat until this time.

- After the 'use by' date food may not look or taste different but it will be unsafe to eat.

'Best before' date

- A 'best before' date is used for low-risk foods or foods which are processed and packaged to have a long shelf life, e.g. UHT milk.

- The date gives the day, month and year.

- After this date foods will start to deteriorate in terms of flavour, colour, texture or taste.

- The date on food products with a shelf life of three months or less must be shown as a day and month.

'Display until' date

- Another date sometimes shown on food products is **'display until'**. This is not a legal requirement.

- The 'display until' date is usually a few days before the 'use by' date so that the consumer has a number of days in which to use the product.

- It also informs the retailer when to remove the product from the shelves or chill/freezer cabinets.

Figure 14.5 *Use by...*

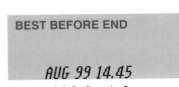

Figure 14.6 *Best before...*

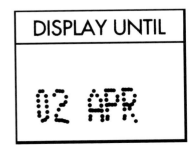

Figure 14.7 *Display until...*

🍴 5 Instructions for use

- Instructions on how to prepare and cook the food are given, e.g.:
  - temperature and cooking time for conventional ovens
  - preparation guidelines and times for cooking in microwave ovens
  - guidelines for cooking from frozen in either conventional ovens or microwaves
  - the defrosting times, cooking times and temperatures as tested by the manufacturer.

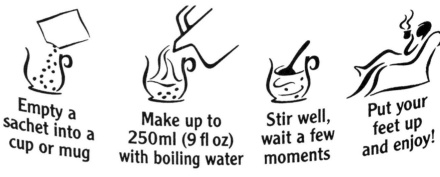

TO SERVE:

Empty a sachet into a cup or mug

Make up to 250ml (9 fl oz) with boiling water

Stir well, wait a few moments

Put your feet up and enjoy!

Figure 14.8 *Instructions on how to serve an instant cup of soup*

Figure 14.9 *The name and address of the manufacturer are given*

🍴 6 Name and address of the manufacturer

- Consumers must be given the name and address of either:
  - the manufacturer, e.g. Heinz, or
  - the supplier/retailer, e.g. Tesco Stores Ltd.
- This information is a point of contact for consumers who wish to know more about the product or to make a complaint.

🍴 7 Place of origin

- This shows the place the food has come from, e.g. 'product of Spain'.

Figure 14.10 *Place of origin*

🍴 8 Weight or volume

- The Weights and Measures Act 1985 makes short weight an offence. Most pre-packed food is required to carry on the container an indication of the net **weight** or **volume**. When sold other than pre-packed, most food has to be sold either by quantity or by number.
- The Act covers both the minimum and the average system of quantity control. The 'average' system of quantity control is mainly for pre-packed goods and is indicated next to the weight declaration on the pack by the symbol 'e'. The seller has to make the quantity known to the purchaser.
- The actual weight of the product must be given, i.e. within a few grams of the weight.
- Weights under 5 g do not have to be stated.
- Some foods are sold in standard amounts.

Figure 14.11 *Weight or volume*

⚬ Other labelling information

- Manufacturers may decide to give extra information. Look to see if you can find any of the following.

1 BAR CODES

- **Bar codes** appear on most food labels.

- An electronic scanner at the checkout reads the bar code.

- The price of the product is recorded and displayed.

- Details can be recorded for stocktaking.

- In the future more information will be stored on the bar code, e.g. production date.

Figure 14.12 *A bar code*

2 LOT OR BATCH MARK

- A **lot or batch mark** helps to identify each stage of the food product production process. It records details such as the date of production, the production line and the packaging system.

- Manufacturers must also be able to trace the making process of goods back to the raw ingredients and their origin. A unique code is used for each product and this is known in the food industry as **traceability**.

DISPLAY UNTIL:	03APR UOWUW
BEST BEFORE:	05APR CLCK6

Figure 14.13 *A batch mark*

3 SPECIAL INFORMATION

- Symbols or word 'flashes' may be printed on the label to give information about:

  - dietary group, e.g. 'suitable for vegetarians'

  - storage, e.g. 'suitable for home freezing'

  - ingredients, e.g.:
    - 'This product contains traces of nuts.'
    - 'Made with 100% chicken breast.'
    - 'Although every care has been taken to remove bones some may remain.'

  - cooking, e.g. 'suitable for microwave'

  - special features, e.g. 'medium hot curry'.

Figure 14.14 *Suitable for vegetarians*

4 OPENING INSTRUCTIONS

- These are often given to prevent spillage or leakage, e.g. 'Cut along dotted line.'

Figure 14.15 *Suitable for home freezing*

Figure 14.16 *Suitable for microwave*

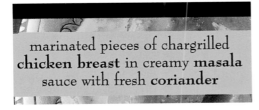

Figure 14.17 *Ingredients with special features*

Figure 14.18 *Ingredients*

RESEALABLE PACK ➤ CUT OR TEAR

Figure 14.19 *Opening instructions*

Figure 14.20 *Waste disposal*

5 ENVIRONMENTAL ISSUES

■ Symbols or statements are used to inform the customer about:

- types of plastics used in packaging

- any recycled materials or the origin of packaging materials

- disposal of packaging by recycling methods.

6 NUTRITIONAL INFORMATION

■ Many manufacturers put **nutritional information** on food product labels, although they are not required to do so by law unless a special claim is made about the product, e.g. 'high in fibre', 'low in fat'.

■ The advantages of stating nutritional information on the label include:

- Consumers know what nutrients are in the product.

- The nutrient content of one food can be compared with another.

- Informed choices can be made.

- Foods which have a specific nutrient content can be selected, e.g. low in sugar.

■ Nutritional information that is stated on labels must comply with EU regulations and be given in one of the following formats.

Group 1: Energy
Protein
Carbohydrate
Fat

Group 2: Energy
Protein
Carbohydrate
Fat
Sugars
Saturates
Fibre
Sodium

Figure 14.21

NUTRITION

TYPICAL COMPOSITION	A 200G (7oz) serving provides	100g (31/2oz) provide
Energy	176kJ/42kcal	88kJ/21kcal
Protein	2.2g	1.1g
Carbohydrate	7.0g	3.5g
of which sugars	6.2g	3.1g
Fat	0.2g	0.1g
of which saturates	trace	trace
Fibre	1.6g	0.8g
Sodium	0g	0g
This can contains approx 2 servings.		

INFORMATION

Figure 14.22

NUTRITION INFORMATION

	As sold 100g provides:	Per 3 Dippers grilled provides:
Energy	1063kJ/255kcal	590kJ/140kcal (Calories)
Protein	12.7g	7.0g
Carbohydrate	14.8g	8.0g
(of which sugars)	0.3g	0.2g
Fat	16.1g	9.0g
(of which saturates)	5.8g	3.2g
Fibre	0.2g	0.1g
Sodium	0.6g	0.4g

■ Additional information about the amounts of polyunsaturates, monounsaturates, starch, cholesterol, vitamins and minerals can be given.

Calibration

■ The values of each nutrient must be given as follows:

- Average amounts present are given in 100 g or 100 ml so that comparisons between different products can be made.

- Energy values are given in kilojoules (kJ) and kilocalories (Kcal).

- Protein, fat and carbohydrate are given in grams (g).

- Fibre is given as non-starch polysaccharide (NSP).

- Sodium is given in grams (g).

- Vitamins and minerals must be shown as a percentage of the reference nutrient intake (RNI) in the product or recommended daily allowance (RDA).

KEY WORDS

These are the key words (highlighted in the text). Tick them if you know what they mean. Otherwise go back and check them again.

legal requirement	**'best before'**	**lot or batch mark**
ingredients	**'display until'**	**traceability**
storage instructions	**weight**	**nutritional**
shelf-life	**volume**	**information**
'use by'	**bar codes**	**calibration**

CHECK YOURSELF QUESTIONS

Q1 A tin of chopped tomatoes in rich tomato juice has the following instructions printed on the label. Give a reason for this.
Preparation guidelines
All appliances vary. The following are guidelines only.
To heat on the hob.
Empty contents of can into a saucepan. Heat gently for 3-4 minutes, stirring occasionally.
DO NOT ALLOW TO BOIL.

Q2 A packet of crisps has a 'best before' date printed on the back of the packet:
06:Mar 99

Why does this product have a 'best before' date?

Q3 A jar of marmalade has this code printed on the lid. Give a reason for this.
Oct 2000
09:03 8331

Q4 A packet of digestive biscuits has these two pieces of information printed on the wrapping:
Ingredients
Wheat flour, vegetable oil and hydrogenated vegetable oil, sugar, wholemeal, cultured skimmed milk, partially inverted sugar, syrup, raising agents (sodium bicarbonate, tartaric acid), salt.
Suitable for vegetarians.

(i) Does the manufacturer have to give both pieces of information?
(ii) Why would the manufacturer put both pieces of information on the label?

Q5 A packet of vacuum-packed Double Gloucester cheese has the following date stamps on the label:
Display until 21st January
Use by 28th January

Why does this product have a 'use by' date?

Answers are on page 243.

Packaging

ᵗ⊚ᵗ What is packaging for?

■ Food packaging and the design of the packaging play an important part in food production. You will find that nearly all the foods we buy today come in some form of packaging. Over the years the materials and methods of packaging have changed as new technology has been introduced.

Figure 15.1 *A grocery shop in the 1940s*

Figure 15.2 *A modern supermarket*

Figure 15.3 *Food products can be packaged in all sorts of ways*

■ Food packaging legislation states that food packaging must not:

- be hazardous to human health
- cause the food to deteriorate
- cause unacceptable changes in the substance or quality of the product.

■ Packaging has a number of important **functions**. It helps to **identify**, **contain** or **protect** food products or ingredients. You will need to be aware of these different functions.

CONTAINING THE PRODUCT

■ Packaging holds the contents together and, when sealed, prevents spillage and loss. The packaged products can then be **transported**, stored and displayed easily and used conveniently.

■ The packaging can be a uniform shape and size, e.g. rectangular or square boxes for cakes, cake mixes and breakfast cereals. These can be further packaged into larger boxes or plastic shrink-wrap for transportation.

■ Sometimes the packaging has to hold difficult or irregular shapes which are not easy to fit, e.g. vegetables and fruit. These are often packed into nylon nets or plastic bags.

- Crates, trays and pallets are used to load and hold packaged foods during transportation. These are often made from rigid plastic to prevent contamination from splinters or staples, which often occurs when wooden or cardboard containers are used.

Figure 15.4 *Food products being transported*

PROTECTION
- The food product must be protected from:

    • **Physical damage**, which can be caused by vibration, collision or being crushed during storage, display or transportation. For example, fragile foods such as eggs are protected by rigid plastic/cardboard boxes. Cornflakes are protected by firm cardboard. Soft fruits are protected in glass jars or metal cans.

    • **Atmospheric conditions**, such as the effect of changes in temperature, light, humidity or air controls. For example, warm temperatures may cause fruit to overripen, bright light may cause vegetables to lose colour, oxygen may cause cut foods to change colour and start to go brown.

    • **Contamination** from chemicals, micro-organisms, insects or rodents. Foods that are contaminated by any of these are unsafe to use.

    • **Tampering**, which is a problem because products can become contaminated if they are opened by mistake and then reclosed. The design of the packaging can help to prevent food products from being tampered with. Tamperproof packaging techniques make it easy to see if the packaging has been opened. Examples include:
        – plastic collars on bottle lids, e.g. sauce bottles
        – film overwraps on cardboard boxes, e.g. on a box of teabags
        – paper strips across jar lids, e.g. on a jar of mayonnaise
        – plastic rings on the caps of screw-top bottles, e.g. lemonade
        – tin foil seals in pourable boxes, e.g. fruit juices.

Figure 15.5 *Tamperproof seals*

IDENTIFICATION
- Information about the product can be printed on the packaging. Labelling information is required by law to describe and inform consumers about products.

- The presentation of the packaging at the point of sale helps to attract customers to buy the product.

- The design of the packaging, which may include the shape, colour, size, etc., is used to identify a specific manufacturer and the product range.

🍽 Materials

- In past times natural materials such as wood and pottery were used to pack and store foods, e.g. apples in wooden crates and honey in stoneware jars. Today several types of material are used, including glass, paper, metal and plastic. These materials are constantly being adapted and improved to produce a wide variety of packaging which often includes a mixture of materials.

Figure 15.6 *Glass is a frequently used packaging material*

GLASS

- Glass bottles are used to package milk, wine, sauces, salad dressings, etc.

- Glass jars are used to package herbs, jam, honey, fruit, cook-in sauces, etc.

- Glass can be:

  - brittle and will often break easily

  - moulded into a variety of shapes

  - transparent so the product can be seen

  - coloured to enhance appearance

  - resistant to high temperatures when contents are added

  - tough and rigid to withstand crushing

  - impermeable to substances which may contaminate the contents

  - **recycled**

  - cheap to produce

  - heavy, giving additional weight to the product.

Figure 15.7 *Metal trays and containers are used to package many foods*

METALS

- Two types of metal are used to make cans and a range of packaging parts, such as tops, screwcaps, bottle tops, trays, foil wrappings and laminates. These two types are **tinplate** and **aluminium**.

- Tinplate and aluminium can be:

  - strong, to retain shape and withstand crushing

  - heat treated to high temperatures

  - impermeable to substances that would contaminate the contents

  - lightweight

  - used in different thicknesses

  - moulded into a variety of shapes.

Figure 15.8 *Plastics are used by many manufacturers*

PLASTICS

- Several types of plastic are used for packaging food. Some are rigid and some are flexible. They include:

  - polyethylene terephthalate, used for bottles to hold liquids

  - polystyrene, used for trays and containers. The polystyrene is expanded and pressed into different shapes to hold liquid or solid foods. It a poor conductor of heat and is often used to make insulated containers for hot drinks and takeaway foods

- polythene, which can be of high density, withstanding high temperatures, e.g. boil in the bag foods, or of low density for use at room temperature or in the refrigerator or freezer. Polythene can also be used as a stretchable film, e.g. cling film. It can also be bonded to another material to act as a lining. This is called **lamination**.

- cellulose film, which is available in a range of colours and is used for many different purposes.

■ Plastic can be:

- moulded into a variety of shapes

- very lightweight

- impermeable to substances that would contaminate the food contents

- difficult to dispose of

- **biodegradable** (these plastics are more expensive)

- sealed under pressure and heat treatment.

PAPER AND PAPERBOARD

■ Paper has been used for packaging for many years and it is still very popular. It can be used for all or parts of the packaging, e.g. as paper bags, labels, greaseproof paper, parchment and cartons.

Figure 15.9 *Paper and card packaging*

■ Paper and paperboard can be:

- made in a variety of thicknesses

- used in sheets for flexible wrapping

- moulded into a variety of shapes, e.g. cartons

- recycled to reduce costs and save natural resources

- coated or laminated

- easy to print on

- lightweight.

▮◉▮ Choosing the right type of food packaging

■ The characteristics of the food determine the type of packaging that is needed. You can check out the characteristics of food products by asking the following questions.

■ Is the food product:

- light or heavy in weight?

- sensitive to light, oxygen, temperature or moisture?

- cheap or expensive to produce?

- dry or wet?

- liquid or solid?

- brittle or rigid?

- stored at an **ambient room temperature**, or does it need chilled or frozen storage?

- capable of a short or long shelf life?

What is the characteristic of the food product?

■ Food manufacturers need to ask these questions and must also consider a range of other factors when choosing the right type of packaging for their product. You should also ask yourself similar questions when taking a close look at packaging during your coursework project. For example:

- Will the packaging help to sell the product?

■ First, the manufacturer will define the **characteristics** of the food product, e.g.:

- weight – light or heavy?

- volume – solid or aerated?

- firmness – fragile or robust?

- keeping quality – short or long shelf life?

- cost – cheap or expensive?

- sensitivity – to oxygen, light or moisture?

- risk factor – high-, medium-, or low-risk food?

- moisture content – wet or dry?

- storage temperature – frozen, chill, room temperature?

- density – solid or liquid?

■ Second, what characteristics are required by the packaging:

- type of protection – rigid, firm, flexible, mouldable?

- size or quantity – large, small, single or double wrapped?

- compatibility – must be a material which will not react with the food

- resistance to temperature change – e.g. plastics suitable for frozen foods or boil in the bag products

- cost of packaging material – cheap, expensive?

What is required of the packaging?

- suitable for storage and cooking – e.g. stored by chilling → cooked by microwave

- method of sealing – airtight, no leakages

- weight of packaging – heavy, e.g. glass, or lightweight, e.g. plastic film

- surface area – for printing information on

- shape and style – tray, bag, carton, jar, drum, tube, can, bottle, sachet

- opening mechanism – to prevent spillage, e.g. ring pull, screwtop, foil cap

- storage mechanism – stackable on shelves?

Third, the marketing aspect of the packaging must be considered. Packaging informs the customer about the product. Factors to consider include:

- information, e.g. pictures printed on the package

- the ability to view the product, e.g. through a cellophane window

- product identity, e.g. value or economy brand (simple yellow, blue and white stripes) or luxury brand (gold or silver)?

- computer graphics, e.g. on a cardboard box of breakfast cereals, the label of tinned foods, the cardboard sleeve around a cook chill product.

What is the marketing concept of the packaging?

	Product Characteristic	Packaging Requirement	Packaging Method
Novelty Birthday Cake	Squashable, expensive, limited shelf life. Moist, special features, e.g. decorations. Not easy to handle.	Moisture barrier. Impact protection, window feature, stable base for ease of serving.	Cardboard box with cellophane window. Covered foil cardboard base for serving.
Figure 15.10 *A novelty birthday cake*			
Teabags	Light, moisture-sensitive, fragile, cheap, long shelf life at ambient temperatures.	Impact protection, moisture barrier. Cheap, prevent leakage of tea particles.	Thin cardboard box, cellophane outer wrapping with peel-back strip.
Figure 15.11 *Teabags are packed to keep out moisture*			
Jam or Marmalade	Moist, sticky, runny, oxygen-sensitive. Fairly expensive, long life at ambient temperatures.	Moisture and oxygen barrier to prevent growth of yeasts and moulds. Impact protection. Firm structure to contain runny texture.	Glass jar can be heated to sterilisation temperature. Screw top lid with seal to provide airtight conditions.
Figure 15.12 *Jam is packed in airtight conditions*			

Table 15.1 *Product characteristics*

🍴 Packaging and the environment

- Many people are concerned about the environment, i.e. **green issues**, and you may be too. Food packaging can cause a number of **environmental** problems because:

  - it uses up natural resources, e.g. oil, trees, metal ore

  - it causes air, land or water pollution

  - it cannot always be recycled and is not biodegradable. It has to be disposed of in landfill sites.

- **Consumers** can reduce waste by:

  - buying re-usable containers, e.g. bags, jars, egg cartons

  - re-using carrier bags, e.g. plastic or thick paper

  - taking waste packaging to recycling centres, e.g. glass, cans, paper

  - buying minimum packaging, e.g. single-wrapped rather than double-wrapped products

  - selecting biodegradable materials wherever possible.

> ⚡ **A* EXTRA**
>
> Try to include labelled sketches or diagrams when answering a question on labelling or packaging, as this shows where information will be found and from what materials the packaging will be made. It also means you have to write less but are able to make it clear to the examiner what you understand and know about packaging and labelling.

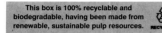

Figure 15.13 *Recyclable packaging*

■ **Manufacturers** can reduce waste by:

- reducing the amount of packaging

- using paper or card that has come from sustainable forests

- avoiding harmful processes, such as bleaching wood pulp with chemicals

- using materials which the consumer can recycle

- printing symbols on the packaging that inform consumers, e.g. recycling logos, plastic identification symbols, anti-litter symbols

- providing information about the packaging materials.

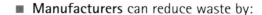 Packaging for takeaway food products

■ Many of us buy takeaway food products and it is particularly important that the packaging of such products can be disposed of easily.

■ This packaging often includes the use of paper sheets, plastic trays, pots and lids or cardboard boxes that aim to:

- protect the food during transportation

- prevent leakage or spillage

- keep the food hot.

■ Over the last few years there has been a huge increase in the range of takeaway food products, e.g. burgers, fish and chips, pizza, kebabs.

Figure 15.14 *Foods packed in vacuum packaging*

■ Manufacturers, retailers and consumers all need to be aware of the environmental issues involved in producing, using and disposing of such a large amount of packaging.

■ Have you noticed that some foods are packed in plastic bags or plastic trays with lids from which the air has been removed or changed to preserve the contents? You need to be aware of these two packaging methods. They are called **vacuum** packing and **modified atmosphere** packaging.

VACUUM PACKAGING

- This has been used for several years now. All the air around the food is removed and the plastic package is sealed.

- The food is kept in **anaerobic** conditions, i.e. there is no oxygen around it.

- This sort of packaging is used for bacon, fish and coffee.

MODIFIED ATMOSPHERE PACKAGING (MAP)

■ This may also be referred to as **controlled atmosphere packaging (CAP)**.

Figure 15.15 *Foods packed in MAP packaging*

■ MAP or CAP preserves food in sealed packs that contain a mixture of three gases:
- oxygen
- nitrogen
- carbon dioxide.

- The process involves:
  - packaging fresh foods in peak condition
  - replacing the air by 'gas flashing' a combination of gases around the food
  - sealing the plastic bag or plastic lid to a food tray by means of a **hermetic** sealing process.
- The new technique of MAP allows:
  - the consumer to see the food product through the clear pack
  - a wide range of foods to be stored in this way, e.g. meat, fish, smoked fish, bacon, salads, fruit, fresh pasta, bread, poppadums
  - an increase in shelf life by retarding microbial activity, e.g. meat up to seven days at chill temperature, bread up to three months at room temperature
  - the colour of the food to stay the same until the pack is opened.
- However, once the packaging is opened the food has a normal shelf life and must be stored accordingly.

GASES USED IN FOOD PACKAGING
- **Carbon dioxide:**
  - retards the growth of bacteria
  - can cause damage to the food if used in too great a quantity
  - is absorbed by the foods, which can cause the packaging to collapse.
- **Oxygen:**
  - helps to retain the colour of the food, e.g. meat stays red
  - retards the action of some micro-organisms
  - can cause oxidation of foods and make them deteriorate.
- **Nitrogen:**
  - is used to replace some of the oxygen
  - reduces the rate of oxidation.
- The ratio of nitrogen, carbon dioxide and nitrogen varies according to the food being packaged.

CHECK YOURSELF QUESTIONS

Q1 Why is it important to package food products or ingredients?

Q2 Why do sandwiches have to be wrapped before being sold?

Q3 Give two reasons why a pizza is often packaged in a cardboard box before being frozen?

Q4 How would a cook-chill lasagne that is to be reheated in a microwave be packaged?

Answers are on page 243.

Sensory analysis

🍽 Using sensory analysis in your coursework

■ Sensory analysis is used to **evaluate** food products. When you use sensory analysis on the food products you design and make you will discover details about their qualities such as:

- flavour and taste
- texture
- appearance – colour, shape, size
- smell or aroma
- sound.

■ Sensory analysis will provide answers to questions about your food products in three main areas:

■ **Description:**

- What does the product taste like?
- What are its sensory characteristics?
- How does a change in production, packaging or storage affect sensory characteristics?

■ **Discrimination:**

- Is this product different from a similar product made by another manufacturer or competitor?
- Would people notice the difference?
- How great is the difference?

■ **Preference or hedonics:**

- How much do people like the food product?
- Which **attributes** are liked?
- Is this an improvement over another product?

🍽 Using sensory analysis in the food industry

■ Sensory analysis is used by the food industry at several stages of product formulation and development.

■ By carrying out sensory analysis manufacturers are able to:

- compare a product with a competitor's product

Figure 16.1 *Sensory analysis being carried out in the food industry*

- improve products by modifying or changing the ingredients
- make judgements about the sensory characteristics of a food product
- check during production that the specification is being met
- monitor quality control by checking regular samples from the production line against the specification
- detect differences between products from different production runs or batches
- profile the characteristics of a new product or a modified product
- describe specific characteristics, e.g. sweetness
- test that the quality of a product is maintained throughout its shelf life
- check that a new product is acceptable to consumers
- demonstrate new products to a marketing or sales team
- promote new or reformulated products to consumers.

■ Sensory analysis is carried out by:
- trained testers in **controlled conditions**

or

- untrained testers – consumers in uncontrolled conditions, e.g. market place, shop or home environment.

■ To obtain reliable results the tests are set up in a controlled way to ensure fair testing. Arrangements could include:
- an environment controlled by lighting and temperature
- an atmosphere free from other smells
- individual booths to reduce influence from other testers
- food samples presented on or in identical sized and shaped plain containers
- a small number of samples presented at one time
- coded samples with random numbers
- correct serving temperature for the food samples
- drinking water or eating a plain cracker biscuit between samples to clear the mouth
- clear instructions for the tester
- straightforward response sheets to record the results.

Figure 16.2 *A sensory analysis testing booth*

¶◉¶ Which senses are used in sensory analysis?

- Your **sensory** organs collect information about the food you eat. Sensory organs are: eyes, nose, tongue, skin and ears. They detect the senses of:

  - **sight** – appearance

  - **smell and taste** – aroma and flavour

  - **touch**, texture and mouthfeel

  - **sound** – noise.

- The characteristics of food that affect our organs of sense are known as **organoleptic** qualities.

SIGHT

- The appearance of food is important because you see the food before you eat it. But what makes food look attractive? Colour, size, shape, age and texture can all make food look more or less appetising.

Colour

- Foods are expected to be specific colours, e.g. tomato soup is usually red, peas are usually green.

- Sometimes artificial colours are used to give improved colours or shades to some foods, e.g. tartrazine (E 102) in soft drinks.

- Some foods are processed to be sold white, e.g. salt, sugar, flour and rice.

Aesthetics

- Food can be made to look appealing by attractive presentation, e.g. garnishes for savoury products, decorations on sweet products, placing products in or on appropriate containers, e.g. plates, dishes, glasses.

HEARING

- Some food products make sounds. These make the food interesting during preparation, cooking, serving or eating, e.g. the crackle of popcorn, the sizzle of bacon, the crunch of crisps, the fizz of sparkling drinks, the crunch of raw carrot.

SMELL AND TASTE

- These two senses work together to develop the flavour of food.

  - Smell is sensed in the upper cavity of the nose. It detects freshness, ripeness and the individual scents of foods, e.g. strawberries, cabbage.

  - Your sense of smell is reduced when you have a cold or flu.

Taste

- Taste buds on the tongue detect four groups of flavours: bitter, sweet, sour, salt

  - The flavours develop when the food is chewed and mixed with saliva.

  - The sensitivity of food is reduced when food is either very hot or very cold.

  - Sensitivity is most distinct when the temperature range is between 22°C and 41°C.

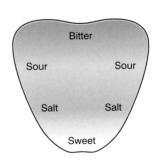

Figure 16.3 *Taste areas on the tongue*

TOUCH

- If you touch or feel food with your fingers you will sense qualities such as softness, stickiness, hardness, etc. The surface of the tongue and other areas of sensitive skin in the mouth also detect different sensations, e.g. moistness, dryness. These qualities are known as **mouthfeel**.

- There are many textures, e.g. gritty, brittle, mushy, crumbly.

Sensory analysis tests

- Sensory analysis tests can be used on food products to establish their most important characteristics. There are several types of sensory analysis test. These meet British Standard BS5929.

PREFERENCE OR ACCEPTANCE TESTS

- These tests would be used to evaluate 'product acceptability' by finding out the opinions, likes and dislikes of the consumer.

- There are no right or wrong answers. The tests gather subjective information about what consumers prefer. To get a reliable result these tests often involve using large numbers of people in market place testing.

- You may already know about two of these tests:

  - paired **preference** test

  - **hedonic ranking test**.

Paired preference test

- A 'tester' is presented with two samples and asked which sample they prefer.

- They may prefer one sample but could find both samples unacceptable.

Hedonic ranking test

- Hedonic ranking indicates consumer preferences. This test does not evaluate the quality of specific product attributes.

- This test finds out the degree of liking for a product from 'extreme like' to 'extreme dislike'.

- A 'tester' is presented with one or more food samples and asked to mark on a five to nine-point scale the point that represents their preference or degree of liking for the product.

- Comments may also be recorded.

- Numerical scales can contain five, seven or nine ranks:

  1 like extremely

  2 like very much

  3 like slightly

  4 like moderately

  5 neither like nor dislike

6 dislike moderately

7 dislike slightly

8 dislike very much

9 dislike extremely

- ■ The choice of test depends on the age of the tester or the type of product being evaluated.

DIFFERENCE TESTS

- ■ You would use these tests to find out if there is a perceptible difference between two or more products. They are **objective** tests. They use comparative judgements to determine:
  - differences in particular sensory characteristics
  - small differences between products.
- ■ Food manufacturers use these sensory analysis tests in product development, e.g.:
  - reducing the fat content in a 'healthy option' product range
  - reducing the fruit content in an economy range of biscuits.
- ■ You will find several types of difference tests:
  - paired comparison tests
  - triangle tests
  - duo-trio tests
  - taste threshold tests
  - two out of five tests.

PAIRED COMPARISON TEST

- ■ A pair of coded samples is presented for the comparison of a specific characteristic, e.g. sweetness.
- ■ This involves fewer samples and less tasting than the triangle test.
- ■ A minimum of 20 tastes will give a useful result.

Triangle test

- ■ Three coded samples are presented to the tester at the same time. Two of the samples are identical, one is different.
- ■ The tester is asked to identify the 'odd one out'.
- ■ Further questions about the samples may be asked.
- ■ A minimum of five 'testers' are required.
- ■ This is a useful test to detect very small differences between a small number of samples.

A* EXTRA

When asked to describe a sensory test, it is often easier to write it as a list of points rather than by descriptive writing.

Always include the correct technical vocabulary and the way in which the test is a fair test.

Ways of recording results are also a means of obtaining more marks.

- Triangle tests are often used during:
  - product development, to see if consumers can tell the difference between the same product made by different manufacturers, e.g. different brands of crisps, cola drinks, biscuits or cheese
  - manufacture, to ensure quality control to make sure that the products from each batch or production run are the same.

Duo–trio test
- You will find that this test is often used in place of the triangle test when less tasting is required. It is particularly useful when strong flavours are involved, e.g. curry, chilli, spicy sausages, etc.
- A control sample is presented to the tester.
- Two further samples are presented together for evaluation. One of these samples is the same as the control, the other is different.
- The tester has to select the sample they feel is different from the control sample.

Two out of five test
- This test is used to see if differences can be detected between two products.
  - Each 'tester' is presented with coded sets of five samples.
  - Three of the samples are the same, and two are different.
  - The 'tester' must select which two are different.
  - The results from each 'tester' are recorded and evaluated to decide if there is a noticeable difference.

Taste threshold test
- This test is occasionally used to find out the lowest or minimum quantity of an ingredient or substance which can be added to a product before a noticeable change occurs, e.g. in flavour, colour, etc.

GRADING TEST
- These test for the degree of intensity of a specific sensory property, e.g. sweetness. The food samples are ranked in order to reflect this or to show consumer preference. You would use these tests to:
  - sort a large number of samples so that a smaller number could be selected from them for a more precise test
  - find out consumer preferences as part of market research
  - obtain rapid results as less skill is required than in other tests.
- You could use three grading tests: **ranking**, **rating** and **profiling**.

Ranking
  - A set of coded samples, arranged in a random order, is presented to the tester.

- The tester has to rank the samples in order of either:
  - a **specified** attribute, e.g. sweetness, saltiness, or
  - a **preference** on a hedonic scale or ranking.

- A minimum of 10 untrained assessors are needed.

- This test is rapid, allowing several samples to be tested at once.

■ When testing the sweetness of yogurt, for example, the descriptor for 5–8 would be sweet and the descriptor for 1–4 would be sour.

8	Extremely	sweet	4	Slightly	sour
7	Very	sweet	3	Moderately	sour
6	Moderately	sweet	2	Very	sour
5	Slightly	sweet	1	Extremely	sour

■ This is an example of a **bi–polar scale**. The statements are two different or opposite characteristics, e.g. dry/juicy; thick/thin; fine/coarse; hard/soft; tough/tender; weak/strong.

Rating
- A tester is presented with a set of coded food products and asked to rate a particular characteristic or preference.

- A minimum of 20 assessors are needed.

- They are asked to rate the products according to a particular scale, e.g. this five-point scale could be used when tasting yogurt:

1 disike a lot

2 dislike a little

3 neither like nor dislike

4 like a little

5 like a lot

or this scale could be used when testing tomato ketchup:

1 much too salty

2 too salty

3 just right

4 too little salt

5 far too little salt

■ This is an example of a **unipolar scale** because all the statements relate to the same characteristic, i.e. salt.

- Rating tests are more informative than ranking tests because the extent of the sensory attribute or preference is assessed rather than just putting them in order.

Profiling tests

- This is also called **sensory profiling**. Sensory profiling is used to obtain a detailed, descriptive evaluation of the differences between products and to find out how much of each difference there is.

- A sensory profile of each product is developed which may include the characteristics of: texture, flavour, aroma, appearance, mouthfeel and sound. These may be assessed separately or together.

- For sensory profiling tests you need:

  - Trained assessors as the tests are more complex than other tests

  - Six or more trained assessors who are presented with a set of coded samples.

  - Each assessor has to rate the intensity on a scale of one to six. (One is lowest; six is highest.)

  - The results from each assessor are added up and the average rating for each **descriptor** is worked out.

  - The results are plotted on a spider diagram or star diagram, to provide a visual product profile.

KEY WORDS

These are the key words (highlighted in the text). Tick them if you know what they mean. Otherwise go back and check them again.

attributes	sound	ranking
controlled conditions	organoleptic	rating
sensory	aesthetics	profiling
sight	mouthfeel	bi-polar scale
smell and taste	preference	sensory profiling
touch	hedonic ranking test	descriptor

CHECK YOURSELF QUESTIONS

Q1 Give three reasons why food manufacturers use sensory analysis during the development of a new bread product.

Q2 Why do trained testers carry out sensory analysis?

Q3 Your sensory organs collect information about the foods you eat. The senses they detect are listed below. Give two sensory descriptors that describe the characteristics associated with each of the senses.
- sight/appearance
- smell
- touch/mouthfeel
- sound
- taste

Q4 Explain why a research and development team of food technologists would use a hedonic ranking test to evaluate a new chocolate cake product.

Q5 During a production run why would a food manufacturer use the triangle test for sensory analysis of custard cream biscuits?

Q6 Profiling is a method of showing test results from rating tests. Explain why a food manufacture would use sensory profiling.

Answers are on page 244.

Exam questions and student's answers

1 This is part of a label from a chilled lemon mousse.

Chilled Lemon Mousse
Low Fat Whipped Lemon Dessert
Ingredients Reconstituted Skimmed Milk, Lemon Juice, Sugar, Skimmed Milk, Vegetable Extract, Cocoa Butter, Lemon Zest, Pork Gelatine, Emulsifier E472b, Modified Maize Starch, Colour E161b, Stabilisers E415, E410, E412

Why are the ingredients on the label listed in this order? (2 marks)

Because, by law the ingredients list must go in order from the heaviest to the lightest. Therefore these products are listed in descending order of weight starting with the greatest and ending with the least.   2/2

2 From the label, name one ingredient which is an additive and explain fully why it has been used. (3 marks)

One additive which is used in the lemon mousse is emulsifier E472b. This is used to prevent the ingredients separating out because an emulsifier stops ingredients like oil and water from separating and keeps them mixed together.   2/3

How to score full marks

1 The student gains full marks for this question. She has shown that she understands the legal requirements of labelling.

2 The student gets two marks out of three for this answer. She has named an additive correctly and has given a correct reason for including it. However, she has omitted the scientific understanding of an emulsifier. To get full marks she needed to say that an emulsifier holds tiny drops of oil suspended in water and this is how separation is prevented.

Other additives, e.g. modified maize starch, colour, stabilisers, could have been given and explained instead of E472b. These would have gained equal marks providing an explanation of their use was given. However, naming more than one additive would not have gained any additional marks. There needed to be a named additive and an explanation of its function.

1 Why is it important that the product label lists all the additives used? (2 marks)

2 In addition to the ingredient information, other points of information are equally important on the label.

3 What are these and how do they help the consumer? (8 marks)

Packaging is necessary for a lemon cheesecake which is to be sold from a chill cabinet.

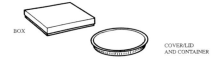

BOX

COVER/LID
AND CONTAINER

Explain the function of the packaging for a cheesecake. (5 marks)

4 Complete the table below.

(a) Name three materials used for packaging a cheesecake product.

(b) State two properties for each packaging material you have suggested which make it suitable for the product. (9 marks)

Part of packaging	Material	Properties of material chosen
Container	Material 1	1 .... 2 ....
Cover/lid	Material 2	1 .... 2 ....
Box	Material 3	1 .... 2 ....

5 Give two environmental problems which result from the use of packaged food. (2 marks)

Answers and comments are on page 225.

COMPLETE EXAM PAPER

Sample Student's answer: Tier H (HIGHER)

I A food manufacturer wants to develop a new range of sweet baked products.

Products already on the market.

During research the design team evaluate similar existing products already on the market. Give five questions the design team might ask about an existing product from looking at the packaging label. **(5 marks)**

1   Does it look appealing to the consumer?

2   Does it contain additives?

3   Does the product look like any picture shown?

4   What kind of sweet baked product is it?

5   How much does it cost?   3/5

Examiner's comments

I The student only scored three marks out of a possible five because some of the answers are vague e.g. 'Does the product look like any picture shown?'

The student has omitted very important points of information about the development of a new product. There is no mention about the type of ingredients which could be used, the nutritional profile which the product needs to meet, the cooking and storage methods which could be considered and any special dietary needs at which the product might be aimed, all of which could be gained from examining the existing products.

2 Nutritional profiles were gathered from products already on the market.

Table to show nutritional information.

Food products per 100 grams	KJ	Carbo-hydrate (g)	Starch (g)	Sugar (g)	Dietary fibre (g)	Protein (g)	Fat (g)	Saturated fat (g)	Sodium (g)
Chocolate biscuits	2,197	67.6	24.2	43.4	3.1	5.7	27.6	17.4	1.6
Sandwich biscuits	2,151	69.3	39.1	30.2	1.2	5.1	25.9	14.8	2.2
Shortbread	2,115	65.5	48.3	17.2	2.1	6.2	26.1	13.6	1.4
Fruit cake	1,490	57.9	14.8	43.1	2.8	5.1	12.9	6.1	2.5
Jam sponge	1,280	64.2	16.5	47.7	1.2	4.2	4.9	2.1	4.2
Jam tart	1,616	62.8	25.3	37.5	1.7	3.5	14.9	n/a	2.3
Nutri-Grain Bars	1,550	69.1	39.9	29.2	3.5	4.1	8.1	1.5	0.3

(a) Sweet baked products are not generally 'healthy options'.

With reference to the table explain this statement. (8 marks)

The statement that they are not generally 'healthy options' is taken from the figures of certain amounts of things in the products. It would appear from this table that sweet baked products contain quite a lot of fat, maybe even high amounts – going up to 27.6 g of fat in a chocolate digestive, although also going down to 8.1 g in Nutri-Grain bars though this could really be considered high amounts just for a snack. They also have quite high amounts of sugar in them, the lowest being shortbread at 17.2 g to jam sponge 47.7 g. These, again, are high amounts for just a snack. Neither large amounts of sugar or fat are considered good for you – rotting teeth and excess body fat are known to result from overdoses of recommended daily amounts. So this is probably why the statement considers them not 'healthy options'. Also perhaps they do not really contain any other valuable mineral or anything not able to be gained from healthier foods. Also we should notice that the fat in the table shows large amounts of it being saturated which is known as not being good for us. 8/8

(b) How are manufacturers adapting their existing cake and biscuit products to meet consumer requirements for a 'healthy' option? (5 marks)

Manufacturers tend to advertise products with less fat – 'virtually fat free', 'half the fat' and '95% fat free'. So this would suggest that they are cutting down on sugars used and perhaps using additives to gain some flavours these could give. They also add things people see as giving the product healthier components and more nutrition, such as nuts. They could be adding additives to do the job of things like fat and sugar. They are also experimenting to find how much they can take out of the recipe without compromising taste and texture. 3/5

Examiner's comments

2 The student has lost marks because her knowledge about fat and sugar is inaccurate. Also no reference has been made to the specific ingredients which would make the product a healthy option. There needed to be some reference to reduced salt or increased starch and dietary fibre, protein or the overall energy value.

3 In the test kitchen when designing a new cake product components must be combined in the correct proportions if the finished product is to be successful.

(a) Complete the table below:

    (i) fill in the correct quantities in grams of fat and sugar;

    (ii) give one different example of a food product made by each method.   **(12 marks)**

Method	Ratio	Flour	Fat	Egg	Sugar	Example
Creaming/all in one	Equal	100 g	100 g	2	100 g	Victoria Sandwich
Rubbing in	8:4:2:3	200 g	100 g	2	90 g	Fruit cake
Whisking	1:2:1	50 g	0 g	2	50 g	Sponge cake/Swiss roll
Melting	8:6:2:8	200 g	150 g	2	200 g	Gingerbread

11/12

(b) The main ingredients in cakes are fat, sugar, eggs, flour, a raising agent and sometimes a liquid. Each ingredient performs an important function.

    Explain the function of each of the ingredients listed.   **(12 marks)**

Name of ingredient	Use of ingredient in preparation and cooking
FAT	Gives the cake flavour and texture. Gives the cake soft tender crumb and richness. Is also a shortening agent. Gives colour – waterproof flour stops it becoming glutenous and stretchy like bread dough.
SUGAR	Gives volume as air particles stick to the sugar crystals. Gives taste and flavour as well as colour – due to Millard reaction.
EGGS	Stabilises the mixture both in the mixing process and in baking. Also acts as a coagulating agent helping to set the cake – correct use doesn't alter flavour.
RAISING AGENT	Gives the cake volume from a chemical reaction causing air in mixture, steam rising giving a nicely shaped cake – Correct use doesn't
FLOUR	Forms the foam structure of the cake. Gives a soft and tender crumb to the cake.
LIQUID	Gives the cake its moisture, as well as acting alongside the raising agent to give volume as it turns to steam and rises.

10/12

Examiner's comments

3 (a) The student has given the wrong answer for the weight of the sugar in the rubbed in mixture. The answer should have been 75 grams not 90 grams

(b) The student has lost marks for the following reasons:
  • A raising agent produces carbon dioxide not air.
  • The carbon dioxide expands on heating making the mixture rise.
  • Flour forms the structure of the cake not the foam structure

Any of the following functions of ingredients could have been accepted.

FAT
• Holds tiny air bubbles which create texture and volume
• Adds colour and flavour, particularly butter and margarine
• Helps increase shelf life
• Produces a cake with a short crumb or rich texture

SUGAR
• With fat helps to hold air in the mixture
• Increases the volume of the cake
• Sweetens the mixture and adds flavour
• Holds the fat in emulsion

EGGS
• Contain the protein albumin which, when beaten, traps air to form a foam adding air to the mixture
• Hold the fat in emulsion once the mixture has been beaten
• Contain lecithin in the egg yolk which helps keep the emulsion stable
• Increase the volume and help to hold air in the mixture
• Add colour and flavour
• Can be a glaze to add shine and colour to the top of the cake
• Help to set the cake due to the coagulation of the protein

RAISING AGENT
• Alters texture
• Produces gas which expands on heating
• Makes cake light and airy
• Makes cake rise
• Might alter taste and colour, e.g. bicarbonate of soda in gingerbread

FLOUR
• Forms the main structure of most cakes
• Soft flour has low gluten content and gives a soft crumb
• Some flours improve texture and colour, e.g. wholemeal
• Is usually the main ingredient and gives the bulk to the cake
• Absorbs fat and liquid during gelatinisation

LIQUID
• Produces steam to help the mixture rise during baking
• Combines with the protein in the flour to develop gluten
• Necessary for gelatinisation of starch to prevent cake having raw taste

4 A food manufacturer decides to develop a range of cake and biscuit products which will be sold from a **vending machine**.

(a) The design team works to a general design specification.

Complete the **five** point specification for a cake or biscuit product for a vending machine.

Do not include packaging material.   (4 marks)

The **first** point has been done for you.

1   long shelf lfe

2   Suitable for falling or being dropped without breaking.

3   Look good and appetising.

4   Taste good and not be too unhealthy.

5   Be cheap and fairly easy to make.   ⁴/₄

(b) A range of cakes and biscuits are needed for the vending machine.

With the aid of a labelled sketch give two different product ideas.   (6 marks)

Design Idea 1   Design Idea 2

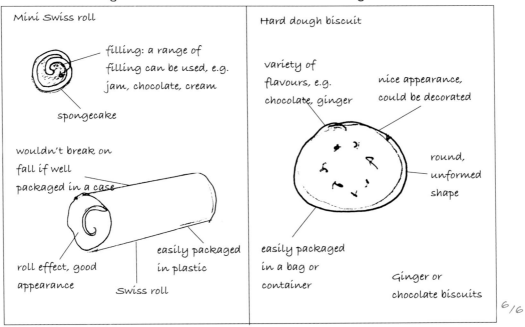

Design Idea 1 — Mini Swiss roll: filling: a range of filling can be used, e.g. jam, chocolate, cream; spongecake; wouldn't break on fall if well packaged in a case; roll effect, good appearance; Swiss roll; easily packaged in plastic.

Design Idea 2 — Hard dough biscuit: variety of flavours, e.g. chocolate, ginger; nice appearance, could be decorated; round, unformed shape; easily packaged in a bag or container; Ginger or chocolate biscuits.

⁶/₆

(c) Choose one of your product ideas for the manufacturer to develop.

Tick your chosen idea

Idea 1

Idea 2 ✓

Explain in detail the reasons for your choice. (4 marks)

A variety of things could be done to a biscuit like this – such things as having chocolate toppings makes the appearance look good. Or interesting flavours such as ginger. Also they can be easily packaged to withstand a drop and not break. They are also of good size, shape and weight to be contained in a small space without jamming the vending machine. Lots of people like biscuits – they won't break and nothing will squish out of them if they fall. Biscuits are considered healthier as there is less fat in a hard biscuit design.

4/4

(d) The test kitchen will develop this idea into a prototype.

With the aid of notes, sketches and charts as appropriate, give detailed information for the development, manufacture and production of your idea.

Do not include packaging detail.

Marks will be awarded for details of:

an annotated sketch of your final product (5 marks)
the **product** specification (5 marks)
ingredients/materials used (3 marks)
production schedules/plan (5 marks)
control checks (2 marks)

Annotated sketch of final product.

lines on biscuit cracked appearance of
biscuit looks good – from cooling of biscuit

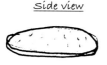

Side view

size to fit in
machine - bitesize

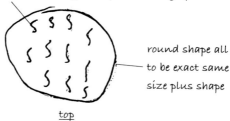

round shape all
to be exact same
size plus shape

top

underneath

5/5

a dark even colour formed from
Millard reaction and caramelisation
and also ginger in the biscuits

Product specification

Each biscuit must:

Be 3cm in diameter.

Be 0.5cm in thickness.

Be of a golden brown colour – no darker or lighter.

Contain 10g flour.

Contain 5g fat.

Contain 2g ginger powder.

Have no more than 4 cracks on surface – each no more than 2mm wide.

Cost no more than 1p to produce.

Look good and appealing.

Be made of highest quality ingredients and manufacture.

Each product:

Will contain 15 biscuits

Cost between 30p and 50p in a vending machine.   5/5

Ingredients/materials used

Ingredients in the biscuit are: flour, small amounts of fat, ginger for flavour and appearance of biscuits, water, some sugar. Also some stabilisers to increase shelf life so the biscuit will not go off in the machine quickly. Some sugar for flavour but not too much to be considered unhealthy.

Average recipe – making 15 biscuits

100g flour

50g fat

40g ginger powder

water – binds ingredients

40g sugar

Scaled up for factory – makes approx. 4000

40kg flour

20kg fat

18kg ginger powder

water

18kg sugar

stabilisers

Would be made in factory on large scale – stabilisers needed when lots of ingredients are used in order to ensure mixture is stable, also to keep it stable.   3/3

Production schedules/plan/control checks

Made in factory – with a mixture of an assembly line, continuous flow, containing machines and humans. Undergoing computer checks as well as visual checks – checking for things such as bacteria, correct cooling temperatures and lengths, size and shape of biscuits.

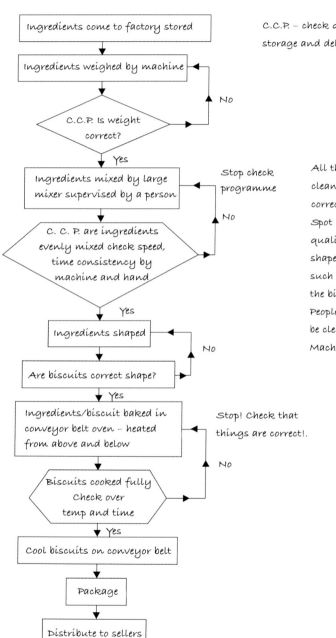

C.C.P. – check quality of ingredients, storage and delivery

All throughout the factory should be clean and efficient and working correctly – with clean environment. Spot checks should be made to check quality such as temperatures, sizes, shapes also to pick up foreign things such as metals, so they don't get into the biscuit and contaminate it. People should wear correct clothing – be clean and fully trained in process. Machinery should be clean.

ㅋ/ㅋ

4 The student has scored high marks for this question for the following reasons:
- The answer shows a general understanding of food product development.
- Good vocabulary used in the design specification.
- Detailed labelled sketches are provided Two completely different product ideas are used not a variation of the same.
- The annotated sketch of the final product is clear. A firm proposal with a clear and appropriate solution has been given. It considers all the necessary factors. The detail of the products can be easily seen.

- The product specification is very detailed and this is where the student shows real understanding.
- One mark was lost on the ingredient information as only the base mixture had been considered.
- A very good production schedule, clearly set out with control points, clear instructions and use of appropriate terminology, processes, timings and health and safety requirements. All these contributed to this very good answer.

---

5 In the test kitchen a prototype cake is made.

For mass production other ingredients may be added.

(a) Choose two of the following ingredients and explain their function. (4 marks)

Glycerine, Salt, Water, Preservatives, Emulsifiers

Preservatives – these increase the shelf life of the product allowing it to be sold for longer and still of high quality with no effect on taste or appearance. Stops the product going off.

Emulsifiers – hold the mixture together and keep large quantities of ingredients, such as are used in mass production, stable so that the mixture is correct and the end result is still all right and correct even though on large scale.

2/4

(b) Manufacturers often use sugar substitutes. Give reasons why sugar substitutes are not always suitable for use in cake production. (3 marks)

Due to the fact the sugar gives the cake extra volume, as when mixing and baking the mixture, air sticks to the fine sugar granules, adding air and giving good volume. Without the sugar air would not be as present and the cake wouldn't have as much volume. Also the taste may be affected as no sugar leaves a strange taste, poor texture, and colour and the cake would be much denser.

3/3

Examiner's comments

5 The student lost marks for the following reasons:

Preservative
There was repetition in the answer and the student omitted to say that a preservative slows down decay.

Emulsifier
The most important fact about an emulsifier is that it keeps fats and oils mixed in water. The student did not show that she understood this in the answer given and consequently lost marks. There was also some confusion over the difference between emulsifiers and stabilisers in the answer given.

COMPLETE EXAM PAPER

6 (a) Explain why a cake manufacturer uses free standing electrical equipment for the production of large quantities of cake mixture.

(4 marks)

Drawing of a free standing electric mixer.

Using things such as a mixer make making the cake a lot easier when large quantities are included. As the process becomes quicker and more efficient, it can evenly mix the ingredients in much less time then a person. Air can be added as needed and control from the different speed settings will get the mixing correct. Having it free standing means it can be controlled by people for as long as necessary and at the speed necessary - also could be programmed.

2/4

(b) What health and safety precautions would need to be followed by people using this equipment?

(6 marks)

Protective eye goggles to prevent things going in their eyes. They should be wearing rubber gloves, only to be worn once to prevent them contaminating ingredients. Also they shouldn't wear outside clothes or shoes that could bring in bacteria. They should be wearing some kind of clean white coat and also have hair tied back under a hat to prevent contamination – maybe wear a mask on their face to stop breathing on and contaminating food.
They should be trained in safety rules when using the equipment and on how to use it so not to spoil food, injure themselves or others or to damage the machine. They would also need to ensure the machine is kept clean and bacteria free.

5/6

Examiner's comments

6 (a) The student only gained two marks out of four for this question because of the very general nature of the answer. The student needed to comment on how a consistent product could be made with the use of electrical equipment, e.g. how the equipment can be used to ensure consistency of volume, aeration, mixing time, mixing speed etc.

(b) The student did not give specific details about the safety requirements of operating the equipment which was needed in order to obtain full marks. For example, some reference should have been made to the use of 'Stop' buttons, regular servicing, safety guards etc.

7 Most food products are packaged for sale.

(a) Explain the functions of food packaging. (5 marks)

To protect food by covering it and preventing tampering or contamination of the product. To keep the food product safe from breaking. Stop foreign bodies getting in. Help to prolong shelf life by keeping oxygen out and prevent food from going stale. Labels can go on the packaging which inform the customer of what it is, the ingredients contained, and perhaps show pictures of the product. Packaging should draw the consumer's eye to the product so that they will buy it – advertise the product and inform the customer.

(b) Name a suitable material for each part of the packaging of jam tarts.

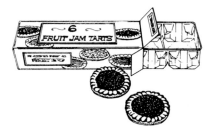

⁵/₅

Material for jam tart container   Foil tin (1 mark)

Reason for choice   Easily shaped to required shape, will hold the jam tart   ¹/₁

easily in place and shape and it is clean and won't pass on bacteria. (2 marks)

¹/₂

Material for inner packaging   Plastic (1 mark)

Reason for choice   Cheap and easily shaped to desired shape – hygienic and   ¹/₁

will help prevent contamination. Stop the tarts from moving and breaking. (2 marks)

²/₂

Material for box   Cardboard (1 mark)

Reason for choice   Cheap and easily shaped – can be printed on so that   ¹/₁

information such as name and label and picture can be on it. (2 marks)

²/₂

c) Strict legal regulations apply to food labelling.

List the information that must be on the label by law. (7 marks)

1   The product's name and explanation
2   Ingredients list
3   Manufacturer's name and address
4   Nutritional information
5   Storage instructions/cooking instructions
6   Best before/sell by date
7   Barcode

⁶/₇

(d) Give **three** items of consumer advice that may also be on the packaging. (3 marks)

1 If a product may contain nuts warnings may be printed clearly for people with allergies.

2 If needed, how the product should be cooked, with time and temperatures.

3 The recommended price – any special offers that are on and what the customer should do if they win, or how to win.

$^1/_3$

Examiner's comments

7 (b) Although this was a good answer, in order to have gained full marks the student needed to give additional information when giving the reasons for choosing various materials for packaging the tarts.

Materials for Tart Container
The statement 'won't pass on bacteria is vague'. A more definite reason is needed, e.g. Foil is light, Tarts can be baked or re-heated in this type of case.

Material for Box
The student should have qualified the term cardboard by stating that it needed to be paperboard or thin card. An additional reason, e.g. can be coated, folded or cheap would have gained full marks.

(c) (d) The student mixed up the answers on 7c and 7d. Nutritional information and bar-code are consumer advice.
Cooking instructions and special claims are required by law.
Additional legal requirements which the student could have given are:
• Special Claims
• Weight or volume.
The examples of Consumer Advice could have included:
• Nutritional Information
• Serving suggestions/portion size
• Guarantees
• Environmental considerations
• Bar-code if related to 'self scan'.

8 (a) (i) What do the initials CAD stand for? (1 mark)

Computer analysed data

0/1

(ii) What do the initials CAM stand for? (1 mark)

Computer analysed mechanism

0/1

(b) With examples, describe ways in which computer technology can help in development and production of a food product. (5 marks)

Computers can help in the development and production of a food product at stages such as quality control. By keeping records and recording information such as temperatures and sizes - like in a biscuit factory - the computer could then give warnings if the oven was becoming too warm or too cold. The computer could also keep track of the quality of the biscuit thickness, size, weight and density to make sure the whole process is correct. It can store these records in little space compared with hand written data and do so for a while. The computer could keep track of a design team's progress - what they've tried - and give print outs of graphs of people's opinions - what things they've done, like how much ingredients used.

The computer could also keep track of orders of ingredients and the delivery and quality of them by on arrival. Also of stock in the warehouse and its rotation. And also perhaps of sales of the product.

5/5

Examiner's comments

8 The answers to part (a) should have been:
(i) computer-aided design
(ii) computer-aided manufacture

9 Sensory testing takes place during the development of a product.

(a) Explain four reasons why sensory testing takes place. (8 marks)

1 To ensure that people actually like the product and think it tastes good and to find out how it could be changed and improved.

2 To check which product people like the most and for what reasons and to see if this is the majority opinion. Paired comparison of two products tested.

3 To check that an assembly line, batch production is producing identical and uniformed products with no variation in taste or appearance that the consumer can see.

4 Check if improvements can be noticed and see if these are liked and to check a product against its specification. If you've added extra nuts can the consumer tell or not, so does it matter and do they still like it? *8/8*

(b) Product profiling was carried out on a final product by trained testers.

The specification stated that the biscuit should be crisp, sweet, nutty, with a soft, toffee filling and a smooth outer coating.

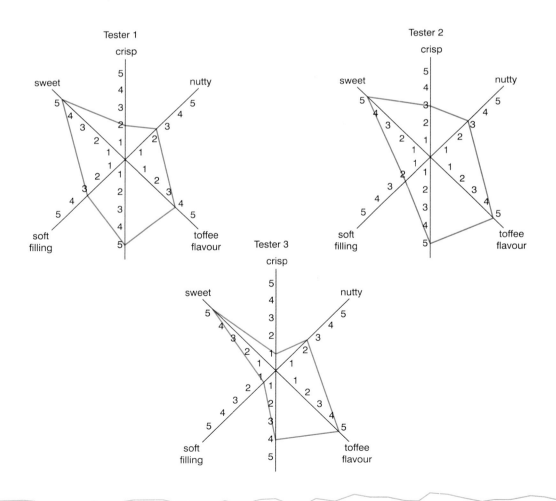

Using the information given on the taster profiles complete the table below.

(i) Identify three characteristics which require improvement.   (3 marks)

(ii) Give **two** improvements for each.   (6 marks)

Characteristic requiring improvement	Improvements
Crisp	1 Removing some fat makes the dough harder, biscuit crisper 2 Bake for longer to make harder and crisper – more dry
Nutty	1 Add more nuts to the ingredients ensure evenly mixed in 2 Add different varieties of nuts to give more nuttier flavours
Soft filling	1 Add more toffee to make a softer filling 2 Try a new filling as well to improve softness

3/3

3/6

Examiner's comments

9 The following improvements could have been mentioned in order to score full marks:

For the biscuit:
  Bake at higher temperature
  Cool completely before storing
  Add a 'crisp' ingredient
  Add a glaze
  Make the biscuit thinner

For the filling:
  Change ingredients
  Add more fat
  Weigh more accurately
  Increase or reduce boiling time

10 Labelling must inform the consumer of any additive. Food manufacturers are allowed to add safe substances to foods if they are needed.

(a) List **five** reasons for using additives. (5 marks)

1 To preserve food for longer
2 Add extra colours
3 Add extra flavours
4 To stabilise the ingredients - hold it all together
5 Emulsifying agent to the ingredients   5/5

(b) What does the 'E' in front of a number mean? (2 marks)

That it is an additive, an emulsifying agent – or an extra ingredient - the number is the designated one given to that product.   0/2

(c) Discuss why there are an increasing number of food manufacturers and retailers selling foods with fewer or no additives in them and the consequences of this action. (10 marks)

Manufacturers and retailers are adding less additives to foods probably due to consumer demand. Some children are allergic to some additives which make them hyperactive so children can't eat them but parents want the children to be able to have these foods – a consequence of this could mean more of the products are sold as they can now be bought by more people. Also consumers demand foods without additives in them as they want to know exactly what they are eating and people often feel that additives contain products that are unsafe even though the government has approved them. They don't want to be eating weird things – so they won't buy things if they feel eating them is unsafe. The manufacturer taking them out means the consumers will buy more of the product again and people will trust them again. But it could also result in a distrust of people in the food industry as it is like admitting the additives were harmful in the first place.

Additives may also be taken out due to government policies finding them unnecessary in the food product or even dangerous. Again this could lead to distrust of food manufacturers making unsafe food or adding unneeded things. However removing unneeded things could result in changes in colour or flavour, which may result in a drop of sales. It's like the situation of the European Union wanting us to take green colouring out of peas - it is needed but people could be allergic to it as well. But lack of colour could make the peas less appealing to look at and sales may drop – the same is relevant with all foods.

Taking additives out could result in change in sales for the good or maybe for the worse if under bad circumstances. But it could also shorten the life of some of the food so we would have to eat things quicker but people don't mind if the food doesn't contain things they don't know they're eating – and it could also change appearance and colour.   10/10

10 (b) The answer should be that it is recognised by the European Union as being on the permitted 'safe' list.

Examiner's comments on complete paper

The student has scored highly on this paper.

STRENGTHS
Good revision carried out.
Good application of knowledge and understanding when given a situation or problem.
Questions read carefully.
Mark allocation was used to generate specific numbers of points for answers.
In the design question (number 4) the student has ensured that all the areas are covered as detailed in the mark allocation.
Good annotation of drawings and sketches showing thoughts and ideas.

WEAKNESSES
Where questions ask for explanation, discussion, description or where there is a need for extended writing, i.e. more than one or two sentences, the student is repetitive and the answers 'ramble on'.
The student could have gained just as many marks by writing much less. Some planning of the answer before beginning to write would have helped.

EXAM PRACTICE: ANSWERS AND COMMENTS

EXAM PRACTICE 1

1 a)

i) Margarine, lard, solid white vegetable fat, e.g. white fat or compound fat, e.g. Trex or a mixture. $^1/_1$

ii) Reason – firm, hard fat to rub into the flour to coat the flour. Margarine adds colour. $^2/_2$

iii) Fat coats the flour grains with fat to stop gluten forming when water is added. This makes sure the pastry has a short crumbly texture. $^3/_3$

iv) Eggs are a protein food. They set when heated. Eggs can set a liquid. The two eggs in the recipe will set the milk. $^3/_3$

> **Examiner's Comments** All the answers are factually correct. The student has a good understanding of the function of ingredients and what happens when they are combined with other ingredients. In question 1 (a) (iv) the term 'coagulate' would help to explain the reason required. Try to use the correct terminology in your answers. It shows depth of understanding and it helps you to be concise with your answers.

1 b)

Vegetarian Option
Broccoli and Blue Cheese Flan
150g broccoli
2 eggs
250ml milk
100g blue cheese, e.g. stilton
25g parmesan cheese
salt and pepper

Value for Money Option
Bacon, Cheese and Vegetable
250ml milk
2 eggs
50g cheddar cheese
4 rashers streaky bacon
1 small onion
1 small leek
25g margarine
salt and pepper

Reasons for Choice
No meat included. Strong flavours from the vegetable and the blue cheese. Good contrast of colour. Unusual combination

Reasons for Choice
Economy priced ingredients often sold with cheaper alternatives, i.e. own brand. Vegetables strong flavours, can be boiled or fried before adding. Bacon adds colour and crisp texture. $^{12}/_{12}$

> **Examiner's Comments** In this type of question you can apply knowledge gained through practical sessions. This student has given correct answers. The basic recipe has been modified in two different ways. For the vegetarian option a meat alternative such as tofu could have been included. The examiner will be looking for a mixture of interesting colours, flavours and textures, combined in a palatable and appetising way.

1 c)

i) Carrot (grated) $^1/_1$
Carrot has a firm, crunchy texture and it gives colour to the coleslaw. $^2/_2$

ii) Courgette $^1/_1$
It can be sliced or cut in strips. The skin can be left on to give colour. $^2/_2$

iii) Sun dried tomatoes $^1/_1$
These are strong flavoured and dark coloured. They are a bit unusual and would be crunchy in the bread. $^2/_2$

> **Examiner's Comments** The student has chosen appropriate vegetables and given good reasons to justify their choice. This type of question gives plenty of scope for the student to select from the wide range of vegetables available. The reason must reflect the characteristics of the vegetable chosen. Marks will be lost if the two do not link together. Again try to explain your answer in sentence form.

EXAM PRACTICE 2

I a)

i) Melting method $^1/_1$

ii) There is a high proportion of sugar, sticky syrup and fat in this recipe. These ingredients are melted in a pan so that they can be easily mixed with the flour and spices. $^1/_1$

Examiner's Comments This is a basic cake method used in recipes with a high proportion of sugar and fat. You will need to know the four basic methods for making cakes, i.e. creamed, rubbed-in, melted, whisked.

I b)

The bicarbonate of soda is a chemical raising agent. When heated in the cake mixture it produces steam and carbon dioxide which makes the mixture rise. $^2/_2$

Examiner's Comments Bicarbonate of soda is the simplest type of raising agent. It does, however, produce sodium carbonate as well as the steam and carbon dioxide. This leaves a dark yellow colour and a sharp taste. Bicarbonate of soda is used mainly in recipes that have strong-flavoured ingredients to disguise it, e.g. ground ginger and golden syrup in this recipe.

I c)

The manufacture should use a cutter, which is shaped so that it will fit closely to each biscuit. Turning the cutter so that it dovetails together will avoid waste. Planning the cutting pattern will also help. Avoid using irregular shapes that create a lot of wasted space on the rolled out biscuit mixture. $^2/_2$

Examiner's Comments There are some good points made in this answer. A manufacturer must avoid wastage. It would also cost time and effort to roll out the biscuit mixture a second time. Very often the mixture becomes firmer or drier when it is rolled again so the aim is to cut out as many biscuits as possible first time. Sketches might have helped the student communicate their ideas about the layout of the cutter on the biscuit mixture.

I d)

i) (This answer would contain diagrams of biscuit shapes to reflect the Olympic games.)

ii) • Ready made icing in tube ready to pipe. This comes in different colours and is very useful for drawing thin lines or for filling in blocks of colours.
  • Coloured sweets – can be bought in the quantity required in the correct size and colour.
  • Ready made marzipan - guaranteed consistency of marzipan mixture used to make individual shaped pieces. It can also be coloured. $^6/_6$

Examiner's Comments The content of the answer offers good reasons for the selection of standard components. The student has written in note form and should really have given a well reasoned answer in sentence form.

EXAM PRACTICE 3

I a)

i) Hazard Analysis Critical Control Points $^2/_2$

ii) It is used for planning how to identify where possible problems would occur in the production of a food product and how these could be prevented. The problems are identified as possible hazards, the effects of the hazards are known as risks and the ways they are stopped are controls. $^2/_2$

Examiner's Comments
i) The student gained full marks for the meaning of HACCP. If part of it had been wrong the student could still have gained one mark.
ii) Despite giving a lot of points the student cannot gain more than the maximum mark of 2.

2

Stages in the production of a frozen chicken pie	Possible Hazards	Controls Used	Quality Control Checks
Collect raw ingredients Temperature control	Cross contamination dry and perishable goods	Separate storage areas for supplier, quality standards	Reputed supplier, visits to
Weigh ingredients	Cross contamination	Separate scales preparation areas	Different storage and
Mix ingredients for pastry	Bacteria present	Correct storage	Stock rotation
Cook chicken	Food poisoning	Cook to 72°C	Food probe
Make white sauce for chicken filling	Raw flavour	Cook to 100°C	Temperature
Combine sauce with chicken and cool	Cross contamination	Cool and store rapidly	Temperature and time
Roll out pastry		Accurate measurement	Computer controlled rollers
Add filling		Portion control	Accurate measurement
Bake	Food Poisoning	Temperature	Food probe
Freeze freezing	Bacterial growth	Time and temperature	Cooling tunnel, quick
Store	Cross contamination Metal detection	Temperature	Thermometers/computer control ⁸/10

Examiner's Comments Although there are gaps in this answer the student has shown understanding of the question and has attempted to give possible hazards and controls for most of the process. The mark allocation for this would have been 8 marks out of 10 for giving a nearly complete answer with some detail.

EXAM PRACTICE 4

1 a) Chilling is a short-term preservation method which prolongs the storage ²/2

b) It is very popular because it does not change the look, appearance or taste of food which other methods of preservation do. ²/2

2 a) Food should be chilled within 30 minutes of it being made. The food must reach its cold temperature within 90 minutes of it being chilled. The critical temperature is between 1 and 3 degrees C. ³/3

b) It is very important that the temperature of a chill cabinet is kept correct. This can be done by using a thermometer in the chill cabinet which can be checked at regular intervals. Also a food probe could be used to check certain products at certain times. If a food probe is used on one of the products the product would then have to be thrown away.

Some chill cabinets are fitted with alarms which will sound if the temperature becomes too low or too high.

Staff are used to check temperatures of chill cabinets and to record these over the day. Sometimes there are small computer-controlled devices in a chill cabinet which record and print the temperature each hour. This means that a careful check can be kept on variations and patterns. ⁵/5

Examiner's Comments The answers to all parts of the question are clear and concise. The answer to question 2 (b) on checking the temperature of the chill cabinet has been done particularly well. Overall the student would have scored full marks for all parts of the question.

EXAM PRACTICE 5

1 By law all of the additives must be listed to ensure that the consumer knows exactly what the product contains. The additives are often hidden factors that cannot initially be seen in the product but some people may be allergic to them and if they are not stated then if the consumer was allergic to them they would be liable to sue the company. 2/2

Examiner's Comments The student gets full marks for this answer as he has mentioned that by law the additives must be named and the reasons for this from a consumer's point of view. Nothing has been omitted.

2 The product packaging must be bright and colourful and attract the consumer because the packaging will basically act as the salesperson. The labelling must have a title and sub heading to tell the customer immediately what the product is. The label must display any special flashes, i.e. fat free, to show the consumer what the product is. If special flashes are present then there must be proof on the label that the special claims are true. This enables the consumer to believe them. The address of the manufacturer must be on the labelling so that if the consumer would like to make any comments or complaints then they can do so.

A bar code is normally present, however that is for the convenience of the shopkeeper for stock keeping and pricing goods. The volume or weight of the food must be given to show the consumer how much they can expect in the product. A nutritional table is also required which is essential for the consumer especially if they are on a diet or have special dietary requirements. The cost is often given. Storage instructions are essential on labelling to ensure no bacteria contaminate the food. Also if the product needs to be cooked or prepared these instructions must be stated to ensure the food is cooked properly by the consumer to prevent food poisoning. 7/8

Examiner's Comments The student gains 7 marks out of 8 for this answer. Many different points of information given on a label are discussed, however the student fails to identify specifically what are legal requirements and what are there for consumer advice, despite referring to these and giving reasons for each piece of information.

3 Packaging is used to protect the cheesecake from being squashed, to prevent people from tampering with it and to protect it from exposure to the air and bacteria. The packaging is also able to give information which is useful to the consumer. It also enables the cheesecake to be stored and stacked in the chill cabinet without being crushed. 5/5

Examiner's Comments
This is a good answer and covers the main functions of packaging. The student would have gained full marks for this answer. Other points which could have been added or used instead would have been:
- preserves/reduces food spoilage
- helps people to choose
- guarantees safety and hygiene
- promotes and advertises the product.

4 (a and b)

Part of Packaging	Material	Properties of material chosen
Container	Material 1 *Rigid foil*	1 *Non Crushable* 2 *Moisture proof*
Cover/lid	Material 2 *Transparent plastic film*	1 *Dust proof* 2 *Stops liquids leaking out*
Box	Material 3 *Thin cardboard*	1 *Protects the cheesecake* *from being crushed* 2 *Information can be printed* *on it* *9/9*

Examiner's Comments
This answer would have gained full marks. The student has used the mark allocation in the margin and ensured that sufficient points have been made to gain the marks needed.

5 i)   *The packaging needs to be recyclable to*
conserve the natural resources of the world.

   ii)   *It can be expensive if it is not able to be*
recycled.   *2/2*

Examiner's Comments
Both these points are relevant and would gain a mark each.

SECTION 11: KNOWLEDGE AND UNDERSTANDING
1 Food commodities (page 78)

Q1 Two main groups of flour are:
- wholemeal flour
  - all the grain is milled, giving a 100% extraction rate
  - contains fibre in its bran content so it has a high NSP (non-starch polysaccharide) content
  - is brown in colour with a nutty flavour.
- white flour
  - the bran and germ, i.e. 30% of the wheat grain, are not milled, giving a 70% extraction rate.
  - contains less fibre so it has a lower NSP (non-starch polysaccharide) content
  - is whitish in colour.

Comments Steel rollers are used in modern roller milling and two types of flour result from the primary processing stages carried out during the roller milling of wheat grains. To produce white flour an extra stage is needed to separate the bran and germ part of the grain from the endosperm which is then milled. There is also a traditional method of milling wheat. This is called stonegrinding. It involves grinding the grains between two rotating heavy circular stones to produce stoneground flour.

Q2 Your answer could include:
- Strong white flour – this has a high gluten content which helps to create high volume, open-textured products, e.g. white bread, Yorkshire pudding.
- Plain white flour – often called all-purpose flour. It contains less gluten and is used for shortcrust pastry, biscuits, and for thickening sauces and gravies.
- Self-raising flour – this has a chemical raising agent evenly mixed into it, e.g. baking powder. It is used to create an aerated texture in cakes, scones, etc.
- Soft cake flour – this has a chemical raising agent evenly mixed into it and it is made from wheat with a lower protein content. Additional sieving in the processing produces a fine soft flour used for sponge cakes.

Comments Gluten is a protein found in wheat flour. It is not present in other cereals, e.g. maize, barley, oats. Gluten is formed from two proteins – glutenin and gliadin. When mixed with water they give the dough an elastic stretchy working characteristic. The mixing and kneading process in bread-making strengthens the gluten. The dough has the capacity to stretch and hold the carbon dioxide produced by the raising agent. Salt also strengthens gluten. It coagulates when baked in a high temperature (e.g. when bread is baked at 220°C) to form a high volume open texture.

Other products such as cakes, rubbed-in pastry such as shortcrust, and some biscuit mixtures do not require this stretchy elastic property. A flour which contains less gluten is needed to provide a short crumbly texture, e.g. shortcrust pastry or shortbread, or a soft fine risen texture, e.g. sponge cakes.

Many products can be developed from a single food commodity. This produces product diversity. Many products are made from processing maize. Can you think of other single food commodities that are processed to make several more food products for us to use?

Q3
- Ingredient list 1 is for tinned baked beans in tomato sauce.
  Function: The sugar is added to sweeten the sauce and counter the sharp (acidic) taste of the vinegar.
- Ingredient list 2 is for a jar of fruit chutney. The sugar is a main ingredient. Note the position of sugar in the list. Refer to Revision Session 14 which explains that ingredients are listed in descending order of weight.
  Function: The sugar has several functions in the chutney:
  - as a preservative to inhibit growth of micro-organisms
  - as sweetener to sweeten the fruit (apples) and to balance the sharp taste of the vinegar
  - as colour – brown sugar is often used in chutney to add flavour and colour.

Comments This is another example of how a single food commodity is used to manufacture products which meet the needs and preferences of consumers. In response to the National Guidelines on Dietary Targets some people try to eat less sugar. As well as cutting out familiar sugary foods such as sweets, cakes, biscuits and sugar added to hot drinks or sprinkled on breakfast cereals, it is necessary to reduce the intake of 'hidden' sugars, i.e. those foods which are not usually linked to sugar, e.g. baked beans, tomato sauce.

2 Characteristics of food materials (page 88)

Q1 i) Rich (sweet) shortcrust pastry base – An egg yolk is added to a 200 g pastry mix. It adds colour and flavour, enriches and helps to bind dry ingredients together.

ii) Lemon filling – 2 egg yolks are added to 250 ml sauce mixture. The egg yolk helps to thicken the liquid because the protein coagulates when added to the hot sauce mixture. Egg yolk also adds colour and flavour.

iii) Meringue topping – 2 egg whites are whisked to make the meringue. The egg white protein albumen stretches to hold air bubbles to make a foam. When baked at 150°C the albumen coagulates to give a solid fine-mesh structure.

Comments Eggs are a very useful and versatile ingredient. They have three main working characteristics: coagulation, foam formation and emulsification

Q2 • Some water in the milk changes to steam and rises from the surface.
• Fat globules rise to the surface and give a pale creamy colour.
• The proteins lactalbumin and lactoglobulin coagulate and form a skin on the top of the milk.
• Small bubbles of air rise to the top and collect under the skin.
• As the milk boils the pressure in the bubbles of steam causes them to rise, forcing the skin upwards and the milk boils over!

Comments Protein coagulates on heating. In the case of milk the proteins form a skin on the top of food products such as custard, sauces and milk puddings. Stirring the milk or milk mixture helps to break up the mass of coagulated proteins.

Q3 The differences between the two types of meat are the amount and type of connective tissue present and the length of the muscle fibres.
• Tray 2 – rump steak consists of short, thin muscle fibres with small amounts of collagen (connective tissue). It is also sliced into thin pieces. It will be tender and only require quick cooking to make it palatable. It does not need to be tenderised.
• Tray 1 – braising steak consists of thicker and longer muscle fibres and a larger amount of connective tissue. It needs to be cooked by a long slow moist method to soften the collagen and elastin and make the muscle fibres tender and palatable.

Comments Meat is muscle tissue made up of long thin muscle fibres held together in bundles by the connective tissue, collagen. Collagen is a water-soluble protein which dissolves during cooking to form gelatine. The connective tissue, elastin, binds the muscles together. Elastin is tougher and less soluble than collagen.

Q4 The muscle fibres are short and there is a smaller amount of the connective tissue collagen to hold the fibres together. There is no tough elastin. This flesh structure does not need long cooking methods to tenderise the muscle fibres. The protein coagulates at 60°C and the collagen is converted to soluble gelatine. Cooking times would be: grilled trout 4 minutes each side; baked halibut 20 minutes.

Comments Fish is similar in structure and composition to lean meat. The flesh is made up of bundles of short muscle fibres held together by collagen, with no tough elastin. Fish is different to meat in that there is very little colour change in fish during cooking, except in shellfish.

Q5 (a) butter or margarine; (b) hard margarine or lard; (c) olive oil; (d) soft margarine; (e) corn oil.

Comments You can work out reasons for your choice:
a) butter or margarine for colour, flavour and ability to hold air
b) solid fat to form a protective layer to prevent gluten forming when water is added

c) olive oil to add flavour and form an oil in water emulsion

d) soft margarine contains some unsaturated fatty acids to give a solid but softer consistency than butter

e) corn oil for heating to a high temperature to seal and cook food for a crisp texture.

Q6 Your answer should include:

a) Wheat is the only cereal that contains the proteins glutenin and gliadin which form gluten when mixed with water. Strong wheat flour has a high gluten content. Gluten stretches to hold air or gas produced by the raising agent, yeast.

b) Cornflour is a starch powder used to thicken a liquid by the process of gelatinisation (i.e. the starch grains absorb liquid, swell, burst and thicken the liquid).

c) Basmati rice is a long-grain rice which has a distinctive smell and flavour. During cooking it softens and cooks to produce light fluffy separate grains.

Comments Cereals are cultivated grasses grown throughout the world for their nutritious edible seeds. They are a staple food in many countries. Cereals are processed to make a vast range of food products.

3 Food processing (page 103)

Q1 Processed foods usually contain more than one ingredient. When the ingredients are mixed together a structure is formed. The structure formed in a food product is known as a colloidal structure. A colloidal structure consists of two parts which are evenly mixed or dispersed into one another. The parts may be liquid, e.g. vinegar, oil, water, milk; solid, e.g. flour particles; or gas, e.g. carbon dioxide, air bubbles.

Comments There are four colloidal structures: emulsions, suspensions, foams and gels. Make sure you know about each one.

Q2 An emulsion is made from two different liquids, e.g. oil and water. But liquids such as oil and water do not mix. They are said to be 'immiscible'. When shaken together the oil breaks into small droplets and mixes into the water, i.e. an emulsion is formed when one liquid mixed into another. If left to stand, the two parts separate, with the oil floating on the water.

Comments The emulsion can be:
• oil in water, e.g. oil beaten into vinegar
• water in oil, e.g. fat-free milk beaten into oil for margarine.

Q3 To stop the two liquids in an emulsion from separating a third substance is added. This is known as an emulsifying agent. The emulsifying agent has one part which attracts to water and one part which attracts to oil.

Comments Egg yolk contains lecithin which is a naturally occurring emulsifying agent. It attracts to both the vegetable oil and the spirit vinegar and holds them together. The mayonnaise is then a stable emulsion, i.e. it will not separate out.

Q4 Yorkshire puddings are made from a batter mix of 100 g flour, 1 egg and 250 ml water/milk, salt and pepper. The liquid first helps to form a suspension when mixed with the flour and egg. When the batter mix is cooked at a high temperature of 210°C, the liquid reaches boiling point and creates steam. The steam forces its way up through the mixture, stretching it and making it rise. As the mixture bakes it sets into a risen shape.

Baked Yorkshire pudding

Steam can get trapped inside the mixture. The steam condenses on cooling and causes the Yorkshire pudding to collapse. This could be the reason or it may be that the Yorkshire pudding was taken out of the oven before the mixture had set and the shape has collapsed.

Comments Emulsifying agents lower the surface tension between two liquids so that they combine and form a stable emulsion. Lecithin in egg yolk also stabilises a creamed cake mixture. In large-scale manufacture artificial stabilisers are used. An example is GMS used to stabilise the emulsion formed from milk and oil in margarine.

Steam is an important raising agent in food products that contain large amounts of liquid, e.g. choux pastry. Two conditions are needed: large amounts of liquid and a high baking temperature to create the steam.

Q5 The advantages of the Chorleywood bread process are that:
- it is mixed by high-speed mechanical mixers in less than five minutes. This speeds up the time taken to make the bread
- less factory space is needed than for traditional bulk fermentation
- it does not require temperature and humidity control conditions
- less space and less time are required, therefore the production costs are less
- it gives a higher yield of bread per unit of flour
- it enables a higher quality bread product to be made, i.e. keeping qualities, volume, texture, colour and cost.

Comments The Chorleywood bread process was developed in 1961. Today most bread is made on large-scale automatic manufacturing plant lines. The stages are monitored and controlled by computers. All this helps to produce consistent high quality bread products every time.

Q6 Bicarbonate of soda is a chemical raising agent. Chemical raising agents produce carbon dioxide in a chemical reaction. Bicarbonate of soda is the simplest form of chemical raising agent. Your advice could include:
- sodium carbonate, steam and carbon dioxide are produced
- the carbon dioxide and steam will aerate the cake mixtures
- the soda leaves a dark yellow colour and a sharp alkaline taste in the mixture
- strong-flavoured ingredients will disguise the yellow tinge and the alkaline taste.

Examples of suitable cake mixtures include parkin and gingerbread. Look at the list of ingredients in this recipe for Cornish ginger biscuits:

Cornish Ginger Biscuits
*1 level teaspoon golden syrup
100 g margarine
100g sugar
1 level teaspoon bicarbonate of soda
125 g plain flour
*1 level teaspoon ground ginger
quarter teaspoon salt
(*flavour masks the use of bicarbonate of soda)

Remember that chemical raising agents must be measured accurately.

Comments There are three types of chemical raising agents:
- bicarbonate of soda
- bicarbonate of soda plus an acid
- baking powder.

The acid neutralises the chemical reaction with bicarbonate of soda and prevents the taste and colour residual left when bicarbonate of soda is used on its own. One example of a recipe is Singin' Hinny, a traditional scone-type recipe:

Singin' Hinny
200 g plain flour
quarter teaspoon bicarbonate of soda
half teaspoon cream of tartar
quarter teaspoon salt
75 g lard
75 g currants
milk

Q7 Egg is a protein. Proteins coagulate when heated. The soluble structure changes to become insoluble, e.g. when egg is cooked as in hard boiled egg. Eggs can be used in combination with other ingredients, e.g. to coagulate and set a liquid. During the cooking of the egg custard mixture at 170°C for 45 minutes the egg/milk mixture sets to form a firm, springy filling.

Comments Eggs can be used to set milk or cream for a filling in savoury flans or quiche. Other proteins also coagulate on heating, e.g:
- gluten protein in bread dough
- milk proteins form a skin on heated milk
- whisked egg white bakes into a solid white hard meringue.

Q8 Some of the ingredients used to make the burgers would be loose or dry ones. They would need to be held or bound together by liquid or egg. The binding ingredient in burgers would need to moisten and bind the ingredients together but it would also need to stop the burgers crumbling when cooked and turned on the barbecue. The egg will coagulate on heating and bind the burger ingredients firmly together.

Comments There are three main properties of the proteins in eggs which enable them to be used in many different ways in food products:
- egg proteins coagulate on heating
- egg proteins stretch when whisked and hold air in the structure to create a foam
- egg yolk protein lecithin is a natural emulsifying agent.

4 Alternative ingredients (page 111)

Q1 Soya lecithin is a protein which is used as an emulsifier to stabilise and improve the consistency of the mallow filling during processing and storage.

Comments Emulsions are substances such as oil and water mixed together. If left to stand, these two liquids would not stay mixed. A third substance is added to hold the two parts together. The 'match maker' is called an emulsifying agent. Other examples of emulsifying agents include:
- lecithin, found naturally in egg yolk, which stabilises mayonnaise and creamed cake mixtures
- glycerol monosterate (GMS) which is used to stabilise a wide range of processed food including margarine. (Refer to Revision Session 3 page 89.)

Q2 White bread is a popular choice for many consumers. Wheat flour often produces a light yellow colouring and therefore bleaching agents used to be added to the bread to make it whiter. However, many people do not like the idea of artificial additives such as bleaching agents being added to bread. So bread manufacturers looked for another way of making white bread. Soya flour bakes white and is a alternative natural bleaching agent. It is combined with wheat flour to produce whiter bread and cakes.

Comments Soya flour helps to improve the overall qualities of bread products by producing a moister, softer crumb, an improvement in crumb colour and more flavour. It also increases the amount of dough and improves the keeping qualities of the finished product.

Q3 Your answer could include the following points:
- TVP is made from soya beans which are processed to resemble the shape and texture of meat.
- Soya beans give a high yield per hectare so they are cheaper to produce than meat. This saving in cost will be reflected in the price of the snack meal.
- TVP can be dried and packaged with a shelf life of about a year. This makes the snack meal a convenient product to store.

Comments You could have included different reasons, e.g. some consumers are vegetarian. This means that they eat a restricted range of animal proteins, i.e. no meat. A plant-based substitute such as TVP would be an acceptable form of protein for a vegetarian.

Q4 Myco-protein is not a suitable meat analogue for vegans. This is because during the final stages of production the myco-protein fibres are bound together with egg white. This binding agent also helps to develop the texture. The myco-protein is then processed into shapes, i.e. cubes, sliced, shredded or minced to produce meat analogues.

Comments Vegans are a specific group of vegetarians who do not eat any animal product such as meat, eggs or milk.

Q5 A meat extender is a meat analogue which is used to 'bulk out' or extend food products. TVP could be used to reduce the cost of a minced beef product, e.g. shepherd's pie, lasagne, minced beef pie. The meat analogue would not totally replace the minced beef. It would be used in a ratio which did not change the characteristic of the food product. TVP has little flavour but it absorbs the flavour of the ingredients it is cooked with, e.g. in this case beef stock, garlic, herbs.

Comments If TVP has been added to a food product, the information on the label must not mislead the consumer, i.e:
- The name of the product must clearly tell consumers what the product is. For example, beef lasagne must contain minced beef. It could not be made just from TVP. If it was it would need to be called beef-flavoured lasagne.
- The list of ingredients would indicate the proportion of beef to TVP as ingredients are listed in descending order of weight. Whichever of these two ingredients (beef or TVP) was there in the larger quantity would be put first in the list. (Refer to Revision Session 14 page 180.)

Q6 Your reasons could include:
- TVP has a bland flavour and the soya mince and onions would not provide an interesting flavour or any colour for the rissoles.
- TVP is best cooked with distinctive-flavoured foods and in this recipe these are Marmite, tomato ketchup, herbs and Worcestershire sauce. These add a distinct savoury flavour to the TVP.
- These ingredients also add a deeper colour to the soya rissole mixture.
- The egg is used to bind the ingredients together. Egg coagulates on heating so the egg will coagulate when the rissoles are cooked by frying in hot oil.

Comments Soya mince is made from defatted soya flour which has been extruded to resemble the shape and texture of pieces of meat.

Q7 Marinated tofu pieces are:
- time-saving – marinating food, i.e. soaking food in flavoured liquid, requires time for the flavour to be absorbed into the product
- pre-cooked and convenient to use as they simply need adding to a recipe and heating through
- easy to use in a range of food products, i.e. stir-fry, casseroles, soup, as an alternative to meat
- a variation on the original plain soya bean curd which has been used for many years in East Asia, China and Japan.

Comments Tofu is a vegetable protein, made from soya beans that are ground to a paste and sieved to produce soya milk. The milk is boiled and cooled to 50°C. Calcium sulphate is added to coagulate the milk. The solid curd is pressed and formed into tofu blocks.

Look back at the list of ingredients. Note the ingredient calcium sulphate, which is a natural coagulant.

5 Manufacturing in quantity (page 114)

Q1 The cake manufacturer uses two suppliers to make sure that they have a constant supply. If one supplier had difficulties, e.g. with obtaining raw ingredients, such as the ground almonds, or with the processing machinery which makes the marzipan, this supplier would not be able to supply the cake manufacturer. But marzipan would still be available from the second supplier.

Comments It is quite common for standard components to be bought from more than one supplier. This follows the traditional saying: 'Don't put all your eggs in one basket.' A constant supply of a standard component must be guaranteed.

Q2 (i) Three advantages could include:
- It saves the time needed to buy and store the raw ingredients for the pastry, e.g. flour, fat.
- It saves preparation time, i.e. no weighing or mixing of the ingredients is necessary.
- It guarantees a consistent result.

(ii) Three disadvantages could include:
- Frozen foods need to be stored at a specific temperature (−18°C). This needs to be planned into the manufacturing schedule.
- Special storage conditions are needed, e.g. a freezer room.
- Frozen pastry takes time to thaw.
- It could be expensive if only bought in small quantities.

Comments Manufacturers need to consider both the advantages and the disadvantages when using standard components. Points to consider include cost, time of storage, ease of use and the quality of the product. Balance the points for with the points against to reach a decision.

Q3 Any three from:
- ready-made pizza bases
- ready-grated mozzarella cheese
- ready-chopped vegetables for the toppings
- ready-made tomato and herb sauce.

Reasons should include a reference to savings in time, cost and labour costs, consistency of result and quality, and storage.

Comments Buying in standard components helps manufacturers to increase production without major investment in:
- equipment for extra production lines
- extra staffing costs
- storage of raw ingredients.

Q4 Standard components kept in stock could include:
- stock cubes: chicken, beef, fish, vegetable flavours. To use in lasagne, chilli, meat or fish pie, etc.
- canned vegetables: tomatoes, kidney beans, sweetcorn. To use in hot main-course meals, salads, etc.
- dried foods: chocolate strands or shapes, chopped nuts, wafer biscuits, sugar strands or shapes. To use to decorate puddings, cakes, ice cream sundaes, etc.

Comments These standard components can be used directly in recipes whenever they are needed. They can be used in a variety of products on different menus. They:
- have a long shelf life
- add variety, colour, flavour and interest to a product
- give consistency of results.

Q5 Several varieties are available, e.g. blackberry and apple, cherry, strawberry, gooseberry. Reasons for use could include:
- Some fruits are only available at certain times of the year, e.g. cherries, strawberries.
- Some fruit takes time to prepare, e.g. stoning cherries, hulling strawberries, peeling apples.
- Consistency of the quality of the filling is guaranteed between different batches.

Comments Canned pie fillings have several advantages. Before choosing the supplier of the pie filling it would be necessary to do a quality check on the pie filling. Check the ratio of solid fruit pieces to fruit sauce. The cheaper pie fillings will contain more fruit sauce. In this context the baker would need to decide how much he or she could afford to pay and what quality he or she wants the individual fruit pies to have.

6 Measurement, ratio and proportion (page 126)

Q1 The manufacturer would probably choose an electronic weighing machine. Some of these record in grams, whilst others record to the decimal point of a gram. The sensor in the electric circuit sends a signal to a digital display unit each time a portion of fruit filling is weighed. The digital display can be situated in a position where it can be easily read.

The reading can also be connected to:
- an alarm system which sounds if incorrect amounts of fruit filling are being deposited
- a computer to monitor the weighing process as part of the quality control procedures.

Comments Accurate weighing of ingredients is vital to the production of consistent and successful results. In the example of the fruit filling going into fruit pies, the weight of the filling is a crucial factor. Too much fruit filling will boil over during cooking. Too little filling causes the finished weight of the pies to be too low. Consumers would complain and the manufacturer would not be complying with the Weights and Measures Regulations 1985.

Q2 No, certainly not. Even though the spices are added in small amounts, i.e. in a much lower ratio to the main ingredients of stock, onion and yogurt, they each have an intense and distinct flavour. Adding too much, too little or the incorrect combination could ruin the overall quality of the curry sauce. The spices would have to be weighed out accurately and in the correct ratio.

Comments In a small-scale sample, using 450 ml of vegetable stock, the spices are added in the following quantities: 10 ml ground coriander, 5 ml fenugreek seeds, 5 ml ground cumin, 10 ml turmeric. A 5-ml measuring spoon could be used to measure them out. An additional point to watch would be to make sure the measure is level and not heaped. In a large-scale manufacturing situation large quantities of the spices would be used. These may be weighed by an electronic weighing machine or, because the spices are dry and powdery, they could be measured by volume in a measuring container. Whichever method is chosen, it must be accurate.

Q3 After the prototype for the chocolate cake had been developed in the test kitchen a manufacturing specification would be compiled. This would be very detailed and contain all the information about the manufacture of the chocolate cake, e.g. ingredients, ratio and proportion of ingredients, finished weight, processes, specific times and temperature schedules, quality control procedures. This gives clear guidance to the production manager who will make sure that the product matches the manufacturing specification.

Comments The manufacturing specification must be strictly adhered to if the final products are going to be of a consistent quality.

Q4 Three modifications or adaptations could include:
- using a mixture of interesting cheeses to flavour the sauce, e.g. Italian three-cheese sauce
- adding a vegetable such as dried porcine, mushroom, asparagus or leek
- using low-fat ingredients, e.g. skimmed milk, low-fat cheese.

The new products could be promoted as a new product range to reflect the changes made, e.g. 'Italian Fare', 'Vegetarian Selection', 'Low-fat Option'.

Comments Changing individual ingredients or putting in additional ingredients will affect the flavour and the texture of the pasta and sauce product. Sample or test recipes need to be made

and the results recorded. Only one variation should be made each time to enable the impact of the change to be assessed. This is known as 'fair testing'.

Q5 Three reasons may include:
i) The yeast is bought in in pre-weighed units of 1 kg. This ensures that an accurate amount of yeast is used in each batch. Pre-weighed ingredients are referred to as standard components.
ii) Fresh yeast is blended with warm liquid just before adding to the flour. It can be used immediately and reduces any waiting time.
iii) Yeast is the raising agent in bread. During the fermentation process yeast produces carbon dioxide. If an incorrect amount of yeast is used in a batch of dough the final bread products would not be satisfactory, i.e:
   - too much yeast – over-risen dough with a large, uneven texture
   - too little yeast – unrisen dough with a close, heavy texture.

Comments The selection, combination and specific quantity of ingredients are very important. Foundation recipes have a designated tolerance and qualities of ingredients above or below this tolerance will affect the quality of the final product. Successful recipe development could include:
- accurately weighing and measuring each ingredient
- combining ingredients in appropriate ratios and proportions
- carrying out fair tests to monitor the affect of recipe amendments.

7 Manufacturing systems (page 135)

Q1 Your answer would need to include some of the following points:
- The number of food products to be made
- how often, e.g. every day, weekly?
- type of equipment available
- cost of the final product
- number of workers available
- level of skill of the workers
- money available for investment in new equipment/machinery.

Comments There are several types of production process systems. They include one-off, batch, mass and continuous-flow production systems. Some of the main points which influence the choice of production method include:

- the number of products to be made, e.g. one hundred, several thousand
- the cost of making the product and the selling price of the product, e.g. an expensive celebration cake or a packet of economy digestive biscuits
- the equipment or money available to set up a production system.

Remember to draw a conclusion from the points you have listed and to give your choice of the most appropriate method of production system.

Q2   Choux-based products could include eclairs, profiteroles, buns.
Variations could be developed by using different toppings, filling and flavours:
- toppings – melted chocolate, coffee icing, dusting with icing sugar
- fillings – fresh cream, fresh cream with fruit filling, e.g. strawberries, fresh cream with vanilla custard, flavoured fresh cream, e.g. vanilla, coffee.

Comments The production system used for the choux pastry is batch production. A small number of similar products are required. Slight adaptations would be made to the base product to meet consumer demand or to create consumer interest. To extend your revision on batch production you could think about:

- some of the other features of batch production systems
- what other base products could be made to complete the range of cream cakes sold in the cake shop each day.

Q3   The 'just in time' system is when food products are made only to order. Nothing is made in advance. The biscuit manufacturer will only manufacture the chocolate digestive biscuits to meet regular orders, i.e. a supermarket may have a regular order every week, or to meet special orders they receive. Reasons for 'just in time' systems include:
- No finished products are put into storage.
- This saves floor space.

- There is no waste because products do not get damaged in storage nor do they pass their 'date marks'.
- Raw materials do not have to be bought in in advance for food products that may never be made.

Comments The 'just in time' system is one of the main features of modern automated manufacture. Manufacturing processes can be organised very quickly in response to orders received. 'Just in time' is also used in other industries, especially the electronics industry, where goods can be damaged and can become outdated if stored for long periods. In the food industry the shelf life of a product is always well defined by 'date marks'.

Q4   Enrobing is coating a food product with another ingredient to give it an outer layer. Reasons for the use of enrobing include:
- To increase a product range, e.g. plain digestive biscuit, milk chocolate-coated digestive biscuit, plain chocolate-coated digestive biscuit.
- To give a contrasting texture, e.g. fish coated with breadcrumbs (soft fish – crispy coating).
- To give contrasting flavours, e.g. chicken coated with batter (e.g. chicken dippers).
- To increase the range of cooking methods which may add texture and flavour, e.g. shallow-fry fish fingers (the crispy, crunchy texture and flavour are changed by frying).
- To allow food to be hand held, e.g. fish or chicken goujons (cut into strips and
- To allow food to be hand held, e.g. fish or chicken goujons (cut into strips and coated with breadcrumbs) for a buffet party (may be served with selections of dips).

Comments Food manufacturers are always looking for new products to develop. Enrobing foods in different coatings is one way of creating new foods or extending an existing product range. You may like to make a list of all the enrobed products you have seen, used or eaten yourself.

Q5   CAM stands for computer-aided manufacture. Your answer would need to show how CAM is used in the food industry by explaining when CAM is used and giving reasons, e.g. for standardising production. Here equipment can be programmed or set to repeat a process time after time with accuracy and precision, e.g. cutting pastry circles, spraying flavourings. Any changes in size or rate of spray are made on the computer and this makes for an accurate and speedy adaptation of the production line

Comments You will need to explain fully each of the examples of the use of CAM that you give. Some production lines may use CAM in individual pieces of equipment, or, alternatively, only parts of the production line may involve CAM. Other production lines, particularly continuous-flow systems, will be fully automated, with a central computer unit.

8 Quality assurance and quality control (page 138)

Q1 Your answer could include:
- concise specification for each raw ingredient and component – this may include weight, size, shape, moisture content, nutritional content, colour, etc.
- sourcing from more than one country if seasonal ingredients are required all year round
- using more than one supplier to make sure that ingredients are always available
- keeping raw materials free from contamination during delivery
- using correct contamination-free storage equipment and areas, e.g. strict control of debagging, deboxing, and environment control conditions
- using supplies in strict rotation.

Comments Remember that quality assurance is applied before, during and after production.
The selection, purchase, delivery and storage of raw ingredients and components are an important part of quality assurance procedures.

Q2 At this stage the quality of design would be guaranteed or assured if the research and development team linked the development of the new product to the needs and preferences of consumers. Your answer could include:
- research and analysis of consumer needs and preferences

- defining a target group of consumers who will buy the product
- writing general design criteria to guide the research and generation of ideas
- writing a design specification to develop critical ideas through to prototypes
- evaluation of the prototypes against the design specification.

Comments It is important to build in quality assurance procedures at the design stage. This makes sure that time, effort and money are not wasted by taking a badly thought out product through to the manufacturing stage. A company could not afford to set up large-scale production lines, buy in bulk ingredients and manufacture large quantities of a product that no one wanted to buy. Quality of design is essential.

Q3 These systems set out guidelines and standards which help companies to achieve the level of quality they require in their food products. The company has to state their plans and actions clearly in manuals or policy documents. These systems involve everyone in the company as being responsible for their part in the production system.

Comments Some food companies try very hard to improve the quality of their food products and to build up a good relationship with consumers.

Q4 Quality assurance is all the procedures that cover the total design and manufacture of a food product. Quality control examines the production of the food product.

Comments Remember that quality control is part of a food manufacturer's quality assurance procedure.

9 Food production systems (page 142)

Q1 (i) Your answer would need to include three stages with temperature controls from production systems you have studied. The following are examples of the type of things you might include:
- ready made pastry for pies and pastries stored at 12°C–15°C
- raw meat and fish stored below 4°C

- cook chill products stored at 0°C–5°C
- bread proved at 40°C and baked at 300°C
- frozen foods stored at –20°C to –25°C
- meat in tomato sauce cooked at 90°C–100°C
- fresh vegetables stored below 8°C.

(ii) Different methods can be used to record, monitor and control temperature e.g:
- a temperature sensor or thermometer used to record the temperature of a freezer chill cabinet or an oven
- a thermostat to keep temperature at a set point or within a range
- a temperature probe to monitor temperature, e.g. throughout a product; at the centre of bread during baking
- a continuous digital display of temperature levels
- connection to a central computer system which will activate an alarm system if the temperature moves out of range
- regular checks by food handlers/ workers, e.g. every hour.

Comments Temperature is critical to food safety. You will find that reference is made to this vital aspect of food production in several areas of study into food technology.

Temperature is critical to:
- the control of the growth of micro-organisms, e.g. during storage
- the prevention and destruction of micro-organisms during preparation, cooking and preservation, e.g. heating food to high temperatures
- the quality of food products, such as texture and palatability, e.g. a starch-based sauce will have an incorrect texture and bland flavour if not heated to 100°C for two minutes to allow gelatinisation of the starch to take place; and fried foods e.g. potato crisps/chips, will not have a crisp texture if the oil or fat has not been heated to a high enough temperature.

Q2   Your answer could include:
- Computers can be programmed to hold very detailed records of each ingredient, e.g. original source, supplier, amount delivered, delivery date and characteristics such as moisture content.
- Electronic sensors can signal the need for ordering more stock.

- This can ensure the automatic use of materials in correct rotation.
- It can control the delivery or flow of ingredients to the production area.
- It provides data for stock taking.
- It allows the storage and retrieval of codes which are allocated to each delivery of raw materials. In the event of problems with a finished product, the raw materials can be traced back. This is known as traceability.

Comments You can now see that computers can be used extensively for the control of stock. Computers are also used for recording and tracking in retail outlets. Bar codes are printed on the packaging of all food products. When products are purchased the bar codes are scanned at the check out. Computers record which products have been sold and how many were sold each day and each week. The information is analysed to find out:
- consumer needs and preferences
- market trends, e.g. seasonal requirements, dietary groups, age groups
- popular and unpopular selling lines.
The computer system can also be used for automatic ordering of new stock which, in the case of large supermarkets, is delivered on a 24-hour schedule.

Q3   Your answer could be in the form of a diagram to show input → process → output.

Comments Remember that a system is a sequence of activities which work together to make a food product. A system has three parts: input, process, output.
   Try to identify the stages of production in a food product that you have designed and made. Put them in a logical order and show the links between each part or particular process.

Q4   Your answer needs to include a flow diagram and a feedback loop.

Comments Don't forget that control and feedback are important in food production systems. Process control monitors the system and information is fed back to make sure all processes are being carried out correctly. This is called feedback. In this example the feedback information would indicate that either:

(i) The oven temperature is incorrect or working at varying levels because some products are undercooked and some are overcooked.

(ii) The conveyor belt is not moving at the correct rate or at a regular rate. A consistent flow rate through the tunnel oven is necessary to make sure that all the products are baked evenly.

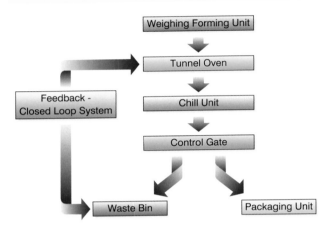

10 Risk assessment (page 148)

Q1 (i) Potential hazards include:
- raw materials being delivered to the factory
- micro-bacterial growth during storage
- contamination from foreign bodies
- cross-contamination from components, e.g. nuts.

(ii) Control measures include:
- detailed specifications given to suppliers of raw materials
- checking goods on delivery, i.e. as to temperature, condition of food, date marks
- sorting food by debagging and putting into containers
- storing all raw materials covered and off the floor
- separating raw and cooked foods
- sieving some foods to check for foreign bodies
- storing at safe temperatures
- strict stock rotation using foods in order of purchase.

Comments You will find that the aim of all the procedures is to identify hazards and prevent them from happening. The first checks involve making sure that the raw materials are not contaminated on arrival. Then methods of handling and storing the foods must be organised to prevent the food becoming contaminated at the factory.

Monitoring may involve:
- regular quality control checks of suppliers
- continuous monitoring of temperatures
- record keeping and recording of suppliers' codes, date marking and stock rotation
- hygiene standards of storage containers and food handlers
- segregation of packaging materials from food materials by use of designated areas or colour coding to prevent cross-contamination
- computer-controlled equipment to display temperatures, atmospheric control, etc.
- sensors – to measure acidity, pH conditions, metal detection, etc.

Q2 Chicken is a high-risk food. The manufacturer will have made sure that the chicken was thoroughly cooked during production of the curry. To eliminate a hazard at the later stage of reheating the curry by the consumer, the manufacturer needs to give clear instructions. All of the curry needs to be heated to above 70°C. To make sure this happens the manufacture gives two critical limits:
- temperature: 190°C, 375°F or Gas Mark 5
- time: 25 minutes.

Comments HACCP is a safety system which applies throughout the entire production of a food product, from raw ingredients to serving. All hazards have to be identified and procedures put in place to eliminate them. Instructions on the label inform the consumer of the final process needed to make sure the food product is presented, served and eaten to the standard intended by the manufacturer.

Q3 The bread is contaminated by a piece of metal. This could have entered the product at these stages:
- delivery of the raw material, i.e. flour
- by dropping off the packaging
- by dropping off a piece of machinery or equipment during processing
- by dropping off a piece of jewellery worn by a food handler.

Comments There are three categories of hazard: microbiological, physical and chemical. Physical hazards include contamination by other materials, such as wood, metal, plastic, etc. The presence of metal in any of the food products can be identified by fitting sensors on the production line.

Q4 The team has to collect, collate and act on the data. The team would usually involve six people representing a range of responsibilities, e.g. quality assurance, engineering, microbiology, production, hygiene. These people need to have a wide knowledge and sound understanding of food processing and food hygiene. Technical data about microbiology, engineering and food processing will be needed to identify hazards accurately and plan preventive and corrective measures.

Comments The HACCP team play an important role in drawing up the arrangements for food safety. A small team of people with different roles and responsibilities has worked well in many food industries applying HACCP. An example of team membership in a food company preparing ready meals is:
- Product Development Manager
- Senior Development Chef
- Technologist
- Process Development Manager
- Process Development Technologist
- Microbiologist.

Q5 Your answer could include these details:
- induction training in personal hygiene is required for new personnel
- all food handlers must meet the personal/hygiene standards set out in regulations on:
  - jewellery
  - gloves
  - handwashing procedure
  - hair and facial hair policy
  - protective clothing
  - changing procedure
- personnel are not permitted to enter the food production plant if suffering from any infection or illness. A 'return to work' policy must be followed when such a person returns to work
- all staff undergo initial training and training updates in personnel hygiene.

Comments The points about personnel hygiene apply to all staff including production workers, management, engineers and visitors and contractors entering or working in the production areas. Checks are made to monitor personnel hygiene standards. This may include visual inspection, hand swabs and factory audits.

11 Food safety and food spoilage (page 161)

Q1 Yeast is used as the raising agent in bread products. Yeast is a living organism which, in the optimum conditions of warm temperatures (25°C–30°C), moisture and food, undergoes a process known as fermentation. The yeast breaks down sugars to produce alcohol and carbon dioxide. In breadmaking the carbon dioxide expands when heated and aerates the dough.

Comments When you make bread you will find that the yeast can be bought in three forms: fresh yeast, dried yeast and easy-blend yeast. Some interesting bread products can be made with yeast, e.g. teacakes, Chelsea buns, bread rolls, croissants, ciabatta, bara brith. However, you must remember that yeast can also cause food spoilage in some foods. This can occur in high-sugar foods, e.g. jam, fruit yogurts.

Q2 Foods can be grouped into three categories of risk: high, medium and low. Foods that have a high protein and moisture content provide ideal conditions for micro-organisms to grow and multiply. Foods considered to be of high risk are raw meat, fish, dairy products, cooked meat and poultry, shellfish, sauces, soups, egg products, cooked rice.

Comments Remember that micro-organisms can cause microbial spoilage which makes foods unfit to eat. Foods can be infected by moulds, yeasts or bacteria. Each type grows in specific conditions. Some bacteria are pathogenic and it is pathogenic bacteria which cause food poisoning. If left unrefrigerated, high-risk category foods provide optimum conditions for the growth of pathogenic bacteria, e.g. food (high protein), moisture and warmth.

Q3 Salmonella bacteria are found in the gut of most animals and birds, particularly chicken, and in raw meat, eggs, seafood and dairy products. If the foods have been prepared or kept in the temperature range of 7°C–45°C, the salmonella bacteria will have multiplied to a level likely to cause food poisoning. The bacteria can be destroyed by high temperatures but if frozen foods are not thawed completely before cooking, the foods may not be cooked thoroughly in the middle. There is also the risk of cross-contamination from infected food handlers or from raw to cooked foods.

Comments *Don't forget that bacteria are microscopic organisms which reproduce by binary fission (cells divide over and over again). They are most active in the optimum conditions of warmth, moisture and oxygen. Several types of bacteria cause food poisoning. Some bacteria are toxic which means that they produce a poisonous substance . These toxins can be harmful and can cause severe symptoms or death, e.g. Clostrichium botulinium.*

Q4 Recent legislation, i.e. the Food Safety Act 1990 and Food Safety (General Food Hygiene) Regulations 1995, have set out specific guidelines to reduce the risks of cross-contamination of food by food handlers. Two examples are:
- food hygiene training. On successful completion of the Food Hygiene Training course, food handlers are awarded the Basic Food Hygiene Certificate.
- personal hygiene standards – food handlers are expected to wear protective workwear and follow guidelines related to all aspects which may cause food to become infected.

Comments *Read through the main points of the existing legislation to make sure that all food is safe to eat. When you visit supermarkets or buy food from restaurants, cafes or takeaway snack bars, look to see how the staff who handle or serve the food meet the requirements for personal hygiene as covered by the food legislation.*

Q5 When the fruit is cut an enzyme called polyphenol reacts in the presence of oxygen to cause a browning reaction. Enzymes are inactivated in acidic conditions and therefore dipping the fruit in the acidic lemon juice reduces the rate of browning.

Comments *Remember that enzymes bring about both desirable and undesirable changes in food. Enzyme reactions are beneficial in bread, brewing and cheese manufacture.*

12 Temperature and preservation (page 171)

Q1 Mayonnaise and salad cream contain high-risk ingredients, e.g. egg and dairy products. They provide ideal conditions for the growth of micro-organisms. They are packaged into sterile jars or bottles and sealed to prevent re-entry of bacteria. When the seal is broken there is a chance that micro-organisms will grow because of the air and warm conditions. Between −1°C to 4°C is the recommended temperature zone for high-risk foods.

Comments *Low temperatures inhibit the growth of micro-organisms. Bacteria, yeasts and moulds are not destroyed but they will remain dormant, i.e. they are prevented from multiplying and contaminating the food. Food poisoning is an illness caused by eating contaminated food. Storing high-risk foods at room temperature is a common cause of food poisoning.*

Q2 Food manufacturers are required by the Food Safety Regulations 1995 to make sure that food is safe to eat. A method of food safety management and risk assessment is done by carrying out HACCP. This identifies critical control points where food safety may be at risk. The storage of chilled foods in chill cabinets and frozen food in freezers are critical control points. The temperature must be maintained within critical limits, e.g. chill cabinets −1 to 4°C; freezer cabinets below −28°C to prevent the growth of micro-organisms.

Comments Different methods can be used to record, monitor and control the temperature of chill cabinets or freezers.

They include:
- a temperature sensor or thermometer to record the temperature
- a thermostat to maintain the temperature at a set point or within a range
- a temperature probe to monitor temperature
- the continuous digital display of the temperature reading
- connection to a central computer system which activates an alarm system if the temperature moves out of the critical range
- regular checks by food handlers/workers of the temperature readings, e.g. every hour.

Q3

Food	Preservation Method	Principle
Raspberries	• canned in sugar syrup • jam • freezing • chilling	Canning at high temperatures High temperatures + sugar Low temperatures $-18°C$ Refrigerate -1 to $4°C$
Tomatoes	• canned in tomato juice • sun dried tomatoes • chutney • bottled tomato sauce	Canning at high temperatures Drying High temperatures, vinegar, sugar + sterilisation. High temperatures
Fish	• canned in tomato sauce or brine/ oil • smoked (kippers or haddock) • freezing (fish or fish products) • modified atmosphere packaging	Canning, high temperatures Smoking process Low temperatures $-18°C$ Mixture of gases in sealed packaging

Comments Many methods are used to preserve large quantities of different foods. Some techniques use the principle of temperature to preserve or extend shelf life. High temperature methods include pasteurisation, sterilisation, ultra-heat treatment, canning, bottling, jamming. Low temperature methods include freezing and chilling. A combination of temperature and a high concentration of salt, sugar or vinegar is used for jam, chutney, canning in brine and pickling.

Q4
- Solid fat, e.g. butter and margarine softens at room temperature and this makes it easy to spread on bread or to cream with sugar in cake mixtures.
- Solid fat, e.g. butter/margarine melts at high temperatures and can be mixed in as a liquid, e.g. melted cake/biscuit mixture.
- Solid fat, e.g. lard melts at very high temperatures. At the very high temperature of 220°C it is used for cooking chipped potatoes. If overheated the fat starts to break down, smoke and will eventually burst into flames.

Comments An increase in temperature causes changes to the physical state of food. The texture, colour or flavour may alter. These changes can be useful as they increase the working characteristics of foods and create more opportunities for variety in food product development.

Q5 The process of irradiation helps to delay the ripening of some foods and also prevents food spoilage, e.g. it:
- stops vegetables sprouting
- delays fruit from ripening
- destroys insects and pests which may damage foods, e.g. rice, wheat
- destroys micro-organisms.

Comments Irradiation means that X-rays are used to preserve food, i.e. rays from radioactive or electron beams are passed through the food. The food has been treated with ionising radiation.

Q6 Your answer could include:
- Chilling, i.e. storing food below 4°C is suitable for high-risk foods. It reduces the risk of food poisoning.
- Chilling is suitable for a wide range of foods. Some of these foods are not suitable for other methods of preservation such as freezing.
- Chilling foods does not change the flavour, colour, texture or shape of the foods and therefore allows their natural characteristics to be maintained.
- Prepared and cooked foods can be stored by chilling. They require little or no preparation so they are very convenient to use.

Comments Chilling is the storage of food at low temperatures which inhibit the growth of micro-organisms and enzyme activity. It is required by law that chilled foods are stored within the temperature range of −1°C to 4°C. Chilled foods must be sold from chill cabinets in shops and stored in a refrigerator at home.

13 Additives (page 179)

Q1 Foods that contain preservatives have an extended shelf life, i.e. they keep for longer periods of time. They do not have to be used immediately. Consumers can shop less frequently which saves time by reducing the number of shopping trips. Food is available out of season and this increases the choice of food products available on a regular basis. Manufacturers can safely transport such foods from other countries and can also transport processed food over long distances to retail outlets.

Comments Preservatives prevent the growth of micro-organisms which can cause food spoilage and lead to food poisoning. Preservatives extend the shelf life of food products.

Q2 The list of ingredients shows that the rice pudding does not contain any additives. The manufacturer is informing the consumer that the product is free from preservatives and that no colours have been added. Consumers who prefer to buy food products with no or few additives would be interested in this product. Some people may be allergic to additives. Sometimes they do not know which additives they are allergic to. It is better for them to be safe by choosing food products that do not contain any additives.

Comments Additives must be declared on the list of ingredients printed on a food label. This is a legal requirement. The ingredients must be listed in descending order of the amount used, and by name or 'E' number.

Note the label also states that this rice pudding contains no gluten. It would therefore be a suitable product for people who require a special diet that is gluten free, i.e. people with coeliac disease.

Q3 Emulsifiers are additives which help to improve the texture and consistency of food. They will help to form an emulsion when the cocoa, milk, sugar, cocoa butter and vegetable fat are mixed together. Emulsifiers help to prevent ingredients separating. The emulsifiers help to give the chocolate a smooth creamy texture. They also help to lengthen the shelf life of the chocolate.

Comments Emulsifiers are used in many foods. Lecithin is a naturally occurring emulsifier found in eggs. It is used to form an emulsion of oil and water in mayonnaise and creamed cake mixtures. Other examples of emulsifiers used in food products include:
- E471 in ice-cream
- E472e in bread mix.

Q4 Colours are added to the custard during processing to:
- make it look attractive
- produce the yellow colour that consumers expect
- make sure that the colour is the same between different batches.

The colours used are curcumin and annatto. These colours come from natural sources. The manufacturer has not added any artificial colours and tells the consumer this by printing this information on the label.

Comments Colours often improve the aesthetic appearance of food products. They do not improve flavour or taste. Some consumers think that colour is not necessary and that it need not be added to foods.

Q5 Flavourings and flavour enhancers are used to add flavours to food products or to restore flavours lost in processing. Artificial flavour enhancers, such as monosodium glutamate (E621), have the ability to make other flavours stronger.

Comments Flavourings and flavour enhancers have to meet the strict requirements of the Food Safety Act 1990 and all other flavouring regulations.

Q6 An important feature of potato products is the shape. The stabiliser is used to maintain the shape and texture of the potato waffle during storage and during the cooking process. Stabilisers help to keep a product in the same condition as when it was produced.

Comments Stabilisers are used in a variety of foods to improve and maintain the consistency of the food during processing, storage and cooking. Another example of a stabiliser is xanthan gum (X415) which is used to stabilise salad dressing, sweet pickle, coleslaw, etc.

14 Product labelling (page 185)

Q1 It is a legal requirement to give instructions to the consumer about how to prepare and cook food products. The instructions may include:
- the method of cooking, e.g on the hob in a saucepan
- the time required to heat, e.g. 3-4 minutes
- any special instructions, e.g. 'Do not boil'.

Comments This type of information helps the consumer to enjoy the product as the manufacturer intended it to be prepared and eaten.

Q2 Crisps are low-risk foods and have a longer shelf life than a food like cheese. They are processed and sealed in a bag. A three-month shelf life is the expected time for safe storage.

Comments A 'best-before' date is another form of date marking. It is a legal requirement for manufacturers to indicate the shelf life of a product and this is used for low-risk foods.

Q3 This is a lot or batch mark. It helps to identify each stage of the production process of the marmalade. It can be used to record details such as the date of production, the production line and the packaging system.

Comments Manufacturers must be able to trace the product back to the raw ingredients. A unique code is used for each product and this is known as 'traceability'.

Q4 (i) No. The list of ingredients is a legal requirement.
The information or symbol showing that the biscuits are suitable for vegetarians is not required by law.

Comments The ingredients are listed in descending order of weight. The main ingredient is shown first.
The information on nutrition and the symbols for specific food groups help the consumer to select food products to suit their specific nutritional requirements, e.g. vegetarians.

Q5 Cheese is a high-risk food and will spoil quickly once the packet is open. The 'use by' date is a clear instruction that the food is safe to eat until this time.

Comments It is a legal requirement to inform the customer of the shelf life of a food product. Date marking is used to indicate how long high-risk food may be kept for.

15 Packaging (page194)

Q1 The desired qualities of food products and ingredients must be preserved during transportation and storage.

Comments Many people think that the function of food packaging is only to make a food product look attractive. The important functions of the packaging are to protect or contain the product or to provide information about the contents.

Q2 The main reason why sandwiches are wrapped is to prevent contamination, i.e. to keep the sandwich in hygienic conditions.

Comments Sandwiches can be wrapped in flexible, stretch-wrap plastic or in rigid plastic containers. The rigid plastic containers will stop the sandwich from being crushed during transportation or while on display.

Q3 The cardboard carton is rigid and will protect the pizza from being damaged or crushed. These cartons will also stack easily in the freezer. Information labels can be printed on the outside of the carton.

Comments Other pieces of packaging may be used but this would increase the cost, e.g. the pizza may be put on a plastic-coated board and it may be overwrapped in a clear thin plastic film. These both protect the pizza and help to keep ingredients such as grated cheese on top of the pizza.

Q4 There would probably be three pieces of packaging:
- a plastic moulded tray to store, cook and serve the lasagne in
- a plastic film cover to seal the tray
- a cardboard outer sleeve to protect the plastic tray and to print information on.

Comments The properties of the materials are:
(i) the plastic for the tray, moulded to shape:
- is resistant to moisture
- is non-toxic
- can be heated in a microwave
- is rigid yet lightweight.
(ii) the plastic for the cover, very thin and lightweight:
- can be pierced to allow steam to escape
- will fuse to the tray to form a seal
- is suitable for use in a microwave.
(iii) the cardboard sleeve
- can be folded to fit the shape of the tray:
- is rigid to prevent crushing
- is easy to print on
- is sometimes made from renewable resources.

16 Sensory analysis (page 202)

Q1 The food manufacturer could use sensory analysis to:
- evaluate existing breads made by other manufacturers
- make judgements about the sensory characteristics of a bread product
- improve the prototype bread product during the development stage by modifying or changing ingredients.

Comments Remember that sensory analysis is used to evaluate food products because it enables the food manufacturer to measure and define sensory qualities. Sensory analysis can be used at several stages of product formulation, development or manufacture.

Q2 Testers can be trained to:
- detect very small differences between products

or
- make an assessment of specific attributes of a food product.

Comments Trained testers regularly carry out sensory analysis in controlled conditions. They contribute to the production of reliable, accurate and unbiased test results.

Untrained testers are often invited to test products in less controlled conditions. They are asked to give general information about the products that they prefer. A balance of consumers may be required, i.e. people of different age, sex or ethnicity. On other occasions a similar group of consumers may be targeted, e.g. teenagers or students.

Q3 Your answer could include two of the following descriptors:

Sense	Descriptor
Sight/appearance	glossy, dark red, golden brown, dull
Sound	sizzling, crackling, bubbling, crunchy
Smell	spicy, fruity, musty,
Taste	sour, sweet, salty, bitter, hot, strong
Touch/mouthfeel	soft, greasy, sticky, hard, gritty, mushy, brittle, crumbly

Comments The characteristics of food that affect the organs of sense are known as organoleptic qualities. These are measured to gather information about the qualities of a food product. The descriptors are used by the trained testers when they record their answers to sensory analysis tests.

Q4 A hedonic ranking test finds out how much consumers like the new chocolate cake product. It does not evaluate the quality or specific attributes of the chocolate cake but shows only if the consumer prefers or likes the product.

Comments For a hedonic ranking test the tester is presented with one or more samples (in this case chocolate cake). They are asked to mark on a five-nine-point scale the point which represents their preference or degree of liking for the product. The scale would range from extremely like to extremely dislike.

This test could be carried out by untrained testers, e.g. shoppers in a supermarket.

Q5 A triangle test is used to detect any differences between the same product. During manufacture it would be used in quality control to make sure that each batch of custard creams is the same or to check that the standard of production is the same at all times.

Comments Triangle testing is one of the 'difference tests'. These tests are used to see if there are any differences between two or more products. They may also be used to tell the difference between the same product made by different manufacturers.

Other difference tests include paired comparison tests, duo-trio tests, two out of five tests, threshold tests.

Q6 Sensory profiling gives a detailed descriptive evaluation about a product. The results for each sample are plotted onto a star diagram or spider diagram. The profile may include characteristics of texture, flavour, aroma, appearance, mouthfeel and sound.

The results can be compared to see what consumers think about the product. The profile can detail a small number of characteristics or more complex descriptions, using up to 15 characteristics for very detailed analysis.

Comments Profiling is a grading test which tests for the degree of intensity of a specific sensory characteristic. For example, a manufacturer may wish to evaluate three different brands of tomato soup. For each sample assessors are asked to rate, on a scale of one to six, the sensory descriptors of sweetness, red colour, tomato flavour, saltiness, creamy, tanginess.

The results are plotted onto a star diagram to provide a visual product profile for each brand of tomato soup. These can be compared and evaluated by the manufacturer. Modifications could then be made to improve their own brand of tomato soup.

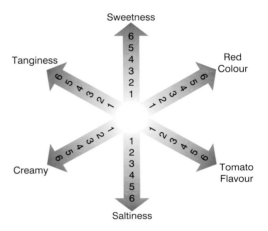

A star diagram which evaluates tomato soup

Published by HarperCollins*Publishers* Ltd
77-85 Fulham Palace Road
London W6 8JB

www.**Collins**Education.com
On-line support for schools and colleges

© HarperCollins*Publishers* Ltd 2003

First published 2001
This new edition published 2003

ISBN-13 978 0 00 720901 9
ISBN-10 0 00 720901 0

Jenny Hotson and Jill Robinson assert the moral right to be identified as the authors of this work.

British Library Cataloguing in Publication Data
A catalogue record for this book is available from the British Library.

Edited by Sue Chapple
Production by Jack Murphy
Series and book design by Sally Boothroyd
Index compiled by Julie Rimington
Printed and bound in Hong Kong by Printing Express Ltd.

Acknowledgements
The Author and Publishers are grateful to the following for permission to reproduce copyright material:
HMSO Figures 11.8 & 11.9
AQA (NEAB): p. 149 Q1 (full course, foundation, 1998 Q7); p. 149 Q2 (short course, higher, 1997 Q6a-b); p. 150 Q1 (short course, foundation, 1997 Q7a-b); p. 172 top Q1 & Q2 (short course, higher, 1997 Q11a-c); pp. 172 bottom Q1 & Q2 (short course, higher, 1997 Q11c-d); p. 204 Q5 & Q6 (short course, higher, 1997 Q9a-c; pp. 205-21 (full course, higher, 1999).
All answers to questions taken from past examination papers are entirely the responsibility of the authors.

The Author and Publishers are grateful to the following for permission to reproduce photographs:
Anthony Blake Photographic Library: 8.3, 1.6 (Milk Marque), 1.7 (Andy Knight), 1.8, 3.5, 3.7, 3.9, 3.10 (Heather Brown), 3.11 (Heather Brown), 3.14, 3.15 (Heather Brown), 3.21 (Charlie Stebbings), 4.1 (Timothy Ball), 4.2 (Maximilian Stock), 4.4 (Gerrit Buntrock), 4.5 (Paola Zucchi), 4.6 (Scott Morrison), 4.7 (top, Robert Lawson, bottom, Philip Wilkins), 4.8 (Graham Kirk), 6.1 (Maximilian Stock), 6.2 (Milk Marque), 6.7, 6.8 (Milk Marque), 6.9, 6.10 (Milk Marque), 6.11 (Tim Hill), 6.12 (Gerrit Buntrock), 6.13 (Milk Marque), 6.14 (Joff Lee), 6.15 (Milk Marque), 6.16 (Maxmilian Stock), 6.17 (Maximilian Stock), 11.5; Beamish 15.1; British Meat 8.2, 16.1, 16.2; British Sugar: 1.4, 1.5; Jane Asher Party Cakes 5.2; Marks & Spencer 8.1; Science Photo Library: 1.3, 6.3, 6.4, 11.1, 11.2, 11.3, 11.10, 11.11, 15.8; Strathaird Ltd. 12.10; Tesco 10.1, 11.12
Extra photographs were taken on behalf of Collins Educational by Martin Sookias and Trevor Clifford.

Illustrations
Dave Mostyn, Geoff Ward, Gecko Ltd

The Authors and Publishers wish to thank all AQA (NEAB) Food technology Centres who have supplied examples of work for this book, including The Broxbourne School, Easingwold School, Northallerton College, Richmond School and Biddick School.

Every effort has been made to contact the holders of copyright material, but if any have been inadvertently overlooked, the Publishers will be pleased to make the necessary arrangements at the first opportunity.

INDEX